The New Tribunals Handbook

The New Tribunals Handbook

by

Richard Blakeley
MA (Cantab); LLM (Harvard)
Christopher Knight
MA (Cantab); BCL (Oxon)
Sarah Love
MA (Oxon); GDL (City)

Consultant Editor
Richard Gordon QC

Bloomsbury Professional

Bloomsbury Professional Ltd, Maxwelton House, 41–43 Boltro Road, Haywards Heath, West Sussex, RH16 1BJ

A CIP Catalogue record for this book is available from the British Library.

ISBN 978 1 84766 535 5

Typeset by Phoenix Photosetting, Chatham, Kent

Printed and bound in Great Britain by CPI Antony Rowe, Chippenham, Wiltshire

Foreword

I am very happy to welcome The New Tribunals Handbook as a valuable and timely addition to the growing body of works on the new tribunal system. The range of subjects covered is a testament to how far we have come since the Leggatt report set out his vision for creating a coherent structure for tribunals, while preserving their distinctive characteristics.

I am conscious that the pace of reform has created its own problems for those who are having to adapt their practices to the new format and procedures. This new work should offer a friendly and manageable guide to the new system. I congratulate the authors on their speedy response to the new developments and wish the project the best of success.

Robert Carnwath

Senior President of Tribunals

Preface

In 1964, the first 'Crown Court Index' by Peter Morrish and Ian McLean was published. It had a simple, alphabetical arrangement with extensive cross-referencing between entries. The work's convenient organisation and ease of navigation made it useful to lawyers and the Bench alike. The work is now entering its 31st edition.

When the new tribunal system created by the Tribunals, Courts and Enforcement Act 2007 came into being in November 2008, Richard Gordon QC realised that a similar work could be of great potential utility, helping the wide range of tribunal users (including practitioners and tribunal personnel, as well as lay tribunal users) to navigate the procedural pitfalls of the new two-tier structure. He envisaged in The New Tribunals Handbook a practical work, which could be used 'on the spot' in hearings and whenever information had to be located quickly.

Since November 2008, the number of Chambers in the two-tier tribunal system has doubled in the First-tier Tribunal from three to six, and increased fourfold in the Upper Tribunal from one to four. The most recent phase of the system's growth involved the creation and expansion of the jurisdiction of the General Regulatory Chamber, followed by the addition of the Immigration and Asylum Chambers in February 2010.

These successive expansions have rendered The New Tribunals Handbook a more voluminous work than we had originally anticipated. However, we have endeavoured to preserve the practicality and accessibility which Richard Gordon first envisaged and have kept these two principles firmly in mind throughout the compilation and drafting of The Handbook. With further planned expansions to the tribunal system, the need for clear practical guidance, including from the tribunals themselves, will only increase if the tribunal system is to remain an accessible jurisdiction that serves its users well.

As well as being easily accessible, we hope that users will also find The Handbook to be comprehensive. We have included the latest versions of the procedural rules for the various Chambers. The law and accompanying procedural rules are stated as at 1 October 2010.

We would like to express our gratitude to Richard Gordon for conceiving of the concept of The Handbook and for acting as our Consultant Editor throughout the preparation of this first edition. We would also like to thank the editorial team at Bloomsbury Professional for their patience in waiting for the concept to be turned into a fully-fledged work as the authors tried to hit the moving target that has been the successive expansions of the tribunal system. While we cannot lay claim to having produced anything comparable to the 'Crown Court Index', we hope nevertheless that The New Tribunals Handbook will be a useful source for practitioners and users alike.

Richard Blakeley

Christopher Knight

Sarah Love

November 2010

CONTENTS

Appendices

Table of Statutes

European Convention on Human Rights is tabled under Sch 1 to the Human Rights Act 1998

Statutes

Table of Statutory Instruments

Table of Cases

ABBREVIATIONS

The following abbreviations will be used throughout:

AAC	Administrative Appeals Chamber of the Upper Tribunal
ADR	Alternative Dispute Resolution
AJTC	Administrative Justice and Tribunals Council
CPR	Civil Procedure Rules
FTTIAC	Immigration and Asylum Chamber of the First-tier Tribunal
GRC	General Regulatory Chamber of the First-tier Tribunal
GRC Rules	Tribunal Procedure (First-tier Tribunal) (General Regulatory Chamber) Rules 2009
The Handbook	The New Tribunals Handbook
HESCC	Health, Education and Social Care Chamber of the First-tier Tribunal
HESCC Rules	Tribunal Procedure (First-tier Tribunal) (Health, Education and Social Care Chamber) Rules 2008
IAC Rules	Asylum and Immigration Tribunal (Procedure) Rules 2005
IAC (Fast Track) Rules	Asylum and Immigration Tribunal (Fast Track Procedure) Rules 2005
Lands Chamber Rules	Lands Tribunal Rules 1996
Leggatt Report	Report of the Review of Tribunals by Sir Andrew Leggatt, 'Tribunals for Users, One System, One Service' (HMSO, 2001)
SEC	Social Entitlement Chamber of the First-tier Tribunal
SEC Rules	Tribunal Procedure (First-tier Tribunal) (Social Entitlement Chamber) Procedural Rules 2008
TCC	Tax and Chancery Chamber of the Upper Tribunal
TC Rules	Tribunal Procedure (First-tier Tribunal) (Tax Chamber) Rules 2009
TCEA 2007	Tribunals, Courts and Enforcement Act 2007
Upper Tribunal Rules or UT Rules	Tribunal Procedure (Upper Tribunal) Rules 2008
UTIAC	Immigration and Asylum Chamber of the Upper Tribunal
WPAFCC	War Pensions and Armed Forces Compensation Chamber
WPAFCC Rules	Tribunal Procedure (First-tier Tribunal) (War Pensions and Armed Forces Compensation Chamber) Rules 2008
The White Book	Lord Justice Walker (ed.), The White Book Service 2010: Civil Procedure (Sweet & Maxwell, 2010)

Abbreviations

The White Paper	White Paper, Transforming Public Services, Complaints, Redress and Tribunals 2004 (Cm 6243)

Note: All procedural rules have been amended since their original enactment. For full references of the statutory instruments listed here see **Procedural rules.**

CONTACT DETAILS

CONTACT INFORMATION FOR THE TRIBUNALS SERVICE AND THE TRIBUNALS

The below contains a list of useful contact numbers and addresses for the various Tribunals falling within the jurisdiction of the Tribunals Service (including some which are not covered in this edition of the Handbook). These are subject to frequent change and parties should note the sender's address in any correspondence received from a particular Tribunal and any address for response set out therein. Parties should also check the website for the relevant Tribunal which can be located at *www.tribunals.gov.uk* in order to ascertain the current contact details. It should be noted that specific contact details were not at the time of writing available for each Tribunal or Chamber covered in this edition of the Handbook; parties are advised to contact the Tribunals Service directly in respect of those Tribunals and Chambers not listed below.

The Tribunals Service

The Tribunals Customer Service Centre is open from 8:30 a.m. to 5:30 p.m. from Monday to Friday and can be contacted by telephone on:

0845 6000 877 (immigration and asylum queries);

0845 795 9775 (employment helpline);

or, in social security and child support cases, a number of regional centres including:

0845 408 3500 (for Birmingham)
0292 066 2180 (for Cardiff)
0141 354 8400 (for Glasgow)
0113 389 6000 (for Leeds)
0151 243 1400 (for Liverpool)
0191 201 2300 (for Newcastle)
0208 652 2300 (for Sutton)

The email address for the **Tribunals Service** is
Customer.Service@tribunals.gsi.gov.uk.

The postal address for the **Tribunals Service** is:

5th Floor
102 Petty France
London
SW1H 9AJ

(Please note that this address should not be used for sending documents or questions in relation to proceedings before a particular tribunal).

Contact Details

The Tribunal Procedure Committee can be contacted at:

Secretary to the Tribunal Procedure Committee
Tribunals Service
Area 2.38
2nd Floor
102 Petty France
London
SW1H 9AJ
Email: tpcsecretariat@justice.gsi.gov.uk

Specific Tribunals

Adjudicator to HM Land Registry

AHMLR
Attn: Margaret Haig (Tribunal Manager)
7th Floor
Victory House
34 Kingsway
London
WC2B 6EX
Tel: 020 3077 5800
Fax: 020 3077 5836
Email: alr@tribunals.gsi.gov.uk

Administrative Appeals Chamber

AAC London
5th Floor
Chichester Rents
81 Chancery Lane
London
WC2A 1DD
Tel: 020 7911 7085
Fax: 020 7911 7093
Email: adminappeals@tribunals.gsi.gov.uk

AAC Wales
Civil Justice Centre
2 Park Street
Cardiff
CF10 1ET
Tel: 02920 662257

AAC Scotland
George House
126 George Street
Edinburgh
EH2 4HH
Tel: 0131 271 4310
Email: ossc@ossc-scotland.org.uk

AAC Northern Ireland
3rd Floor
Bedford House
16–22 Bedford Street
Belfast
BT2 7FD
Tel: 02890 728736

Asylum support cases

First-tier Tribunal (Asylum Support)
Anchorage House
2nd Floor
2 Clove Crescent
East India Dock
London
E14 2BE
Tel: 020 7538 6171
Freephone (for appellants only): 0800 3897913
Fax: 020 7538 6200

Care standards Cases

Tribunals Service, Care Standards
Mowden Hall
Staindrop Road
Darlington
DL3 9BG
Tel: 01325 392712
Fax: 01325 391045
Email: cst@tribunals.gsi.gov.uk

Charity cases

First-tier Tribunal (Charity) Manager
Tribunals Operational Support Centre
PO Box 9300
Leicester
LE1 6ZX
Tel: 0845 6000 877
Fax: 0116 249 4253
Email: CharityTribunal@tribunals.gsi.gov.uk

Claims management services cases

First-tier Tribunal (Claims Management Services)
45 Bedford Square
London
WC1B 3DN
Tel: 020 7612 9700

Consumer credit cases

First-tier Tribunal (Consumer Credit)
45 Bedford Square
London
WC1B 3DN
Tel: 020 7612 9700
Fax: 020 7436 4151
Email: consumercreditappeals@tribunals.gsi.gov.uk

Criminal injuries compensation cases
Glasgow (for all enquires except relating to judicial review)

Tribunals Service - Criminal Injuries Compensation
Wellington House
134–136 Wellington Street
Glasgow
G2 2XL
Tel: 0141 354 8555
Fax: 0141 354 8556
London (for enquiries relating to judicial review)

Tribunals Service – Criminal Injuries Compensation
5th Floor
Fox Court
14 Grays Inn Road
London
WC1X 8HN
Tel: 0203 206 0664
Fax: 0203 206 0652
enquiries-cicap@tribunals.gsi.gov.uk

Employment Appeal Tribunal

EAT London
Audit House
58 Victoria Embankment
London
EC4Y 0DS
Tel: 020 7273 1041
Fax: 020 7273 1045
Email: londoneat@tribunals.gsi.gov.uk

EAT Edinburgh
52 Melville Street
Edinburgh
EH3 7HF
Tel: 0131 225 3963
Fax: 0131 220 6694
Email: edinburgheat@tribunals.gsi.gov.uk

Environment cases

First-tier Tribunal (Environment)
PO Box 9300
Leicester
LE1 8DJ
Tel: 0845 600 0877
Fax: 01162 494253
Email: regulatoryappeals@tribunals.gsi.gov.uk

Estate agents appeals

First-tier Tribunal (Estate Agents)
45 Bedford Square
London
WC1B 3DN
Tel: 020 7612 9700
Fax: 020 7436 4151
Email: estateagentsappeals@tribunals.gsi.gov.uk

Gambling Appeals

Gambling Appeals Tribunal
Attn: Tribunal Manager
Tribunals Operational Support Centre
PO Box 9300
Leicester
LE1 6ZX
Tel: 0845 6000 877
Fax: 0116 249 4253
Email: gat@tribunals.gsi.gov.uk

Gender Recognition Panel

Gender Recognition Panel
PO Box 9300
Leicester
LE1 6ZX
Tel: 0845 355 5155
Email: grpenquiries@tribunals.gsi.gov.uk

Contact Details

Immigration and Asylum Chamber (First-tier Tribunal)
Correspondence for all out of country appeals should be lodged at:

First-tier Tribunal (Immigration and Asylum Chamber)
PO Box 7866
Loughborough
United Kingdom
LE11 2XZ

Appeal forms for out of country appeals should be lodged at:

First-tier Tribunal (Immigration and Asylum Chamber)
PO Box 6987
Leicester
United Kingdom
LE1 6ZX

Appeal forms & correspondence for In Country appeals should continue to be lodged at:

First-tier Tribunal (Immigration and Asylum Chamber)
Administrative Support Centre
Birmingham
P.O. Box 14619
Birmingham
B16 6FQ
OR 0121 450 6391

All telephone enquires should be made using the following number:

0845 6000 877

Immigration and Asylum Chamber (Upper Tribunal)
Appeals forms should be sent to:

First-tier Tribunal (Immigration and Asylum Chamber)
IA Field House
15 Breams Buildings
London
EC4A 1DZ
Or to Upper Tribunal (Immigration and Asylum Chamber) at the same address.

All telephone enquires should be made using the following number:

0845 6000 877

All other correspondence should be sent to:

Upper Tribunal (Immigration and Asylum Chamber)
Arnhem Support Chamber
PO Box 6987
Leicester
LE1 6ZX

Immigration Services cases

First-tier Tribunal (Immigration Services)
Victory House
7th Floor,
Victory House
30–34 Kingsway London
WC2B 6EX
Tel: 020 3077 5860
Fax: 020 3077 5836
Email: imset@tribunals.gsi.gov.uk

Information rights

First-tier Tribunal (Information Rights)
General Regulatory Chamber
Arnhem House Support Centre
PO BOX 9300
Leicester
Leicestershire
LE1 8DJ
Tel: 0845 600 0877
Fax: 0116 249 4253
Email: informationtribunal@tribunals.gsi.gov.uk

Lands Chamber (Upper Tribunal)

The Lands Tribunal
43–45 Bedford Square
London
WC1B 3AS
Tel: 020 7612 9710
Fax: 020 7612 9723
lands@tribunals.gsi.gov.uk
DX: 149065 Bloomsbury 9

Local government standards cases

First-tier Tribunal (Local Government Standards in England)
Tribunal Service
York House
31–36 York Place
Leeds
West Yorkshire
LS1 2ED
Tel: 01133 896086/01133 896013
Fax: 01133 896002
Email: ap-enquiries@tribunals.gsi.gov.uk

Mental Health Cases

First-tier Tribunal (Mental Health)
PO BOX 8793
5th Floor
Leicester
LE1 8BN
DX743090 LEICESTER 35
Tel: 0116 249 7088/0845 2232022

Primary health lists cases

Primary Health Lists
Mowden Hall
Staindrop Road
Darlington
DL3 9BG
Tel: 01325 391130
Fax: 01325 391045

Proscribed Organisations Appeal Commission

Proscribed Organisations Appeal Commission
PO Box 36469
London
EC4A 1WR
Tel: 0845 6000 877
Fax: 020 7073 4122

Reserve Forces Appeal Tribunal

Secretary of Tribunals
Reserve Forces Appeal Tribunals (RFAT)
Tribunals Service
Alexandra House
14–22 The Parsonage
Manchester
M3 2JA
Tel: 0161 833 6100
Fax: 0161 832 0249
Email: rfat@tribunals.gsi.gov.uk

Social Security and Child Support Cases

Social Security and Child Support Cases are dealt with by a number of local tribunals at various locations around the United Kingdom. Below are the principal centres:

Birmingham

Tribunals Service
SSCSA
Administrative Support Centre
PO Box 14620
B16 6FR
Tel: 0845 408 3500
Fax: 0121 634 7201
Email: ASCBirmingham@tribunals.gsi.gov.uk

Cardiff
Eastgate House
Newport Road
Cardiff
CF24 0YP
Tel: 02920 662 180
Fax: 02920 440 596
Email: SSCSA-Cardiff@tribunals.gsi.gov.uk

Glasgow
Wellington House
134-136 Wellington Street
Glasgow
G2 2XL
Tel: 0141 354 8400
Fax: 0141 354 8463
Email: SSCSA-Glasgow@tribunals.gsi.gov.uk

Contact Details

Leeds
York House
York Place
Leeds
LS1 2ED
Tel: 0113 389 6000
Fax: 0113 389 6001
Email: SSCSA-Leeds@tribunals.gsi.gov.uk

Liverpool
36 Dale Street
Liverpool
L2 5UZ
Tel: 0151 243 1400
Fax: 0151 243 1401
Email: SSCSA-Liverpool@tribunals.gsi.gov.uk

Newcastle
Manorview House
Kings Manor
Newcastle upon Tyne
NE1 6PA
Tel: 0191 201 2300
Fax: 0191 201 2357
Email: SSCSA-Newcastle@tribunals.gsi.gov.uk

Nottingham
ASC
54 Hagley Road
PO Box 14620
B16 6FR
Tel: 0845 408 3500
Fax: 0121 450 6392
Email: mailto:ASCBirmingham@tribunals.gsi.gov.uk

Sutton
Copthall House
9 The Pavement
Grove Road
Sutton
SM1 1DA
Tel: 0208 652 2300
Fax: 0208 652 2381
Email: SSCSA-Sutton@tribunals.gsi.gov.uk

Special Educational Needs and Disability cases

There are two centres in England and Wales dealing with special educational needs and disability cases:

Darlington:

Special Educational Needs & Disability
2nd Floor Old Hall
Mowden Hall
Staindrop Road
DL3 9BG
Tel: 01325 392760
Fax: 01325 391080 or 01325 391310
Email: sendistqueries@tribunals.gsi.gov.uk

Wales:

Special Educational Needs & Disability
Unit 32
Ddole Road
Enterprise Park
Llandridnod Wells
Powys
LD1 6PF
Tel: 01597 829 800

Special Immigration Appeals Commission

The Special Immigration Appeals Commission
PO Box 36469
London
EC4A 1WR
Tel: 0845 6000 877
Fax: 020 7073 4122

Tax Chamber

First-tier Tribunal (Tax)
Tribunals Service – Tax
2nd Floor
54 Hagley Road
Birmingham
B16 8PE
Tel: 0845 223 8080
Email: taxappeals@tribunals.gsi.gov.uk

Tax and Chancery Chamber

The Upper Tribunal, Tax and Chancery Chamber
45 Bedford Square
London
WC1B 3DN
Tel: 0207 612 9700
Email: financeandtaxappeals@tribunals.gsi.gov.uk

Transport cases

First-tier Tribunal (Transport)
Victory House
7th Floor,
Victory House
30-34 Kingsway
London
WC2B 6EX
Tel: 020 3077 5860
Fax: 020 3077 5836
Email: transport@tribunals.gsi.gov.uk

War Pensions and Armed Forces Compensation Chamber

War Pensions & Armed Forces Compensation Chamber
Tribunal Manager
5th Floor
Fox Court
14 Gray's Inn Road
London
WC1X 8HN
Tel: 020 3206 0701
Fax: 020 3206 0702
Email: pensions.appeal@tribunals.gsi.gov.uk

1 Administrative Appeals Chamber

COMPOSITION AND LOCATION

1.1 The Administrative Appeals Chamber ('AAC') is one of the four Chambers of the Upper Tribunal (see **Upper Tribunal**).

1.2 There are offices of the AAC in both London and Edinburgh. Full-time judges sit in London, Edinburgh Belfast, Cardiff, Leeds and Manchester; though oral hearings may be held at other centres where circumstances make that necessary.

Judges

1.3 The AAC is headed by a Chamber President and is presided over by the Senior President. It is the largest chamber in terms of both workload and the number of judges. The AAC consists of specialist judges who decide applications for permission to appeal and appeals on points of law from decisions of First-tier Tribunals. Many of its judges will be drawn from the High Court.

1.4 Upper Tribunal judges normally sit on their own to hear cases and most of their cases are decided without oral hearings. For a list of the matters which are to be decided by more than one judge, see *Practice Statement, Composition of tribunals in relation to matters that fall to be decided by the Administrative Appeals Chamber of the Upper Tribunal on or after 18 January 2010*, 14 January 2010, or the relevant subsection of **Constitution and composition of the Upper Tribunal**.

Registrars

1.5 There is a small team of in-house lawyers called Registrars who assist the Upper Tribunal judges. They deal with matters of procedure before an Upper Tribunal judge decides whether to give permission for an appeal to be made. Registrars may also deal with matters such as directing submissions from parties and directing hearings, until the case is ready to be decided by the Upper Tribunal judge. They also undertake research for Upper Tribunal judges.

1.6 Any party may ask an Upper Tribunal judge to reconsider any decision that a Registrar makes on a procedural matter within 14 days of notification of the decision (Upper Tribunal Rules 2008, r 4(3).

1.7 Registrars cannot make decisions on permission to appeal or decide an appeal. Such decisions can only be made by Upper Tribunal judges.

PROCEDURAL RULES

1.8 Proceedings before the AAC are governed by the Upper Tribunal Rules as amended. The Upper Tribunal Rules are reproduced at Appendix 8. See **Upper Tribunal procedural rules**.

1.9 Administrative Appeals Chamber

APPELLATE JURISDICTION AND POWERS

1.9 At present, the AAC hears appeals from:

- the General Regulatory Chamber (with the exception of charities appeals);
- the Social Entitlement Chamber;
- the Health, Education and Social Care Chamber;
- the War Pensions and Armed Forces Compensation Chamber;
- the Mental Health Review Tribunal for Wales;
- the Special Educational Needs Tribunal for Wales; and
- the Pensions Appeal Tribunal (Scotland).

1.10 The AAC also hears:

- references under the Forfeiture Act 1982, s 4;
- appeals under the Pensions Appeal Tribunals Act 1943, s 5 from the Pensions Appeal Tribunal (Northern Ireland);
- appeals under the Safeguarding Vulnerable Groups Act 2006, s 4; and
- appeals against decisions of the Traffic Commissioners made under the Public Passenger Vehicles Act 1981.

1.11 Most appeals are on points of law alone (TCEA 2007, s 11). The AAC also has jurisdiction to judicially review procedural decisions of First-tier Tribunals where there is no right of appeal and criminal injuries compensation appeals decided by the First-tier Tribunal as well as all other judicial review cases transferred to the Upper Tribunal which have not been specifically allocated to the Tax and Chancery Chamber (see **Judicial Review in the Upper Tribunal, Upper Tribunal, and Tax and Chancery Chamber**).

APPEALS AND REFERENCES TO THE AAC

1.12 See **Appeals and references to the Upper Tribunal.**

2 Administrative Justice And Tribunals Council

THE COUNCIL ON TRIBUNALS

2.1 The Administrative Justice and Tribunals Council ('AJTC') was set up under Chapter V of the TCEA 2007 to replace the previous supervisory body for tribunals, the Council on Tribunals (see TCEA 2007, ss 44 and 45).

2.2 The Council on Tribunals operated under the Tribunals and Inquiries Act 1992 ('TIA 1992') with a stated statutory purpose to keep under review and report on the constitution and working of the tribunals under its supervision. The Council's aim was to ensure that tribunals and inquiries met the needs of users through the provision of an open, fair, impartial, efficient, timely and accessible service. Accordingly, the Council was to consider and report on matters referred to it under the TIA 1992 with respect to tribunals and to consider and report on the administrative procedures of statutory inquiries. In practice this involved making mainly general recommendations on the procedure and composition of tribunals (see *White Paper, Transforming Public Services, Complaints, Redress and Tribunals 2004* (Cm 6243), para 11.2 ('The White Paper'). The Council was also under a statutory duty to make an annual report about its work, which was to be laid before Parliament.

2.3 Sir Andrew Leggatt recommended placing the Council at the heart of the proposed tribunal reforms by enhancing its role (see *The White Paper*, paras 11.3–11.10). These proposals were accepted and taken forward by the government (see *The White Paper*, paras 11.11–11.15) and formed TCEA 2007, ss 44 and 45 and Sch 7.

THE ADMINISTRATIVE JUSTICE AND TRIBUNALS COUNCIL

The AJTC's role

2.4 The AJTC's role in relation to the supervision of tribunals is similar to that previously exercised by the Council on Tribunals. However, its remit is broader in a number of important respects: the AJTC is charged with keeping the administrative justice system as a whole under review. It is tasked with considering how to make the system more accessible, fair and efficient, and advising the Lord Chancellor, the Scottish Ministers, Welsh Ministers and the Senior President accordingly. The AJTC's wider administrative justice role is concerned with ensuring that the relationships between the courts, tribunals, ombudsmen and alternative dispute resolution routes satisfactorily reflect the needs of tribunal users (see explanatory notes to TCEA 2007, paras 28–29).

Composition of the AJTC

2.5 The AJTC consists of a minimum of 10 and maximum of 15 members, together with the Parliamentary Commissioner for Administration. The members of the AJTC are to be appointed by the Lord Chancellor, together with the Scottish Ministers and Welsh Ministers (each with the concurrence of the others) (TCEA 2007, Sch 7, para 1). They may be removed only on grounds of inability or misbehaviour (TCEA 2007, Sch 7, para 3). One member is to be appointed Chairman by the Lord Chancellor (TCEA 2007, Sch 7, para 2). The current Chairman is former Information Commissioner, Richard Thomas CBE. There are Scottish and Welsh Committees of the AJTC (TCEA 2007, Sch 7, para 4). A full list of the AJTC members is available at www.ajtc.gov.uk.

Functions of the AJTC

2.6 The AJTC's functions can broadly be split into those functions relating to the administrative justice system as a whole, those relating to tribunals, and those relating to statutory inquiries. The last of these functions falls outside the scope of this Handbook and will not be considered here (see TCEA 2007, Sch 7, para 15).

2.7 In respect of administrative justice, the AJTC is responsible for keeping the system under review (TCEA 2007, Sch 7, para 13). This function extends to the overall system by which decisions of an administrative or executive nature are made in respect of a particular person, including the procedures for making such decisions, the law under which such decisions are made, and the systems for resolving dispute in relation to such decisions.

2.8 The AJTC is to advise the Lord Chancellor, the Scottish and Welsh Ministers and the Senior President on the development of the administrative justice system and make such reports and proposals as it thinks are necessary in relation to its areas of responsibility. It may also propose further areas for research.

2.9 With respect to tribunals generally, the AJTC's responsibility is to 'listed tribunals' which means the First-tier Tribunal and Upper Tribunal (TCEA 2007, Sch 7, paras 14 and 25). The AJTC is to keep the constitution and working of listed tribunals under review and report on those tribunals. The AJTC may of its own initiative consider and report on any other matter relating to listed tribunals generally, or a particular listed tribunal that the AJTC considers is of special importance. The AJTC may also scrutinise and comment on existing or proposed legislation relating to tribunals, including the procedural rules. Indeed, there is an express statutory obligation incumbent upon Ministers to consult the AJTC prior to the exercise by the Minister of a power to make, approve or confirm procedural rules for any listed tribunals (save where such rules are made by the Tribunal Procedure Committee) (TCEA 2007, Sch 7, para 24).

2.10 The AJTC has a duty to make an annual report on its proceedings (TCEA 2007, Sch 7, para 21). In a similar fashion to the Law Commission, the AJTC must formulate a programme of the work that it plans to undertake (TCEA 2007, Sch 7, para 20).

2.11 The AJTC's members have a right to attend proceedings before any listed tribunal even if those proceedings take place in private or do not involve an oral hearing (TCEA 2007, Sch 7, para 22).

2.12 In March 2010 the AJTC published a draft list of ten principles of administrative justice for consultation. These provide a valuable indicator of how the AJTC sees its role. They are that:

A good administrative justice system should—

1. make users central – and always keep their needs in mind;
2. lead to just and timely outcomes – correct decisions within timescales which meet the needs of users;
3. ensure its decisions comply with the law;
4. demonstrate independence and openness – in internal review, complaint-handling and appeals;
5. treat people fairly and respectfully – having regard to individual circumstances
6. work proportionately and efficiently – in offering routes to redress, in procedural requirements and in delivering value for money;
7. be coherent and consistent – in treating similar circumstances in a similar way;
8. keep people informed and empowered – providing information, advice, help from others and in appropriate cases, representation;
9. adopt high standards of behaviour – in governance and in dealings with users;
10. value continuous learning – organisationally and in policy-making.

Although somewhat vague, these principles espoused by the AJTC reflect laudable aims, which it is to be hoped the new tribunals structure meets.

3 Alternative Dispute Resolution

GENERAL AVAILABILITY OF ALTERNATIVE DISPUTE RESOLUTION

3.1 TCEA 2007 envisages that recourse may generally be had to forms of ADR before the First-tier Tribunal and Upper Tribunal.

3.2 TCEA 2007 accordingly echoes the recognition in the Civil Procedure Rules that mediation and other forms of ADR are being increasingly used in the justice system and can in many cases achieve more efficient and effective justice, with the added benefits of reducing costs for the parties and the justice system, and in many cases avoiding the pressure and stress that appearing in a court or tribunal can cause. The intention behind increased ADR in the tribunal system is to achieve earlier resolution of disputes, in particular against a background of a strong system of precedent and guidance cases (see **Guidance Cases**). The aim is to 'further push the centre of gravity of administrative justice from the generation of formal legal disputes towards an expanded sphere of early intervention, ADR and settlement': Buck, 'Precedent in Tribunals' (2006) 25 CJQ 458, 465.

3.3 One statutory duty of the Senior President of Tribunals is to have regard to 'the need to develop innovative methods of resolving disputes that are of a type that may be brought before tribunals' under TCEA 2007, s 2(3)(d).

3.4 In TCEA 2007 the term 'mediation' is preferred to ADR. However, given the range of meanings that 'mediation' can bear, the two must be considered synonymous (the relevant explanatory note to TCEA 2007 states that 'the term mediation can encompass a broad spectrum of activity': paragraph 153). Section 24 of TCEA 2007 enables and empowers the making of tribunal procedural rules in respect of mediation. In this way, ADR is given a defined statutory basis against which rules and practice directions can be enacted.

3.5 In making such rules and directions, TCEA 2007 prescribes that the rule-making body must have regard to the principles that:

- mediation of matters in dispute between parties to proceedings is to take place only by agreement between those parties (s 24(1)(a));
- where parties to proceedings fail to mediate, or where mediation between parties to proceedings fails to resolve disputed matters, the failure is not to affect the outcome of the proceedings (s 24(1)(b)).

ADR IN SPECIFIC TRIBUNALS

3.6 The procedural rules enacted in respect of most of the various Chambers of the First-tier Tribunal and the Upper Tribunal each contain a specific provision dealing with ADR. This is found at rule 3(1) of the various relevant procedural rules and provides as follows:

> 3.—(1) The Tribunal should seek, where appropriate,—
>
> (a) to bring to the attention of the parties the availability of any appropriate alternative procedure for the resolution of the dispute; and

(b) if the parties wish and provided that it is compatible with the overriding objective, to facilitate the use of the procedure.

3.7 Perhaps unsurprisingly the rules governing the Immigration and Asylum Chamber of the First-tier Tribunal do not contain an equivalent rule 3(1), although, oddly, appeals to the IAC of the Upper Tribunal are not exempted from the Upper Tribunal Rules 2008, r 3(1).

3.8 It has long been held that engagement in ADR can be a good reason to extend time in the context of judicial review cases (see *R (Cowl) v Plymouth City Council* [2001] EWCA Civ 1935, [2002] 1 WLR 803) and there is no reason why it should not be just as relevant under the TCEA regime. In the event that the parties agree to pursue ADR, an application should be made promptly to the relevant Chamber to seek directions for a stay if the parties agree to pursue ADR.

APPROPRIATENESS OF ADR

3.9 Given the wide-ranging subject-matter jurisdiction possessed by the tribunals system as a whole, it is obvious that ADR will not be appropriate in a large number of cases. It is unlikely to be possible to specify the circumstances in which ADR will or will not be appropriate. What can be said is that many appeals to the First-tier Tribunal concerning, for example, the withdrawal or refusal of the entitlement to some benefit or the imposition of a penalty will be unlikely to be resolved through ADR (in part because of statutory restrictions on the decision making body being appealed). Indeed, the citizen-State nature of the disputes to be heard by the tribunals would seem to limit the availability of effective ADR in many cases.

3.10 Some commentators have noted the tension between the emphasis on ADR in TCEA 2007 and the litigation strategy of various decision-making bodies whose decisions will be the subject of appeals to the tribunals. In respect of appeals to First-tier Tax Chamber and then to the Tax and Chancery Chamber of the Upper Tribunal, HMRC's Litigation and Settlements Strategy (www.hmrc.gov.uk/practitioners/lss.pdf) sets out the factors that HMRC should take into account when considering whether to settle cases. This includes an expectation that HMRC should seek full value from settlement where there is a strong case and encourages a focus on the wider impact of cases as well as their individual value. It has been noted that these principles 'may place HMRC in a position that is insufficiently flexible to make ADR worthwhile in some cases, in particular if HMRC are pursuing a point because of its wider impact rather than its importance to the taxpayer in question.' (Gething et al, 'Transformation of the Tax Tribunal' [2009] British Tax Review 250, 262).

3.11 It is suggested here that parties appearing before any of the Chambers of the First-tier Tribunal should consider whether ADR would be appropriate in their case. Particular regard should be had to the utility of ADR in cases involving monetary sums. That is not to say that ADR will take place in all jurisdictions covered by the tribunals structure; and TCEA 2007 neither intended nor envisaged such an inflexible approach (see explanatory notes, paragraph 153). However, as an advantage of the tribunals structure is meant to be speed and greater cost-effectiveness it is to be hoped that public bodies will be quick to display the spirit envisaged by TCEA 2007.

REFUSAL TO PARTICIPATE IN ADR

3.12 It has been queried whether a tribunal might demand reasons from a party which unreasonably refused to participate in ADR ([2009] British Tax Review 250, 262). At present, it appears unlikely that reasons will be demanded for a refusal to participate in ADR. In particular, none of the present Tribunal rules or practice directions provides for the imposition of sanctions on a party that unreasonably refuses to participate in ADR. Such sanctions would likely only sound in costs, as any substantive sanction would likely be contrary to TCEA 2007, s 24(1)(b) (set out above, and providing that a failure to mediate is not to affect the outcome of proceedings). In court proceedings a failure to use ADR can affect a party's ability to recover or liability to pay costs (*Halsey v Milton Keynes General NHS Trust* [2004] EWCA Civ 576, [2004] 1 WLR 3002). Several Chambers of the First-tier Tribunal may award costs in circumstances in which one party acts unreasonably in bringing or conducting proceedings (see **Costs**). As the costs position in the Upper Tribunal typically mirrors that of the First-tier Tribunal which made the decision under appeal, the Upper Tribunal will frequently have this power also. A party's failure to use ADR could in some cases amount to a sufficiently unreasonable act as to trigger a liability to pay costs. This will particularly be so where it is the State party that has refused to participate in ADR and has insisted on litigating proceedings that it has subsequently lost.

4 Appeals And References To The Upper Tribunal

PERMISSION TO APPEAL

4.1 A party wishing to appeal a decision of another tribunal to the Upper Tribunal has a right to appeal on a point of law, but that right may only be exercised with permission (TCEA 2007, s 11(1)–(3)). Permission is required from either the tribunal making the decision against which the party wishes to appeal or from the Upper Tribunal following a successful application for permission (TCEA 2007, s 11(4)). For a discussion of what constitutes a point of law, see **Fact and law in Tribunal decisions**.

APPLICATION TO THE UPPER TRIBUNAL FOR PERMISSION TO APPEAL

4.2 The procedure for applying for permission to appeal to the Upper Tribunal is set out in the Upper Tribunal Rules 2008, as amended. The Rules do not apply to proceedings in the Lands Chamber (see **Lands Chamber** and **Lands Chamber procedural rules**). The following discussion applies to appeals and references to the Administrative Appeals Chamber, the Immigration and Asylum Chamber and the Tax and Chancery Chamber of the Upper Tribunal. The Upper Tribunal Rules are reproduced at **Appendix 8**.

4.3 A party may apply to the Upper Tribunal for permission to appeal only if he has first made an application for permission to appeal to the tribunal which made the decision being challenged and that application was refused or not admitted (Upper Tribunal Rules, r 21(2)) (see **Appeals from the First-tier Tribunal**).

Time limit for applying for permission to appeal to the Upper Tribunal

4.4 An application for permission to appeal to the Upper Tribunal must be made by the appellant in writing, and received by the Upper Tribunal no later than one month after the date on which the tribunal sent notice of its refusal of permission to appeal to the appellant (Upper Tribunal Rules, r 21(3)(b)).

4.5 The time limit for applying to the Upper Tribunal for permission to appeal may be extended on an application by the appellant (Upper Tribunal Rules, r 5(3)(a)) (see **Extensions of time**).

4.6 The time limit for an application for permission to appeal a decision under the Safeguarding Vulnerable Groups Act 2006, s 4 must be received by the Upper Tribunal no later than three months after the date on which written notice of the decision being challenged was sent to the appellant (Upper Tribunal Rules, r 21(3)(a)).

4.7 Immigration and asylum cases have different time limits on appeals. Any appeal must be made no later than seven working days after the date on which written notice of the decision being challenged was sent to the appellant, or four working days if it is a fast track case where the appellant is in the UK (Upper Tribunal Rules, r 21(3)(aa)). The time limit is 56 days if the appellant is outside the UK (Upper Tribunal Rules, r 21(3)(ab)). Those time limits are shortened to five working days, two working days and 28 days respectively if notice is sent electronically or served personally (Upper Tribunal Rules, r 21(3A)). (It is important to note the, unexplained, difference in using 'working days' or simply 'days' in the application of these time periods).

4.8 Compliance with the above time limits is likely to prove very important and the Upper Tribunal is required to refuse applications made out of time unless it considers it appropriate to grant an extension of time under r 5(3)(a) of the Upper Tribunal Rules (Upper Tribunal Rules, r 21(6)(b)).

4.9 If the appellant provides the application for permission to appeal to the Upper Tribunal outside of the prescribed time limit (or any time limit ordered by the Upper Tribunal in accordance with r 5(3)(a) of the Upper Tribunal Rules), the application must include a request for an extension of time and state the reasons why the application was not provided in time (Upper Tribunal Rules, r 21(6)(a)). If this rule is not complied with, the Upper Tribunal must refuse the application for permission to appeal.

4.10 If the appellant's application for permission to appeal to the tribunal which made the decision under challenge (see **Appeals from the First-tier Tribunal**) was refused or not admitted because it was made out of time, the application to the Upper Tribunal must state the reasons why that application was not made in time (Upper Tribunal Rules, r 21(7)(a)). The Upper Tribunal must only admit such an application if it considers that it is in the interests of justice to do so (Upper Tribunal Rules, r 21(7)(b)).

Content of an application for permission to appeal

4.11 The application must state (Upper Tribunal Rules, r 21(4)):

- the name and address of the appellant;
- the name and address of the appellant's representative (if any);
- an address where documents for the appellant may be sent or delivered;
- details, including the full reference (see **Citation and reporting**) of the decision being challenged;
- the grounds on which the appellant relies;
- whether the appellant wants the application to be dealt with at an oral hearing (see **Hearings**); and
- if the application being made is out of time or the application to the tribunal which made the decision being appealed was refused or not admitted because it was made out of time, the reasons why the application was made out of time (Upper Tribunal Rules, r 21(6) and (7)).

4.12 Along with the application for permission to appeal to the Upper Tribunal, the appellant must provide a copy of (Upper Tribunal Rules, r 21(5)):

- any written record of the decision being appealed;

- any separate written statement of reasons for that decision; and
- if the application is for permission to appeal against a decision of another tribunal, the notice of refusal of permission to appeal, or notice of refusal to admit the application for permission to appeal, from that other tribunal.

The test to be applied

4.13 The test to be applied on an application for permission to appeal to the Upper Tribunal is, unhelpfully, not set out by legislation or practice direction. The failure to specify a permission test is both unfortunate and likely to be productive of uncertainty and consequent case law. However, it is suggested here that the criteria to be applied by the Upper Tribunal when determining an application must logically, in the absence of any statutory stipulation to the contrary, be the same as the test to be applied by the First-tier Tribunal when dealing with the application for permission to appeal against its own ruling.

4.14 Accordingly, the test to be applied by the Upper Tribunal when determining an application for permission to appeal to the Upper Tribunal is whether there is a reasonable prospect of success, or if there is some other compelling reason for the appeal to be heard. It appears from the case law of the Administrative Appeals Chamber that the tribunal is looking at levels of arguability in determining permission applications, but without setting out a specific test. The proposed test is dealt with elsewhere in the Handbook (see **Appeals from the First-tier Tribunal**). This test differs from that to be applied by the Upper Tribunal when it determines applications for permission to appeal from its own decisions as the permissible appeals from the Upper Tribunal have been narrowly prescribed by statutory instrument (see **Appeals from the Upper Tribunal**).

Refusal of permission to appeal

4.15 If the Upper Tribunal refuses permission to appeal, it must give written notice of this fact to the appellant and state its reasons for refusing the application for permission (Upper Tribunal Rules, r 22(1)). There is no requirement that the Upper Tribunal communicate its refusal of an application for permission appeal to any other party involved in the proceedings.

4.16 In respect of applications for permission to appeal against a decision of the General Regulatory Chamber, the Health, Education and Social Care Chamber, the Tax Chamber, the Mental Health Review Tribunal for Wales or the Special Educational Needs Tribunal for Wales and applications for permission to appeal under the Safeguarding Vulnerable Groups Act 2006, s 4, if the Upper Tribunal refuses permission to appeal or gives permission only on limited grounds or subject to conditions, the appellant may apply for the decision to be reconsidered at an oral hearing (Upper Tribunal Rules, r 22(4)). An application for an oral hearing in such circumstances must be made in writing and received by the Upper Tribunal within 14 days of the date on which the Upper Tribunal gave written notice to the appellant of its decision in respect of the appellant's application for permission to appeal (Upper Tribunal Rules, r 22(5)).

4.17 Appeals And References To The Upper Tribunal

Grant of permission to appeal

4.17 If the Upper Tribunal grants an appellant permission to appeal, it must send written notice of the permission to each party, together with the reasons for any limitations or conditions or limits on the grant of permission (Upper Tribunal Rules, r 22(2)(a)).

4.18 Unless the Upper Tribunal directs otherwise, the application for permission to appeal will stand as the notice of appeal (see below). The Upper Tribunal must therefore send a copy of the application for permission to appeal together with the attendant documents submitted by the appellant to each respondent (Upper Tribunal Rules, r 22(2)(b)).

4.19 If the Upper Tribunal deems it appropriate, it may determine the appeal without obtaining any further response from the parties, providing the appellant and each respondent consents to this course of action (Upper Tribunal Rules, r 22(2)(c)).

4.20 It will be at the discretion of the Tribunal as to whether or not to permit a new point to be raised on appeal which was not argued below. This is a perfectly obvious proposition which needs no authority to be cited for it. It is particularly important that the Upper Tribunal retain a sense of flexibility about new points, given that many of those before it will be unrepresented, or perhaps represented for the first time only on appeal. Given that the appeal is on a point of law it will often be the case that the appellant wishes to challenge the legality of the First-tier Tribunal's decision on a ground which he or she did not deal with at the time because he or she did not realise it was going to be an issue. While running new factual grounds will be less likely to find favour, it will be important that the Upper Tribunal does not limit itself in a manner reminiscent of the appellate courts; the Tribunals are designed to be more flexible and informal. It is suggested here that the discretion to refuse to take new points ought to be generally constrained to cases in which it is bordering on an abuse of process, or where the new issue is not, or is only tangentially, relevant.

NOTICE OF APPEAL

4.21 A notice of appeal is required in three circumstances (Upper Tribunal Rules, r 23(1)):

- in proceedings on appeal to the Upper Tribunal for which permission to appeal is not required (except proceedings under rr 26A and 26B);
- if a tribunal other than the Upper Tribunal has given permission for the appellant to appeal to the Upper Tribunal;
- if the Upper Tribunal has given permission to appeal but has directed that the application for permission does not stand as the notice of appeal.

4.22 The appellant must provide a notice of appeal to the Upper Tribunal within one month of receiving notice from the Tribunal granting permission to appeal (whether this is the Upper Tribunal or the Tribunal making the decision being appealed), or from the decision to which the appeal which does not require permission relates (Upper Tribunal Rules, r 23(2)). When the Upper Tribunal receives the notice of appeal it must send a copy of the notice and any accompanying documents to each respondent (Upper Tribunal Rules, r 23(6)).

4.23 As with applications for permission to appeal (see above), if the appellant provides the notice of appeal to the Upper Tribunal outside of the one month time limit (or any extended time limit prescribed by the Upper Tribunal under r 5(3)(a) of the Upper Tribunal Rules), the notice of appeal must include a request for an extension of time and state the reasons why the notice of appeal was not provided in time. In such circumstances, unless the Upper Tribunal extends time under r 5(3)(a) of the Upper Tribunal Rules it must not admit the notice of appeal (Upper Tribunal Rules, r 23(5)).

4.24 The notice of appeal must state (Upper Tribunal Rules, r 23(3)):

- the name and address of the appellant;
- the name and address of the appellant's representative (if any);
- an address where documents for the appellant may be sent or delivered;
- details, including the full reference (see **Citation and reporting**) of the decision being challenged;
- the grounds on which the appellant relies;
- whether the appellant wants the application to be dealt with at an oral hearing (see **Hearings**); and
- In cases in which the Upper Tribunal has granted permission to appeal, the Upper Tribunal's case reference.

4.25 Where permission to appeal has been granted by a tribunal other than the Upper Tribunal, the notice of appeal must be accompanied by (Upper Tribunal Rules, r 23(4)):

- any written record of the decision being appealed;
- any separate written statement of reasons for that decision; and
- the notice of permission to appeal from the Tribunal granting permission.

Responding to the notice of appeal

4.26 A respondent will usually have the right to respond to the notice of appeal, unless the Upper Tribunal directs otherwise (Upper Tribunal Rules, r 24(1A)). Any response must be in writing and received by the Upper Tribunal no later than one month after the respondent has received a copy of the notice of appeal from the Upper Tribunal or, if the Upper Tribunal directs that the application for permission stands as the notice of appeal, no later than one month after the date on which the Upper Tribunal sent notice to the respondent that it had granted permission to appeal (Upper Tribunal Rules, r 24(2)). When the Upper Tribunal receives a written response to the notice of appeal it must send a copy of the response and any accompanying documents to the appellant and each other party (Upper Tribunal Rules, r 24(5)).

4.27 The response must state (Upper Tribunal Rules, r 24(3)):

- the name and address of the respondent;

- the name and address of the respondent's representative (if any);
- an address where documents for the respondent may be sent or delivered;
- whether the respondent opposes the appeal;
- the grounds on which the respondent relies, including (in the case of an appeal against the decision of another tribunal) any grounds on which the respondent was unsuccessful in the proceedings which are the subject of the appeal, but intends to rely in the appeal; and
- whether the respondent wants the case to be dealt with at a hearing.

4.28 As with applications for permission to appeal (see above), if the respondent provides its written response to the Upper Tribunal outside of the one month time limit (or any extended time limit prescribed by the Upper Tribunal under r 5(3)(a) of the Upper Tribunal Rules), the notice of appeal must include a request for an extension of time and state the reasons why the response was not provided in time (Upper Tribunal Rules, r 24(4)). Unlike applications for permission to appeal and notices of appeal received out of time, it does not appear that the Upper Tribunal is obliged to refuse to accept a response to a notice of appeal received out of time unless it extends time under r 5(3)(a) of the Upper Tribunal Rules.

NATURE OF THE APPEAL BEFORE THE UPPER TRIBUNAL

4.29 Appeals before the Upper Tribunal are against decisions of the First-tier Tribunal. The question the Upper Tribunal asks is not whether the First-tier Tribunal was right but rather whether an error of law was committed which vitiates that decision (see further **Fact and law in Tribunal decisions**). The Upper Tribunal is not tasked with repeating the exercise already performed by the First-tier Tribunal (see *Gover v Propertycare Ltd* [2006] EWCA Civ 286, [2006] ICR 1073 at [8] per Buxton LJ). This does not mean however that the hearing on appeal must focus solely on the decision of the First-tier Tribunal and neglect consideration of the original decision that was itself the subject of the case before the First-tier Tribunal (see *Osmani v Camden LBC* [2004] EWCA Civ 1706; [2005] HLR 22 at [34] per Auld LJ). Indeed, the courts have been mindful not to indulge in the drawing of over-semantic distinctions between appeals, reviews and rehearings (see *El Du Pont De Nemours & Co v ST Dupon* [2003] EWCA Civ 1368, [2006] 1 WLR 2793 at [84]–[98] per May LJ in the context of appeals under the Trade Marks Acts 1938 and 1994).

4.30 An appeal lies against a decision (which means the judgment or order: *Onslow v Commissioners of Inland Revenue* (1890) LR 25 QBD 465; and *R (Jones) v Ceredigion County Council* [2007] UKHL 24, [2007] 1 WLR 1400 at [14]–[18] per Lord Bingham) and not against the underlying reasoning or findings, though it is usually this that makes the decision incorrect (*Lake v Lake* [1955] P 336). The Upper Tribunal will typically (though not always) only have jurisdiction to decide issues relating to the particular decision under appeal (*Re W (Permission to appeal)* [2007] EWCA Civ 786, [2008] 1 FLR 406 and see **Guidance cases**). This does not mean that the Upper Tribunal must limit itself to the grounds on which the decision of the First-tier Tribunal was based. Whether or not this is correct depends on the purpose of the underlying legislation and the particular appellate jurisdiction being exercised (see *Joyce v Secretary of State for Health* [2008] EWHC 1891 (Admin), [2009] PTSR 266 [60]-[70] per Goldring J). The Upper Tribunal can of course deal with issues that are ancillary or incidental to the grounds of appeal (*Commissioners of Revenue and Customs v Vodafone* [2006] EWCA Civ 1132, (2006) STC 1530).

REFERENCES UNDER THE FORFEITURE ACT 1982

4.31 If an question arises under the Forfeiture Act 1982, s 4, the person to whom the application of or the relevant benefit of advantage has been made must refer the question to the Upper Tribunal (Upper Tribunal Rules, r 26(1)).

4.32 Any reference under the Forfeiture Act must be in writing and include (Upper Tribunal Rules, r 26(2)):

- a statement of the question to be determined by the Upper Tribunal;
- a statement of the relevant facts;
- the grounds upon which the reference is made; and
- an address for sending documents to the person making the reference and each respondent to the reference.

4.33 When the Upper Tribunal receiving a written reference under the Forfeiture Act it must send a copy and any accompanying documents to each respondent (Upper Tribunal Rules, r 26(3)).

4.34 A respondent to a reference has the same rights to respond to a reference under the Forfeiture Act as if it were a notice of appeal (Upper Tribunal Rules, r 26(4)). A respondent must therefore adhere to the rules set out above in respect of responses to a notice of appeal (see above and Upper Tribunal Rules, r 24). A right of reply to any response also lies in accordance with the rules set out above in respect of the appellant's right to respond to a written response to a notice of appeal (see above and Upper Tribunal Rules, r 25).

CASES TRANSFERRED OR REFERRED TO THE UPPER TRIBUNAL, APPLICATIONS MADE DIRECTLY TO THE UPPER TRIBUNAL AND PROCEEDINGS WITHOUT NOTICE TO A RESPONDENT

4.35 The preceding procedural rules do not automatically apply to a case which is transferred or referred to the Upper Tribunal from the First-tier Tribunal, or to a case (other than under the Forfeiture Act) which is begun directly in the Upper Tribunal. Instead, the Upper Tribunal must give directions as to the procedure to be followed, which may include applying some or all of the ordinary rules (Upper Tribunal Rules, r 26A).

FINANCIAL SERVICES CASES

4.36 Financial services cases are governed by the Upper Tribunal Rules, Sch 3 (r 26B) and cover a reference notice made in respect of: (a) a decision of the Financial Services Authority; (b) a decision of the Bank of England; (c) a decision of the Pensions Regulator; or (d) a decision of a person relating to the assessment of any compensation or consideration under the Banking (Special Provisions) Act 2008 or the Banking Act 2009.

4.37 Where a reference notice is signed and sent by the applicant to be received by the Upper Tribunal not later than 28 days after notice was given of the decision in respect of which the reference is made, the reference notice must cover:

(a) the name and address of the applicant;

(b) the name and address of the applicant's representative (if any);

(c) if no representative is named under sub-paragraph (b), an address where documents for the applicant may be sent or delivered; and

(d) the issues that the applicant wishes the Upper Tribunal to consider.

4.38 The applicant must send to the Tribunal a copy of the relevant decision and must send a copy of the reference to the respondent (Upper Tribunal Rules, Sch 3, para 2).

4.39 The Tribunal will keep a publicly available register of all such references made to it (Upper Tribunal Rules, Sch 3, para 3).

5 Appeals From The First-Tier Tribunal

See: **Appeals and References to the Upper Tribunal; Review, correction and setting aside of Tribunal decisions.**

APPEALING DECISIONS OF THE FIRST-TIER TRIBUNAL

5.1 A party wishing to appeal a decision of the First-tier Tribunal to the Upper Tribunal has a right to appeal on a point of law, but that right may only be exercised with permission TCEA 2007, s 11(1)–(3)). Permission is required from either the Chamber of the First-tier Tribunal making the decision against which the party wishes to appeal or from the Upper Tribunal following the refusal of permission by the First-tier Tribunal (TCEA 2007, s 11(4)).

Appeal lies against decisions of the First-tier Tribunal

5.2 An appeal lies against a decision (which means the judgment or order: *Onslow v Commissioners of Inland Revenue* (1890) LR 25 QBD 465; and *R (Jones) v Ceredigion County Council* [2007] UKHL 24, [2007] 1 WLR 1400 at [14]–[18] per Lord Bingham) and not against the underlying reasoning or findings, though it is usually this that makes the decision incorrect (*Lake v Lake* [1955] P 336; if the Tribunal wishes a particular finding to be appealed, it may make a declaration in its order embodying that finding: *Compagnie Noga D'importation Et D'Exportation SA v Australia and New Zealand Banking Group Ltd* [2002] EWCA Civ 1142, [2003] 1 WLR 307). The Upper Tribunal will typically (though not always) only have jurisdiction to decide issues relating to the particular decision under appeal (*Re W (Permission to appeal)* [2007] EWCA Civ 786, [2008] 1 FLR 406 and see **Guidance cases**). This does not mean that the Upper Tribunal must limit itself to the grounds on which the decision of the First-tier Tribunal was based. Whether or not this is correct depends on the purpose of the underlying legislation and the particular appellate jurisdiction being exercised (see *Joyce v Secretary of State for Health* [2008] EWHC 1891 (Admin), [2009] PTSR 266 [60]–[70] per Goldring J). The Upper Tribunal can of course deal with issues that are ancillary or incidental to the grounds of appeal (*Commissioners of Revenue and Customs v Vodafone* [2006] EWCA Civ 1132, (2006) STC 1530).

5.3 As a right of appeal can only be conferred by statute (*Evans v Bartlam* [1937] AC 473; *Lane v Esdaile* [1891] AC 210), it lies only against those decisions of the First-tier Tribunal specified by statute. By virtue of TCEA 2007, s 11, appeals lie against all decisions of the First-tier Tribunal except those specified as excluded decisions by the Lord Chancellor under the power conferred by TCEA 2007, s 11(5). The decisions specified as being so excluded are numerous and as such are set out elsewhere in the Handbook (see **Excluded appeals**). The right of appeal arises against any other decision of the Tribunal including, it is suggested, decisions entered by way of consent order (see **Consent orders**) and decisions to strike out a case (*Synergy Child Services Ltd v Ofsted* [2009] UKUT 125 (AAC)).

5.4 Appeals From The First-Tier Tribunal

Who may seek permission to appeal?

5.4 It is typically only the unsuccessful party before the First-tier Tribunal that may apply to appeal. However, there are circumstances in which the successful party may challenge the decision. These arise only exceptionally and seem to extend only to cases in which the parts of the First-tier Tribunal's decision are severable, for example a finding on jurisdiction (which the successful party lost) and a finding on the merits (which the successful party won) and the issue on which the successful party lost raises a fundamental legal issue (see *Secretary of State for Work and Pensions v Morina* [2007] EWCA Civ 749, [2007] 1 WLR 3033) or cases in which a successful public body seeks to appeal rulings that are unnecessary or which create procedural or substantive uncertainty and it is in the public interest that such an appeal be allowed (see *Office of Communications v Floe Telecom Ltd* [2009] EWCA Civ 47).

5.5 In certain (though rare) circumstances an individual who was not a party to the original decision may seek permission to appeal where their interests are adversely affected by the outcome of the decision. Whether such a person applied to be added as a party in the proceedings below is relevant to the exercise of the discretion whether to grant permission to appeal, but it does not follow from the fact that such an application would have failed that permission to appeal should be refused. If the Tribunal considers that the applicant individual has no real interest in the case it should refuse permission even if the appeal would have a real prospect of success (*George Wimpey UK Ltd v Tewkesbury Borough Council* [2008] EWCA Civ 12, [2008] 1 WLR 1649).

Grounds of appeal

5.6 A party wishing to appeal a decision of the First-tier Tribunal to the Upper Tribunal may only do so on grounds that the Tribunal has erred in law (TCEA 2007, s 11(1)–(3)). For a discussion of what constitutes a point of law, see **Fact and law in Tribunal decisions**.

APPLICATION FOR PERMISSION TO THE FIRST-TIER TRIBUNAL

The need for an application to the First-tier Tribunal

5.7 The statutory right of appeal to the Upper Tribunal against decisions of the First-tier Tribunal is not conditional upon the making of an unsuccessful application for permission to the First-tier Tribunal. However, the Upper Tribunal Rules provide that such an application must first be made Upper Tribunal Rules 2008, r 21(2). A failure first to apply for permission from the First-tier Tribunal can be waived by the Upper Tribunal (Upper Tribunal Rules, r 7(2)(a); see **Failures to comply**). This mirrors the practice under the CPR: where a party fails to apply to the lower court for permission to appeal it suffers no sanction if the decision to appeal to a higher court is subsequently taken by that higher court.

5.8 It is suggested here that the Upper Tribunal's power to waive will be exercised relatively sparingly in cases in which the appellant was professionally represented before the First-tier Tribunal and/or had the right to appeal adequately drawn to its attention by the First-tier Tribunal. The Court of Appeal has held that 'in the vast majority of cases, practitioners should follow the guidance contained in the notes [in the *White Book*] to the rule [CPR, r 52.3(2)] and apply to the trial judge at the point of judgment.' (*T (A Child)* [2002] EWCA Civ 1736, [2003] 1 FLR 531 at [12]–[13] per Thorpe LJ) The notes referred to and endorsed by the Court of Appeal provide in relevant part:

> 'Despite the lack of compulsion [to apply to the lower court for permission], a litigant with arguable grounds for appeal would generally be well advised to apply for permission to the lower court at the time of judgment for five reasons:
>
> (a) The judge below is fully seized of the matter and so the application will take minimal time. Indeed the judge may have already decided that the case raises questions fit for appeal.
>
> (b) An application at this stage involves neither party in additional costs.
>
> (c) No harm is done if the application fails. The litigant enjoys two bites at the cherry.
>
> (d) If the application succeeds and the litigant subsequently decides to appeal, he avoids the expensive and time-consuming permission stage in the appeal court.
>
> (e) No harm is done if the application succeeds, but the litigant subsequently decides not to appeal.' (*White Book* 2010, paragraph 52.3.4).

Time for making an application for permission to appeal

5.9 If the decision of the First-tier Tribunal is given at a hearing, the application for permission to appeal should be made orally at that hearing. However, a written application must be made under the procedural rules, unless the Tribunal orders otherwise. For the purposes of making a written application for permission to appeal, time does not start to run until the latest of:

- The party's receipt of the Tribunal's written reasons for the decision;
- The party's receipt of amended reasons for a decision, or correction of the decision following a review;
- The party's receipt of notification that an application for the decision to be set aside has been unsuccessful.

GRC Rules, r 42(2); HESCC Rules, r 46(2); SEC Rules, r 38(3); TC Rules, r 39(2); WPAFCC Rules, r 36(2)). These rules do not apply to cases heard in the FTTIAC.

5.10 If, in proceedings before the Social Entitlement Chamber or the War Pensions and Armed Forces Compensation Chamber, a party applies for permission to appeal when the Tribunal has not given a written statement of reasons for its decision, the application for permission to appeal will be treated as an application for a written statement of reasons if no such application for a written statement has been made (see **Reasons**). Unless the Tribunal decides to give permission, the application is not to be treated as an application for permission to appeal. If however, an application for a written statement of reasons has been made and refused on grounds of delay, the Tribunal must only admit the application for permission if it considers that it is in the interests of justice to do so (SEC Rules, r 38(7); WPAFCC Rules, r 36(6)).

5.11 Following receipt of the above notifications, a written application for permission to appeal must be made and received by the First-tier Tribunal within the prescribed time limit. The time limits by Chamber are as follows:

- General Regulatory Chamber: 28 days
- Health, Education and Social Care Chamber: 28 days
- Social Entitlement Chamber: 1 month
- Tax Chamber: 56 days
- War Pensions and Armed Forces Compensation Chamber: 42 days
- Immigration and Asylum Chamber (in country appeals): 5 days
- Immigration and Asylum Chamber (out of country appeals): 28 days
- Immigration and Asylum Chamber (fast track appeals): 2 days

(GRC Rules, r 42(2); HESCC Rules, r 46(2); SEC Rules, r 38(3); TC Rules, r 39(2); WPAFCC Rules, r 36(2); IAC Rules, r 24(2)–(3); IAC (Fast Track) Rules, r 17(1)).

5.12 If an appeal is made out of time, the person seeking permission to appeal must include a request for an extension of time and state the reasons why the application was not provided in time. If the First-tier Tribunal does not extend the time for making the application under rule 5(3) of the relevant procedural rules it must not admit the application (GRC Rules, r 42(4); HESCC Rules, r 46(4); SEC Rules, r 38(5); TC Rules, r 39(4); WPAFCC Rules, r 36(4); IAC Rules, r 24(4)). It is self-evident from the foregoing that applications for leave to appeal should be made within the prescribed time limits, which are not ungenerous. The test for extension is, in the context of immigration and asylum cases, arguably broader than that under the Nationality, Immigration and Asylum Act 2002, s 103A(4)(b) which applied a 'reasonably practicable' test.

Content of an application for permission to appeal

5.13 An application for permission to appeal must:

- Identify the decision of the First-tier Tribunal to which it relates;
- Identify the alleged error or errors of law in the decision; and
- State the result the party making the application is seeking.

(GRC Rules, r 42(5); HESCC Rules, r 46(5); SEC Rules, r 38(6); TC Rules, r 39(5); WPAFCC Rules, r 36(5); IAC Rules, r 24(5))

GRANT OR REFUSAL OF PERMISSION TO APPEAL

Constitution of the First-tier Tribunal

5.14 The constitution of the First-tier Tribunal when determining whether or not an application for permission to appeal should be allowed varies according to the Chamber in which the case is being heard. This is dealt with in detail elsewhere in the Handbook (see **Constitution and composition of the First-tier Tribunal**). As a general principle, and save where it would be inexpedient, the Tribunal determining an application for permission will be constituted of one or more of the members or judges of the Tribunal that made the decision in respect of which permission to appeal is sought.

Power to treat the application as one for review

5.15 Upon receipt of an application for permission to appeal, the First-tier Tribunal is obliged to consider whether to review its decision. Regard must be had to whether this would be consistent with the overriding objective. If the Tribunal decides not to review the decision, or does so and takes no action, the Tribunal must then consider whether to give permission to appeal in relation to the decision or part of it (GRC Rules, r 43(1)–(2); HESCC Rules, r 47(1)–(2); SEC Rules, r 39(1)–(2); TC Rules, r 40(1)–(2); WPAFCC Rules, r 37(1)–(2); IAC Rules, r 25(1)–(2)) (see **Review, correction and setting aside of Tribunal decisions**).

The test to be applied on an application for permission

5.16 The test to be applied on an application to the First-tier Tribunal for permission to appeal its decision to the Upper Tribunal is not specified by statute. It is suggested here that the relevant criteria are those that typically apply to appeals within the courts system: is there a reasonable prospect of success on appeal and/or should the appeal be allowed for some other compelling reason.

5.17 These criteria have been said by the Court of Appeal to be 'clear-cut and easy to apply' (*CMA CGM SA v Beteiligungs-KG MS 'Northern Pioneer' Schiffahrtgesellschaft mbH & Co* [2002] EWCA Civ 1878, [2003] 1 WLR 1015 at [23]). This is not always the case; however, the broad principles are clear.

5.18 The meaning of 'some other compelling reason' is dealt with elsewhere in the Handbook (see **Appeals from the Upper Tribunal**). This entry will focus on the test of 'reasonable prospect of success'. In some cases this will be a simple criterion to apply: the First-tier Tribunal may be obviously right or obviously wrong. It may seem highly unlikely that the First-tier Tribunal would consider itself obviously wrong, however, the same test is to be applied by the Upper Tribunal which may well reach this view.

5.19 In other cases, the application of the test will be less clear; in particular where an application for permission is made orally and immediately following the Tribunal reaching or announcing its substantive decision.

5.20 In such a case, it is suggested that the test to be applied is akin to that applied in respect of an application for summary judgment: does the appellant have a real prospect of success? Indeed, the correct approach has been laid down by the Court of Appeal as follows:

'The Court will only refuse leave if satisfied that the applicant has no realistic prospect of succeeding on the appeal. This test is not meant to be any different from that which is sometimes used, which is that the applicant has no arguable case. Why however this court has decided to adopt the former phrase is because the use of the word "realistic" makes it clear that a fanciful prospect or an unrealistic argument is not sufficient'

(*Smith v Cosworth Casting Processes Ltd* [1997] 1 WLR 1538 per Lord Woolf MR; and see in the context of summary judgment *Swain v Hillman* [2001] 1 All ER 91, endorsed in the context of permission to appeal by Brooke LJ in *Tanfern Ltd v Cameron-MacDonald (Practice Note)* [2000] 1 WLR 1311 at [21]).

5.21 Finally, it should be noted that though 'some other compelling reason to appeal' does not encompass cases raising an important point of principle or practice in the context of appeals from the Upper Tribunal (see **Appeals from the Upper Tribunal**), this limitation should not apply in respect of applications for permission to the Upper Tribunal in the First-tier Tribunal and Upper Tribunal. It is suggested here that the First-tier Tribunal and Upper Tribunal are able to grant permission to appeal to the Upper Tribunal if a case involves an important point of principle or practice (see **Appeals from the Upper Tribunal; Guidance cases**) or if the Upper Tribunal is bound by authority that may be incorrectly decided in light of further developments and an appeal to the Upper Tribunal is needed in order that the case be considered by a higher court (see *Beedell v West Ferry Printers Ltd* [2001] EWCA Civ 400, [2001] ICR 962).

Grant or refusal of permission

5.22 The First-tier Tribunal must send a record of its decision on the permission application to the parties as soon as practicable (GRC Rules, r 43(3); HESCC Rules, r 47(3); SEC Rules, r 39(3); TC Rules, r 40(3); WPAFCC Rules, r 37(3)).

5.23 In immigration and asylum cases the Tribunal must make a decision within 10 days of receipt of the permission application (IAC Rules, r 25(3)). The procedure in an asylum case is that the Tribunal sends the decision documents to the Secretary of State, who must then serve them on the appellant within 28 days (IAC Rules, r 27(2)), with an obligation on the Tribunal to serve on the appellant if the Secretary of State fails to notify it of compliance (r 27(2)). In a fast track case the Tribunal must send the appellant its decision and reasons within one business day (IAC (Fast Track) Rules, r 18).

5.24 If the Tribunal refuses permission to appeal, it must send to the parties a statement of reasons for such refusal and notify the unsuccessful party of its right to apply to the Upper Tribunal for permission to appeal and the time within which and the method by which such an application must be made (GRC Rules, r 43(4); HESCC Rules, r 47(4); SEC Rules, r 39(4); TC Rules, r 40(4); WPAFCC Rules, r 37(4)) (see **Appeals and references to the Upper Tribunal**).

5.25 If the Tribunal grants permission to appeal, it may do so in respect of all or part of the decision, and may grant permission to appeal on limited grounds. However, if the Tribunal grants permission to appeal in respect of only part of a decision or grants permission on limited grounds, it must send to the parties a statement of reasons for refusing permission in respect of the remainder of the decision or for granting permission on limited grounds. The Tribunal must also notify the unsuccessful party of its right to apply to the Upper Tribunal for permission to appeal in respect of the remainder of the decision or the other grounds advanced before the First-tier Tribunal (GRC Rules, r 43(5); HESCC Rules, r 47(5); SEC Rules, r 39(5); TC Rules, r 40(5); WPAFCC Rules, r 37(5)).

ONWARD APPEALS – PRE- AND POST-TRANSFER

First-tier Tribunal

5.26 War Pensions and Armed Forces Compensation Chamber (established November 2008)

Tribunal	Previous onward appeal	New onward appeal	Basis of appeal to UT
Pension Appeals Tribunal (England and Wales)	Pensions Appeal Tribunal (War Pensions Administrative Provisions Act 1919, s 8(2))	Administrative Appeals Chamber (Upper Tribunal)	Point of law (right of appeal to UT extended to include appeal against assessment of award. Previous appeal only against entitlement decision with JR against assessment)

5.27 Health, Education and Social Care Chamber (established November 2008)

Tribunal	Previous onward appeal	New onward appeal	Basis of appeal to UT
Care Standards Tribunal (except appeals under Safeguarding Vulnerable Groups Act 2006, s 4)	High Court (Protection of Children Act 1999, s 9(6))	Administrative Appeals Chamber (Upper Tribunal)	Point of law
Mental Health Review Tribunals for England	No right of appeal; case stated procedure or judicial review by High Court	Administrative Appeals Chamber (Upper Tribunal)	Point of law
Special Educational Needs & Disability Tribunal	High Court (Tribunals and Inquiries Act 1992, s 11)	Administrative Appeals Chamber (Upper Tribunal)	Point of law
Family Health Services Appeals Authority	High Court (Tribunals and Inquiries Act 1992, s 11)	Administrative Appeals Chamber (Upper Tribunal)	Point of law

5.28 General Regulatory Chamber (established September 2009)

Tribunal	**Previous onward appeal**	**New onward appeal**	**Basis of appeal to UT**
Charity Tribunal	High Court (Charities Act 1993, s 2(c))	Tax and Chancery Chamber (Upper Tribunal)	Point of law
Consumer Credit Appeals Tribunal	Court of Appeal (Consumer Credit Act 1974, s 41A)	Administrative Appeals Chamber (Upper Tribunal)	Point of law
Estate Agents Appeals Panel	High Court (Estate Agents Act 1979, s 7)	Administrative Appeals Chamber (Upper Tribunal)	Point of law
Transport Tribunal (appeals against decisions of the Driving Standards Agency)	Court of Appeal (Transport Act 1985, Sch 4, para 14)	Administrative Appeals Chamber (Upper Tribunal)	Point of law
Gambling Appeals Tribunal – transfer date: Jan 2010	High Court (Gambling Act 2005, s 145)	Administrative Appeals Chamber (Upper Tribunal)	Point of law
Claims Management Services Tribunal – transfer date: Jan 2010	Court of Appeal (Compensation Act 2006, s 13)	Administrative Appeals Chamber (Upper Tribunal)	Point of law
Information Tribunal (except appeals against national security certificates) – transfer date: Jan 2010	High Court (Data Protection Act 1998, s 49)	Administrative Appeals Chamber (Upper Tribunal)	Point of law
Immigration Services Tribunal – transfer date: Jan 2010	No right of appeal; judicial review to the High Court	Administrative Appeals Chamber (Upper Tribunal)	Point of law
Adjudication Panel for England – transfer date: Jan 2010	High Court (Local Government Act 2000, ss 78 and 79)	Administrative Appeals Chamber (Upper Tribunal)	Point of law, and wider appeal rights for a person penalised by a decision

Note – Under Local Government Act 2000, ss 78 and 78B there is an appeal right on any grounds against a decision by an interim case tribunal drawn from the Adjudication Panel for England (see **Local authority standards cases**) to impose a suspension, or against the length of suspension, or against any adverse decision of a case tribunal. Once the jurisdiction has transferred into the First-tier Tribunal the breadth of available appeal rights have been maintained by retaining an appeal right against these matters on any grounds other than a point of law, in addition to the appeal right on a point of law at TCEA 2007, s 11.

5.29 Tax Chamber (established April 2009, at the same time as other changes to the tax appeals system by HMRC)

Tribunal	Previous onward appeal	New onward appeal	Basis of appeal to UT
General Commissioners of Income Tax Special Commissioners of Income Tax VAT & Duties Tribunals Section 706 Tribunal Section 704 Tribunal	High Court (Taxes Management Act 1970, s 56) (Taxes Management Act 1970, s 56) (Tribunals and Inquiries Act 1992, s 11) (Tribunals and Inquiries Act 1992, s 11)	Tax and Chancery Chamber (Upper Tribunal)	Point of law, and wider appeal rights against the amount of certain penalties

Note – Various pieces of tax legislation provide for penalties which can be appealed to the First-tier Tribunal (formerly the General or Special Commissioners). Unlike other cases in the tax jurisdiction these can only be dealt with by the First-tier Tribunal at first-instance; they cannot be transferred up to the Upper Tribunal if they are complex. There is, however, an appeal right to the Upper Tribunal against the amount of the penalty in addition to the normal s 11 appeal on a point of law. This is to maintain the breadth of the previous appeal right to the High Court against these penalties.

5.30 Social Entitlement Chamber (established November 2008)

Tribunal	Previous onward appeal	New onward appeal	Basis of appeal to UT
Social Security and Child Support Appeal Tribunals	Social Security/Child Support Commissioners (Social Security Act 1998, s 14/Child Support Act 1991, s 24)	Administrative Appeals Chamber (Upper Tribunal)	Point of law; Under the Tax Credit Act 2002,Sch 2, para 2(2) or 4(1) and Child Trust Funds Act 2004, s 21(10)
Criminal Injuries Compensation Panel	No right of appeal; judicial review by High Court	No right of appeal; judicial review by Administrative Appeals Chamber (Upper Tribunal)	Point of law
Asylum Support Tribunal	No right of appeal; judicial review by High Court	No right of appeal; judicial review by the High Court	Point of law

5.31 Appeals From The First-Tier Tribunal

5.31 Immigration & Asylum Chamber (established February 2010)

Tribunal	Previous onward appeal	New onward appeal	Basis of appeal to UT
Asylum and Immigration Tribunal	Reconsideration by AIT and review by High Court (Nationality, Immigration and Asylum Act 2002, s 103A)	Immigration & Asylum Chamber (Upper Tribunal)	Point of law

6 Appeals From The Upper Tribunal

RIGHT OF APPEAL FROM THE UPPER TRIBUNAL

The right of appeal

6.1 A party may appeal against an unfavourable decision of the Upper Tribunal to the Court of Appeal (or the Court of Session in Scotland). This right is set out in the TCEA 2007, s 13. By virtue of s 13(1) and (2), any party has a right of appeal on any point of law arising from a decision made by the Upper Tribunal (other than an excluded decision, on which see below).

6.2 The right of appeal may only be exercised with the permission of the Upper Tribunal or the appellate court (TCEA 2007, s 13(3), (4)).

The test for the grant of permission

6.3 Appeals from the Upper Tribunal lie on a point of law only. Further, TCEA 2007, s 13(6) empowers the Lord Chancellor to restrict appeals to the Court of Appeal to cases where:

- The proposed appeal would raise some important point of principle or practice; or
- There is some other compelling reason for the appeal to be heard.

This is a narrow test which equates appeals from the Upper Tribunal with second appeals from the High Court or county court (see Access to Justice Act 1999, s 55(1)).

6.4 The Lord Chancellor signalled his intention to exercise the power under TCEA 2007, s 13(6) as early as the publication of *Transforming Tribunals* (CP30/07, paragraph 178). Indeed, by virtue of the Appeals from the Upper Tribunal to the Court of Appeal Order 2008, SI 2008/2834 the Lord Chancellor exercised the power under TCEA 2007, s 13(6). The Order came into force on 3 November 2008 and by paragraph 2 provided that:

> Permission to appeal to the Court of Appeal in England and Wales or leave to appeal to the Court of Appeal in Northern Ireland shall not be granted unless the Upper Tribunal or, where the Upper Tribunal refuses permission, the relevant appellate court, considers that—
>
> (a) the proposed appeal would raise some important point of principle or practice; or
>
> (b) there is some other compelling reason for the relevant appellate court to hear the appeal.

6.5 It should be noted that the Order does not apply to appeals to the Court of Session. However, by virtue of Part XIV of the Scottish statutory instrument Act of Sederunt (Rules of the Court of Session Amendment No 5) (Miscellaneous) 2008, SI 2008/349, rule 41.59 aligns the position in Scotland in respect of appeals from the Upper Tribunal with that of the rest of the United Kingdom.

Restricting permission to appeal: the appellate court's resources and seniority

6.6 The reasoning behind restricting the grant of permission to appeal in respect of second appeals has been highlighted by the Court of Appeal in cases under CPR, r 52.13 (second appeals) as being to ensure the appropriate distribution of judicial resources and to recognise the appropriate position and seniority of the Court of Appeal in the judicial hierarchy. In the Court of Appeal *Practice Note Tanfern Ltd v Cameron-MacDonald* [2000] 1 WLR 1311, Brooke LJ for a unanimous court noted (at [44]) that: 'judges of the quality of Lords Justices of Appeal were a scarce and valuable resource, and that it was important that they were used effectively and only on work which was appropriate to them'. This was echoed in *Clark (Inspector of Taxes) v Perks* [2001] 1 WLR 17, in which the Court of Appeal stated (at [17]) that the second appeal rules were designed "to use the time and resources of the judges of the Court of Appeal, and of the lawyers and staff who support them, on matters which really merit the attention of a court of this stature in the judicial hierarchy.'

6.7 The emphasis of the Court of Appeal on its place within the judicial hierarchy is particularly important given the intent underlying the reforms to the tribunals system. The Upper Tribunal is intended to be an expert tribunal staffed by specialist judges in its subject-matter jurisdiction. The Court of Appeal is thus entitled to take a robust view as to the correctness of the Upper Tribunal's decisions and preserve the resources of the Court of Appeal (see the similar deference given to factual decisions of the Technology and Construction Court: *Skanska Construction UK Ld v Egger (Barony)* [2002] EWCA Civ 1914; *Yorkshire Water Services v Taylor Woodrow Construction Northern Ltd* [2005] EWCA Civ 894, [2005] BLR 395). As Carnwath LJ has noted (writing extra-judicially): 'If the Upper Tribunal is doing its job properly, its decisions should come to be regarded as sufficiently expert and authoritative for onward appeals to be rare, particularly given the hands-off approach advocated in recent House of Lords decisions.' ('Tribunal justice - a new start' [2009] PL 48, 68).

Deference to the Tribunal decision

6.8 There is a long line of authority now established that the appellate courts will show significant deference to the expertise of the decision-making tribunal both as the finder of fact and as the body with expertise in the relevant area of law. See, for example:

> '...This is an expert tribunal charged with administering a complex area of law in challenging circumstances. To paraphrase a view I have expressed about such expert tribunals in another context, the ordinary courts should approach appeals from them with an appropriate degree of caution; it is probable that in understanding and applying the law in their specialised field the tribunal will have got it right: see *Cooke v Secretary of State for Social Security* [2002] 3 All ER 279, para 16. They and they alone are the judges of the facts. It is not enough that their decision on those facts may seem harsh to people who have not heard and read the evidence and arguments which they have heard and read. Their decisions should be respected unless it is quite clear that they have misdirected themselves in law. Appellate courts should not rush to find such misdirections simply because they might have reached a different

conclusion on the facts or expressed themselves differently…':*AH (Sudan) v Secretary of State for the Home Department* [2007] UKHL 49, [2008] 1 AC 678 at [30] per Baroness Hale (asylum and immigration);

'It is also important that such appeal structures have a link to the ordinary court system, to maintain both their independence of government and the sponsoring department and their fidelity to the relevant general principles of law. But the ordinary courts should approach such cases with an appropriate degree of caution. It is quite probable that on a technical issue of understanding and applying the complex legislation the Social Security Commissioner will have got it right. The Commissioners will know how that particular issue fits into the broader picture of social security principles as a whole. They will be less likely to introduce distortion into those principles. They may be better placed, where it is appropriate, to apply those principles in a purposive construction of the legislation in question. They will also know the realities of tribunal life. All of this should be taken into account by an appellate court when considering whether an appeal will have a real prospect of success.': *Cooke v Secretary of State for Social Security* [2001] EWCA Civ 734, [2002] 3 All ER 279 at [16] per Hale LJ (social security).

And see also *Napp Pharmaceutical Holdings Limited v Director General of Fair Trading* [2002] EWCA Civ 796, [2002] 4 All ER 376; and *National Grid plc v Gas & Electricity Markets Authority* [2010] EWCA Civ 114 at [23]-[26] per Richards LJ (competition law); *Hooper v Secretary of State for Work and Pensions* [2007] EWCA Civ 495 at [40]-[41] per Dyson LJ; and *Hinchy v Secretary of State for Work and Pensions* [2005] UKHL 16, [2005] 1 WLR 967 at [30] per Lord Hoffmann (criticising, interestingly, a decision of Carnwath LJ for insufficient respect having been paid to the Social Security Commissioners) (social security).

6.9 Although the First-tier Tribunal and the Upper Tribunal are amalgamations of different specialist bodies, their division into Chambers means that they retain distinct expertise in particular areas of law. It is unlikely that the higher courts will be anything other than extremely slow to move away from the deference set down in the jurisprudence of Baroness Hale and others. However, deference will have to be earned. As one commentator has put it, 'the success of the Upper Tribunal as an authoritative and expert judicial body will be the key to the success of the Government's reforms': Radcliffe, 'The Tribunals Revolution' [2007] JR 197 at [37]. There is certainly no doubt that those involved in the system have every intention of seeing the Upper Tribunal maintain and develop the existing status. Carnwath LJ has, extra-judicially, ended an article ([2009] PL 48, 69) in the following way:

'Recent House of Lords case law points the way for the Upper Tribunal to assert the leading role in laying down guidelines on law, principle and practice, on issues peculiar to the specialist jurisdictions under its care. There is scope for rethinking the traditional allocation, as between courts and tribunals, of responsibilities for definitive interpretation of substantive law, including human rights law, in specialist fields.'

Meaning of important point of principle or practice

6.10 Appeals from the Upper Tribunal are on the same footing as second appeals from the courts to the Court of Appeal. In this respect, guidance as to when permission will be granted can be drawn from the cases in which the courts have had to apply the test set down in CPR, r 52.13.

6.11 The courts have adopted a narrow meaning of 'important point of principle or practice'. Indeed, this has typically been confined to an important point of principle or practice which has not yet been determined. As the Court of Appeal held in *Uphill v BRB (Residuary) Ltd* [2005] EWCA Civ 60, [2005] 1 WLR 2070 at [18] per Dyson LJ: '…it is clear that the reference … to "an important point of principle or practice" is to an important point of principle or practice that has not yet been established. The distinction must be maintained between (a) establishing and (b) applying an established principle or practice correctly…'. Thus permission will not be granted to appeal against a decision as to the application of a particular principle or practice, if the meaning and extent of that principle or practice has been established at Court of Appeal level or higher, even where the application of that principle appears to have been wrong.

Meaning of some other compelling reason

6.12 The Court of Appeal has adopted a robust attitude to the grant of permission in respect of second appeals even when faced with appeals which would appear to have a strong prospect of success. In *B (A Child)* [2009] EWCA Civ 545; [2009] 2 FLR 632, Wall LJ held (at [11]) that: 'Were either arguability or even a strong prospect of success to constitute a compelling reason for a second appeal, there would be no difference between first and second appeals, and the Statute would be deprived of its meaning and effect. … The strength of the case does not of itself provide a compelling reason to hear an appeal.'

6.13 Though not of itself determinative, the prospects of success are highly relevant and in *Uphill*, Dyson LJ (at [24]) held that the possibility of success was 'a good starting point'.

6.14 It is important to note that the Court of Appeal has (rightly) been reluctant to limit or prescribe those reasons which will be sufficiently compelling. Examples include:

- cases in which the 'complexity of the challenge to the judge's order is such that it cannot properly be examined without hearing a full appeal. Complexity of this order can in my judgment constitute a "compelling reason" for the grant of permission, including permission for a second appeal' (*esure Insurance Ltd v Direct Line Insurance plc* [2008] EWCA Civ 842, [2009] Bus LR 438 at [65] per Arden LJ);
- appeals concerning 'the effect of a decision relating to the welfare or future upbringing of a child' (*B (A Child)* at [14]);
- cases which may have a wide impact beyond their immediate facts (*Cramp v Hastings BC* [2005] EWCA Civ 1005, [2005] 4 All ER 1014, at [34] per Brooke LJ);
- cases involving a large amount of public money (*Cramp v Hastings BC*, at [66] per Brooke LJ); and
- cases in which the two lower courts have reached different conclusions (*B (A Child)* at [14], though expressed with some hesitation).

The inclusion from February 2010 of the Immigration and Asylum Chamber of the Upper Tribunal has meant that the restrictive test for onward appeals is now applicable to that category of case too. This is a significant change and a potentially much more restrictive one. It has been argued strongly by Sir Richard Buxton (extra-judicially on behalf of the Joint Council for the Welfare of Immigrants) that the application of s 13(6) to immigration and asylum cases will amount to a 'serious injustice'. He argues that good faith and good practice ought to prevent the government from withholding appeal rights, in particular, where a principle has been wrongly applied leading to a breach of the UK's international obligations under the Refugee Convention and the European Convention on Human Rights: 'Application of Section 13(6) of the Tribunals, Courts and Enforcement Act 2007 to Immigration Appeals from the Proposed Upper Tribunal' [2009] JR 225. It appears, however, that the government did not find this argument compelling. It will be for practitioners to convince the Court of Appeal that compliance with the UK's international obligations is a compelling reason for leave to appeal to be granted.

Excluded decisions

6.15 Appeals to the Court of Appeal (or Court of Session) against certain decisions of the Upper Tribunal are excluded under TCEA 2007, s 13(8) and Orders enacted by the Lord Chancellor thereunder. See **Excluded appeals**.

The relevant appellate court

6.16 As noted above, the relevant appellate court will differ depending on the jurisdiction in which the proceedings are located. TCEA 2007, s 13(11)–(13), specifies the relevant appellate court for an appeal from the Upper Tribunal, being the Court of Appeal in England and Wales, the Court of Session in Scotland, and the Court of Appeal in Northern Ireland.

6.17 By virtue of TCEA 2007, s 13(11), the Upper Tribunal must, before deciding any application made for permission to appeal, determine and specify which appellate court is the relevant court. The exercise of this function will typically be straightforward; however, s 13(11) is designed to deal with situation in which it is not obvious which is the appropriate appellate court. These will typically be where the appeal is in respect of linked cases which began in different locations or cases in which an appellant has moved (for example) from Scotland to England.

The relevant party

6.18 By virtue of TCEA 2007, s 13(14), the Lord Chancellor may specify who may or may not be treated as being a party to a case for the purposes of appealing a decision of the Upper Tribunal. At present, some rights of appeal under social security legislation to the Social Security and Child Support Commissioners are not limited to the claimant and the Secretary of State, but may include trade unions and claimants' spouses.

APPLICATIONS FOR PERMISSION TO APPEAL

The test to be applied on the application for permission to appeal

6.19 See above.

Procedure for applying for permission to appeal

6.20 An application for permission to appeal must be made in writing to the Upper Tribunal (Upper Tribunal Rules, r 44). The Rules do not apply to proceedings in the Lands Chamber (see **Lands Chamber procedural rules**), but the practical effect is precisely the same. An application for permission must be made to the Upper Tribunal (TCEA 2007, s 13(5)). This is important as an application to the Court of Appeal cannot be made without the party having first applied to the Upper Tribunal for permission. This is to be contrasted with appeals to the Upper Tribunal, as the Upper Tribunal can waive a failure first to apply to the First-tier Tribunal for permission (see **Appeals from the First-tier Tribunal** and **Failures to comply**).

6.21 By virtue of the Upper Tribunal Rules, r 44(7), the application must:

- identify the decision of the Upper Tribunal to which it relates;
- identify the alleged error or errors of law in the decision; and
- state the result the party making the application is seeking.

Given the test to be applied on an application for permission, the appellant should also state why the case is an appropriate one to be heard by a higher court and should specify the important point of practice or principle raised by the case and/or why it is said there is a compelling reason for allowing permission to appeal.

Time for applying for permission

6.22 The application must be received by the Upper Tribunal within one month of the latest of the date the Upper Tribunal sent the appellant (Upper Tribunal Rules, r 44(4)):

- written notice of the decision;
- notification of amended reasons for, or correction of, the decision following a review; or
- notification that an application for the decision to be set aside has been unsuccessful.

6.23 There is a three-month time limit for appeals against (Upper Tribunal Rules, r 44(2), (3)):

- a decision in a social security and child support case (as defined in the SEC Rules) (see **Social security and child support cases**);
- a decision in proceedings in the War Pensions and Armed Forces Compensation Chamber of the First-tier Tribunal (see **War Pensions and Armed Forces Compensation Chamber**);
- a decision of a Pensions Appeal Tribunal for Scotland or Northern Ireland;
- proceedings under the Forfeiture Act 1982 (see **Administrative Appeals Chamber**).

A financial services case carries a 14-day time limit (Upper Tribunal Rules, r 44(3D)).

6.24 An in-country immigration and asylum case carries a 12-day time limit (10 working days if notified electronically or in person) (Upper Tribunal Rules, r 44(3B)(a)(i) and (3C)(a)), unless the appellant is in detention, when the time limit is seven working days (five working days if notified electronically or in person) (Upper Tribunal Rules, r 44(3B)(a)(ii) and (3C)(b)).

6.25 A case arising from an immigration and asylum decision made in respect of a person outside of the UK carries a 38-day time limit (10 working days if notified electronically or in person) (Upper Tribunal Rules, r 44(3B)(b) and (3C)(c)).

6.26 To avoid any anomaly arising from the limits being 12 days or 10 working days (which could be significant over, for example, Christmas), Presidential Guidance No 1 of 2010 has been issued for the Immigration and Asylum Chamber instructing judges to treat applications made within 12 working days as cases in which a waiver should be made by the Tribunal.

6.27 If the application for appeal is made out of time, the application must include a request for an extension of time and state the reasons why the notice was not provided in time (Upper Tribunal Rules, r 44(6) (see **Extensions of time**).

6.28 Unless the Upper Tribunal extends time for the application under the Upper Tribunal Rules, r 5(3)(a) (power to extend time) the Upper Tribunal must refuse the application (Upper Tribunal Rules, r 44(6)(b)).

Upper Tribunal's consideration of application for permission to appeal

6.29 On receiving the application for permission, the Upper Tribunal may decide instead to review the decision in accordance with the Upper Tribunal Rules, r 46, but only if (Upper Tribunal Rules, r 45(1)):

- in making its decision the Upper Tribunal overlooked a legislative provision or binding authority which could have had a material effect on the decision; or
- since the decision was made a court has made a binding decision which could (had it been made prior to the decision) have had a material effect on the decision.

6.30 If the Upper Tribunal does not review the decision or reviews only part of it, it must then turn to consider whether to give permission to appeal in relation to all of part of the decision. The decision should be made promptly, and the Upper Tribunal must send a written record of its decision to the partiers as soon as practicable (Upper Tribunal Rules, r 45(2), (3)).

6.31 If permission to appeal is refused in whole or in part, the written decision must contain a statement of reasons and notify the appellant of its right to make an application for permission to appeal to the relevant appellate court (see above for meaning of 'relevant appellate court') and specify the time within which, and the method by which, such application must be made (Upper Tribunal Rules, r 45(4), (5)).

6.32 The procedure for onward appeals to the Court of Appeal will be governed by CPR Part 52. Therefore, unless the Upper Tribunal directs otherwise the application for permission to appeal must be made within 21 days of the Upper Tribunal's decision refusing permission to appeal in whole or in part (CPR r 52.4(2)). Parties should refer to the provision of Part 52 and the relevant practice direction for details of the procedural requirements for appellants and respondents in appeals to the Court of Appeal.

PROCEEDINGS ON APPEAL

6.33 By virtue of TCEA 2007, s 14 the relevant appellate court may, if it finds that the Upper Tribunal made an error of law, set aside the decision of the Upper Tribunal and either remit the case to the Upper Tribunal (or such other lower tribunal as is appropriate) or re-make the decision itself.

6.34 If the appellate court remits the case to the Upper Tribunal, it may give such directions as it thinks appropriate (including as to the composition of the panel to hear the remitted case). The Upper Tribunal may in turn remit the case to such other lower tribunal as is appropriate (TCEA 2007, s 14(3), (5), (6)).

6.35 If the appellate court determines that it should re-make the decision, it may make any decision which the Upper Tribunal (or the appropriate lower tribunal) itself could have made and make such findings of fact as it considers appropriate (TCEA 2007, s 14(4)).

Onward Appeals – pre and post transfer

Appeals from the Upper Tribunal

6.36 Administrative Appeals Chamber (established November 2008)

Tribunal	Previous onward appeal	New onward appeal	Basis of onward appeal
Social Security/Child Support Commissioners	Court of Appeal (Social Security Act 1998, s 15/ Child Support Act 1991, s 25)	Court of Appeal	Point of law
Care Standards Tribunal (appeals under Safeguarding Vulnerable Groups Act 2006, s 4)	Court of Appeal (Safeguarding Vulnerable Groups Act 2006, s 4)	Court of Appeal	Point of law
Transport Tribunal (appeals against decisions of Traffic Commissioners)	Court of Appeal (Transport Act 1985, Sch 4, para 14)	Court of Appeal	Law and fact
Information Tribunal - appeals against national security certificates under the Data Protection Act 1998, s 28, and the Freedom of Information Act 2000, s 60 – transfer date: Jan 10	No onward appeal	No onward appeal (excluded decision under TCEA 2007, s 13(8))	N/A

Note - Appeals to the Upper Tribunal from Traffic Commissioners' decisions may be made on points of law and fact. This replicates the appeal rights when the appeals were dealt with by the Transport Tribunal

6.37 Tax and Chancery Chamber (established April 2009)

Tribunal	Previous onward appeal	New onward appeal	Basis of onward appeal
Financial Services & Markets Tribunal	Court of Appeal (Financial Services & Markets Act 2000, s 137)	Court of Appeal	Point of law
Pensions Regulator Tribunal	Court of Appeal (Pensions Act 2004, s 104)	Court of Appeal	Point of law

6.38 Lands Chamber (established April 2009)

Tribunal	Previous onward appeal	New onward appeal	Basis of onward appeal
Lands Tribunal	Court of Appeal (s 3(4) Lands Tribunal Act 1949)	Court of Appeal	Point of law

Note on Lands Chamber:

The Lands Chamber has taken on the functions of the former Lands Tribunal only. The Chamber deals with a mixture of first instance and onward appeals. All appeals from the Chamber are on point of law only (no change from pre-transfer). Some appeals to the Chamber from the Valuation and Leasehold Valuation Tribunals are not restricted to points of law and may be brought on fact and law as many of the issues are valuation questions.

6.39 Immigration & Asylum Chamber (established February 2010)

Tribunal	Previous onward appeal	New onward appeal	Basis of onward appeal
Asylum and Immigration Tribunal – reconsiderations	Court of Appeal (Nationality, Immigration and Asylum Act 2002, s 103B)	Court of Appeal	Point of law

7 Arbitration

7.1 The TCEA 2007, Sch 5, para 14 provides for the making of procedural rules in respect of the applicability of arbitration to proceedings before the First-tier Tribunal and Upper-Tribunal. In particular, TCEA 2007 states that rules can be made providing for Part 1 of the Arbitration Act 1996 not to apply in proceedings before the First-tier Tribunal and Upper Tribunal, save insofar as the First-tier Tribunal or Upper Tribunal acts as the arbitrator.

7.2 In line with TCEA 2007, Sch 5, para 14, the procedural rules for the Chambers of the First-tier Tribunal and Upper Tribunal specify that Part 1 of the Arbitration Act is to be disapplied.

7.3 This provision is found at rule 3(2) of the relevant procedural rules (with the exception of the IAC Rules and the Lands Chamber Rules) and simply states: 'Part 1 of the Arbitration Act 1996 does not apply to proceedings before the Tribunal'.

7.4 The effect of the above is that any arbitration agreement between the relevant parties to a dispute will not be binding and operative upon the parties in so far as proceedings before the First-tier Tribunal or Upper Tribunal are concerned.

7.5 Given that the vast majority of proceedings before the First-tier Tribunal and Upper Tribunal involve non-commercial claims between private parties and state parties, the existence of an arbitration agreement between the parties is in any event unlikely. However, as a result of the exclusion of arbitration by the relevant procedural rules, a party will not be in breach of any such agreement by commencing proceedings before the First-tier Tribunal or Upper Tribunal. Likewise, the First-tier Tribunal and Upper Tribunal are under no obligation to stay proceedings (as would be a court under the Arbitration Act 1996, s 9) on the application of a party alleging that a dispute within the relevant tribunal's jurisdiction should proceed to arbitration.

7.6 In the event that parties are subject to an otherwise relevant arbitration clause and wish to resolve their dispute outside of the tribunals system, the parties should consider making an application to the relevant tribunal for a stay to pursue mediation or alternative dispute resolution (see **Alternative Dispute Resolution**).

7.7 Uniquely, the Lands Chamber may act as an arbitrator under the Lands Tribunal Act 1949, s 1(5). This will arise where parties have contractually agreed to use the Lands Chamber as a form of dispute resolution, and those disputes will usually involve valuation of land, but not necessarily so. The Lands Chamber must agree to accept the reference. The Lands Chamber Rules apply certain provisions of the Arbitration Act 1996 to these proceedings (Lands Chamber Rules, r 26), namely s 8 (whether agreement discharged by death of a party); s 9 (stay of legal proceedings); s 10 (reference of interpleader issue to arbitration); s 12 (power of court to extend time for beginning arbitral proceedings, etc.); s 23 (revocation of arbitrator's authority); s 57 (correction of award or additional award) in so far as it relates to costs and so that the reference to 'award' shall include a reference to any decision of the Tribunal;

and s 60 (agreement to pay costs in any event). Any person making a reference to the Lands Chamber shall supply the relevant agreement containing the arbitration clause (r 26A).

8 Assessors

See also **Evidence; Experts**

APPOINTMENT OF AN ASSESSOR

8.1 Assessors are a form of expert, appointed by a Tribunal to assist it with those parts of proceedings in respect of which specialist expertise is required.

8.2 The TCEA 2007, s 28(1) empowers the First-tier Tribunal and Upper Tribunal to appoint an assessor in certain circumstances. It provides that:

- If it appears to the First-tier Tribunal or the Upper Tribunal that a matter before it requires special expertise not otherwise available to it, it may direct that in dealing with that matter it shall have the assistance of a person or persons appearing to it to have relevant knowledge or experience.
- The Lord Chancellor may establish panels of persons deemed suitable to be assessors, though the Tribunal need not invariably select from these panels (TCEA 2007, s 28(3)).

8.3 Given the wide subject matter jurisdiction of the First-tier Tribunal, there will be many cases in which the Tribunal may conceivably consider having recourse to an assessor in particular in medical, social security and land valuation contexts. However, similar comments were made following the suggestion by Lord Woolf in his Access to Justice report that more use might be made of expert assessors beyond the traditional use in Admiralty and patents proceedings (*Access to Justice: Final Report*, paragraphs 13.58–13.60). No significant observable expansion of the use of assessors has been noted following the enactment of the CPR (see Dwyer, 'The Future of Assessors Under the CPR' [2006] CJQ 219).

The role of an assessor

8.4 The assessor's principal role is to help the Tribunal to understand:

- the effect and meaning of technical evidence within the assessor's area of specialism; and
- the balance of the evidence in light of the technical evidence within the assessor's area of specialism.

8.5 The assessor's role need not be a passive one. That is to say, an assessor is not required to sit back and wait to be consulted by the Tribunal. He or she 'may, in proper cases, suggest to the [Tribunal] questions which the [Tribunal] might [itself] put to an expert witness with a view to testing the witness's view or to making plain his meaning.': *Richardson v Redpath Brown and Co Ltd* [1944] AC 62, 70 per Viscount Simon LC. Similarly, an assessor may suggest relevant facts that the Tribunal should investigate further.

8.6 The role of an assessor must be distinguished from that of an expert witness, including a single joint expert (on which see **Experts**). The difference is a fundamental one: an assessor does not give evidence (*R v Deputy Industrial*

Injuries Commissioner, ex p Jones [1962] 2 QB 677, 689); he or she merely helps the Tribunal understand the evidence that has been given. As a corollary, an assessor is not sworn and there is no right to question an assessor (though it is suggested here that the Tribunal may in its discretion permit such questioning to take place).

8.7 The assessor's role must also be distinguished from that of the Tribunal itself. Though it can be said that the assessor is part of the Tribunal (Dwyer, p 220), or at least that he or she has a judicial role (*The White Book 2010*, paragraph 35.15.4), this is not entirely clear on the authorities (and for a different view see Jacobs, *Tribunal Practice and Procedure*, paragraph 8.72, citing *R(I) 14/51*). The best answer at present is probably that an assessor is not part of the Tribunal, at least in the normal sense. Indeed, the assessor has no right to be privy to the Tribunal's deliberations (*R(I) 14/51*, at [7]). Whether strictly speaking an assessor is part of the Tribunal or not , it is clear that they 'take no part in the judgment whatever; they are not responsible for it, and have nothing to do with it': *The Beryl* [1884] PD 137, 141, per Brett MR. For this reason, the Tribunal must take care that it does not place undue weight on the assessor's advice when reaching its decision and must itself independently assess all the evidence in light of the assessor's advice (see for example, *Owners of SS Australia v Owners of Cargo of SS Nautilus* [1927] AC 145).

Procedural considerations

8.8 It is consistent with natural justice that the parties are able to make submissions as to those points in respect of which the Tribunal might benefit from the assistance of the assessor's advice. The Tribunal should be mindful of adopting a procedure that maximises the opportunity for the assessor to assist the Tribunal.

8.9 With this in mind, it is perhaps self-evident that the assessor should be present at any oral hearing that takes place (*ex p Jones* at 687). If there is only a paper hearing, the assessor must have access to all the relevant documents and evidence in order that he or she can advise the Tribunal adequately (*ex p Jones* at 686).

8.10 It is equally consistent with natural justice that the advice given by an assessor is made available to the parties in order that they can make appropriate submissions upon it (*Watson v General Medical Council* [2005] EWHC 1896 (Admin), [2006] ICR 113; *The Global Mariner v Atlantic Crusader* [2005] EWHC 380 (Admlty), [2005] 1 Lloyd's Rep 699 at [66]–[68] per Gross J). However, it is not invariably the case that an assessor's advice must be disclosed to the parties (see for example *Ahmed v Governing Body of the University of Oxford* [2002] EWCA Civ 1907, [2003] 1 WLR 995). As a rule of thumb, if the Tribunal is to be directed on the law, this should be given in open court; if the advice tends towards or is in the nature of expert evidence it should normally be disclosed to the parties; where a corporate judicial decision is made, the detail of the discussion should normally remain confidential (*Ahmed v Governing Body of the University of Oxford* [2002] EWCA Civ 1907; [2003] 1 WLR 995, at [33]). The authority cited for this final category of corporate judicial decisions by the Court of Appeal in *Ahmed* is *Roylance v General Medical Council* [2000] 1 AC 311. However, Roylance did not involve an assessor at all and was about the confidentiality of discussions of a regulatory decision-making panel during its decision-making process in the context of a bias challenge. It may be that the third category set out in *Ahmed* will need revisiting, but in principle it is difficult to see why the judicial decision-making process should not remain confidential.

9 Asylum Support Appeals

See also **Social Entitlement Chamber; Social Entitlement Chamber procedural rules**

ASYLUM SUPPORT APPEALS IN THE FIRST-TIER TRIBUNAL

9.1 The First–tier Tribunal (Asylum Support) was set up to consider appeals from decisions made by the United Kingdom Border Agency, ('UKBA') under the provisions for support arrangements for asylum seekers and their dependants contained in the Immigration and Asylum Act 1999.

9.2 UKBA considers whether an applicant meets the test of 'destitution' and determines to what extent support should be provided. This support includes, for example, the provision of accommodation and cash for essential needs. If UKBA refuses to provide support or decides to stop or withdraw existing support, an asylum seeker can appeal to the First-tier Tribunal against its decision.

9.3 Since 3 November 2008, asylum support appeals have fallen within the jurisdiction of the Social Entitlement Chamber (see **Social Entitlement Chamber**). The SEC Rules define asylum support cases as being:

> '...proceedings concerning the provision of support for an asylum seeker, a failed asylum seeker or a person designated under section 130 of the Criminal Justice and Immigration Act 2008 (designation), or the dependents of any such person'.

9.4 Section 130 of the Criminal Justice and Immigration Act 2008 deals with the designation of foreign criminals who are liable to deportation but cannot be removed as to do so would be in contravention of that person's human rights and the designation of dependents of such foreign criminals.

9.5 The SEC does not deal with asylum claims or any other immigration matters. It only considers asylum support appeals, that is to say, appeals against a refusal or a termination of support made by the UKBA.

PROCEDURE IN ASYLUM SUPPORT APPEALS

9.6 The procedure in asylum support appeals follows that set out in the SEC Rules and is set out elsewhere in this Handbook (see **Social Entitlement Chamber procedural rules**). This entry will deal with those provisions of the SEC Rules that apply differently in asylum support appeals than in other cases before the SEC. In particular, parties should note the expedited manner with which asylum support appeals are dealt. This substantially reduces the time for appeal and response from those applicable in other SEC cases.

Notice of appeal

9.7 In asylum support cases, the appellant must start proceedings by sending or delivering a notice of appeal to the SEC.

9.8 Appellants and their representatives should note the stringent time limit for appealing a decision of the UKBA: the notice of appeal must be received by the within 3 days after the date on which the appellant received written notice of the decision being challenged (SEC Rules, r 22(1)). The notice of appeal must be on the approved form, which is provided on the Tribunal's website: *Practice Direction, First-tier Tribunal, Social Entitlement Chamber, Asylum Support Cases* (30 October 2008) at paragraph 3.

9.9 Where the notice of appeal is sent by first class post it is taken to have been received two working days (as defined in SEC Rules, r 12(3), ie, not including Saturdays and Sundays etc) after the day on which it was sent: *Practice Direction* at paragraphs 2 and 4. This application of 'working days' is not applied to responses from UKBA, which must be within three days.

9.10 The notice of appeal should contain the usual information (see SEC Rules, r 22 and **Social Entitlement Chamber procedural rules**). In addition, in asylum support cases, the notice of appeal must also:

- state whether the appellant will require an interpreter at any hearing, and specify the language or dialect required; and
- state whether the appellant intends to attend or be represented at any hearing.

9.11 In accordance with the expedited nature of asylum support appeals, the SEC must send a copy of the notice of appeal and accompanying documents to each other party on the day that it receives the notice of appeal or as soon as reasonably practicable on the following day (see SEC Rules, r 22(7)(a)).

UKBA's response

9.12 When UKBA receives the notice of appeal from the SEC in an asylum support case, it must provide a written response to the SEC within three days after the date on which the SEC received the notice of appeal (SEC Rules, r 24(1)(a)).

9.13 The time limit for responding starts to run from the time at which the SEC receives the notice of appeal and not from the time at which the decision-maker receives the notice of appeal. As the SEC need not necessarily send the notice of appeal to the UKBA until the day after it is received, the three day time limit will frequently be a two day time limit.

Calculation of time

9.14 In order to mitigate the potential harshness of the expedited timetable in asylum support cases, the SEC Rules do not prescribe that any act to be done on a particular day be done by 5pm on that day as is typically the case (SEC Rules, r 12). It appears that, for example, a response from UKBA that is received before midnight on the day three days after the date on which the SEC received the notice of appeal will be within time for the purpose of the SEC Rules.

Notice of hearings

9.15 In asylum support cases, the SEC must give notice of a hearing to the parties of at least one day, and not more than five days (SEC Rules, r 29(2)(a)). It appears that the SEC retains a residual discretion in asylum support cases to give shorter notice with the consent of the parties or in urgent or exceptional cases (SEC Rules, r 29(2)(b)). However, it is difficult to envisage circumstances in which this discretion could be exercised in asylum support cases. Hearings at less than one day's notice are unlikely to be practical or produce satisfactory outcomes in many cases.

Notice of decisions

9.16 In asylum support cases, the SEC must give its decision orally at a hearing or send a decision notice to the parties on the day that the decision is made (SEC Rules, r 33(3)).

Appeal and review of SEC decisions in asylum support cases

9.17 It is important for appellants and advocates to note that there is no right of appeal to the Upper Tribunal in asylum support cases (SEC Rules, r 38(1); and see the Appeals (Excluded Decisions) Order 2009, SI 2009/275 at paragraph 2). However, the decisions of the SEC in asylum support cases are subject to judicial review in the High Court. The exclusion of asylum support cases from the jurisdiction of the Upper Tribunal makes no practical sense, and it is to be hoped that the anomaly will be corrected.

9.18 As a corollary of there being no right of onward appeal, parties are unable to apply to the SEC for review of its decision in asylum support cases (SEC Rules, r 40(1)).

Composition of the Tribunal in asylum support cases

9.19 All asylum support cases before the SEC must be decided by one judge (*Practice Statement, Composition of tribunals in relation to matters that fall to be decided in asylum support cases in the Social Entitlement Chamber on or after 3 November 2008*, 30 October 2008, paragraph 3).

10 Bringing Proceedings In The First-Tier Tribunals

FIRST-TIER TRIBUNAL – TYPES OF PROCEEDINGS

10.1 There are a number of different types of proceedings in the First-tier Tribunals (see **First-tier Tribunal**) and the method of bringing those proceedings will differ according to the nature of the proceedings and the particular Chamber in which the proceedings are being brought (see, respectively, **Chambers; General Regulatory Chamber; Health, Education And Social Care Chamber; Immigration and Asylum Chamber (First-tier Tribunal); Social Entitlement Chamber; Tax Chamber**, and **War Pensions And Armed Forces Compensation Chamber**).

10.2 In outline, there are many different types of proceedings which have to be brought in a particular way in the First-tier Tribunals. These are currently:

- Appeals in the GRC (other than charities cases).
- Appeals in the GRC in charities cases.
- Applications for leave in the HESCC (except for mental health cases).
- Applications which do not require leave in the HESCC (except for mental health cases).
- Applications and references in mental health cases in the HESCC.
- Appeals in the IAC.
- Fast-track appeals in the IAC.
- Appeals in the SEC.
- Applications and appeals in the TC.
- Appeals in the WPAFCC.

Appeals in the General Regulatory Chamber (other than charities cases)

10.3 Under the GRC Rules, r 22(1)(b) an appellant must start proceedings by sending or delivering an notice of appeal to the Tribunal so that it is received within 28 days after notice of the act or decision to which the proceedings relate was sent to the appellant.

10.4 Different time limits (see **Time limits**) are applied by r 22(6) to the following types of case in the GRC:

(a) in an appeal against a refusal or revocation of a licence to give driving instruction, within 14 days of the date on which notice of the decision was sent to the appellant;

(b) in an appeal under the Data Protection Act 1998, s 28(4) or the Freedom of Information Act 2000, s 60(1) (including that subsection as applied and modified by regulation 18 of the Environmental Information Regulations 2004), at any time during the currency of the disputed certificate to which it relates;

(c) in an appeal under the Data Protection Act 1998, s 28(6) or the Freedom of Information Act 2000, s 60(4) (including that subsection as applied and modified by Environmental Information Regulations 2004, SI 2004/3391 reg 14), within 28 days of the date on which the claim was made that the certificate applies to the information or data in question;

(d) in the case of a reference from an ethical standards officer made in accordance with the Local Government Act 2000, ss 63(3)(b) or 65(4), within 28 days of the completion of the report made in accordance with ss 63(3)(a) and 65(1) of that Act; or

(e) in the case of a reference from a Standards Committee under the Local Government Act 2000 within 28 days of the meeting which decided to make such a reference.

10.5 The notice of appeal must (see GRC Rules, r 22(2)) include the following details:

(a) the name and address of the appellant;

(b) the name and address of the appellant's representative (if any);

(c) an address where documents for the appellant may be sent or delivered;

(d) the name and address of any respondent;

(e) details of the decision or act, or failure to decide or act, to which the proceedings relate;

(f) the result the appellant is seeking;

(g) the grounds on which the appellant relies; and

(h) any further information or documents required by an applicable practice direction.

10.6 In addition, the appellant must send with the notice of appeal a copy of any written record of any decision under challenge, and any statement of reasons for that decision that the appellant has or can reasonably obtain (GRC Rules, r 22(3)).

10.7 If (GRC Rules, r 22(4)) the appellant provides the notice of appeal to the Tribunal later than the time required by the rules or later than any extension of time granted by the Tribunal (see **Extensions of time**) then:

(a) the notice of appeal must include a request for an extension of time and the reason why the notice of appeal was not provided in time; and

(b) unless the Tribunal extends time for the notice of appeal the Tribunal has no power to admit the notice of appeal.

10.8 When the Tribunal receives the notice of appeal it will – other than in national security cases covered by GRC Rules, r 19(2) – send a copy of the notice of appeal and any accompanying documents to each other party (GRC Rules, r 22(5)).

The notice of appeal form is available from the Tribunal's website.

Appeals in the General Regulatory Chamber in charities cases

10.9 A charities case means an appeal or application in respect of a decision, order or direction of the Charity Commission, or a reference under the Charities Act 1993, Sch 1D (GRC Rules, r 1(3)).

10.10 Under r 26(1) GRC Rules an appellant must start any other proceedings by sending or delivering an notice of appeal to the Tribunal so that it is received:

(a) if the appellant was the subject of the decision to which the proceedings relate, within 42 days of the date on which notice of the decision was sent to the appellant; or

(b) if the appellant was not the subject of the decision to which the proceedings relate, within 42 days of the date on which the decision was published.

10.11 The notice of appeal must (see GRC Rules, r 26(2)) include the following details:

(a) the name and address of the appellant;

(b) the name and address of the appellant's representative (if any);

(c) an address where documents for the appellant may be sent or delivered;

(d) the basis on which the appellant has standing to start proceedings before the Tribunal;

(e) the name and address of any respondent;

(f) details of the decision or act, or failure to decide or act, to which the proceedings relate;

(g) the result the appellant is seeking;

(h) the grounds on which the appellant relies; and

(i) any further information or documents required by an applicable practice direction.

10.12 In addition, the appellant must send with the notice of appeal a copy of any written record of any decision under challenge, and any statement of reasons for that decision that the appellant has or can reasonably obtain (GRC Rules, r 26(3)).

10.13 If (GRC Rules, r 26(5)) the appellant provides the notice of appeal to the Tribunal later than the time required by the rules or later than any extension of time granted by the Tribunal (see **Extensions of time**) then:

(a) the notice of appeal must include a request for an extension of time and the reason why the notice of appeal was not provided in time; and

(b) unless the Tribunal extends time for the notice of appeal the Tribunal has no power to admit the notice of appeal.

10.14 The appellant must send or deliver a copy of the notice of appeal and any accompanying documents to the respondent at the same time as it provides the notice of appeal to the Tribunal (GRC Rules, r 26(6)).

10.15 If the notice of appeal relates to a reference under the Charities Act 1993, Sch 1D (GRC Rules, r 26(4)):

(a) if the appellant is the Charity Commission, it must send evidence of the Attorney General's consent to the reference with the notice of appeal; and

(b) on receiving the notice of appeal the Tribunal must publish details of the reference and information as to how a person likely to be affected by the reference can apply to be added as a party to the proceedings.

The notice of appeal form is available from the Tribunal's website.

Applications for leave other than mental health cases in the HESCC

10.16 Applications for leave in certain classes of case (see Tribunal Procedure (First-tier Tribunal) (Health, Education and Social Care Chamber) Rules 2008 ('HESCC Rules'), r 19(1)) must give full reasons must why the applicant considers that the Tribunal should give leave (see HESCC Rules, r 19(2)(a)). The classes of case (which are currently all in respect of the HESCC's social care jurisdiction) to which this requirement applies are applications under (respectively):

(a) the Protection of Children Act 1999, s 4(1)(b) (appeal against a decision not to remove the applicant from the list kept under s 1 of that Act);

(b) the Protection of Children Act 1999, s 4(2) (application to have the issue of the applicant's inclusion in the list kept under s 1 of that Act determined by the Tribunal);

(c) the Care Standards Act 2000, s 86(1)(b) (appeal against a decision not to remove the applicant from the list kept under s 81 of that Act);

(d) the Care Standards Act 2000, s 86(2) (application to have the issue of the applicant's inclusion in the list kept under s 81 of that Act determined by the Tribunal); and

(e) the Criminal Justice and Court Services Act 2000, s 32 (application to have the issue of the continuation of a disqualification order determined by the Tribunal).

10.17 The form used is the same application notice as for other social care applications in the HESCC which do not require leave (but which also has a statement of reasons section for these types of applications). In addition, the time limits for bringing these proceedings are governed by the same provisions (see below and **Time limits**).

10.18 Once the application has been lodged, the Tribunal will consider it and (unless it gives directions under HESCC Rules, r 19(3)) communicate its decision. If leave is granted then the Tribunal will give directions as to the future conduct of the proceedings (HESCC Rules, r 19(4)).

Applications which do not require leave (other than mental health cases) in the HESCC

10.19 Under HESCC Rules, r 20(1) an applicant must start any other proceedings (other than mental health) before this arm of the Tribunal by sending or delivering an application notice to the Tribunal so that it is received—

(a) if a specific time for providing the application notice is specified in the Schedule to HESCC Rules (see **Time limits**) within that time; or

(b) otherwise within 28 days after notice of the act or decision to which the proceedings relate was sent to the applicant.

This requirement applies generally to care standards and special educational needs cases as do the provisions set out immediately below.

10.20 The application notice must (see HESCC Rules, r 20(2)) be signed by the applicant and must include the following details:

(a) the name and address of the applicant;

(b) the name and address of the applicant's representative (if any);

(c) an address where documents for the applicant may be sent or delivered;

(d) the name and address of any respondent;

(e) details of the decision or act, or failure to decide or act, to which the proceedings relate;

(f) the result the applicant is seeking;

(g) the grounds on which the applicant relies; and

(h) any further information or documents required by an applicable practice direction.

10.21 In addition, the applicant must (see HESCC Rules, r 20(3)) send with the application notice a copy of any written record of any decision under challenge, and any statement of reasons for that decision that the applicant has or can reasonably obtain.

10.22 If (HESCC Rules, r 20(4)) the applicant provides the application notice to the Tribunal later than the time required by the rules or later than any extension of time granted by the Tribunal (see **Extensions of time**) then:

(a) the application notice must include a request for an extension of time and the reason why the application notice was not provided in time; and

(b) unless the Tribunal extends time for the application notice the Tribunal has no power to admit the application notice.

10.23 In proceedings under Suspension Regulations in care standards cases (see HESCC Rules, r 20(5)) the applicant must send or deliver a copy of the application notice and any accompanying documents to the respondent at the same time as it provides the application notice to the Tribunal.

10.24 However, in all other proceedings than suspension proceedings, when the Tribunal receives the application notice it will (see HESCC Rules, r 20(6)) send a copy of the application notice and any accompanying documents to each other party.

10.25 Specially designed notices of application have been drafted for the two different types of tribunal (Care Standards and Special Educational Needs and Disability) to which these requirements apply and which are available from the Tribunal's website.

Applications and references in mental health cases in the HESCC

10.26 In mental health cases proceedings are commenced by application or reference in the HESCC which replaces the former mental health review tribunals (see

Mental health cases).

10.27 By HESCC Rules, r 32(1) an application or reference must be—

(a) made in writing;

(b) signed (in the case of an application, by the applicant or any person authorised by the applicant to do so); and

(c) sent or delivered to the Tribunal so that it is received within the time specified in the Mental Health Act 1983 or the Repatriation of Prisoners Act 1984 (see **Time limits**).

10.28 If possible (see HESCC Rules, r 32(2)) an application must include—

(a) the name and address of the patient;

(b) if the application is made by the patient's nearest relative, the name, address and relationship to the patient of the patient's nearest relative;

(c) the provision under which the patient is detained, liable to be detained, subject to guardianship, a community patient or subject to after-care under supervision;

(d) whether the person making the application has appointed a representative or intends to do so, and the name and address of any representative appointed;

(e) the name and address of the responsible authority in relation to the patient.

10.29 Subject to the power in HESCC Rules, r 14(2) to withhold evidence likely to cause harm (see **Mental health cases**) when the Tribunal receives a document from any party it must send a copy of that document to each other party (HESCC Rules, r 32(3)).

10.30 If the patient is a conditionally discharged patient (as defined in the Mental Health Act 1983) the Secretary of State must send or deliver a statement containing the information and documents required by the relevant practice direction to the Tribunal so that it is received by the Tribunal as soon as practicable and in any event within six weeks after the Secretary of State received a copy of the application or a request from the Tribunal (HESCC Rules, r 32(4)).

10.31 In proceedings under the Mental Health Act 1983, s 66(1)(a) (application for admission for assessment), on the earlier of receipt of the copy of the application or a request from the Tribunal, the responsible authority must (see HESCC Rules, r 32(6)) send or deliver to the Tribunal—

(a) the application for admission;

(b) the medical recommendations on which the application is founded;

(c) such of the information specified in the relevant practice direction as is within the knowledge of the responsible authority and can reasonably be provided in the time available; and

(d) such of the documents specified in the relevant practice direction as can reasonably be provided in the time available.

10.32 Otherwise (see HESCC Rules, r 32(6)) the responsible authority must send or deliver a statement containing the information and documents required by the relevant practice direction to the Tribunal so that it is received by the Tribunal as soon as practicable and in any event within three weeks after the responsible authority received a copy of the application or reference. If the patient is a restricted patient the responsible authority must (see HESCC Rules, r 32(7)) also send the statement to the Secretary of State, and the Secretary of State must send a statement of any further relevant information to the Tribunal as soon as practicable and in any event—

(a) in proceedings under the Mental Health Act 1983, s 75(1), within two weeks after the Secretary of State received the relevant authority's statement; or

(b) otherwise, within three weeks after the Secretary of State received the relevant authority's statement.

10.33 By HESCC Rules, r 32(8) if the Secretary of State wishes to seek the approval of the Tribunal under the Mental Health Act 1983, s 86(3), the Secretary of State must refer the patient's case to the Tribunal and the provisions of the HESCC Rules applicable to references under the 1983 Act apply to such proceedings.

10.34 By HESCC Rules, r 33 when the Tribunal receives the stipulated information it must give notice of the proceedings—

(a) where the patient is subject to the guardianship of a private guardian, to the guardian;

(b) where there is an extant order of the Court of Protection, to that court;

(c) subject to a patient with capacity to do so requesting otherwise, where any person other than the applicant is named by the authority as exercising the functions of the nearest relative, to that person;

(d) where a health authority, Primary Care Trust, National Health Service trust or NHS foundation trust has a right to discharge the patient under the provisions of the Mental Health Act 1983, s 23(3), to that authority or trust; and

(e) to any other person who, in the opinion of the Tribunal, should have an opportunity of being heard.

10.35 Before the hearing there must be a medical examination (see **Mental health cases**).

10.36 A specially designed notice of application has been drafted for use in mental health cases which is available from the Tribunal's website.

Appeals in the FTTIAC

10.37 An appeal to the Tribunal must be filed by delivery by post, via a document exchange service, by fax or by email under Asylum and Immigration Tribunal (Procedure) Rules 2005 ('IAC Rules'), r 55 (IAC Rules, r 6(2)).

10.38 An appellant who is in detention under the Immigration Acts, or a person who has been the subject of a decision whilst out of the UK, may file a notice of appeal under IAC Rules, r 55 or by serving it personally the person having custody of him, or the entry clearance officer, respectively (IAC Rules, r 6(3),(4)). The custodian must forward on the notice of appeal to the

Tribunal within two days having endorsed the date of service on him (IAC Rules, r 6(5)). The entry clearance officer must do likewise, forwarding on the notice of appeal as soon as is reasonably practicable and in any event within days, including a copy of the decision papers (IAC Rules, r 6(6)).

10.39 The time limits within which the notice of appeal must be filed are different depending upon the type of case, and the rules in IAC Rules, r 7 are set out in full:

> '(1) A notice of appeal by a person who is in the United Kingdom must be given—
>
> (a) if the person is in detention under the Immigration Acts when he is served with notice of the decision against which he is appealing, not later than 5 days after he is served with that notice; and
>
> (b) in any other case, not later than 10 days after he is served with notice of the decision.
>
> (2) A notice of appeal by a person who is outside the United Kingdom must be given—
>
> (a) if the person—
>
> (i) was in the United Kingdom when the decision against which he is appealing was made; and
>
> (ii) may not appeal while he is the United Kingdom by reason of a provision of the 2002 Act, not later than 28 days after his departure from the United Kingdom; or
>
> (b) in any other case, not later than 28 days after he is served with notice of the decision.
>
> (3) Where a person—
>
> (a) is served with notice of a decision to reject an asylum claim; and
>
> (b) on the date of being served with that notice does not satisfy the condition in section 83(1)(b) of the 2002 Act, but later satisfies that condition,
>
> paragraphs (1) and (2)(b) apply with the modification that the time for giving notice of appeal under section 83(2) runs from the date on which the person is served with notice of the decision to grant him leave to enter or remain in the United Kingdom by which he satisfies the condition in section 83(1)(b).'

(References above to the '2002 Act' are to the Nationality, Immigration and Asylum Act 2002).

10.40 The notice of appeal must be in the official form, available from the Tribunal's website, and must contain the following information (IAC Rules, r 8(1)) as well as having been signed by the appellant or his representative (IAC Rules, r 8(3), (4)):

(a) state the name and address of the appellant; and

(b) state whether the appellant has authorised a representative to act for him in the appeal and, if so, give the representative's name and address;

(c) set out the grounds for the appeal;

(d) give reasons in support of those grounds; and

(e) so far as reasonably practicable, list any documents which the appellant intends to rely upon as evidence in support of the appeal.

10.41 The notice of appeal must be accompanied by the notice of decision appealed against, or the reasons why it is not practicable to provide the notice of decision where it is not practicable to provide it (IAC Rules, r 8(2)).

10.42 If the appellant files the notice of appeal outside the time limit he must apply for an extension of time, providing reasons why he failed to comply and written evidence in support of those reasons (IAC Rules, r 10(1)). If no extension is applied for the Tribunal may extend time of its own initiative, or it may notify the appellant that it proposes to treat the appeal as being out of time (IAC Rules, r 10(2)). Upon notification the appellant has three days (10 days if outside the UK) from the notification to respond challenging the calculation of time or providing special circumstances as to the failure to request an extension (IAC Rules, r 10(3)–(4)).

10.43 Where the notice of appeal was given out of time, the Tribunal may extend the time for appealing if satisfied that by reason of special circumstances it would be unjust not to do so (IAC Rules, r 10(5)). However, the decision on any extension will be taken on the papers alone (IAC Rules, r 10(6)). It will then be for the Tribunal to notify the appellant of its decision and the reasons for it.

10.44 Where an extension of time is sought, or is necessary, in a case where the appellant is to be removed from the UK within five days of the notice of appeal the Tribunal must make a decision under IAC Rules, r 10 before the removal date if reasonably practicable to do so. This includes the ability to shorten time limits found in IAC Rules, r 10 (IAC Rules, r 11).

10.45 The Tribunal will serve the notice of appeal on the respondent as soon as reasonably practicable, unless the respondent has forwarded the notice to the Tribunal (IAC Rules, r 12).

Fast-track appeals in the FTTIAC

10.46 The fast-track rules apply where the appellant is in detention under the Immigration Acts at a place specified in the IAC (Fast Track) Rules, Sch 2 when he was served with notice of the immigration decision against which he is appealing, and has been continuously in detention under the Immigration Acts at a place or places specified in Schedule 2 since that notice was served on him (IAC (Fast Track) Rules, r 5).

10.47 In such a case, the following IAC Rules apply which were set out above: IAC Rules, rr 6(1)–(3), 8, 10(1) (IAC (Fast Track) Rules, r 6). A custodian served with a notice of appeal under IAC Rules, r 6(3)(b) must forward it to the Tribunal immediately having endorsed it (IAC (Fast Track) Rules, r 7).

10.48 A person who wishes to appeal must give a notice of appeal not later than two days after the day on which he is served with notice of the immigration decision against which he is appealing (IAC (Fast Track) Rules, r 8(1)). Where a notice of appeal is given outside the time limit the Tribunal must not extend the time for appealing unless it is satisfied that, because of circumstances outside the control of the person giving notice of appeal or his representative, it was not practicable for the notice of appeal to be given within that time limit (IAC (Fast Track) Rules, r 8(2)). Any issue of timeliness will be decided as a preliminary issue at the hearing, and if the decision is that the appeal is out of time the Tribunal must not go on to hear the substantive appeal and instead notify the parties of its decision and summary reasons within one day (IAC (Fast Track) Rules, r 12(1), (3)).

Appeals in the SEC

10.49 The SEC deals with three classes of case. These are: (i) asylum support appeals against decisions made by the UK Border Agency, (ii) appeals from decisions of the Criminal Injuries Compensation Authority and (iii) disputes over social security and child support (see **Social Entitlement Chamber**).

10.50 The SEC Rules have slightly different rules for bringing asylum support and criminal injuries compensation appeals from those applicable to social security and child support disputes.

Asylum support and criminal injuries compensation cases

10.51 An appellant must (see SEC Rules, r 22(2) and see, also, **Time limits**) start asylum support and criminal injuries compensation appeals by sending or delivering a notice of appeal to the Tribunal so that it is received—

(a) in asylum support cases, within three days after the date on which the appellant received written notice of the decision being challenged;

(b) in criminal injuries compensation cases, within 90 days after the date of the decision being challenged.

10.52 The notice of appeal (SEC Rules, r 22(3)) must be in English or Welsh, must be signed by the appellant and must state—

(a) the name and address of the appellant;

(b) the name and address of the appellant's representative (if any);

(c) an address where documents for the appellant may be sent or delivered;

(d) the name and address of any respondent;

(e) details (including the full reference) of the decision being appealed; and

(f) the grounds on which the appellant relies.

10.53 The appellant must (see SEC Rules, r 22(4)) provide with the notice of appeal—

(a) a copy of any written record of the decision being challenged;

(b) any statement of reasons for that decision that the appellant has or can reasonably obtain;

(c) any documents in support of the appellant's case which have not been supplied to the respondent; and

(d) any further information or documents required by an applicable practice direction.

10.54 In asylum support cases the notice of appeal must also (SEC Rules, r 22(5))—

(a) state whether the appellant will require an interpreter at any hearing, and if so for which language or dialect; and

(b) state whether the appellant intends to attend or be represented at any hearing.

10.55 If the appellant provides the notice of appeal to the Tribunal later than the time required by SEC Rules (see above and **Time limits**) (or by an extension of time allowed under SEC Rules, r 5(3)(a), see **Extensions of time**) then (SEC Rules, r 22(6)):

(a) the notice of appeal must include a request for an extension of time and the reason why the notice of appeal was not provided in time; and

(b) unless the Tribunal extends time for the notice of appeal under rule 5(3)(a) (power to extend time) the Tribunal must not admit the notice of appeal.

10.56 The Tribunal must (SEC Rules, r 22(7)) send a copy of the notice of appeal and any accompanying documents to each other party—

(a) in asylum support cases, on the day that the Tribunal receives the notice of appeal, or (if that is not reasonably practicable) as soon as reasonably practicable on the following day;

(b) in criminal injuries compensation cases, as soon as reasonably practicable after the Tribunal receives the notice of appeal.

10.57 A specially designed notice of appeal has been drafted for use in asylum support cases which is available from the Tribunal's website.

Social security and child support disputes

10.58 Except in references under the Child Support Act 1991 and proceedings under the Tax Credits Act 1991, Sch 2, para 3, an appellant must (see SEC Rules, r 23(2)) start proceedings by sending or delivering a notice of appeal to the decision maker so that it is received within the time specified in SEC Rules, Sch 1 (see **Time limits**). However, by SEC Rules, r 23(4), where an appeal is not made within that time it will be treated as having been made in time if the decision maker does not object save (see SEC Rules, r 23(5)) no appeal may be made more than 12 months after the time specified in Schedule 1. The Tribunal is, exceptionally, specifically barred from extending time or waiving a failure to comply with the time limits where it is more than 12 months after the expiry of the time limit (SEC Rules, r 23(8)).

10.59 If (SEC Rules, r 23(3)) the appellant provides the notice of appeal to the decision maker later than the time stipulated in SEC Rules the notice of appeal must include the reason why the notice of appeal was not provided in time.

10.60 The notice of appeal must be in English or Welsh, must be signed by the appellant and must (see SEC Rules, r 23(6)) state—

(a) the name and address of the appellant;

(b) the name and address of the appellant's representative (if any);

(c) an address where documents for the appellant may be sent or delivered;

(d) details of the decision being appealed; and

(e) the grounds on which the appellant relies.

10.61 The decision maker must (SEC Rules, r 23(7)) refer the case to the Tribunal immediately if—

(a) the appeal has been made after the time specified in Schedule 1 and the decision maker objects to it being treated as having been made in time; or

(b) the decision maker considers that the appeal has been made more than 12 months after the time specified in Schedule 1.

10.62 Quite what the purpose of referral to the Tribunal is in circumstances where, because of SEC Rules, r 23(8), the Tribunal cannot do anything about the claim being 12 months out of time is unclear. Presumably it will allow the Tribunal to resolve any issue as to whether the claim was out of time or not and to make relevant directions.

10.63 No specific form is necessary for social security and child support disputes although a form is obtainable from the office making the decision that is sought to be appealed.

10.64 Cases to which references under the Child Support Act 1991 and proceedings under the Tax Credits Act 1991, Sch 2, para 3 apply are dealt with under SEC Rules, r 26. A reference or an information must be made in writing to the Tribunal (SEC Rules, r 26(2), (3)).

10.65 The reference or information must (SEC Rules, r 26(4)) include:

(a) an address where documents for the person starting proceedings may be sent or delivered;

(b) the names and addresses of the respondents and their representatives (if any); and

(c) a submission on the issues that arise for determination by the Tribunal.

10.66 The Tribunal must also be provided with a copy of any relevant document in the possession of the appellant, unless a practice direction directs otherwise, and both the application and accompanying documents should be sent to all other parties, subject to any obligation of confidentiality under SEC Rules, r 19(3) (SEC Rules, r 26(5), (6)). The respondent has one month to send any further relevant documentation and/or a written submission to the Tribunal (SEC Rules, r 26(7)).

Applications and appeals in the Tax Chamber

10.67 Under the Tribunal Procedure (First-tier Tribunal) (Tax Chamber) Rules 2009 ('TC Rules'), r 20(1) where any enactment provides for a person to make or notify an appeal to the Tribunal, the appellant must start proceedings by sending or delivering a notice of appeal to the Tribunal within any time limit imposed by that enactment (see **Time limits**).

10.68 The notice of appeal must (see TC Rules, r 20(2)) include the following details:

(a) the name and address of the appellant;

(b) the name and address of the appellant representative (if any);

(c) an address where documents for the appellant may be sent or delivered;

(d) the name and address of any respondent;

(e) details of the decision or act, or failure to decide or act, to which the proceedings relate;

(f) the result the appellant is seeking; and

(g) the grounds on which the appellant relies.

10.69 In addition, the appellant must (TC Rules, r 20(3)) send with the notice of appeal a copy of any written record of any decision under challenge, and any statement of reasons for that decision that the appellant has or can reasonably obtain.

10.70 If (TC Rules, r 20(4)) the appellant provides the notice of appeal to the Tribunal later than the time required by the rules or later than any extension of time granted by the Tribunal (see **Extensions of time**) then:

(a) the notice of appeal must include a request for an extension of time and the reason why the notice of appeal was not provided in time; and

(b) unless the Tribunal extends time for the notice of appeal the Tribunal has no power to admit the notice of appeal.

10.71 Where the relevant enactment provides for a person or persons to make an originating application or reference to the Tribunal, the appellant must start proceedings by providing an application notice or notice of reference to the Tribunal within any time limit imposed by that enactment (TC Rules, r 21(1)). In other respects, the procedural rules under TC Rules, r 21 are equivalent to those under TC Rules, r 20, except that there need not be a respondent to the application.

10.72 Where the relevant enactment provides that no appeal may proceed when the sum claimed by HMRC remains outstanding unless HMRC or the Tribunal consents the appellant must file a notice of appeal which also provides (TC Rules, r 22(2)):

(a) a statement as to whether the appellant has paid the amount in dispute;

(b) if the appellant has not paid the amount in dispute, a statement as to the status or outcome of any application to HMRC for consent to the appeal proceeding; and

(c) if HMRC have refused such an application, an application to the Tribunal for consent to the appeal proceeding.

10.73 The Tribunal must stay proceedings until the application for consent has been determined (TC Rules, r 22(4)).

10.74 Following receipt by the Tribunal the case will be allocated to one of the TC categories of case: default paper, basic, standard or complex (TC Rules, r 23(1), (2)) (see **Tax Chamber**).

10.75 The various relevant forms are available from the Tribunal's website.

Appeals in the WPAFC

10.76 This chamber hears appeals from ex-servicemen or women who have had claims for a war pension rejected by the Secretary of State (see **War Pensions and Armed Forces Compensation Chamber**).

10.77 An appellant is required (WPAFCC Rules, r 21(1)) to start proceedings by sending or delivering a notice of appeal to the decision maker so that it is received within the stipulated time limits (see also, **Time limits**). These are:

(a) in proceedings under the Pensions Appeal Tribunals Act 1943, s 5(1), within three months after the date on which written notice of the decision being challenged was sent to the appellant; or

(b) in other cases under the Pensions Appeal Tribunals Act 1943, within six months after the date on which written notice of the decision being challenged was sent to the appellant.

10.78 If (WPAFCC Rules, r 21(2)) the appellant provides the notice of appeal to the decision maker later than the stipulated times then the notice of appeal must include the reason why the notice of appeal was not provided in time.

10.79 Where an appeal is not made within the stipulated time it will be treated as having been made in time if the decision maker does not object (WPAFCC Rules, r 21(3)). But (WPAFCC Rules, r 21(4)) no appeal may be made more than 12 months after the stipulated time. The Tribunal is, exceptionally, specifically barred from extending time or waiving a failure to comply with the time limits where it is more than 12 months after the expiry of the time limit (WPAFCC Rules, r 21(7)).

10.80 The notice of appeal must be in English or Welsh, must be signed by the appellant and must state the following (WPAFCC Rules, r 21(5))—

(a) the name and address of the appellant;

(b) the name and address of the appellant's representative (if any);

(c) an address where documents for the appellant may be sent or delivered;

(d) details (including the full reference) of the decision being appealed; and

(e) the grounds on which the appellant relies.

10.81 By WPAFCC Rules, r 21(6) the decision maker must refer the case to the Tribunal immediately if—

(a) the appeal has been made after the stipulated time and the decision maker objects to it being treated as having been made in time; or

(b) the decision maker considers that the appeal has been made more than 12 months after the stipulated time.

10.82 As in the SEC, quite what the purpose of referral to the Tribunal is in circumstances where, because of WPAFCC Rules, r 21(7), the Tribunal cannot do anything about the claim being 12 months out of time is unclear. Presumably it will allow the Tribunal to resolve any issue as to whether the claim was out of time or not and to make relevant directions.

10.83 By WPAFCC Rules, r 22(1) if the decision maker revises the decision challenged—

(a) the proceedings shall proceed as if they had been brought in relation to the revised decision; and

(b) the appellant may make representations in relation to the revised decision within 42 days of the date on which notice of the revised decision was sent to the appellant.

10.84 The appeal will (see WPAFCC Rules, r 22(2), (3)) lapse if the appellant—

(a) does not wish to proceed with the appeal and notifies the Tribunal accordingly; or

(b) does not make representations within 42 days or has no representations to make and has so informed the Tribunal.

A specially designed notice of appeal (PAT 1) has been drafted for use in was pension appeal cases and is available from the Tribunal's website.

11 Care Standards Cases

See also **Administrative Appeals Chamber; Health, Education and Social Care Chamber; Health, Education and Social Care Chamber procedural rules.**

JURISDICTION IN CARE STANDARDS CASES

11.1 Care standards cases consist of appeals against decisions to restrict or bar an individual from working with children or vulnerable adults and decisions to cancel, vary or refuse registration of certain health, childcare and social care provision.

Jurisdiction of the Health, Education and Social Care Chamber

11.2 Care standards cases are heard by the HESCC. By virtue of paragraph 5 (as amended) of the First-tier Tribunal and Upper Tribunal (Chambers) Order 2008, SI 2008/2684, the HESCC was assigned the following functions falling within the rubric of 'care standards':

- hearing applications or appeals against decisions or determinations related to work with children or vulnerable adults;
- hearing appeals against decisions related to registration in respect of provision of health or social care;
- an application in respect of, or an appeal against a decision related to, the provision of health care or health services;
- hearing appeals against decisions related to registration in respect of social workers and social care workers; and
- hearing appeals against decisions related to the provision of childcare.

11.3 The HESCC accordingly hears the following care standards cases:

— Appeals against decisions of the Secretary of State for Education and Skills to:
  - Include an individual's name on the list kept under the Protection of Children Act 1999 ('PCA 1999'), s 1 of individuals who are unsuitable to work with children (the 'Protection of Children Act List');
  - Restrict or prohibit someone from teaching or otherwise working with children in schools or other education establishments; and
  - Cancel the registration of an independent school (see **Schools registration cases**);

— Appeals against decisions of the Secretary of State for Health to:
  - Include an individual's name on the list kept under the Care Standards Act 2000 ('CSA 2000'), s 81 of individuals who are considered unsuitable to work with vulnerable adults (the 'Protection of Vulnerable Adults List');

11.4 **Care Standards Cases**

— Appeals against decisions of the Care Quality Commission and the Welsh Assembly Government in respect of:

- Care homes;
- Residential Family Centres;
- Domiciliary Care Agencies;
- Nurses Agencies;
- Fostering Agencies and Voluntary Adoption Agencies;
- The registration of private and voluntary healthcare provision such as independent hospitals, clinics and medical agencies; and
- NHS providers in respect of regulations on healthcare associated infections;

— Appeals against decisions of the Chief Inspector of Schools in England (Ofsted) and the Welsh Assembly Government in respect of the:

- Registration under the Early Years Childcare Register;
- Registration under the General Childcare Register;
- Disqualification and refusal to waive disqualification from registration as a child minder or day care provider;
- Registration of Children's homes; and;
- A refusal to waive disqualification of a person from providing, managing or having a financial involvement in a children's home or; being employed in a children's home;

— Appeals against decisions of the General Social Care Council and the Care Council Wales in respect of:

- The registration of social workers; and
- The registration of social care workers.

— Applications:

- by individuals to have their names removed from the Protection of Children Act List and the Protection of Vulnerable Adults List, provided the relevant minimum period of time has elapsed
- by individuals prohibited from teaching, acting as a proprietor of an independent school or working in schools or further education institutions to have the ban lifted, provided the relevant minimum period time has elapsed;
- by individuals subject to a court order disqualifying them from working with children for the revocation of that disqualification provided the relevant minimum period time has elapsed;

(where the minimum time period is five years if the individual was under 18 when subject to the relevant measure or 10 years in all other cases).

Jurisdiction of the Administrative Appeals Chamber

11.4 The Administrative Appeals Chamber of the Upper Tribunal hears all appeals against decisions of the HESCC on a point of law, where permission is granted by either the HESCC (after a refusal to review the decision) or by the AAC itself (see **Appeals and references to the Upper Tribunal**).

The AAC also hears direct appeals against decisions of the Independent Safeguarding Authority ('ISA') to bar them from working with children and/or vulnerable adults or a decision not to remove an individual's name from the relevant list of barred individuals. The HESCC does not have jurisdiction to hear such appeals which must be brought before the AAC.

Procedure in care standards cases before the HESCC

The HESCC rules

11.5 All care standards cases before the First-tier Tribunal are conducted in accordance with the HESCC Rules. These are set out elsewhere in this Handbook (see **Health, Education and Social Care Chamber procedural rules**). This entry will deal with those provisions of the HESCC Rules that apply differently in care standards cases than in other cases before the HESCC. Parties and their representatives should note that the majority of the HESCC Rules apply equally regardless of the type of case brought before the HESCC.

Care standards cases requiring leave from the Tribunal to bring proceedings

11.6 Rule 19 of the HESCC Rules specifies the procedure for seeking leave of the HESCC to bring certain appeals and applications in care standards cases.

11.7 The circumstances in which leave is required are (HESCC Rules, r 19(1)):

- an appeal under PCA 1999, s 4(1)(b) against a decision not to remove the applicant from the Protection of Children Act List;
- an application under PCA 1999, s 4(2) by an applicant provisionally included on the Protection of Children Act List to have the issue of his or her inclusion determined by the HESCC;
- an appeal under CSA 2000, s 86(1)(b) against a decision not to remove the applicant from the Protection of Vulnerable Adults List;
- an application under CSA 2000, s 86(2) by an applicant provisionally included on the Protection of Vulnerable Adults List to have the issue of his or her inclusion determined by the HESCC;
- an application made under the Criminal Justice and Courts Services Act 2000 ('CJCA 2000'), s 32 by an applicant who is subject to an order disqualifying him or her from working with children under CJCA 2000, ss 26 and 26 (due to the applicant's having committed an offence against a child), to have the issue of his or her disqualification determined by the HESCC.

11.8 An application for leave must give full reasons as to why the applicant considers the HESCC should give leave and comply with the HESCC Rules, r 20. Rule 20 sets out the requirements for an application notice as if the application for leave were itself by way of application notice (see the following section).

11.9 Care Standards Cases

Care standards cases not requiring leave

11.9 In all care standards cases not falling within HESCC Rules, r 19 summarised above the applicant must start proceedings by sending or delivering an application notice to the HESCC (HESCC Rules, r 20(1)). For the time by which this must be done, see the following section of this entry.

11.10 The application notice must contain (HESCC Rules, r 20(2), (3)):

- the name and address of the appellant;
- the name and address of the appellant's representative (if any);
- an address where documents for the appellant may be sent or delivered;
- the name and address of any respondent;
- details of the decision or act, or failure to decide or act, which is under appeal or to which the proceedings relate;
- the result the appellant is seeking;
- the grounds on which the appellant relies;
- any further information or documents required by a practice direction; and
- any copy or written record of any decision which is being challenged and any statement of reasons for the decision which the appellant has or can reasonably obtain.

11.11 If the appeal is made out of time, the appeal notice must include a request for an extension of time under HESCC Rules, r 5(3)(a) giving reasons why it was not provided in time (HESCC Rules, r 20(4)(a)). Unless the HESCC extends time under r 5(3)(a), the HESCC must not admit the application notice (HESCC, r 20(4)(b)).

Time limits for applications and responses in care standards cases

11.12 The time limit by which an application notice must be sent or delivered to the HESCC depends on the underlying legislative provision giving rise to the right to appeal to the HESCC. In any case not set out in the table below an application notice must be received by the Tribunal within 28 days after notice of the act or decision to which the proceedings relate was sent to the applicant (HESCC Rules, r 20(1)(b)).

11.13 The time limit by which the relevant respondent must respond also varies depending on the underlying legislative framework. In any case not set out in the table below a response must be received by the Tribunal within 21 days after the date on which the respondent received the application notice (HESCC Rules, r 21(1)(b)).

11.14 The time limits are as follows (Schedule to the HESCC Rules):

Type of proceedings	**Time for application notice**	**Time for response**
Under Suspension Regulations (suspension of registration as a childcare provider)	10 working days after written notice of the decision was sent to the applicant	three working days after the respondent received the application notice

Type of proceedings	Time for application notice	Time for response
Under the Children Act 1989, s 79M, except against a notice under section 79L(1)(a) of that Act (notice of intention to refuse an application for registration for childminding or providing day care) Under the School Standards and Framework Act 1998, Shc 26,para 10 (appeal against a decision of the Chief Inspector for Wales) Under the Care Standards Act 2000, s 68 (appeal against a decision of the Council) except an appeal against a refusal under section 58 of that Act (refusal of an application to be included on a register of social workers) Under the Childcare Act 2006, s 74(1)(b)–(e) and (2) (appeal against steps taken by the Chief Inspector except refusal of application for registration or against a prescribed determination)	28 days after written notice of the decision was sent to the applicant	20 working days after the respondent received the application notice
Under the Care Standards Act 2000, s 21 (refusal or cancellation of registration, or variation of conditions of registration, by registration authority or by order of a justice of the peace) Under the Health and Social Care Act 2008, s 32 (appeal against a decision of the Care Quality Commission or an order of a justice of the peace cancelling registration) Under the Education Act 2002, s 166 (appeal against steps taken by the registration authority) Under the Education and Skills Act 2008, s 124 (appeal against removal of a registered independent educational institution from the register)	28 day time limits are set out in the Care Standards Act 2000, s 21(2), the Education Act 2002, s 166(2) and the Health and Social Care Act 2008, s 32(2) and the Education and Skills Act 2008, s 124	20 working days after the respondent received the application notice
Under the Children Act 1989, s 65A (refusal to give consent for a person who is disqualified from fostering a child privately to carry on, be otherwise concerned in the management of, have any financial interest in, or be employed in, a children's home) Under the Children Act 1989, s 79M against a notice under 79L(1)(a) of that Act (notice of intention to refuse an application for registration for childminding or for providing day care) Under the Protection of Children Act 1999, s 4 (inclusion of a person on a list of individuals who are considered unsuitable to work with children, a refusal to remove a person from such list, or determination of inclusion on the list where a person has been provisionally included on the list for more than nine months) *continued overleaf*	three months after written notice of the decision was sent to the applicant	20 days after the respondent received the application notice

11.14 Care Standards Cases

Type of proceedings	Time for application notice	Time for response
Under the Care Standards Act 2000, s 68 where the appeal is against a refusal under section 58 of that Act (refusal of an application to be included on a register of social workers) Under the Care Standards Act 2000, s 86 (inclusion of a person on a list of individuals who are considered unsuitable to work with vulnerable adults, a refusal to remove a person from such list, or determination of inclusion on the list where a person has been provisionally included on the list for more than 9 months) Under the Education (Prohibition from Teaching or Working with Children) Regulations 2003 (decision to give a direction, or a refusal to revoke a direction, prohibiting or restricting a person from working in education or in a job which brings them regularly into contact with children) Under the Childcare Act 2006, s 74(1)(a) (refusal of registration as a childcare provider)		
Under regulations made under the National Health Service Act 1977, s 28X (decision contingently to remove a person from a list maintained by a Primary Care Trust or Local Health Board of persons authorised to perform primary medical, dental or ophthalmic services, or local pharmaceutical services)	(a) for the first application in relation to a decision, three months after the decision was made; (b) for any further application in respect of the same decision, six months after the Tribunal made its last determination in relation to that decision; (c) for any further application in respect of the same decision where the parties apply jointly to the Tribunal with a view to seeking— (i) the same variation of conditions, (ii) the same imposition of different conditions, or (iii) for the contingent removal to be revoked,	21 days after the respondent received the application notice

Type of proceedings	Time for application notice	Time for response
	one month after the Tribunal made its last determination in relation to that decision.	
Under the Education Act 1996, Part 4 and Sch 27 (provision of education to a child with special educational needs)	two months after written notice of the decision was sent to the applicant	30 working days after the respondent received the application notice
Under the Disability Discrimination Act 1995, s 281 (disability discrimination in the education of a child)	six months after the decision or act complained of	30 working days after the respondent received the application notice

Suspension Regulations cases

11.15 Care standards cases under the Suspension Regulations – being any regulations which provide for a right of appeal against a decision to suspend, or not to lift the suspension of, a person's registration as a childcare provider (see the Childcare Act 2006, s 69 and The Child Minding and Day Care (Suspension of Registration) (England) Regulations 2003, SI No 2003/332, reg 8) (HESCC Rules, r 1(3)) – are subject to the same procedural rules as other care standards cases, subject to minor exceptions which place Suspension Regulations proceedings on an accelerated timetable.

11.16 These exceptions are:

- the time for bringing an application under the Suspension Regulations (see above);
- the time for responding to such an application (see above);
- that the applicant must send or deliver a copy of the application notice and any accompanying documents to the respondent at the same time as it sends or delivers the application notice to the HESCC (HESCC Rules, r 20(5));
- that the HESCC must give the parties at least three working days notice of any hearing (to be contrasted with the usual period of 14 working days) (HESCC Rules, r 25(2)(a));
- that the HESCC must provide a decision notice to the parties together with its written reasons within three working days of the hearing (HESCC Rules, r 30(3)).

Procedure in care standards cases before the Upper Tribunal

Upper Tribunal Rules

11.17 All care standards cases before the Administrative Appeals Chamber of the Upper Tribunal are conducted in accordance with the Upper Tribunal Rules. These are set out elsewhere in this Handbook (see **Upper Tribunal**

procedural rules). The Upper Tribunal Rules apply equally to all care standards cases on appeal to the Upper Tribunal.

Care standards cases commenced before the Administrative Appeals Chamber

11.18 This section deals with appeals to the AAC under the Safeguarding Vulnerable Groups Act 2006, s 4 in respect of decisions of the Independent Safeguarding Authority to include the appellant's name on the ISA Children's List, the ISA Adults List, the Protection of Children Act List, the Protection of Vulnerable Adults List or against a decision to restrict or prohibit the appellant's employment as a teacher or otherwise work with children in schools or further education institutions. Such appeals are commenced before the ACC and do not involve the First-tier Tribunal. An appeal against a decision of the ISA can only be brought with the permission of the AAC.

11.19 The procedure for applying for permission to appeal to the AAC is set out elsewhere in this Handbook and will not be repeated (see **Appeals and references to the Upper Tribunal**). For present purposes it suffices to note those provisions of the Upper Tribunal Rules solely concerned with care standards cases. There are three such provisions, the first two of which are of particular importance for appellants.

11.20 Rule 21(3)(a) of the Upper Tribunal Rules varies the usual one month time limit for applying for permission to appeal to the AAC for appeals under Safeguarding Vulnerable Groups Act 2006, s 4. A party wishing to appeal against a decision of the ISA must do so no later than three months after the date on which written notice of the decision being challenged was sent to him or her.

11.21 Upper Tribunal Rules, r 22 deals with the AAC's decision in respect of permission to appeal. Upper Tribunal Rules, r 22(3)(b) applies in circumstances in which the AAC determines an application for permission to appeal against a decision of the ISA without a hearing. If the AAC does so, and either refuses permission to appeal or gives permission on limited grounds or subject to conditions, the appellant, by virtue of Upper Tribunal Rules, r 22(3)(b) and 22(4) has a right to apply for the decision to be reconsidered at an oral hearing. An application for reconsideration at a hearing must be made in writing and received by the AAC within 14 days after the date on which the appellant was informed of the AAC's decision on the application for permission to appeal (Upper Tribunal Rules, r 22(5)).

11.22 Finally, under Upper Tribunal Rules, r 20(1), in appeals against a decision of the ISA the Secretary of State has the power to pay such allowances for the purpose of or in connection with the attendance of persons at hearings as the Secretary of State may determine.

12 Case Management Powers

See also **Directions; Overriding objective; Procedural rules.**

DISCRETION TO REGULATE OWN PROCEDURE

12.1 The First-tier Tribunal and Upper Tribunal have a wide-ranging discretion to regulate their own procedure. This is to be welcomed, given the varied subject-matter of the cases which will be brought before the tribunals generally and before specific Tribunals (see for example the varied subject-matter jurisdiction of the General Regulatory Chamber and the Health, Education and Social Care Chamber).

12.2 The Tribunal's power to regulate its own procedure is typically given effect by r 5(1) of the relevant tribunal procedural rules. This power is subject to the provisions of TCEA and to the overriding objective (see **Overriding objective**).

THE OVERRIDING OBJECTIVE

12.3 The conduct of proceedings before the Tribunals, and the exercise of any case management powers, is to be conducted in accordance with the overriding objective. This is discussed in more detail elsewhere in the Handbook (see **Overriding objective**).

12.4 In brief summary, acting in accordance with the overriding objective requires case management decisions to be taken in a manner which will best lead to the just resolution of proceedings, and involves consideration of whether exercising any particular case management power will:

- Be proportionate to the importance of the case, the complexity of the issues, the anticipated costs and the resources of the parties;
- Avoid unnecessary formality;
- Allow appropriate flexibility with regard to the particular subject-matter of proceedings and the identity/capacity of the parties;
- Ensure that parties are able to participate fully in the proceedings;
- Effectively utilise the Tribunal's expertise; and
- Avoid delay.

AVAILABLE CASE MANAGEMENT POWERS

12.5 The case management powers available to the First-tier and Upper Tribunal and the type of orders and direction which can be made by the Tribunals are, by virtue of the wide procedural discretion discussed above, not limited. Some of the case management powers possessed by the Tribunals are enumerated in what is typically r 5(3) of the relevant Tribunal procedural rules. Rule 5(3) is non-exhaustive and must be read alongside the remainder of the procedural rules for the relevant Tribunal. This pattern is not followed in the Immigration and Asylum Chamber of the First-tier Tribunal, whose Rules provide the power to make directions on a more limited, non-exhaustive, list in r 45. There appears to be no equivalent single case management power provision in the Lands Chamber Rules. The following discussion is without prejudice to the individual attributes of the procedures in the FTTIAC and the Lands Chamber.

12.6 The following is a non-exhaustive list of the case management powers of the First-tier and Upper Tribunal and the types of order which it can make. The First-tier Tribunal and the Upper Tribunal may:

- extend or shorten the time for complying with any rule, practice direction or direction (see **Extensions of time**);
- consolidate or hear together two or more sets of proceedings or parts of proceedings raising common issues, or treat a case as a lead case (it should be noted that there is no provision in the Health, Education and Social Care Chamber Rules, r 5(3) providing for the HESCC to treat a case as lead case (see **Health, Education and Social Care Chamber procedural rules**));
- permit or require a party to amend a document;
- permit or require a party or another person to provide documents, information, evidence or submissions to the Tribunal or a party (see **Documents; Evidence**);
- deal with an issue in the proceedings as a preliminary issue;
- hold a hearing to consider any matter, including a case management issue (see **Hearings**);
- decide the form of any hearing;
- adjourn or postpone a hearing;
- require a party to produce a bundle for a hearing;
- stay (or, in Scotland, sist) proceedings;
- strike out a party's case (see **Striking out**);
- substitute, add or remove a party (see **Parties**);
- make an order for costs (see **Costs**);
- transfer proceedings to another court or tribunal if that other court or tribunal has jurisdiction in relation to the proceedings and—
  - because of a change of circumstances since the proceedings were started, the Tribunal no longer has jurisdiction in relation to the proceedings; or
  - the Tribunal considers that the other court or tribunal is a more appropriate forum for the determination of the case;
- suspend the effect of its own decision pending the determination by the Tribunal or the Upper Tribunal of an application for permission to appeal against, and any appeal or review of, that decision (see **Appeals from the First-tier Tribunal and Appeals to the Upper Tribunal**) or in the Upper Tribunal pending an appeal or review of the Upper Tribunal's decision;

- in the Upper Tribunal, in an appeal, or an application for permission to appeal, against the decision of another tribunal, suspend the effect of that decision pending the determination of the application for permission to appeal, and any appeal;
- in the Upper Tribunal, require any other tribunal whose decision is the subject of proceedings before the Upper Tribunal to provide reasons for the decision, or other information or documents in relation to the decision or the proceedings in that tribunal;
- direct, in the Upper Tribunal, that a fast track immigration or asylum case cease to be treated as a fast track case if: the parties consent; the Tribunal is satisfied that there are exceptional circumstances which suggest that the appeal or application could not be justly determined if it were treated as a fast track case; or the Secretary of State has failed to comply with a rule or direction and the other party would be prejudiced if the appeal or application were treated as a fast track case;
- direct, in a financial services case in the Upper Tribunal, that the effect of the decision in respect of which the reference has been made is to be suspended pending the determination of the reference, if it is satisfied that to do so would not prejudice the interests of any persons (whether consumers, investors or otherwise) intended to be protected by that notice; or the smooth operation or integrity of any market intended to be protected by that notice (except that this power does not apply to a reference in respect of a Pensions Regulator decision).

12.7 Some guidance has recently been provided by the Administrative Appeals Chamber of the Upper Tribunal in *MA v Secretary of State for Work and Pensions* [2009] UKUT 211 (AAC) on the appropriate principles to be considered in applications for an adjournment. The *MA* case concerned an appeal from the Social Entitlement Chamber where a request at the hearing for an adjournment to collect medical evidence was refused. On appeal, the AAC stressed the need to make case management decisions by reference to the overriding objective (see **Overriding objective**), and went on to provide principles for adjournment applications:

> 'The starting point is the reason for the application. In this case, it was to obtain further evidence. A tribunal is always entitled to consider whether this evidence is likely to be helpful. In making its assessment, it is relevant to take into account: (i) the evidence that is already before the tribunal; (ii) the evidence that is likely to be obtained if the proceedings are adjourned; (iii) how long it will take to obtain it; and (iv) whether the tribunal could use its expertise to compensate for the lack of additional evidence.' (at [15])
>
> 'Parties are under a duty to co-operate with the tribunal generally. That involves ensuring as far as possible that their case is ready by the time of the hearing.' (at [20])
>
> 'The interests of the claimant are likely to be resolved when considering the value of an adjournment. As to the other party, this is likely to be Secretary of State in a social security case. The Secretary of State is not a contentious party to the proceedings. By virtue of that status and the duty to co-operate, the Secretary of State's only interest is in assisting

> the tribunal to ensure that it makes the correct decision in fact and law on the claimant's entitlement to benefit… It will surely be exceptional for an adjournment that would otherwise be granted to be refused solely on account of the needs of the system as a whole.' (at [21]–[23])

The judge went on to find that there had been no error of law in refusing the adjournment (at [24]):

> 'I can find no significant error in the tribunal's approach to the case. It took account of the grounds for the application and made an assessment of the likely value that would be obtained by an adjournment. That was the key consideration. Its analysis is rational. It took advantage of the tribunal's flexibility in using its members' combined special expertise to avoid delay and to allow the claimant full and effective participation in the proceedings. All of those factors are within the scope of the overriding objective. By using its expertise, it reconciled fairness and efficiency with making the proceedings accessible to a claimant whose evidence was not complete.'

The principles set out in *MA* will be of significant analogous use in other appeals relating the exercise of case management powers.

13 Chambers

DIVISION OF FIRST-TIER TRIBUNAL AND UPPER TRIBUNAL INTO CHAMBERS

Rationale for the Chambers structure

13.1 The TCEA 2007, s 7 and Sch 4 make provision for the organisation of the First-tier and Upper Tribunal into Chambers.

13.2 It is through this division of the First-tier and Upper Tribunal into Chambers that the jurisdictional boundaries of the tribunals system are established and the procedural rules for the First-tier Tribunal and Upper Tribunal can be made sufficiently flexible to deal with the wide variety of different jurisdictions being brought within the new system. The system of Chambers makes it possible to assimilate the myriad subject-matters dealt with by previous tribunals into the two tribunal system.

13.3 The Chambers system is intended to boost the efficacy of the tribunal system and avoid the dilution of expertise which would occur (with consequent damage to the level of service provided to the public) if all judges and members could deal with all kinds of case (TCEA Explanatory Notes, paragraph 78). The Chambers system ensures that similar work is dealt with by judges and members with the relevant skills to deal with it.

Machinery for division of tribunals

13.4 TCEA 2007, s 7 gives the Lord Chancellor the power, exercised with the concurrence of the Senior President (see **Senior President**), to make provision for the organisation of each of the First-tier and Upper Tribunal into a number of Chambers. TCEA 2007, s 7(9) provides for the Senior President and the Lord Chancellor together to be able to vary by order the distribution of functions between the Chambers in either the First-tier Tribunal or the Upper Tribunal, whether on a functional or geographical basis, or a combination of the two.

Chamber Presidents

13.5 TCEA 2007, s 7(2)–(4) provide that for each Chamber within the First tier Tribunal and Upper Tribunal there must be a person (or two persons) to preside over that Chamber. A person cannot be the Chamber President of more than one Chamber within the First-tier Tribunal at the same time. Likewise, a person cannot preside over more than one Chamber within the Upper Tribunal at the same time, although they can preside over one Chamber of the First-tier Tribunal and over one Chamber of the Upper Tribunal at the same time.

13.6 Schedule 4 to TCEA 2007 makes provision for the appointment of Chamber Presidents. By virtue of TCEA 2007, Sch 4, paras 1 and 5, the eligibility requirements to be a Chamber President or a Deputy Chamber President are identical to those for appointment as a judge of the Upper Tribunal (see TCEA 2007, Sch 3).

13.7 The Chamber President is a judicial leadership role involving particular skills and experience in addition to the requirements to be satisfied to be a judge within the tribunals system. Pursuant to TCEA 2007, Sch 4, para 2, a Chamber President may (although need not) be drawn from the judiciary of the High Court or the Court of Session in Scotland or Court of Appeal in Northern Ireland. Prior to making an appointment from the High Court (or other relevant) judiciary, the Lord Chancellor must consult the Senior President of Tribunals and seek a nomination of a suitable candidate from the Lord Chief Justice of England and Wales or Northern Ireland, or the Lord President of the Court of Session. If no suitable candidate is forthcoming, selection will be made by the Judicial Appointments Commission (see the Constitutional Reform Act 2005, Sch 14, Part 3 as amended by TCEA 2007, Sch 8, para 66).

13.8 A Chamber President may delegate the functions of his office to any judge or other member of the First-tier or Upper Tribunal, or to a member of staff (TCEA 2007, Sch 4, para 4) or to a Deputy Chamber President if one is appointed under TCEA 2007, Sch 4, para 5. The appointment process for Deputy Chamber Presidents is the same as that for Chamber Presidents.

13.9 The most important duty of a Chamber President is set out in TCEA 2007, Sch 4, para 7, which obliges a Chamber President to make arrangements for the issuing of guidance on changes to the law and practice relating to the jurisdictions assigned to his or her Chamber. These procedural guidelines are intended to supplement the formal rules of the Chamber.

CURRENT CHAMBERS

13.10 The Upper Tribunal is divided into four Chambers:

- The Administrative Appeals Chamber (see **Administrative Appeals Chamber**) dealing (in summary) with onward appeals from all the First–tier Tribunals (except the Tax Chamber, the Immigration and Asylum Chamber and charities cases from the General Regulatory Chamber); appeals from the Mental Health Review Tribunal, (Wales); and Special Educational Needs Tribunal (Wales); appeals from the Pensions Appeal Tribunal (Scotland); appeals under the Pensions Appeal Tribunals Act 1943, s 5 from the Pensions Appeal Tribunal (Northern Ireland); appeals under the Safeguarding Vulnerable Groups Act 2006, s 4; references under the Forfeiture Act 1982; appeals from the Traffic Commissioners and most judicial review matters;
- The Tax and Chancery Chamber (see **Tax and Chancery Chamber**) dealing with onward appeals from the Tax Chamber of the First-tier Tribunal and the charities cases from the General Regulatory Chamber; appeals formerly heard by the Financial Services and Markets Tribunal; appeals formerly heard by the Pensions Regulator Tribunal and some judicial review matters.
- The Lands Chamber (see **Lands Chamber**) dealing with certain disputes concerning land, particularly the valuation of land, adopting the jurisdiction of the old Lands Tribunal;
- The Immigration and Asylum Chamber (see **Immigration and Asylum Chamber (Upper Tribunal)**) dealing with onward appeals

from the Immigration and Asylum Chamber of the First-tier Tribunal on immigration and asylum matters.

13.11 At the time of writing, the First-tier Tribunal is divided into six Chambers:

- The General Regulatory Chamber (see **General Regulatory Chamber**), which has jurisdiction over:
  - dealing with charity cases (see **Charity cases**);
  - appeals in claims management services cases where a sanction has been imposed or authorisation refused by the Claims Management Regulator (see **Claims management cases**);
  - consumer credit appeals (see **Consumer Credit appeals**);
  - appeals from environmental sanctions imposed under the Regulatory, Enforcement and Sanctions Act 2008 (see **Environment appeals**);
  - estate agents appeals (see **Estate agents appeals**);
  - appeals against the decisions of the Gambling Commission (see **Gambling appeals**);
  - appeals against decisions of the Immigration Services Commissioner (see **Immigration services appeals**);
  - information rights cases (see **Information rights cases**);
  - local government standards cases (see **Local government standards cases**); and
  - certain transport cases (see **Transport cases**).
- The Health, Education and Social Care Chamber (see **Health, Education and Social Care Chamber**) which has jurisdiction in respect of:
  - appeals against a decision related to children with special educational needs, claims of disability discrimination in the education of a child and appeals against a decision related to an independent school (see **Special educational needs and disability cases** and **Schools registration cases**);
  - applications or appeals against a decision or determination related to work with children or vulnerable adults (see **Care standards cases**);
  - an appeal against a decision related to registration in respect of provision of health or social care (see **Care standards cases**);
  - an appeal against a decision related to registration in respect of social workers and social care workers (see **Care standards cases**);
  - appeal against a decision related to the provision of childcare (see **Care standards cases**);
  - applications and references by and in respect of patients under the provisions of the Mental Health Act 1983 or paragraph 5(2)

of the Schedule to the Repatriation of Prisoners Act 1984 (see **Mental health cases**).

- The Immigration and Asylum Chamber (see **Immigration and Asylum Chamber (First-tier Tribunal)**), which has jurisdiction over applications and appeals in respect of decisions relating to a person's immigration or asylum status.
- The SEC (see **Social Entitlement Chamber**) which has jurisdiction over appeals:
  - in asylum support cases (see **Asylum support appeals**);
  - in criminal injuries compensation cases (see **Criminal injury compensation appeals**);
  - regarding entitlement to, payments of, or recovery or recoupment of payments of, social security benefits, child support, vaccine damage payment, tax credits and child trust funds or entitlement to be credited with earnings or contributions (see **Social security and child support cases**);
  - regarding payments in consequence of diffuse mesothelioma;
  - regarding a certificate or waiver decision in relation to NHS charges; and
  - against a decision as to whether an accident was an industrial accident.
- The TC (see **Tax Chamber**) dealing with taxation cases and in particular cases formerly dealt with by:
  - the Special and General Commissioners for Income Tax;
  - the VAT and Duties Tribunal;
  - the tribunal established under the Income and Corporation Taxes Act 1988, s 706; and
  - the tribunal established under the Income Tax Act 2007, s 704.
- The WPAFCC (see **War Pensions and Armed Forces Compensation Chamber**) which has all functions relating to appeals under the War Pensions (Administrative Provisions) Act 1919 and the Pensions Appeal Tribunals Act 1943.

13.12 There are various other tribunals and panels which form part of the Tribunals Service but which are yet to be assimilated into Chambers. It is expected that this process will continue as the collective experience of the system progresses and in particular in response to (TCEA Explanatory Notes, paragraph 84):

- the transfer of functions of other tribunals to the First-tier or Upper Tribunals;
- changes in original decisions (for example as the social security benefit system evolves);
- the creation of new areas of appeal (for example as has recently occurred in connection with the regulation of licensed gambling); or
- in relation to the prevalence of a particular jurisdiction at a point in time, and other business and user needs.

13.13 It is envisaged that this will involve any or all of the following (TCEA Explanatory Notes, paragraph 84):

- the establishment of new Chambers;
- the addition of jurisdictions to existing Chambers; and
- the transfer of functions and/or jurisdictions between Chambers.

13.14 One important pillar of the Tribunal Service is the employment jurisdiction, covered by the Employment Tribunals and the Employment Appeal Tribunal. There are no current plans to bring these within the TCEA regime as it is felt that the employment jurisdiction is currently functioning well. It also does not match the general rule of the other tribunals of concerning citizen-State disputes. The position of the employment jurisdiction will be kept under review.

14 Charity Cases

CHARITY TRIBUNAL

14.1 Charity cases were previously dealt with by the Charity Tribunal, an independent body set up under the Charities Act 2006. The Charity Tribunal's principal functions were:

- to hear appeals against the decisions of the Charity Commission (the regulator and registrar of charities in England and Wales);
- to hear applications for review of decisions of the Charity Commission;
- to consider references from the Attorney General or the Charity Commission on points of law.

14.2 From 1 September 2009, the Charity Tribunal was abolished and its functions were transferred to the First-tier Tribunal, with charities cases to be heard by the General Regulatory Chamber (see **General Regulatory Chamber**). By virtue of paragraph 2 of the Transfer of Functions of the Charity Tribunal Order 2009, SI 2009/1834 the functions of the Charity Tribunal were transferred to the First-tier Tribunal and the Upper Tribunal, with the question as to which one of them is to exercise the function in a particular case being determined by, or under, tribunal procedure rules (see below). For a helpful overview and analysis of the First-tier Tribunal's role and jurisdiction in charity cases, see Morris 'The First-tier Tribunal (Charity): Enhanced Access to Justice for Charities or a case of David versus Goliath?' [2010] CJQ 491.

CHARITIES CASES BEFORE THE GRC

Procedural rules in charities cases

14.3 Procedure in charities cases is governed by the General Regulatory Chamber Rules. These are dealt with in detail elsewhere in the Handbook (see **General Regulatory Chamber procedural rules**). This entry will deal only with the provisions of the GRC Rules that apply specifically in charities cases.

Bringing an appeal against the decision of the Charity Commission

14.4 The appellant starts proceedings before the GRC in a charities case by sending or delivering to the GRC a notice of appeal so that it is received within 42 days of the date on which notice of the decision being appealed was sent to the appellant (GRC Rules, r 26(1)(a)). If the appellant was not the subject of the decision to which the proceedings relate, the notice of appeal must be received by the Tribunal within 42 days of the date on which the decision was published (GRC Rules, r 26(1)(b)).

14.5 If the appeal is lodged out of time, the notice of appeal must include a request for an extension of time and state why the notice of appeal was not provided in time. Unless the GRC extends time for the notice of appeal under GRC Rules, r 5(3)(a) (power to extend time) it must not admit the notice of appeal (GRC Rules, r 26(5)) (see **Extensions of time**).

14.6 The notice of appeal must include (GRC Rules, r 26(2)):

- the name and address of the appellant;
- the name and address of the appellant's representative (if any);
- an address where documents for the appellant may be sent or delivered;
- the basis on which the appellant has standing to start proceedings before the GRC;
- the name and address of any respondent;
- details of the decision or act, or failure to decide or act, to which the proceedings relate;
- the result the appellant is seeking;
- the grounds on which the appellant relies; and
- a copy of any written record of the decision being challenged, and any statement of reasons for that decision that the appellant has or can reasonably obtain (GRC Rules, r 26(3)).

14.7 If the notice of appeal relates to a reference under Schedule 1D of the Charities Act 1993 and the appellant is the Charity Commission, it must send evidence of the Attorney General's consent to the reference with the notice of appeal and on receiving the notice of appeal the GRC must publish details of the reference and information as to how a person likely to be affected by the reference can apply to be added as a party to the proceedings (GRC Rules, r 26(4)).

14.8 The notice of appeal must be sent by the appellant to the respondent at the same time as it is provided to the GRC (GRC Rules, r 26(6)).

Response

14.9 In charities cases, the respondent party must send or deliver to the GRC a response to the notice of appeal within 28 days after the date on which the respondent received the notice of appeal (GRC Rules, r 27(1)).

14.10 The response must include or enclose (GRC Rules, r 27(2)–(5)):

- the name and address of the respondent;
- the name and address of the respondent's representative (if any);
- an address where documents for the respondent may be sent or delivered;
- a statement as to whether the respondent opposes the appellant's case and, if so, any grounds for such opposition which are not contained in another document provided with the response;
- a statement as to whether the respondent would be content for the case to be dealt with without a hearing if the GRC considers it appropriate;
- a copy of any written record of the decision being challenged, and any statement of reasons for that decision, that the appellant did not provide with the notice of appeal and the respondent has or can reasonably obtain;
- the documents relied upon by the respondent when reaching the decision;

- any other documents which the respondent considers could adversely affect its case or support the appellant's case. Respondent parties should note that this is a more extensive disclosure obligation than that which pertains under non-charities cases before the GRC (see GRC Rules, r 23).

Respondents in charities cases should be alert to the need to satisfy this duty and to consider carefully whether there are documents in its possession or control that are helpful to the appellant.

14.11 If the respondent provides the response to the GRC out of time, the response must include a request for an extension of time and the reason why the response was not provided in time (GRC Rules, r 27(6)) (see **Extensions of time**).

14.12 The respondent must send or deliver a copy of the response and any accompanying documents to each other party at the same time as it provides the response to the GRC (GRC Rules, r 27(7)).

Appellant's reply

14.13 The appellant party in charities cases has the option of putting in a written reply to the respondent's response (GRC Rules, r28(1)) and may submit a list of documents additional to those listed in the appeal notice or the response (GRC Rules, r 28(4)). Copies of any additional documents must be sent to the respondent at the same time as the appellant provides its reply to the GRC (GRC Rules, r 28(5)).

14.14 The reply must be sent to the GRC no later than 28 days after the respondent sent the appellant its response (GRC Rules, r 28(2)). If the appellant provides its reply out of time, the reply must include a request for an extension of time and state why it response was not provided in time (GRC Rules, r 28(3)) (see **Extensions of time**).

Secondary disclosure by the respondent

14.15 In the event that the appellant submits a reply under the GRC Rules, r 28, the respondent becomes under an obligation to make secondary disclosure under r 29.

14.16 Within 14 days of the appellant's reply, the respondent must send or deliver to the GRC a list of any further material which might reasonably be expected to assist that appellant's case as disclosed by that appellant's reply and was not included in a list of documents provided by the respondent with the response (GRC Rules, r 29(1)).

14.17 If the respondent provides the list to the GRC later than the time required, the response containing the list must include a request for an extension of time and state why the response was not provided in time (GRC Rules, r 29(2)). The list must be delivered to each other party at the same time as it is provided to the GRC (GRC Rules, r 29(3)).

Provision of disclosed documents

14.18 If any party has provided a list of documents at the response, reply, or secondary disclosure stages, that party must provide any other party with a copy of any document specified in the list or make such a document available for reading or copying within seven days of receiving a request from another party that a copy or the document be provided or made available (GRC Rules, r 30).

Involvement of the Attorney General under section 2D of the Charities Act 1993

14.19 If the GRC directs that all the necessary papers in proceedings be sent to the Attorney General under the Charities Act 1993, s 2D(2) and (3), the Attorney General must notify the GRC whether he or she intends to intervene in the proceedings within 28 days of receiving the papers (GRC Rules, r 31(1)).

14.20 The Attorney General may at any time notify the GRC that he or she intends to intervene in the proceedings on his or her own initiative (GRC Rules, r 31(2)).

14.21 In the event that the GRC requests that the Attorney General argue a question in relation to the proceedings under the Charities Act 1993, s 2D(4)(b), the GRC must provide to the Attorney General (GRC Rules, r 31(3)):

- a statement of the question;
- an account of the proceedings to date;
- the reasons the GRC considers it necessary to have the question fully argued by the Attorney General; and
- copies of the documents the Tribunal considers necessary to enable the Attorney General to decide whether it is appropriate to argue the question.

14.22 If the Attorney General notifies the GRC that the Attorney General intends to intervene in, or to argue a question in relation to, proceedings under the Charities Act 1993, s 2D(4), the GRC must hold a case management hearing (GRC Rules, r 31(4)).

Hearings and decisions in charities cases

14.23 The procedure for and at hearings in charities cases and the rules in respect of decisions of the GRC in charities cases are the same as in other cases before the GRC and are accordingly dealt with elsewhere in the Handbook (see **General Regulatory Chamber procedural rules**; **Hearings**; and **Decisions**).

Referral to the Upper Tribunal

14.24 In a charities case the Tribunal may refer the case or a preliminary issue in the case to the Chamber President with a request that it be transferred to the Upper Tribunal for determination. The Chamber President may then direct the transfer if the Chamber President of the Upper Tribunal agrees (GRC Rules, r 19).

Appeals from the First-tier Tribunal

14.25 Unlike almost all GRC cases, charities cases are not appealed to the Administrative Appeals Chamber of the Upper Tribunal. Instead, any appeal on a point of law goes to the Tax and Chancery Chamber of the Upper Tribunal (see **Tax and Chancery Chamber**). The procedural rules governing appeals are the same in both Upper Tribunal chambers and are dealt with elsewhere (see **Appeals and references to the Upper Tribunal**).

15 Citation And Reporting

15.1 The citation of decisions of the First-tier Tribunals and Upper Tribunal is governed by the Senior President's *Practice Statement on the Form of Decisions and Neutral Citation*, 31 October 2008.

NEUTRAL CITATION

15.2 Each decision of the Upper Tribunal will be issued with a unique number by the Upper Tribunal Office at the request of a party. In the First-tier Tribunal requests for a unique number for a decision should be made to the relevant Chamber President.

15.3 Unique numbers will only be issued in respect of First-tier decisions by the Upper Tribunal Office. If a request is made to the relevant First-tier Chamber President, the President will, if he or she considers it appropriate, then refer the decision to the Upper Tribunal to determine whether a unique number should be issued.

15.4 Decisions are cited as follows:

- Upper Tribunal (Administrative Appeals Chamber): [2010] UKUT 1 (AAC)
- Upper Tribunal (Immigration and Asylum Chamber): [2010] UKUT 2 (IAC)
- Upper Tribunal (Lands Chamber): [2010] UKUT 3 (LC)
- Upper Tribunal (Tax and Chancery Chamber): [2010] UKUT 4 (TCC)
- First-tier Tribunal (General Regulatory Chamber): [2010] UKFTT 1 (GRC)
- First-tier Tribunal (Health Education and Social Care Chamber): [2010] UKFTT 2 (HESC)
- First-tier Tribunal (Immigration and Asylum Chamber): [2010] UKFTT 3 (IAC)
- First-tier Tribunal (Social Entitlement Chamber): [2010] UKFTT 4 (SEC)
- First-tier Tribunal (Tax Chamber): [2010] UKFTT 5 (TC)
- First-tier Tribunal (War Pensions and Armed Forces Compensation Chamber): [2010] UKFTT 6 (WPAFCC)

REPORTING

15.5 When a decision is selected for reporting it is given a new number beginning with an 'R': eg C[CASE CODE]/[NUMBER]/[DATE] is reported as R([CASE CODE]) [NUMBER]/[DATE] (NB the two numbers will not be the same). The case code will be preserved.

15.6 As is typically the case, a decision should be reported if it decides a difficult issue, contributes to the coherent development or operation of the law or gives practical guidelines to decision-makers or other tribunals. The Administrative Appeals Chamber publishes, through HM Stationery Office, the Administrative Appeals Chamber Reports with the leading decisions of the Chamber from the year. These decisions are also set out on the Chamber's website.

15.7 In the Upper Tribunal, decisions by single judges may be reported if they are of precedential value. Of relevance to this determination will be whether the decision is the first concerning a particular issue or extends existing principles to new areas of the Tribunal's jurisdiction, whether it resolves a conflict of authority or settles a point which was previously in doubt, and whether it modifies a previous reported decision.

15.8 Decisions of three-judge panels of the Upper Tribunal will typically be reported in the absence of exceptional reasons for not doing so.

15.9 Decisions on permission to appeal are only reported if they contain useful analysis or statements of principle.

16 Claims Management Services Cases

THE CLAIMS MANAGEMENT SERVICES TRIBUNAL

16.1 The jurisdiction of the Claims Management Services Tribunal was established by the Compensation Act 2006, s 12 to administer appeals relating to decisions of the Claims Regulator. It extended only to England and Wales. Its principal subject-matter jurisdiction was to hear appeals from business and individuals who provide claims management services in areas such as:

- Personal injury, including work-related injury, disease or disability;
- Criminal injuries compensation;
- Industrial Injuries Disablement Benefit;
- Employment;
- Housing disrepair; and
- Financial products and services.

16.2 From 18 January 2010, the Claims Management Services Tribunal was abolished and its functions were transferred to the General Regulatory Chamber (see **General Regulatory Chamber**) as a regulatory body covered by the First-tier Tribunal and Upper Tribunal (Chambers) Order 2008, SI 2008/2684 (as amended), paragraph 5B(a).

REGULATION OF CLAIMS MANAGEMENT SERVICES

16.3 The substantive content of the regulation of claims management services is outside of the scope of this book. In brief summary, a large number of claims management companies began to operate from around 2000 in response to legal and regulatory changes including the relaxing of the rules prohibiting conditional fees. The manner of this operation began to cause concern that consumers and litigants were being denied access to justice and compensation. Following the report of the Better Regulation Task Force it was decided that the Secretary of State for Justice should act as the Regulator with regulation and monitoring ultimately to pass to the Legal Services Board.

16.4 As a result claims management services are principally regulated by the Compensation Act 2006 and the Compensation (Claims Management Services) Regulations 2006, SI 2006/3322 which set out most of the detail of the regulatory scheme and the requirements that have to be met in order to obtain authorisation to carry out claims management services.

16.5 The Regulator makes rules covering the conduct of authorised persons and regulatory fees. The Regulator is presently the Secretary of State for Justice and all decisions of the Regulator are made in his name. Day-to-day responsibility for claims management services regulation lies with the Head of Claims Management Regulation, a senior civil servant in the Ministry of Justice. The authorisation and monitoring process is conducted by a Monitoring and Compliance Unit.

16.6 The essence of the regulation is that businesses that provide claims management services must be authorised, exempt or subject to a waiver. Authorised persons are then subject to the Conduct of Authorised Persons Rules 2007 which are in two parts. The general rules cover:

- requirements for businesses to certify that they comply with the rules;
- financial requirements;
- arrangements in respect of enforcement, discipline and provision of information;
- arrangements for the provision of information to the Regulator; and
- arrangements for exempt introducers.

16.7 The Client Specific Rules cover:

- advertising, marketing and soliciting business;
- taking on business; and
- representing a client.

16.8 The Complaints Handling Rules 2006 set out the requirements that authorised businesses must meet for dealing with complaints by clients and require that authorised businesses have a publicised written policy for handling complaints which meets certain standards. The Client Account Rules 2006 set out the requirements for maintaining client accounts that must be met by those authorised businesses that handle client money.

16.9 The Compensation Act 2006 regulates:

- advertising for, or otherwise seeking out, persons who may have a cause of action;
- advising a claimant or potential claimant in relation to his claim or cause of action;
- referring details of a claim or claimant, or a cause of action or potential claimant, to another person, including a person having the right to conduct litigation;
- investigating, or commissioning the investigation of, the circumstances, merits or foundation of a claim, with a view to the use of the results in pursuing the claim;
- representation of a claimant.

PROCEDURAL RULES FOR CLAIMS MANAGEMENT SERVICES CASES

16.10 Procedure in claims management services cases are governed by the General Regulatory Chamber Rules and are dealt with in detail in the GRC entry (see **General Regulatory Chamber procedural rules**). There are no special provisions relating only to claims management services cases and the procedural rules do not differ significantly from those under the old Tribunal. In particular, the time limit for filing a notice of appeal against a decision of the Claims Regulator to the GRC is also 28 days (GRC Rules, r 22(1)(b)).

16.11 An appeal against a decision of the GRC lies to the Administrative Appeals Chamber of the Upper Tribunal on a point of law only where permission is granted either by the GRC (after a refusal to review the decision) or by the AAC itself (see **Appeals and references to the Upper Tribunal**).

17 Consent Orders

POWER TO MAKE CONSENT ORDERS

17.1 There is no provision in the TCEA 2007 enabling the First-tier Tribunal and Upper Tribunal to enter judgment by way of a consent order. However, the relevant procedural rules provide for this.

17.2 The Upper Tribunal is empowered to make consent orders under the Upper Tribunal Rules, r 39 and the Lands Chamber Rules, r 51.

17.3 Likewise, the Chambers of the First-tier Tribunal have the power to make consent orders and so dispose of proceedings: see GRC Rules, r 39; HESCC Rules, r 29; SEC Rules, r 32; TC Rules, r 34; and WPAFCC Rules, r 30. There is no equivalent provision in the IAC Rules.

17.4 The *pro forma* provision in the various Tribunal procedural rules provides:

(1) The Tribunal may, at the request of the parties but only if it considers it appropriate, make a consent order disposing of the proceedings and making such appropriate provision as the parties have agreed.

(2) Notwithstanding any other provision of these Rules, the Tribunal need not hold a hearing before making an order under paragraph (1), or provide reasons for the order.

17.5 Rule 51 of the Lands Chamber Rules is in the following form: 'Where the parties to proceedings have agreed the terms of an order to be made by the Tribunal, particulars of those terms signed by all the parties or by their representatives shall be sent to the registrar and an order may be made by the Tribunal in accordance with those terms in the absence of the parties.'

DISCRETION TO MAKE CONSENT ORDERS

17.6 The Upper Tribunal and the First-tier Tribunal will only make a consent order if it considers that it is appropriate to do so.

17.7 The following are factors that will go to the Tribunal's discretion or ability to make a consent order:

- The Tribunal should not (and arguably must not) make an order that would otherwise be outside of its jurisdiction. This is because the consent order power is encapsulated in Tribunal procedural rules which cannot expand the substantive jurisdiction of the relevant Tribunal;
- It is not clear how far this doctrine extends. As consent orders are based upon contractual agreement between the parties (which contract then takes effect and is replaced by the court's order; see *Siebe Gorman and Co Ltd v Pneupac Ltd* [1982] 1 WLR 185), it is unclear why, as a matter of principle, for example a Tribunal that would not otherwise have the power to make an award of costs (or could not do so in particular circumstances) would not be able to make an order by consent which provided for the payment of one party's legal costs by the other. It is probably the case that a consent order can be considered as being

severable, with bits that strictly are outside of the jurisdiction of the Tribunal being contractual undertakings only (*Jenkins v Livsey* [1985] AC 424, 444 per Lord Brandon) and the rest being enforceable as a court order;

- It will not ordinarily be appropriate for a Tribunal to make an order which cannot be supported on the facts. However, it may only be in a limited number of circumstances where the Tribunal is sufficiently confident as to the underlying factual basis of the dispute to express an opinion on this either way and to determine that a consent order would not be appropriate;
- It is suggested that the Tribunal will be rightly wary of making an order by consent, at least without any further consideration, where the order is adverse to the appellant individual, and particularly so in categories of case where the law is complex (such as social security) and/or the individual may be in a vulnerable position (such as mental health);
- The Tribunal will have regard to whether or not its order will be enforceable (on which see below and **Enforcement**) in particular where the order contains an undertaking by one party for example to reconsider the decision under appeal;
- It has been suggested by Jacobs (*Tribunal Practice and Procedure* (2009), paragraph 14.63) that it will not be appropriate to make a consent order in respect of the 'public' purpose of an appeal. That is to say, where a provision in the consent order would be one which furthers a public purpose such as ensuring public confidence in the administration of justice it may not be appropriate to enter an order by consent (on the distinction between public and private elements of an appeal see the Bowman Committee, *Review of the Court of Appeal (Civil Division)*, 1997, chapter 1). Whether or not this factor will bite in a particular case will depend on how broadly a given 'public' provision in a consent order is drawn. It is suggested that it will rarely be appropriate for a broad policy or procedural undertaking to be given by a public body and judicially approved through a consent order.

FORM OF CONSENT ORDERS

17.8 Though the Civil Procedure Rules do not govern proceedings before the First-tier and Upper Tribunal, consent orders drawn up between the parties should accord to the basic requirements of form set out in CPR, r 40.6(7) which provides that:

(a) the order which is agreed by the parties must be drawn up in the terms agreed;

(b) it must be expressed as being 'By Consent';

(c) it must be signed by the legal representative acting for each of the parties to whom the order relates or … by the party if he is a litigant in person.

17.9 Parties to judicial review proceedings in the Upper Tribunal should however be mindful of the Practice Direction to Part 54 of the CPR which sets out a more involved procedure for the provision of a consent order which finally disposes of a claim judicial review. In accordance with paragraph 17 of the Practice Direction to Part 54, the parties should provide two copies of a document which:

- sets out the terms of the proposed order;
- contains a short statement of the factual matters relied upon as justifying the making of the order;
- contains a brief summary of any authorities and statutory provisions relied upon as justifying the making of the order; and
- is signed by the parties

together with copies of the authorities and provisions relied upon.

17.10 It is expected that the Upper Tribunal will then, as is the case under CPR, PD54 para 17, consider the documents referred to above and will make the order under r 39 of the Upper Tribunal Rules if satisfied that the order should be made. If not so satisfied, a hearing date will be set and the claim for judicial review will proceed to be heard by the Upper Tribunal.

NO REQUIREMENT FOR A HEARING OR REASONS

17.11 As noted above, the First-tier or Upper Tribunal need not hold a hearing before making a consent order, nor does the Tribunal need to give any reasons for its agreement to make the order. However, where there is any doubt as to whether or not an order should be made by consent, it is suggested here that it will be appropriate to hear submissions, in particular when it might be said that the order was adverse to an appellant individual.

ENFORCEMENT OF CONSENT ORDERS

17.12 A consent order made by a Tribunal must be enforced in the normal way (see **Enforcement**). As most Tribunals do not have enforcement powers and none are conferred by TCEA 2007, enforcement must be effected in the High Court or county court. Pursuant to TCEA 2007, s 27, judgments of a Tribunal in England and Wales under which a sum of money is payable are now enforceable as if they were judgments of the county court or High Court of England and Wales (like provisions also apply for Scotland and Northern Ireland).

17.13 Alternatively, in a case of non-compliance with a consent order of a Tribunal, the (express or implied) existence of a liberty to apply would arguably entitle an aggrieved party to go back before the Tribunal and ask it to set aside its previous decision. This applies only to the extent that a consent order can be said to be considered a 'decision' of the Tribunal. It is suggested here that consent orders are and should properly be considered as encapsulating a decision of the Tribunal not least because such orders are not made as a matter of course but only when the Tribunal considers in appropriate to do so

(Jacobs questions whether or not this is the case: see *Tribunal Procedure and Practice* (2009), paragraph 14.48).

APPEALING OR SETTING ASIDE OF CONSENT ORDERS

17.14 Consent orders may be challenged by appeal or by an application to the Tribunal to set aside the consent order (see above and *de Lasala v de Lasala* [1980] AC 546 PC, 561 per Lord Diplock).

17.15 Generally, an appeal against a consent order will be difficult unless one of the following principles applies:

- the order was procured by fraud (a party making false statements in order to secure a consent order may be guilty of contempt (*Kirk v Walton* [2008] EWHC 1780 (QB); [2009] 1 All ER 257);
- if the order was agreed in the face of a mistake by a party going to the very heart of the agreement (*de Lasala* [1980] AC 546 PC, 561);
- exceptionally, if the order is void for uncertainty (*Times Newspapers v Fitt* [1981] ICR 637);
- if a Tribunal considered it appropriate on enquiry to make the award but one party fails to make full and frank disclosure and the Tribunal would have reached a substantially different result had it known the true position (*Jenkins v Livsey* [1985] AC 424, 438–445 per Lord Brandon).

17.16 It may be appropriate for a Tribunal to set aside a consent order for non-compliance where the conditions for setting aside are met (see **Review, correction and setting aside of Tribunal decisions**). The more common method of dealing with non-compliance is to rely on its status as a judgment of the county or High Courts under TCEA 2007, s 27, but this will only be applicable where the consent order required the payment of a sum of money. Although monetary awards will form the vast bulk of Tribunal decisions – other than those reached under the judicial review jurisdiction for which separate provision is made in TCEA 2007, ss 15(3) and 16(7) – where a consent order is made it is much more likely than in the ordinary run of Tribunal litigation that there may be an agreement to do, or refrain from doing, something. This is a significant potential lacuna, and ought itself to be indicative to the Tribunal that a setting-aside power should be available to avoid the injustice of a party agreeing a consent order and then refusing to comply with it. If the non-compliant party is the public authority it may well be possible to judicially review their failure to comply (either in the Upper Tribunal or the High Court) as unlawful and unreasonable, but this will be costly and an additional layer of litigation. If the non-compliant party is an individual, the choice is likely to be between attempting a claim for breach of contract (which has difficulty both in legal theory and practice) or applying to the Tribunal to set aside the order. It may only be possible for this to be done if an express provision for liberty to apply is built into the order; otherwise this may go beyond the jurisdiction of the Tribunal which will typically lack the power to enforce its own orders. Where a party has some concern that the order may not be complied with it would be sensible to request the inclusion of a liberty to apply provision which makes allowance for the Tribunal to consider setting aside the consent order and proceeding to reach a formal decision.

18 Constitution And Composition Of The First-Tier Tribunal

See **First-tier Tribunal; Chambers.**

18.1 The constitution and composition of the various Chambers of the First-tier Tribunal varies according to Chamber and according to the subject-matter of the proceedings and is determined by reference to the Practice Statements made by the Senior President under the First-tier Tribunal and Upper Tribunal (Composition of Tribunal) Order 2008, SI 2008/2835.

18.2 Particular types of qualification for non-lawyer members of the Tribunals are set out in The Qualifications for Appointment of Members to the First-tier Tribunal and Upper Tribunal Order 2008, SI 2008/2692 (referred to below as the '2008 Order').

THE GENERAL REGULATORY CHAMBER

18.3 The constitution and composition of the GRC in respect of any decision that disposes of proceedings or determines a preliminary issue is laid down by the Practice Statement dated 1 October 2010: *Composition of tribunals in relation to matters that fall to be decided by the General Regulatory Chamber on or after 1 September 2010* (the 'GRC Practice Statement').

Composition in specific cases

18.4 In charities cases (see **Charity cases**) the Tribunal is constituted of one, two or three members of the GRC as determined by the Chamber President. Each member of the Tribunal must be either a judge or other member who has substantial experience in a charity or not-for-profit organisation (GRC Practice Statement, paragraph 4).

18.5 In claims management cases (see **Claims management cases**) and local authority standards cases (see **Local authority standards cases**), the Tribunal is constituted of one judge and one or two other members of the GRC. If the Chamber President considers it appropriate, cases can be heard by one judge sitting alone (GRC Practice Statement, paragraphs 5, 10).

18.6 In consumer credit appeals cases (see **Consumer credit appeals**) and estate agents appeals (see **Estate agents appeals**), the Tribunal is constituted of one judge and one or two other members of the GRC (GRC Practice Statement, paragraphs 6, 8). The two other members must have substantial experience in (or more) of:

- the regulatory field;
- consumer affairs;
- an industry, trade or business sector and the matters that are likely to arise as issues in the course of disputes with regulators of such industries.

(See the 2008 Order, paras 2(4)(e), (f) and (g))

18.7 In environment cases (see **Environment cases**), the Tribunal is constituted of one judge or one judge and one or two other members where each other member has knowledge and experience of environmental matters (GRC Practice Statement, paragraph 7).

18.8 In gambling appeals cases (see **Gambling appeals**) the Tribunal is constituted of one, two or three judges as determined by the Chamber President (GRC Practice Statement, paragraph 9).

18.9 In information rights cases (see **Information rights cases**) the Tribunal is constituted of one judge and two other members each of which has substantial experience of data protection or freedom of information rights (GRC Practice Statement, paragraph 11).

18.10 In immigration services cases (see **Immigration services cases**) the Tribunal is constituted of one judge and two other members each of which has substantial experience in immigration services or the law and procedure relating to immigration (GRC Practice Statement, paragraph 12).

18.11 In transport cases (see **Transport cases**) the Tribunal is constituted of one judge and one or two other members where each other member has substantial experience in transport operations and its law and practice (GRC Practice Statement, paragraph 13).

Provisions applicable to all cases

18.12 Following a decision by the GRC disposing of proceedings, any decision taken by the GRC:

- under the Tribunal Procedure (First-tier Tribunal) (General Regulatory Chamber) Rules 2009 ('GRC Rules'), r 5(3)(l) suspending the effect of that decision pending a review of that decision or pending determination of permission to appeal; or
- reviewing that decision under TCEA 2007, s 9

must be decided by one judge unless the Chamber President considers it appropriate that it is decided by:

- the same members of the Tribunal as made that original decision; or
- a fully constituted Tribunal compromised of different members of the GRC to those which made that original decision (GRC Practice Statement, paragraph 14).

18.13 Any other decision, including decisions as to directions and decisions striking out a case under r 8 of the GRC Rules must be made by one judge (GRC Practice Statement, paragraph 14). Though the GRC Practice Statement does not contain wording to this effect, it is unlikely that the intention of paragraph 14 was that a decision striking out a case must be invariably made by one judge; if such a decision is made at a hearing, the Tribunal must be fully constituted as set out above.

18.14 In respect of GRC Tribunals consisting of more than one member, the judge will be the presiding member of the Tribunal. If the Tribunal contains more than one judge, the presiding member will be chosen by the Chamber President (GRC Practice Statement, paragraph 16).

THE HEALTH, EDUCATION AND SOCIAL CARE CHAMBER

18.15 The constitution and composition of the HESCC in respect of any decision that disposes of proceedings or determines a preliminary issue is laid down by the Practice Statement dated 16 December 2009: *Composition of tribunals in relation to matters that fall to be decided by the Health, Education and Social Care Chamber on or after 18 January 2010* (the 'HESCC Practice Statement').

Composition in specific cases

18.16 In primary health lists cases (see **Primary health lists cases**) the Tribunal is composed of three members, being: one judge, one other member who is a registered medical practitioner, registered dentist, registered optometrist, or a pharmacologist, and one other member who has substantial experience of health matters. Alternatively, where the Chamber President considers it appropriate the member with experience of health matters can be substituted for another judge (HESCC Practice Statement, paragraph 3).

18.17 In mental health cases (see **Mental health cases**) the Tribunal is composed of three members, being: one judge, one other member who is a registered medical practitioner, and one other member who has substantial experience of health or social care matters (HESCC Practice Statement, paragraph 4). The member who is a registered medical practitioner constitutes the 'appropriate member of the Tribunal' that is to conduct a medical examination of the patient under HESCC Rules, r 34.

18.18 In special educational needs or disability discrimination in schools cases (see **Special educational needs and disability cases**) the Tribunal is constituted of one judge and two other members having substantial experience of educational, child care, health or social care matters (HESCC Practice Statement, paragraph 6).

Composition in all other cases

18.19 In all other cases, the HESCC is constituted of either:

- one judge and two other members where each other member has substantial experience of one or more of educational, child care, health or social care matters; or
- where the Chamber President considers it appropriate, two judges and one other member who has substantial experience of one or more of educational, child care, health or social care matters (HESCC Practice Statement, paragraph 7).

Provisions applicable in all cases

18.20 The judge member of the HESCC will be the presiding member of the Tribunal. If the Tribunal contains more than one judge, the presiding member will be chosen by the Chamber President (HESCC Practice Statement, paragraph 8).

18.21 Following a decision by the HESCC disposing of proceedings, any decision taken by the HESCC:

- under the HESCC Rules, r 5(3)(l) suspending the effect of that decision pending a review of that decision or pending determination of permission to appeal;
- setting aside that decision under the HESCC Rules, r 45;
- in respect of permission to appeal that decision under the HESCC Rules, r 47;
- in special educational needs cases, reviewing that decision under the HESCC Rules, r 48; or
- reviewing that decision under the HESCC Rules, r 49 or TCEA 2007, s 9

must be decided by one judge unless the Chamber President considers it appropriate that it is decided by:

- the same members of the Tribunal as made that original decision; or
- a fully constituted Tribunal compromised of different members of the HESCC to those which made that original decision (HESCC Practice Statement, paragraph 9).

18.22 Any other decision, including decisions as to directions and decisions striking out a case under r 8 of the HESCC Rules must be made by one judge, except where a decision striking out a case is made at or following a hearing (HESCC Practice Statement, paragraph 10).

IMMIGRATION AND ASYLUM CHAMBER

18.23 The constitution and composition of the FTTIAC is governed by the Practice Statement dated 10 February 2010: *Immigration and Asylum Chambers of the First-tier Tribunal and the Upper Tribunal* (the 'IAC Practice Statement').

18.24 The composition arrangements for the FTTIAC are quite detailed and worth repeating in full from paragraph 2.1 of the IAC Practice Statement:

- Whether notice of appeal given in time/whether to extend time for appealing (except where Asylum and Immigration Tribunal (Procedure) Rules 2005 ('IAC Rules'), r 11 applies)/refusal to accept notice of appeal (IAC Rules, r 9): one judge.
- Whether to extend time for appealing where IAC Rules, r 11 applies (special provisions for imminent removal cases): one judge, from those approved by the Senior President to make such decisions.
- All appeals or other matters which are not specified below: one judge or a panel of two or three members, at least one of whom must be a judge and no more than one of whom may be an other member.
- The giving of any directions under IAC Rules, r 45(6): the Chamber President.
- The giving of any other directions (whether or not at case management review or other hearings): one judge.
- Appeals which are to be determined without a hearing: one judge.

- Applications for bail and other bail matters: one judge.
- Issue of a witness summons: one judge.
- Any determination that an appeal be dismissed as abandoned or finally determined: one judge.
- Review under IAC Rules, r 60(1A) and any resulting action under that paragraph: the Chamber President.
- Applications for permission to appeal to Upper Tribunal: one judge, from those approved by the Senior President to deal with such applications.
- Review under TCEA 2007, s 9 of a decision (consequent on an application for permission to appeal) and any resulting action under that section: one judge, from those approved by the Senior President to deal with s 9 matters.

18.25 However, the giving of directions, bail matters, witness summonses or the dismissal of an appeal may be dealt with by the members of the panel as a whole which is sitting in the case (IAC Practice Statement, paragraph 2.2).

THE SOCIAL ENTITLEMENT CHAMBER

Composition in social security and child support cases

18.26 The constitution and composition of the SEC in respect of any decision that disposes of proceedings or determines a preliminary issue in social security and child support cases is laid down by the Practice Statement dated 30 October 2008: *Composition of tribunals in social security and child support cases in the Social Entitlement Chamber on or after 3 November 2009* (the 'Social Security Practice Statement').

18.27 Where the appeal relates to relates to an attendance allowance or a disability living allowance under Part III of the Social Security Contributions and Benefits Act 1992, the Tribunal is constituted of:

- one judge;
- one other member who is a registered medical practitioner;
- and one other member who is experienced in dealing with the physical or mental needs of disabled persons because they either work with disabled persons in a professional or voluntary capacity or are themselves disabled (see 2008 Order, paragraph 2(3)).

(Social Security Practice Statement, paragraph 4).

18.28 In respect of the following appeals the Tribunal is constituted of one judge and one other member who is a registered medical practitioner:

- appeals involving a personal capability assessment as defined in the Social Security (Incapacity for Work) (General) Regulations 1995, SI 1995/311 reg 2(1):
- appeals involving a limited capability for work assessment as defined in the Employment and Support Allowance Regulations 2008, SI 2008/794, r 2(1);

- appeals involving the determination of limited capability for work-related activity within the meaning of the Employment and Support Allowance Regulations 2008, regs 34 and 35;
- appeals made under the Social Security (Recovery of Benefits) Act 1997, s 11(1)(b);
- appeals raising issues relating to severe disablement allowance under the Social Security Contributions and Benefits Act 1992, s 68 or industrial injuries benefit under Part V of that Act (except for an appeal solely concerned with the making of a declaration of an industrial accident under the Social Security Act 1998, s 29(2));
- appeals made under the Vaccine Damage Payments Act 1979, s 4;
- appeals against a certificate of NHS charges under the Health and Social Care (Community Health and Standards) Act 2003, s 157(1);
- appeals arising under Part IV of the Child Maintenance and Other Payments Act 2008.

(Social Security Practice Statement, paragraph 5).

18.29 In any other case, the Tribunal will consist of one judge (Social Security Practice Statement, paragraph 6).

18.30 The constitution of the SEC in respect of the appeals listed above is variable at the discretion of the Chamber President (Social Security Practice Statement, paragraphs 7–8) (or a judge to whom the Chamber President has delegated the relevant function, see Social Security Practice Statement, paragraph 9). In particular:

- where the appeal may require the examination of financial accounts, the Chamber President may direct that the Tribunal contains an accountant (see 2008 Order, paragraph 2(i) for the qualifications accepted as rendering someone 'an accountant' for these purposes) (Social Security Practice Statement, paragraph 7a);
- where the complexity of the medical issues raised by an appeal demands it, the Chamber President may direct that the Tribunal contain an additional member who is a registered medical practitioner;
- the Chamber President may in any event direct that there be added any further Tribunal judge or member as he or she considers appropriate for the purposes of providing further experience for that judge or member or for assisting the Chamber President in the monitoring of standards of decision-making;
- where the Chamber President considers that a particular case only raises questions of law and that to decide the matter does not require the expertise of any of the non-judge members of the Tribunal, the Chamber President may direct that the Tribunal consists of a sole judge, or a judge plus any member whose experience and qualifications are necessary to decide the matter.

This is provided that in all cases, the number of members on the Tribunal does not exceed three (Social Security Practice Statement, paragraph 3).

Directions by the Chamber President that members be 'added' to the Tribunal cannot take the total number of members above three and accordingly such a direction cannot be made in respect of appeals relating to an attendance allowance or a disability living allowance under Part III of the Social Security Contributions and Benefits Act 1992 as these appeals must in any event be heard by a prescribed three-member panel (see above and Social Security Practice Statement, paragraph 4).

Composition in asylum support appeals

18.31 All asylum support cases before the SEC (see **Asylum support appeals**) must be decided by one judge (Practice Statement dated 30 October 2008: *Composition of tribunals in relation to matters that fall to be decided in asylum support cases in the Social Entitlement Chamber on or after 3 November 2008*, paragraph 3).

Composition in criminal injuries compensation appeals

18.32 In criminal injuries compensation cases (see **Criminal injuries compensation appeals**) any matter falling to be decided by the SEC at a hearing must be decided by two or three members each of whom is either a judge of another member who is appropriately qualified (Practice Statement dated 30 October 2008: *Composition of tribunals in relation to matters that fall to be decided in criminal injury compensation cases in the Social Entitlement Chamber on or after 3 November 2008*, paragraph 3 ('Criminal Injuries Practice Statement')). To be appropriately qualified, the member must satisfy one or more of the following criteria:

- The member is a registered medical practitioner;
- The member is a registered nurse;
- The member is a registered dentist;
- The member is a clinical psychologist;
- The member is a pharmacologist;
- The member is an accountant;
- The member is experienced in dealing with the physical or mental needs of disabled persons because he or she works with disabled persons in a professional or voluntary capacity or is disabled;
- The member has substantial experience of educational, child care, health, or social care matters; or
- The member has substantial experience of dealing with victims of violent crime.

(See 2008 Order, paragraphs 2(2)(a)–(d), (f), (i), 2(3), (2)(4)(b), (c)).

18.33 In criminal injuries compensation cases falling to be decided otherwise than at a hearing must be decided by one member who is a judge or who has any of the qualifications set out above (Criminal Injuries Practice Statement, paragraph 5).

Provisions applicable in all cases

18.34 Only the Chamber President may designate a case a lead case under r 18 of the SEC Rules (or otherwise) (Social Security Practice Statement, paragraph 10).

18.35 Decisions on permission to appeal under the Tribunal Procedure (First-tier Tribunal) (Social Entitlement Chamber) Procedural Rules 2008 ('SEC Rules'), r 39 or reviews of a decision under the SEC Rules, r 40 or TCEA 2007, s 9 must be carried out by a single salaried Tribunal judge and preferably by the salaried judge who constituted or was a member of the Tribunal who made the decision unless this would be impracticable or cause undue delay (Social Security Practice Statement, paragraph 11).

18.36 The judge member of the SEC will be the presiding member of the Tribunal. If the Tribunal contains more than one judge, the presiding member will be chosen by the Chamber President (Social Security Practice Statement, paragraph 12). The presiding member may regulate the procedure of the Tribunal and it will be for him or her to give any written statement of reasons under the SEC Rules, r 34(2) (Social Security Practice Statement, paragraph 13).

18.37 In cases involving a medical or physical examination in accordance with the SEC Rules, r 25, the 'appropriate member' of the Tribunal is the member who is a registered medical practitioner (Social Security Practice Statement, paragraph 14).

18.38 These rules appear only in the Social Security Practice Statement without repetition in the other SEC Practice Statements and without express indication of their application to cases not about social security or child support. However, the SEC Rules which the Practice Statement refers to apply in all SEC hearings and there is no logical reason why they should be restricted to certain types of case only.

TAX CHAMBER

18.39 The composition of the Tax Chamber is determined in accordance with the Practice Statement dated 27 August 2009: *Composition of tribunals in relation to matters that fall to be decided by the Tax Chamber of the First-tier Tribunal and the Tax and Chancery Chamber of Upper Tribunal on or after 1 September 2009*, ('Tax Practice Statement').

18.40 Members of the Tax Chamber consist of judges and other members (Tax Practice Statement, paragraph 1). The other members must meet one or more of the following criteria:

- The member is a pharmacologist;
- The member is an accountant;
- The member is a member or Fellow of the Royal Institution of Chartered Surveyors;
- The member has substantial experience in tax matters and related tax procedures; or
- The member has substantial experience n a business, trade or not-for-profit organisation.

(See 2008 Order, paragraphs 2(2)(f)–(i), 2(4)(h)–(i)).

Composition in specific cases

18.41 The composition of the Tax Chamber is determined by the level of case before it (see **Tax Chamber** for more details):

- In a default paper case, a decision must be made by one judge or other member (Tax Practice Statement, paragraph 3);
- In a basic case:
  - a decision that disposes of proceedings or determines a preliminary issue made at or following a hearing must be made by either one or two members each of whom is a judge or other member. In exceptional cases in which the Chamber President considers it appropriate, a basic case may be determined by a panel of three judges or members (Tax Practice Statement, paragraph 4);
  - any other decision, including the giving of directions or striking out a case under the TC Rules, r 8 (except a decision to strike out at, or following, a hearing) must be made by one judge, or one other member of the Tax Chamber who has been designated by the Chamber President to make such decisions (Tax Practice Statement, paragraph 6).
- In a standard or complex case:
  - a decision that disposes of proceedings or determines a preliminary issue made at or following a hearing must be made by one judge or one judge and one or two members each of whom is a judge or other member as determined by the Chamber President (Tax Practice Statement, paragraph 7);
  - any other decision, including the giving of directions or striking out a case under the TC Rules, r 8 (except a decision to strike out at, or following, a hearing) must be made by one judge (Tax Practice Statement, paragraph 9).

Provisions applicable to all cases

18.42 Where the tribunal consists of a judge and another member or other members, the judge will be the presiding member. Where more than one judge is to decide the matter, the presiding member will be chosen by the Chamber President (Tax Practice Statement, paragraphs 5, 8).

18.43 Following a decision by the Tax Chamber disposing of proceedings, any decision taken by the Tax Chamber:

- under the TC Rules, r 5(3)(l) suspending the effect of that decision pending a review of that decision or pending determination of permission to appeal;
- setting aside that decision under the TC Rules, r 38;
- in respect of permission to appeal that decision under the TC Rules, r 40;
- reviewing that decision under the TC Rules, r 41 or TCEA 2007, s 9;

must be decided by one judge unless the Chamber President considers it appropriate that it is decided by:

- the same members of the Tribunal as made that original decision; or
- a fully constituted Tribunal compromised of different members to those which made that original decision (Tax Practice Statement, paragraph 10).

The War Pensions and Armed Forces Compensation Chamber

18.44 The constitution and composition of the WPAFCC is governed by the Practice Statement dated 30 October 2008: *Composition of tribunals in relation to matters that fall to be decided by the War Pensions and Armed Forces Compensation Chamber on or after 3 November 2008* (the 'WPAFCC Practice Statement').

18.45 A decision by the WPAFCC that disposes of proceedings or determines a preliminary issue at or following a hearing must be made by a three (or exceptionally four) member Tribunal consisting of:

- one judge; and
- one other member who has substantial experience of service in Her Majesty's naval, military or air forces or who is a transferred-in other member from the Pensions Appeal Tribunal and is not a registered medical practitioner; and
- one other member who is a registered medical practitioner or, in a particular case, or class of case, where the Chamber President considers it appropriate in order for the Tribunal to decide the matter, two other members each of whom is a registered medical practitioner.

(WPAFCC Practice Statement, paragraph 3).

18.46 The presiding member will be the judge (WPAFCC Practice Statement, paragraph 4).

18.47 Following a decision by the WPAFCC disposing of proceedings, any decision taken by the WPAFCC:

- under the Tribunal Procedure (First-tier Tribunal) (War Pensions and Armed Forces Compensation Chamber) Rules 2008 ('WPAFCC Rules'), r 5(3)(l) suspending the effect of that decision pending a review of that decision or pending determination of permission to appeal;
- setting aside that decision under the WPAFCC Rules, r 35;
- in respect of permission to appeal that decision under the WPAFCC Rules, r 37; or
- reviewing that decision under the WPAFCC Rules, r 39 or TCEA 2007, s 9;

must be decided by one judge unless the Chamber President considers it appropriate that it is decided by the same members of the Tribunal as made that original (WPAFCC Practice Statement, paragraph 5).

18.48 Any other decision, including the giving of directions or striking out a case under the WPAFCC Rules, r 8 (except a decision to strike out at, or following, a hearing) must be made by one judge (WPAFCC Practice Statement, paragraph 6).

18.49 In cases involving a medical examination in accordance with the WPAFCC Rules, r 24, the 'appropriate member' of the Tribunal is the member who is a registered medical practitioner (WPAFCC Practice Statement, paragraph 7).

19 Constitution And Composition Of The Upper Tribunal

See **Chambers; Upper Tribunal.**

19.1 The constitution and composition of the various Chambers of the Upper Tribunal varies according to Chamber and according to the subject-matter of the proceedings and is determined by reference to the Practice Statements made by the Senior President under the First-tier Tribunal and Upper Tribunal (Composition of Tribunal) Order 2008, SI 2008/2835.

19.2 Particular types of qualification for non-lawyer members of the Tribunals are set out in The Qualifications for Appointment of Members to the First-tier Tribunal and Upper Tribunal Order 2008, SI 2008/2692 (referred to below as the '2008 Order').

THE ADMINISTRATIVE APPEALS CHAMBER

19.3 The constitution and composition of the AAC is determined by the Practice Statement dated 1 October 2010: *Composition of tribunals in relation to matters that fall to be decided by the Administrative Appeals Chamber of the Upper Tribunal on or after 1 October 2010* (the 'AAC Practice Statement').

19.4 Proceedings before the AAC are to be determined by a single judge of the Upper Tribunal subject to the following exceptions:

– where the Senior President of Tribunals or the Chamber President considers that the matter involves a question of law of special difficulty or an important point of principle or practice, the matter will be decided by two or three judges of the Upper Tribunal (the Senior President and Chamber President have a general discretion to direct that a case be heard by two or three judges when in their view this is appropriate);

– where the matter is the determination of an appeal brought under the Safeguarding Vulnerable Groups Act 2006, s 4 (see **Care standards cases**) (otherwise than by the striking out of the appeal under the Tribunal Procedure (Upper Tribunal) Rules 2008 ('Upper Tribunal Rules'), r 8 (see **Striking out**)), the matter will be decided by:

  - one judge and two other members of the Upper Tribunal; or
  - where the Senior President or Chamber President considers that the matter involves a question of law of special difficulty or an important point of principle or practice, or that it is otherwise appropriate, two judges and one other member of the Upper Tribunal;

– where the matter is the determination of an appeal against the decision of a Traffic Commissioner (see **Transport cases**) and the Senior President of Tribunals or Chamber President considers it appropriate the matter is to be decided by:

  - one judge and one other member of the Upper Tribunal; or
  - where the Senior President or Chamber President considers that the matter involves a question of law of special difficulty or an

important point of principle or practice, or that it is otherwise appropriate, two judges and one other member of the Upper Tribunal.

- where the matter is the determination of a national security certificate the matter is to be decided by three judges who, prior to 18 January 2009 (*sic* – the Practice Statement says 2009 but it must mean 2010), were designated under paragraph 2(1) of Schedule 18 to the Data Protection Act 1998;
- where the matter is the determination of an appeal transferred to the Upper Tribunal from the First-tier Tribunal by the General Regulatory Chamber, and the Senior President or Chamber President considers it appropriate, the matter is to be decided by:
  - one judge and one other member of the Upper Tribunal; or
  - where the Senior President or Chamber President considers that the matter involves a question of law of special difficulty or an important point of principle or practice, or that it is otherwise appropriate, two judges and one other member of the Upper Tribunal.

(See AAC Practice Statement, paragraph 3).

19.5 Decisions in respect of any ancillary matters arising for determination in the above cases prior to the making of a decision which disposes of the proceedings may be decided by the presiding member or by all the members. If the ancillary matter is to be determined without a hearing, it may be determined by a judge or Registrar nominated by the Chamber President or presiding member (AAC Practice Statement, paragraph 9).

19.6 In cases brought under the Safeguarding Vulnerable Groups Act 2006, s 4, the 'other members of the Tribunal' referred to above must satisfy the following criteria:

- The other member of the Tribunal must have experience in the provision of services provided by local authorities under the Adoption Act 1976 or the Children Act 1989 or which are similar to such services, and experience in relevant social work; or
- The member must have:
  - experience in the provision of services by a Health Authority, a Special Health Authority, a National Health Service trust, an NHS foundation trust or a Primary Care Trust; or
  - experience in the provision of education in a school or in an institution within the further education sector; or
  - experience of being employed by a local education authority in connection with the exercise of its functions under Part I of the Education Act 1996.

  and must have:

  - experience in the conduct of disciplinary investigations; or
  - experience on an Area Child Protection Committee, or similar experience; or

- experience of taking part in child protection conferences or in child protection review conferences, or similar experience; or
- experience in negotiation the conditions of service of employees.

(See AAC Practice Statement, paragraphs 4, 5, 6 and 7).

19.7 In respect of the determination of an appeal against the decision of a Traffic Commissioner, the 'other members of the Tribunal' must have substantial experience in transport operations and its law and practice (AAC Practice Statement, paragraph 4A).

19.8 In respect of the determination of an information rights appeal transferred by the General Regulatory Chamber, the 'other members of the Tribunal' must have substantial experience of data protection or of freedom of information (including environmental information) rights (AAC Practice Statement, paragraph 4B).

19.9 If the Tribunal consists of more than one judge, the presiding member will be the senior judge as determined by the Senior President or Chamber President. If the Tribunal consists of a judge and two other members of the Tribunal, the judge will be the presiding member (AAC Practice Statement, paragraph 8).

19.10 Where the Upper Tribunal has given a decision that disposes of proceedings, a number of consequential matters must be decided by the same member or members of the Upper Tribunal as gave that decision (AAC Practice Statement, paragraph 10). The following decisions must be decided by an identically constituted Tribunal as made that first decision:

- applications under the Upper Tribunal Rules, r 5(3)(l) suspending the effect of that decision pending a review of that decision or pending determination of permission to appeal;
- applications setting aside that decision under the Upper Tribunal Rules, r 43;
- in respect of permission to appeal that decision under the Upper Tribunal Rules, r 45; or
- reviewing that decision under the Upper Tribunal Rules, r 46 or the Tribunals, Courts and Enforcement Act 2007 ('TCEA 2007'), s 10;
- in respect of a decision made under the Forfeiture Act 1982, reviewing that decision under the Upper Tribunal Rules, r 47.

19.11 If it would be impracticable or would cause undue delay for the above decisions to be made by an identically constituted Tribunal as made the first decision the position changes. In such cases, where the initial decision was made by more than one member of the AAC, the decisions listed above must be made by the presiding member or any other judge from that constitution if available. In all other cases, the decisions listed above must be made by another judge of the Upper Tribunal nominated by the Chamber President (AAC Practice Statement, paragraph 11).

IMMIGRATION AND ASYLUM CHAMBER

19.12 The constitution and composition of the IAC, Upper Tribunal, is governed by the Practice Statement dated 10 February 2010: *Immigration and Asylum*

Chambers of the First-tier Tribunal and the Upper Tribunal (the 'IAC Practice Statement').

19.13 The ordinary rule in the UTIAC is that matters are decided by a single judge (IAC Practice Statement, paragraph 6.1). Exceptions to this are:

- Where the matter involves a question of law of special difficulty or an important point of principle or practice, or otherwise appropriate, the Senior President or Chamber President may decide that a panel or two or three judges should hear the matter (IAC Practice Statement, paragraph 6.2).
- The Senior President or Chamber President may decide that a panel of one judge and two other members, or two judges and one other member, is appropriate (IAC Practice Statement, paragraph 6.3).
- An application for permission to appeal to the Upper Tribunal is to be decided by one Upper Tribunal judge, from those approved by the Senior President or the Chamber President (IAC Practice Statement, paragraph 6.4).
- Although any procedural or ancillary matter arising in cases falling under one of the above exceptions may be decided by any judge (IAC Practice Statement,paragraph 6.5).

LANDS CHAMBER

19.14 The constitution and composition of the Land Chamber is determined by the Practice Statement dated 9 June 2009: *Composition of tribunals in relation to matters that fall to be decided by the Lands Chamber of the Upper Tribunal on or after 1 June 2009* (the 'Lands Chamber Practice Statement').

19.15 Matters decided by the Lands Chamber are typically decided by one, two or three members of the Tribunal as determined by the Chamber President (Lands Chamber Practice Statement, paragraph 3). A matter may be decided solely by members of the Tribunal who are 'other members' of the Tribunal. Other members are not judges but must be a member or Fellow of the Royal Institution of Chartered Surveyors (see the 2008 Order, paragraph 2(2)(h)).

19.16 Where the Lands Chamber gives a decision disposing of proceedings, determination of an application for a review of the decision or for permission to appeal under Part 8A of the Lands Tribunal Rules 1996 ('Lands Chamber Rules') or TCEA 2007, s 10, it must be decided by the same members of members of the Tribunal that gave that original decision (Lands Chamber Practice Statement, paragraph 5) unless this is impractical or would cause undue delay in which case the matter must be decided by:

- the presiding member or any other judge from the Tribunal that made the original decision if available; or
- another judge of the Upper Tribunal nominated by the Chamber President (Lands Chamber Practice Statement, paragraph 6).

19.17 Where more than one member of the Lands Chamber is to decide a matter, the presiding member is the Chamber President where he or she is one of the members, or, if the President is not a member of the Tribunal deciding the matter, any member nominated by the Chamber President.

TAX AND CHANCERY CHAMBER

19.18 The constitution and composition of the Tax and Chancery Chamber is determined by the Practice Statement dated 27 August 2009: *Composition of tribunals in relation to matters that fall to be decided by the Tax Chamber of the First-Tier Tribunal and the Tax and Chancery Chamber of Upper Tribunal on or after 1 September 2009* ('TCC Practice Statement').

19.19 A decision that disposes of proceedings or determines a preliminary issue made at, or following, a hearing must be made by:

- one judge; or
- one judge and one or two members each of whom is a judge or other member as determined by the Chamber President (TCC Practice Statement, paragraph 11).

19.20 Members of the TCC consist of judges and other members (TCC Practice Statement, paragraph 1). The other members must meet one or more of the following criteria:

- The member is a pharmacologist;
- The member is an accountant;
- The member is a member or Fellow of the Royal Institution of Chartered Surveyors;
- The member has substantial experience in tax matters and related tax procedures; or
- The member has substantial experience n a business, trade or not-for-profit organisation.

(See 2008 Order, paragraphs 2(2)(f)–(i), 2(4)(h)–(i)).

19.21 Any decision other than one that disposes of proceedings or determines a preliminary issue made at, or following, a hearing, including one giving directions or one striking out a case under the Upper Tribunal Rules, r 8 (except at, or following, a hearing) (TCC Practice Statement, paragraph 13).

19.22 Where the TCC has given a decision that disposes of proceedings a number of consequential matters must be decided by the same member or members of the TCC as gave that decision (TCC Practice Statement, paragraph 14). The following decisions must be decided by an identically constituted Tribunal as made that first decision:

- applications under the Upper Tribunal Rules, r 5(3)(l) suspending the effect of that decision pending a review of that decision or pending determination of permission to appeal;
- applications setting aside that decision under the Upper Tribunal Rules, r 43;
- in respect of permission to appeal that decision under the Upper Tribunal Rules, r 45; or
- reviewing that decision under the Upper Tribunal Rules, r 46 or TCEA 2007, s 10.

19.23 If it would be impracticable or would cause undue delay for the above decisions to be made by an identically constituted Tribunal as made the first decision, the position changes. In such cases, where the initial decision was made by more than one member of the TCC, the decisions listed above must be made by the presiding member or any other judge from that constitution if available. In all other cases, the decisions listed above must be made by another judge of the Upper Tribunal nominated by the Chamber President (TCC Practice Statement, paragraph 15).

19.24 The presiding member of the TCC will be the judge member of the Tribunal or if more than one judge is to decide the matter the 'presiding member' will be chosen by the Chamber President (TCC Practice Statement, paragraph 12).

20 Consumer Credit Cases

JURISDICTION TO HEAR CONSUMER CREDIT APPEALS CASES

Consumer Credit Appeal Tribunal

20.1 The Consumer Credit Appeals Tribunal ('CCAT') was established from 6 April 2008 by the Consumer Credit Act 2006 which amended and updated the Consumer Credit Act 1974 (see the Consumer Credit Act 1974, s 40A).

20.2 The CCAT heard appeals arising out of the decisions of the OFT taken pursuant to the OFT's administration of the licensing regime for traders in the consumer credit or consumer hire business. The OFT grants consumer credit licenses to those it consider suitable under the licensing regime established by the Consumer Credit Act 1974 and in accordance with the criteria set out in the 1974 Act.

20.3 The CCAT also heard appeals against decisions of the OFT under the Money Laundering Regulations 2007, SI 2007/2157.

20.4 Typical appeals included appeals against decisions of the OFT:

- Refusing to issue, renew or vary a licence under the Consumer Credit Act;
- Excluding an individual from a group licence;
- Compulsorily varying, suspending or revoking a standard or group licence;
- Refusing to end the suspension of a licence in accordance with the terms of an application;
- Imposing or refusing to withdraw a consumer credit prohibition order or restriction;
- Refusing to register or cancelling the registration of an applicant under the Money Laundering Regulations;
- Imposing a penalty under the Money Laundering Regulations.

The CCAT was obliged to maintain a register (the 'Register') of appeals to the Tribunal and of its decisions disposing of appeals. The Register must be reasonably accessible to the public without charge (Consumer Credit Appeals Tribunal Rules 2008, SI 2008/668 (the 'CCAT Rules'), r 14).

Transfer of functions to the General Regulatory Chamber

20.5 As of 1 September 2009, the jurisdiction of the CCAT was transferred to the General Regulatory Chamber (see **General Regulatory Chamber**) by The Transfer of Functions of the Consumer Credit Appeals Tribunal Order 2009, SI 2009/1835.

PROCEDURE IN CONSUMER CREDIT CASES

The GRC Procedure

20.6 From 1 September 2009, with the transfer of the CCAT's jurisdiction to the GRC, consumer credit cases will follow the procedure for all cases other than charity cases before the GRC (see **General Regulatory Chamber procedural rules**). There are no separate provisions in the GRC Rules for consumer credit cases.

Specific features of consumer credit cases

20.7 The CCAT Rules do not differ markedly from the Tribunal Procedure (First-tier Tribunal) (General Regulatory Chamber) Rules 2009 ('GRC Rules') and the transfer of the CCAT's functions to the GRC has been unproblematic. Those familiar with the operation of the CCAT Rules should however note the following four points.

20.8 First, the CCAT was obliged to maintain the Register containing particulars of appeal to, and decisions of (including the final determination) the CCAT (CCAT Rules, r 14(1)). The Register was to be reasonably accessible to any person without charge (CCAT Rules, r 14(2)). The GRC Rules contain no equivalent requirement to maintain the Register, but it is the practice of the First-tier Tribunal (Consumer Credit) to in fact keep such a Register. The Register is available on the Tribunal's website, along with the Register of the CCAT.

20.9 Secondly, unlike before many First-tier Tribunals (and other finance tribunals), the CCAT Rules did not provide that the appellant may file a reply in response to the Regulator's statement of case. Under the GRC Rules, however, the appellant does have such a right and may reply to the OFT's response by way of written submission and provision of further documents (GRC Rules, r 24(1)).

20.10 Thirdly, the direct right of appeal from decisions of CCAT to the Court of Appeal or Court of Session (as applicable) (the Consumer Credit Act 1974, s 41A) is abolished. Parties unhappy with a decision of the GRC must proceed by way of appeal on a point of law to the Administrative Appeals Chamber of the Upper Tribunal (see **Appeals from the First-tier Tribunal** and **Appeals and references to the Upper Tribunal**).

20.11 Finally, parties should note the slightly differing rules as to costs as between the CCAT and the GRC. In proceedings before the CCAT, costs were available under paragraph 15 of Schedule 1A to the Consumer Credit Act 1974 (not the CCAT Rules) where: (a) the Tribunal disposes of an appeal or an appeal is withdrawn before the Tribunal disposes of it, and (b) the Tribunal thinks that a party to the appeal acted vexatiously, frivolously or unreasonably in bringing the appeal or otherwise in relation to the appeal, it may order that party to pay to the other party the whole or a part of the costs incurred by the other party in relation to the appeal. The GRC may only make an award for costs in consumer credit cases in two circumstances:

- under TCEA, s 29(4) in respect of wasted costs; or
- if the GRC considers that a party has acted unreasonably in bringing, defending or conducting the proceedings (see **Costs**).

21 Costs

GENERAL POWER TO AWARD COSTS

21.1 Prior to the enactment of the TCEA 2007, the power of many tribunals to award costs was extremely limited, with enabling legislation often containing no or a limited power as to costs (absent a power in enabling legislation, no tribunal may award costs: *Jones v Department of Employment* [1989] QB 1, 25 per Slade LJ). This has been changed by TCEA 2007, s 29, which gives the First-tier Tribunal and Upper Tribunal a general discretionary power to award costs.

21.2 TCEA 2007, s 29 provides that all costs (in Scotland, expenses) of and incidental to proceedings before the First-tier Tribunal and Upper Tribunal shall be in the discretion of the tribunal in which the proceedings take place. Section 29(2) gives the tribunal full power to determine by whom and to what extent such costs are to be paid.

COSTS IN THE FIRST-TIER TRIBUNAL

Tribunal procedural rules as to costs

21.3 Whilst TCEA 2007, s 29 creates a broad discretionary power for tribunals to award costs, it was never intended that this should apply across all jurisdiction or in all Chambers (see TCEA Explanatory Notes, paragraph 116). Section 29(3) thus stipulates that the general discretion to award costs is subject to Tribunal procedure rules. This gives flexibility to the new system to determine where a costs regime would be appropriate and what limits are appropriate. Reference must be made to the relevant procedural rules in each Chamber or Tribunal.

Costs in the General Regulatory Chamber

21.4 By virtue of the Tribunal Procedure (First-tier Tribunal) (General Regulatory Chamber) Rules 2009 ('GRC Rules'), r 10(1), the General Regulatory Chamber may only make an award for costs in three circumstances:

- under TCEA 2007, s 29(4) in respect of wasted costs (see below);
- if the GRC considers that a party has acted unreasonably in bringing, defending or conducting the proceedings;
- in cases in which the Charity Commission or Information Commissioner is the respondent and a decision, direction or order of the Charity Commission or Information Commissioner is the subject of the proceedings, where the Tribunal considers that the decision, direction or order was unreasonable.

21.5 An order for costs may be made by the GRC on application by a party or of its own initiative (GRC Rules, r 10(2)) but must not be made unless the paying party is first given the opportunity to make representations (GRC Rules, r 10(5)(a)). If the paying party is an individual, the GRC must have regard to the individual's financial means (GRC Rules, r 10(5)(b)).

21.6 A party applying for an order for costs do so in writing, with a copy of the application being provided to the Tribunal and to the party against whom it is proposed the order be made (GRC Rules, r 10(3)(a)). The application must be accompanied with a schedule of costs such as would allow the GRC to summarily assess those costs (GRC Rules, r 10(3)(b)). The application must be made within 14 days of the date on which the GRC sends to the applying party the decision notice which finally disposes of all issues in the proceedings (GRC Rules, r 10(4)).

21.7 The amount of costs to be paid may be ascertained by (GRC Rules, r 10(6)):

- summary assessment;
- agreement of a specified sum by the paying person and the person entitled to receive the costs; or
- assessment of the whole or a specified part of the costs incurred by the receiving party, if not agreed. The GRC may at its discretion specify that such an assessment is to take place on the indemnity basis.

21.8 If costs are to be ascertained by assessment, either the paying or receiving party may apply to the county court for a detailed assessment of cost in accordance with the Civil Procedure Rules (GRC Rules, r 10(7)(a)). If the order is for expenses in Scotland, the application should be made to the Auditor of the Court of Session (GRC Rules, r 10(7)(b)). In Northern Ireland, applications should be made to the county court for the costs to be taxed (GRC Rules, r 10(7)(c)).

Costs in the Health, Education and Social Care Chamber

21.9 By virtue of the HESCC Rules, r 10(1), the Health, Education and Social Care Chamber may only make an award for costs in two circumstances:

- under TCEA 2007, s 29(4) in respect of wasted costs (see below);
- if the HESCC considers that a party has acted unreasonably in bringing, defending or conducting the proceedings.

21.10 It should be noted that it is not usually the practice to award costs in cases involving children, even if such costs are available in principle (*Gojkovic v Gojkovic (No. 2)* [1992] Fam 40; although an award will be made where a party has behaved unreasonably: *R v R (Costs: Child Case)* [1997] 2 FLR 95).

21.11 In mental health cases, the HESCC may make a costs award in respect of wasted costs (see below). However, in mental health cases, the HESCC has no power to make any other cost order, including an order against a party if the HESCC considers it has acted unreasonably in bringing, defending or conducting the proceedings (HESCC Rules, r 10(2)).

21.12 An order for costs may be made by the HESCC on application by a party or of its own initiative (HESCC Rules, r 10(3)) but must not be made unless the paying party is first given the opportunity to make representations (HESCC Rules, r 10(6)(a)). If the paying party is an individual, the HESCC must have regard to the individual's financial means (HESCC Rules, r 10(6)(b)).

21.13 A party applying for an order for costs do so in writing, with a copy of the application being provided to the Tribunal and to the party against whom it is proposed the order be made (HESCC Rules, r 10(4)(a)). The application must be accompanied with a schedule of costs such as would allow the

HESCC to summarily assess those costs (HESCC Rules, r 10(4)(b)). The application must be made within 14 days of the date on which the HESCC sends the decision notice which finally disposes of all issues in the proceedings (HESCC Rules, r 10(5)).

21.14 The amount of costs to be paid may be ascertained by (HESCC Rules, r 10(7)):

- summary assessment;
- agreement of a specified sum by the paying person and the person entitled to receive the costs; or
- assessment of the whole or a specified part of the costs incurred by the receiving party, if not agreed. The HESCC may at its discretion specify that such an assessment is to take place on the indemnity basis.

21.15 If costs are to be ascertained by assessment, either the paying or receiving party may apply to the county court for a detailed assessment of costs in accordance with the Civil Procedure Rules (HESCC Rules, r 10(8)).

Costs in the Immigration and Asylum Chamber

21.16 The IAC Rules, r 23A expressly provides that the FTTIAC may not make an award of costs or expenses under TCEA 2007, s 29.

Costs in the Social Entitlement Chamber

21.17 The SEC Rules, r 10 expressly provides that the Social Entitlement Chamber has no power to make an award in respect of costs or expenses.

Costs in the Tax Chamber

21.18 By virtue of the TC Rules, r 10(1), the Tax Chamber may only make an award for costs in three circumstances:

- under TCEA 2007, s 29(4) in respect of wasted costs (see below);
- if the Tax Chamber considers that a party or their representative has acted unreasonably in bringing, defending or conducting the proceedings; or
- in cases which have been allocated as a Complex case under TC Rules, r 23 (see **Tax Chamber**) in which the taxpayer has not sent a written request to the Tax Chamber within 28 days of receiving notice that the case had been allocated as a Complex case that the proceedings be excluded from potential liability for costs or expenses.

21.19 These provisions permit greater flexibility on costs recovery than was possible before the General and Special Commissioners.

21.20 An order for costs may be made by the Tax Chamber on application by a party or of its own initiative (TC Rules, r 10(2)) but must not be made unless the paying party is first given the opportunity to make representations (TC Rules, r 10(5)(a)). If the paying party is an individual, the Tax Chamber must have regard to the individual's financial means (TC Rules, r 10(5)(b)).

21.21 A party applying for an order for costs do so in writing, with a copy of the application being provided to the Tribunal and to the party against whom it is proposed the order be made (TC Rules, r 10(3)(a)). The application must be accompanied with a schedule of costs such as would allow the Tax Chamber to summarily assess those costs (TC Rules, r 10(3)(b)). The application must be made no later than 28 days after the date on which the Tax Chamber sends to the applying party the decision notice which finally disposes of all issues in the proceedings or a notice of withdrawal under r 17 which ends proceedings (TC Rules, r 10(4)).

21.22 The amount of costs to be paid may be ascertained by (TC Rules, r 10(6)):

- summary assessment;
- agreement of a specified sum by the paying person and the person entitled to receive the costs; or
- assessment of the whole or a specified part of the costs incurred by the receiving party, if not agreed. The Tax Chamber may at its discretion specify that such an assessment is to take place on the indemnity basis.

21.23 If costs are to be ascertained by assessment, either the paying or receiving party may apply to the county court, High Court or the Costs Office of the Supreme Court (as specified in the order) for a detailed assessment (TC Rules, r 10(7)(a)). The assessment will take place in accordance with the Civil Procedure Rules as if those rules had applied throughout the proceedings. If the order is for expenses in Scotland, the application should be made to the Auditor of the Court of Session (TC Rules, r 10(7)(b)). In Northern Ireland, applications should be made to the Taxing Office of the High Court of Northern Ireland (TC Rules, r 10(7)(c)).

21.24 Ministerial statements have set out the policy of HMRC in relation to costs recovery, suggesting that HMRC are to waive costs in the Upper Tribunal or above, particularly where HMRC was the appellant. Relevant factors will be financial hardship, clarification of a wider point of law and the efficient collection of revenue. HMRC will usually come to any arrangement in advance of the hearing: *Hansard*, HC Vol. 490, col.29WS (27 March 2009) (Stephen Timms); HL Vol. 709, col.60WS (30 March 2009) (Lord Myners).

Costs in the War Pensions and Armed Forces Chamber

21.25 The WPAFCC Rules, r 10 expressly provides that the War Pensions and Armed Forces Compensation Chamber has no power to make an award in respect of costs, although no mention is made of expenses because the Tribunal hears only English and Welsh cases.

COSTS IN THE UPPER TRIBUNAL

21.26 The costs position in the Upper Tribunal typically mirrors that in the lower tribunal from which the case is being heard on appeal. The Lands Chamber of the Upper Tribunal is dealt with separately below.

21.27 By virtue of the Tribunal Procedure (Upper Tribunal) Rules 2008 ('Upper Tribunal Rules'), r 10 the Upper Tribunal has the power to make an order for costs in the following circumstances:

- to the extent and in the circumstances that the tribunal from which the proceedings were transferred or referred by or are on appeal from had the power to make an order in respect of costs (Upper Tribunal Rules, r 10(1)(b));
- in proceedings transferred by or on appeal from the Tax Chamber of the First-tier Tribunal (Upper Tribunal Rules, r 10(1)(a));
- in judicial review proceedings (Upper Tribunal Rules, r 10(3)(a));
- if it considers that a wasted costs order under TCEA 2007, s 29(4) is appropriate (see below) (Upper Tribunal Rules, r 10(3)(c));
- if it considers that a party or its representative has acted unreasonably in bringing, defending or conducting the proceedings (Upper Tribunal Rules, r 10(3)(d));
- if, in a financial services case, it considers that the decision in respect of which the reference was made was unreasonable (Upper Tribunal Rules, r 10(3)(e));
- in a national security appeal, if it considers a wasted costs order is appropriate, or there has been unreasonable conduct; if, where there has been a certificate it may order costs against the Minister when the certificate has been quashed or withdrawn; and if where the case is an application for a certificate a costs order may be made against any party losing the appeal to the Upper Tribunal in whole or in part (see Upper Tribunal Rules, rr 10(1)(aa) and10(1A)).

21.28 An order for costs may be made by the Upper Tribunal on application by a party or of its own initiative (Upper Tribunal Rules, r 10(4)) but must not be made unless the paying party is first given the opportunity to make representations (Upper Tribunal Rules, r 10(7)(a)). In the case of an order for costs against an individual in judicial review proceedings or due which is being made under rule 10(3)(d) due to that individual's unreasonable conduct, the Upper Tribunal must have regard to the individual's financial means (Upper Tribunal Rules, r 10(7)(b)).

21.29 A party applying for an order for costs must do so in writing, with a copy of the application being provided to the Upper Tribunal and to the party against whom it is proposed the order be made (Upper Tribunal Rules, r 10(5)(a)). The application must be accompanied with a schedule of costs such as would allow the Upper Tribunal to summarily assess those costs (Upper Tribunal Rules, r 10(5)(b)). The application must be made within one month of the date on which the Upper Tribunal sends a decision notice finally disposing of all issues in the proceedings or notice of a withdrawal which ends the proceedings (Upper Tribunal Rules, r 10(6)).

21.30 The amount of costs to be paid may be ascertained by (Upper Tribunal Rules, r 10(8)):

- summary assessment by the Upper Tribunal;

- agreement of a specified sum by the paying person and the person entitled to receive the costs; or
- assessment of the whole or a specified part of the costs incurred by the receiving party, if not agreed. The Upper Tribunal may at its discretion specify that such an assessment is to take place on the indemnity basis.

21.31 If costs are to be ascertained by assessment, either the paying or receiving parties may apply to the High Court or the Costs Office of the Supreme Court (as specified in the order) for the assessment of costs. The assessment will take place in accordance with the Civil Procedure Rules as if those rules had applied throughout the proceedings (Upper Tribunal Rules, r 10(9)(a)). If the order is for expenses in Scotland, the application should be made to the Auditor of the Court of Session (Upper Tribunal Rules, r 10(9)(b)). In Northern Ireland, applications should be made to the Taxing Office of the High Court of Northern Ireland (Upper Tribunal Rules, r 10(9)(c)).

21.32 There is no single provision in the Lands Tribunal Rules 1996 ('Lands Chamber Rules') which provides a costs award power, but it is clear from the Rules that the Tribunal has the power to make any award of costs it feels appropriate in all the circumstances. Action taken by the Tribunal which could be said to be out of the ordinary course usually has an express provision permitting consequential costs awards to be made: see, for example, r 8(7) (statement of case not in accordance with rule); r 36(2) (additional grounds of appeal permitted); r 38(7) (interlocutory applications); r 39(5) (pre-trial reviews); r 42(6) (adjournments); r 46(2) (failure to comply with Rules); r 49(2) (hearings in default). Provision for the taxation of costs, determined by the registrar and appealable to the Tribunal, is made in r 52. Where the simplified procedure is used the Tribunal may ordinarily not make an award of costs unless it is an exceptional case, or an appropriate settlement offer was refused, and if an award of costs is made it must not exceed what would be awarded in the county court (r 28(11)). The simplified procedure costs rules do not apply in cases to which s 4 of the Land Compensation Act 1961 or subsections (6) and (7) of s 175 of the Commonhold and Leasehold Reform Act 2002 apply (r 28(11)).

WASTED COSTS

21.33 TCEA 2007, s 29(4) makes provision for the relevant tribunal to make an order disallowing any wasted costs or ordering that a legal or other representative pay a sum in respect of wasted costs.

21.34 Wasted costs are defined as any costs incurred by a party (TCEA 2007, s 29(5)):

- as a result of any improper, unreasonable or negligent act or omission on the part of any legal or other representative or any employee of such a representative; or
- which, in the light of any such act or omission occurring after they were incurred, the relevant Tribunal considers it is unreasonable to expect that party to pay.

21.35 As set out above, the GRC, the HESCC and the Tax Chamber have the power to make an order for wasted costs. Such an order is an exceptional one and the legal representative against whom an order is made should always be given an opportunity to make representations as to why the order is not justified or should not be made (*Re Wiseman Lee (Solicitors) (wasted costs order) (No 5 of 2000)* [2001] EWCA Crim 707, (2001) Sol Jo LB 119).

21.36 In determining whether or not to make an order for wasted costs, the Tribunal should apply a three-stage test and ask:

- Had the legal representative of whom complaint was made acted improperly, unreasonably or negligently?
- If so, did such conduct cause the applicant to incur unnecessary costs?
- If so, was it, in all the circumstances, just to order the legal representative to compensate the applicant for the whole or part of the relevant costs?

(*Allen v Unigate Dairies Ltd*; *Ridehalgh v Horsefield*; *Philex plc v Golban*; *Watson v Watson*; *Antonelli v Wide Gery Farr (A Firm)* [1994] Ch 205).

21.37 In answering the first of these questions, it has been held that 'improper' conduct covers but is not limited to conduct which would ordinarily be held to justify disbarment, striking off, suspension from practice or other serious professional penalty. It also extends to conduct that could be fairly stigmatised as being improper according to the general consensus of professional and judicial opinion, whether or not this fell outside some procedural rules or professional code of conduct (see *Ridehalgh v Horsefield* and Cook, *Cook on Costs 2010*, (Lexis Nexis 2010) paragraph 32.9).

21.38 'Unreasonable' conduct covers conduct which was vexatious or designed to harass the other side, rather than advance the resolution of the case. Conduct of this nature will be 'unreasonable' whether or not it arises out of a desire to succeed on behalf of the client and not from any improper motive. Equally, conduct will not be unreasonable simply because it leads to an unsuccessful outcome for the client or because other professionals would have been more cautious or not proceeded with a case in the circumstances. In this respect, the touchstone of unreasonableness has been correctly described as follows: 'The acid test is whether the conduct permitted of a reasonable explanation. It is not unreasonable to be optimistic.' (Cook, *Cook on Costs 2010*, (Lexis Nexis 2010) paragraph 32.9).

21.39 Conduct amounting to 'negligence' for these purposes is not to be equated with there being cause of action by the applicant against his lawyer (such a test could clearly not apply to an application for a wasted costs order brought by an applicant against the other party's lawyer, there being no duty of care in such circumstances). However, the courts have firmly discountenanced any suggestion that an applicant for a wasted costs order needed to prove less than he would had to prove in an action for negligence. The Court of Appeal in *Ridehalgh v Horsefield* adopted the test set out by the House of Lords in *Saif Ali v Sydney Mitchell & Co* [1980] AC 198, 217 per Lord Diplock to the effect that negligence in this context will mean some 'advice, acts or omissions in the course of their professional work which no member of the profession who is reasonably well-informed and competent would have done or omitted to do' (see further the notes to CPR, r 48.7 in the *White Book*).

21.40 An application for wasted costs should only be made after the full hearing of the proceedings (save in exceptional circumstances) (*Filmlab Systems International Ltd v Pennington* [1995] 1 WLR 673).

21.41 The application should almost always be made by an aggrieved party: the Tribunal should be slow to raise the possibility of such an application itself, this is because in this would render the Tribunal 'both the prosecutor and the adjudicator and difficult and embarrassing issues on costs could arise if an order were not made' (Cook, *Cook on Costs 2010*, (Lexis Nexis 2010) paragraph 32.17).

21.42 The burden of proof that a wasted costs order is justified is on the applicant party seeking the order. It is not for the respondent to prove to the contrary. The applicant must also be able to point to costs that have in fact been wasted as a result of the conduct alleged (*Brown v Bennett* [2002] 1 WLR 713).

22 Criminal Injury Compensation Appeals

JURISDICTION

22.1 The Social Entitlement Chamber hears appeals against decisions of the Criminal Injuries Compensations Authority ('CICA') in respect of the Criminal Injuries Compensation Scheme.

22.2 Proceedings before the Tribunal are governed by the Tribunal Procedure (First-tier Tribunal) (Social Entitlement Chamber) Procedural Rules 2008 ('SEC Rules') (see **Social Entitlement Chamber procedural rules** and Appendix 5).

THE CRIMINAL INJURIES COMPENSATION SCHEME

22.3 The scheme currently in force is the Criminal Injuries Compensation Scheme 2008 (the '2008 Scheme') as made by the Secretary of State under the Criminal Injuries Compensation Act 1995.

22.4 An application for compensation to CICA will be determined by a claims officer and written notification of the decision will be sent to the applicant or applicant's representative. The applicant then has 90 days in which to communicate written acceptance of the award to CICA (paragraph 50(1) of the 2008 Scheme).

REVIEW OF A DECISION BY CICA

22.5 An applicant may seek review of any decision of a claims officer under the 2008 Scheme (2008 Scheme, paragraph 58):

- not to waive or extend the time in which an applicant has to make an application for compensation (see the 2008 Scheme, paragraph 18) or apply for review of a decision (see the 2008 Scheme, paragraph 59);
- not to re-open a case (see the 2008 Scheme, paragraphs 56–57);
- to withhold or make an award or to make a reduced award (see the 2008 Scheme, paragraphs 53–54);
- to require repayment of an award (see the 2008 Scheme, paragraph 49); or
- to withdraw an award (see the 2008 Scheme, paragraph 50(1)).

22.6 An application for the review of a decision by a claims officer must be made in writing to CICA and must be supported by reasons (2008 Scheme, paragraph 59).

22.7 An application for review must be received by CICA within 90 days of the date the decision to be reviewed was issued (2008 Scheme, paragraph 59).

APPEAL TO THE FIRST-TIER TRIBUNAL

22.8 An applicant who is dissatisfied with the outcome of a review can appeal CICA's decision to the Social Entitlement Chamber of the First-tier Tribunal.

An appeal does not lie unless a review has been requested and CICA has made a decision upon that review.

22.9 Where the appeal concerns a decision not to re-open a case under paragraphs 56 or 57 of the 2008 Scheme, and the application for re-opening was made more than two years after the date of the final decision, the First-tier Tribunal must be satisfied that the renewed application can be considered without a need for further extensive enquiries by the CICA (2008 Scheme, paragraph 62).

TIME FOR MAKING AN APPEAL

22.10 An appellant must start proceedings by sending or delivering a notice of appeal to the Social Entitlement Chamber so that it is received by the Tribunal within 90 days after the date of the review decision being appealed (SEC Rules, r 22(2)(b)).

22.11 If the appellant provides the notice of appeal to the SEC outside of the prescribed time limit, the notice of appeal must include a request for an extension of time and state the reasons why the notice of appeal was not provided in time (SEC Rules, r 22(6)). If this rule is not complied with, it appears that the First-tier Tribunal must refuse to admit the appeal. If the appellant does comply with the rule, the Upper Tribunal must nonetheless refuse to admit the appeal unless it extends time for the application under the SEC Rules, r 5(3)(a) (see **Extensions of time**).

Notice of appeal

22.12 A notice of appeal in criminal injury compensation cases must be in writing, in English or Welsh and must be signed by the appellant (SEC Rules, r 22(3)).

22.13 A notice of appeal must state (SEC Rules, r 22(3)):

- the name and address of the appellant;
- the name and address of the appellant's representative (if any);
- an address where documents for the appellant may be sent or delivered;
- the name and address of any respondent;
- details (including the full reference) of the decision being appealed; and
- the grounds on which the appellant relies.

22.14 The appellant must also provide (SEC Rules, r 22(4)):

- a copy of any written record of the decision being challenged;
- any statement of reasons for that decision that the appellant has or can reasonably obtain;
- any documents in support of the appellant's case which have not been supplied to the respondent; and

The SEC must then send a copy of the notice of appeal and any accompanying documents to each other party as soon as reasonably practicable after receiving the notice of appeal (SEC Rules, r 22(7)(b)).

RULES OF PROCEDURE OF THE FIRST-TIER TRIBUNAL

22.15 See **Social Entitlement Chamber procedural rules** and **Case management powers.**

THE OUTCOME OF A CRIMINAL INJURY COMPENSATION APPEAL

22.16 The orders made by the SEC upon the determination of a criminal injury compensation appeal are dependent upon the provision of the 2008 Scheme in respect of which the review decision under appeal was taken.

22.17 In respect of appeals against a decision taken on review under paragraph 58(1)(a) (not to waive or extend the time limit in paragraphs 18 or 59 of the 2008 Scheme), (b) (not to re-open a case) or (f) (to withdraw an award) of the 2008 Scheme, the SEC will, if it allows the appeal, direct CICA to act as follows:

- In a case where the appeal was against a decision not to waive the time limit in paragraph 18 of the 2008 Scheme (time limit for making an application for compensation), to arrange for the application for compensation to be dealt with under the 2008 Scheme as if the time limit had been waived by a claims officer (2008 Scheme, paragraph 63(2));
- In a case where the appeal was against a decision not to extend the time limit in paragraph 59 of the 2008 Scheme (time limit for bringing a review), to conduct a review under paragraph 60 of the 2008 Scheme (2008 Scheme, paragraph 63(3));
- In a case where the appeal was against a decision not to re-open a case, to re-open the case under paragraphs 56 and 57 of the 2008 Scheme (2008 Scheme, paragraph 63(4));
- In a case where the appeal was against a decision to withdraw an award under paragraph 50(1), to allow the applicant a further period of 90 days in which either to accept the award or seek a review on other grounds (2008 Scheme, paragraph 63(5)).

22.18 In respect of appeals against a decision taken on review under paragraph 58(1)(c) (to withhold an award), (d) (to make an award or reduced award) or (e) (to require repayment of an award) of the 2008 Scheme, the SEC will, if it allows the appeal, make such direction as it thinks appropriate as to the decision to be made by a claims officer on the application for compensation (2008 Scheme, paragraph 64).

22.19 In respect of appeals against a decision taken on review under paragraph 58(1)(c) (to withhold an award), (d) (to make an award or reduced award) or (e) (to require repayment of an award) of the 2008 Scheme, the SEC also has the power to order an interim payment on application or adjournment (2008 Scheme, paragraph 65(a)).

22.20 In the event that an appeal against a decision taken on review under paragraph 58(1)(c) (to withhold an award), (d) (to make an award or reduced award) or (e) (to require repayment of an award) of the 2008 Scheme is found to be frivolous or vexatious, the SEC may reduce the amount of compensation to be awarded by such amount as it in its discretion considers appropriate (2008 Scheme, paragraph 65(b)).

HEARINGS IN CRIMINAL INJURY COMPENSATION APPEALS

See generally **Hearings**.

22.21 The Social Entitlement Chamber may make a decision which disposes of a criminal injury compensation appeal without a hearing (SEC Rules, r 27(4)).

22.22 If the SEC makes a decision disposing of a criminal injury compensation appeal without a hearing, any party may make a written application to the Tribunal for the decision to be reconsidered at a hearing (SEC Rules, r 27(4)(b)).

22.23 An application for a reconsideration hearing must be in writing and received by the SEC one month after the date on which the Tribunal sent notice of its decision to the party making the application (SEC Rules, r 27(6).

22.24 An application for a hearing may not be made in relation to the following decisions in criminal injury compensation appeals (SEC Rules, r 27(5)):

- a decision by the Tribunal not to extend a time limit;
- a decision by the Tribunal not to set aside a previous decision;
- a decision by the Tribunal not to allow an appeal against a decision not to extend a time limit; or
- a decision by the Tribunal not to allow an appeal against a decision not to reopen a case.

The hearing must be held in private unless the appellant has consented to a public hearing and the Tribunal considers that it is in interests of justice for the hearing to be in public (SEC Rules, r 30(2). In effect, it will be for the appellant to request a public hearing from the Tribunal.

22.25 The Tribunal may meet the reasonable expenses incurred by the appellant, or any person who attends a hearing to give evidence, in attending the hearing; or incurred by the appellant in connection with any arrangements made by the Tribunal for the inspection of the appellant's injury (SEC Rules, r 20).

APPEALS FROM THE FIRST-TIER TRIBUNAL

22.26 A criminal injury compensation case cannot be appealed to the Upper Tribunal and the Social Entitlement Chamber cannot be asked to review its own decision (SEC Rules, rr 38(1) and 40(1)). If it is thought that the Tribunal has erred in law the proper course of action is to judicially review the Social Entitlement Chamber in the Administrative Appeals Chamber of the Upper Tribunal (see **Judicial review in the Upper Tribunal**).

23 Decisions

See also **Reasons; Review, correction and setting aside of tribunal decisions.**

DECISIONS OF THE FIRST-TIER AND UPPER TRIBUNAL

23.1 Decisions of the First-tier and Upper Tribunal may be given orally at a hearing (see **Hearings**) or in writing. This is so whether or not the decision is one as to directions or one involving the substantive merits of the proceedings between the parties. The relevant Tribunal may also give a decision orally at a hearing when this disposes of the proceedings, though it is to be expected that in many cases the Tribunal will reserve judgment, particularly given the requirements for Tribunals to give reasons for many of their decisions (see **Reasons**).

23.2 Where a decision is one which finally disposes of all issues in proceedings, the relevant Tribunal must, as soon as reasonably practicable after making its decision, provide to each party:

- a decision notice stating the Tribunal's decision;
- written reasons for the decision (see **Reasons**);
- notification of any rights of review or appeal against the decision, and the time within which and the manner in which such right of review or appeal must be exercised.

The requirement to provide written reasons does not apply to a decision that finally disposes of proceedings if that decisions was taken in respect of an application for the correction, review or setting aside of a decision (see below and **Review, correction and setting aside of tribunal decisions**).

DECISIONS BY CONSENT

23.3 The First-tier and Upper Tribunal may, at the request of the parties and subject to the Tribunal's discretion, give any decision with the consent of the parties. The Tribunals may make such a consent order where this disposes of the proceedings and can make any other appropriate order or direction as the parties have agreed (see **Consent orders**).

CONTESTING THE DECISION OF THE TRIBUNAL

23.4 There are a number of routes by which a disappointed party can contest a decision of the First-tier Tribunal and Upper Tribunal.

23.5 Where the decision contains an error as a result of a clerical mistake or accidental slip or omission, the Tribunal may itself correct this error (see **Review, correction and setting aside of tribunal decisions**).

23.6 A disappointed party may apply for the relevant Tribunal to review its decision. Such a review will typically only be undertaken if there is an attendant application for permission to appeal and in cases in which the Tribunal is satisfied there is an error of law in the decision (see **Review, correction and setting aside of tribunal decisions**).

23.7 A disappointed party may also apply for permission to appeal to the Upper Tribunal against a decision of the First-tier Tribunal (see **Appeals from the First-tier Tribunal**), or the Court of Appeal or Court of Session against a decision of the Upper Tribunal (see **Appeals from the Upper Tribunal**).

DECISIONS OF PARTICULAR CHAMBERS

23.8 The rules and requirements in respect of decisions of the First-tier Tribunal and the Upper Tribunal are generally standardised and provide for decisions to be given in the manner discussed above.

Upper Tribunal

23.9 The relevant provisions are found in the Upper Tribunal Rules (as amended), rr 39 and 40 These do not generally differ from the standard practice and requirements discussed above, except that special provision is made for national security appeals. The Lands Chamber is governed by separate rules, but which apply in the standard way (Lands Tribunal Rules 1996 ('Lands Chamber Rules'), r 50). The Upper Tribunal Rules do provide specific rules for the asylum cases where the appellant is in the UK. In those circumstances, the decision notice is sent to the Secretary of State as soon as is reasonably practicable, who must send it on to the appellant within 30 days, notifying the Tribunal as soon as is reasonably practicable of having done so. If, 31 days after having sent the decision to the Secretary of State, the Tribunal has not been so notified it must send the decision to the appellant itself (Upper Tribunal Rules, r 40A).

General Regulatory Chamber

23.10 The relevant provisions are found at the GRC Rules, rr 37 and 38 and they do not differ from the standard practice and requirements discussed above.

Health, Education and Social Care Chamber

23.11 In cases other than mental health cases, the relevant provisions are found in the HESCC Rules, rr 29 and 30. These do not differ from the standard practice and requirements discussed above, except that in proceedings under Suspension Regulations, the documents and information must be provided at the hearing or sent within three working days after the hearing (r 30(3)).

23.12 In mental health cases, the position is slightly different. The relevant rules are rr 41 and 42 of the HESCC Rules. These rules follow the standard practice discussed above but also stipulate a time limit within which a decision notice, written reason and notification of the right of appeal must be provided by the HESCC. The notice and reasons must be provided:

- in respect of proceedings under the Mental Health Act 1983, s 66(1)(a), either at the hearing or within three working days after the hearing; and
- in all other mental health cases, either at the hearing or within seven days after the hearing.

23.13 Rule 42 of the HESCC Rules deals with provisional decisions and provides that a decision with recommendations under the Mental Health Act 1983, s 72(3)(a) or 72(3A)(a) or a deferred direction for conditional discharge under s 73(7) of the Mental Health Act 1983 is a decision which is to be taken as finally disposing of proceedings. Such a decision is thus one in respect of which the HESCC is under an obligation to give written reasons within the time limits in r 41.

Immigration and Asylum Chamber

23.14 The FTTIAC has a different set of procedures which apply to proceedings before it, governed by the IAC Rules. The FTTIAC must provide written reasons for its determination and must serve those reasons on every party within 10 days of the day on which the hearing of the appeal finished, or within 10 days of the date of the determination of the appeal on paper (IAC Rules, r 22). However, where the appellant is in the UK and the appeal relates to a claim for asylum, the FTTIAC is under the same time limits but sends its determination to the Secretary of State, who must send them on to the appellant within 28 days (or the date on which the Secretary of State applies for permission to appeal, whichever is the sooner), notifying the Tribunal as soon as is reasonably practicable of having done so. If, 29 days after having sent the decision to the Secretary of State, the Tribunal has not been so notified it must send the decision to the appellant itself (IAC Rules, r 23(4)–(6)).

23.15 In a fast track appeal, governed by the Asylum and Immigration Tribunal (Fast Track Procedure) Rules 2005 ('IAC (Fast Track) Rules'), the FTTIAC must provide written reasons for its determination and must serve those reasons on every party within two days of the day on which the hearing of the appeal finished, or within two days of the date of the determination of the appeal on paper (IAC Fast Track Rules, r 14).

Social Entitlement Chamber

23.16 The relevant provisions are found in the SEC Rules, rr 32–34. These rules make provisions different to those set out above only in so far as there is no general duty to give reasons for decisions incumbent upon the SEC.

23.17 Under SEC Rules, r 34(1), reasons must be given in asylum support cases which dispose of proceedings within 3 days of any hearing or, if the case is decided without a hearing, on the day the decision is made. In all other cases the SEC has a discretion as to whether or not to give reasons. Under r 34(3)–(5), a party has a right to apply for a written statement of reasons for a decision of the SEC finally disposing of proceedings. The application must be made within one month of the date on which the SEC provided its decision notice to the party applying for a statement of reasons. The SEC is obliged to allow any such application (SEC Rules, r 34(5)), provided that it is received on time and subject to its right to withhold any information likely to cause harm. The SEC must provide a written statement of its reasons to each party within one month of receipt of the application or as soon as reasonably practicable thereafter.

Tax Chamber

23.18 The relevant provisions are found at TC Rules, r 35. The practice in the Tax Chamber is consistent with the standard practice set out above. There is a time limit for the provision of the decision notice: this must be done within 28 days of the making of any decision which finally disposes of all issues in proceedings (TC Rules, r 35(2)).

23.19 The decision notice, by virtue of TC Rules, r 35(3) (unless the parties agree it is unnecessary) must:

- contain a summary of the findings of fact and reasons for the decision; or
- be accompanied by full written findings of fact and reasons for the decision.

23.20 If the Tax Chamber provides no findings and reasons, or summary findings and reasons only, a party to the proceedings may apply for full written findings and reasons. A party wishing to appeal against a decision of the Tax Chamber must in such circumstances make an application for full written findings and reasons prior to making an application for permission to appeal (TC Rules, r 35(4)). The application for full written findings and reasons must be made in writing within 28 days of the date after which the Tax Chamber provided its decision notice (TC Rules, r 35(5)). The Tax Chamber is obliged to allow any such application, provided it is received in time and subject to its right to withhold any information likely to cause harm. The Tax Chamber must send a full written statement of findings and reasons to each party within 28 days of receipt of the application or as soon as practicable thereafter (TC Rules, r 35(5)).

War Pensions and Armed Forces Compensation Chamber

23.21 The relevant provisions are found in the WPAFCC Rules, rr 30–32. As with the Social Entitlement Chamber, there is no general duty to give reasons for decisions incumbent upon the WPAFCC.

23.22 Under WPAFCC Rules, r 32(1), the WPAFCC has a discretion as to whether or not to give reasons for a decision finally disposing of proceedings. Under WPAFCC Rules, r 32(2)–(4), a party has a right to apply for a written statement of reasons for a decision of the WPAFCC finally disposing of proceedings. The application must be made within 42 days of the date on which the WPAFCC provided its decision notice to the party applying for a statement of reasons. The WPAFCC is obliged to allow any such application (WPAFCC Rules, r 32(4)), provided that it is received on time and subject to its right to withhold any information likely to cause harm. The WPAFCC will then have one month (or as soon as reasonably practicable thereafter) to provide a written statement of its reasons to each party.

24 Directions

See also **Case management powers; Failures to comply.**

DIRECTIONS IN THE FIRST-TIER TRIBUNAL AND UPPER TRIBUNAL

24.1 The First-tier Tribunal and Upper Tribunal have a wide procedural discretion and are empowered to regulate their own procedure as appropriate (see **Case management powers**). The relevant Tribunal may accordingly give such directions as it sees fit in relation to the conduct or disposal of proceedings.

PROCEDURE FOR THE GIVING OF DIRECTIONS

Procedural rules

24.2 The applicable procedural rules (see **Procedural rules**) for most of the Chambers of the First-tier Tribunal and the Upper Tribunal (see **Chambers**) contain a rule as to the procedure for applying for and giving directions as rule 6. The rule is expressed in uniform language across the Chambers and in both the First-tier and Upper Tribunals, except that there is no direct comparator in the Immigration and Asylum Chamber (although there is a power of the Tribunal to give directions in the IAC Rules, r 45) and in the Lands Chamber of the Upper Tribunal the terminology is of interlocutory applications for directions under Lands Chamber Rules, r 38.

Applications for directions

24.3 By virtue of r 6(1), the relevant Tribunal may give directions on its own initiative (except in the Lands Chamber) or on application by one of the parties.

24.4 Any party wishing to apply for directions otherwise than at a hearing (at which this may be done orally) (but can only apply in writing in the Lands Chamber) should:

- send a written application to the relevant Tribunal (or the registrar of the Lands Chamber: Lands Chamber Rules, r 38);
- state as precisely as possible the direction sought;
- state as fully as possible the reasons why it is appropriate that the requested direction be made (see r 6(2), (3) of the applicable procedural rules).

Notice to other parties of the application

24.5 It appears that any application for directions may be made without notice to the other party and the procedural rules contain no express general rule mandating that applications for directions are made on notice. It is however expressly provided that the relevant Tribunal must notify other parties in respect of certain applications unless the Tribunal considers there is good reason not to do so (for example, in respect of an application to withhold a document from disclosure under what is typically r 14 of the applicable procedural rules; see **Documents**).

Determination of an application for directions

24.6 The relevant Tribunal may determine on the basis of the application referred to above that it is appropriate to make the order sought, or such other order as the Tribunal in its discretion deems appropriate.

24.7 Alternatively, the Tribunal may decide that it is desirable that it has the benefit of submissions from the other parties to the case, and may, in its discretion invite written submissions in respect of whether a particular directions order should be made (in accordance with what is typically r 5(3)(d) of the relevant procedural rules).

24.8 The Tribunal may also, at its discretion, direct that a hearing should be held in order to determine whether the directions order should be made (in accordance with what is typically r 5(3)(f) of the relevant procedural rules). In accordance with the overriding objective, it is to be expected that hearings in respect of discrete case management issues will be relatively rare, as a disproportionate use of time and resources.

The order for directions

24.9 By virtue of r 6(4) of the applicable procedural rules, the relevant Tribunal must typically send written notice to each other party to the case and any other affected person of any order for direction that is made. This is subject to a general discretion in r 6(4) not to notify any or all other parties or affected persons if there is good reason not to do so. There is no discretion in the Immigration and Asylum Chamber, which must inform the parties orally or in writing of any directions made (IAC Rules, r 45(3)).

Challenging an order for directions

24.10 Unless the relevant Tribunal exercises its power not to notify a particular party of an order for directions, any party which has been notified of the Tribunal's order may challenge that order. The notified party thus has liberty to apply for another direction amending, suspending or setting aside the first direction pursuant to r 6(5) of the applicable procedural rules. There does not appear to be such a provision for challenge in the Immigration and Asylum Chamber, so any dispute over a direction which discloses an error of law may have to be judicially reviewed in the Upper Tribunal.

24.11 Such applications should, as with any originating application for directions, be in writing, stating the reasons why the first direction should be so amended, suspended or set aside.

FAILURE TO COMPLY WITH AN ORDER FOR DIRECTIONS

24.12 If a party fails to comply with a direction of the First-Tier or Upper Tribunals, this does not automatically render the irregular action taken by that party void. The relevant Tribunal may in its discretion waive the failure to comply if this appears to be just in the circumstances. Alternatively, the Tribunal may impose such sanctions or requirements as it deems just in the circumstances (see **Failures to comply** for the procedural provisions).

25 Documents

SENDING AND DELIVERY OF DOCUMENTS

25.1 Rules on the sending of documents to other parties to proceedings before the First-tier Tribunal and Upper Tribunal and to the Tribunals themselves are set out in the Upper Tribunal Rules, r 13 and those of each of the Chambers of the First-tier Tribunal (see **Chambers**). Any references to r 13 in this entry are to the procedural rules of the relevant Chamber of the First-Tier Tribunal or the Upper Tribunal. The format of the rules in the Lands Chamber of the Upper Tribunal and the Immigration and Asylum Chamber of the First-tier Tribunal differs from the others, and reference will be made to those rules where the content differs from r 13.

Sending documents to other parties

25.2 The electronic sending of documents is encouraged by the tribunal system and as such, if a party provides a fax number, email address or other details for the electronic transmission of documents to them, that party must accept delivery of documents by that method and is deemed to have consented to the acceptance of delivery of documents by that method (r 13(2)).

25.3 However, if the relevant tribunal or a party sends a document to another party or the tribunal by email or any other electronic means of communication, the recipient may request that the sender provide a hard copy of the document to the recipient. The recipient must make such a request as soon as reasonably practicable after receiving the document electronically (r 13(4)).

25.4 A party is also able to refuse to accept delivery of documents electronically or by any other form of communication other than pre-paid post or delivery by hand (which a party cannot refuse to accept). Thus if a party informs both the relevant tribunal and all other parties that such a form of communication should not be used to provide documents to that party, that form of communication must not be so used (r 13(3)).

25.5 In respect of pre-paid post or delivery by hand, the tribunal and each party may assume that the address provided by a party or its representative is and remains the address to which documents should be sent or delivered until receiving written notification to the contrary (r 13(5)). Any document to be served on any person under the Lands Chamber Rules shall be deemed to have been served if sent by pre-paid post to that person at his given address for service (Lands Tribunal Rules 1996 ('Lands Chamber Rules'), r 54(3)). In the FTTIAC until a party or representative notifies the Tribunal of a change of address, any document served on him at the most recent address which he has notified to the Tribunal shall be deemed to have been properly served on him, although if the respondent is aware of a change of address he must inform the Tribunal of that change (Asylum and Immigration Tribunal (Procedure) Rules 2005 ('IAC Rules'), r 56).

25.6 In the FTTIAC, if any document is served on a person who has notified the Tribunal that he is acting as the representative of a party, it shall be deemed to have been served on that party (IAC Rules, r 55(4)). The IAC Rules also provide deemed service dates, which are important to the often short time limits applied:

(a) where the document is sent by post or document exchange from and to a place within the UK, on the second day after it was sent;

(b) where the document is sent by post or document exchange from or to a place outside the UK, on the twenty-eighth day after it was sent; and

(c) in any other case, on the day on which the document was sent or delivered to, or left with, that person.

(d) Or, in the case of personal service upon the decision-maker, the date of personal delivery (IAC Rules, r 55(5)–(6)).

Sending documents to the tribunals

25.7 Any document to be provided to the First-tier Tribunal and Upper Tribunal must by virtue of r 13(1) be:

- sent by pre-paid post or delivered by hand to the address specified for the proceedings;
- sent by fax to the number specified for the proceedings; or
- sent or delivered by such other method as the First-tier or Upper Tribunal may permit or direct.

USE OF DOCUMENTS AND INFORMATION

25.8 The First-tier Tribunals and Upper Tribunal are empowered to control the use of documents and information both within the relevant proceedings and any collateral use or publication. Rule 14 of the procedural rules for the Chambers of the First-tier Tribunal (see **Chambers**) and the Upper Tribunal set down this power. The rules do however vary between the various Chambers of the First-tier Tribunal and Upper Tribunal though it is suggested here that the difference in wording as between the various rules is unlikely to lead to a different application of the Tribunals' powers in practice. No equivalent provisions appear in the rules of the Lands Chamber of the Upper Tribunal or the Immigration and Asylum Chamber of the First-tier Tribunal.

Use of documents and information in the HESCC, SEC and WPAFCC

25.9 The HESCC, the SEC and the WPAFCC have (save for one exception relating to mental health cases which does not apply to the SEC or the WPAFCC) identical provisions in their respective procedural rules dealing with the use of documents and information.

25.10 By virtue of r 14(1), the Tribunals are empowered to make any order prohibiting the disclosure or publication of:

- specified documents or information relating to the proceedings; or
- any matter likely to lead members of the public to identify any person whom the relevant tribunal considers should not be identified.

An order may only be made under r 14 if the relevant Tribunal is satisfied (the burden being on the party resisting disclosure) both that (r 14(2)):

- such disclosure would be likely to cause that person or some other person serious harm; and
- having regard to the interests of justice, that it is proportionate to give such a direction.

25.11 The relevant Tribunal may make such an order of its own initiative or on the application of another party. If a party wishes to apply for an order under r 14, it must (r 14(3)):

- exclude the relevant document or information from any documents that will be provided to the other party or parties to the proceedings; and
- provide the excluded document or information to the relevant Tribunal together with written reasons as to why it should be excluded from disclosure or publication such as to enable the relevant Tribunal to determine whether the conditions in r 14(2) (above) are met.

25.12 As an alternative to prohibiting disclosure entirely, the Tribunal may order in the case of a party who is represented that the documents or information be disclosed only to the party's representative. It may do so only if satisfied that (r 14(5), (6)):

- disclosure to the representative would be in the represented party's interests; and
- the representative will not directly or indirectly disclose the document or information to any other person (without the consent of the relevant Tribunal).

25.13 Ordinarily, the public authority will have taken the view itself that if it cannot disclose information confidential to a third party to the appellant it can disclose to the appellant's solicitor. The Upper Tribunal has indicated in a mental health case about disclosure of medical records that it will be in 'quite exceptional circumstances' that such disclosure is not possible of the authority's own volition: *Dorset Healthcare NHS Trust v MH* [2009] UKUT 4 (AAC); [2009] PTSR 1112 at [28]. Where an application has to be made to the Tribunal it will ordinarily be decided on the day of the substantive hearing: *MH* at [32]–[34].

25.14 In HESCC and Upper Tribunal (on which see below), information about mental health cases and the names of any persons concerned in such cases are automatically restrained from publication and must not be made public unless the tribunal gives a direction to the contrary (HESCC Rules, r 14(7); Upper Tribunal Rules, r 14(7)).

Use of documents and information in the Upper Tribunal and General Regulatory Chamber

25.15 Rule 14 in the General Regulatory Chamber Rules is entitled 'Prevention of disclosure or publication of documents and information'. However, it takes largely the same form as the 'Use of documents and information' provisions in the HESCC, SEC and WPAFCC Rules. Rule 14 of the Upper Tribunal Rules, as amended, more closely resembles that of the Tribunal Procedure (First-tier Tribunal) (General Regulatory Chamber) Rules 2009 ('GRC Rules') than the Tribunals already discussed in this entry.

25.16 Documents

25.16 To this end:

- The GRC and Upper Tribunal are empowered to prohibit the disclosure or publication of specified documents or information relating to the proceedings or any matter likely to lead members of the public to identify any person whom the GRC or Upper Tribunal considers should not be identified (GRC Rules, r 14(1); Upper Tribunal Rules, r 14(1)).
- Such an order may only be made under r 14 if the GRC or Upper Tribunal is satisfied both that such disclosure would be likely to cause that person or some other person serious harm; and that, having regard to the interests of justice, it is proportionate to make such an order (GRC Rules, r 14(2); Upper Tribunal Rules, r 14(2)).
- A party applying for an order under r 14 must exclude the relevant document or information from that provided to another party, and must provide the excluded document or information to the GRC or Upper Tribunal together with written reasons as to why it should be excluded from disclosure or publication (GRC Rules, r 14(3); Upper Tribunal Rules, r 14(3)).
- The GRC or Upper Tribunal may order in the case of a party who is represented that the documents or information be disclosed only to the party's representative if satisfied that disclosure to the representative would be in the represented party's interests and the representative will not directly or indirectly disclose the document or information to any other person (without the relevant Tribunal's consent) (GRC Rules, r 14(4), (5); Upper Tribunal Rules, r 14(5), (6)).

25.17 Further, the GRC and Upper Tribunal are expressly empowered to give a direction that certain documents or information must or may be disclosed to the GRC or Upper Tribunal on the basis that it will not disclose such documents or information to other persons, or specified other persons (GRC Rules, r 14(6); Upper Tribunal Rules, r 14(8)). Again, as noted above, though this power is not expressly contained in the procedural rules of the Tribunals already discussed in this entry, it is highly likely that those Tribunals also have the power to make such an order, given the wide case management powers and procedural discretion afforded to the First-tier Tribunal. If a party wishes to apply for such an order it may withhold the relevant document or information from the other parties until the GRC or Upper Tribunal has had an opportunity to rule on the application (GRC Rules, r 14(7); Upper Tribunal Rules, r 14(9). In the GRC, such an application will be 'on notice' to the extent that, unless it considers there is good reason not to do so, the GRC will notify any other parties that the application has been made (GRC Rules, r 14(8)) There is no like provision in the amended Upper Tribunal Rules, though it is expected that the Upper Tribunal will determine in its discretion whether other parties should be notified of the application.

25.18 In cases involving matters relating to national security, the GRC and Upper Tribunal are under a duty to ensure that information is not disclosed that is contrary to the interests of national security (GRC Rules, r 14(9); Upper Tribunal Rules, r 14(10)).

25.19 Finally, as with the Tribunals already discussed, the GRC and Upper Tribunal are under a duty to conduct proceedings (including the recording of decisions and reasons appropriately), so as not to undermine the effect of any order made under r 14 of the GRC or Upper Tribunal Rules or the duty in cases involving matters of national security (GRC Rules, r 14(10); Upper Tribunal Rules, r 14(11)).

Use of documents and information in the Tax Chamber

25.20 Rule 14 of the Tribunal Procedure (First-tier Tribunal) (Tax Chamber) Rules 2009 ('TC Rules') is very brief, and provides only that the Tax Chamber may make an order prohibiting the disclosure or publication of:

- specified documents or information relating to the proceedings (TC Rules, r 14(a)); or
- any matter likely to lead members of the public to identify any person whom the Tribunal considers should not be identified (TC Rules, r 14(b)).

25.21 However, given the wide case management powers and the power of the Tax Chamber to control its own procedure (TC Rules, r 5(1)), it is to be expected that the Tax Chamber will exercise similar controls over the use of documents and information as are set out more explicitly in the procedural rules of the other Chambers. That r 14(a) is so broad reinforces this likelihood. Parties before the Tax Chamber should therefore bear in mind the control mechanisms and limits on disclosure which are available in the tribunals discussed earlier in this entry when considering whether to make an application under r 14 of the TC Rules and on what basis.

26 Enforcement

ENFORCEMENT POWERS OF THE FIRST-TIER TRIBUNAL AND UPPER TRIBUNAL

26.1 The First-tier Tribunal and Upper Tribunal have no enforcement powers of their own, and none is conferred by the provisions of the TCEA 2007.

ENFORCEMENT OF MONETARY AWARDS

26.2 Previously, a successful claimant before a tribunal was required to register his judgment in the county courts in order to be able to proceed to enforce payment of a monetary sum due thereunder. However, pursuant to TCEA 2007, s 27, judgments of a Tribunal in England and Wales under which a sum of money is payable are now enforceable as if they were judgments of the county court or High Court of England and Wales (like provisions also apply for Scotland and Northern Ireland).

26.3 This reform simplifies enforcement by providing for enforcement either in the county court or High Court, whereas previously although most tribunal awards were enforced through the county courts, some were enforced solely through the High Court.

26.4 Importantly, TCEA 2007 removes the need for registration of unpaid awards in the county court or the High Court and provides that they can be enforced as if they bear the right to a warrant of execution. Successful claimants before the First-tier Tribunal or Upper Tribunal will therefore be able to proceed immediately to the county court or High Court for enforcement without the need for any further steps. This direct route to enforcement equalises the position between tribunal users and other civil claimants and is to be welcomed.

26.5 Furthermore, TCEA 2007 also provides (see paragraph 55 of Schedule 8) for unpaid awards of the First-tier Tribunal and Upper Tribunal to be entered on the Register of Judgments, Orders and Fines in accordance with the Courts Act 2003, s 98. The Register is a useful weapon in encouraging voluntarily compliance with court orders as it can be searched by banks, building societies, and credit companies.

26.6 Outside of judicial review cases in the Upper Tribunal (see below) no provision is made by TCEA 2007 for the enforcement of a Tribunal decision which is not for a sum of money. This will not usually be a problem, as the overwhelming majority of cases will be ones in which either a sum of money is sought, or where, for example, in immigration and asylum cases, the only party against which a decision might be given is a public authority which can normally be expected to comply with Tribunal decisions. Non-monetary enforcement ought, however, to be monitored to see if there is a *lacuna* in the legislation which creates a genuine practical problem.

ENFORCEMENT OF JUDGMENTS IN JUDICIAL REVIEW CASES

26.7 Where the Upper Tribunal exercises its judicial review functions (see **Judicial review in the Upper Tribunal**) any award made for damages, restitution or recovery of a sum due made in favour of a claimant is enforceable as if it were an award of the High Court (TCEA 2007, s 16(7)) or the Court of Session as applicable (TCEA 2007, s 21(4)). Where the Upper Tribunal makes a mandatory order, a prohibiting order, a quashing order, a declaration or an injunction that judgment too is enforceable as though it were a judgment of the High Court (TCEA 2007, s 15(3)(b)) or Court of Session (TCEA 2007, s 21(4)).

PART 4 OF TCEA 2007

26.8 The enforcement aspects of TCEA (see TCEA 2007, ss 95–105) will also apply to successful claimants before the First-tier Tribunal and Upper Tribunal. They are designed to render the process of obtaining information about judgment debtors far simpler. TCEA 2007 empowers the courts to obtain information about the debtor, as claimants will be able to make information requests under the provisions contained in Part 4 of TCEA 2007. This will enable claimants to identify (with the court's assistance) what kind of court action it would be appropriate to take to recover their judgment debt. However, at the time of writing, these provisions are not in force and it is now thought that Part 4 will never be implemented.

27 Environment Cases

LEGISLATIVE BACKGROUND

27.1 Following a review conducted by Professor Richard Macrory entitled *Regulatory Justice: Making Sanctions Effective* (November 2006) for the Department of Business, Innovation and Skills the Government enacted the Regulatory, Enforcement and Sanctions Act 2008. This provided a general enabling power (in s 36) to make orders providing for the application of new civil sanctions across any area of administrative decision-making. The sanctions fall under four general categories: fixed monetary penalties (ss 39–41); discretionary notices (ss 42–45); stop notices (ss 46–49); and enforcement undertakings (s 50). Where one of these sanctions has been imposed there is to be a right of appeal to the First-tier Tribunal: s 54(1).

27.2 The primary area in which the 2008 Act has been used to date is in relation to environmental issues. On 6 April 2010 the Environmental Civil Sanctions (England) Order 2010, SI 2010/1157 ('the 2010 Order') and the Environmental Sanctions (Miscellaneous Amendments) (England) Regulations 2010, SI 2010/1159 ('the 2010 Regulations') came into force. Between them, these two pieces of legislation put in place a whole scheme of sanctions for environmental protection. It is expected that equivalent legislation will be enacted by the Welsh Assembly in the near future.

27.3 The regulators authorised to issue sanctions are the Environment Agency and Natural England (article 2 of the 2010 Order). Wales will have an additional regulator: the Countryside Council for Wales. It is possible that local authorities will also be given the powers of regulators in the future. The civil sanctions which are introduced under the 2010 Order and may be imposed by the regulators are as follows:

- **Compliance notice:** A requirement to take specified steps within a stated period to secure that an offence does not continue or happen again.
- **Restoration notice:** A requirement to take specified steps within a stated period to secure that the position is, so far as possible, restored to what it would have been if no offence had been committed.
- **Enforcement undertaking:** These enable a person, which a regulator reasonably suspects of having committed an offence, to give an undertaking to a regulator to take one or more corrective actions set out in the undertaking.
- **Fixed monetary penalty ('FMP'):** A requirement to pay a monetary penalty of a fixed amount.
- **Variable monetary penalty ('VMP'):** A requirement to pay a monetary penalty of an amount determined by the regulator reflecting the circumstances of the offence.
- **Third party undertaking:** These enable a person who has received a regulator's notice of intent to impose a variable monetary penalty, for example, to give a commitment to take action to benefit a third party affected by the non-compliance.

- **Stop notice:** A requirement for a person to stop carrying on an activity described in the notice until it has taken steps to come back into compliance.
- **Enforcement cost recovery notice:** These enable the regulator to recover its costs after issuing a fixed monetary penalty or enforcement undertaking.

27.4 An appeal may be heard in the Tribunal against any of these types of sanction except an enforcement undertaking, which as it is an undertaking which a party makes of its own volition (albeit with the threat of sanctions), is not an appropriate matter for appeal. However, appeals may be heard against the refusal of the regulator to issue a completion certificate for an enforcement undertaking or stop notice. Any compensation decision of the regulator may also be appealed.

27.5 Under the 2010 Order and the 2010 Regulations, sanctions (although not necessarily all types in all cases) may be issued for breaches of the following legislation. Further legislation will doubtless be added in the future:

- Destructive Imported Animals Act 1932
- Hill Farming Act 1946
- Pests Act 1954
- Weeds Act 1959
- Salmon and Freshwater Fisheries Act 1975
- Wildlife and Countryside Act 1981
- Salmon Act 1986
- Environmental Protection Act 1990
- Water Resources Act 1991
- Water Industry Act 1991
- Deer Act 1991
- Land Drainage Act 1991
- Protection of Badgers Act 1992
- Environment Act 1995
- Water Act 2003
- Sludge (Use in Agriculture) Regulations 1989, SI 1989/1263
- Environmental Protection (Disposal of Polychlorinated Biphenyls and other Dangerous Substances) (England and Wales) Regulations 2000, SI 2000/1043
- Control of Pollution (Oil Storage) (England) Regulations 2001, SI 2001/2954
- Water Resources (Environmental Impact Assessment) (England and Wales) Regulations 2003, SI 2003/164
- Hazardous Waste (England and Wales) Regulations 2005, SI 2005/894

- Environmental Impact Assessment (Agriculture) (England) (No. 2) Regulations 2006, SI 2006/2522
- Producer Responsibility Obligations (Packaging Waste) Regulations 2007, SI 2007/871
- Transfrontier Shipment of Waste Regulations 2007, SI 2007/1711
- Nitrate Pollution Prevention Regulations 2008, SI 2008/2349

JURISDICTION OVER ENVIRONMENT CASES

27.6 As of 6 April 2010 appeals against a sanction imposed by an environmental regulator fall under the jurisdiction of the General Regulatory Chamber of the First-tier Tribunal, which will sit anywhere in the UK. The procedure is governed by the Tribunal Procedure (First-tier Tribunal) (General Regulatory Chamber) Rules 2009, SI 2009/1976 ('GRC Rules') as amended. There are no special provisions in the GRC Rules for environment cases and for details of the rules see **General Regulatory Chamber procedural rules**.

27.7 An appeal against a decision of the GRC will lie to the Administrative Appeals Chamber of the Upper Tribunal (see **Appeals from the First-tier Tribunal**).

APPEALS TO THE GRC

27.8 The 2010 Order requires the regulator to prove any relevant offence to the criminal standard, and where there is no offence the Tribunal shall determine the burden of proof. All notices are suspended pending an appeal, with the exception of stop notices (see below), which the Tribunal may vary or suspend. The Tribunal has the power to withdraw, confirm or vary the requirement or notice, or take any steps the regulator could have taken, or remit the matter to the regulator (article 10 of the 2010 Order).

27.9 The grounds of appeal against a fixed monetary penalty final notice are that the decision was: based on an error of fact, wrong in law, unreasonable or for any other reason (article 8 of Schedule 1 to the 2010 Order). The same grounds apply to appeals against final variable monetary penalty notices, compliance notices, restoration notices and third party undertakings (article 8 of Schedule 2 to the 2010 Order).

27.10 An appeal against a stop notice may be on the grounds that the decision was based on an error of fact, was wrong in law, was unreasonable, that any step notified is unreasonable, that the person served had not committed an offence and would not have committed an offence had the stop notice not been served, that the person served would not because of a defence been liable to be convicted of any offence had the stop notice not been served, or any other reason (article 3 of Schedule 3 to the 2010 Order).

27.11 The failure to issue a completion certificate in respect of a stop notice or an enforcement undertaking may be appealed on the grounds that it was based on an error of fact, was wrong in law, was unfair or unreasonable, or was wrong for any other reason (article 4(5) of Schedule 3 and article 5(5) of Schedule 4 to the 2010 Order).

27.12 Any decision to award or not to award compensation for loss suffered by the imposition of a stop notice may be appealed on the grounds that it was unreasonable, based on incorrect facts or for any other reason (article 5(2) of Schedule 3 to the 2010 Order).

STOP NOTICES AND FAST TRACK APPEALS

27.13 The Senior President of Tribunals has issued a Practice Direction in relation to stop notices: *Fast Track Process for Appeals against Stop Notices before the First-tier Tribunal in the General Regulatory Chamber*, 9 April 2010. This recognises the need for stop notice appeals to be heard and determined expeditiously. Time limits for the response of the respondent, and any reply of the appellant, are reduced to seven days (paragraphs 3–4). The parties must also indicate to the Tribunal within seven days of the response if they wish the matter to be determined at an oral hearing, otherwise it will be determined on the papers (paragraph 5). Where an oral hearing is requested the Tribunal should list it not earlier than four weeks after the request and not later than six weeks. Where less than 14 days notice of the hearing is possible that notice should be given as the case is urgent (paragraph 6).

27.14 A final bundle must be circulated 10 days prior to the hearing. A pre-hearing review by telephone conference will take place five days prior to the hearing. Written submissions must be circulated three days prior. All documents should be filed electronically where possible (paragraphs 7–10).

27.15 The Tribunal will aim to announce its judgment within 24 hours of the hearing and provide written reasons within 21 days (paragraph 11).

28 Estate Agents Appeals

ESTATE AGENTS APPEALS PANEL

28.1 The Estate Agents Appeals Panel ('EAAP') was previously appointed by the Secretary of State for Business, Enterprise and Regulatory Reform (as it then was) to hear appeals to the Secretary of State under the Estate Agents Act 1979 against decisions and orders of the Office of Fair Trading ('OFT') prohibiting a person from acting as an estate agent or warning orders in respect of an estate agent's failure to comply with his or her or its obligations under the 1979 Act.

28.2 From 1 September 2009, the Estate Agents Appeals Panel was abolished and its functions were transferred to the General Regulatory Chamber (see **General Regulatory Chamber**). By virtue of article 2 of the Transfer of Functions (Estate Agents Appeals and Additional Scheduled Tribunals) Order 2009, SI 2009/1836 the function of the Secretary of State to decide appeals under s 7(1) of the Estate Agents Act 1979 was transferred to the First-tier Tribunal.

ESTATE AGENTS APPEAL CASES BEFORE THE GRC

Procedural Rules on Estate Agents Appeal cases

28.3 Procedure in estate agents appeal cases will be governed by the GRC Rules and are dealt with in detail in the GRC entry (see **General Regulatory Chamber procedural rules**). As these differ in some marked respects from the previous rules applicable in estate agents appeal cases, they will be discussed in some detail.

Starting an estate agents appeal case – procedure prior to the hearing

28.4 The appellant agent must start proceedings before the GRC by delivering to the Tribunal a notice of appeal within 28 days of the date on which notice of the OFT's decision or warning order (GRC Rules, r 22(1)(b)).

28.5 The GRC has the power to extend the time limit for making an appeal and/or to permit appeals to be heard out of time (GRC Rules, rr 5(3), 22(4) (see **Extensions of time**). The EAAP had no such power and from the appellant's point of view this is to be welcomed.

28.6 Following receipt of the notice of appeal (which will be sent by the GRC under r 22(5)), the OFT has 28 days to respond, setting out whether the appeal is opposed and on what grounds and whether the OFT would be content for the case to be determined without a hearing (GRC Rules, r 23).

28.7 The appellant agent then has the opportunity to provide further written submission and documents in reply to the OFT's response.

The nature of the appeal

28.8 Before the EAAP, the nature of the appeal was in the nature of a rehearing. The EAAP thus did not embark upon an inquiry as to whether the OFT's adjudicating officer reached the correct conclusion on the evidence before him/her at the time of the decision. Rather, the EAAP asked whether on the evidence before the panel at the date of the hearing, the appellant agent was fit and proper person to carry on work as an estate agent.

28.9 However, the GRC Rules are silent on the general nature of appeals to the GRC and there are no specific provisions dealing with estate agents appeal cases. In the absence of specific guidance as to the nature of an estate agents' appealing hearing before the GRC, it is to be expected that the GRC hearing will have the appropriate regard to the previous practice of the EAAP and that such appeals will continue to be in the nature of a rehearing. This has the attendant benefit for the appellant agent that he/she is permitted to (and should) adduce further evidence as to fitness to practise which was not before the OFT's adjudicator. Indeed, the GRC is permitted to admit any evidence whether or not that evidence was available to any previous relevant decision maker (GRC Rules, r 15(2)(a)(ii)).

Hearings before the GRC

28.10 The GRC, as with the EAAP, has a wide procedural discretion to conduct hearings in such manner as it see fit, subject of course to any relevant guidance, the GRC Rules and the provisions of the Tribunals, Courts and Enforcement Act 2007 ('TCEA 2007'). Hearings before the GRC are described in more detail in **Hearings**.

28.11 Hearings should be in public save where the GRC considers it necessary that the hearing or part of it should be held in private (GRC Rules, r 35). The parties will likely be given an opportunity to make submissions as to the need for and appropriateness of holding a hearing in private.

28.12 Hearings before the EAAP typically avoided unnecessary formality, though it will remain to be seen whether this continues before the GRC. Given the breadth of the GRC's subject-matter jurisdiction, it is suggested that the GRC will, out of consistency, take a more formal approach than the EAAP. As with the EAAP, evidence before the GRC will typically not be given on oath, though the GRC has the power to require any party to swear an oath or give an affirmation (GRC Rules, r 15(2)–(3)).

28.13 If a party who has been notified of the hearing (or reasonable steps have been taken to notify that party) fails to attend, the GRC may proceed to determine the appeal in that party's absence (GRC Rules, r 36).

DECISIONS IN ESTATE AGENTS APPEAL CASES

28.14 The GRC may give its decision orally at the hearing but must in all cases provide to each party as soon as reasonably practicable (GRC Rules, r 38):

- A decision notice stating the decision;
- Written reasons for the decision; and
- Notification of any right to appeal and the time within which and manner in which the right of appeal may be exercised.

28.15 This differs markedly from former procedure. Previously, following a hearing the EAAP would write a report and make recommendations to the Secretary of State who would (save in exceptional cases) accept and follow the recommendations of the EAAP. The Secretary of State would then give directions as to the outcome of the appeal and send these, together with a copy of the EAAP's report to both parties.

Costs

28.16 The GRC may only award costs in two circumstances in estate agents appeals (GRC Rules, r 10(1)):

- under TCEA 2007, s 29(4) in respect of wasted costs; or
- if it considers that a party has acted unreasonably in bringing, defending or conducting the proceedings.

28.17 This is to be contrasted with the previous position, whereby the successful party was generally awarded its costs by the Secretary of State.

28.18 Given the consequences for an individual agent of a negative decision by the OFT, it is unlikely that, save in cases of unreasonable conduct at the hearing or in which the appellant agent gives manifestly unreliable or untruthful evidence, a costs order will be made against the appellant agent (see **Costs**).

29 Excluded Appeals

STATUTORY BASIS FOR EXCLUDED APPEALS

Appeals from the First-tier Tribunal

29.1 Certain appeals to the Upper Tribunal from the First-tier Tribunal are excluded by the TCEA 2007, s 11(5) (see **Appeals from the First-tier Tribunal**).

29.2 By virtue of TCEA 2007, s 11(5)(f), the Lord Chancellor has the power to specify that a decision be an excluded appeal for the purposes of TCEA 2007, s 11, but, by virtue of s 11(6), only if:

- In respect of decisions of that description, there is a right to appeal to a court, the Upper Tribunal or any other tribunal from the decision and that right is, or includes, something other than a right (however expressed) to appeal on any point of law arising from the decision; or
- Decisions of that description are made in carrying out a function transferred under TCEA 2007, s 30 and prior to the transfer of the function there was no right to appeal from decisions of that description.

Thus an appeal being designated as an excluded appeal does not necessarily mean that no appeal lies to the Upper Tribunal or other appellate body, only that that right of appeal is otherwise than a right of appeal on a point of law under TCEA 2007, s 11. Parties must consult the relevant underlying legislation under which they wish to appeal in order to ascertain whether there is in fact a right of appeal, to which body that right lies and on what basis.

Appeals from the Upper Tribunal

29.3 Certain appeals to the Court of Appeal or Court of Session are excluded by TCEA 2007, s 13(8) (see **Appeals from the Upper Tribunal**).

29.4 By virtue of TCEA 2007, s 13(8)(f), the Lord Chancellor has the power to add to the list of excluded appeals. However, the Lord Chancellor's power is subject to s 13(9) which provides that the power to designate a category of decision as excluded can only be undertaken for one of two purposes:

- To preserve existing appeal rights where those rights are, or include, something other than a right of appeal on a point of law; or
- To preserve the existing position in cases where there is currently no appeal right.

Thus an appeal being designated as an excluded appeal does not necessarily mean that no appeal lies to the Court of Appeal or Court of Session, only that that right of appeal is otherwise than a right of appeal on a point of law under TCEA 2007, s 13. Parties must consult the relevant underlying legislation under which they wish to appeal in order to ascertain whether there is in fact a right of appeal, to which body that right lies and on what basis.

EXCLUDED APPEALS

Appeals from the First-tier Tribunal

29.5 Appeals from the First-tier Tribunal to the Upper Tribunal against certain decisions of the First-tier Tribunal are excluded under TCEA 2007, s 11(5):

- any decision of the First-tier Tribunal on an appeal against a review made under the Criminal Injuries Compensation Act 1995, s 5(1)(a) (see **Criminal injury compensation cases**);
- any decision of the First-tier Tribunal on an appeal made in exercise of a right conferred by the Victims of Overseas Terrorism Compensation Scheme in compliance with the Crime and Security Act 2010, s 52(3);
- a decision on an appeal against a national security certificate under the Data Protection Act 1998, s 28(4) or (6) or the Freedom of Information Act 2000, s 60(1) or (4);
- a decision of the First-tier Tribunal under TCEA 2007, s 9:
- to review, or not to review, an earlier decision of the Tribunal;
- to take no action, or not to take any particular action, in the light of a review of an earlier decision of the Tribunal;
- to set aside an earlier decision of the tribunal;
- to refer, or not to refer, a matter to the Upper Tribunal; or
- a decision of the First-tier Tribunal that is set aside under TCEA 2007, s 9 (including a decision set aside after proceedings on an appeal under this section have been begun).

29.6 Pursuant to the power conferred by TCEA 2007, s 11(5)(f), the Lord Chancellor has enacted the Appeals (Excluded Decisions) Order 2009, SI 2009/275 and the Tribunals, Courts and Enforcement Act 2007 (Miscellaneous Provisions) Order 2010, SI 2010/41 amending it. By virtue of the 2009 Order as amended, no right to appeal to the Upper Tribunal arises in respect of the following decisions (as noted above, parties should consult the relevant legislation to determine whether an alternative route of appeal exists):

- any decision on an appeal under s 103 of the Immigration and Asylum Act 1999;
- a decision under paras 22, 23, 24, 29, 30, 31, 32 and 33 of Sch 2 to the Immigration Act 1971;
- any decision under ss 20(7), (8B) or (8G)(b) (power to call for documents of taxpayer and others), 20B(1B) or (6) (restrictions on powers under ss 20 and 20A) or 20BB(2)(a) (falsification etc. of documents) of the Taxes Management Act 1970;
- any decision under ss 35A(2) (variation of undertakings), 79A(2) (variation of undertakings) or 219(1A) (power to require information) of the Inheritance Tax Act 1984;
- any decision under ss 152(5) (notification of taxable amount of certain benefits) or 215(7) (advance clearance by Board of distributions and payments) of the Income and Corporation Taxes Act 1988;

- any decision under s 138(4) of the Taxation of Chargeable Gains Act 1992 (procedure for clearance in advance);
- any decision under s 187(5) or (6) (returns and information) of, or para 3(2) or 6(2) of Sch 21 (restrictions on powers under section 187) to, the Finance Act 1993;
- any decision under para 91(5) of Sch 15 to the Finance Act 2000 (corporate venturing scheme: advance clearance);
- any decision under para 88(5) of Sch 29 to the Finance Act 2002 (gains and losses from intangible fixed assets: transfer of business or trade);
- any decision under paras 2, 4, 7, 9, 10, 11 or 24 of Schedule 13 to the Finance Act 2003 (stamp duty land tax: information powers);
- any decision under ss 306A (doubt as to notifiability), 308A (supplemental information), 313B (reasons for non-disclosure: supporting information) or 314A (order to disclose) of the Finance Act 2004;
- any decision under s 697(4) of the Income Tax Act 2007 (opposed notifications: determinations by tribunal);
- any decision under reg 10(3) of the Venture Capital Trust (Winding up and Mergers) (Tax) Regulations 2004, SI 2004/2199 (procedure for Board's approval);
- any decision under regs 5A (doubt as to notifiability), 7A (supplemental information), 12B (reasons for non-disclosure: supporting information) or 12C (order to disclose) of the National Insurance Contributions (Application of Part 7 of the Finance Act 2004) Regulations 2007, SI 2007/785;
- any procedural, ancillary or preliminary decision made in relation to an appeal against a decision under s 40A of the British Nationality Act 1981, ss 82, 83 or 83A of the Nationality, Immigration and Asylum Act 2002, or reg 26 of the Immigration (European Economic Area) Regulations 2006, SI 2006/1003.

Appeals from the Upper Tribunal

29.7 Appeals to the Court of Appeal (or Court of Session) against certain decisions of the Upper Tribunal are excluded under TCEA 2007, s 13(8):

- a decision on an appeal against a national security certificate under the Data Protection Act 1998, s 28(4) or (6) or the Freedom of Information Act 2000, s 60(1) or (4);
- a decision on an application for permission to appeal (under TCEA 2007, s 11(4)(b));
  - a decision under TCEA 2007, s 10;
  - to review, or not to review, an earlier decision of the Tribunal;
  - to take no action, or not to take any particular action, in the light of a review of an earlier decision of the Tribunal, or
  - to set aside an earlier decision of the Tribunal,

– a decision that is set aside under TCEA 2007, s 10 (including a decision set aside after proceedings on an appeal to the Court of Appeal or Court of Session under TCEA 2007, s 13 have been begun).

29.8 Pursuant to the power under TCEA 2007, s 13(8)(f), the Lord Chancellor has enacted several orders designating certain decisions as excluded decisions for the purposes of the appeal rights under TCEA 2007 (see The Appeals (Excluded Decisions) Order 2008, SI 2008/2707 and the Appeals (Excluded Decisions) (Amendment) Order 2008, SI 2008/2780 both of which are now revoked). The relevant order presently in force is the Appeals (Excluded Decisions) Order 2009, SI 2009/275 and the Tribunals, Courts and Enforcement Act 2007 (Miscellaneous Provisions) Order 2010, SI 2010/41 amending it.

29.9 By virtue of the 2009 Order the Lord Chancellor has designated a variety of decisions under taxation legislation as excluded decisions in respect of which there is no right of appeal to the Court of Appeal or the Court of Session under TCEA 2007, s 13, just as there is no right of appeal under s 11 above (as noted above parties should consult the relevant legislation to determine whether an alternative route of appeal exists):

- any decision under ss 20(7), (8B) or (8G)(b) (power to call for documents of taxpayer and others), 20B(1B) or (6) (restrictions on powers under ss 20 and 20A) or 20BB(2)(a) (falsification etc. of documents) of the Taxes Management Act 1970;
- any decision under ss 35A(2) (variation of undertakings), 79A(2) (variation of undertakings) or 219(1A) (power to require information) of the Inheritance Tax Act 1984;
- any decision under ss 152(5) (notification of taxable amount of certain benefits) or 215(7) (advance clearance by Board of distributions and payments) of the Income and Corporation Taxes Act 1988;
- any decision under s 138(4) of the Taxation of Chargeable Gains Act 1992 (procedure for clearance in advance);
- any decision under s 187(5) or (6) (returns and information) of, or paras 3(2) or 6(2) of Sch 21 (restrictions on powers under section 187) to, the Finance Act 1993;
- any decision under para 91(5) of Sch 15 to the Finance Act 2000 (corporate venturing scheme: advance clearance);
- any decision under para 88(5) of Sch 29 to the Finance Act 2002 (gains and losses from intangible fixed assets: transfer of business or trade);
- any decision under paras 2, 4, 7, 9, 10, 11 or 24 of Sch 13 to the Finance Act 2003 (stamp duty land tax: information powers);
- any decision under ss 306A (doubt as to notifiability), 308A (supplemental information), 313B (reasons for non-disclosure: supporting information) or 314A (order to disclose) of the Finance Act 2004;
- any decision under s 697(4) of the Income Tax Act 2007 (opposed notifications: determinations by tribunal);
- any decision under reg 10(3) of the Venture Capital Trust (Winding up and Mergers) (Tax) Regulations 2004, SI 2004/2199 (procedure for Board's approval);

- any decision under regs 5A (doubt as to notifiability), 7A (supplemental information), 12B (reasons for non-disclosure: supporting information) or 12C (order to disclose) of the National Insurance Contributions (Application of Part 7 of the Finance Act 2004) Regulations 2007, SI 2007/785;
- any procedural, ancillary or preliminary decision made in relation to an appeal against a decision under s 40A of the British Nationality Act 1981, ss 82, 83 or 83A of the Nationality, Immigration and Asylum Act 2002, or reg 26 of the Immigration (European Economic Area) Regulations 2006, SI 2006/1003.

30 Experts

See also **Evidence; Assessors.**

EXPERT EVIDENCE

Power to control admissibility of expert evidence

30.1 The First-tier Tribunal and the Upper Tribunal have wide powers to control the admissibility of evidence (see **Case management powers and Directions**). These explicitly extend to a power to give directions concerning the admissibility of expert evidence (Upper Tribunal Rules, r 15(1)(c); GRC Rules, r 15(1)(e); HESCC Rules, r 15(1)(c); SEC Rules, r 15(1)(c); TC Rules, r 15(1)(c); WPAFCC Rules, r 15(1)(c). See also the relevant provision in the Lands Chamber of the Upper Tribunal: Lands Chamber Rules, r 42. There is no equivalent provision in the Immigration and Asylum Chamber of the First-tier Tribunal).

30.2 The power to admit expert evidence is typically expressed as follows:

> "Without restriction on the general powers in rule 5(1) and (2) (case management powers), the Tribunal may give directions as to…
>
> …
>
> Whether the parties are permitted or required to provide expert evidence, and if so whether the parties must jointly appoint a single expert to provide such evidence…"

The exception to this formulation is the SEC Rules, which omit any mention of single joint experts. There is no apparent reason for this omission and it is clear from the broad discretionary case management powers possessed by the Social Entitlement Chamber that it has the power to restrict expert evidence to evidence from a single joint expert in appropriate cases. The Lands Chamber of the Upper Tribunal has different, detailed provision which will be addressed separately.

Expert witnesses in the Lands Chamber

30.3 In the Lands Chamber expert witnesses are provided for in the Lands Chamber Rules, r 42, except that r 42 does not apply to right of light applications (see **Lands Chamber**). Furthermore, the Senior President of Tribunals has issued *Interim Practice Directions and Guidance for the Lands Chamber* (13 May 2009), which deals with expert witnesses at some length.

30.4 Rule 42(2) permits one expert witness per side as the general rule, except in mineral valuation or business disturbance cases in which two experts per side is permitted (r 42(3)). A party may apply to the Tribunal to call more than one expert witness (r 42(4)). Within 28 days of receiving a request from registrar to the Tribunal a party shall provide to the Tribunal and the other parties copies of the expert witness's report, including every plan and valuation of the land or property to which the proceedings relate (which shall include full particulars and computations in support of the valuation) which it is proposed to put in evidence; and the full particulars of any comparators being relied upon or a statement that no comparators will be referred to (r 42(5)). Attempts to rely on documents not provided prior to the hearing, and applications for additional experts, may cause the Tribunal to adjourn the hearing with punishment in costs (r 42(6)).

30.5 There is no mention of joint experts in r 42, but the Practice Direction requires that where there is more than one expert in a case the experts should take steps before preparing or exchanging their reports to agree all matters of fact relevant to their reports, including the facts relating to any comparable transaction on which they propose to rely, any differences of fact, and any plans, documents or photographs on which they intend to rely in their reports (paragraph 17.3). An expert who wishes to respond to the report of another expert should do so in a separate, supplementary report (paragraph 17.7). After exchange, the Tribunal will normally order the experts to meet to reach agreement as to facts, to agree any relevant plans, photographs, etc, to identify the issues in the proceedings and, where possible, to reach agreement on an issue. They may be directed to prepare a statement for the Tribunal showing those facts and issues on which the experts agree and those facts and issues on which they disagree and a summary of their reasons for disagreeing. Any agreement reached between the experts will not bind the parties unless they choose to be bound (paragraphs 17.11–17.12). Computer valuations should use common models between the experts, and which can be provided to the Tribunal (paragraph 17.13).

30.6 The expert witness report should be addressed to the Tribunal. It will not be privileged against disclosure, although the Tribunal will only order disclosure if it is satisfied that there are reasonable grounds to consider the statement of instructions given to be inaccurate or incomplete. It should contain the following information (paragraphs 17.4–17.6):

(a) details of the expert's qualifications;

(b) details of any literature or other material on which the expert has relied in making the report;

(c) who carried out any inspection or investigations which the expert has used for the report and whether or not the investigations have been carried out under the expert's supervision;

(d) the qualifications of the person who carried out any such inspection or investigations, and

(e) where there is a range of opinion on the matters dealt with in the report

(i) summarise the range of opinion, and

(ii) give reasons for his own opinion;

(f) a summary of the conclusions reached;

(g) a statement that the expert understands his or her duty to the Tribunal and has complied with that duty;

(h) a statement setting out the substance of all material instructions (whether written or oral). The statement should summarise the facts and instructions given to the expert which are material to the opinions expressed in the report or upon which those opinions are based; and

(i) be verified by a statement of truth.

30.7 Within 28 days of service of the expert's report, another party (for whom the witness was not instructed) may send to the expert written questions for the purposes of clarification. The Tribunal may order that the questions be answered and if they are not, may direct that the report cannot be relied upon as evidence, or that the instructing party cannot recover the costs of the expert (paragraphs 17.8–17.9). Any party may rely on a disclosed expert report (paragraph 17.10).

30.8 Paragraph 17.2 on the duties of expert witnesses in the Lands Chamber is worth quoting in full:

> 'It is the duty of an expert to help the Tribunal on matters within his or her expertise. This duty overrides any obligation to the person from whom they have received instructions or by whom they are paid. The evidence should be accurate and complete as to relevant fact, and should represent the honest and objective opinion of the witness. If a professional body has adopted a code of practice and professional conduct dealing with the giving of evidence, then the Tribunal will expect a member of that body to comply with the provisions of the code in the preparation and presentation of their evidence.'

Definition of expert evidence

30.9 There is a well-established distinction between expert and non-expert witnesses that is encapsulated in the Civil Evidence Act 1972, s 3. A discussion of the scope of expert evidence, the issues on which experts are entitled to give evidence and opine and the weight to be attributed to such evidence is outside the scope of the this book. For a comprehensive discussion of this issue see: James, *Expert Evidence Law and Practice* (3rd edn, 2009, Sweet and Maxwell).

30.10 For present purposes it suffices to note that an expert's evidence is necessarily founded on his or her training and experience in particular field investing him or her with specialist knowledge and experience outside the ken of the inexpert individual. In this respect, experts are not permitted to give evidence on matter within ordinary human experience (*R v Turner* [1975] QB 834). An expert is accordingly a person with a high degree of skill and knowledge in a particular subject and who is able to assist the Tribunal by the preparation of a written report and, if necessary, the giving of oral evidence (see the commentary to CPR rr 35.1 and 35.2 in the White Book). One distinction between their evidence and that of inexpert others is that 'the advantage of a particular skill or training … not only enables them to form opinions and to draw inferences from observed facts, but also to identify facts which may be obscure or invisible to a lay witness.': *Phipson on Evidence* (17th edn, 2009, Sweet and Maxwell) paragraph 33-10.

Exercise of the power to admit expert evidence

30.11 The admission of expert evidence in court litigation is far from routine and it is to be expected that the position with regard to tribunals will be no different; this is not least because many of the Chambers are constituted of specialised members with extensive experience in the relevant field. Parties should evaluate carefully whether or not to adduce expert evidence in light of the rules on costs before the First-tier Tribunal and Upper Tribunal and the limited circumstances in which costs will be recovered (typically where the other party has acted unreasonably; see **Costs**).

30.12 Where a party wishes to adduce expert evidence it is incumbent upon that party to discharge the burden of demonstrating to the Tribunal that it will provide assistance (*Clarke (Executor of the Will of Francis Bacon) v Marlborough Fine Art (London) Ltd* [2002] EWHC 11 (Ch)). The Tribunal will be mindful of the need to control the inappropriate use of experts to bolster cases where their use provides no material assistance to the Tribunal (see eg *Thermos v Aladdin Sales & Marketing Ltd* [2000] FSR 420).

30.13 It is suggested here that the principal factors that will weigh with a Tribunal in determining whether or not to admit expert evidence are:

- As with all questions of admissibility, particularly in respect of evidence of opinion, the relevance of the expert evidence;
- Whether the evidence goes to an issue that is central to the proceedings or only peripheral;
- The complexity of the issues raised by the case;
- The relative expertise of the Tribunal;
- The likely cost of obtaining the expert evidence;
- The effect of obtaining and adducing the expert evidence on the time in which the proceedings can be determined;
- The value of the claim to the parties (both monetarily, personally and professionally – see *S (by her Mother and litigation friend DS) v Chesterfield and North Derbyshire Royal Hospital NHS Trust* [2003] EWCA Civ 1284 at [19] per Brooke LJ).

30.14 A party wishing to adduce expert evidence should also apply to do so promptly. The courts have been increasingly reluctant to admit late expert evidence or evidence that has been raised for the first time close to trial, save in exceptional cases (*Baron v Lovell* [1999] CPLR 630, CA; *Holmes v SGB Services Plc* [2001] EWCA Civ 354).

Single joint experts

30.15 As set out above, the various procedural rules give the First-tier Tribunal and Upper Tribunal the power to order that expert evidence be given by way of a single joint expert. In many cases directing that expert evidence is to be given in this fashion will be in accordance with the overriding objective and will be equitable, in that the costs can be shared by both parties as such costs are unlikely to be recovered in any event (see CPR r 35.8(5) and **Costs**).

30.16 The starting point under the CPR is that there should be no more than one expert in a particular speciality unless necessary for some real purpose (Lord Woolf's Final Report on Access to Justice, chapter 13, paragraph 11). Parties wishing to instruct more than one such expert must accordingly give cogent reasons as to why a single joint expert is necessary in their particular case.

This is particularly so in smaller proceedings in which it is important to keep costs in perspective (*Field v Leeds City Council* [2001] CPLR 129, CA).

30.17 In accordance with the overriding objective, many of the factors of relevance to the Tribunal's decision as to whether to order a single joint expert will be those set out above in respect of whether to admit expert evidence at all. Further, the Tribunal will have regard to the additional costs of instructing more than one expert and the need to ensure equality of arms. This latter consideration will be particularly powerful in cases in which one party's witnesses of fact are also experts in the relevant field (*S v Chesterfield and North Derbyshire Royal Hospital NHS Trust* [2003] EWCA Civ 1284 at [43] (3) per Kennedy LJ).

30.18 A party who is dissatisfied with a single joint expert may put further questions to the expert or apply to adduce a report from a new expert. However, the courts have been surprisingly willing to accede to such applications and will normally permit a party to instruct his own expert where he has 'reasonable grounds' for challenging the single joint expert's opinion and for taking that course (*Layland v Fairview New Homes* [2002] EWHC 1350 (Ch); [2003] CPLR 19 at [30] per Neuberger J). A party wishing to make such an application should apply promptly after receipt of the single joint expert's report and must provide cogent reasons as to why a new expert is required and that the ordering of a new report will not be disproportionate or unjust (*Cosgrove v Pattison* [2001] CPLR 177, ChD).

DUTIES OF EXPERTS

30.19 The Protocol for the Instruction of Experts (annexed to CPR Part 35) sets out the duties of expert witnesses in civil proceedings before the courts. It is suggested here that these duties apply equally to experts properly called and giving evidence as such in proceedings before the First-tier Tribunal and Upper Tribunal. Reference is made here to experts properly called in order to distinguish experts from inexpert witnesses who may nonetheless give opinion evidence before a Tribunal which may well be held inadmissible before a court. The duties set out in the Protocol for the Instruction of Experts are unlikely to apply to such witnesses. However, as the dividing line between expert and inexpert witnesses is blurry, parties should be mindful of the duties imposed by the Protocol, which provides:

> 4.1 Experts always owe a duty to exercise reasonable skill and care to those instructing them, and to comply with any relevant professional code of ethics. However when they are instructed to give or prepare evidence for the purpose of civil proceedings in England and Wales they have an overriding duty to help the court on matters within their expertise (CPR 35.3). This duty overrides any obligation to the person instructing or paying them. Experts must not serve the exclusive interest of those who retain them.
>
> 4.2 Experts should be aware of the overriding objective that courts deal with cases justly. This includes dealing with cases proportionately, expeditiously and fairly (CPR 1.1). Experts are under an obligation to assist the court so as to enable them to deal with cases in accordance with the overriding objective. However the overriding objective does

not impose on experts any duty to act as mediators between the parties or require them to trespass on the role of the court in deciding facts.

4.3 Experts should provide opinions which are independent, regardless of the pressures of litigation. In this context, a useful test of 'independence' is that the expert would express the same opinion if given the same instructions by an opposing party. Experts should not take it upon themselves to promote the point of view of the party instructing them or engage in the role of advocates.

4.4 Experts should confine their opinions to matters which are material to the disputes between the parties and provide opinions only in relation to matters which lie within their expertise. Experts should indicate without delay where particular questions or issues fall outside their expertise.

4.5 Experts should take into account all material facts before them at the time that they give their opinion. Their reports should set out those facts and any literature or any other material on which they have relied in forming their opinions. They should indicate if an opinion is provisional, or qualified, or where they consider that further information is required or if, for any other reason, they are not satisfied that an opinion can be expressed finally and without qualification.

4.6 Experts should inform those instructing them without delay of any change in their opinions on any material matter and the reason for it.

4.7 Experts should be aware that any failure by them to comply with the Civil Procedure Rules or court orders or any excessive delay for which they are responsible may result in the parties who instructed them being penalised in costs and even, in extreme cases, being debarred from placing the experts' evidence before the court. In *Phillips v Symes* [2004] EWHC 2330 (Ch); [2005] 1 WLR 2043 Peter Smith J held that courts may also make orders for costs (under section 51 of the Senior Courts Act 1981) directly against expert witnesses who by their evidence cause significant expense to be incurred, and do so in flagrant and reckless disregard of their duties to the court.

FORM OF EXPERT EVIDENCE

30.20 Expert evidence will usually be by way of written report (CPR r 35.5(1)). The contents of an expert's report in litigation before the courts are set out in the Practice Direction to Part 35 and should be followed by experts before the First-tier Tribunal and Upper Tribunal. The relevant paragraphs provide:

2.1 An expert's report should be addressed to the court and not to the party from whom the expert has received his instructions.

2.2 An expert's report must:

(1) give details of the expert's qualifications;

(2) give details of any literature or other material which the expert has relied on in making the report;

(3) contain a statement setting out the substance of all facts and instructions given to the expert which are material to the opinions expressed in the report or upon which those opinions are based;

(4) make clear which of the facts stated in the report are within the expert's own knowledge;

(5) say who carried out any examination, measurement, test or experiment which the expert has used for the report, give the qualifications of that person, and say whether or not the test or experiment has been carried out under the expert's supervision;

(6) where there is a range of opinion on the matters dealt with in the report—

(a) summarise the range of opinion, and

(b) give reasons for his own opinion;

(7) contain a summary of the conclusions reached;

(8) if the expert is not able to give his opinion without qualification, state the qualification; and

(9) contain a statement that the expert understands his duty to the court, and has complied and will continue to comply with that duty.

2.3 An expert's report must be verified by a statement of truth as well as containing the statements required in paragraph 2.2(8) and (9) above.

2.4 The form of the statement of truth is as follows: 'I confirm that insofar as the facts stated in my report are within my own knowledge I have made clear which they are and I believe them to be true, and that the opinions I have expressed represent my true and complete professional opinion.'

30.21 In accordance with the overriding objective, oral testimony by expert witnesses should be necessary only in a limited number of cases where the Tribunal feels unable without oral evidence to determine which of the accounts of disagreeing experts should be preferred.

30.22 As set out elsewhere in the Handbook (see **Witnesses**) the First-tier Tribunal and the Upper Tribunal has the power to compel witnesses by way of summons to attend a hearing and to give evidence and answer questions. This power is not limited to lay witnesses and extends to any expert that has given evidence for one or both parties. It is to be expected that the power to summons an expert will be used extremely sparingly. However, the courts have been willing to do so where necessary, including in cases where this would take the witness away from other important work (*Lilly ICOS Ltd v Pfizer Ltd (No. 2)* [2002] EWCA Civ 2; [2002] 1 WLR 2253).

31 Extensions Of Time

See also **Case management powers**, **Directions** and **Time limits**

POWER TO EXTEND TIME

31.1 The First-tier Tribunal and Upper Tribunal have a wide procedural discretion in relation to the directions (see **Directions**) that they are empowered to make and have a similarly wide discretion in respect of case management (see **Case management powers**).

31.2 The power to extend (or shorten) the time limit for compliance with any rule, practice direction or direction is contained at r 5(3)(a) of the procedural rules for each of the Chambers of the First-tier Tribunal and of the Upper Tribunal (see **Chambers** and **First-tier Tribunal**).

31.3 In the Lands Chamber of the Upper Tribunal an application may be made for any time limit in the Rules to be extended, subject to any conditions imposed by the registrar. The registrar may make an extension even if applied for outside of the primary time limit (Lands Chamber Rules, r 35). On application, or of its own motion, the Lands Chamber may make an urgency direction shortening existing time limits (Lands Chamber Rules, r 35A).

31.4 The Immigration and Asylum Chamber of the First-tier Tribunal has the power to make directions which specify the length of time allowed for anything to be done or which vary any time limit in these Rules or in directions previously given by the Tribunal for anything to be done by a party (including, where the Tribunal considers that there are exceptional reasons for doing so, extending a time limit which has expired) (IAC Rules, r 45(4)).

31.5 This power is to be exercised in accordance with the overriding objective (see **Overriding objective**) and, particularly in the cases of extensions of time for bringing an application or appeal before a tribunal, must only be exercised if it would be in the interests of justice to do so.

APPLICATIONS TO EXTEND TIME

31.6 Unless made orally at hearing, a party wishing to apply for a direction to extend time should do so in writing, stating the reasons why an extension of time is required and why it is just that the First-tier Tribunal or Upper Tribunal should, in its discretion, make the order sought.

APPLICATIONS, APPEALS ETC. MADE OUT OF TIME

31.7 Though certain of the procedural rules for various tribunals provide that an application or appeal or some other submission made out of time will be deemed to contain an attendant application to extend time, this is only rarely the case and is not common practice in the First-tier Tribunal or Upper Tribunal. For example the Upper Tribunal Rules, r 22(6) provides that an application for permission to appeal to the Upper Tribunal must contain an application for an extension of time if made out of time. Similarly, the GRC Rules, rr 22(4)(a) and 23(5) provide respectively that an appeal notice or response received out of time must contain an application for an extension of time.

31.8 Parties should thus be astute to ensure that any application or appeal made out of time contains a request for an extension of time under the appropriate procedural rule (in the case of the First-tier and Upper Tribunal, r 5(3)(a) of the relevant procedural rules) together with the reasons why the application or appeal is being made out of time and the reasons why the Tribunal should exercise its discretion in the party's favour.

31.9 In the FTTIAC it is vitally important to note that late notices of appeal against an immigration or asylum decision are governed by the IAC Rules, r 10. A late notice must include an application for an extension of time, and the test applied by the FTTIAC is whether they are 'satisfied that by reason of special circumstances it would be unjust not' to extend time (IAC Rules, r 10(5)). This rule was applicable under the previous tribunal system and detailed guidance was given on the circumstances in which an extension would be given in *BO and Others (Extension of time for appealing) Nigeria* [2006] UKAIT 35; [2006] Imm AR 441, which was recently applied and added to in *TR v Asylum and Immigration Tribunal* [2010] EWHC 2055 (Admin). Practitioners should refer to those two authorities when considering an application for an extension under IAC Rules, r 10, bearing in mind that an application for an extension must be considered on the papers only (IAC Rules, r 10(6)).

32 Evidence

See also **Assessors; Documents; Experts; Witnesses**

ADMITTING AND EXCLUDING EVIDENCE IN THE TRIBUNALS

32.1 A full examination of the law of evidence is beyond the scope of the Handbook. This entry sets out the basic provisions common to the First-tier and Upper Tribunals, discusses their application and sets out exceptions relating to particular Chambers.

32.2 It suffices to note here that the key basis of English law's approach to evidence is that evidence is admissible when it is sufficiently relevant, but that it is admissible only insofar as it is not excluded by a rule of law or as a matter of discretion. It is open to the Tribunal to consider material which may prove to be inadmissible at a later stage (*Barings plc v Coopers and Lybrand* [2001] EWCA Civ 1163; [2001] CPLR 451). Whether evidence is 'relevant' tends to be easier to recognise than to describe, but an early text on the subject defines relevance as 'any two facts to which it is applied are so related to each other that according to the common course of events one either taken by itself or in connection with other facts proves or renders probable the past, present or future existence or non-existence of the other' (Stephen, *Digest of the Law of Evidence* (1876, Macmillan), article 1). In the ordinary civil courts there is a discretion, not found at common law, to exclude evidence (CPR r 32.1(2)), which has been described as a case management power to prevent cases getting out of hand (*Post Office Counters Ltd v Mahida* [2003] EWCA Civ 1583 at [24] per Hale LJ).

32.3 The TCEA 2007, Sch 5, para 10 provides for the making of rules about evidence. Each of the Tribunal Procedural Rules contains such rules. Rule 15(2) of the GRC Rules is in the same terms as the equivalent provisions in the rules of the other First-tier Tribunal Chambers (subject to the Chamber-specific rules set out below) and the Upper Tribunal. (The IAC Rules and the Lands Chamber Rules are structured differently and are dealt with below). It provides:

(2) The Tribunal may—

(a) admit evidence whether or not—

(i) the evidence would be admissible in a civil trial in the United Kingdom; or

(ii) the evidence was available to a previous decision maker; or

(b) exclude evidence that would otherwise be admissible where—

(i) the evidence was not provided within the time allowed by a direction or a practice direction;

(ii) the evidence was otherwise provided in a manner that did not comply with a direction or a practice direction; or

(iii) it would otherwise be unfair to admit the evidence.

32.4 Rule 15(2) gives the Chambers of the First-tier Tribunal and the Upper Tribunal a wide power to determine which evidence will be admissible. This power is wider than that in the civil courts more generally, as the Tribunals are permitted to receive otherwise inadmissible evidence.

32.5 As the touchstone of admissibility will usually be the relevance of the evidence sought to be admitted, it may be that the power to admit otherwise inadmissible evidence is not one to which the Tribunal will often need to resort. There will be few circumstances in which the Tribunal will wish to admit irrelevant evidence, but the flexibility given to the Tribunal is important to a system of dispute resolution designed to be user-friendly, straight-forward to understand and responsive to particular circumstances. Where the Tribunal admits evidence that would not otherwise be admissible, it should justify this decision by reference to principles of fairness and natural justice and to the overriding objective (see **Overriding objective**).

32.6 The Tribunal, as a public authority for the purposes of the Human Rights Act 1998, does not have the power to admit evidence if to do so would infringe the human rights of a party (for example under Article 6 of the ECHR). For this reason, the rules of legal professional privilege apply in proceedings before the Tribunal and the Tribunal cannot override their operation, although there may on occasion be debate about whether the evidence is properly covered by the scope of the privilege. The Administrative Appeals Chamber of the Upper Tribunal has confirmed (contrary to the slightly ambiguous tone in Jacobs, *Tribunal Practice and Procedure* (2009) at paragraphs 10.48–10.54) that legal professional privilege (arising out of the relationship of legal advisor and client) and litigation privilege (covering documents produced in contemplation of legal proceedings) apply to the Tribunals, which cannot override the privilege: *LM v London Borough of Lewisham* [2009] UKUT 204 (AAC) at [24], [30]. Similarly, the Tribunal cannot compel any person to give evidence or produce any document that the person could not be compelled to give or produce on a trial of an action (see eg GRC Rules, r 16(3); Tribunal Procedure (First-tier Tribunal) (Health, Education and Social Care Chamber) Rules 2008 ('HESCC Rules'), r 16(3); Asylum and Immigration Tribunal (Procedure) Rules 2005 ('IAC Rules'), r 51(2); Tribunal Procedure (First-tier Tribunal) (Social Entitlement Chamber) Procedural Rules 2008 ('SEC Rules'), r 16(3); Tribunal Procedure (First-tier Tribunal) (Tax Chamber) Rules 2009 ('TC Rules'), r 16(3); Tribunal Procedure (First-tier Tribunal) (War Pensions and Armed Forces Compensation Chamber) Rules 2008 ('WPAFCC Rules'), r 16(3); Tribunal Procedure (Upper Tribunal) Rules 2008 ('Upper Tribunal Rules'), r 16(3)). It is impossible to envisage any Tribunal requiring a party to proceedings before it to take any step contrary to the protections of legal professional/litigation privilege, let alone the other main forms of privilege: the privilege against self-incrimination (see *Rank Film Distributors Ltd v Video Information Centre* [1982] AC 380) and 'without prejudice' privilege (see *Rush and Tomkins Ltd v Greater London Council* [1989] AC 1280 and the recent decision of the Supreme Court in *Oceanbulk Shipping & Trading*

SA v TMT Asia Ltd [2010] UKSC 44). The Court of Appeal has recently confirmed that legal professional privilege only applies between clients and their lawyers. It does not extend to accountants, even when giving advice on tax law: *R(Prudential) v Pandelfo* [2010] EWCA Civ 1094. This will be especially important in the Tax Chamber.

32.7 The Tribunals' case management powers (eg in the GRC under GRC Rules, r 15(1)) permit the Tribunals to give directions and to control:

- Disclosure (see **Documents**);
- Statements of agreed matters;
- The issues on which it requires evidence;
- The nature of the evidence it requires;
- Whether the parties are permitted or required to provide expert evidence and the nature of that evidence (see **Experts**);
- The number of witnesses whose evidence may be put forward (see **Witnesses**);
- The manner in which evidence is to be provided;
- The time at which evidence is to be provided.

32.8 The Tribunals can police compliance with directions and orders by the imposition of sanctions on parties including refusing to admit evidence and in extreme cases striking out of appeals or responses (see **Failures to comply**). In respect of witness evidence, the First-tier Tribunal may refer to the Upper Tribunal, and ask the Upper Tribunal to exercise its power under TCEA 2007, s 25 in relation to any failure by a person to comply with a requirement imposed by the Tribunal (GRC Rules, r 7(3); HESCC Rules, r 7(3); SEC Rules, r 7(3); TC Rules, r 7(3); WPAFCC Rules, r 7(3). See Upper Tribunal Rules, r 7(3)–(4) for the conduct of the referral):

- to attend at any place for the purpose of giving evidence;
- otherwise to make themselves available to give evidence;
- to swear an oath in connection with the giving of evidence;
- to give evidence as a witness;
- to produce a document; or
- to facilitate the inspection of a document or any other thing (including any premises).

32.9 The above powers will be used in combination to control the evidence that is put before the Tribunal. In exercising these powers, the principal factors that the Tribunal will take into account, and those that parties and their representatives should address when making submissions as to the admissibility of evidence, are as follows:

- As noted above, the touchstone of admissibility is relevance;
- The Tribunal will however be guided throughout by the overriding objective and the importance of doing justice in a particular case (see the factors set out by Lord Bingham in *O'Brien v Chief Constable of South Wales Police* [2005] UKHL 26; [2005] 2 AC 534 at [5]–[6]);

- The Tribunal will usually exclude evidence that is irrelevant (ie not probative of a material fact);
- The Tribunal will usually exclude evidence that is immaterial;
- The Tribunal may exclude evidence that is repetitive of other evidence given;
- The Tribunal ought ordinarily to exclude evidence which is prejudicial rather than probative, or where it would be unfair to admit it (see, for example, *Snowball v Gardner Merchant Ltd* [1987] ICR 719);
- The Tribunal will have regard to the timing of the evidence, whether it is late and whether the party seeking to adduce it has complied with the Tribunal's own rules and directions. For guidance on how the First-tier Tribunal should approach the admissibility of late evidence see *HJ v London Borough of Brent* [2010] UKUT 15 (AAC) at [13]–[20];
- The Tribunal will always have regard to the effect that admission (or otherwise) of the evidence on the proceedings. Evidence that is significant or highly probative will usually be admitted even if adduced late or by a party that has not complied with the relevant rules. If necessary, an adjournment will be granted so as to mitigate any potential unfairness to the other parties;
- The Tribunal will have regard to how the evidence was obtained. If evidence has been obtained illegally, the Tribunal must seek to balance two conflicting interests: the interests of the public that in litigation the truth should be revealed and the interests of the public that the courts should not acquiesce in, let alone encourage, a party to use unlawful means to obtain evidence (see *Jones v University of Warwick* [2003] EWCA Civ 151, per Lord Woolf CJ at [2]). In *Jones* Lord Woolf CJ held (at [22]) that: 'The central question in every case where a complaint is made as to the method of obtaining evidence, and the use to which it is put, is whether the trial as a whole is fair.'
- The Tribunal will also have regard to the burden on the parties and the Tribunal of admitting the evidence (*O'Brien*, at [6]). If admission of evidence is going to result in considerably increased costs or unacceptable delay, or will unduly lengthen proceedings, then the Tribunal will need to balance these undesirable consequences against the probative value and importance of the evidence in question.

EVIDENCE IN PARTICULAR TRIBUNALS

32.10 Although the rules of evidence across the Tribunals are broadly the same, there are some differences between the Chambers and some occasional divergence from the position of the GRC set out above.

Health, Education and Social Care Chamber

32.11 There are no references in the HESCC Rules, r 15(1) to exchanging lists of documents for inspection as that form of disclosure exercise is not standard practice in the HESCC. Nor are statements of agreed matters mentioned. The Tribunal has the power in special educational needs cases (see **Special**

educational needs and disability cases) to require the parent, or other person responsible for, the child at issue in the proceedings to make available the child for examination or assessment by a qualified person, or to require the relevant school to permit the qualified person access to the school and the child for the purpose of an assessment of the child or the provisions made for the child (HESCC Rules, r 15(4)). If access is denied by the required person without good reason the Tribunal may consider that that person had failed to co-operate with the Tribunal, which may lead to an adverse result (HESCC Rules, r 15(5)). This stops short of providing for adverse findings or inferences but is evidently aimed at ensuring assessments are able to be carried out for the Tribunal.

Immigration and Asylum Chamber (First-tier Tribunal)

32.12 The IAC Rules are not structured in the same way as those of the other First-tier Tribunals. Consequently, the rules on evidence are found in the IAC Rules, r 51. However, the approach of the FTTIAC is very similar to the other Chambers. Oral, documentary or other evidence of any relevant fact may be given, even if that evidence would be inadmissible in a court of law (IAC Rules, r 51(1)). The Tribunal cannot compel a witness or party to give evidence or a document which they could not be compelled to give in an ordinary civil court (IAC Rules, r 51(2)). The Tribunal itself may require a witness to give evidence on oath, without having to refer the matter to the Upper Tribunal (IAC Rules, r 51(3)). The Tribunal require the original of a document to be produced when only a copy is put into evidence (IAC Rules, r 51(5)).

32.13 A stricter position on late evidence is taken in the FTTIAC. Any written evidence which is served outside of the directed time limits must not be considered by the Tribunal unless there is good reason to do so (IAC Rules, r 51(4)). Reversing what is, in effect, a presumption of admissibility this rule is necessary because of the often tight time limits imposed in immigration and asylum cases.

32.14 In an appeal against the refusal of entry clearance or the refusal of a certificate of entitlement the Tribunal is only entitled to consider only the circumstances appertaining at the time of the decision (the Nationality, Immigration and Asylum Act 2002, s 85(5)) and must only consider evidence which complies with that restriction (IAC Rules, r 51(6)). With the exception of forged documents – which the Nationality, Immigration and Asylum Act 2002, s 108 requires the Tribunal to investigate in private without reference to the party putting forward the forgery – the IAC must not take account of evidence which has not been made available to all parties (IAC Rules, r 51(7)).

Social Entitlement Chamber

32.15 There are no references in the SEC Rules, r 15(1) to exchanging lists of documents for inspection as that form of disclosure exercise is not standard practice in the SEC. Nor are statements of agreed matters mentioned. Otherwise, the rules on evidence in the SEC are as set out above.

Tax Chamber

32.16 There are no references in the TC Rules, r 15(1) to exchanging lists of documents for inspection as that form of disclosure exercise is not standard practice in the TC. Nor are statements of agreed matters mentioned and in r 15(2)(a) there is no reference to the material available to the previous decision-maker. It is hard to see how the latter omission will alter the power of the Tribunal to hear evidence which was not before HMRC if it wishes to do so. Otherwise, the rules on evidence in the TC are as set out above.

War Pensions and Armed Forces Compensation Chamber

32.17 There are no references in the WPAFCC Rules, r 15(1) to exchanging lists of documents for inspection as that form of disclosure exercise is not standard practice in the WPAFCC. Nor are statements of agreed matters mentioned. Otherwise, the rules on evidence in the WPAFCC are as set out above.

Upper Tribunal

32.18 There are no references in the Upper Tribunal Rules, r 15(1) to exchanging lists of documents for inspection as that form of disclosure exercise is not standard practice in the Upper Tribunal. Nor are statements of agreed matters mentioned. There are, however, additional rules to deal with fresh evidence in immigration and asylum cases which was not before the IAC at first instance. Any party wishing to rely on such evidence must notify the Upper Tribunal and any other party indicating the nature of the evidence and explaining why it was not submitted below (Upper Tribunal Rules, r 15(2A)(a)). When deciding whether to admit the evidence the Upper Tribunal must consider whether there has been unreasonable delay in the production of the evidence (Upper Tribunal Rules, r 15(2A)(b)).

32.19 In the Senior President's *Practice Directions – Immigration and Asylum Chambers of the First-tier Tribunal and Upper Tribunal*, 10 February 2010 great stress is placed on the compliance with r 15(2A) 'in every case'. If no specific direction is given, the notice should be served as soon as practicable after the grant of permission (paragraph 4.1). The party notifying the Tribunal should clarify whether the new evidence relates to the error of law said to have been made by the First-tier Tribunal, or to any re-making of the decision by the Upper Tribunal, and whether the evidence is in oral or documentary form (paragraphs 4.2–4.3). If oral, a time estimate should be provided (paragraph 4.5). In a fast track appeal the parties should attend the hearing with all witnesses and evidence available and necessary for setting aside and re-making the decision (paragraphs 4.7, 3.8).

Lands Chamber (Upper Tribunal)

32.20 The rules of evidence in the Lands Chamber are substantially different from the other Chambers and are found primarily in the Lands Chamber Rules, rr 33–34. Evidence may be given orally and is given on oath or affirmation, although evidence by affidavit requires the consent of the parties or the order of the Tribunal (Lands Chamber Rules, r 33(1)). The Tribunal may require the personal attendance of any witness at any stage of the proceedings for examination or cross-examination (Lands Chamber Rules, r 33(2)). Nothing in the Civil Evidence Act 1972 prevents expert evidence from being given before the Tribunal by any party even if no application has been made to the

Tribunal for a direction as to the disclosure of that evidence to any other party to the proceedings (Lands Chamber Rules, r 33(4)).

32.21 The Senior President of Tribunals has issued *Interim Practice Directions and Guidance for the Lands Chamber* (13 May 2009). This stresses that evidence is given on oath or affirmation (despite the more cautious wording in r 33(1)); that all witnesses should provide a written statement verified by a statement of truth in the form set out in paragraph 16.1; that the statement will stand as evidence in chief, but that oral evidence may be given to amplify or deal with new developments; and that any such additional evidence should be notified in advance to the other parties and if it is not the Tribunal may take that into account when deciding whether to permit the evidence to be given (paragraph 16.2).

32.22 The Tribunal (or its registrar) may, on the application of a party or of its own motion, order any party (Lands Chamber Rules, r 34(1)):

(a) to deliver to the registrar any document or information which the Tribunal may require and which it is in the power of the party to deliver;

(b) to afford to every other party to the proceedings an opportunity to inspect those documents (or copies of them) and to take copies;

(c) to deliver to the registrar an affidavit or make a list stating whether any document or class of document specified or described in the order or application is, or has at any time been in his possession, custody or power and stating when he parted with it;

(d) to deliver to the registrar a statement in the form of a pleading setting out further and better particulars of the grounds on which he intends to rely and any relevant facts or contentions;

(e) to answer interrogatories on affidavit relating to any matter at issue between the applicant and the other party;

(f) to deliver to the registrar a statement of agreed facts, facts in dispute and the issue. or issues to be tried by the Tribunal; or

(g) to deliver to the registrar witness statements or proofs of evidence.

A party shall have at least 14 days from the date of the direction in which to comply with the direction of the Tribunal (Lands Chamber Rules, r 34(2)).

32.23 In the simplified procedure strict rules of evidence shall not apply to the hearing and evidence shall not be taken on oath unless the Tribunal orders otherwise (Lands Chamber Rules, r 28(10)).

33 Fact and Law in Tribunal Decisions

DISTINCTION BETWEEN FACT AND LAW

33.1 Reasoned decisions from the First-tier Tribunal and Upper Tribunal will typically contain a statement of the facts found or relied upon, the legal provisions or principles applied and the Tribunal's conclusion of the application of the relevant provisions or principles to the facts as found.

33.2 Appeals to the Upper Tribunal and to the Court of Appeal or Court of Session lie only in respect of errors of law (TCEA 2007, ss 11 and 13). It is therefore important to distinguish between fact and law when identifying whether a decision of the First-tier Tribunal or Upper Tribunal is susceptible to appeal.

33.3 The distinction between fact and law is often a blurry one, and an issue may often be a mixed one of both fact and law. However, the distinction must be respected as this boundary specifically delineates that appellate competence of the Upper Tribunal and appeal courts. It is not appropriate for a tribunal whose jurisdiction is limited to consideration of errors of law to extend the meaning or range of issues that can be qualified as such (see *Varndell v Kearney & Trecker Marwrin Ltd* [1983] ICR 683, 695 per Eveleigh LJ). Similarly, the Upper Tribunal or appellate court must take care not to extend its interference with the decisions of the tribunals below so that it has the practical consequence of removing the appropriate discretion given to such Tribunals (*Re J (A Child) (Custody Rights; Jurisdiction)* [2005] UKHL 40; [2006] 1 AC 80 at [12] per Baroness Hale).

33.4 For present purposes, it is important to note the following:

- Though it is difficult to draw a clear line between law and fact in a number of cases, a potential appellant should endeavour if possible to distil a pure question of law from any mixed question of fact and law as it is arguable that the Upper Tribunal has no jurisdiction to consider the question until it has performed this exercise and extracted such a question (*O'Kelly v Trusthouse Forte Plc* [1984] QB 90 at 122H–123A per Lord Donaldson MR; and see *MT (Algeria) v Secretary of State for the Home Department* [2007] EWCA Civ 808; [2008] QB 533 at [97]).
- The courts have interpreted the distinction between law and fact in a manner which is 'designed to give a greater degree of latitude to tribunals where there is room for difference of opinion. The rule is, in effect, that the application of a legal definition or principle to ascertained fact is erroneous in point of law only if the conclusion reached by the tribunal is unreasonable.' (see Wade and Forsyth, *Administrative Law* (2004, 9th edn), p 944). For an example of the unreasonableness approach in action in respect of the General Commissioners of Tax see *Marson v Morton* [1986] STC 463 (HC), 470 per Browne-Wilkinson VC.
- The traditional position is therefore that the appellate tribunal or court be satisfied that there must have been a misdirection on a question of law before it can intervene (*O'Kelly v Trusthouse Forte Plc* [1984] QB 90 at 123B–C).

- There has always been scope for the courts so to intervene where, having considered the facts, the court concludes that 'the true and only reasonable conclusion contradicts the determination' of the tribunal below (*Edwards v Bairstow* [1956] AC 14, 36 per Lord Radcliffe). Similarly, an inference drawn from primary facts by the lower tribunal may be disturbed on appeal if that inference is not supported by the primary facts (*Furniss v Dawson* [1984] AC 474, 527 per Lord Brightman).
- However, the courts have recently appeared willing to adopt a more flexible and pragmatic approach to the distinction between law and fact (see the speech of Lord Hoffmann in *Moyna v Secretary of State for Work and Pensions* [2003] UKHL 44; [2003] 1 WLR 1929).
- Lord Hoffmann said: 'In any case in which a tribunal has to apply a standard with a greater or lesser degree of imprecision and to take a number of factors into account, there are bound to be cases in which it will be impossible for a reviewing court to say that the tribunal must have erred in law in deciding the case either way' (*Moyna* [2003] UKHL 44; [2003] 1 WLR 1929 at [20]).
- There is nonetheless room for flexibility in the application of the fact/law distinction which allows classification of a question of fact as one of law if it is arguably one which 'judges can answer better than juries'; or conversely, that a question of law can be treated as one of fact because it is considered 'inexpedient' for an appellate tribunal to have to form an independent judgment (see the analysis by the Senior President, Sir Robert Carnwath, in 'Tribunal justice – a new start' [2009] PL 48, 62–63).
- This movement away from rigid classification based on the objective nature of the finding made has been confirmed, and arguably extended, so that whether a question is one of fact or law now depends 'upon whether as a matter of policy one thinks that it is a decision which an appellate body with jurisdiction limited to errors of law should be able to review.' (see *Lawson v Serco Ltd* [2006] UKHL 3; [2006] 1 All ER 823, at [34] per Lord Hoffmann).
- Parties should bear in mind that there will nonetheless remain 'question[s] of degree on which the decision of the primary fact-finder is entitled to considerable respect' (*Lawson v Serco Ltd* [2006] UKHL 3; [2006] 1 All ER 823 at [34] per Lord Hoffmann).
- Despite the existence of some flexibility, the Court of Appeal has affirmed in strong terms the need for appellate tribunals to 'be rigorous in letting only issues of law go through to the second stage' (*Krasniqi v Secretary of State for the Home Department* [2006] EWCA Civ 391 at [10] per Sedley LJ, and [41] per Chadwick LJ).
- The judicial review jurisdiction of the Upper Tribunal against procedural decisions of the First-tier Tribunal will also allow the Upper Tribunal to intervene where there has been a mistake of fact as defined in *E v Secretary of State for the Home Department* [2004] EWCA Civ 49; [2004] QB 1044 at [66] per Carnwath LJ. For the appeal to fall within this definition:
  - there must have been a mistake as to an existing fact (including the availability of evidence);

- the fact or evidence must be 'established', in the sense of being uncontentious and objectively verifiable;
- the appellant must not have been responsible for the mistake; and
- the mistake must have played a material (but not necessarily decisive) part in the reasoning under challenge.

33.5 In cases in which an unequivocally 'pure' question of law does not arise (as is often the case in 'classification' cases in which a tribunal is required to determine whether a particular set of facts falls within a statutory definition), appellants seeking permission to appeal or arguing that an appealable question has arisen out of the decision of the First-tier Tribunal should emphasise *inter alia*:

- the policy reasons for allowing an appeal on the particular question;
- the utility of an appeal, in particular in respect of developing areas of law or cases in which guidance from the Upper Tribunal would be beneficial;
- the reasons why it will not be inexpedient to allow an appeal on the particular question; and
- the competency of the Upper Tribunal to decide the question – in particular, that the Upper Tribunal is in effect a specialist intermediate appeal tribunal between the First-tier Tribunal and the Court of Appeal. Therefore, even though the appeal jurisdiction of the Upper Tribunal is limited to errors of law, it 'should be permitted to venture more freely into the "grey area" separating fact from law, than an ordinary court. Arguably, "issues of law" in this context should be interpreted as extending to any issues of general principle affecting the specialist jurisdiction' (see 'Tribunal justice – a new start' [2009] PL 48, 64).
- It is also worth remembering that in at least some of the jurisdictions now encompassed by the TCEA 2007, an appeal used to lie as of right to the courts (such as in tax cases to the High Court). Now, an appeal will only progress if permission to appeal is granted by either the First-tier Tribunal or the Upper Tribunal. On that basis, if the Tribunal is of the opinion that, but for its uncertainty over whether the error is one of law, it would otherwise have given leave in the case, it is suggested here that leave should be given. The permission stage will operate as a sufficient control mechanism to ensure that neither the Upper Tribunal, nor the Court of Appeal, is swamped by undesirable factual appeals. A more lenient approach to defining errors of law can be adopted without the risk of the floodgates being overwhelmed.

33.6 In response to an application for permission, the notice of appeal, or at the appeal hearing itself if any, respondents should emphasise, *inter alia*:

- the indissolubility of finding and questions of fact from those of law so as to prevent the formation of a sufficiently 'pure' question of law;
- the inexpediency of allowing an appeal;
- the absence of utility of allowing an appeal on the particular question;

- the relative competence of the First-tier Tribunal to decide the question; and
- that it is clear in any event that appellate Tribunals should approach the decisions of specialist tribunals with 'an appropriate degree of caution' (see *Cooke v Secretary of State for Social Security* [2001] EWCA Civ 734; [2002] 3 All ER 279 at [5]–[17] per Hale LJ) even where a question of law is involved, and that a degree of latitude is given to such tribunals and their views must be given weight ('Tribunal justice – a new start' [2009] PL 48, 63).

EXAMPLE ERRORS OF LAW

33.7 It is beyond the scope of the Handbook to enumerate every form that an error of law in a tribunal decision may take (see also: Jacobs, *Tribunal Practice and Procedure* (2009), paragraphs 4.262–4.344). The Court of Appeal has however given some broad guidance which is instructive.

33.8 In *R (Iran) v Secretary of State for the Home Department* [2005] EWCA Civ 982; [2005] Imm AR 535, at [9]–[10], Brooke LJ gave the following examples under the heading 'The jurisdiction to correct errors of law: examples of errors of law commonly encountered':

> '[9] ...
>
> i) Making perverse or irrational findings on a matter or matters that were material to the outcome ("material matters");
>
> ii) Failing to give reasons or any adequate reasons for findings on material matters;
>
> iii) Failing to take into account and/or resolve conflicts of fact or opinion on material matters;
>
> iv) Giving weight to immaterial matters;
>
> v) Making a material misdirection of law on any material matter;
>
> vi) Committing or permitting a procedural or other irregularity capable of making a material difference to the outcome or the fairness of the proceedings;
>
> vii) Making a mistake as to a material fact which could be established by objective and uncontentious evidence, where the appellant and/or his advisers were not responsible for the mistake, and where unfairness resulted from the fact that a mistake was made.
>
> [10] Each of these grounds for detecting an error of law contain the word "material" (or "immaterial"). Errors of law of which it can be said that they would have made no difference to the outcome do not matter...'

33.9 To this may be added:

- A tribunal acting outside its jurisdiction whether in the sense of its subject-matter jurisdiction, the scope of its authority or the exercise of its powers over parties and remedies;

- A tribunal being improperly constituted according to the relevant practice statement or statute (*De Haney v Brent MIND* [2003] EWCA Civ 1637; [2004] ICR 348) (see **Constitution and composition of the First-Tier Tribunal** and **Constitution and composition of the Upper Tribunal**);
- A tribunal hearing a case not properly brought before it (including where incorrect or improper notice or listing has taken place);
- A tribunal making a finding based on material on which the parties had no opportunity to make submissions;
- A tribunal failing to give adequate reasons where required (see **Reasons**);
- A tribunal making a finding of fact in respect of which there is no evidence at all or drawing an inference unsupported by evidence;
- A tribunal making an irrational or perverse finding of fact (this will constitute an error of law only where there is a very strong or overwhelming case to support the conclusion that the Tribunal's decision was perverse: see eg *Connex South Eastern Ltd v Bangs* [2005] EWCA Civ 14; [2005] ICR 763; for the advantage of a trial judge hearing the evidence over the appellate tribunal see *Assicurazioni Generali SpA v Arab Insurance Group* [2002] EWCA Civ 1642; [2003] 1 WLR 577).

Exceptions in the Upper Tribunal

33.10 Although TCEA 2007, s 11 imposes a general rule that an appeal to the Upper Tribunal can only be on the basis of an error of law, not every case in the Upper Tribunal will be brought under s 11. The Upper Tribunal has, in certain categories of case, a first-instance jurisdiction direct from the primary decision-maker. For example, much of the work of the Lands Chamber of the Upper Tribunal is direct first appeals, although certain tribunals not yet within the scope of the TCEA are subject to appeals to the Lands Chamber (see **Lands Chamber**) in an equivalent to the ordinary procedure. Alternatively, a case may have been transferred from the First-tier Tribunal to the Upper Tribunal because of its difficulty. Consequently, there will be hearings in the Upper Tribunal in which it is necessary to adduce factual evidence, and for the Upper Tribunal to make factual findings.

33.11 In an appeal from the First-tier Tribunal, the Upper Tribunal has the power to make any decision the First-tier Tribunal could have made, including making such findings of fact as are appropriate (TCEA 2007, s 12(4)). However, an appeal is not a rehearing. It is therefore probable that the ability to make fresh findings of fact is 'limited to identifying or placing appropriate weight on the relevant facts or drawing appropriate inferences from them...In other words, if the facts before the Upper Tribunal are capable of supporting two or more reasonable conclusions it may be open to the Upper Tribunal to substitute its preferred conclusion for that of the First-tier Tribunal' (Gething & Barker, 'The Upper Tribunal's power to make determinations of fact on appeal from the First-tier Tribunal' [2009] British Tax Review 351, 356).

34 Failures to Comply

FAILURES TO COMPLY WITH RULES AND DIRECTIONS

34.1 The term failure to comply is used here to refer to a party's failure to comply with and/or satisfy its obligations under:

- a provision of the relevant procedural rules in the First-tier or Upper Tribunal in which the proceedings are taking place;
- an applicable practice direction; or
- a direction of the First-tier or Upper Tribunal.

34.2 The procedural rules for the various Chambers of the First-tier Tribunal (see **Chambers and First-tier Tribunal**) and for the Upper Tribunal contain provisions dealing with the effects and consequences attendant upon a failure to comply with the above rules and directions. In the Chambers of the First-tier and Upper Tribunal this is typically to be found at r 7 of the relevant procedural rules. The effect of r 7 is set out below, with references to the appropriate procedural rules, noting any differences between them. The Immigration and Asylum Chamber has a different structure to its rules so that failures to comply are dealt with under the IAC Rules, r 59. In the Upper Tribunal, the Lands Chamber is governed by the Lands Chamber Rules, which, again, have a different structure.

FAILURES TO COMPLY IN THE FIRST-TIER TRIBUNAL

Irregular actions not automatically void

34.3 If a party fails to comply with a relevant rule or direction, this does not automatically render the irregular action taken by that party void. The First-tier Tribunal has a general discretion to waive the failure to comply if this appears to be just in the circumstances. This aspect of r 7 is consistent across the First-tier Tribunal and is found at r 7(1) and 7(2)(a) of the procedural rules for each Chamber of the First-tier Tribunal. Failures to comply do not render appeals automatically void in the FTTIAC, unless the Tribunal so orders (IAC Rules, r 59(1)(a)).

Available sanctions

34.4 Alternatively, if the First-tier Tribunal does not consider it just to waive the failure to comply, it may impose such sanction or requirements as it in its discretion determines is just. The First-tier Tribunal must exercise its powers to impose sanctions in accordance with the overriding objective to deal with cases fairly and justly (see **Overriding objective**).

34.5 The FTTIAC does not have an enumerated list of indicative sanctions but it does have a general power to make any order or take any step it considers appropriate to remedy the error (IAC Rules, r 59(1)(b)). The FTTIAC is also governed by the overriding objective (IAC Rules, r 4). In particular, the IAC Rules provide that a determination of an appeal shall not be rendered void by the hearing or the determination having taken place or been delivered outside of a specified time limit (IAC Rules, r 59(2)).

34.6 The sanctions envisaged by r 7 include:

- requiring the failure to be remedied (r 7(2)(b) of each of the Chambers' procedural rules);
- exercising its power to strike out a party's case (see **Striking Out**) (r 7(2)(c) of each of the Chambers' procedural rules);
- in the GRC and TC, restricting a party's participation in the proceedings (GRC Rules, r 7(2)(e) and TC Rules, r 7(2)(d));
- in the HESCC, restricting a party's participation in the proceedings except in mental health cases (HESCC Rules, r 7(2)(e));
- referring a question to the Upper Tribunal under the power contained in r 7(3) (GRC Rules, r 7(2)(d), HESCC Rules, WPAFCC Rules, and SEC Rules; TC Rules, r 7(2)(e)).

Though the SEC Rules and WPAFCC Rules do not expressly convey a power to restrict a party's participation in proceedings, r 7 is not expressly an exhaustive list of sanctions and it is suggested that the SEC and the WPAFCC has such a power. This view is reinforced by the existence of a power to restrict participation in any proceedings (save in mental health cases) in the Upper Tribunal (see below).

Referring a question to the Upper Tribunal concerning a failure to comply

34.7 The First-tier Tribunal may ask the Upper Tribunal to exercise its powers under the TCEA 2007, s 25. Section 25 provides that the Upper Tribunal has the same powers as the High Court (in England and Wales and in Northern Ireland) or the Court of Session (in Scotland) in respect of:

- the attendance and examination of witnesses;
- the production and inspection of documents; and
- all other matters incidental to the Upper Tribunal's functions.

34.8 The First-tier Tribunals may thus refer questions to the Upper Tribunal and ask it to exercise its powers of compulsion over witnesses and documents in respect of failures to comply with directions by the First-tier Tribunal that a person (r 7(3) of the procedural rules of each of the First-tier Tribunal Chambers):

- attend at any place for the purpose of giving evidence;
- otherwise make themselves available to give evidence;
- swear an oath in connection with the giving of evidence;
- give evidence as witness;
- produce a document; or
- facilitate the inspection of a document or any other thing (including any premises).

This power is not expressly reflected in the IAC Rules, but the Upper Tribunal has the same powers in relation to the IAC as to the other Chambers and there is no reason to suppose it is not a power which is encompassed by the more general provision set out above. In the case of some of the circumstances in which a reference to the Upper Tribunal would be made the IAC Rules grant the power to the FTTIAC in any event, such as requiring an oath to be sworn (IAC Rules, r 51(3)).

FAILURES TO COMPLY IN THE UPPER TRIBUNAL

Irregular actions not automatically void

34.9 As with proceeding before the First-tier Tribunal, if a party fails to comply with a relevant rule or direction of the Upper Tribunal, this does not automatically render the irregular action taken by that party void. The Upper Tribunal has a general discretion to waive the failure to comply if this appears to be just in the circumstances (Upper Tribunal Rules, r 7(1), r 7(2)(a)). The same is true in the Lands Chamber (Lands Chamber Rules, r 47).

Available sanctions

34.10 Alternatively, if the Upper Tribunal does not consider it just to waive the failure to comply, it may impose such sanction or requirements as it in its discretion determines is just. The Upper Tribunal must exercise its powers to impose sanctions in accordance with the overriding objective to deal with cases fairly and justly (see **Overriding objective**).

34.11 The sanctions envisaged by r 7 include:

- requiring the failure to be remedied (Upper Tribunal Rules, r 7(2)(b));
- exercising its power to strike out a party's case (see **Striking Out**) (Upper Tribunal Rules, r 7(2)(c));
- except in mental health, immigration or asylum cases, restricting a party's participation in the proceedings (Upper Tribunal Rules, r 7(2)(b)).

In the Lands Chamber the procedural rules are more specific. Where a party has failed to send a document within the required time limit the Tribunal may direct that it be sent, adjourn any scheduled hearing and make an award of costs reflecting the failure (Lands Chamber Rules, r 46(1)). Where a party has failed to pursue proceedings with due diligence, or otherwise failed to comply with the Lands Chamber Rules the Tribunal may – of its own motion, or on an application by another party – order that the proceedings be heard, order that the proceedings be dismissed, order that a party be debarred from taking any future part, or make any other order which seems appropriate, including as to costs. The Tribunal cannot make such an order without having heard from the parties (Lands Chamber Rules, r 46(2)). If an order is made under r 46(2) by the registrar rather than the Tribunal, a party has the right to appeal to the Tribunal within seven days (Lands Chamber Rules, rr 46(3) and 38(9)).

Questions referred by the First-tier Tribunal concerning a failure to comply

34.12 As noted above, the First-tier Tribunal may ask the Upper Tribunal to exercise its powers under TCEA 2007, s 25. Section 25 provides the Upper Tribunal with the powers of the High Court or Court of Session to require the attendance and examination of witnesses and the production and inspection of documents, and all other matters incidental to the Upper Tribunal's functions.

34.13 If such a question is referred, the Upper Tribunal may exercise its power under TCEA 2007, s 25 in respect of the failure to comply as if the requirement had been imposed by the Upper Tribunal itself (Upper Tribunal Rules, r 7(3), (4)).

35 Financial Services Cases

35.1 There are two primary types of financial services cases: those previously heard by the Financial Services and Markets Tribunal, and those previously heard by the Pensions Regulator Tribunal.

THE FINANCIAL SERVICES AND MARKETS TRIBUNAL

35.2 The Financial Services and Markets Tribunal ('FSMT') was established by the Financial Services and Markets Act 2000 (the 'FSMA 2000'), s 132. The FSMT heard references arising from decision notices issued by the Financial Services Authority ('FSA'), the Bank of England and compensation and consideration assessors acting under the Banking (Special Provisions) Act 2008 and the Banking Act 2009. The jurisdiction of the FSMT extended to the whole of the United Kingdom (see explanatory notes to the Financial Services and Markets Tribunal Rules 2001, SI 2001/2476).

35.3 Decision notices from the FSA cover a wide range of regulatory and disciplinary matters which include:

- The grant or revocation of permission for the carrying out of regulated activities or the imposition of requirements on a person's permission, including requirements for a firm to maintain particular resource levels;
- Penalties for market abuse in breach of the FSA Code of Market Conduct;
- Disciplinary statements and/or penalties directed at persons found to be in breach of the requirements of the FSMA 2000;
- Refusals to admit securities to the official list or decisions to suspend securities from the official list;
- Censuring or imposing a penalty on issuers in breach of the listing rules.

35.4 The firm or the individual to whom a decision notice is addressed had the right to refer the matter to the FSMT which would proceed to determine the appropriate action for the FSA to take (FSMA 2000, pre-amendment, s 133(4)).

THE PENSIONS REGULATOR TRIBUNAL

35.5 The Pensions Regulator Tribunal ('PRT') was established by the Pensions Act 2004, s 102 and had jurisdiction to hear references from a determination notice or a final notice made by the Pensions Regulator. The Regulator's objectives are to protect the benefits of members of pension schemes, encourage good pension-scheme practice and reduce risk of Government bailouts (Pensions Act 2004, s 5). The notices issued by the Regulator could impose:

- A financial penalty;
- The suspension or prohibition of a trustee;
- The imposition of a contribution notice;

- An order winding up a scheme; or
- An order freezing a scheme.

35.6 The PRT was not a tribunal of general jurisdiction. Only types of notice specifically permitting a reference in the 2004 Act could be referred to the PRT.

ALLOCATION OF JURISDICTION OF FSMT AND PRT TO UPPER TRIBUNAL

35.7 The First-tier Tribunal and Upper Tribunal (Chambers) Order 2008, SI 2008/2684 as amended, allocated in art 8(1)(aa) appeals against decisions of the FSA, the Bank of England and compensation and consideration assessors under the Banking (Special Provisions) Act 2008, and in art 8(1)(ab) appeals against decisions of the Pensions Regulator, to the Tax and Chancery Chamber of the Upper Tribunal (see **Tax and Chancery Chamber**). This transfer of functions took effect on 6 April 2010, when the FMST and the PRT (except for Northern Ireland) were abolished: see the Transfer of Tribunal Functions Order 2010, SI 2010/22.

35.8 The 2010 Order substantially amends the provisions of FSMA 2000 which had previously provided for an appeal to the FSMT. Section 132 has been removed, and s 133 has been amended. The Upper Tribunal is given the power to suspend the effect of an appealed decision pending the Tribunal's decision (s 133(3)); the Tribunal may consider any relevant evidence, even if it post-dates the decision challenged (s 133(4)); and the Tribunal must decide what the appropriate course of action for the decision-maker to take is, although it may not direct the FSA to do anything which would otherwise have required a fresh decision notice (ss 133(5) and 133A(2)).

Procedure

35.9 Procedure is now governed by the Upper Tribunal Rules (see **Appeals and references to the Upper Tribunal**, **Upper Tribunal**, and **Upper Tribunal procedural rules**).

35.10 The amended s 133(3) is recognised in Upper Tribunal Rules, r 5(5), giving the Tribunal the power to suspend the effect of a decision which is being appealed, where the Tribunal is satisfied that the interests of any persons (whether consumers, investors or otherwise) intended to be protected and the smooth operation or integrity of any market intended to be protected is not prejudiced. This power does not apply to decisions of the Pensions Regulator (Upper Tribunal Rules, r 5(6)).

35.11 The bringing of a reference in financial services cases is governed by Schedule 3 to the Upper Tribunal Rules (r 26B). Where a reference notice is signed and sent by the applicant to be received by the Tribunal not later than 28 days after notice was given of the decision in respect of which the reference is made, the reference notice must cover:

(a) the name and address of the applicant;

(b) the name and address of the applicant's representative (if any);

(c) if no representative is named under sub-paragraph (b), an address where documents for the applicant may be sent or delivered; and

(d) the issues that the applicant wishes the Upper Tribunal to consider.

35.12 The applicant must send to the Tribunal a copy of the relevant decision and must send a copy of the reference to the respondent (Upper Tribunal Rules, Sch 3, para 2).

35.13 The Tribunal will keep a publicly available register of all such references made to it (Upper Tribunal Rules, Sch 3, para 3), as the FSMT and PRT were required to do.

35.14 The respondent must deliver its response within 28 days, identifying the statutory provision for the referred action, the reasons for the referred action and all facts and matters the respondent relies upon, including a list of all documents which support and undermine the decision. These are to be sent to the applicant at the same time as the Tribunal (Upper Tribunal Rules, Sch 3, para 4). The same rules apply to any reply that the applicant wishes to make (Upper Tribunal Rules, Sch 3, para 5). Following receipt of the reply, if the respondent considers that it has any further material which might assist the applicant's case, it must send a list of that material to the Tribunal and the applicant within 14 days (Upper Tribunal Rules, Sch 3, para 6).

35.15 Lengthy and detailed provisions are made in Upper Tribunal Rules, Sch 3, para 7 providing for exceptions to the disclosure obligations. These include where disclosure would be contrary to the public interest or the commercial interests of other persons, whilst not significantly aiding the applicant's case. The Upper Tribunal has the power to consider whether or not to make directions in such cases.

35.16 Where a reference was made by a third party in a third party rights case under FSMA 2000, s 393, the Upper Tribunal Rules, (Sch 3, para 9) make minor modifications to the applicable procedure to take account of that alteration of the normal bi-partite dispute.

35.17 Where a party wishes to appeal against the decision of the Upper Tribunal, the application notice must be received by the Tribunal within 14 days of the date on which the Tribunal sent written notice of the decision, or notification of its amended reasons or decision following a review, or notification that an application to set aside a decision was unsuccessful (Upper Tribunal Rules, r 44(3D)). Parties should note that this is a substantially shorter time period than the month that is normally allowed.

35.18 The Tribunal has the power to award costs against the regulator where it considers that the decision in respect of which a reference was made was unreasonable (Upper Tribunal Rules, r 10(3)(e)).

36 First-Tier Tribunal

See also **Chambers; Upper Tribunal**

THE FIRST-TIER TRIBUNAL

36.1 The TCEA 2007 provides a new unified structure to what was previously an incoherent and ad hoc tribunals system by creating two new generic tribunals, the First-tier Tribunal and the Upper Tribunal (see **Upper Tribunal**). Section 3 of TCEA 2007 provides for the creation of a First-tier Tribunal consisting of judges (who are legally qualified members of the tribunal) and other members (with relevant expertise in the jurisdictions covered by the tribunal), and presided over by the Senior President of Tribunals (see **Constitution and composition of the First-tier Tribunal**).

36.2 The First-tier Tribunal's main function is to hear appeals against decisions of the Government and other public bodies in the areas in which it has been given jurisdiction. By virtue of TCEA 2007, s 11, a right to appeal to the Upper Tribunal lies from most decisions of the First-tier Tribunal (see **Appeals from the First-Tier Tribunal** and **Appeals and references to the Upper Tribunal**). Appeals lie to the Upper Tribunal only on a point of law. The First-tier Tribunal has the role of being the fact-finding Tribunal as well as being the legal arbiter of disputes. For many users of the Tribunal system, the First-tier Tribunal, located in a huge number of centres around the country, will be the only contact they have or need to have with the new TCEA 2007 structure.

36.3 The First-tier Tribunal is intended to be flexible and to evolve as the system matures. In particular, in order to avoid a return to a proliferation of tribunals each with bespoke rules, the First-tier Tribunal is intended not only to be able to absorb the jurisdictions of a large number of existing tribunals (it is intended that the First-tier Tribunal will eventually exercise the jurisdictions exercised by most of the tribunal jurisdictions administered by central government) but also to be ready to take on any new appeal right or jurisdiction created by Parliament.

As a creature of statute, the First-tier Tribunal has no inherent powers: *MH v Nottinghamshire County Council* [2009] UKUT 178 (AAC).

JURISDICTIONS COVERED BY THE FIRST-TIER TRIBUNAL

36.4 The First-tier Tribunal currently has jurisdiction over a range of appeals formerly heard by:

- the Asylum Support Tribunal;
- the Asylum and Immigration Tribunal;
- the Care Standards Tribunal;
- the Charity Tribunal;
- the Claims Management Services Tribunal;

- the Consumer Credit Appeals Tribunal;
- the Criminal Injuries Compensation Panel;
- the Estate Agents Appeals Panel;
- the Family Health Services Appeals Authority;
- the Gambling Appeals Tribunal;
- the General and Special Commissioners of Income Tax;
- the Immigration Services Tribunal;
- the Information Tribunal;
- Local Government Standards in England;
- the Mental Health Review Tribunal;
- the Pensions Appeals Tribunals (England and Wales);
- the Social Security and Child Support Appeals Tribunal;
- the Special Educational Needs and Disability Tribunal;
- (parts of) the Transport Tribunal; and
- the VAT and Duties Tribunals.

CHAMBERS OF THE FIRST-TIER TRIBUNAL

36.5 In order to facilitate the smooth operation of the First-tier Tribunal, it is presently divided into six Chambers (see **Chambers**):

- the General Regulatory Chamber, dealing with charity cases (see **Charity cases**), claims management services appeals (see **Claims management services cases**), consumer credit appeals (see **Consumer Credit appeals**), environment cases (see **Environment cases**), estate agents appeals (see **Estate agents appeals**), gambling appeals (see **Gambling appeals**), immigration services appeals (see **Immigration services cases**), information rights cases (see **Information rights cases**), Local government standards in England cases (see **Local government standards cases**) and certain transport cases (see **Transport cases**).
- the Health, Education and Social Care Chamber (see **Health, Education and Social Care Chamber**) dealing with care standards cases (see **Care standards cases**), special education needs and disability cases (see **Schools**), mental health cases (see **Mental health cases**) and primary health list cases (see **Primary health list cases**);
- the Immigration and Asylum Chamber (see **Immigration and Asylum Chamber (First-tier Tribunal)**) dealing with all immigration and asylum decisions on appeal;
- the Social Entitlement Chamber (see **Social Entitlement Chamber**) dealing with asylum support cases (see **Asylum support appeals**), Criminal injuries compensation cases (see **Criminal injury compensation appeals**) and social security and child support cases (see **Social Security and Child Support cases**);

- the Tax Chamber (see **Tax Chamber**) dealing with taxation cases; and
- the War Pensions and Armed Forces Compensation Chamber (see **War Pensions and Armed Forces Compensation Chamber**) dealing with war pensions and armed forces compensation cases.

36.6 It is through this division of the First-tier and Upper Tribunal into Chambers that the jurisdictional boundaries of the tribunals system are established and the procedural rules for the First-tier Tribunal and Upper Tribunal can be made sufficiently flexible to deal with the wide variety of different jurisdictions being brought within the new system. The system of Chambers makes it possible to assimilate the myriad subject-matters dealt with by previous tribunals into the two tribunal system. It is likely that a Lands and Housing Chamber, with a route of onward appeal to the Lands Chamber of the Upper Tribunal, will be the next addition to the First-tier Tribunal.

37 Gambling Appeals

See also **General Regulatory Chamber; General Regulatory Chamber procedural rules**

LEGISLATIVE BACKGROUND

37.1 The Gambling Appeals Tribunal ('GAT') was an independent body set up by the Gambling Act 2005, s 141 to hear appeals against the decisions of the Gambling Commission.

37.2 The Gambling Commission issues operating licences to companies engaged in the business of gambling, as well as personal functional and personal management licences to people in key management positions. Licence holders and applicants had a right of appeal to the GAT against the decisions of the Gambling Commission relating to their existing licence or licence application.

37.3 In particular, the GAT had jurisdiction to hear:

- Appeals against decisions not to issue or renew an operating or personal licence;
- Appeals against decisions to attach a condition to a personal or operating licence;
- Appeals against decisions to refuse to continue the effect of an operating licence when a new controller takes over;
- Appeals against decisions to refuse to vary an operating or personal licence;
- Appeals against a notification to lapse an operating or personal licence due to mental or physical incapacity;
- Appeals following a review to: (i) attach a warning; (ii) attach an additional condition to a licence; (iii) remove or amend a condition attached to a licence; and (iv) make, amend or remove an exclusion for remote licences);
- Appeals following a review to suspend a licence;
- Appeals following a review to revoke a licence;
- Appeals following a review to impose a financial penalty on an operating or personal licence; and
- Appeals against a decision to void a bet.

TRANSFER OF FUNCTIONS TO THE GENERAL REGULATORY CHAMBER

37.4 As of 18 January 2010, the jurisdiction of the GAT was transferred to the General Regulatory Chamber of the First-tier Tribunal (see **General Regulatory Chamber**) under the Transfer of Tribunal Functions Order 2010, SI 2010/22, art 2(1)(c).

VENUE

37.5 Hearings in the First-tier Tribunal (Gambling) are normally held in London, Birmingham, Manchester, Leeds, Glasgow and Cardiff. However, a hearing can be arranged at another venue if necessary.

PROCEDURE IN GAMBLING APPEALS

The GRC Procedure

37.6 Since 18 January 2010, with the transfer of the GAT's jurisdiction to the GRC, Gambling Appeals follow the procedure for all cases other than charity cases before the GRC. The GRC Rules are covered in detail elsewhere in this Handbook (see **General Regulatory Chamber procedural rules**).

37.7 The GRC Rules apply unmodified to gambling appeals. Parties should note GRC Rules, r 19A(1) (applicable solely to gambling appeals), which provides that the GRC may suspend the effect of a decision of the Gambling Commission (whether or not it has already taken effect) while an appeal against that decision could be brought within the time limit or has been brought but has yet to be finally determined or withdrawn.

Special features of gambling appeals

37.8 The Gambling Appeals Tribunal Rules 2006, SI 2006/3293 (the 'GAT Rules') did not differ markedly from the GRC Rules and accordingly, the transfer of the GAT's functions to the GRC has been unproblematic. There are however four features of note.

37.9 First, there is a slight but important difference in the time limit for the bringing of an appeal against a decision of the Gambling Commission. An appeal to the GAT had to be brought within one month of the date of decision under the Gambling Act 2005, s 142. However, an appeal to the GRC must be brought within 28 days of the date that notice of the decision was sent to the appellant (GRC Rules, r 22(1)(b)). Section 142 of the 2005 Act has been repealed by the Transfer of Tribunals Functions Order 2010, SI 2010/22. Both the GAT and GRC had or have the power to extend time, but this is a change to be noted because if an appeal is sent to the GRC out of time without a request for an extension the GRC is obliged to dismiss it (GRC Rules, r 22(4)(b)).

37.10 Second, the GAT was obliged to maintain a register containing particulars of appeal to, and decisions of (including the final determination) the GAT (the 'Register') (GAT Rules, r 33(1)). The Register was to be reasonably accessible to any person without charge (GAT Rules, r 33(2)). The GRC Rules contain no provision for the maintenance of a public register, but it appears from the website of the Gambling sub-division of the GRC that the Register will nonetheless be maintained and made available through the website.

37.11 Third, the right of appeal from the GAT to the High Court is abolished. Parties unhappy with a decision of the GRC must proceed by way of appeal to the Administrative Appeals Chamber of the Upper Tribunal.

37.12 Fourth, parties should note the differing rules as to costs as between the GAT and the GRC. In proceedings before the GAT, costs were available against the Gambling Commission on the basis that the Gambling Commission's decision or action under appeal was unreasonable to the extent that no reasonable person having the Gambling Commission's powers and being subject to its duties could have made that decision or taken that action (GAT Rules, r 28(3)). The GRC may only make an award for costs (see **Costs**) in gambling appeals in two circumstances:

- under TCEA 2007, s 29(4) in respect of wasted costs; or
- if the GRC considers that a party has acted unreasonably in bringing, defending or conducting the proceedings.

37.13 It is also important to note that an appeal to the GRC is subject to the payment of a fee, as it was in the GAT, unless the appellant is in receipt of qualifying benefits. Those fees are set out in the First-tier Tribunal (Gambling) Fees Order 2010, SI 2010/42 and, at the time of writing, are very high going up to £13,070 in respect of a casino operating licence.

38 General Regulatory Chamber

THE GENERAL REGULATORY CHAMBER

38.1 The General Regulatory Chamber was the fifth Chamber to be added to the First-tier Tribunal and assumed jurisdiction over a number of subject matters on 1 September 2009. The GRC is and was intended to be the most flexible and wide-ranging of the Chambers and it is anticipated that many further jurisdictions will be added to the GRC over the coming years. This flexibility is reflected in the definition of its jurisdiction. Under article 5B of the First-tier Tribunal and Upper Tribunal (Chambers) Order 2008, SI 2008/2684 (as amended) the GRC is simply assigned the following functions:

(a) proceedings in respect of the decisions and actions of regulatory bodies which are not assigned to the HESCC;

(b) matters referred to the First-tier Tribunal under Schedule 1D to the Charities Act 1993; and

(c) the determination of remuneration for carrying mail-bags in a ship or aircraft.

Jurisdictions transferred to the GRC on 1 September 2009

38.2 Since 1 September 2009, the GRC has jurisdiction to hear the following cases:

- Charity cases formerly falling within the jurisdiction of the Charity Tribunal (see **Charity cases**);
- Consumer credit appeal cases formerly heard by the Consumer Credit Appeals Panel (see **Consumer credit appeals**);
- Estate agents appeal cases formerly heard by the Estate Agents Appeal Panel (see **Estate agents appeals**).

The above Tribunals were abolished with the transfer of their functions to the GRC.

38.3 From 1 September 2009, the GRC also began to hear appeals and claims which were formerly heard by the Transport Tribunal (see **Transport cases**). However, only certain of the Transport Tribunal's functions were transferred to the GRC; the Transport Tribunal retains an independent existence. In this respect, the main caseload of the GRC will consist of appeals against decisions of the Driving Standards Agency. Appeals against decisions of the Traffic Commissioner are heard directly by the Administrative Appeals Chamber of the Upper Tribunal. The Transport Tribunal continues to hear appeals under the Transport (Scotland) Act 2001.

Jurisdictions transferred to the GRC from 18 January 2010

38.4 Since 18 January 2010, the GRC has had jurisdiction to hear the following cases:

- Local authority standards cases formerly falling within the jurisdiction of the Adjudication Panel for England (see **Local authority standards cases**);

- Appeals by the providers of claims management services against decisions of the statutory regulator (currently the Secretary of State for Justice) that were formerly heard by the Claims Management Services Tribunal (see **Claims management cases**);
- Gambling cases formerly heard by the Gambling Appeals Tribunal (see **Gambling appeals**);
- Appeals by the providers or users of immigration services against decisions of the statutory regulator (the Immigration Services Commissioner) that were formerly heard by the Immigration Service Tribunal (see **Immigration services cases**);
- Freedom of information and data protection cases formerly heard by the Information Tribunal (see **Information rights cases**), except that appeals under the Data Protection Act 1998, s 28 and the Freedom of Information Act 2000, s 60 will be transferred directly to the Upper Tribunal.

Jurisdiction transferred to the GRC from 6 April 2010

38.5 From 6 April 2010, the GRC has had jurisdiction to hear appeals against new civil sanctions made in respect of certain environmental offences under the Regulatory Enforcement and Sanctions Act 2008 and issued by the regulators (the Environment Agency and Natural England) (see **Environment cases**).

Possible future additions to the GRC's jurisdiction

38.6 In *Transforming Tribunals: Implementing Part 1 of the Tribunals, Courts and Enforcement Act 2007*, (Ministry of Justice Consultation Paper, CP 30/07) it was suggested that the functions of the following tribunals were suitable for transfer into the GRC (Annex C, p.72):

- Aircraft & Shipping Tribunal;
- Antarctic Act Tribunal;
- Chemical Weapons Licensing Appeal Tribunal;
- Foreign Compensation Commission;
- Insolvency Practitioners Tribunal;
- Mines and Quarries Tribunal;
- NHS Medicines Appeal Tribunal;
- Plant Varieties and Seeds Tribunal;
- Sea Fish License Tribunal.

These may well be brought into the GRC's jurisdiction in due course.

Procedure in the GRC

38.7 Proceedings before the GRC are governed by the Tribunal Procedure (First-Tier Tribunal) (General Regulatory Chamber) Rules 2009, SI 2009/1976 as amended (the 'GRC Rules'). These Rules provide detailed procedural guidance on how cases are to be brought and regulated in the full range of

GRC jurisdictions and are discussed in detail elsewhere in this Handbook (see **General Regulatory Chamber procedural rules**). The GRC Rules are set out in Appendix 1.

38.8 For more specific discussion of matters falling within the jurisdiction of the GRC, see: **Case management powers**; **Costs**; **Directions**; **Documents**; **Evidence**; **Extensions of time**; **Parties**; **Representation**; **Striking out**; **Time limits**; **Withdrawal of proceedings**; and **Witnesses**.

39 General Regulatory Chamber Procedural Rules

See **General Regulatory Chamber; Procedural rules**

PROCEDURE BEFORE THE GENERAL REGULATORY CHAMBER

39.1 Procedure before the GRC is governed by the GRC Rules which came into force on 1st September 2009 as amended by the Tribunal Procedure (Amendment) Rules 2010, SI 2010/43.

39.2 The majority of provisions of the GRC Rules apply equally to all types of case within the GRC's jurisdiction. However, there are a number of provisions specifically dealing with charity cases and transport cases. These will be referred to in passing in this entry of the Handbook but are not covered explicitly. A party or representative appearing in the GRC in a charity or transport case should read this section in conjunction with the entries on charities cases (see **Charity cases**) and transport cases (see **Transport cases**).

The overriding objective

39.3 The GRC Rules provide that proceedings before the GRC are to be conducted in accordance with the overriding objective (GRC Rules, r 2) (see **Overriding objective**). This objective is, as with the Civil Procedure Rules, to deal with cases fairly and justly. What constitutes dealing with a case fairly and justly will of course be entirely dependent on the particular circumstances of the case before the GRC, which enjoys a wide-ranging discretion to regulate its own procedure.

39.4 However, some guidance is given. The GRC Rules, r 2 expands upon the definition of the overriding objective and provides that dealing with cases fairly and justly includes:

- dealing with the case in ways which are proportionate to the importance of the case, the complexity of the issues, the anticipated costs and the resources of the parties;
- avoiding unnecessary formality and seeking flexibility in the proceedings;
- ensuring, so far as practicable, that the parties are able to participate fully in the proceedings;
- using any special expertise of the Tribunal effectively; and
- avoiding delay, so far as compatible with proper consideration of the issues.

The GRC must seek to give effect the overriding objective when exercising any power under the GRC Rules or interpreting any rule or practice direction.

GENERAL POWERS OF THE GRC

Case management powers

39.5 The GRC has a wide procedural discretion and is empowered to regulate its own procedure as it sees fit (GRC Rules, r 5(1)). The GRC may give such directions as it deems appropriate in relation to the conduct or disposal of proceedings and may do so at any time (GRC Rules, r 5(1)–(3)).

39.6 The case management powers of the GRC are set out in more detail elsewhere in the Handbook (see **Case management powers**). Of note, the GRC may:

- extend or shorten the time for complying with any rule, practice direction or direction, unless such extension or shortening would conflict with a provision of another enactment containing a time limit (GRC Rules, r 5(3)(a)) (see **Extensions of time**);
- direct that a failure to comply with a rule or practice direction will result in a party's case being struck out (GRC Rules, r 8(1)) (see **Striking out**);
- permit or require a party or another person to provide documents, information or submissions to the GRC or any other party (GRC Rules, r 5(3)(d)) (see **Documents**; **Submissions**);
- deal with an issue in the proceedings as a preliminary issue (GRC Rules, r 5(3)(e));
- hold a hearing to consider any matter, including a case management issue (GRC Rules, r 5(3)(f));
- decide the form of any hearing (GRC Rules, r 5(3)(g) (see **Hearings**));
- add, substitute or remove a party (GRC Rules, r 9) (see **Parties**);
- stay proceedings (GRC Rules, r 5(3)(j));
- strike out a party's case (GRC Rules, r 8);
- specify a case as lead case and giving directions staying other cases before the GRC giving rise to common or related issues of fact or law (GRC Rules, r 18);
- suspend the effect of its own judgment pending a review or an appeal (GRC Rules, r 5(3)(l)).

Directions

39.7 The GRC may give directions on its own initiative or on application by one of the parties (GRC Rules, r 6). A party wishing to apply for directions otherwise than at a hearing (at which this may be done orally) should send a written application to the Tribunal stating the direction sought and the reasons why it is appropriate that the requested order be made (GRC Rules, r 6(2), (3)).

39.8 The GRC may decide in its discretion to invite submissions from the other parties to the case (GRC Rules, r 5(3)(d)) or hold a hearing to determine whether the directions order sort should be made (GRC Rules, r 5(3)(f)).

39.9 In any event, unless the GRC exercises its power not to notify a particular party of a directions decision (GRC Rules, r 6(4)), which it is expected will be exercised extremely rarely, a party notified of the GRC's order has liberty to apply for another direction amending, suspending or setting aside the first direction (GRC Rules, r 6(5)). Such an application should also be in writing, stating the reasons why the first direction should be so amended, suspended or set aside.

Failure to comply with rules and directions

39.10 If a party fails to comply with a provision of the GRC Rules, a practice direction or a direction of the GRC this does not automatically render the irregular action taken by that party void. The GRC has a general discretion to waive the failure to comply if this appears to be just in the circumstances (GRC Rules, r 7(1), (2)(a)) (see **Failures to comply**).

39.11 Alternatively, the GRC may impose such sanction or requirement as it in its discretion determines is just, including (see GRC Rules, r 7(2), (3); r 8):

- requiring the failure to be remedied;
- exercising its power to strike out a party's case (see below);
- barring or restricting a party's participation in the proceedings;
- referring a question to the Upper Tribunal and asking the Upper Tribunal to exercise its powers under the TCEA 2007, s 25 in relation to failures to comply with directions by the GRC that a person give evidence, swear an oath, or produce a document, or facilitate the inspection of a document or any other thing.

The GRC must exercise its powers to impose sanctions in accordance with the overriding objective to deal with cases fairly and justly.

Power to strike out a party's case

(See generally **Striking out**)

39.12 The power to strike out a party's case applies equally to appellant and respondent. The relevant rules do however use differing terminology in respect of the two parties (see GRC Rules, r 8(7)): referring to the striking out of proceedings against the appellant and to barring the respondent from taking part in the proceedings. The practical effect of the two will however typically be identical, in that the striking out of the appellant's case determines the case against him and the barring of a respondent from taking further part in the proceedings permits the GRC to determine summarily any or all issues against the respondent (GRC Rules, r 8(8)). Here, the more familiar terminology of striking out will be retained in respect of both appellant and respondent.

39.13 The GRC has a broad power to strike out a party's case (or part thereof) if it considers that it is in the interests of justice to do so. There are however two limited circumstances in which a party's case must be struck out or will be struck out automatically.

39.14 As to the former, the GRC must strike out the whole or a part of the proceedings if it does not have jurisdiction and does not exercise its power to transfer the proceedings to another court or tribunal (GRC Rules, r 8(2); and see GRC Rules, r 5(3)(k)(i)).

39.15 As to the latter, all or part of a party's case will be struck out automatically if it fails to comply with a direction of the GRC which stated that failure to comply would result in all or part of the case being struck out (GRC Rules, r 8(1)).

39.16 The GRC may strike out all or part of a party's case if:

- the party has failed to comply with a direction which stated that failure to comply could lead to the striking out of the proceedings or part of them;
- the appellant has failed to co-operate with the GRC to such an extent that it cannot deal with the proceedings fairly and justly; or
- the Tribunal considers there is no reasonable prospect of a party's case, or part of it, succeeding.

39.17 Save in respect of strike out following a failure to comply with a direction, the GRC must not strike out all or part of a party's case without first giving that party an opportunity to make representations as to why the GRC should not strike out its case (GRC Rules, r 8(4)).

39.18 If a party's case or part of it is struck out automatically or by the GRC under r 8(1) or (3)(a) for a failure to comply with a direction, that party may apply for the case to be reinstated and to be permitted to take further part in the proceedings (GRC Rules, r 8(5)). The application must be made in writing and received by the Tribunal within 28 days of the party being notified of the striking out of all or part of its case (GRC Rules, r 8(6)).

39.19 The effect of striking out all of the appellant's case necessarily determines the appeal against him. However, it appears that the GRC retains a discretion in respect of the effect of the striking out of a respondent's case and the barring of the respondent from taking further part in proceedings. GRC Rules, r 8(8) provides that if a respondent has been barred from taking further part in proceedings, the GRC 'need not consider any response or other submission made by that respondent' and 'may summarily determine any or all issues against that respondent'. The wording of r 8(8) implies a discretion to determine the appeal against the appellant notwithstanding that the respondent's case has been struck out. The circumstances in which this will be exercised will be rare. However, it is suggested that there may be cases in which the respondent has failed to comply with a direction to an extent that it is inappropriate to lift the bar to participation and reinstate its case, but that nonetheless the appeal is sufficiently weak that it must be determined against the appellant in any event.

DISCLOSURE

39.20 There is no prescribed formal disclosure procedure in cases before the GRC and in accordance with its wide case management powers under the GRC Rules, r 5, the GRC can specify in its discretion what disclosure should take place and when. The GRC may give directions as to the exchange between parties of lists of documents which are relevant to the appeal, or relevant to particular issues, and for the inspection of such documents (GRC Rules, r 15(1)(a)).

39.21 If an order for disclosure is made, a party wishing to withhold disclosure of otherwise disclosable documents or information may apply for a direction that the documents or information be withheld from the other party or parties. The first party must exclude the relevant document or information from any documents that will be provided to the other party and provide the GRC with the document or information together with the reasons as to why the first party submits the document or information should be excluded from disclosure (GRC Rules, r 14(2)–(4)). The first party may similarly apply for an order that the excluded document or information be disclosed to the GRC but not to the other party (GRC Rules, r 14(6)–(8)).

39.22 The GRC may also of its own initiative or on the application of a party, order any person to produce a document in its possession or control which relates to an issue in the proceedings provided that the document is one which that person could be compelled to produce at the trial of an action in a court of law (GRC Rules, r 16(1)(b), (3)).

EVIDENCE AND SUBMISSIONS BEFORE THE GRC

39.23 The GRC has a wide discretion as to the directions it may make in respect of the evidence to be admitted and the submissions it will hear. The GRC will typically give directions as to the issues on which it requires evidence and submissions (GRC Rules, r 15(1)(c)) and the nature of the evidence and submissions it requires (GRC Rules, r 15(1)(d)).

39.24 In particular, the GRC may give directions in respect of:

- The time at which evidence and submissions are to be given; (GRC Rules, r 15(1)(h)) (see **Evidence; Submissions**);
- Whether evidence is to be given orally or by written witness statement (GRC Rules, r 15(1)(g)) (see **Witnesses**);
- Whether evidence is to be given on oath (GRC Rules, r 15(3));
- Any limit on the number of witnesses (GRC Rules, r 15(1)(f));
- Whether the parties are permitted or required to provide expert evidence, and if so whether the parties must jointly appoint a single expert to provide such evidence (GRC Rules, r 15(1)(e)) (see **Experts**).

39.25 The GRC is permitted to admit any evidence whether or not that evidence would be admissible in a civil trial in England and Wales and whether or not it was available to any previous relevant decision maker (GRC Rules, r 15(2)(a)).

39.26 Likewise, the GRC has a broad discretion to exclude evidence which would usually and otherwise be admissible where it is of the opinion that it would be unfair to admit the evidence (GRC Rules, r 15(2)(b)(iii). Evidence may also be excluded where it is provided out of time or in a manner which does not comply with a direction or practice direction (GRC Rules, r 15(2)(b)(i), (ii)).

39.27 The GRC also has the power to summon any person to attend as a witness at a hearing or order that any person answer specified questions, provided that the person could be could be compelled to give that evidence in a court of law in the part of the United Kingdom where the GRC proceedings are due to be determined (GRC Rules, r 16).

BRINGING AN APPEAL BEFORE THE GRC

Appeal notice

39.28 In most cases, an appellant must start proceedings before the GRC by sending a notice of appeal to the GRC so that it is received within 28 days of the date on which notice of the decision was sent to the appellant (GRC Rules, r 22(1)(b)). In certain cases a different specific time limit is set out in r 22(6) of the GRC Rules (see **Bringing proceedings in the First-tier Tribunal**).

39.29 The notice must include (GRC Rules, r 22(2),(3)):

- the name and address of the appellant;
- the name and address of the appellant's representative (if any);
- an address where documents for the appellant may be sent or delivered;
- the name and address of any respondent;
- details of the decision or act, or failure to decide or act, which is under appeal or to which the proceedings relate;
- any copy or written record of any decision which is being challenged and any statement of reasons for the decision which the appellant has or can reasonably obtain;
- the result the appellant is seeking;
- the grounds on which the appellant relies; and
- any further information or documents required by a practice direction.

39.30 If the appeal is made out of time, the appeal notice must include a request for an extension of time under GRC Rules, r 5(3)(a) giving reasons why it was not provided in time (GRC Rules, r 22(4)(a)) (see **Extensions of time**). Unless the GRC extends time under r 5(3)(a), the GRC must not admit the notice of appeal.

Staying the decision subject to appeal

39.31 Where specifically provided for in primary legislation, the GRC may stay or suspend certain decisions which are the subject of appeal. A person who wishes the GRC to decide whether that substantive decision should be stayed or suspended must make a written application with the same contents as an ordinary application notice (see above) (GRC Rules, r 20). If the GRC grants a stay or suspension of the substantive decision, it may do so subject to such conditions as it sees fit and may give directions as to the further conduct of the appeal or the substantive decision (GRC Rules, r 20(4)).

Response to the notice of appeal

39.32 Each respondent to an appeal must put in a response to the notice of appeal within 28 days of the date on which the respondent receives the notice of appeal (GRC Rules, r 23(1)(b)). The time for responding to a notice of appeal in a transport case is 14 days (GRC Rules, r 23(1)(a)) (see **Transport cases**).

39.33 The response must include (GRC Rules, r 23(2)–(4)):

- the name and address of the respondent;
- the name and address of the respondent's representative (if any);
- an address where documents for the respondent may be sent or delivered;
- any further information or documents required by a practice direction or direction;

- whether the respondent would be content for the case to be dealt with without a hearing if the Tribunal considers it appropriate;
- a statement as to whether the respondent opposes the appellant's case and the grounds for that opposition;
- any copy or written record of any decision which is being challenged and any statement of reasons for the decision which the appellant has not provided and which the respondent has or can reasonably obtain.

39.34 If the response is made out of time, the response must include a request for an extension of time together with the reasons why the response was not provided in time (GRC Rules, r 23(5)) (see **Extensions of time**).

39.35 The respondent must send the response and any accompanying documents to each other party at the same time as it sends the response to the GRC (save in transport cases, where the GRC sends the copy to the other parties) (GRC Rules, r 23(6), (7)).

Appellant's reply

39.36 The appellant has a right to reply to the respondent's response by way of written submission and provision of further documents (GRC Rules, r 24(1)). Any reply and accompanying documents must be sent to the GRC within 14 days of the date on which the respondent (or the Tribunal in a transport case) sent the response to the appellant. If the reply is made out of time, the reply must include a request for an extension of time together with the reasons why the response was not provided in time (GRC Rules, r 24(3)).

39.37 The appellant must send a copy of any reply and accompanying documents to each other party at the same time as it sends the reply to the GRC (save in transport cases, where the GRC sends the copy to the other parties) (GRC Rules, r 23(4), (5)).

HEARINGS BEFORE THE GRC

(See **Hearings**)

39.38 Each party is entitled to attend any hearing that is held and to send written representations to the GRC and each other party prior to the hearing (GRC Rules, r 33(1)).

39.39 This entitlement is subject to the GRC's power to exclude (GRC Rules, r 35(4)):

- any person whose conduct the GRC considers is disrupting or is likely to disrupt the hearing;
- any person whose presence the GRC considers is likely to prevent another person from giving evidence or making submission freely;
- any person who the GRC considers should be excluded in order to give effect to orders preventing or limiting the disclosure of documents and information under rule 14;
- any person where the purpose of the hearing would be defeated by the attendance of that person;
- any witness prior to giving his evidence.

39.40 Hearings must be held in public unless the GRC directs that a hearing or part of it is to be held in private in which case the GRC may issue directions as to who is to attend the hearing or part of it (GRC Rules, r 35(1)–(3)).

39.41 A party may appoint a representative (whether legally qualified or not) to represent that party in the proceedings (GRC Rules, r 11(1)). The party must notify the GRC and each other party of any representative's name and address (GRC Rules, r 11(2)). A representative may do anything required to be done by a party (save for signing a witness statement, or, if the representative is not legally qualified, sending a notification of representation under r 11(2)). Other parties may send any document required to be sent to the represented party to that party's representative and are permitted to assume that the representative remains authorised until being notified to the contrary (GRC Rules, r 11(4)).

39.42 With the GRC's permission, a party may be represented at a hearing by a person of whom the GRC has not been notified (GRC Rules, r 11(5)).

Dispensing with the need for a hearing

39.43 The GRC must hold a hearing before making a decision which disposes of proceedings unless:

- each party has consented to the mater being determined without a hearing; and
- the GRC is satisfied that it can properly determine the issues without a hearing. (GRC Rules, r 32(1))

39.44 The GRC does not need to hold a hearing, prior to refusing to correct, set aside or review its own decision; the GRC may also strike out a party's case under GRC Rules rule 8 without holding a hearing (GRC Rules, r 32(2), (3)).

39.45 If the Tribunal determines a preliminary issue in an appeal in accordance with the GRC Rules, r 5(3)(e) and the determination of the preliminary issue leaves no further issue to be determined, the GRC may dispose of the proceedings without any further hearing (GRC Rules, r 32(4)).

Hearings in a party's absence

39.46 If a party fails to attend a hearing the GRC may proceed in its absence (GRC Rules, r 36) if:

- the GRC is satisfied that the party has been notified of the hearing or that reasonable steps have been taken to notify the party of the hearing; and
- it is in the interests of justice to proceed with the hearing.

DECISIONS OF THE GRC

(See **Decisions**)

39.47 The GRC may dispose of proceedings by consent order if the parties agree and the GRC considers it in the interests of justice to do so (GRC Rules, r 37) (see **Consent Orders**).

39.48 The GRC may give any decision orally at a hearing or reserve its judgment (GRC Rules, r 38(1)).

39.49 As soon as reasonably practicable after making a decision which finally disposes of all issues in the proceedings, the GRC must provide each party with (GRC Rules, r 38(2):

- a decision notice stating the GRC's decision;
- written reasons for the decision; and
- notification of any right of appeal against the decision and the time within which, and manner in which, such right of appeal may be exercised.

When sending its decision notice and written reasons, the GRC must take account of any order made under r 14 preventing or limiting the disclosure of documents and written reasons (GRC Rules, r 38(2)).

39.50 The GRC may also give reasons for decisions which do not finally dispose of proceedings (GRC Rules, r 38(3)).

Setting aside a decision of the GRC

39.51 Under GRC Rules, r 41, the GRC may set aside all or part of a decision disposing of proceedings and retake that decision or part of it if it is in the interests of justice to do so and:

- a document relating to the proceedings was not sent to, or was not received at an appropriate time by, a party or a party's representative; and/or
- a document relating to the proceedings was not sent to the Tribunal at an appropriate time; and/or
- a party, or a party's representative, was not present at a hearing related to the proceedings; and/or
- there has been some other procedural irregularity in the proceedings.

A party who wishes to apply for a decision to be set aside must do so in writing within 28 days of the date on which the GRC notified the party of its decision (GRC Rules, r 41(3)).

Reviews and appeals from decisions of the GRC

39.52 An appeal against a decision of the GRC to the Upper Tribunal lies on a point of law only under TCEA 2007, s 11(see **Appeals and references to the Upper Tribunal**) with permission of the GRC or the Upper Tribunal (the Administrative Appeals Chamber in cases except charities cases, which are appealed to the Tax and Chancery Chamber).

39.53 A party seeking permission to appeal must submit a written application to the GRC setting out (GRC Rules, r 42(5)):

- the decision of the Tribunal to which it relates;
- the alleged error or errors of law in the decision; and
- the result the party making the application is seeking.

39.54 The application for permission must be sent to the Tribunal no later than 28 days after the latest of the dates that the GRC sent the party who intends to appeal (GRC Rules, r 42(1)–(3)):

- written reasons for the decision;
- notification of amended reasons for, or correction of, the decision following a review (see below); or
- notification that an application for the decision to be set aside has been unsuccessful (providing that the application was made in time under GRC Rules, r 41 (or the extended time limit if the GRC grants an extension).

39.55 If the party seeking permission to appeal fails to provide the written application to the GRC within the 28 day time limit stipulated by GRC Rules, r 42(2) (or the extended time limit if the GRC grants an extension), the application must include a request for an extension of time and state the reasons why the application was not made in time (GRC Rules, r 42(4)(a)). Unless the GRC grants the request for an extension of time under r 5(3)(a), it must refuse the application for permission to appeal (GRC Rules, r 42(4)(b)).

39.56 After receiving the application for permission, the GRC must, before proceeding to determine whether permission should be granted first consider, whether in accordance with the overriding objective, it should exercise its discretion to review the decision in accordance with GRC Rules, r 44 (see below) (GRC Rules, r 43(1)). If the GRC decides not to review the decision, or does review the decision but decides to take no action, the GRC must then proceed to determine the application for permission (GRC Rules, r 43(2)).

39.57 The GRC must send a record of its decision to the parties as soon as practicable (GRC Rules, r 43(3)). If permission is refused, the GRC must provide a statement of reasons and notify the disappointed party of its right to apply to the Upper Tribunal for permission, setting out the time within which and the method by which, an application to the Upper Tribunal must be made (GRC Rules, r 43(4)). If the GRC gives permission to appeal on limited grounds only, it must notify the party of its right to pursue its appeal to the Upper Tribunal in respect of those grounds on which permission to appeal was refused (GRC Rules, r 43(5)).

Review of a decision of the GRC

39.58 Under GRC Rules, r 44 and TCEA 2007, s 9 the GRC may, on an application for permission to appeal, instead undertake a review of its decision. It may do so if satisfied that there was an error of law in its decision (GRC Rules, r 44(1)).

39.59 The GRC must notify the parties in writing of the outcome of any review, and of any right of appeal in relation to the outcome (GRC Rules, r 44(2)).

39.60 If the GRC takes any action in relation to a decision following a review without first giving every party an opportunity to make representations, the notice given following the review must reflect this and state that any party which did not have an opportunity to make representations may apply for such action to be set aside and for the decision to be reviewed again (GRC Rules, r 44(3)).

COSTS

39.61 The successful party has no right to its costs in proceedings before the GRC. The Tribunal may make an order in respect of costs only in two circumstances in non-charity cases (see **Charity cases**) (GRC Rules, r 10):

- an order for wasted costs under TCEA 2007, s 29(4) (see **Costs**); and/or
- if the GRC considers that a party has acted unreasonably in bringing, defending or conducting the proceedings.

39.62 The GRC may make a costs order on its own initiative or on the written application of a party, such application to be sent to the GRC and the party against whom it is proposed an order should be made together with a schedule of costs (GRC Rules, r 10(2),(3)).

39.63 An application for a costs order under GRC Rules, r 10 may be made at any time during the proceedings, but no later than 14 days after the date on which the GRC notifies the applicant of a decision which finally disposes of all issues in the proceedings (GRC Rules, r 10(4)).

39.64 No costs order may be made without the GRC first giving the party against whom that order is to be made an opportunity to make representations (GRC Rules, r 10(5)(a)). If the party against whom an order is sought is an individual, the GRC must consider that person's financial means when determining whether it is appropriate to make an adverse costs order against that individual (GRC Rules, r 10(5)(b)).

39.65 The amount of costs to be paid may be summarily assessed, be agreed between the parties or by detailed assessment if not agreed (GRC Rules, r 10(6),(7)).

39.66 In proceedings in England and Wales the GRC may order costs to be assessed on the indemnity basis if justified in the circumstances (GRC Rules, r 10(7)(a)). The threshold test for an award of indemnity costs is whether the case is taken away from the norm. That is to say, whether the conduct in the proceedings of the party against whom an adverse costs order is sought was out of the ordinary such that it is just to make an award of costs on the indemnity basis.

40 Guidance Cases

GUIDANCE CASES IN THE UPPER TRIBUNAL

40.1 The function of the Upper Tribunal is to act as a specialist appellate tribunal (see **Upper Tribunal**). In this regard, an important part of the function of the Upper Tribunal is to achieve legal and practical consistency across the tribunal system. The establishment of a two tier tribunal system has provided an opportunity to develop the guidance role across the whole tribunal system (see Carnwarth, 'Tribunal Justice: a new start' [2009] PL 48, 59) and to reduce the potential for injustice which resulted from the adoption of disparate approaches to similar questions across the previous tribunals system. Although tribunals do not have the power to issue practice directions without specific statutory authority – which, under the TCEA 2007 belongs to the Senior President – that does not prevent them from issuing guidance as to how the law, rules and practice directions ought generally to be interpreted: *Bovale Ltd v Secretary of State for Communities and Local Government* [2009] EWCA Civ 171; [2009] 3 All ER 340 at [36] per Waller & Dyson LJJ.

40.2 In this regard, the Upper Tribunal will, as part of its functions, provide precedential guidance on particular issues in appropriate cases. This extends not only to issues of law but also to general issues of principle or practice, including as to the application of the law to common factual situations encountered regularly in a particular jurisdiction of the First-tier Tribunal. Examples include the decision of the Lands Tribunal in *Earl Cadogan v Sportelli* [2007] EWCA Civ 1042; [2008] 2 All ER 220 giving guidance as to appropriate valuation practice in leasehold enfranchisement; the decision of the Administrative Appeals Chamber ('AAC') in *Dorset Healthcare NHS Foundation Trust v MH* [2009] UKUT 4 (AAC); [2009] PTSR 1112 giving guidance both as to the status of decisions of a three-member panel of the Upper Tribunal and as to the proper approach to requests in mental health cases for disclosure of documents in which confidential third-party material is contained within a patient's medical records; and the decision of the AAC in case CCS/2314/2008 [2009] UKUT 3 (AAC) giving guidance as to the criteria to be applied by the Social Entitlement Chamber when determining habitual residence in child support cases.

40.3 The envisaged issuing of factual precedents and guidance has developed out of the practice of the (former) Asylum and Immigration Tribunal ('AIT') in asylum appeals. The AIT issued 'country guidance' cases in which it provided an assessment of the political and social conditions in a given country so as to provide a starting point for the assessment of asylum claims. This served to ensure that a consistent approach was adopted at AIT level to the assessment of claims from each particular country. The totality of the available evidence as to conditions could be assessed at AIT level and an assessment undertaken, rather than subjecting part of that same evidence to repeated assessment at a lower judicial level. It is this type of practice and guidance (endorsed at Court of Appeal level: *S v Secretary of State for the Home Department* [2002] EWCA Civ 539; [2002] INLR 416; *R (Iran) v Secretary of State for the Home Department* [2005] EWCA Civ 982; [2005] Imm AR 535) that the Upper Tribunal will seek to emulate (see further 'Tribunal Justice: a new start' [2009] PL 48, 60). The Upper Tribunal will be 'in a unique position to provide a lead by producing precedents that will clarify and develop substantive law in the various tribunal jurisdictions and also provide case law and guidance to clarify procedures' (Buck, 'Precedent in Tribunals and the Development of Principles' (2006) 25 CJQ 458, 482).

LEAD CASES

40.4 All Chambers of the First-tier Tribunal, with the exception of the HESCC, have the power to designate particular cases as 'lead cases'. These are not strictly speaking guidance cases in the manner referred to above. However, lead cases share a similar aim to guidance cases: they achieve earlier exit and resolution points for a number of other cases and avoid the need for extensive litigation in cases which turn on the same legal or factual principles as other pending cases (see Buck, 'Precedent in Tribunals and the Development of Principles' (2006) 25 CJQ 458, 465). Lead cases will be of particular benefit to tribunals which face issues which are complex and subject to detailed changes which affect large numbers of people, such as those concerning social security and tax. In such fields, it has long been the practice to use a test case to determine the preliminary issue of principle before that outcome is applied to the many other cases answered by it.

40.5 The power to designate cases as lead cases is found in rule 18 of the applicable procedural rules in the relevant Chamber of the First-tier Tribunal (again, with the exception of the HESCC); the IAC also has a differently worded rule and will be addressed again at paragraph 40.10.

40.6 In accordance with r 18(1), if two or more cases have been started before the relevant Chamber, the Chamber has yet to make a decision disposing of the proceedings, and, crucially, the cases give rise to common or related issues of fact or law, the Chamber may direct that one (or more) of the cases be specified as a lead case (or lead cases) and will simultaneously stay the other related cases pending determination of the lead case(s) (see r 18(2)).

40.7 The decision in the lead case(s) will then bind the parties in all related cases (r 18(3)), subject to the right of any such party to apply within 28 days of its being notified of the decision in the lead case(s), for a direction that the decision in the lead case(s) does not apply to that particular party in a related case (r 18(4)).

40.8 Following the determination of the lead case(s), the relevant Tribunal must give directions in respect of the stayed cases, providing either for their disposal or for such further directions as may be appropriate (r 18(5)).

40.9 In the event that a lead case lapses or is withdrawn before its determination, the relevant Tribunal must specify whether or not one (or more) of the stayed cases is to assume the role of the lead case(s) and must give directions as to whether any direction in respect of the related cases should be set aside or amended (r 18(6)).

40.10 In the FTTIAC, the Tribunal may direct that two or more pending cases be heard together if some common question of fact or law arises; they relate to the persons of the same family; or it is desirable to hear the appeals together for some other reasons (Asylum and Immigration Tribunal (Procedure) Rules 2005 ('IAC Rules'), r 20).

40.11 Guidance Cases

40.11 It is also possible for the Lands Chamber of the Upper Tribunal to select a test case where all the parties agree (Lands Chamber Rules, r 31). This power may be of greater use to the Lands Chamber than other Chambers of the Upper Tribunal because, at the moment, it does not have cases filtered by a First-tier Tribunal.

41 Health, Education and Social Care Chamber

COMPOSITION AND LOCATION

41.1 The HESCC is one of six Chambers that collectively comprise the First-tier tribunal (see **First-tier Tribunal** and **Chambers**).

41.2 The HESCC is, like the Upper Tribunal and other Chambers of the First-tier Tribunals, presided over by the Senior President. The HESCC itself has a Chamber President and comprises judges and other members, in accordance with the TCEA 2007, s 4.

41.3 Each of the four separate divisions that comprise the HESCC (the Care Standards Tribunal, the Mental Health Tribunal, the Primary Health Lists Tribunal and the Special Educational Needs and Disability Tribunal) has its own members and judges, although judges may be internally transferred between the different HESCC divisions. Under the Transfer of Tribunal Functions Order 2008, SI 2008/2833, persons who, before 3 November 2008, were office-holders in the previous tribunals became transferred-in judges or other members of the First-tier Tribunal (as appropriate).

41.4 The HESCC has a network of hearing venues throughout the United Kingdom.

APPELLATE JURISDICTION AND POWERS

41.5 The HESCC has, by article 5 of the First-tier Tribunal and Upper Tribunal (Chambers) Order 2008, SI 2008/2684 as amended, been assigned all functions relating to:

- an appeal against a decision related to children with special educational needs;
- a claim of disability discrimination in the education of a child;
- an application or an appeal against a decision or determination related to work with children or vulnerable adults;
- an appeal against a decision related to registration in respect of provision of health or social care;
- an application in respect of, or an appeal against a decision related to, the provision of health care or health services;
- an appeal against a decision related to registration in respect of social workers and social care workers;
- an appeal against a decision related to the provision of childcare;
- an appeal against a decision related to an independent school or other independent educational institution; and
- applications and references by and in respect of patients under the provisions of the Mental Health Act 1983 or paragraph 5(2) of the Schedule to the Repatriation of Prisoners Act 1984.

41.6 The HESCC may hear appeals on both fact and law.

41.7 Health, Education and Social Care Chamber

41.7 For more detail on the jurisdiction of the individual divisions of the HESCC see: **Care standards cases; Mental health appeals; Primary health lists cases; Schools registration cases; Special education needs and disability cases;** and **Social care cases.**

PROCEDURAL RULES

41.8 Proceedings before the HESCC are governed by the HESCC Rules. The HESCC Rules are reproduced at Appendix 2. See **Health, Education and Social Care Chamber procedural rules** for details of the provisions.

42 Health, Education and Social Care Chamber Procedural Rules

See also **Procedural rules**.

STATUTORY INSTRUMENT

42.1 Proceedings before the HESCC are governed by the HESCC Rules. The HESCC Rules are reproduced at Appendix 2. See also **Health, Education and Social Care Chamber**.

STRUCTURE

42.2 The HESCC Rules are broadly similar in structure to the rules of the other Chambers of the First-tier Tribunal, save that instead of containing only the usual four parts ('Introduction', 'General powers and provisions', 'Proceedings before the Tribunal' and 'Correcting, setting aside, reviewing and appealing Tribunal decisions'), Part 3 deals with 'Proceedings before the Tribunal other than in mental health cases' while Part 4 deals with 'Proceedings before the Tribunal in mental health cases'.

APPEALING TO THE HESCC

See **Bringing proceedings in the First-tier Tribunals**.

42.3 As explained above, the HESCC comprises four different types of tribunals for hearing different types of proceedings. The procedure for bringing each type is set out in the specific entry for that type. See, respectively, **Care standards cases; Mental health cases; Primary health lists cases; Schools registration cases** and **Special educational needs and disability cases**. What follows below is a general overview setting out the similarities and differences between the three types of proceeding.

Procedure in care standards and special educational needs and disability cases

42.4 Proceedings are started by way of application notice (HESCC Rules, r 20), except for certain types of care standards cases which require leave from a judge before the First-tier Tribunal can hear the appeal. These cases are started by way of application for leave (HESCC Rules, r 19).

42.5 The time limits for sending or delivering the application notice or application for leave vary from case to case. In general, other than those types of case for which there are specific time limits in the Schedule to the HESCC Rules, the time limit is 28 days from the notice of the act or decision to which the proceedings relate (HESCC Rules, r 20(1)(b)).

42.6 An application notice or application for leave must be signed by the applicant and must include (HESCC Rules, r 20(2)):

- the name and address of the applicant;

- the name and address of the applicant's representative (if any);
- an address where documents for the applicant may be sent or delivered;
- the name and address of any respondent;
- details of the decision or act, or failure to decide or act, to which the proceedings relate;
- the result the applicant is seeking;
- the grounds on which the applicant relies; and
- any further information or documents required by an applicable practice direction.

42.7 If the appellant provides the application notice or application for leave to the Tribunal outside of the prescribed time limit, the application notice or application for leave must include a request for an extension of time and the reason why the application was out of time (HESCC Rules, r 20(4)(a)). The Tribunal must not admit the application unless it extends time (HESCC Rules, r 20(4)(b)).

Procedure in mental health cases

42.8 For mental health cases, the application or reference must be made in writing, signed by the applicant or authorised person and sent or delivered to the Tribunal so that it is received within the time specified in the Mental Health Act 1983 or the Repatriation of Prisoners Act 1984 (HESCC Rules, r 32(1)).

42.9 An application must, if possible, include (HESCC Rules, r 32(2)):

- the name and address of the patient;
- if the application is made by the patient's nearest relative, the name, address and relationship to the patient of the patient's nearest relative;
- the provision under which the patient is detained, liable to be detained, subject to guardianship, a community patient or subject to after-care under supervision;
- whether the person making the application has appointed a representative or intends to do so, and the name and address of any representative appointed;
- the name and address of the responsible authority in relation to the patient.

HEARINGS IN THE HESCC

See **Hearings**.

42.10 For mental health cases, the Tribunal must not dispose of proceedings without a hearing (HESCC Rules,r 35(1)). For other cases, the Tribunal must hold a hearing before making a decision which disposes of proceedings unless all parties consent to, or do not object to, the matter being decided without a hearing and the Tribunal considers that it is able to decide the matter without a hearing (HESCC Rules, r 23(1)).

42.11 For mental health cases, special educational needs cases and disability discrimination in schools cases, all hearings must be held in private unless the Tribunal considers that it is in the interests of justice for the hearing to be held in public (HESCC Rules, rr 26(1) and 38(1)). For all other cases, all hearings must, unless the Tribunal directs otherwise, be held in public (HESCC Rules, r 26(1)).

APPEALS FROM THE HESCC

42.12 Appeals from the HESCC lie to the Administrative Appeals Chamber of the Upper Tribunal (see **Administrative Appeals Chamber** and **Upper Tribunal**).

Time for making an appeal

See **Time limits** and **Extensions of time.**

42.13 An application for permission to appeal must be made in writing to the First-tier Tribunal (HESCC Rules, r 46(1)) within one month of the latest of the dates that the Tribunal sends (as applicable):

- written reasons for its decisions;
- notification of amended reasons for, or correction of, the decision following a review; or
- notification that an application to set aside the decision was unsuccessful (HESCC Rules, r 46(3)).

42.14 If the party seeking to appeal sends or delivers the application out of time, the application must include a request for an extension of time and the reason why the application notice was not provided in time. The Tribunal must not admit the application unless it extends time (HESCC Rules, r 46(4)).

Application for permission

42.15 An application for permission to appeal must (HESCC Rules, r 46(5)):

- identify the decision of the Tribunal to which it relates;
- identify the alleged error or errors of law in the decision; and
- state the result the party making the application is seeking.

Consideration by the First-tier Tribunal

42.16 On receiving an application for permission to appeal, the Tribunal must first consider whether to review its own decision (HESCC Rules, r 47(1)). If the Tribunal decides not to review the decision, or reviews the decision and decides to take no action in relation to it, the Tribunal must then consider whether to give permission to appeal (HESCC Rules, r 47(2)).

42.17 The Tribunal must send a record of its decision to the parties as soon as practicable (HESCC Rules, r 47(3)). If permission is refused, the Tribunal must send with the record of its decision a statement of its reasons and notification of the right to apply to the Upper Tribunal and the procedure and time limits for making such an application (HESCC Rules, r 47(4)). This also applies in respect of any grounds on which permission was refused, if permission was granted on limited grounds only (HESCC Rules, r 47(5)).

42.18 In relation to renewing the application for permission before the Upper Tribunal, see **Appeals and references to the Upper Tribunal**.

42.19 In addition to the right to apply for permission to appeal, there is also a right, in special educational needs cases, to apply to the First-tier Tribunal for review of the decision (HESCC Rules, r 48). Such an application may be made in writing if circumstances relevant to the decision have changed since the Tribunal's decision was made (HESCC Rules, r 48(2)). The application must be made so that it is received within 28 days after the date on which the Tribunal sent the decision notice recording its decision to the party making the application (HESCC Rules, r 48(3)). If the application is made later, the application must include a request for an extension of time and the reason why the application notice was not provided in time. The Tribunal must not admit the application unless it extends time (HESCC Rules, r 48(4)).

43 Hearings

See also **Evidence**; **Representation**.

HEARINGS IN THE FIRST-TIER AND UPPER TRIBUNAL

43.1 Each of the applicable sets of procedural rules for the Chambers of the First-tier and Upper Tribunals makes provision for the circumstances in which hearings may or must be held and as to the procedure governing such hearings. The provisions of those rules are mostly uniform across the Chambers and will be set out together below with any differences being noted. The provisions of the procedural rules concerned with hearings must be read subject to the Tribunal's general wide case management powers and discretion to regulate their own procedure (see **Case management powers** and **Directions**).

43.2 The standard Procedural Rules define 'hearing' as meaning an oral hearing, but also as including a hearing conducted in whole or in part by video link, telephone or other means of instantaneous two-way electronic communication (at r 1(3) of the relevant Rules).

DECISION WITH OR WITHOUT A HEARING

The power to hold and dispense with a hearing

43.3 The First-tier and Upper Tribunals have a general discretion as to whether or not to hold a hearing in respect of directions and case management decisions, as well as in respect of substantive questions which do not dispose of the proceedings. All references to decisions made 'without a hearing' are to decisions made without an oral hearing. There must always be at least a paper hearing at which a tribunal meets to consider the papers (*R v Housing Appeal Tribunal* [1920] 3 KB 334, 340 per Lord Reading CJ); this should not be done by the members of the tribunal in isolation (*R v Army Board of the Defence Council, ex p Anderson* [1992] QB 169, 187).

43.4 In respect of any decision which disposes of the proceedings, the First-tier Tribunal must hold a hearing, unless:

- Each party has consented to the matter being determined without a hearing; and
- The Tribunal is satisfied that it can properly determine the issues without a hearing.

The conditions for dispensing with a hearing are cumulative and, notwithstanding the parties' consent to an application or appeal being determined on paper, the relevant tribunal is required to undertake an independent assessment of whether it is appropriate to determine the proceedings without a hearing (GRC Rules, r 32(1); HESCC Rules, r 23(1); SEC Rules, r 27(1); TC Rules, r 29(1); WPAFCC Rules, r 25(1)).

43.5 A different regime applies in the Immigration and Asylum Chamber of the First-tier Tribunal. Every appeal must be determined at an oral hearing unless the appeal is statutorily treated as lapsed, abandoned, determined or withdrawn (IAC Rules, r 15(1)). However, the FTTIAC may determine an appeal without a hearing if (IAC Rules, r 15(2)):

- all the parties to the appeal consent;
- the appellant is outside the United Kingdom or it is impracticable to give him notice of a hearing and, in either case, he is unrepresented;
- the appellant is outside the United Kingdom and his representative's address for service is outside the United Kingdom;
- a party has failed to comply with the Rules or a direction of the Tribunal, and the Tribunal is satisfied that in all the circumstances, including the extent of the failure and any reasons for it, it is appropriate to determine the appeal without a hearing; or
- the Tribunal is satisfied, having regard to the material before it and the nature of the issues raised, that the appeal can be justly determined without a hearing. In this scenario the Tribunal must give the parties notice of its intention and permit written representations on whether a hearing should occur.

43.6 The FTTIAC has the power to order a case management hearing or a hearing of a preliminary issue, and it can order that a hearing be conducted or evidence given or representations made by video link or by other electronic means (IAC Rules, r 45(4)(d), (h)).

43.7 The Upper Tribunal has a general discretion as to whether or not to hold a hearing and may make any decision without a hearing (Upper Tribunal Rules, r 34(1)). In determining whether or not to hold a hearing to consider any matter, and in deciding upon the form of that hearing, the Upper Tribunal must have regard to any views expressed by the parties (Upper Tribunal Rules, r 34(2)). The rule does not require the Upper Tribunal to seek the views of the parties, and so, it is advisable that a party wishing to have an oral hearing on any matter before the Upper Tribunal makes this view known at the earliest appropriate point.

43.8 The Lands Chamber of the Upper Tribunal may order that a case be determined without an oral hearing where the parties consent. If it has so ordered, it may on application or of its own motion, re-order an oral hearing at any time (Lands Chamber Rules, r 27(1), (5)).

Exercise of the discretion

43.9 In determining whether or not an issue can properly be determined by the First-tier Tribunal without a hearing, and whether the Upper Tribunal should exercise its discretion to dispense with or hold an oral hearing, the Tribunal will have regard to the overriding objective and the need to ensure that the matter is heard fairly.

43.10 Neither fairness nor Article 6 of the European Convention on Human Rights demands that there be an oral hearing in every case (*Lloyd v McMahon* [1987] 1 AC 625; *R v Army Board of the Defence Council, ex p Anderson* [1992] QB 169, 187 per Taylor LJ; *Jussila v Finland* (2006) 45 EHRR 892 at [40]-[48]; *Håkansson and Sturesson v Sweden* (1990) 13 EHRR 1 at [66]; *Lundenvall v Sweden (Application No 38629/97)* 12 November 2002 at [34]). This is particularly true in respect of cases before administrative tribunals (*R (Ewing) v Department for Constitutional Affairs* [2006] EWHC 504 (Admin); [2006] 2 All ER 993 at [32] per Sullivan J). Indeed, consideration of the overriding objective may lead the tribunal to conclude that proportionate case management requires that a matter be determined solely on the papers (*Collier v Williams* [2006] EWCA Civ 20; [2006] 1 WLR 1945 at [34]). However, it will be particularly appropriate to hold an oral hearing where there are contested issues of fact (see *R (Thompson) v Law Society* [2004] EWCA Civ 167; [2004] 1 WLR 2522 at [51] per Clarke LJ; *R (West) v Parole Board* [2005] UKHL 1; [2005] 1 WLR 350 at [31], [35] per Lord Bingham).

Exceptions

43.11 A Chamber of the First-tier Tribunal need not hold a hearing prior to a decision refusing to correct, set aside or review its own decision (GRC Rules, r 32(2); HESCC Rules, rr 23(2) and 35(2); SEC Rules, r 27(2); TC Rules, r 29(2); WPAFCC Rules, r 25(2)). Likewise, the First-tier Tribunal may strike out a party's case in accordance with r 8 of its procedural rules without holding a hearing (GRC Rules, r 32(3); HESCC Rules, r 23(3) (not mental health cases); SEC Rules, r 27(3); TC Rules, r 29(3); WPAFCC Rules, r 25(3)).

43.12 If, following a hearing on a preliminary issue which disposed of that issue, the General Regulatory Chamber considers that no issue remains for decision, the GRC can dispose of the case without a further hearing (GRC Rules, r 32(4)).

43.13 The Health, Education and Social Care Tribunal must not dispense of a mental health case without holding an oral hearing (HESCC Rules, r 35(1)).

43.14 The Social Entitlement Chamber hearing a criminal injuries compensation case (see **Criminal injury compensation appeals**) need not hold a hearing prior to making a decision disposing of proceedings (SEC Rules, r 27(4)(a)). However, if the SEC does so, any party may apply to the SEC for the decision to be reconsidered at a hearing (SEC Rules, r 27(4)(b)). This does not apply to decisions not to extend a time limit or not to set aside a previous decision, nor does it apply to appeals against such decisions (SEC Rules, r 27(5)). The time limit for an application for reconsideration at a hearing is one month from the date on which the Tribunal sent notice of the decision to the party applying for reconsideration (SEC Rules, r 27(6)).

RIGHT TO ATTEND

43.15 Each party is entitled to attend any hearing that is held (Upper Tribunal Rules, r 35(1); GRC Rules, r 33(1)(a); HESCC Rules, rr 24(a) and 36; SEC Rules, r 28; TC Rules, r 30; WPAFCC Rules, r 26).

43.16 In a national security appeal in the Upper Tribunal, the relevant Minister is entitled to attend the hearing (Upper Tribunal Rules, r 35(2)). In the Tax Chamber, where proceedings are without notice to the respondent under r 19 there is no entitlement for the respondent to attend (TC Rules, r 30). Additionally, the GRC Rules include an entitlement for any party to send written representations (GRC Rules, r 33(1)(b)), and the GRC has the power to permit or request any person to attend the hearing or make written representations (GRC Rules, r 33(2)).

43.17 A party's representative may attend any hearing either on the basis that a duly appointed representative may do anything that a party may do (except sign a witness statement) or under the express provisions providing for parties to be accompanied by a representative not notified to the Tribunal (with the Tribunal's permission) (see **Representation**) (Upper Tribunal Rules, r 11(3), (5); GRC Rules, r 11(3), (5); HESCC Rules, r 11(3), (5); SEC Rules, r 11(5), (7); TC Rules, r 11(3), (5); WPAFCC Rules, r 11(4), (6). See also IAC Rules, r 48(5) and Lands Chamber Rules, r 37).

43.18 This entitlement is subject to the First-tier Tribunal and Upper Tribunal's discretionary power to exclude:

- any person whose conduct the Tribunal considers is disrupting or is likely to disrupt the hearing;
- any person whose presence the Tribunal considers is likely to prevent another person from giving evidence or making submission freely;
- any person who the Tribunal considers should be excluded in order to give effect to orders preventing or limiting the disclosure of documents and information under r 14 of the relevant procedural rules (see **Documents**);
- any person where the purpose of the hearing would be defeated by the attendance of that person;
- any witness prior to giving his evidence (see **Witnesses**);
- in the Tax Chamber and Upper Tribunal, a person under the age of 18 (TC Rules, r 32(4)(d); Upper Tribunal Rules, r 37(4)(e)), or in the HESCC in a special educational needs or disability case, a child (HESCC Rules, r 26(5)(e)).

(Upper Tribunal Rules, r 37(4), (5); GRC Rules, r 35(4), (5); HESCC Rules rr 26(5), (6) and 38(4), (5); SEC Rules, r 30(5), (6); TC Rules, r 32(4), (5); WPAFCC Rules, r 28(4), (5)).

HEARINGS IN A PARTY'S ABSENCE

43.19 It has long been established that it is not necessary for the parties to the proceedings to be present in order for there to be a validly constituted hearing (*R v Income Tax Special Commissioners, ex p Elmhirst* [1936] 1 KB 487, 500 per Lord Wright MR). This is reflected in the various procedural rules which provide the First-Tribunal and Upper Tribunal may proceed in the absence of a party who fails to attend provided that:

- the Tribunal is satisfied that the party has been notified of the hearing or that reasonable steps have been taken to notify the party of the hearing; and
- it is in the interests of justice to proceed with the hearing.

(Upper Tribunal Rules, r 38; GRC Rules, r 36; HESCC Rules, r 27 (not mental health cases); SEC Rules, r 31; TC Rules, r 33; WPAFCC Rules, r 29).

43.20 In mental health cases, the Health, Education and Social Care Chamber may not proceed in with a hearing in the absence of the patient unless there has been a medical examination of the patient by the Tribunal in accordance with the HESCC Rules, r 34 and the Tribunal is satisfied that patient has either chosen not to attend or is unable to attend for reasons of ill health (HESCC Rules, r 39). The Tribunal may proceed in the absence of a party other than the patient if the normal conditions – notification and interests of justice – are met (HESCC Rules, r 39(1)).

43.21 In the FTTIAC the Tribunal may only hear an appeal in the absence of a party or his representative if satisfied that the party or representative was given notice of the hearing and that there is no good reason for them not to have attended (IAC Rules, r 15(1)). Where that provision does not apply, the Tribunal may hear an appeal in the absence of a party if satisfied that:

- his representative is present;
- the party is outside the UK;
- the party is suffering from a communicable disease or is at risk of turning violent or disorderly;
- the party is unable to attend for a good reason (eg illness);
- the party is unrepresented and it is impracticable to give him notice; or
- the party has notified the Tribunal that he does not wish to attend the hearing (IAC Rules, r 15(2)).

43.22 In the Lands Chamber, the Tribunal may determine an appeal or application in the absence of any party on such terms as to costs as it sees fit (Lands Chamber Rules, r 49(1), (2)). If the non-attending party applies to the Tribunal within seven days of the decision and the Tribunal is satisfied that the party had good reason for not attending, the Tribunal may set aside its decision on such terms as to costs as the Tribunal deems appropriate (Lands Chamber Rules, r 49(3)).

PUBLIC OR PRIVATE HEARINGS

The general position

43.23 Hearings must be held in public unless the First-tier Tribunal or Upper Tribunal directs that a hearing or part of it is to be held in private, in which case the relevant Tribunal may issue directions as to who is to attend the hearing or part of it (Upper Tribunal Rules, r 37(1)–(3); GRC Rules, r 35(1)–(3); HESCC Rules, r 26(1)–(3) (except mental health cases); SEC Rules, r 30(1), (3), (4); TC Rules, r 32(1)–(3) and WPAFCC Rules, r 28(1)–(3)).

Tribunal specific exceptions

43.24 The default position in mental health cases (see **Mental health cases**) before the HESCC is that hearings will be held in private (HESCC Rules, r 38(1)). The HESCC has a discretion in the interests of justice to permit mental health cases to be heard in public. In determining whether to hold a hearing in a mental health case in public, the HESCC must consider the patient's safety and the potential impact on the patient's condition of the hearing being held in public. In this regard, the extent to which reporting can be controlled is important. If the patient applies for the hearing to be in public, the HESCC must evaluate the patient's understanding of the request as well as the wider public interest (see *R (Mersey Care NHS Trust) v Mental Health Review Tribunal* [2004] EWHC 1749 (Admin); [2005] 1 WLR 2469).

43.25 Detailed guidance was given by a three-judge panel of the AAC (including the Senior President) on the correct approach to mental health hearings in public or private in *AH v West London Mental Health Review Tribunal and the Secretary of State for Justice* [2010] UKUT 264 (AAC). The AAC confirmed that it had jurisdiction to hear an appeal against a decision of the HESCC refusing an application to hold the hearing in public (at [14]–[15]). The AAC considered the jurisprudence on the right to a public hearing, and noted that applications for public hearings in mental health cases are very rare (at [24]). The question which the HESCC should ask when dealing with an application are (at [29]):

- Is it consistent with the subjective and informed wishes of the applicant (assuming he is competent to make an informed choice)?
- Will it have an adverse effect on his mental health in the short or long term, taking account of the views of those treating him and any other expert views?
- Are there any other special factors for or against a public hearing?
- Can practical arrangements be made for an open hearing without disproportionate burden on the authority?

43.26 The HESCC was criticised by the AAC for failing to recognise that a public hearing is the starting point, and any exception to that must be justified in the circumstances of the case (at [41]–[43]). The AAC adjourned its own final decision in order to receive evidence on three points: the potential use of the patient appearing via video-link at a public hearing off-site; how regular a problem public hearings are in mental health cases; and how other jurisdictions deal with similar problems (at [50]–[52]).

43.27 In criminal injuries compensation cases before the SEC, hearing must be in private unless the appellant has consented to the hearings being in public and the SEC is satisfied that it is in the interest of justice to for the hearing to be held in public (SEC Rules, r 30(2)).

43.28 The Tax Chamber has a discretion to order that a hearing be held in private in the circumstances defined in the TC Rules, r 32(2):

- in the interests of public order or national security;
- in order to protect a person's right to respect for their private and family life;
- in order to maintain the confidentiality of sensitive information;
- in order to avoid serious harm to the public interest; or
- because not to do so would prejudice the interest of justice.

It has been stated that the Tax Chamber will order that a hearing be made in private if one of the five conditions are satisfied (see Jacobs, *Tribunal Practice and Procedure* (2009), paragraph 8.37). However, the five factors are themselves expressed in vague terms and it is suggested here that r 32(2) is intended merely to provide guidance to the Tax Chamber in the exercise of its discretionary powers. In practice a hearing will be held in private whenever the Tribunal in its discretion considers that one of the conditions is met and that this justifies the hearing being in private. This conclusion is reinforced by the ease with which it could be said some of the factors – in particular, maintaining the confidentiality of 'sensitive' information – are met. It should not be forgotten that the mandatory general rule is for hearings to take place in public. That position should not lightly be departed from by the Tax Chamber.

43.29 The Immigration and Asylum Chamber holds hearings in public, with a number of exceptions (IAC Rules, r 54(1)). Those exceptions, where proceedings are held in private, are:

- allegations of forged documents under the Nationality, Immigration and Asylum Act 2002, s 108 where both the public and a party and/or his representative may be excluded (IAC Rules, r 54(2));
- in the interests of public order or national security (IAC Rules, r 54(3)(a));
- to protect the private life of a party or the interests of a minor (IAC Rules, r 54(3)(b)); or
- to ensure that publicity does not prejudice the interests of justice where the Tribunal is satisfied that it is strictly necessary to do so (IAC Rules, r 54(4)).

43.30 In Lands Chamber of the Upper Tribunal, the default position is that hearings are held in public. In compulsory purchase cases, a public hearing is mandatory. Hearings will be held in private if the Tribunal is sitting as an arbitrator by consent of the parties, and may be private (or partly private) in cases of confidential matters or national security where the Tribunal is satisfied that it is just and reasonable to be private (Lands Chamber Rules, r 5(1), (1A)).

43.31 In the Upper Tribunal, apart from an instruction to consider holding a hearing in private in a national security certificate appeal case (Upper Tribunal Rules, r 37(2A)). The above tribunal-specific exceptions to the general rule that hearings are to be held in public do not apply to those cases on appeal in Upper Tribunal. The Upper Tribunal retains a discretion to determine whether a hearing should be held in private. The general position is that all hearings before the Upper Tribunal must be held in public (Upper Tribunal Rules, r 37(1)). Given that the Upper Tribunal hears only appeals on points of law, it is to be expected that it will be necessary to hold a hearing in private for less frequently than will be the case for a First-tier Tribunal hearing sensitive factual evidence. However, it is suggested here that the Upper Tribunal will display some deference to a determination of the First-Tier Tribunal that a hearing should be held in private, and is likely seriously to consider holding an appeal hearing in private where the hearing was in private below.

44 Immigration and Asylum Chamber (First-tier Tribunal)

COMPOSITION AND LOCATION

44.1 The FTTIAC is one of six Chambers that collectively comprise the First-tier Tribunal (see **First-tier Tribunal** and **Chambers**). The FTTIAC came into existence, replacing the Asylum and Immigration Tribunal ('AIT'), on 15 February 2010.

44.2 The FTTIAC is, like the Upper Tribunal and other Chambers of the First-tier Tribunal, presided over by the Senior President. The FTTIAC itself has a Chamber President. The FTTIAC comprises immigration judges and non-legal members, in accordance with the TCEA, s 4. Most matters that fall to be decided by the FTTIAC may be decided by one First-tier judge (who, in some cases, must be from a list of those approved by the Senior President to make decisions of the kind in question). The two exceptions to this are the giving of directions to extend time in an individual case or class of cases (under IAC Rules, r 45(6)) and the decision to review and set aside any order, decision notice or determination made by the Tribunal under the IAC Rules, r 60(1A). Both of these decisions are to be taken by the Chamber President. See **Constitution and composition of the First-tier Tribunal** for further details.

44.3 The FTTIAC has a number of hearing centres throughout the United Kingdom.

APPELLATE JURISDICTION AND POWERS

44.4 The FTTIAC has, by article 2 of the Transfer of Functions of the Asylum and Immigration Tribunal Order 2010, SI 2010/12, been assigned all functions of the AIT, which the same article abolished. Those functions are, in essence, to hear appeals against decisions made by the Home Office (specifically, its agency the UK Border Agency) in relation to matters of asylum, immigration and nationality (see the First-tier Tribunal and Upper Tribunal (Chambers) Order 2008, SI 2008/2684 (as amended), art 5C).

44.5 The decisions against which there exists a right of appeal to the FTTIAC are contained in ss 82-83A of the Nationality, Immigration and Asylum Act 2002 ('NIAA 2002'), ss 82–83A. The main types of decision against which the FTTIAC hears appeals are:

- refusals of asylum in the UK;
- refusals of entry to, or leave to remain in, the UK; and
- decisions to deport from the UK.

44.6 The FTTIAC may hear appeals on both fact and law. The grounds on which an appeal may lie against the various types of appealable decision are contained in NIAA 2002, s 84.

44.7 Appeals from the FTTIAC go to the Immigration and Asylum Chamber of the Upper Tribunal (see **Immigration and Asylum Chamber (Upper Tribunal)**).

44.8 In addition to its appellate jurisdiction, the FTTIAC also has jurisdiction to hear certain bail applications by persons detained under the Acts referred to in the Asylum and Immigration (Treatment of Claimants, etc) Act 2004, s 44(1).

PROCEDURAL RULES

44.9 Proceedings before the FTTIAC are governed by the IAC Rules and the IAC (Fast Track) Rules. These sets of rules were in use by the previous AIT but have been amended to reflect the AIT's incorporation into the new two-tier tribunals system. The Tribunals Service website page for the FTTIAC contains consolidated versions of both rules which are in force as of 15 February 2010. These consolidated versions are reproduced at Appendices 3 and 4. See also **Immigration and Asylum Chamber (First-tier Tribunal) procedural rules**.

45 Immigration and Asylum Chamber (First-tier Tribunal) Procedural Rules

See also **Procedural rules.**

STATUTORY INSTRUMENTS

45.1 Proceedings before the FTTIAC are governed by the IAC Rules and the IAC (Fast Track) Rules. These rules were in use by the previous AIT but have been amended to reflect the AIT's incorporation into the new two-tier tribunals system. The Tribunals Service website page for the FTTIAC contains consolidated versions of both sets of rules which are in force as of 15 February 2010. These consolidated versions are reproduced at Appendices 3 and 4. See also **Immigration and Asylum Chamber.**

45.2 The IAC Rules and IAC (Fast Track) Rules are supplemented by a Practice Statement and a Practice Direction, both made by the Senior President on 10 February 2010. Although both documents have parts which apply to the Immigration and Asylum Chamber (Upper Tribunal), they are annexed to this entry for convenience.

STRUCTURE

45.3 Reflecting their different and older origins as procedural rules of the AIT, the IAC Rules do not follow the same structure as the procedural rules of other First-tier Tribunal Chambers. Part 1 contains introductory provisions; Part 2 concerns 'Appeals to the Tribunal'; Part 3 deals with 'Appeals to the Upper Tribunal'; and Part 4 concerns bail applications. Part 5 contains general provisions concerning directions, witness summonses, address for service, etc.

45.4 The IAC (Fast Track) Rules follow the structure of the main Rules, save that instead of concerning bail applications, Part 4 concerns 'General Provisions' and Part 5 contains the procedure for removing pending proceedings from the fast track. Each of Parts 2–4 of the IAC (Fast Track) Rules explains which cases that part applies to and then sets out the respects in which the main Rules are modified for cases to which the fast track procedure applies.

APPEALING TO THE FTTIAC

See **Bringing proceedings in the First-tier Tribunals.**

Ordinary and fast track procedures

45.5 The procedural rules governing an appeal to the FTTIAC are contained in the IAC Rules (also known as the 'Principal Rules'). However, the Principal Rules are modified by the IAC (Fast Track) Rules, to provide for an expedited procedure for appellants detained at certain immigration removal centres.

45.6 Rule 5 of the IAC (Fast Track) Rules explains that an appeal falls within the scope of Part 2 of the Fast Track Rules, and is thus subject to the fast track procedure, when the appellant was in detention under the Immigration Acts at one of the places set out in Sch 2 to the Fast Track Rules when he was served with notice of the immigration decision against which he is appealing and has been so continuously since the notice was served on him. Rule 15 of the IAC (Fast Track) Rules contains analogous provisions for appeals from the FTTIAC to the Immigration and Asylum Chamber of the Upper Tribunal.

45.7 The Tribunal has the power to disapply the fast track procedure if:

- all parties consent;
- the Tribunal is satisfied that there are exceptional circumstances which mean that the appeal could not otherwise be determined justly; or
- the respondent has failed to comply with a rule or direction and holding the appellant to the fast track procedure would mean the appellant was prejudiced by that failure (IAC (Fast Track) Rules, r 30(1)).

45.8 If the fast track procedure ceases to apply, whether by reason of the appellant leaving continuous detention or the Tribunal making an order under the IAC (Fast Track) Rules, r 30(1), the Principal Rules apply from that date (IAC (Fast Track) Rules, r 31(2)). Where time has already started to run under a Fast Track Rules provision, the time limit changes to that in the Principal Rules (IAC (Fast Track) Rules, r 31(3)).

45.9 The subsections below set out the relevant rules for each stage of the proceedings under the Principal Rules and then any modifications under the Fast Track Rules.

45.10 There are also special time limits and procedures applicable to asylum appeals for appellants in the UK. These are dealt with in a separate subsection below.

Time for making an appeal

See **Time limits** and **Extensions of time**.

45.11 Under the Principal Rules, an appellant who is in the UK has five days from the date on which he is served with notice of the decision being challenged if he is in detention under the Immigration Acts at the time or 10 days otherwise (IAC Rules, r 7(1)).

45.12 An appellant who is outside the UK has 28 days from when he was served with notice (IAC Rules, r 7(2)(b)) unless he was in the UK when the decision was made but was unable to appeal from in the UK by reason of a provision of the Nationality, Immigration and Asylum Act 2002 ('NIAA 2002'), in which case the 28 days run from the date of departure from the UK (IAC Rules, r 7(2)(a)).

45.13 If an appellant who is served with notice of a decision to reject an asylum claim and who has not, on the date of receiving that notice, been granted leave to enter or remain in the UK for a period exceeding one year is subsequently granted such leave, the time limits above are modified to run from the date on which he is served with notice of the decision granting leave to enter or remain (IAC Rules, r 7(3)).

45.14 Under the Fast Track Rules, the time limit is shortened to not later than two days after the day of being served with notice of the decision being challenged

(IAC (Fast Track) Rules, r 8(1)). The Tribunal must not extend this time limit unless it is satisfied that, because of circumstances outside the control of the appellant or his representative, it was not practicable for the notice of appeal to be given with the time limit (IAC (Fast Track) Rules, r 8(2)).

45.15 If a notice of appeal is given outside the relevant time limit, it must include an application for an extension of time, giving a statement of the reasons for the lateness and accompanying this with any written evidence relied on in support of those reasons (IAC Rules, r 10(1)). This requirement applies to both ordinary and fast track appeals (see IAC (Fast Track) Rules, r 6(c)).

45.16 In the case of ordinary appeals, should a late notice not include an application to extend time, the Tribunal has the power to extend the time for appealing if it is satisfied that, by reason of special circumstances, it would be unjust not to do so (IAC Rules, r 10(5)). This power may be exercised of the Tribunal's own initiative. Should the Tribunal receive a late notice with no application to extend and not decide to exercise its r 10(5) power to extend of its own initiative, the Tribunal must notify the appellant that it proposes to treat his notice of appeal as being out of time (IAC Rules, r 10(2)). It is then open to the appellant to contend that the notice of appeal was, in fact, given in time or that there were special circumstances for the lateness which could not reasonably have been stated in the notice of appeal and to file with the Tribunal written evidence in support of that contention (IAC Rules, r 10(3)). Any such evidence must be filed no more than three days after the notification if the appellant is in the UK and no more than 10 days after, otherwise (IAC Rules, r 10(4)).

45.17 The Tribunal must decide any issue as to whether the notice was given in time or whether to extend time as a preliminary decision, without a hearing, and may take into account only the matters in the notice of appeal, any evidence by the appellant of reasons for lateness or special circumstances and any other relevant matters of fact within the knowledge of the Tribunal (IAC Rules, r 10(6)). Any such decision must be given by way of written notice, including reasons (which may be in summary form) (IAC Rules, r 10(6A)). The Tribunal must serve this notice on the parties (IAC Rules, r 10(7)). However, if it decides to refuse an extension in an appeal relating in whole or in part to an asylum claim by an appellant in the UK then the Tribunal is only obliged to serve on the respondent, which then has to serve on the appellant within 28 days and notify the Tribunal as soon as practicable when and how this was done (IAC Rules, r 10(8)). If the Tribunal does not receive such notification within 29 days, the duty to serve on the appellant as soon as reasonably practicable falls back on the Tribunal (IAC Rules, r 10(9)).

45.18 Special provisions regarding timing and extensions apply if a late notice of appeal is received and the respondent notifies the Tribunal that removal directions have been issued against the appellant to remove him from the UK within five calendar days of the notice date (IAC Rules, r 11(1)). In such cases, the Tribunal must, if reasonably practicable, make any decision about timing and extensions under IAC Rules, r 10 before the removal (IAC Rules, r 11(2)). The Tribunal may notify the appellant of its intention to treat his notice as out of time orally (including by telephone), shorten the time for him to give evidence in response and direct that any such evidence is to be given orally (including requiring the evidence to be given by telephone) (IAC Rules, r 11(3)).

45.19 In appeals to which the fast track procedure applies, there is no provision for the Tribunal to decide to extend time or to reconsider whether a notice of appeal was given in time if the appellant does not make a reasoned application for an extension. Any applications for extension or issues as to timeliness are to be determined as a preliminary issue at the main hearing (IAC (Fast Track) Rules, r 12(1)). Where the Tribunal determines that the appeal is out of time and does not extend time, it must take no further action in relation to the notice of appeal, save for serving on every party written notice (including reasons, which may be in summary form) within one day of making the decision (IAC Rules, r 12(3)).

Notice

45.20 A notice of appeal in FTTIAC cases must be made on a form approved for the purpose by the Senior President. Unlike notices of appeal to other Chambers of the First-tier Tribunal, there is no express requirement in the Principal Rules that the notice be written in English or Welsh and the notice may be signed by the appellant's representative or the appellant (although if the representative signs, he must certify that he has completed the notice in accordance with the appellant's instructions) (IAC Rules, r 8(3), (4)).

45.21 The notice of appeal must (IAC Rules, r 8(1)):

(a) state the name and address of the appellant;

(b) state whether the appellant has authorised a representative to act for him in the appeal and, if so, the representative's name and address;

(c) set out the grounds for the appeal;

(d) give reasons in support of those grounds; and

(e) so far as reasonably practicable, list any documents which the appellant intends to rely upon as evidence in support of the appeal.

45.22 The notice must be accompanied by the notice of the decision being challenged or, if it is not practicable to do so, the reasons why not (IAC Rules, r 8(2)).

45.23 The form, contents and materials accompanying the notice of appeal are unchanged under the Fast Track Rules, which provide for IAC Rules, r 8 to apply in its entirety to fast track appeals.

45.24 In relation to the giving of the notice of appeal, this should ordinarily be done by filing the notice with the Tribunal (IAC Rules, r 6(2); see IAC Rules, r 55(1), as to the methods of filing). But if the appellant is in detention under the Immigration Acts at the time, he may serve it on the person having custody of him (IAC Rules, r 6(3)(b)) or, if he is outside the UK and wishes to appeal against the decision of an entry clearance officer, may serve on the officer (IAC Rules, r 6(4)(b)). The Fast Track Rules provide that if service on the custodian is used, the custodian must endorse on the notice of appeal the date of service and forward it to the Tribunal immediately (IAC (Fast Track) Rules, r 7).

45.25 Save for situations in which the notice of appeal is served directly on an entry clearance officer, under IAC Rules, r 6(4)(b), the Tribunal in ordinary appeals has to serve the notice of appeal on the respondent as soon as is reasonably practicable (IAC Rules, r 12). In fast track appeals, the Tribunal must serve the notice immediately (IAC (Fast Track) Rules, r 9).

45.26 The Tribunal may not accept a notice of appeal where: (i) there is no relevant decision or (ii) the notice concerns a refusal of an application for entry clearance which was not made for a purpose falling within NIAA 2002, s 88A(1)(a) or (b) (ie, visiting a person of a class or description prescribed by regulations or entering as a dependant of a person in circumstances prescribed by regulations) and the notice of appeal does not rely on either of the grounds specified in NIAA 2002, s 88A(3)(a) (namely, unlawfulness under the Race Relations Act 1976, s 19B or breach of the applicant's Convention rights) (IAC Rules, r 9(1), (1A)).

45.27 Where the Tribunal does not accept a notice of appeal, it must notify the appellant and take no further action (IAC Rules, r 9(2)). The Practice Statement, paragraph 3.3, clarifies that such a decision is a procedural or preliminary decision. The Tribunal is required to scrutinise a notice of appeal as soon as practicable after it has been given (Practice Statement, paragraph 3.2).

45.28 If it transpires, at a hearing, that the notice of appeal relates to a decision against which there is, in fact, no right of appeal in the circumstances, the Tribunal must so find (albeit in the form of a determination, not a notice under IAC Rules, r 9): Practice Statement, paragraph 3.4. The fact that a hearing date was set does not mean that the appeal must be treated as valid.

45.29 In both ordinary and fast track cases, the appellant may vary his grounds of appeal only with the permission of the Tribunal (subject to NIAA 2002, s 85(2), which concerns situations in which an appellant is required by the Secretary of State for the Home Department or an immigration officer to state additional grounds for his application to enter or remain in the UK) (IAC Rules, r 14).

Response by the decision maker

45.30 When the decision maker is served with a copy of a notice of appeal, it must (unless it has already done so) file with the First-tier Tribunal a copy of (IAC Rules, r 13(1)):

- the notice of the decision under challenge and any other document served on the appellant giving reasons for that decision;
- any statement of evidence form completed by the appellant and record of an interview with the appellant in relation to the decision under challenge;
- any other unpublished document which is referred to in a document mentioned in the first bullet point above or relied upon by the decision maker; and
- the notice of any other immigration decision made in relation to the appellant in respect of which he has a right of appeal under NIAA 2002, s 82.

45.31 In ordinary cases, the decision maker must file these documents in accordance with any directions given by the Tribunal or, in the absence of any such directions, no later than 2pm on the business day before the earliest date appointed for any hearing of or in relation to the appeal (IAC Rules, r 13(2)). In cases where the Tribunal considers the timeliness of a notice of appeal as a preliminary issue under IAC Rules, r 10, the decision maker must file the documents in question as soon as reasonably practicable after being served with a decision of the Tribunal allowing the appeal to proceed, and in any event not later than 2pm on the business day before the earliest date appointed for any hearing of or in relation to the appeal following that decision (IAC Rules, r 13(3)).

45.32 In fast track cases, IAC Rules, r 13(2), (3) are not relevant because, as said above, the Tribunal cannot consider timeliness of the notice of appeal as a preliminary decision without a hearing. In such cases, the decision maker must file the relevant documents not later than two days after the day on which the Tribunal serves him with the notice of appeal (IAC (Fast Track) Rules, r 10).

45.33 In both fast track and ordinary cases, the decision maker must serve on the appellant a copy of all of the relevant documents, except for those which it has already sent him (IAC Rules, r 13(4)).

Asylum appeals

45.34 In appeals under NIAA 2002, s 82 where the appellant is in the UK and the appeal relates, in whole or in part, to an asylum claim, the procedures and time limits above are modified. Where the appeal is to be considered by the Tribunal at a hearing, the hearing must be fixed for a date not more than 35 days after the later of: (i) the date on which the Tribunal receives the notice of appeal, or (ii) the date on which the Tribunal serves on the appellant preliminary notice of a decision on timeliness under IAC Rules, r 10 (IAC Rules, r 23(2)(a)). (It should be noted that the reference to a 'hearing' does not include a case management review or other preliminary hearing: IAC Rules, r 23(7)). Where the appeal is to be determined without a hearing, the Tribunal must determine it not more than 35 days after the later of those dates (IAC Rules, r 23(2)(b)). However, if the respondent does not file the documents which he is required to file under the IAC Rules within the appropriate time, the 35-day time limits do not apply and the Tribunal may vary any hearing date fixed within 35 days if it is satisfied that it would be unfair to the appellant to proceed with the hearing on the date fixed (IAC Rules, r 23(3)).

45.35 The Tribunal must serve its determination on the respondent by sending it not later than 10 days after the hearing finishes, or (if there is no hearing) after the appeal is determined (IAC Rules, r 23(4)). The respondent must then serve the determination on the appellant not later than 28 days after receiving it from the Tribunal – unless the respondent makes an application for permission to appeal against the decision of the Tribunal (in which case the determination must be sent, delivered or personally served not later than the date on which the respondent makes the application) (IAC Rules, r 23(5)(a)). The respondent must, as soon as practicable after serving the determination on the appellant, notify the Tribunal on what date and by what means it was served (IAC Rules, r 23(5)(b)). If the respondent does not do so within 29 days after the Tribunal serves the determination on it, the Tribunal must serve the determination on the appellant as soon as reasonably practicable thereafter (IAC Rules, r 23(6)).

HEARINGS IN THE FTTIAC

See **Hearings**.

45.36 In most full hearings before the FTTIAC, the directions that the Tribunal will give with notice of the hearing are for:

- the appellant to serve the witness statements on which he intends to rely, a bundle of the documents he relies on, a skeleton argument and a chronology of events no later than five working days before the full hearing (or 10 days if the appellant is outside the UK) (Practice Direction, paragraph 7.5(a)); and
- the respondent to serve his bundle of documents relied on no later than five working days before the full hearing (Practice Direction, paragraph 7.5(b)).

45.37 In the case of fast-track cases, these materials will usually be served at the hearing or, if practicable, the business day immediately before (Practice Direction, paragraph 2.1).

When an appeal must or may be determined at a hearing

45.38 The First-tier Tribunal must consider every appeal at a hearing except where the appeal (IAC Rules, r 15):

- lapses pursuant to NIAA 2002, s 99 (because a certificate has been issued by the Secretary of State or an immigration officer);
- is treated as abandoned pursuant to NIAA 2002, s 104(4) (because the appellant began his appeal in the UK then left the UK);
- is treated as finally determined pursuant to NIAA 2002, s 104(5) (because a deportation order is made against the appellant); or
- is withdrawn by the appellant or treated as withdrawn in accordance with IAC Rules, r 17 (because the decision maker notifies the Tribunal that the decision has been withdrawn or because the appellant dies before the appeal is determined and the Tribunal directs that the appeal shall be treated as withdrawn).

45.39 In ordinary appeals, in addition to the above, the Tribunal may determine an appeal without a hearing if all of the parties consent (IAC Rules, r 15(2)(a)); if the appellant is outside the UK or it is impracticable to give him notice and, in either case, he is unrepresented (IAC Rules, r 15(2)(b)); if the appellant is outside the UK and his representative's address for service is outside the UK (IAC Rules, r 15(2)(ba)); or if a party has failed to comply with a provision of the rules or a direction of the Tribunal, or to provide a satisfactory explanation for not including the notice of the decision under challenge with the notice of appeal (IAC Rules, r 8(2)(b)), and the Tribunal is satisfied that in all the circumstances (including the extent of and any reasons for the failure) that it is appropriate to determine the appeal without a hearing (IAC Rules, r 15(2)(c)). The Tribunal may also determine an appeal without a hearing if it is satisfied, having regard to the material before it and the issues raised, that the appeal can be justly determined without a hearing (IAC Rules, r 15(2)(d)) – but only if the Tribunal first gives the parties notice of its intention to determine the appeal on the papers and an opportunity to make written representations as to whether there should be a hearing (IAC Rules, r 15(3)).

45.40 In fast track appeals, in addition to the list of the situations set out in paragraph 45.38 above, the Tribunal must also have a hearing if: (i) the Tribunal adjourns the hearing under the IAC (Fast Track) Rules, rr 28 or 30(2)(a). Rule 28 entitles the Tribunal to adjourn where there is insufficient time; where a party has not been served with notice of the hearing in accordance with the IAC (Fast Track) Rules; where the Tribunal is satisfied on the evidence that the appeal cannot be justly determined on the date listed but there is an identifiable future date no more than 10 days after the listed date by which it can be justly determined; or where the Tribunal makes an order under r 30. Rule 30 concerns transfers out of the fast track procedure.

When an appeal may be heard in the absence of a party

45.41 In both ordinary and fast track cases, the Tribunal may hear an appeal in the absence of a party or his representative if it is satisfied that the party/representative has been given notice of the date, time and place of the hearing and there is no good reason for his absence (IAC Rules, r 19(1)).

45.42 Where the above does not apply, the Tribunal may nevertheless hear an appeal in the absence of a party if satisfied that:

- a representative of the party is present at the hearing;
- the party is outside the UK;
- the party is suffering from a communicable disease or there is a risk of him behaving in a violent or disorderly manner;
- the party is unable to attend the hearing because of illness, accident or some other good reason;
- the party is unrepresented and it is impracticable to give him notice of the hearing; or
- the party has notified the Tribunal that he does not wish to attend the hearing.

Hearing appeals together

45.43 When two or more appeals are pending at the same time, the Tribunal may direct them to be heard together if it appears that (IAC Rules, r 20):

- some common question of fact or law arises in each of them;
- they relate to decisions or action taken in respect of persons who are members of the same family; or
- for some other reason it is desirable for the appeals to be heard together.

45.44 Fast track appeals may be heard together, as long as all of the appeals in question fall within the scope of the fast track rules (IAC (Fast Track) Rules, r 6(g)).

Adjourning hearings

45.45 In ordinary appeals, a party may apply for an adjournment of a hearing in the appeal. A party making such an application must notify all other parties of the application, if practicable, and show good reason why an adjournment is necessary (IAC Rules, r 21(a) and(b)). Any fact or matter relied upon in support of the application should be supported by evidence (IAC Rules, r 21(c)). Except in fast track cases, in which an application may be made at the hearing, applications must be made no later than one clear working day before the hearing date (Practice Direction, paragraphs 9.7 and 9.1). Any late application must be made at the hearing, with the party or his representative seeking the amendment in attendance (Practice Direction, paragraph 9.4). Only in the most exceptional circumstances will a late application for an adjournment be considered without such attendance (Practice Direction, paragraph 9.5).

45.46 The Tribunal must not adjourn a hearing on such an application unless it is satisfied that the appeal cannot otherwise be justly determined (IAC Rules, r 21(2)). In particular, the Tribunal must not adjourn a hearing to allow the applicant more time to produce evidence unless it is satisfied that the evidence relates to a matter in dispute in the appeal; it would be unjust to determine the appeal without giving the applicant further opportunity to produce the evidence; and, where the applicant has already failed to comply with directions for the production of the evidence, he has provided a satisfactory explanation for that failure (IAC Rules, r 21(3)).

45.47 Where the hearing is adjourned, the Tribunal will fix a new hearing date which is no later than is strictly required by the circumstances necessitating the adjournment (IAC Rules, r 21(4)(b)). The IAC Rules prescribe a period of within 28 days of the original hearing date, unless the Tribunal is satisfied that there are exceptional circumstances which mean that the appeal cannot be heard justly within that time (IAC Rules, r 21(4)(a)).

Case management review hearings and directions

45.48 Where an appellant is present in the UK and has a right of appeal while in the UK, the Tribunal may direct that a case management review hearing ('CMR') be held in his appeal (Practice Direction, paragraph 7.1). Although not a full hearing, a CMR is a hearing in the appeal like any other; the case may be determined if the appellant does not appear and is not represented (Practice Direction, paragraph 7.2).

45.49 In addition to the information in the notice of appeal, the appellant must provide the Tribunal and the decision maker at the CMR with (Practice Direction, paragraph 7.3):

- particulars of any application to vary his grounds of appeal;
- particulars of any amendment to the reasons in support of his grounds;
- particulars of any witnesses to be called or whose written statement or report is to be relied on at the full hearing; and
- the draft of any directions that he is requesting the Tribunal to make at the CMR.

45.50 The decision maker must also provide to the Tribunal and the appellant a draft of any directions that he is requesting, as well as any amendment which has been or is proposed to be made to the notice of decision under challenge or to any document served on the appellant giving reasons for the decision (Practice Direction, paragraph 7.4).

DISPOSITION OF APPEALS BY THE FTTIAC

See **Decisions, Withdrawal of proceedings.**

Determinations

45.51 As explained above, there are limited circumstances in which the Tribunal may proceed to a determination of an appeal without a hearing.

45.52 Except in asylum cases (which are covered below), where the Tribunal determines an appeal it must serve on every party a written determination containing its decision and the reasons for it (IAC Rules, r 22(1)).

45.53 If the appeal is considered at a hearing, the Tribunal must send its determination not later than ten days after the hearing finishes; otherwise, not later than ten days after the determination (IAC Rules, r 22(2)).

45.54 In fast track appeals, where the Tribunal determines an appeal it must give a written determination with reasons (IAC (Fast Track) Rules, r 14(1)). If the appeal is considered at a hearing, this determination must be served on all parties to the appeal not later than two days after the day on which the appeal hearing finishes; otherwise, not later than two days after the determination (IAC (Fast Track) Rules, r 14(2)).

Certifications of pending appeals

45.55 The Secretary of State may certify, under NIAA 2002, s 97, that a decision to exclude or remove a person from the UK was taken in the interests of national security of the relationship between the UK and another country (NIAA 2002, s 97(1)(a)) or that the decision was taken in accordance with a direction of the Secretary of State which identifies the person to whom the decision relates and which is given wholly or partly on one of the same grounds (NIAA 2002, s 97(1)(b)). The Secretary of State may also certify that the decision is or was taken wholly or partly in reliance on information which in his opinion should not be made public in the interests of national security, in the interests of the relationship between the UK and another country, or otherwise in the public interest (NIAA 2002, s 97(3)). In any of these cases, the certification prevents an appeal being brought under NIAA 2002, ss 82–83A against the decision.

45.56 Similarly, in relation to decisions to refuse a person leave to enter the UK or entry clearance, under NIAA 2002, s 98 the Secretary of State may certify that the decision is or was taken by him, wholly or partly on the ground that the exclusion or removal from the UK of the person in question is conducive to the public good (NIAA 2002, s 98(2)(a)), or in accordance with a direction by him which identifies the person in question and which is given wholly or partly on one of the same grounds (NIAA 2002, s 98(2)(b)). In these cases, an appeal generally may not be brought (although NIAA 2002, s 98(4), (5) provide for limited exceptions).

45.57 If a certificate under NIAA 2002, ss 97 or 98 is issued, the Secretary of State or immigration officer who issues that certificate must file notice of the certification with the Tribunal (IAC Rules, r 16(1)). The Tribunal must notify the parties and refrain from taking further action in relation to the appeal (IAC Rules, r 16(2)).

Withdrawals and abandonments of pending appeals

45.58 In addition to proceeding to a determination or being certified, an appeal may also be withdrawn or abandoned.

45.59 An appellant may withdraw his appeal at a hearing or at any time, by filing written notice with the Tribunal (IAC Rules, r 17(1)). An appeal is treated as withdrawn if the respondent notifies the Tribunal that the challenged decision has been withdrawn (IAC Rules, r 17(2)). Where an appellant dies before his appeal has been determined, the Tribunal may either direct that the appeal be treated as withdrawn or, where the Tribunal considers it necessary, direct that the personal representative of the appellant may continue proceedings in his place (IAC Rules, r 17(2A)).

45.60 If an appeal is withdrawn or treated as withdrawn, the Tribunal must serve notice on the parties (IAC Rules, r 17(3)).

45.61 An appeal brought by a person in the UK shall be treated as abandoned if the appellant leaves the UK (NIAA 2002, s 104(4)). An appeal by a person brought in the UK shall also be treated as abandoned if the appellant is granted leave to enter or remain in the UK (NIAA 2002, s 104(4A)), albeit subject to exceptions if the appellant wishes to pursue his appeal on certain grounds, which are set out in NIAA 2002, s 104(4B), (4C). In addition, appeals in respect of certain types of immigration decision – namely:

- refusal of leave to enter;
- refusal of a certificate of entitlement to a right of abode;
- refusal to vary leave to enter or remain (if the result is that the appellant has no leave to enter or remain);
- variation of leave to enter or remain (if the effect is that the appellant has no leave to enter or remain);
- revocation of indefinite leave to enter or remain – shall be treated as finally determined if a deportation order is made against the appellant. Finally, an appeal brought by a person who is subsequently issued with one of the appropriate documents specified in paragraph 4(2) of Schedule 2 to the Immigration (European Economic Area) Regulations 2006, SI 2006/1003 shall be treated as abandoned.

45.62 If any party in an appeal is pending before the Tribunal is aware that one of the events listed in the previous paragraph (ie, an event that would lead to an appeal being treated as abandoned or finally determined) has taken place, he must notify the Tribunal (IAC Rules, r 18). Where the event is that the appellant has been granted leave to enter or remain in the UK, he must file a notice with the Tribunal if he wishes to pursue his appeal on the basis of one of the grounds in the exceptions (insofar as the appeal is brought on that ground).

45.63 If the ground is that in NIAA 2002, s 104(4B) (namely breach of the UK's obligations under the Refugee Convention), the appellant must have been granted leave to enter or remain in the UK for a period exceeding 12 months and has 28 days from the date on which he receives notice of the grant of leave to file the notice (IAC Rules, r 18(1A)(a)).

45.64 If the exception is that in NIAA 2002, s 104(4C) (namely discrimination by a public authority contrary to the Race Relations Act 1976, s 19B), the appellant has 28 days from the date on which he receives notice of the grant of leave to enter or remain to file the notice (IAC Rules, r 18(1A)(b)).

45.65 Failure to comply with these time limits will mean that the appeal is treated as abandoned (IAC Rules, r 18(1B)). The respondent must be served with a copy of the notice at the same time (IAC Rules, r 18(1C)). The Tribunal will also notify the appellant of the date on which it received the notice and send a copy of the notice of receipt to the respondent (IAC Rules, r 18(1F), (1G)).

45.66 The notice filed under IAC Rules, r 18(1A), must state the following:

- the appellant's full name and date of birth;
- the Tribunal's reference number;
- the Home Office reference number, if applicable;
- the Foreign & Commonwealth Office reference number, if applicable
- the date on which the appellant was granted leave to enter or remain in the UK (which, in the case of a NIAA 2002 , s 104(4B) appeal, must be for more than 12 months);
- that the appellant wishes to pursue the appeal insofar as it is brought on the ground specified in the relevant exception.

45.67 Where an appeal is treated as abandoned or finally determined, the Tribunal must serve notice of this on the parties and take no further action in relation to the appeal (IAC Rules, r 18(2)).

APPEALS FROM THE FTTIAC

45.68 Appeals from the FTTIAC lie to the Immigration and Asylum Chamber of the Upper Tribunal (see **Appeals from the First-tier Tribunal, Immigration and Asylum Chamber (Upper Tribunal)** and **Upper Tribunal**).

Time for making an appeal

See **Time limits** and **Extensions of time**.

45.69 An application for permission to appeal must be made in writing to the First-tier Tribunal (IAC Rules, r 24(1)). For ordinary cases, the application must be sent or delivered to the Tribunal so that it is received no later than five days after the date on which the party making the application is deemed to have been served with written reasons for the decision (IAC Rules, r 24(2)), unless the appellant is outside the UK, in which case the time is 28 days (IAC Rules, r 24(3)).

45.70 In fast track cases, the application must be received no later than two days after the date on which the party is served with written reasons (IAC (Fast Track) Rules, r 17(1)).

45.71 In either case, if the application is not made within time, the Tribunal may extend the time for appealing if it is satisfied that there are special circumstances that would make it unjust not to do so; if not, it must not admit the application (IAC Rules, r 24(4); IAC (Fast Track) Rules, r 17(2)).

Application for permission

45.72 An application for permission to appeal must (IAC Rules, r 24(5)):

- identify the decision of the first-tier tribunal to which it relates;
- identify the alleged error or errors of law in the decision; and
- state the result the party making the application is seeking.

Consideration by the First-tier Tribunal

45.73 On receiving an application for permission to appeal, the First-tier Tribunal must first consider whether to review its own decision (IAC Rules, r 25(1)). If the First-tier Tribunal decides not to review the decision, or reviews the decision and decides to take no action in relation to it, the First-tier Tribunal must then consider whether to give permission to appeal (IAC Rules, r 25(2)). The First-tier Tribunal must make its decision as to review or appeal no later than 10 days after receiving the application (IAC Rules, r 25(3)).

45.74 The FTTIAC must send written reasons for its decision to the parties. If permission is refused, the FTTIAC must send with the reasons of its decision notification of the right to apply to the Upper Tribunal and the procedure and time limits for making such an application (IAC Rules, r 25(4)). This also applies in respect of any grounds on which permission was refused, if permission was granted on limited grounds only (IAC Rules, r 25(5)).

45.75 So far as the grounds for review are concerned, the Tribunal may only undertake a review of its decision if it is satisfied that there was an error of law (IAC Rules, r 26(1)). The First-tier Tribunal is likely to adopt this course only if it is satisfied that (Practice Statement, paragraph 4.2):

- the effect of any error of law has been to deprive a party before the First-tier Tribunal of a fair hearing or other opportunity for his case to be put to and considered by the Tribunal; or
- there are highly compelling reasons why the matter should be re-decided by the First-tier Tribunal.

45.76 The Tribunal must notify the parties of the outcome of any review and of any right of appeal (save in asylum cases, where the notices are sent to the Secretary of State first) (IAC Rules, r 26(2)). If the Tribunal takes an action following a review without first giving all parties an opportunity to make representations, the notice given must state that any party which did not have an opportunity to make representations may apply for the action to be set aside and the decision re-reviewed (IAC Rules, r 26(3)).

45.77 For fast track cases, the Tribunal is not obliged to consider whether to review its decision first (IAC (Fast Track) Rules, r 16(b)) and the Tribunal must send the parties written reasons for its decision not later than one business day after receiving the application (IAC (Fast Track) Rules, r 18).

45.78 In asylum appeals for which the appellant is in the UK at the time of the appeal, a modified notification procedure applies: see IAC Rules, r 27(2). The Tribunal must send the notification of the outcome of the review or appeal to the Secretary of State, who must then serve them on the appellant not later than 28 days after receiving them. The Secretary of State must then notify the Tribunal as soon as practicable on what date and by what means he served the appellant. If he does not notify within 29 days after the Tribunal sends the documents, the Tribunal must serve the documents on the appellant as soon as reasonably practicable.

45.79 In relation to renewing the application for permission before the Upper Tribunal, see **Appeals from the First-tier Tribunal** and **Appeals and references to the Upper Tribunal**.

BAIL APPLICATIONS TO THE FTTIAC

45.80 As well as hearing appeals against immigration and asylum decisions, the FTTIAC may also hear bail applications by those detained under the Immigration Acts.

Application for bail

45.81 An application to be released on bail must be made by filing with the Tribunal an application notice in an approved form, containing the following details (IAC Rules, r 38(2)):

- the applicant's full name, date of birth and date of arrival in the UK;
- the address of his place of detention;
- whether an appeal by him to the Tribunal is pending;
- the address where the applicant will reside if his application for bail is granted (or, if such an address cannot be given, the reason why not);
- where the applicant is aged 18 or over, whether he will, if required, agree as a condition of bail to co-operate with electronic monitoring under the Asylum and Immigration (Treatment of Claimants, etc) Act 2004, s 36;
- the amount of the recognizance in which he will agree to be bound;
- the full names, addresses, occupations and dates of birth of any persons who have agreed to act as sureties and the amounts of recognizances in which they will agree to be bound;
- the grounds on which the application is made (and, where a previous application has been refused, full details of any change in circumstances which has occurred since); and
- whether an interpreter will be required at the hearing, and in respect of what language or dialect.

Hearing of bail applications

45.82 If a bail application is filed the Tribunal must serve a copy on the Secretary of State as soon as reasonably practicable and fix a hearing (IAC Rules, r 39(1)). If practicable, the application must be listed for hearing within three working days of receipt by the Tribunal of the notice of application (Practice Direction, paragraph 13.1).

45.83 If the Secretary of State wishes to contest the application, he must file with the Tribunal and serve on the applicant a written statement of his reasons not later than 2pm on the business day before the hearing (or, if he was served less than 24 hours before the hearing, as soon as reasonably practicable) (IAC Rules, r 39(2)).

45.84 The Tribunal must serve written notice of its decision on the parties and the person with custody of the applicant. Where bail is granted, the notice must include the conditions of bail and the amount(s) in which the applicant and any sureties are to be bound (IAC Rules, r 39(4)) and where refused, the reasons for the refusal (IAC Rules, r 39(5)). Any recognizance or surety must be in writing, stating: (i) the amount by which the person agrees to be bound and (ii) that he has read and understood the bail decision and agrees to pay that amount of money if the applicant fails to comply with the bail conditions (IAC Rules, r 40(1)). The recognizance must be signed and filed with the Tribunal (IAC Rules, r 40(2)).

45.85 If bail is granted the person with custody of the applicant must release him upon being served with a copy of the decision and being satisfied that any recognizances required as a condition have been entered into (IAC Rules, r 41).

Annex 1

PRACTICE DIRECTIONS (IMMIGRATION AND ASYLUM CHAMBERS OF THE FIRST-TIER TRIBUNAL AND THE UPPER TRIBUNAL)

10 February 2010, Senior President of Tribunals

PART 1 PRELIMINARY

1 Interpretation, etc.

1.1 In these Practice Directions:-

"the 2002 Act" means the Nationality, Immigration and Asylum Act 2002;

"the 2007 Act" means the Tribunals, Courts and Enforcement Act 2007;

"adjudicator" means an adjudicator appointed, or treated as appointed, under section 81 of the 2002 Act (as originally enacted);

"AIT" means the Asylum and Immigration Tribunal;

"CMR hearing" means a case management review hearing;

"fast track appeal" means an appeal to which Part 2 of the Fast Track Rules applies;

"Fast Track Rules" means the Asylum and Immigration Tribunal (Fast Track Procedure) Rules 2005;

"First-tier rule", followed by a number, means the rule bearing that number in the Asylum and Immigration Tribunal (Procedure) Rules 2005;

"IAT" means the Immigration Appeal Tribunal;

"Practice Statements" means the Practice Statements - Immigration and Asylum Chambers of the First-tier Tribunal and the Upper Tribunal (dated 10 February 2010); and "Practice Statement", followed by a number, means the Statement bearing that number in the Practice Statements;

"Transfer of Functions Order" means the Transfer of Functions of the Asylum and Immigration Tribunal Order 2010 (SI/2010/21);

"The Tribunal" means the Immigration and Asylum Chamber of the First-tier Tribunal or of the Upper Tribunal, as the case may be;

"UT rule", followed by a number, means the rule bearing that number in the Tribunal Procedure (Upper Tribunal) Rules 2008.

1.2 Except where expressly stated to the contrary, any reference in these Practice Directions to an enactment is a reference to that enactment as amended by or under any other enactment.

1.3 Other expressions in these Practice Statements have the same meanings as in the 2007 Act.

1.4 These Practice Directions come into force on 15 February 2010.

1.5 These Practice Directions apply, as appropriate, in relation to transitional cases to which Schedule 4 to the Transfer of Functions Order applies; and references to the First-tier Tribunal and the Upper Tribunal shall be construed accordingly.

PART 2 PRACTICE DIRECTIONS FOR THE IMMIGRATION AND ASYLUM CHAMBER OF THE FIRST-TIER TRIBUNAL

2 Standard directions in fast track appeals

2.1 In the case of a fast track appeal, the parties must respectively serve the material specified in Practice Direction 7.5(a) and (b) either at the hearing or, if practicable, on the business day immediately preceding the date of the hearing.

2.2 Subject to the exception mentioned in Practice Direction 7.7, witness statements served in pursuance of paragraph 2.1 shall stand as evidence-in-chief at the hearing.

PART 3 PRACTICE DIRECTIONS FOR THE IMMIGRATION AND ASYLUM CHAMBER OF THE UPPER TRIBUNAL

3 Procedure on appeal

3.1 Where permission to appeal to the Upper Tribunal has been granted, then, unless and to the extent that they are directed otherwise, for the purposes of preparing for a hearing in the Upper Tribunal the parties should assume that:-

(a) the Upper Tribunal will decide whether the making of the decision of the First-tier Tribunal involved the making of an error on a point of law, such that the decision should be set aside under section 12(2)(a) of the 2007 Act;

(b) except as specified in Practice Statement 7.2 (disposal of appeals by Upper Tribunal), the Upper Tribunal will proceed to re-make the decision under section 12(2)(b)(ii), if satisfied that the original decision should be set aside; and

(c) in that event, the Upper Tribunal will consider whether to re-make the decision by reference to the First-tier Tribunal's findings of fact and any new documentary evidence submitted under UT rule 15(2A) which it is reasonably practicable to adduce for consideration at that hearing.

3.2 The parties should be aware that, in the circumstances described in paragraph 3.1(c), the Upper Tribunal will generally expect to proceed, without any further hearing, to re-make the decision, where this can be undertaken without having to hear oral evidence. In certain circumstances, the Upper Tribunal may give directions for the giving of oral evidence at the relevant hearing, where it appears appropriate to do so. Such directions may be given before or at that hearing.

3.3 In a case where no oral evidence is likely to be required in order for the Upper Tribunal to re-make the decision, the Upper Tribunal will therefore expect any documentary evidence relevant to the re-making of the decision to be adduced in accordance with Practice Direction 4 so that it may be considered at the relevant hearing; and, accordingly, the party seeking to rely on such documentary evidence will be expected to show good reason why it is not reasonably practicable to adduce the same in order for it to be considered at that hearing.

3.4 If the Upper Tribunal nevertheless decides that it cannot proceed as described in paragraph 3.1(c) because findings of fact are needed which it is not in a position to make, the Upper Tribunal will make arrangements for the adjournment of the hearing, so that the proceedings may be completed before the same constitution of the Tribunal; or, if that is not reasonably practicable, for their transfer to a different constitution, in either case so as to enable evidence to be adduced for that purpose.

3.5 Where proceedings are transferred in the circumstances described in paragraph 3.4, any documents sent to or given by the Tribunal from which the proceedings are transferred shall be deemed to have been sent to or given by the Tribunal to which those proceedings are transferred.

3.6 Where such proceedings are transferred, the Upper Tribunal shall prepare written reasons for finding that the First-tier Tribunal made an error of law, such that its decision fell to be set aside, and those written reasons shall be sent to the parties before the next hearing.

3.7 The written reasons shall be incorporated in full in, and form part of, the determination of the Upper Tribunal that re-makes the decision. Only in very exceptional cases can the decision contained in those written reasons be departed from or varied by the Upper Tribunal which re-makes the decision under section 12(2)(b)(ii) of the 2007 Act.

3.8 Unless directed otherwise, the parties to any fast track appeal which is before the Upper Tribunal will be expected to attend with all necessary witnesses and evidence that may be required if the Upper Tribunal should decide that it is necessary to set aside the decision of the First-tier Tribunal and re-make the decision. It will be unusual for the Upper Tribunal to adjourn or transfer, but, if it does so, paragraph 3.6 and 3.7 will, so far as appropriate, apply.

3.9 In this Practice Direction and Practice Direction 4, "the relevant hearing" means a hearing fixed by the Upper Tribunal at which it will consider if the First-tier Tribunal made an error of law.

3.10 Without prejudice to the generality of paragraph 1.5, where, by virtue of any transitional provisions in Schedule 4 to the Transfer of Functions Order, the Upper Tribunal is undertaking the reconsideration of a decision of the AIT, references in this Practice Direction and Practice Direction 4 to the First-tier Tribunal shall be construed as references to the AIT.

4 Evidence

4.1 UT rule 15(2A) imposes important procedural requirements where the Upper Tribunal is asked to consider evidence that was not before the First-tier Tribunal. UT rule 15(2A) must be complied with in every case where permission to appeal is granted and a party wishes the Upper Tribunal to consider such evidence. Notice under rule 15(2A)(a), indicating the nature of the evidence and explaining why it was not submitted to the First-tier Tribunal, must be filed with the Upper Tribunal and served on the other party within the time stated in any specific directions given by the Upper Tribunal; or, if no such direction has been given, as soon as practicable after permission to appeal has been granted.

4.2 A party who wishes the Upper Tribunal to consider any evidence that was not before the First-tier Tribunal must indicate in the notice whether the evidence is sought to be adduced:-

(a) in connection with the issue of whether the First-tier Tribunal made an error of law, requiring its decision to be set aside; or

(b) in connection with the re-making of the decision by the Upper Tribunal, in the event of the First-tier Tribunal being found to have made such an error.

4.3 The notice must clearly indicate whether the party concerned wishes the evidence to be considered at the relevant hearing and state whether the evidence is in oral or documentary form.

4.4 Where a party wishes, in the circumstances described in paragraph 4.2(b), to adduce only documentary evidence, Practice Direction 3.3 will apply.

4.5 Where a party wishes, in the circumstances described in paragraph 4.2(b), to adduce oral evidence at the relevant hearing, the notice must explain why it is considered desirable to proceed in such a manner and give details of the oral evidence and a time estimate.

4.6 Where the Upper Tribunal acts under Practice Direction 3 to adjourn or transfer the hearing, it shall consider any notice given under UT rule 15(2A) and give any directions arising therefrom, if and to the extent that this has not already been done.

4.7 This Practice Direction does not apply in the case of a fast track appeal (as to which, see Practice Direction 3.8).

5 Pursuing appeal after grant of leave

5.1 This Practice Direction applies where:-

(a) an appeal would otherwise fall to be treated as abandoned pursuant to section 104(4A) of the 2002 Act because the appellant is granted leave to remain in the United Kingdom; but

(b) the appellant wishes, in pursuance of section 104(4B) or (4C), to pursue the appeal, insofar as it is brought on asylum grounds or on grounds of unlawful discrimination.

5.2 Where this Practice Direction applies, the appellant must comply with the following requirements (which are the relevant practice directions for the purposes of UT rule 17A(3)).

5.3 Where section 104(4B) of the 2002 Act (asylum grounds) applies, the notice required by UT rule 17A(3) to be sent or delivered to the Upper Tribunal must state:-

(a) the appellant's full name and date of birth;

(b) the Tribunal's reference number;

(c) the Home Office reference number, if applicable;

(d) the Foreign and Commonwealth Office reference number, if applicable;

(e) the date on which the appellant was granted leave to enter or remain in the United Kingdom for a period exceeding 12 months; and

(f) that the appellant wishes to pursue the appeal in so far as it is brought on the ground specified in section 84(1)(g) of the 2002 Act which relates to the Refugee Convention.

5.4 Where section 104(4C) of the 2002 Act (grounds of unlawful discrimination) applies, the notice required by UT rule 17A(3) to be sent or delivered to the Upper Tribunal must state:-

(a) the appellant's full name and date of birth;

(b) the Tribunal's reference number;

(c) the Home Office reference number, if applicable;

(d) the Foreign and Commonwealth Office reference number, if applicable;

(e) the date on which the appellant was granted leave to enter or remain in the United Kingdom; and

(f) that the appellant wishes to pursue the appeal in so far as it is brought on the ground specified in section 84(1)(b) of the 2002 Act which relates to section 19B of the Race Relations Act 1976 (discrimination by public authorities).

5.5 Where an appellant has sent or delivered a notice under UT rule 17A(3), the Upper Tribunal will notify the appellant of the date on which it received the notice.

5.6 The Upper Tribunal will send a copy of the notice issued under paragraph 5.5 to the respondent.

5.7 In this Practice Direction:-

"appellant" means the party who was the appellant before the First-tier Tribunal; and

"respondent" means the party who was the respondent before the First-tier Tribunal.

PART 4 PRACTICE DIRECTIONS FOR THE IMMIGRATION AND ASYLUM CHAMBER OF THE FIRST-TIER TRIBUNAL AND THE UPPER TRIBUNAL

6 Form of notice of appeal etc.

6.1 The form of notice approved for the purpose of:-

(a) First-tier rule 8 (notice of appeal);

(b) First-tier rule 24 (application for permission to appeal to the Upper Tribunal);

(b) First-tier rule 38 (application for bail); and

(d) UT rule 21 (application to the Upper Tribunal for permission to appeal).

as the case may be, is the appropriate form as displayed on the Tribunal's website at the time when the notice is given, or that form with any variations that circumstances may require.

7 Case management review hearings and directions

7.1 Where the Tribunal so directs, a CMR hearing will be held in the case of an appeal where the party who is or was the appellant before the First-tier Tribunal:-

(a) is present in the United Kingdom; and

(b) has a right of appeal whilst in the United Kingdom.

7.2 It is important that the parties and their representatives understand that a CMR hearing is a hearing in the appeal and that the appeal may be determined under the relevant Procedure Rules if a party does not appear and is not represented at that hearing.

7.3 In addition to any information required by First-tier rule 8 (form of contents and notice of appeal), the appellant before the First-tier Tribunal must provide that Tribunal and the respondent at the CMR hearing with:-

(a) particulars of any application for permission to vary the grounds of appeal;

(b) particulars of any amendments to the reasons in support of the grounds of appeal;

(c) particulars of any witnesses to be called or whose written statement or report is proposed to be relied upon at the full hearing; and

(d) the draft of any directions that the appellant is requesting the Tribunal to make at the CMR hearing.

7.4 In addition to any documents required by relevant Procedure Rules, the party who is or was the respondent before the First-tier Tribunal must provide the Tribunal and the other party at the CMR hearing with:-

(a) any amendment that has been made or is proposed to be made to the notice of decision to which the appeal relates or to any other document served on the person concerned giving reasons for that decision; and

(b) a draft of any directions that the Tribunal is requested to make at the CMR hearing.

7.5 In most cases, including those appeals where a CMR hearing is to be held, the Tribunal will normally have given to the parties the following directions with the notice of hearing:-

(a) not later than 5 working days before the full hearing (or 10 days in the case of an out-of-country appeal) the appellant shall serve on the Tribunal and the respondent:

(i) witness statements of the evidence to be called at the hearing, such statements to stand as evidence in chief at the hearing;

(ii) a paginated and indexed bundle of all the documents to be relied on at the hearing with a schedule identifying the essential passages;

(iii) a skeleton argument, identifying all relevant issues including human rights claims and citing all the authorities relied upon; and

(iv) a chronology of events;

(b) not later than 5 working days before the full hearing, the respondent shall serve on the Tribunal and the appellant a paginated and indexed bundle of all the documents to be relied upon at the hearing, with a schedule identifying the relevant passages, and a list of any authorities relied upon.

7.6 At the end of the CMR hearing, the Tribunal will give the parties any further written directions relating to the conduct of the appeal.

7.7 Although in normal circumstances a witness statement should stand as evidence-in-chief, there may be cases where it will be appropriate for appellants or witnesses to have the opportunity of adding to or supplementing their witness statements.

7.8 In addition to the directions referred to above, at the end of the CMR hearing the Tribunal will also give to the parties written confirmation of:-

(a) any issues that have been agreed at the CMR hearing as being relevant to the determination of the appeal; and

(b) any concessions made at the CMR hearing by a party.

8 Trial bundles

8.1 The parties must take all reasonably practicable steps to act in accordance with paragraph 8.2 to 8.6 in the preparation of trial bundles for hearings before the Tribunal.

8.2 The best practice for the preparation of bundles is as follows:-

(a) all documents must be relevant, be presented in logical order and be legible;

(b) where the document is not in the English language, a typed translation of the document signed by the translator, and certifying that the translation is accurate, must be inserted in the bundle next to the copy of the original document, together with details of the identity and qualifications of the translator;

(c) if it is necessary to include a lengthy document, that part of the document on which reliance is placed should, unless the passages are outlined in any skeleton argument, be highlighted or clearly identified by reference to page and/or paragraph number;

(d) bundles submitted must have an index showing the page numbers of each document in the bundle;

(e) the skeleton argument or written submission should define and confine the areas at issue in a numbered list of brief points and each point should refer to any documentation in the bundle on which the appellant proposes to rely (together with its page number);

(f) where reliance is placed on a particular case or text, photocopies of the case or text must be provided in full for the Tribunal and the other party; and

(g) large bundles should be contained in a ring binder or lever arch file, capable of lying flat when opened.

8.3 The Tribunal recognises the constraints on those representing the parties in appeals in relation to the preparation of trial bundles and this Practice Direction does not therefore make it mandatory in every case that bundles in exactly the form prescribed must be prepared. Where the issues are particularly complex it is of the highest importance that comprehensive bundles are prepared. If parties to appeals fail in individual cases to present documentation in a way which complies with the direction, it will be for the Tribunal to deal with any such issue.

8.4 Much evidence in immigration and asylum appeals is in documentary form. Representatives preparing bundles need to be aware of the position of the

Tribunal, which may be coming to the case for the first time. The better a bundle has been prepared, the greater it will assist the Tribunal. Bundles should contain all the documents that the Tribunal will require to enable it to reach a decision without the need to refer to any other file or document. The Tribunal will not be assisted by repetitious, outdated or irrelevant material.

8.5 It may not be practical in many appeals to require there to be an agreed trial bundle but it nevertheless remains vital that the parties inform each other at an early stage of all and any documentation upon which they intend to rely.

8.6 The parties cannot rely on the Tribunal having any prior familiarity with any country information or background reports in relation to the case in question. If either party wishes to rely on such country or background information, copies of the relevant documentation must be provided.

9 Adjournments

9.1 Applications for the adjournment of appeals (other than fast track appeals) listed for hearing before the Tribunal must be made not later than 5.00p.m. one clear working day before the date of the hearing.

9.2 For the avoidance of doubt, where a case is listed for hearing on, for example, a Friday, the application must be received by 5.00p.m. on the Wednesday.

9.3 The application for an adjournment must be supported by full reasons and must be made in accordance with relevant Procedure Rules.

9.4 Any application made later than the end of the period mentioned in paragraph 9.1 must be made to the Tribunal at the hearing and will require the attendance of the party or the representative of the party seeking the adjournment.

9.5 It will be only in the most exceptional circumstances that a late application for an adjournment will be considered without the attendance of a party or representative.

9.6 Parties must not assume that an application, even if made in accordance with paragraph 9.1, will be successful and they must always check with the Tribunal as to the outcome of the application.

9.7 Any application for the adjournment of a fast track appeal must be made to the Tribunal at the hearing and will be considered by the Tribunal in accordance with relevant Procedure Rules.

9.8 If an adjournment is not granted and the party fails to attend the hearing, the Tribunal may in certain circumstances proceed with the hearing in that party's absence.

10 Expert evidence

10.1 A party who instructs an expert must provide clear and precise instructions to the expert, together with all relevant information concerning the nature of the appellant's case, including the appellant's immigration history, the reasons why the appellant's claim or application has been refused by the respondent and copies of any relevant previous reports prepared in respect of the appellant.

10.2 It is the duty of an expert to help the Tribunal on matters within the expert's own expertise. This duty is paramount and overrides any obligation to the person from whom the expert has received instructions or by whom the expert is paid.

10.3 Expert evidence should be the independent product of the expert uninfluenced by the pressures of litigation.

10.4 An expert should assist the Tribunal by providing objective, unbiased opinion on matters within his or her expertise, and should not assume the role of an advocate.

10.5 An expert should consider all material facts, including those which might detract from his or her opinion.

10.6 An expert should make it clear:-

(a) when a question or issue falls outside his or her expertise; and

(b) when the expert is not able to reach a definite opinion, for example because of insufficient information.

10.7 If, after producing a report, an expert changes his or her view on any material matter, that change of view should be communicated to the parties without delay, and when appropriate to the Tribunal.

10.8 An expert's report should be addressed to the Tribunal and not to the party from whom the expert has received instructions.

10.9 An expert's report must:-

(a) give details of the expert's qualifications;

(b) give details of any literature or other material which the expert has relied on in making the report;

(c) contain a statement setting out the substance of all facts and instructions given to the expert which are material to the opinions expressed in the report or upon which those opinions are based;

(d) make clear which of the facts stated in the report are within the expert's own knowledge;

(e) say who carried out any examination, measurement or other procedure which the expert has used for the report, give the qualifications of that person, and say whether or not the procedure has been carried out under the expert's supervision;

(f) where there is a range of opinion on the matters dealt with in the report:

(i) summarise the range of opinion, so far as reasonably practicable, and

(ii) give reasons for the expert's own opinion;

(g) contain a summary of the conclusions reached;

(h) if the expert is not able to give an opinion without qualification, state the qualification; and

(j) contain a statement that the expert understands his or her duty to the Tribunal, and has complied and will continue to comply with that duty.

10.10 An expert's report must be verified by a Statement of Truth as well as containing the statements required in paragraph 10.9(h) and (j).

10.11 The form of the Statement of Truth is as follows:-

"I confirm that insofar as the facts stated in my report are within my own knowledge I have made clear which they are and I believe them to be true, and that the opinions I have expressed represent my true and complete professional opinion".

10.12 The instructions referred to in paragraph 10.9(c) are not protected by privilege but cross-examination of the expert on the contents of the instructions will not be allowed unless the Tribunal permits it (or unless the party who gave the instructions consents to it). Before it gives permission the Tribunal must be satisfied that there are reasonable grounds to consider that the statement in the report or the substance of the instructions is inaccurate or incomplete. If the Tribunal is so satisfied, it will allow the cross-examination where it appears to be in the interests of justice to do so.

10.13 In this Practice Direction:-

"appellant" means the party who is or was the appellant before the First-tier Tribunal; and

"respondent" means the party who is or was the respondent before the First-tier Tribunal.

11 Citation of unreported determinations

11.1 A determination of the Tribunal which has not been reported may not be cited in proceedings before the Tribunal unless:-

(a) the person who is or was the appellant before the First-tier Tribunal, or a member of that person's family, was a party to the proceedings in which the previous determination was issued; or

(b) the Tribunal gives permission.

11.2 An application for permission to cite a determination which has not been reported must:-

(a) include a full transcript of the determination;

(b) identify the proposition for which the determination is to be cited; and

(c) certify that the proposition is not to be found in any reported determination of the Tribunal, the IAT or the AIT and had not been superseded by the decision of a higher authority.

11.3 Permission under paragraph 11.1 will be given only where the Tribunal considers that it would be materially assisted by citation of the determination, as distinct from the adoption in argument of the reasoning to be found in the determination. Such instances are likely to be rare; in particular, in the case of determinations which were unreportable (see Practice Statement 11 (reporting of determinations)). It should be emphasised that the Tribunal will not exclude good arguments from consideration but it will be rare for such an argument to be capable of being made only by reference to an unreported determination.

11.4 The provisions of paragraph 11.1 to 11.3 apply to unreported and unreportable determinations of the AIT, the IAT and adjudicators, as those provisions apply respectively to unreported and unreportable determinations of the Tribunal.

11.5 A party citing a determination of the IAT bearing a neutral citation number prior to [2003] (including all series of "bracket numbers") must be in a position to certify that the matter or proposition for which the determination is cited has not been the subject of more recent, reported, determinations of the IAT, the AIT or the Tribunal.

11.6 In this Practice Direction and Practice Direction 12, "determination" includes any decision of the AIT or the Tribunal.

12 Starred and Country Guidance determinations

12.1 Reported determinations of the Tribunal, the AIT and the IAT which are "starred" shall be treated by the Tribunal as authoritative in respect of the matter to which the "starring" relates, unless inconsistent with other authority that is binding on the Tribunal.

12.2 A reported determination of the Tribunal, the AIT or the IAT bearing the letters "CG" shall be treated as an authoritative finding on the country guidance issue identified in the determination, based upon the evidence before the members of the Tribunal, the AIT or the IAT that determine the appeal. As a result, unless it has been expressly superseded or replaced by any later "CG" determination, or is inconsistent with other authority that is binding on the Tribunal, such a country guidance case is authoritative in any subsequent appeal, so far as that appeal:-

(a) relates to the country guidance issue in question; and

(b) depends upon the same or similar evidence.

12.3 A list of current CG cases will be maintained on the Tribunal's website. Any representative of a party to an appeal concerning a particular country will be expected to be conversant with the current "CG" determinations relating to that country.

12.4 Because of the principle that like cases should be treated in like manner, any failure to follow a clear, apparently applicable country guidance case or to show why it does not apply to the case in question is likely to be regarded as grounds for appeal on a point of law.

13 Bail applications

13.1 An application for bail must if practicable be listed for hearing within three working days of receipt by the Tribunal of the notice of application.

13.2 Any such notice which is received by the Tribunal after 3.30p.m. on a particular day will be treated for the purposes of this paragraph as if it were received on the next business day.

13.3 An Upper Tribunal judge may exercise bail jurisdiction under the Immigration Act 1971 by reason of being also a First-tier judge.

13.4 Notwithstanding paragraph 13.3, it will usually be appropriate for a bail application to be made to an Upper Tribunal judge only where the appeal in question is being heard by the Upper Tribunal, or where a hearing before the Upper Tribunal is imminent. In case of doubt, a potential applicant should consult the bails section of the First-tier Tribunal.

14 This Practice Direction is made by the Senior President of Tribunals with the agreement of the Lord Chancellor. It is made in the exercise of powers conferred by the Tribunals, Courts and Enforcement Act 2007.

Annex 2

PRACTICE STATEMENTS (IMMIGRATION AND ASYLUM CHAMBERS OF THE FIRST-TIER TRIBUNAL AND THE UPPER TRIBUNAL)

10 February 2010, Senior President of Tribunals

PART 1 PRELIMINARY

1. Interpretation, etc.

1.1 In these Practice Statements:

"the 2007 Act" means the Tribunals, Courts and Enforcement Act 2007;

"the 2008 Order" means the First-tier Tribunal and Upper Tribunal (Composition of Tribunal) Order 2008;

"Chamber President" means the President of the Immigration and Asylum Chamber of the First-tier Tribunal or of the Upper Tribunal, as the case may be;

"CMR hearing" means a case management review hearing;

"First-tier rule", followed by a number, means the rule bearing that number in the Asylum and Immigration Tribunal (Procedure) Rules 2005;

"First-tier judge" means a judge of the First-tier Tribunal;

"other member" means a person who, immediately before the repeal by the Transfer of Functions Order of section 5(2)(d) of the 2007 Act, was a member of the Upper Tribunal by reason of that enactment;

"Practice Directions" means the Practice Directions - Immigration and Asylum Chambers of the First-tier Tribunal and the Upper Tribunal (dated 10 February 2010); and "Practice Direction", followed by a number, means the Direction bearing that number in the Practice Directions;

"Senior President" means the Senior President of Tribunals;

"Transfer of Functions Order" means the Transfer of Functions of the Asylum and Immigration Tribunal Order 2010 (SI/2010/21);

"The Tribunal" means the Immigration and Asylum Chamber of the First-tier Tribunal or of the Upper Tribunal, as the case may be;

"Upper Tribunal judge" means a judge of the Upper Tribunal;

"UT Rules" means the Tribunal Procedure (Upper Tribunal) Rules 2008; and "UT rule", followed by a number, means the rule bearing that number in the UT Rules.

1.2 Other expressions used in these Practice Statements have the same meanings as in the 2007 Act.

1.3 Any reference in these Practice Statements to an enactment is a reference to that enactment as amended by or under any other enactment.

1.4 These Practice Statements come into force on 15 February 2010.

1.5 These Practice Statements apply, as appropriate, in relation to transitional cases to which Schedule 4 to the Transfer of Functions Order applies; and references to the First-tier Tribunal and the Upper Tribunal shall be construed accordingly.

PART 2 PRACTICE STATEMENTS FOR THE IMMIGRATION AND ASYLUM CHAMBER OF THE FIRST-TIER TRIBUNAL

(for paragraph 2 see **Constitution and composition of the First-tier Tribunal**)

3 Where the Tribunal may not accept a notice of appeal

3.1 First-tier rule 9 (where the Tribunal may not accept a notice of appeal) imposes a duty on the Tribunal not to accept an invalid notice of appeal (in the circumstances described in rule 9(1A)) and to serve notice to this effect on the person who gave the notice of appeal and on the respondent.

3.2 The Tribunal will scrutinise a notice of appeal as soon as practicable after it has been given. First-tier rule 9 makes no provision for the issue of validity to be determined by means of a hearing or by reference to any representations of the parties.

3.3 Once the Tribunal has served the notice described in paragraph 3.1, First-tier rule 9 provides that the Tribunal must take no further action in relation to the notice of appeal. The decision under First-tier rule 9 is, accordingly, a procedural or preliminary decision.

3.4 The fact that a hearing date may have been given to the parties does not mean that the appeal must be treated as valid. Accordingly, if at a hearing (including a CMR hearing) it transpires that the notice of appeal does not relate to a decision against which there is, in the circumstances, an exercisable right of appeal, the Tribunal must so find, but it will do so in the form of a determination, rather than by means of a notice under First-tier rule 9.

4 Review of decision of First-tier Tribunal

4.1 On an application to the First-tier Tribunal for permission to appeal under section 11 of the 2007 Act (right to appeal to Upper Tribunal) on a point of law arising from a decision, the First-tier Tribunal may review that decision pursuant to First-tier rule 26, only if it is satisfied that there was an error of law in that decision.

4.2 Following such a review, the First-tier Tribunal may (subject to section 9(10)) set the decision aside under section 9(4)(c) and re-decide the matter concerned under section 9(5)(a). The First-tier Tribunal is, however, likely to adopt this course only if it is satisfied that:-

(a) the effect of any error of law has been to deprive a party before the First-tier Tribunal of a fair hearing or other opportunity for that party's case to be put to and considered by the First-tier Tribunal; or

(b) there are highly compelling reasons why the matter should be re-decided by the First-tier Tribunal. (Such reasons are likely to be rare.)

4.3 Nothing in this Practice Statement affects the operation of First-tier rule 60 (correction of orders and determinations).

5 Record of proceedings

5.1 The Tribunal shall keep a record of proceedings of any hearing and attach that record to the Tribunal's case file.

PART 3 PRACTICE STATEMENTS FOR THE IMMIGRATION AND ASYLUM CHAMBER OF THE UPPER TRIBUNAL

(for paragraph 6 see **Constitution and composition of the Upper Tribunal**)

7 Disposal of appeals in Upper Tribunal

7.1 Where under section 12(1) of the 2007 Act (proceedings on appeal to the Upper Tribunal) the Upper Tribunal finds that the making of the decision concerned involved the making of an error on a point of law, the Upper Tribunal may set aside the decision and, if it does so, must either remit the case to the First-tier Tribunal under section 12(2)(b)(i) or proceed (in accordance with relevant Practice Directions) to re-make the decision under section 12(2)(b)(ii).

7.2 The Upper Tribunal is likely on each such occasion to proceed to re-make the decision, instead of remitting the case to the First-tier Tribunal, unless the Upper Tribunal is satisfied that:-

(a) the effect of the error has been to deprive a party before the First-tier Tribunal of a fair hearing or other opportunity for that party's case to be put to and considered by the First-tier Tribunal; or

(b) there are highly compelling reasons why the decision should not be re-made by the Upper Tribunal. (Such reasons are likely to be rare.)

PART 4 PRACTICE STATEMENTS FOR THE IMMIGRATION AND ASYLUM CHAMBERS OF THE FIRST-TIER TRIBUNAL AND THE UPPER TRIBUNAL

8 Presiding member

8.1 Where more than one member of the Tribunal is to decide a matter, the presiding member for the purposes of article 7 of the 2008 Order and this Practice Statement is:-

(a) the judge; or

(b) the senior judge, where the Tribunal contains more than one judge.

9 Transfer of proceedings

9.1 Where:-

(a) the Tribunal ("the original Tribunal") has started to hear an appeal but has not completed the hearing or given its determination; and

(b) the Chamber President decides that it is not practicable for the original Tribunal to complete the hearing or give its determination without undue delay, the Chamber President may direct the appeal to be heard by a differently constituted Tribunal ("the new Tribunal").

9.2 Where an appeal has been transferred under paragraph 9.1:-

(a) any documents sent to or given by the original Tribunal shall be deemed to have been sent to or given by the new Tribunal; and

(b) the new Tribunal will deal with the appeal as if it had been commenced before it.

9.3 Without prejudice to paragraph 9.1, the Chamber President may transfer proceedings in the circumstances described in Practice Direction 3 (procedure on appeal); and paragraph 9.2(a) shall apply in the case of such a transfer as it applies in the case of a transfer under paragraph 9.1.

10 Format etc of determinations

10.1 In order to ensure consistency in the formatting of determinations, every determination of the Tribunal must:-

(a) state in the heading whether the appeal is being determined following a hearing or without a hearing;

(b) be laid out in sequentially numbered paragraphs; and

(c) be signed and dated at its end or employ such electronic or other methods as the Senior President or the Chamber President may approve for signifying that the determination is finalised.

10.2 Since Article 8 of the 2008 Order provides that the decision of the majority is the decision of the Tribunal (and that the presiding member has a casting vote), where the jurisdiction of the Tribunal is exercised by more than one member the resulting determination or other decision will not express any dissenting view or indicate that it is that of a majority.

11 Reporting of determinations

11.1 This Practice Statement is to be read in conjunction with Practice Direction 11 (citation of unreported determinations) and Practice Statement – Form of decisions and neutral citation First-tier Tribunal and Upper Tribunal on or after 3 November 2008 (31 October 2008).

11.2 The decision whether to report a determination is that of the Tribunal and it is not perceived to be an issue in which the parties to the appeal have an interest.

11.3 A determination is reportable only if it follows a hearing or other consideration where the jurisdiction of the Tribunal was exercised by the Senior President, the Chamber President or an Upper Tribunal judge (whether or not sitting alone and, in the case of an Upper Tribunal judge, whether sitting as such or as a First-tier judge).

11.4 A determination which is reportable but not in fact reported will be anonymised (where appropriate), treated as an unreported determination for the purposes of the Tribunal's website and entered as such on that website.

11.5 Determinations not falling within paragraph 11.3 are unreportable. They will be sent to the parties (in accordance with the relevant Procedure Rules) but will not be published or archived in publicly accessible form.

11.6 The Tribunal's website is the only official source of the determinations of the Tribunal.

11.7 In this Practice Statement:-

"determination" includes any decision of the Tribunal; and

"Upper Tribunal judge" does not include a deputy judge of the Upper Tribunal.

Annex 3

PRACTICE DIRECTION (FIRST-TIER TRIBUNAL: MENTAL HEALTH CASES)

30 October 2008, Senior President of Tribunals

1. This Practice Direction applies to a "mental health case" as defined in Rule 1(3) the Tribunal Procedure (First-tier Tribunal) (Health, Education and Social Care Chamber) Rules 2008 ("the 2008 Rules").

2. For the purposes of this Practice Direction, a patient is an "in-patient" if at the time of the application or referral he is receiving in-patient treatment for mental disorder, even if it is being given informally or under an application, order or direction other than that to which the Tribunal application or reference relates.

CONTENTS OF STATEMENTS FROM THE RESPONSIBLE AUTHORITY AND SECRETARY OF STATE

3. The responsible authority must send a statement to the Tribunal and, in the case of a restricted patient other than a conditionally discharged patient, to the Secretary of State, so that it is received by the Tribunal as soon as is practicable and in any event within three weeks after the responsible authority received a copy of the application or reference.

4. If the patient is a conditionally discharged patient, the Secretary of State must send or deliver a statement to the Tribunal so that it is received by the Tribunal as soon as practicable, and in any event within 6 weeks after the Secretary of State received a copy of the application or a request from the Tribunal.

5. If the patient is neither a conditionally discharged patient, nor a community patient subject to supervised community treatment, nor a patient subject (or to be subject) to after-care under supervision, the statement to the Tribunal must contain the information, documents and reports specified in paragraphs 8(a) to (e) below.

6. If the patient is a conditionally discharged patient, the statement to the Tribunal must, where possible, contain the reports specified in paragraphs 8(c) and (d) below.

7. If the patient is a community patient subject to supervised community treatment the statement to the Tribunal must contain the reports specified in paragraph 8(f) below.

8. The information, documents and reports referred to above are:

   a. the information about the patient set out at Section B below;

   b. the documents concerning the patient set out at Section C below;

   c. the clinician's report set out at Section D below;

   d. the social circumstances report set out at Section E below;

   e. if the patient is an in-patient, the nursing report set out at Section F below;

f. the reports set out in Section H below.

9. Where the patient is a restricted patient, the Secretary of State must send to the Tribunal as soon as practicable and in any event within 3 weeks after the Secretary of State received the responsible authority's statement (within 2 weeks in proceedings under section 75(1) of the Mental Health Act 1983), a statement containing the information set out at Section G below.

10. If the patient is subject (or to be subject) to after-care under supervision, the statement must include the information, documents and reports specified in the Annex to this Practice Direction.

SECTION B. INFORMATION ABOUT THE PATIENT

11. The statement provided to the Tribunal must, in so far as it is within the knowledge of the responsible authority, include the following information:

a. the patient's full name (and any alternative names used in his patient records);

b. the patient's date of birth, age and usual place of residence;

c. the patient's first language and, if it is not English, whether an interpreter is required, and if so in which language;

d. if the patient is deaf whether the patient will require the services of a British Sign Language interpreter, or a Relay Interpreter;

e. the date of admission or transfer of the patient to the hospital in which the patient is detained or liable to be detained, or of the reception of the patient into guardianship, together with details of the application, order or direction that constitutes the original authority for the detention or guardianship of the patient, including the Act of Parliament and the section of that Act by reference to which detention was authorised and details of any subsequent renewal of or change in the authority for detention;

f. details as applicable of the hospital at which the patient is detained or liable to be detained, or the place where the patient is living if received into guardianship;

g. details of any transfers under section 19 or section 123 of the Mental Health Act 1983 since the application, order or direction was made;

h. where the patient is detained or liable to be detained in an independent hospital, details of any NHS body that funds or will fund the placement;

i. where relevant, the name and address of the local social services authority and NHS body having the duty under section 117 of the Mental Health Act 1983 to provide after-care services for the patient (or which would have it were the patient to leave hospital);

j. the name of the patient's responsible clinician and the period which the patient has spent under the care of that clinician;

k. the name of any care co-ordinator appointed for the patient;

l. except in the case of a restricted patient, the name and address of the patient's nearest relative or of the person exercising that function, and whether the patient has requested that this person is not consulted or kept informed about their care or treatment;

m. the name and address of any person who plays a significant part in the care of the patient but who is not professionally concerned with it;

n. where the patient is subject to the guardianship of a private guardian, the name and address of that guardian;

o. the name and address of any deputy or attorney appointed under the Mental Capacity Act 2005;

p. details of any registered lasting power of attorney made by the patient that confers authority to make decisions about his personal welfare, and the donee(s) appointed by him;

q. details of any registered lasting or enduring power of attorney made by the patient that confers authority to make decisions about his property and affairs, and the donee(s) appointed by him; and

r. details of any existing advance decisions to refuse treatment for mental disorder made by the patient.

SECTION C. DOCUMENTS CONCERNING THE PATIENT

12. If the Tribunal so directs, copies of the following documents must be included in the statement provided to the Tribunal if they are within the possession of the responsible authority (otherwise they must be made available to the Tribunal if requested at any other time by the Tribunal):

a. the application, order or direction that constitutes the original authority for the patient's detention or guardianship under the Mental Health Act 1983, together with all supporting recommendations, reports and records made in relation to it under the Mental Health (Hospital, Guardianship and Treatment) Regulations 2008;

b. a copy of every Tribunal decision, and the reasons given, since the application, order or direction being reviewed was made or accepted; and

c. where the patient is liable to be detained for treatment under section 3 of the Mental Health Act 1983, a copy of any application for admission for assessment that was in force immediately prior to the making of the section 3 application.

SECTION D. CLINICIAN'S REPORT

13. The statement provided to the Tribunal must include an up-to-date clinical report prepared for the Tribunal.

14. Unless it is not reasonably practicable, the report must be written or counter-signed by the patient's responsible clinician.

15. This report must describe the patient's relevant medical history, to include:

a. full details of the patient's mental state, behaviour and treatment for mental disorder;

b. in so far as it is within the knowledge of the person writing the report a statement as to whether the patient has ever neglected or harmed himself, or has ever harmed other persons or threatened them with harm, at a time when he was mentally disordered, together with details of any neglect, harm or threats of harm;

c. an assessment of the extent to which the patient or other persons would be likely to be at risk if the patient is discharged by the Tribunal, and how any such risks could best be managed;

d. an assessment of the patient's strengths and any other positive factors that the Tribunal should be aware of in coming to a view on whether he should be discharged; and

e. if appropriate, the reasons why the patient might be treated in the community without continued detention in hospital, but should remain subject to recall on supervised community treatment.

SECTION E. SOCIAL CIRCUMSTANCES REPORT

16. The statement provided to the Tribunal must, include an up-to-date social circumstances report prepared for the Tribunal.

17. This report must include the following information:

a. the patient's home and family circumstances;

b. in so far as it is practicable, and except in restricted cases, a summary of the views of the patient's nearest relative, unless (having consulted the patient) the person compiling the report thinks it would be inappropriate to consult the nearest relative;

c. in so far as it is practicable, the views of any person who plays a substantial part in the care of the patient but is not professionally concerned with it;

d. the views of the patient, including his concerns, hopes and beliefs in relation to the Tribunal proceedings and their outcome;

e. the opportunities for employment and the housing facilities available to the patient;

f. what (if any) community support is or will be made available to the patient and its effectiveness, if the patient is discharged from hospital;

g. the patient's financial circumstances (including his entitlement to benefits);

h. an assessment of the patient's strengths and any other positive factors that the Tribunal should be aware of in coming to a view on whether he should be discharged; and

i. an assessment of the extent to which the patient or other persons would be likely to be at risk if the patient is discharged by the Tribunal, and how any such risks could best be managed.

SECTION F. IN-PATIENT NURSING REPORT

18. This report must include in relation to the patient's current in-patient episode, full details of the following:

a. the patient's understanding of and willingness to accept the current treatment for mental disorder provided or offered;

b. the level of observation to which the patient is subject;

c. any occasions on which the patient has been secluded or restrained, including the reasons why seclusion or restraint was considered to be necessary;

d. any occasions on which the patient has been absent without leave whilst liable to be detained, or occasions when he has failed to return when required, after being granted leave of absence; and

e. any incidents where the patient has harmed himself or others, or has threatened other persons with violence.

19. A copy of the patient's current nursing plan must be appended to the report.

SECTION G. THE SECRETARY OF STATE'S STATEMENT (RESTRICTED PATIENTS ONLY)

20. In cases involving a restricted patient, the Secretary of State must provide a statement to the Tribunal containing any written comments he wishes to make upon the statement he has received from the responsible authority, together with any further information relevant to the application as may be available to him.

21. In addition, the Secretary of State must provide to the Tribunal the following further information:

a. a summary of the offence or alleged offence that resulted in the patient being detained in hospital subject to a restriction order or, in the case of a patient subject to a restriction or limitation direction, that resulted in him being remanded in custody, kept in custody or sentenced to imprisonment;

b. a record of any other criminal convictions or findings recorded against the patient;

c. full details of the history of the patient's liability to detention under the Mental Health Act 1983 since the restrictions were imposed.

SECTION H. PATIENTS RECEIVING SUPERVISED COMMUNITY TREATMENT (SCT)

Clinical Reports

22. The statement provided to the Tribunal must include an up-to-date clinical report prepared for the Tribunal.

23. Unless it is not reasonably practicable to do so, the report must be written or counter-signed by the patient's responsible clinician.

24. This report must include:

a. details of the original authority for the patient's supervised community treatment under the Mental Health Act 1983;

b. the name of the patient's responsible clinician and the length of time the patient has been under their care;

c. full details of the patient's mental state, behaviour and treatment for mental disorder, and relevant medical history;

d. in so far as it is within the knowledge of the person writing the report, a statement as to whether the patient has ever neglected or harmed himself, or has ever harmed other persons or threatened them with harm, at a time when he was mentally disordered, together with details of any neglect, harm or threats of harm;

e. an assessment of the extent to which the patient or other persons would be likely to be at risk if the patient is discharged by the Tribunal, and how any such risks could best be managed;

f. an assessment of the patient's strengths and any other positive factors that the Tribunal should be aware of in coming to a view on whether he should be discharged;

g. the reasons why the patient can be treated as a community patient without continued detention in hospital, and why it is necessary that the responsible clinician should be able to exercise the power under section 17E(1) of the Mental Health Act 1983 to recall the patient to hospital; and

h. details of any specific conditions in force regarding the patient under section 17B of the Mental Health Act 1983.

Social Circumstances Report

25. The statement provided to the Tribunal must include an up-to-date social circumstances report prepared for the Tribunal.

26. This report must include the following information:

a. the patient's home and family circumstances;

b. in so far as it is practicable a summary of the views of the patient's nearest relative, unless (having consulted the patient) the person compiling the report thinks it would be inappropriate to consult the nearest relative;

c. the views of any person who plays a significant part in the care of the patient but is not professionally concerned with it;

d. the views of the patient, including his concerns, hopes and beliefs in relation to the Tribunal;

e. the opportunities for employment, or for occupation and the housing facilities available to the patient;

f. the effectiveness of the community support available to the patient; or the likely effectiveness of the community support which would be available to the patient if discharged from supervised community treatment;

g. details of the patient's financial circumstances (including his entitlement to benefits);

h. an assessment of the patient's strengths and any other positive factors that the Tribunal should be aware of in coming to a view on whether he should be discharged;

i. an account of the patient's progress while a community patient, and any conditions or requirements to which he is subject under the community treatment order, and details of any behaviour that has put him or others at risk of harm; and

j. an assessment of the extent to which the patient or other persons would be likely to be at risk if the patient remains a community patient.

ANNEX: PATIENTS WHO ARE, OR WILL BE, SUBJECT TO AFTER-CARE UNDER SUPERVISION

27. The statement provided to the Tribunal must include;

    a. the details of the after-care services being (or to be) provided under section 117 of the Mental Health Act 1983;

    b. details of any requirements imposed (or to be imposed) on the patient under section 25D of the Mental Health Act 1983;

    c. the information about the patient specified in Section I below;

    d. the documents concerning the patient specified in Section J below;

    e. the reports specified in Section K below.

SECTION I. INFORMATION ABOUT THE PATIENT

28. The statement provided to the Tribunal must include, in so far as it is within the knowledge of the responsible authority, the following information;

    a. the patient's full name, date of birth, age and address;

    b. the date of the acceptance of the supervision application in respect of the patient;

    c. any reclassification of the form of mental disorder from which the patient is recorded as suffering in the supervision application reported in accordance with section 25F(1) of the Mental Health Act 1983;

    d. the name and address of the person who is (or is to be) the patient's responsible clinician and the period (if any) during which he has been in charge of the patient's medical treatment;

    e. the name and address of the person who is (or is to be) the patient's supervisor;

    f. where a registered medical practitioner other than the patient's responsible clinician is or has recently been largely concerned in the treatment of the patient, details of the name and address of that practitioner and the period which the patient has spent under his care;

    g. the name and address of any place where the patient (if he has been discharged) is receiving medical treatment;

    h. the name and address of the hospital where the patient was detained or liable to be detained when the supervision application was made;

    i. the dates of any previous tribunal hearings in relation to the patient since he became subject to after-care under supervision, the decisions reached at such hearings and the reasons given;

    j. details of any proceedings in the Court of Protection and of any receivership order made in respect of the patient;

    k. the name and address of the patient's nearest relative or of any other person who is exercising that function;

    l. the name and address of any other person who takes a close interest in the patient.

SECTION J. DOCUMENTS CONCERNING THE PATIENT

29. Copies of the following documents must be made available to the Tribunal if they are within the possession of the responsible authority;

    a. the original supervision application;

    b. any report furnished under section 25G(3)(b) of the Mental Health Act 1983 in relation to renewal of the supervision application;

    c. any record of modification of the after-care services provided.

SECTION K. REPORTS

Clinical report

30. The statement provided to the Tribunal must include an up-to-date clinician report prepared for the Tribunal.

31. Unless it is not reasonable practicable, the report must be written or countersigned by the patients responsible clinician.

32. This report must describe the patient's relevant medical history and contain a full report on the patient's mental condition.

Supervisor's Report

33. Where the patient is subject to after-care under supervision the statement provided to the Tribunal must include an up-to-date report prepared for the Tribunal by the patient's supervisor.

34. This report must include the following information:

    a. the patient's home and family circumstances, including the attitude of the patient's nearest relative or the person so acting and the attitude of any person who plays a substantial part in the care of the patient but is not professionally concerned with any of the after-care services provided to the patient;

    b. his progress in the community whilst subject to after-care under supervision including an assessment of the effectiveness of that supervision.

Social Circumstances Report

35. Where the patient has not yet left hospital the statement provided to the Tribunal must include an up-to-date social circumstances report prepared for the Tribunal.

36. This report must include the following information:

    a. the patient's home and family circumstances, including the attitude of the patient's nearest relative or the person so acting;

    b. the opportunities for employment or occupation and the housing facilities which would be available to the patient upon his discharge from hospital;

    c. the availability of community support and relevant medical facilities;

    d. the financial circumstances of the patient.

37. This Practice Direction is made by the Senior President of tribunals with the agreement of the Lord Chancellor. It is made in the exercise of powers conferred by the Tribunals, Courts and Enforcement Act 2007.

46 Immigration and Asylum Chamber (Upper Tribunal)

JURISDICTION OF THE IMMIGRATION AND ASYLUM CHAMBER

46.1 The Immigration and Asylum Chamber of the Upper Tribunal is presided over by a Chamber President and is under the ultimate supervision of the Senior President (see **Senior President**). It has one main type of jurisdiction: it hears appeals against decisions of the Immigration and Asylum Chamber of the First-tier Tribunal and cases which have been referred to the Upper Tribunal from the Immigration and Asylum Chamber of the First-tier Tribunal ('FTTIAC'). These categories are straightforward and encompass proceedings which the First-tier Tribunal decides to refer to the Upper Tribunal because of their complexity, either of law or of fact.

46.2 The jurisdiction of the Chamber is governed by the First-tier Tribunal and Upper Tribunal (Chambers) Order 2008, SI 2008/2684 (as amended), art 9A.

VENUE

46.3 The Immigration and Asylum Chamber is based in London but can hear cases in venues around the country if necessary.

PROCEDURE

46.4 The Immigration and Asylum Chamber is governed by the ordinary Upper Tribunal rules of procedure. These are the Tribunal Procedure (Upper Tribunal) Rules 2008, SI 2008/2684 (as amended) ('Upper Tribunal Rules') (see **Upper Tribunal procedural rules**).

46.5 There are a number of specific provisions in the Upper Tribunal Rules which deal with immigration and asylum appeals. These largely replicate the procedural provisions of the FTTIAC (see **Immigration and Asylum Chamber (First-tier Tribunal) procedural rules**) and provide equivalent protections in the Upper Tribunal. Those provisions will not be set out here, but are described in the various entries of this Handbook.

47 Immigration Services Cases

LEGISLATIVE BACKGROUND

47.1 The Immigration Services Commissioner and the Immigration Services Tribunal ('IST') was created by Part V of the Immigration and Asylum Act 1999. The Commissioner was to regulate the provision of immigration advice and services, which only qualified persons are permitted to provide (Immigration and Asylum Act 1999, s 84).

47.2 A qualified person must be registered with the Commissioner, be authorised to practice in the law under one of the professional regulatory bodies (such as the Law Society or the Bar Council), be an equivalent qualified lawyer in another EEA state, or be working for or under such a person (Immigration and Asylum Act 1999, s 84(2)). The Commissioner keeps and maintains a register of those persons registered with the Commissioner, or persons who are exempt from the requirements (Immigration and Asylum Act 1999, s 85).

47.3 The purpose of the Commissioner is to ensure that those who provide immigration advice and services (Immigration and Asylum Act 1999, s 83(5)):

- are fit and competent to do so;
- act in the best interests of their clients;
- do not knowingly mislead any court, tribunal or adjudicator in the United Kingdom;
- do not seek to abuse any procedure operating in the United Kingdom in connection with immigration or asylum (including any appellate or other judicial procedure);
- do not advise any person to do something which would amount to such an abuse.

47.4 Users of the immigration system are encouraged to complain to the Commissioner about poor advice or inadequate service, failure to take proper instructions, making false claims of success, charging unreasonable fees and/or charging for work not done, encouraging the making of false or misleading statements, missing deadlines or failing to appear in court. The Commissioner will investigate complaints made against persons registered with the Commissioner, and complaints against solicitors or barristers will be investigated by the regulatory bodies of the professions.

47.5 The following types of appeal from decisions of the Commissioner were heard by the IST:

- *Refusal to register.* A decision to refuse an application by a person or body to be registered as a qualified person to provide immigration advice or immigration services under the Immigration and Asylum Act 1999, Sch 6, para 1;
- *Withdrawal of exemption.* A decision to withdraw a certificate of exemption given under the Immigration and Asylum Act 1999, s 84(4);

- *Limited registration.* A decision to register a qualified person with limited effect under the Immigration and Asylum Act 1999, Sch 6, para 2(2);
- *Refusal to continue registration.* A decision to refuse an application for continued registration or cancel a registration made under the Immigration and Asylum Act 1999, Sch 6, para 3;
- *Registration variation.* A decision to vary a registration made under the Immigration and Asylum Act 1999, Sch 6, para 3(6);
- *Registration variation.* A decision to vary a registration made under the Immigration and Asylum Act 1999 (as amended by the Nationality, Immigration and Asylum Act 2002, s 140), Sch 6, para 3A; or
- Disciplinary charges laid by the Commissioner under paragraph 9(1)(e) of Schedule 5 to the Immigration and Asylum Act 1999.

47.6 The IST came into being on 30 October 2000 and its procedure was governed by The Immigration Services Tribunal Rules 2000, SI 2000/2739 (as amended by SI 2002/1716).

TRANSFER OF JURISDICTION

47.7 The jurisdiction of the IST is now encompassed by the General Regulatory Chamber, with effect from 18 January 2010: The Transfer of Tribunal Functions Order 2010, SI 2010/22, art 2(1)(d). The First-tier Tribunal (Immigration Services) will normally sit in Victory House in London, but can sit at other venues if necessary.

47.8 The procedure is governed by the Tribunal Procedure (First-tier Tribunal) (General Regulatory Chamber) Rules 2009, SI 2009/1976 (the 'GRC Rules') as amended. For details of the rules see **General Regulatory Chamber procedural rules**.

47.9 The only special provision for immigration services cases is found in the GRC Rules, r 19A(2) which provides that the GRC may direct that while the appeal is pending the relevant decision shall have no or only limited effect. If such a direction is made the Tribunal must consider any application by the Commissioner to vary or cancel the direction (GRC Rules, r 19A(3)). The Tribunal has the power to vary or cancel any interim direction made by the Commissioner (GRC Rules, r 19A(4)). This power will only be necessary where the appeal, or the hearing of the application, is brought outside of the time limit for the appeal (28 days, as it was in the IST). This is because a decision of the Commissioner is not to have effect while the period within which an appeal may be brought against the decision is running (Immigration and Asylum Act 1999, s 87(3A) as amended by the 2010 Order).

47.10 The IST Rules are not drastically different from the GRC Rules, but users are recommended to consult the various relevant sections of this Handbook to ensure that time limits and other procedural requirements are met.

47.11 Appeals from the GRC will lie to the Administrative Appeals Chamber of the Upper Tribunal on a point of law (see **Appeals from the First-tier Tribunal** and **Administrative Appeals Chamber**).

48 Information Rights Cases

LEGISLATIVE BACKGROUND

48.1 Information rights cases cover a wider area than simply freedom of information. Three pieces of legislation create relevant appeal rights: the Data Protection Act 1998 ('DPA 1998'), the Freedom of Information Act 2000 ('FOIA 2000'), and the Environmental Information Regulations 2004, SI 2004/3391 ('EIR'). Appeal rights exist in the following types of information rights cases:

- An appeal to quash a national security certificate issued by a Minister under DPA 1998, s 28(2) (DPA 1998, s 28(4));
- An appeal for a determination that a national security certificate does not relate to particular personal data (DPA 1998, s 28(6));
- An appeal against an enforcement notice, an information notice, or a special information notice served by the Information Commissioner's Office ('ICO') (DPA 1998, s 48(1));
- An appeal against the refusal of the ICO to cancel or vary an enforcement notice (DPA 1998, s 48(2));
- An appeal against a statement of urgency contained in an ICO notice (DPA 1998, s 48(3));
- An appeal by a data controller against an ICO determination under DPA 1998, s 45(1) that particular data is not being processed only for special purposes (DPA 1998, s 48(4));
- An appeal against an ICO decision notice under FOIA 2000, s 50(3)(b) following a complaint that a public authority had failed to deal with a request for information in accordance with Part I of FOIA 2000 (FOIA 2000, s 57(1));
- An appeal by a public authority against an information notice or enforcement notice from the ICO (FOIA 2000, s 57(2));
- An appeal by the ICO or other party whose request has been affected by a Minister's issue of a national security certificate under FOIA 2000, ss 23(2) or 24(3) (FOIA 2000, s 60(1));
- An appeal on the grounds that a national security certificate issued under FOIA 2000, s 24(3) does not apply to the particular information in question as claimed by the public authority holding it (FOIA 2000, s 60(4));
- An appeal against ICO decision notices, information notices and enforcement notices in respect of requests for environmental information (EIR, reg 18);
- An appeal relating to a Ministerial certificate of national security made under EIR,reg 15 (EIR, reg 18(7));
- An appeal against a decision or determination of the ICO made under the Privacy and Electronic Communications (EC Directive) Regulations 2003, SI 2003/2426.

48.2 Originally named the Data Protection Tribunal – established under the Data Protection Act 1984 – the Information Tribunal was the judicial body responsible for almost all information and data-related appeals from decisions of the ICO. The ICO remains the required first port-of-call for information complaints. Procedure in the Information Tribunal was governed by the Information Tribunal (Enforcement Appeals) Rules 2005, SI 2005/14 (as amended by SI 2005/450).

TRANSFER OF JURISDICTION

48.3 The jurisdiction of the Information Tribunal is now mostly encompassed by the General Regulatory Chamber, with effect from 18 January 2010: The Transfer of Tribunal Functions Order 2010, SI 2010/22, art 2(3). However, some cases are heard directly by the Administrative Appeals Chamber of the Upper Tribunal ('AAC'). Tribunal procedure rules are to determine, by art 2(3), which types of cases are assigned to the GRC, and which to the AAC.

48.4 Appeals from the GRC will lie to the Administrative Appeals Chamber of the Upper Tribunal on a point of law (see **Appeals from the First-tier Tribunal** and **Administrative Appeals Chamber**).

48.5 The procedure is governed by the Tribunal Procedure (First-tier Tribunal) (General Regulatory Chamber) Rules 2009, SI 2009/1976 (the 'GRC Rules') as amended. For details of the rules see **General Regulatory Chamber procedural rules**. Proceedings before the Upper Tribunal are governed by the Tribunal Procedure (Upper Tribunal) Rules 2008, SI 2008/2684 ('the Upper Tribunal Rules') as amended (see **Upper Tribunal procedural rules**).

National security certificate cases

48.6 At present the only types of case which are mandatorily transferred from the GRC to the AAC are national security certificate cases arising under an appeal under DPA 1998, s 28 or FOIA 2000, s 60 (including that section as applied and modified by EIR, reg 18). GRC Rules, r 19(1A).

48.7 In a mandatorily transferred national security case, the Upper Tribunal Rules apply. Schedule 2 to the Upper Tribunal Rules sets out the procedure. Within 42 days of receiving a copy of the notice of appeal from the Upper Tribunal, the Minister must send to the Tribunal a copy of the certificate and a response to the notice of appeal (Upper Tribunal Rules, Sch 2, para 3).

48.8 Where the appeal is under DPA 1998, s 28(4) or FOIA 2000, s 60(1) the Minister must set out:

- a summary of the circumstances relating to the issue of the certificate;
- the reason for the issue of the certificate;
- the grounds on which the relevant Minister relies in opposing the appeal; and
- a statement of the evidence on which the relevant Minister relies in support of those grounds (Upper Tribunal Rules, Sch 2, para 4).

48.9 Where the appeal is under DPA 1998, s 28(6) or FOIA 2000, s 60(4) the Minister must set out:

- the extent to which the relevant Minister intends to support or oppose the appeal;
- the grounds on which the relevant Minister relies in supporting or opposing the appeal; and
- a statement of the evidence on which the relevant Minister relies in support of those grounds (Upper Tribunal Rules, Sch 2, para 5).

48.10 The Tribunal will provide a copy of the response to the parties and the ICO, as well as other relevant Ministers, but the responding Minister may object (within the same 42 day time limit) to the response being provided on grounds of national security giving his reasons and a suitably redacted response which can be circulated (Upper Tribunal Rules, Sch 2, paras 6–8). Any step that the Tribunal intends to take must be notified to the Minister first, who may object within 14 days if that step will cause information otherwise exempt to be made public (Upper Tribunal Rules, Sch 2, para 9). A hearing to consider the objection will be held in the absence of the other parties (Upper Tribunal Rules, Sch 2, para 10).

48.11 The Minister is entitled to attend the hearing (Upper Tribunal Rules, r 35(2)) and the AAC will consider whether to hold the hearing in private (Upper Tribunal Rules, r 37(2A)) bearing in mind its obligation not to disclose material contrary to national security (Upper Tribunal Rules, r 14(10)). The Tribunal's reasons for its decision will be communicated to the Minister and the ICO as well (Upper Tribunal Rules, r 39(5)). In the AAC a costs order can be made in a national security case for wasted costs; if a party or representative has acted unreasonably in bringing, defending or conducting the proceedings; against the Minister if a certificate is quashed; and against the losing party where the appeal is against the application of a certificate (Upper Tribunal Rules, r 10(1A)).

Ordinary information rights cases

48.12 By virtue of the GRC Rules, r 19 the First-tier Tribunal may, in its discretion, transfer any other information rights case directly to the AAC, either in whole or only a preliminary issue (GRC Rules, r 19(2)). Such a transfer will ordinarily only be made where there are special features in the case, such as being of considerable public importance or involving complex, sensitive or unusual issues. Either the parties may request a transfer, or the GRC may transfer the case of its own motion, although the parties will ordinarily be invited to make observations on a proposed transfer: see **GRC and AAC Joint Office Note 2 – Discretionary Transfers of Information Rights Appeals.**

48.13 There are some specific provisions for information rights cases in the GRC. Costs will only be awarded against the ICO if the decision, direction or order of the ICO was made unreasonably (GRC Rules, r 10(1)(c)). In an information rights case, GRC Rules, r 18A applies and the Tribunal may make an entry direction requiring the occupier of premises to permit the entry of another person to inspect or examine relevant equipment or materials, which includes methods of personal data storage and deletion. Any direction must specify the date and time of entry and give seven days notice, and it may not require a person to do anything a court could not so order (GRC Rules, r 18(4)–(6)).

48.14 A notice of appeal under DPA 1998, s 28(4) or FOIA, s 60(1) may be made at any time during the currency of the certificate in question (GRC Rules, r 22(6)(b)), and under DPA 1998, s 28(6) or FOIA 2000, s 60(4) within 28 days of the date on which the claim was made that the certificate applies to the information or data in question (GRC Rules, r 22(6)(c)).

48.15 Practitioners should be aware of the GRC Practice Note entitled *Protection of Confidential Information in Information Rights Appeals before the First-tier Tribunal in the General Regulatory Tribunal on or after 18 January 2010*, 1 February 2010, which contains useful guidance from the GRC on the general principles it will adopt in relation to confidential information.

49 Judicial Review Grounds and Principles

See **Judicial review in the Upper Tribunal**.

INTRODUCTION

49.1 It is beyond the scope of this Handbook to provide a full and complete guide to every aspect and ground of judicial review. Readers should consult specialist books on judicial review for further and more detailed guidance, particularly in respect of the specific type of case in which the challenge arises. Judicial review is a procedure of considerable historic vintage which saw a huge resurgence in the 1960s and 1970s as the courts began to accept the importance of public law matching the boundaries of the administrative State. As the mainstay of the business of the Administrative Court, there is a constant growth of judicial review case law which applies and interprets existing grounds, and which develops the scope and content of administrative law. The application of the ordinary principles of judicial review by the Upper Tribunal will not be straightforward. Users of the Upper Tribunal will usually need some form of legal advice as to how to best present a judicial review challenge which focuses on errors of law and does not slide into the substitution of judgment by the Tribunal. Although it is expected that High Court judges will hear the vast majority of judicial review challenges in the Upper Tribunal that may, in time, change and not all members of the Tribunal judiciary will be as used to the principles applied day in and day out by the Administrative Court. TCEA 2007 will involve an interesting learning process for all.

49.2 There are certain principles of judicial review which guide the application of the various grounds for review. These principles must be considered first. Individual grounds for judicial review will be discussed in the subsequent section, but the application of those grounds can only be sensibly be discussed when the underlying principles of judicial review are understood.

49.3 In this entry, 'the Tribunal' means the Upper Tribunal unless the context makes clear otherwise. It is important to remember that references to the decision-maker will include, for the purposes of the Upper Tribunal, some public authorities (such as the Criminal Injuries Compensation Authority) but also the First-tier Tribunal taking decisions which cannot be appealed. The circumstances in which judicial review in the Upper Tribunal can take place are much more limited than in the Administrative Court (see **Judicial review in the Upper Tribunal**), and 'decision-maker' refers to the body being judicially reviewed in the Tribunal. The subject of a judicial review is usually assumed to be a decision, but it may also be an act or omission, or a provision in secondary legislation (including the procedural rules of the Chambers).

PRINCIPLES OF JUDICIAL REVIEW

49.4 The following principles of judicial review will be discussed below:

- The balance to be struck between protecting individual rights and recognising the importance of good administration;

- Judicial review is not an appeal;
- The respect shown to the primary fact-finder;
- Challenges must be material and genuine;
- The standard of review varies depending on the type of challenge.

This is not an exhaustive list, but it provides an indication of the types of concerns which underpin the exercise of judicial review by the courts and, now, the Upper Tribunal.

Striking a balance

49.5 Public law is about the correction of legal wrongs by public authorities and the protection of the legal rights which belong to persons affected by the decisions of public authorities. However, there is an additional dimension to public law which takes it beyond simply the determination of individual rights in particular cases. Public law is there to regulate the actions of the State, while also recognising that it is in the interests of all those for whom the State acts that the State is not prevented from taking the decisions which need to be taken. This does not permit public authorities to act unlawfully, but the courts recognise that conducting good administration can be difficult and is invariably conducted with finite resources. Those resources will not always be best spent defending judicial review cases.

49.6 Consequently, a balance must be struck between ensuring public authorities act lawfully and within their proper remit and ensuring that administration is not unduly restricted. Control mechanisms exist for the courts to aid good administration. For example, an applicant seeking judicial review must get permission to proceed from the Tribunal (see **Judicial review in the Upper Tribunal**); the challenge must be material and genuine; the Tribunal will show respect for decisions which are outside its usual remit or expertise; relief is at the discretion of the Tribunal; and in cases which come closest to challenging the substance of the decision the Tribunal will adopt a standard of review which provides the decision-maker with leeway and the opportunity to choose between different reasonable responses.

49.7 The balance to be struck between individual rights and good administration is often difficult, and often implicit rather than explicit. Recognising that balancing act is essential to understanding the role of the courts and the Upper Tribunal in judicial review cases.

Review not appeal

49.8 The classic formula adopted by the courts is that 'judicial review is quite different from an appeal. It is concerned with the legality rather than the merits of the decision with the jurisdiction of the decision-maker and the fairness of the decision-making process rather than whether the decision was correct': *Kemper Reinsurance Company v Minister of Finance* [2000] 1 AC 1, PC, 14. This formulation can be unhelpful. An appeal in the Upper Tribunal, or in the Court of Appeal from the Upper Tribunal, is an appeal on a point of law only, and that is actually not very different from judicial review. What the usual formula of 'review not appeal' is aimed at is the type of appeal which involves a rehearing of the facts, or the reconsideration of the factual findings of the lower court or tribunal. The formulation of the Privy Council which focuses on legality rather than merits is generally correct – and commonly used: *R v Secretary of State for Education and Employment ex p M* [1996] ELR 162, 205 per Simon Brown LJ – but can be unhelpful when the case is one of substantive review, where the Tribunal will consider the merits of the decision adopted in a limited manner.

49.9 Probably the most accurate formulation is that the courts on a judicial review are concerned not to substitute their own judgment for that of the decision-maker. This is true even in substantive review cases, where the court may find that the decision adopted fell outside the bounds of reasonable responses the decision-maker could make, but does not go on to order that the decision-maker retake the decision to produce one specific result (although, of course, if there were only two choices and one is held unlawful that is the practical outcome). The Tribunal will be reluctant to substitute its own judgment for that of the primary decision-maker because it has not been allocated that function by Parliament. Although the Upper Tribunal contains specialist judges it is not directly responsible for balancing the different administrative concerns with which Parliament has tasked a particular decision-maker. The courts are rightly reluctant to override that legislative choice. Judicial review 'is not intended to take away from those authorities the powers and discretions properly vested in them by law and to substitute the courts as the bodies making the decisions. It is intended to see that the relevant authorities use their powers in a proper manner': *R v Chief Constable of North Wales Police ex p Evans* [1982] 1 WLR 1155, 1160 per Lord Hailsham LC.

Respect to fact-finder

49.10 A particularly important example of the 'review not appeal' or no 'substitution of judgment' approach is that the courts and the Tribunal must show real respect for the findings of fact of the initial decision-maker: *R v Hillingdon London Borough Council ex p Puhlhofer* [1986] AC 484, 518 per Lord Brightman. This will be particularly important where the fact-finder is the First-tier Tribunal. Restraint in respect of facts in judicial review challenges is based on two pillars.

49.11 First, as a matter of principle, the decision-maker has been allocated by Parliament, and the courts should be slow to appropriate to themselves that function (see above). Secondly, as a matter of practice, the court or Tribunal conducting the judicial review will not have had the benefit of hearing the witnesses live, or seeing all the evidence in documentary form, or having had the evidence presented to it and challenged in submissions. It would simply not be possible for the Tribunal to reach a different conclusion on the credibility of a witness to, say, the First-tier Tribunal which heard that witness, unless the conclusion drawn was perverse.

49.12 Difficulties may be raised where it is unclear whether an issue is one of fact or law, but these will turn on the particular context (see **Fact and law in Tribunal decisions**).

Material and genuine

49.13 The potential for disruption of the administrative process by judicial review is significant. The courts are consequently alive to the need to ensure that only genuine disputes are aired in judicial review proceedings:

- The error complained of must be material, in that it must have made a difference to the decision reached: *Simplex GE (Holdings) Ltd v Secretary of State for the Environment* (1989) 57 P & CR 306, CA, 327 per Purchas LJ, 329 per Staughton LJ.
- The claimant must have suffered some sort of injustice or prejudice worthy of the grant of relief: *R (Garg) v Criminal Injuries Compensation Authority* [2007] EWCA Civ 797 at [44] per Smith LJ.
- Judicial review ought not to be a futile endeavour, such as where it has been overtaken by events like a change in the relevant legislation: for example, see *R (Edwards) v Environment Agency* [2008] UKHL 22; [2008] 1 WLR 1587 at [65] per Lord Hoffmann.
- Thus, in 'a cause where there is an issue involving a public authority as to a question of public law, your Lordships have a discretion to hear the appeal, even if by the time the appeal reaches the House there is no longer a lis to be decided which will directly affect the rights and obligations of the parties *inter se*... The discretion to hear disputes, even in the area of public law, must, however, be exercised with caution and appeals which are academic between the parties should not be heard unless there is a good reason in the public interest for doing so': *R v Secretary of State for the Home Department, ex p Salem* [1999] 1 AC 450, 456–457 per Lord Slynn; *Rusbridger v Attorney General* [2003] UKHL 38; [2004] 1 AC 357 at [35] per Lord Hutton.
- It is not generally appropriate to launch judicial review proceedings prematurely, before there is a final decision to challenge, or the act complained of has taken place: *R v Hammersmith and Fulham London Borough Council, ex p Burkett* [2002] UKHL 23; [2002] 1 WLR 1593 at [42]–[43] per Lord Steyn.

Standard of review

49.14 The standard of review is the level of intensity with which the Tribunal will scrutinise the decision, and that level of scrutiny will depend on the ground of review which is invoked. Essentially – although not absolutely precisely – one can draw a distinction between grounds which challenge the substantive decision taken and those which challenge some aspect of the process or basis of the decision. By substantive decision, what is meant is whether the choice of the decision-maker was right on the facts of the case – ie, where a choice was made between different options, was it the right choice? Another way of putting the distinction is to ask whether the issue challenged is one of law (a matter for the Tribunal to determine finally) or of administrative discretion (a matter which the Tribunal will be slow to disturb).

49.15 Judicial review has, traditionally, been wary of interfering with whether the decision-maker got the decision substantively correct, and this is reflected in the standard of review the courts adopt. In contrast, the courts have been much more willing to consider the propriety of the process adopted by the decision-maker, and the basis on which the decision was made, with a consequent stringency of the standard. Let us consider this category first.

49.16 If the complaint is one about the fairness of the procedures adopted by the decision-maker – for example, that the claimant was denied the right to an oral hearing, or no reasons were given, or that the decision-maker was biased – the Tribunal will determine what, in all the circumstances of the case, procedural fairness required the decision-maker to adopt. If the decision-maker fell short of those procedures then the decision will have been reached unfairly and the Tribunal will (subject to its discretion) order relief. The standard of review is therefore one of correctness: either the decision-maker acted fairly according to the proper approach or it did not. Procedural fairness is a question of law:

> '[W]hether a tribunal...was acting in breach of the principles of natural justice is essentially a question of law': *Gillies v Secretary of State for Work and Pensions* [2006] UKHL 2; [2006] 1 WLR 781 at [6] per Lord Hope.

> 'Where it is alleged that a lower tribunal has acted in breach of the rules of fairness or natural justice the court is not confined to reviewing the reasoning of the tribunal on Wednesbury principles. It must make its own independent judgment...Furthermore, the question whether there has been a breach of those principles is one of law, not fact': *R (Mahfouz) v General Medical Council* [2004] EWCA Civ 233 at [19] per Carnwath LJ.

49.17 If the complaint is that the decision-maker made an error of law in making its decision that complaint goes to the basis of the decision itself. An error of law might be that the decision-maker misinterpreted a statutory provision, or did not follow a binding judgment of a higher court, or simply that it applied the law incorrectly. Questions of law are self-evidently within the expertise of the courts and the Upper Tribunal. There can only be one right answer: was the decision lawful or unlawful? If the decision was unlawful, for whatever reason, the Tribunal will (subject to its discretion) order relief. The standard of review is therefore one of correctness: either the decision-maker acted lawfully according to what the Tribunal determines the law is, or it did not:

> 'A tribunal either misdirects itself in law or not according to whether it has got the law right or wrong, and that depends on what the law is and not on what a lay tribunal might reasonably think it was. In this field there are no marks for trying hard but getting the answer wrong': *R v Central Arbitration Committee ex p BTP Tioxide Ltd* [1981] ICR 843, 856 per Forbes J.

49.18 There is one exception to the correctness standard of review for errors of law. Where the court has defined a particular statutory term but that definition is itself open to a range of meanings then providing the decision maker has remained within that spectrum the court will not interfere: *R v Monopolies and Mergers Commission, ex p South Yorkshire Transport Ltd* [1993] 1 WLR 23, HL.

49.19 However, a different standard of review is applied by the courts in cases where the judicial review challenge is to the substance of the decision itself – ie, not that the process was unfair, or that the decision-maker misunderstood the law, but that the decision taken was not right, that it made no sense, that it was not reasonable. The decision-maker had more than one choice and he chose the wrong one, alleges the claimant. These substantive challenges bring the Tribunal much closer to turning judicial review into a form of appeal. To avoid collapsing that distinction, the Tribunal will apply a standard of review which is harder for a claimant to meet successfully. This is known as *Wednesbury* unreasonableness, because it found its modern exposition in Associated *Provincial Picture Houses Ltd v Wednesbury Corpn* [1948] 1 KB 223, CA. Lord Greene MR, at 230, described the test in the following manner:

> 'It is true to say that, if a decision on a competent matter is so unreasonable that no reasonable authority could ever have come to it, then the courts can interfere. That, I think, is quite right; but to prove a case of that kind would require something overwhelming, and, in this case, the facts do not come anywhere near anything of that kind... [Counsel's] proposition that the decision of the local authority can be upset if it is proved to be unreasonable, really meant that it must be proved to be unreasonable in the sense that the court considers it to be a decision that no reasonable body could have come to. It is not what the court considers unreasonable, a different thing altogether.'

49.20 The notion that a decision is so unreasonable that no reasonable authority could have come to it is not an easy test to meet. However, *Wednesbury* unreasonableness is not just a standard of review: it is itself a ground of review. The test of reasonableness will be discussed in more detail as a ground below. What is important to note as a matter of principle is that where it is the substance of the decision which is being challenged, the discretionary choice of the decision-maker, *Wednesbury* provides the usual standard of review.

49.21 There are exceptions to *Wednesbury* unreasonableness in substantive challenges. First, reasonableness does not necessarily mean the same thing in every type of case. It is a sliding scale and can be adjusted to make the test harder or easier depending on the context (see below). Secondly, a challenge based upon a human right, set out in the European Convention on Human Rights and incorporated into English law in Sch 1 to the Human Rights Act 1998 ('HRA'), will invariably be a substantive challenge. The standard of review in HRA cases is not *Wednesbury*, but proportionality. Proportionality is a more structured and more intensive form of review, and applies to each Convention right, although it may mean different things in the context of different rights. Some areas of the Tribunal's work will involve regular invocation of the HRA and it is to be expected that proportionality will be a regular feature of the Tribunal's work (see below and **Proportionality**).

GROUNDS OF JUDICIAL REVIEW

49.22 The most famous description of the leading categories of judicial review comes from *Council of Civil Service Unions v Minister for the Civil Service* [1985] AC 374, HL, 410–411 per Lord Diplock:

> 'Judicial review has I think developed to a stage today when without reiterating any analysis of the steps by which the development has come about, one can conveniently classify under three heads the grounds upon which administrative action is subject to control by judicial review. The first ground I would call "illegality," the second "irrationality" and the third "procedural impropriety." That is not to say that further development on a case by case basis may not in course of time add further grounds. I have in mind particularly the possible adoption in the future of the principle of "proportionality"...

> By "illegality" as a ground for judicial review I mean that the decision-maker must understand correctly the law that regulates his decision-making power and must give effect to it. Whether he has or not is par excellence a justiciable question to be decided, in the event of dispute, by those persons, the judges, by whom the judicial power of the state is exercisable.
>
> By "irrationality" I mean what can by now be succinctly referred to as "Wednesbury unreasonableness" (*Associated Provincial Picture Houses Ltd v Wednesbury Corporation* [1948] 1 KB 223). It applies to a decision which is so outrageous in its defiance of logic or of accepted moral standards that no sensible person who had applied his mind to the question to be decided could have arrived at it. Whether a decision falls within this category is a question that judges by their training and experience should be well equipped to answer...
>
> I have described the third head as "procedural impropriety" rather than failure to observe basic rules of natural justice or failure to act with procedural fairness towards the person who will be affected by the decision. This is because susceptibility to judicial review under this head covers also failure by an administrative tribunal to observe procedural rules that are expressly laid down in the legislative instrument by which its jurisdiction is conferred, even where such failure does not involve any denial of natural justice'.

49.23 Lord Diplock's tripartite classification remains the standard starting point today, although it requires some development because there are numerous grounds and sub-grounds upon which a judicial review challenge may be brought. Only the most common, and particularly relevant to the work of the Tribunal, will be considered here. They are:

- Illegality/error of law;
- Error of fact;
- Improper purposes;
- Irrelevant considerations;
- Fettering of discretion;
- Equality of treatment;
- Legitimate expectation;
- Irrationality/unreasonableness;
- Procedural impropriety/unfairness;
- Review under the HRA 1998.

Illegality/error of law

49.24 The use of error of law can be ambiguous. In its broader sense, both the content of this category and all the subsequent categories are species of errors of law. Thus, when TCEA 2007 gives the power to appeal on the basis of an error of law it includes all of the following grounds (and others besides). However, illegality also has a narrower sense, namely an error of law which does not fall into a separate category. It is both a blanket term, and the label for the category into which everything not otherwise allocated falls.

49.25 The idea can also be summed up as whether or not the public authority has acted *ultra vires*: outside its lawful powers. A decision challenged may contain an error of law because it is inconsistent with the proper interpretation of primary legislation, secondary legislation, European Union law, international law (when domestically applicable), or some aspect of the common law, including binding judicial decisions. The decision-maker may not have had the jurisdiction to make the decision or take the action that it did. Indeed, on orthodox public law principles, an error of law means that there was no jurisdiction: *Anisminic v Foreign Compensation Commission* [1969] 2 AC 147 (see, in respect of the Upper Tribunal itself, **Upper Tribunal**).

49.26 Illegality or error of law is the broadest and most inclusive ground of judicial review. Anyone wishing to bring judicial review proceedings in the Tribunal should identify the particular error of law complained of, but if it does not appear to fall within one of the categories dealt with below it is perfectly proper to frame the complaint as one about illegality, an error of law or *ultra vires*.

Error of fact

49.27 The error of fact jurisdiction has three main aspects. First, the Tribunal may judicially review a decision where there has been a mistake of fact as defined in *E v Secretary of State for the Home Department* [2004] EWCA Civ 49; [2004] QB 1044 at [66] per Carnwath LJ, namely where the following conditions are fulfilled:

- there has been a mistake as to an existing fact (including the availability of evidence);
- the fact or evidence is 'established', in the sense of being uncontentious and objectively verifiable;
- the appellant was not responsible for the mistake; and
- the mistake played a material (but not necessarily decisive) part in the reasoning under challenge.

49.28 Secondly, the Tribunal may judicially review a decision which is dependent on the existence of one or more precedent facts, ie a fact must exist before the jurisdiction of the decision-maker is triggered. They are objective factual questions appropriate for review: *R v Secretary of State for the Home Department, ex p Khawaja* [1984] AC 74.

49.29 Thirdly, a factual conclusion or finding which has no basis is reviewable. It is not properly an error of fact but a species of irrationality, but is included here for the sake of completeness. The idea is illustrated by the following dictum of Lord Millett:

> 'A decision may be quashed if it is based on a finding of fact or inference from the facts which is perverse or irrational; or there was no evidence to support it; or it was made by reference to irrelevant factors or without regard to relevant factors. It is not necessary to identify a specific error of law; if the decision cannot be supported the court will infer that the decision-making authority misunderstood or overlooked relevant

evidence or misdirected itself in law. The court cannot substitute its own findings of fact for those of the decision-making authority if there was evidence to support them; and questions as to the weight to be given to a particular piece of evidence and the credibility of witnesses are for the decision-making authority and not the court': *Begum v Tower Hamlets London Borough Council* [2003] UKHL 5; [2003] 2 AC 430 at [99].

Improper purposes

49.30 The illegality of a public authority using a power given to it for a purpose other than the intended purpose is well-established. Bad faith is an obvious example of an improper purpose but is extremely rare and not advisable to allege without clear evidence.

49.31 Examples of improper purposes are: a decision on the designation of council houses for sale taken purely to provide an electoral advantage for the decision-maker (*Porter v Magill* [2001] UKHL 67; [2002] 2 AC 357 at [19] per Lord Bingham); the revocation of television licences bought in advance at a cheaper rate before a price increase took effect (*Congreve v Home Office* [1976] QB 629); the refusal to refer a complaint to an inquiry because of the fear of political embarrassment as a result (*Padfield v Minister of Agriculture, Fisheries and Food* [1968] AC 997).

49.32 Public authorities are required to promote the purpose of the legislation granting them a particular power, not to use that power to frustrate the purpose: *Padfield* [1968] AC 997 at 1030 per Lord Reid; *R (Hooper) v Secretary of State for Work and Pensions* [2005] UKHL 29; [2005] 1 WLR 1681 at [123] per Lord Brown.

49.33 Where there is more than one purpose, only one of which is improper, it is sufficient that the improper purpose materially influenced the relevant decision: *R v Inner London Education Authority, ex p Westminster City Council* [1986] 1 WLR 28, 49 per Glidewell J.

Irrelevant considerations

49.34 Another well-established species of illegality is where a public authority materially fails to take into account all relevant considerations, or materially takes into account an irrelevant one. What is relevant or irrelevant will, of course, depend closely on the circumstances of the case and cannot be easily predicted here.

49.35 Various factors which might be separate grounds for judicial review may also bear on relevancy. For example, consideration of human rights concerns will ordinarily be relevant (*R v Secretary of State for the Home Department, ex p Bugdaycay* [1987] AC 514); a legitimate expectation will be relevant (*R (Bibi) v Newham London Borough Council* [2001] EWCA Civ 607; [2002] 1 WLR 237 at [49] per Schiemann LJ); and available resources may or may not be relevant (compare *R v Gloucestershire County Council, ex p Barry* [1997] AC 584 with *R v East Sussex County Council, ex p Tandy* [1998] AC 714).

49.36 A distinction is drawn between considerations which are statutorily expressly or impliedly relevant – which the court will enforce to a correctness standard – and considerations which are discretionary and the decision-maker is not obliged to apply – which the court will assess by reference to the *Wednesbury* standard of review: *Creednz Inc v Governor-General* [1981] 1 NZLR 172; *In re Findlay* [1985] AC 318.

49.37 The weight given to a relevant consideration by the decision-maker is a matter for the decision-maker and may be challenged only under the Wednesbury standard of review: *Tesco Stores Ltd v Secretary of State for the Environment* [1995] 1 WLR 759, HL, 764 per Lord Keith, 780 per Lord Hoffmann.

49.38 It is worth noting that it will often be possible to characterise an alleged error of law as a matter of irrelevant consideration, or as a matter of improper purpose, without a clear distinction between the two. This has long been the case in public law and has not been resolved largely because it rarely matters in practice.

Fettering of discretion

49.39 A decision-maker is not permitted to fetter his or her discretion

> 'The general rule is that anyone who has to exercise a statutory discretion must not 'shut his ears to an application'...I do not think there is any great difference between a policy and a rule. There may be cases where an officer or authority ought to listen to a substantial argument reasonably presented urging a change of policy. What the authority must not do is to refuse to listen at all': *British Oxygen Co. Ltd v Board of Trade* [1971] AC 610, 625 per Lord Reid.

49.40 The fettering of discretion should be considered in four separate categories. (Knight, 'A Framework for Fettering' [2009] JR 43).

49.41 The first involves an allegation of a fettering of discretion in the exercise of a common law power, whether under the prerogative or some other source. Such cases are not subject to the classic authorities on fettering which have arisen in a statutory context. (*R (Elias) v Secretary of State for Defence* [2006] EWCA Civ 1293; [2006] 1 WLR 3213 at [191]–[192] per Mummery LJ). The exercise of such non-statutory powers is unlikely to arise in the context of the tribunals system.

49.42 Secondly, in cases where primary legislation requires the existence of a policy, that action will be reviewable only on *Wednesbury* unreasonableness grounds. The statutory context can override the application of the normal fettering case law: *R (Nicholds) v Security Industry Authority* [2006] EWHC 1792 (Admin); [2007] 1 WLR 2067.

49.43 The third, and more common, case than that seen in *Nicholds* is where the decision-maker is given a discretion by statute (often to grant a licence or not), and it is open to the decision-maker to conduct the process in the light of a policy which is considered to be appropriate given the statutory scheme. It is in this situation that the approach of *British Oxygen* comes into play. Note that it might be unlawful not to have a policy at all: *R v NW Lancashire HA, ex p A* [2000] 1 WLR 977, CA, 991 per Auld LJ. Decision-makers will adopt policies which fall foul of the fettering rules. They may adopt a method of deciding cases which does not allow for the exercise of discretion such as where a council decided to issue no permits despite a power to do so (*R v London County Council, ex p Corrie* [1918] 1 KB 68); they may decide cases according to a rule of thumb without using discretion (*R v Greater*

Birmingham Appeal Tribunal, ex p Simper [1974] QB 543); or declare that they are not prepared to alter a policy in the light of a difficult case (*R v Torquay Licensing Justices, ex p Brockman* [1951] 2 KB 784). These policies are subject to challenge. It is sensible to see this category of stated policies which admit of no exception as fettering in law.

49.44 Fourth, if a decision-maker can fetter his discretion in law, he can also fetter his discretion in fact. By this it is meant that the policy itself may be lawful in that it provides for consideration of exceptional circumstances, but that in practice the policy is applied as a blanket rule. One example of dealing with the formalistically flexible policy is for the courts to require the decision-maker to have actually envisaged the exceptional circumstances which the policy allows for: *R (Rogers) v Swindon NHS PCT* [2006] EWCA Civ 392; [2006] 1 WLR 2649 at [62] per Sir Anthony Clarke MR. Fettering in fact is a vital category of review. Were one left only with fettering in law judicial review would be a question of form and not substance.

Equality of treatment

49.45 It is a principle of public law that like cases should be treated alike, and vice versa. The like cases expression is a form of ensuring equality and non-discrimination: 'I accept that it would be unfair of the Secretary of State not to treat like cases alike in the sense of discriminating against someone upon inadequate grounds': *R (Zeqiri) v Secretary of State for the Home Department* [2002] UKHL 3; [2002] INLR 291 at [56] per Lord Hoffmann. Different cases may be treated differently, providing that there is justification for doing so. Indeed, unlike cases must be treated differently: *R (Kaur) v Ealing London Borough Council* [2008] EWHC 2062 (Admin).

49.46 If a decision is based on a policy or criteria which are too vague or uncertain then it may be unlawful: *R (Grogan) v Bexley NHS Care Trust* [2006] EWHC 44 (Admin).

49.47 Decision-makers are expected to act consistently: 'It is generally desirable that decision-makers, whether administrative or judicial, should act in a broadly consistent manner': *R (O'Brien) v Independent Assessor* [2007] UKHL 10; [2007] 2 AC 312 at [30] per Lord Bingham.

49.48 As a guard against arbitrariness, a decision-maker may be expected to follow the findings of another body. An example of this was the refusal of the Secretary of State to follow the factual findings of the Parliamentary Commissioner for Administration of maladministration in relation to occupational pension schemes of public bodies wound up by the government, restating his own otherwise rational interpretation. The Court of Appeal held that the Secretary of State must have a good reason (rather than simply a not irrational one) for departing from the ombudsman's findings: *R (Bradley) v Secretary of State for Work and Pensions* [2008] EWCA Civ 36; [2009] QB 114.

Legitimate expectation

49.49 The case law on legitimate expectation is complicated and involves several different strands. It is unlikely to prove relevant in many judicial review challenges to the First-tier Tribunal, so its sphere of application in the Upper Tribunal will be small. Consequently, the discussion here will be brief.

49.50 A legitimate expectation must be founded upon an undertaking, by representation, policy, promise or a practice. In *R v North and East Devon Health Authority, ex p Coughlan* [2001] QB 213 the court identified (at [57]) three possible outcomes in a case where a claimant has a legitimate expectation that he or she would be treated in one way and the public body wishes now to treat him or her in a different way. The court may decide that: (a) the authority is only required to give its previous policy weight, but not more, in which case the court's review of the decision will be on *Wednesbury* grounds; or that (b) the promise or practice induces a legitimate expectation of consultation or other procedural protection (*AG of Hong Kong v Ng Yuen Shiu* [1983] 2 AC 629, 638 per Lord Fraser), which will accordingly be required unless there is an overriding reason otherwise; or that (c) a lawful promise or practice has induced a legitimate expectation of a benefit which is substantive, not simply procedural, in which case to frustrate the expectation may in some circumstances be regarded as so unfair as to amount to an abuse of power. In the first two categories of case the court's role is a conventional role of review (on grounds of rationality in the first, procedural fairness in the second), whereas in the third the court's task was to determine whether there was a sufficient overriding interest to justify a departure from the previous promise or practice, weighing the two considerations against each other (at [57]–[58]). (See *R (Bancoult) v Secretary of State for Foreign and Commonwealth Affairs (No 2)* [2008] UKHL 61; [2008] 3 WLR 955 at [177] per Lord Mance).

49.51 A substantive legitimate expectation arises when there is 'a specific undertaking, directed at a particular individual or group, by which the relevant policy's continuance is assured': *R (Bhatt Murphy (a firm)) v The Independent Assessor* [2008] EWCA Civ 755 at [43] per Laws LJ.

49.52 The standard of review to be applied to the different types of legitimate expectations is not necessarily consistent. As discussed above, in procedural expectation cases the standard of review will be the same as procedural unfairness cases: the correctness standard. In the *Coughlan* category (a) *Wednesbury* review applies. However, for other substantive expectation cases the Court of Appeal in *Coughlan* applied a test which came very close to proportionality, and in *R (Abdi & Nadarajah) v Secretary of State for the Home Department* [2005] EWCA Civ 1363 at [68]–[69] Laws LJ argued that the appropriate standard of review for all legitimate expectation cases is proportionality. There are difficulties of applying proportionality to procedural expectation cases in particular (see Elliott, 'Legitimate Expectations and the Search for Principle: Reflections on Abdi & Nadarajah' [2006] JR 281; and Knight, 'The Test That Dare Not Speak its Name: Proportionality Comes out of the Closet?' [2007] JR 117) and Laws LJ was less wide-ranging in *Bhatt Murphy* at [30]. It is probably the case that in substantive legitimate expectation cases the standard of review is proportionality, or some form of it, but the issue awaits clarification (see **Proportionality**).

Irrationality/unreasonableness

49.53 The nature of the *Wednesbury* unreasonableness test, as classically described, is set out above as the standard of review in substantive judicial review challenges. However, irrationality or unreasonableness is also a ground of judicial review in itself. If a public authority has made a decision in the exercise of its discretion which is thought to be so unreasonable that no reasonable public authority would have made it then it may be reviewed on that basis.

49.54 The precise formulation of the reasonableness test has altered slightly since *Wednesbury* itself. Lord Diplock's phrasing in CCSU is set out above, and in *R v Chief Constable of Sussex, ex p International Trader's Ferry* [1999] 2 AC 418, 452 the test was described by Lord Cooke as 'whether the decision in question was one which a reasonable authority could reach'. This less extreme formula encapsulates how the test is actually applied much more effectively than focussing on whether the decision was so unreasonable the decision-maker could not possibly have reached that decision. The question is whether the decision made falls inside or outside the range of reasonable responses, as delimited by the courts.

49.55 The application of the ordinary *Wednesbury* test can be difficult to predict. There can be a strong suspicion of reverse engineering on the part of the courts, whereby the court decides whether or not it thinks the decision is wrong, or oppressive, or ill-thought out, or unfair, or illogical and then it characterises the decision as irrational. On the other hand, there are many examples of the courts stressing that while the decision is not one that the court itself would have adopted, it remains a reasonable choice for the decision-maker. Reliance on *Wednesbury* unreasonableness leaves much in the discretion of the individual tribunal, and if it is possible to frame a judicial review challenge on some other error of law basis (such as irrelevancy or improper purposes) that will normally be preferable.

49.56 *Wednesbury* is not a monolithic test. It is a sliding scale, dependent upon context (*R v Department for Education and Employment, ex p Begbie* [2000] 1 WLR 1115, CA, 1130 per Laws LJ). In cases which involve human, constitutional or fundamental rights (to the extent that those are different, and to the extent that they are engaged at common law outside of the HRA), the Tribunal will apply 'anxious scrutiny'. This means that the more substantial the interference with a right, the more the court will require by way of justification before it is satisfied that the decision is reasonable in the sense outlined above: *R v Ministry of Defence, ex p Smith* [1996] QB 517, CA. The courts have adopted a broad-brush approach to when a case involves such rights, and it is not necessary to show the application of an ECHR right, or a direct common law equivalent.

49.57 If rights cases will involve an anxious scrutiny version of reasonableness, there are other types of case in which the courts will be especially slow to interfere on irrationality grounds. These tend to be cases in which the subject-matter is outside the expertise of the court and well within the expertise of the decision-maker, such as macro-economic policy (*R v Secretary of State for the Environment, ex p Nottinghamshire County Council* [1986] AC 240), national security (*Secretary of State for the Home Department v Rehman* [2001] UKHL 47; [2003] 1 AC 153), and decisions having had the approval of Parliament (*R v Secretary of State for the Environment, ex p Hammersmith and Fulham London Borough Council* [1991] 1 AC 521). However, in none of these areas may the court abrogate its responsibility to consider the matter or simply rubber-stamp the decision of the public authority.

49.58 A court may find delegated legislation, or part thereof, to have been made irrationally, even where it has been approved by Parliament under the affirmative resolution procedure: *R (Asif Javed) v Secretary of State for the Home Department* [2001] EWCA Civ 780; [2002] QB 129.

Procedural impropriety/unfairness

49.59 Lord Diplock's third head of procedural impropriety is also known as procedural unfairness and natural justice. What natural justice requires will always be dependent on the statutory and factual context. There are many aspects of procedural fairness, the main ones of which are:

- The right to a fair hearing. This may not necessarily be an oral hearing (*Lloyd v McMahon* [1987] 1 AC 625), but encompasses the right to make representations to the decision-maker. There is no requirement that a hearing, even an oral hearing, must follow the model of a court (*Bushell v Secretary of State for the Environment* [1981] AC 75, 95 per Lord Diplock).
- The right to be informed of any case against the intended recipient of the decision (*Ridge v Baldwin* [1964] AC 40). This may not mean the full case, and it may be sufficient to disclose the basic reasons or gist of the case (*R v Gaming Board for Great Britain, ex p Benaim & Khaida* [1970] 2 QB 417; *Bushell v Secretary of State for the Environment* [1981] AC 75, 96 per Lord Diplock).
- Whether or not there is a right to legal representation and/or cross-examination of witnesses, and what rules of evidence apply, will depend upon the context (*R v Board of Visitors of HM Prison Maze, ex p Hone* [1988] AC 379; *R v Board of Visitors of Hull Prison, ex p St Germain (No 2)* [1979] 1 WLR 1401, CA; *R (Roberts) v Parole Board* [2005] UKHL 45; [2005] 2 AC 738).
- The right to adequate consultation before a decision is taken. Consultation should be at the formative stage; there should be sufficient reasoning to enable informed responses; there should be adequate time for a response; and the responses should be conscientiously taken into account: *R v London Borough of Barnet, ex p B* [1994] ELR 357, CA, 370–372 per Auld LJ.
- There is no general duty on administrative decision-makers to give reasons (*Stefan v General Medical Council* [1999] 1 WLR 1293, PC, 1300 per Lord Clyde; *R (Hasan) v Secretary of State for Trade and Industry* [2008] EWCA Civ 1311), although a duty is in fact imposed in more and more categories of case (*R v Home Secretary, ex p Doody* [1994] AC 531; *R (Wooder) v Feggetter* [2002] EWCA Civ 554; [2003] QB 219). The First-tier Tribunal is generally under a duty to give reasons for its decisions (see **Reasons**).
- A decision-maker who is actually biased will breach natural justice. Such cases are extremely rare.
- A decision-maker who is a party to the matter, or who has a direct interest (usually pecuniary, but not necessarily) in the matter, is automatically disqualified from making the decision (*R v Bow Street Magistrates, ex p Pinochet (No 2)* [2000] 1 AC 119; *Dimes v Proprietors of Grand Junction Canal* (1852) 3 HL Cas 759).

- Where a fair-minded and informed observer who is fully aware of the context and facts would conclude that there is a real possibility that the decision-maker was biased, that decision-maker should not make the decision. Justice must be done, and be seen to be done (*Porter v Magill* [2001] UKHL 67; [2002] 2 AC 357 at [103] per Lord Hope; *R v Abdroikov* [2007] UKHL 37; [2007] 1 WLR 2679; *Taylor v Lawrence* [2002] EWCA Civ 90; [2003] QB 528). For the inter-relationship of apparent bias and possible pre-determination of the decision see *Condron v National Assembly for Wales* [2006] EWCA Civ 1573.

The Human Rights Act 1998

49.60 It is well beyond the scope of this Handbook to provide anything but the most basic summary of the HRA1998. The judges of the Upper Tribunal will already be used to the HRA 1998 having an impact on the substantive areas of law covered by the tribunal system, and the relevance of the HRA 1998 will only increase. In terms of a judicial review challenge, the main route by which the HRA will apply will be HRA 1998, s 6.

49.61 HRA 1998, s 6 is, in essence, a new ground of illegality. All public authorities are required to act compatibility with the Articles of the ECHR which are incorporated by domestic law in Sch 1 to the HRA 1998. If it is thought that a public authority, including the First-tier Tribunal, has failed to act compatibly a challenge may be brought by judicial review on the basis that the duty in HRA 1998, s 6(1) has been breached.

49.62 A breach under HRA 1998, s 6 may arise in a number of ways. The decision-maker may:

- Have failed to follow the consistent jurisprudence of the European Court of Human Rights (to which the courts and Tribunal must have regard under HRA 1998, s 2);
- Have acted in accordance with a statutory provision which is incompatible with the ECHR, but which can be interpreted in a manner which is compatible using HRA 1998, s 3;
- Have failed to act compatibly with a substantive ECHR right.

49.63 A person making a claim under the HRA must be a victim of the unlawful act under the meaning of ECHR, Article 34 (HRA 1998, s 7(1), (7)) and HRA proceedings must be brought within one year, although time may be extended (HRA 1998, s 7(5)). It is possible to claim damages for the breach of an ECHR right under s.8, although the courts have interpreted this restrictively (*R (Greenfield) v Secretary of State for the Home Department* [2005] UKHL 14; [2005] 1 WLR 673).

49.64 The Tribunal is not permitted to make a declaration of the incompatibility of primary legislation with an ECHR right under HRA 1998, s 4 and has no jurisdiction over a case which seeks such a declaration, whether or not that is the only relief sought: Lord Judge CJ, *Direction – Classes of case specified under s18(6) TCEA 2007*, 29 October 2008, paragraph 3 (see **Judicial review in the Upper Tribunal**).

49.65 The substantive ECHR rights incorporated into UK law in Sch 1 to the HRA 1998 are:

- Article 2 (right to life);
- Article 3 (prohibition of torture);
- Article 4 (prohibition of slavery);
- Article 5 (right to liberty);
- Article 6 (right to a fair trial);
- Article 7 (no punishment without law);
- Article 8 (right to respect for private and family life);
- Article 9 (freedom of thought, conscience and belief);
- Article 10 (freedom of expression);
- Article 11 (freedom of assembly and association);
- Article 12 (right to marry);
- Article 14 (prohibition of discrimination);
- Article 1 of Protocol 1 (protection of property);
- Article 2 of Protocol 1 (right to education);
- Article 3 of Protocol 1 (right to free elections).

49.66 The standard of review under a HRA 1998, s 6 claim for an infringement of an ECHR right is proportionality (*R v Secretary of State for the Home Department, ex p Daly* [2001] UKHL 26; [2001] 2 AC 532 at [27] per Lord Steyn). Even anxious scrutiny *Wednesbury* review is insufficiently intensive (*Smith & Grady v UK* (1999) 29 EHRR 493).

49.67 The proportionality test adopted by the English courts under the HRA 1998 has been set out by the Privy Council in *de Freitas v Permanent Secretary of Ministry of Agriculture, Fisheries, Lands and Housing* [1999] 1 AC 69, 80 as a carefully structured analysis. The court must ask three questions, namely whether:

(i) the legislative objective is sufficiently important to justify limiting a fundamental right;

(ii) the measures designed to meet the legislative objective are rationally connected to it; and

(iii) the means used to impair the right or freedom are no more than is necessary to accomplish the objective.

49.68 The House of Lords in *Huang v Secretary of State for the Home Department* [2007] UKHL 11; [2007] 2 AC 167 at [19] added the following fourth step, that the analysis must:

> 'always involve the striking of a fair balance between the rights of the individual and the interests of the community which is inherent in the whole of the Convention. The severity and consequences of the interference will call for careful assessment at this stage.'

49.69 The precise application and nature of the proportionality test will differ under each ECHR right, because the wording of each right is different. That difference of wording is extremely important, if sometimes overlooked by busy courts happy to simply apply the standard test. Certainly the proportionality structure set out above is the default position, but practitioners must be prepared to adapt the structure to the particular right in issue, which may require greater or lesser degrees of intensity of scrutiny (see **Proportionality**).

49.70 Much ink has been spilled on the subject of margins of appreciation for, discretionary areas of judgment for and deference to the decision-maker. It is not possible to traverse that ground here. What is undoubtedly the case is that the courts are willing to afford the decision-maker a degree of latitude in the choices that were made, and that degree will vary depending on the context of the case, including the importance of the right, the level of interference, the relative institutional competence of the decision-maker and the court, and the democratic basis for the decision. However, in *Huang* the House of Lords, after noting some of the factors relied upon in the case, held (at [16]) that:

> 'The giving of weight to factors such as these is not, in our opinion, aptly described as deference: it is performance of the ordinary judicial task of weighing up the competing considerations on each side and according appropriate weight to the judgment of a person with responsibility for a given subject matter and access to special sources of knowledge and advice. That is how any rational judicial decision-maker is likely to proceed.'

This should be the approach of the Upper Tribunal (see **Proportionality**).

50 Judicial Review in the Upper Tribunal

ROLE OF JUDICIAL REVIEW IN THE UPPER TRIBUNAL

50.1 Judicial review is a process whereby the acts or decisions of bodies exercising public functions are supervised by the High Court. Most judicial review cases are heard by the Administrative Court, a specialised court which is part of the Queen's Bench Division of the High Court.

50.2 However, as part of its jurisdiction as a superior court of record, the Upper Tribunal (see **Upper Tribunal**) has a specific statutory power to conduct judicial review of certain decisions or actions. In practice this power is usually exercised by the Administrative Appeals Chamber of the Upper Tribunal, but some specific judicial review cases, primarily against financial decision-makers, are allocated to the Tax and Chancery Chamber (see **Administrative Appeals Chamber, Tax and Chancery Chamber** and **Upper Tribunal**). Judicial review cases in the Administrative Appeals Chamber are ordinarily heard by the Senior President, the Chamber President or by a High Court Judge perhaps sitting with one or more judges of the Upper Tribunal.

50.3 The power of the Administrative Appeals Chamber to hear judicial review applications is, at present, linked to classes of case which are linked to subjects already within the scope of the jurisdiction of the Upper Tribunal (see **Upper Tribunal**).

UPPER TRIBUNAL'S POWER TO GRANT JUDICIAL REVIEW

50.4 The Upper Tribunal's judicial review jurisdiction is governed by the TCEA 2007, s 15.

50.5 TCEA 2007, s 15(1) provides that the Upper Tribunal may, in certain circumstances, grant: (i) a mandatory order; (ii) a prohibiting order; (iii) a quashing order; (iv) a declaration; (v) an injunction. These are the same orders as the Administrative Court is empowered to make in judicial review cases before it. By TCEA 2007, s 15(3) such orders have the same effect as they would have if granted by the High Court and are enforceable in the same way as they would be if made by the High Court.

50.6 In deciding whether to make such orders, the Upper Tribunal is required by TCEA 2007, s 15(4), (5) to apply the same principles as the High Court would apply on an application for judicial review.

50.7 Where a quashing order is made, the Upper Tribunal may in addition, by virtue of TCEA 2007, s 17(1), remit the matter concerned to the court, tribunal or authority that made the decision which is the subject of the order, or it may substitute its own decision for the decision in question. However, a substituted decision may only be made (see TCEA 2007, s 17(2)) where: (i) the decision in question was made by a court or tribunal; (ii) on the basis of error of law and (iii) without such error there would only have been one decision that the court or tribunal could have reached.

50.8 It has been held by the Administrative Appeals Chamber in a special educational needs case, where an appeal was pending before the Health, Education and Social Care Chamber of the First-tier Tribunal, that the

Upper Tribunal has power to order interim relief when exercising its judicial review jurisdiction: *R (JW) v The Learning Trust* [2009] UKUT 197 (AAC) at [26]. However, the statutory context in special educational needs cases meant the jurisdiction to order interim relief should be exercised with considerable restraint and only in exceptional circumstances: *The Learning Trust* at [29]. The First-tier Tribunal has no jurisdiction to order interim relief: *The Learning Trust* at [23].

CIRCUMSTANCES IN WHICH JUDICIAL REVIEW MAY BE DETERMINED BY THE UPPER TRIBUNAL

50.9 The judicial review powers of the Upper Tribunal may only be used if either:

(i) certain conditions are satisfied under TCEA 2007, s 18; or

(ii) the case has been transferred to the Upper Tribunal under TCEA 2007, s 19.

50.10 TCEA 2007, s 18 specifies the following four conditions, each of which must be satisfied:

(i) The application must be seeking a form of relief listed in TCEA 2007, s 15 (see above); permission to apply for judicial review; an award of damages or restitution under TCEA 2007, s 16(6) (see **Judicial review procedure in the Upper Tribunal**); or costs or interest (TCEA 2007, s 18(4));

(ii) The application must not call into question anything done by the Crown Court (TCEA 2007, s 18(5));

(iii) The application must fall within a specified category of case made by virtue of a Direction made by the Lord Chief Justice (or person nominated by the Lord Chief Justice) under Part 1 of Schedule 2 to the Constitutional Reform Act 2005 (TCEA 2007, s 18(6)); and

(iv) The judge hearing the case must be a High Court or Court of Appeal judge in England, Wales or Northern Ireland (or the equivalent thereof in Scotland) or such other person as has been agreed by the Lord Chief Justice, the Lord President, or the Lord Chief Justice of Northern Ireland and the Senior President of Tribunals (TCEA 2007, s 18(8)).

50.11 TCEA 2007, s 19 provides for the mandatory transfer of an application for judicial review commenced in the High Court to the Upper Tribunal (including applications for permission to apply for judicial review). In England and Wales, the transfer mechanism has been achieved by TCEA 2007, s 19 introducing a new s 31A into the Senior Courts Act 1981. (The separate provisions for Northern Ireland, introducing a new s 25A into the Judicature (Northern Ireland) Act 1978 , and for Scotland in TCEA 2007, ss 20, 21 will not be addressed here). Four conditions must each be satisfied for transfer to be required. They are:

(1) The application must seek nothing other than that set out in TCEA 2007, s 18(4) (Senior Courts Act 1981, s 31A(4));

(2) The application must not call into question anything done by the Crown Court (Senior Courts Act 1981, s 31A(5));

(3) The application must fall within a specified category of case made by virtue of a Direction made by the Lord Chief Justice (or person nominated by the Lord Chief Justice) under Part 1 of Schedule 2 to the Constitutional Reform Act 2005 (Senior Courts Act 1981, s 31A(6));

(4) The application must not call into question: (i) any decision made under the Immigration Acts; (ii) the British Nationality Act 1981; (iii) any statutory instrument under either the Immigration Acts or the British Nationality Act 1981; or (iv) any other current provision of law which determines British citizenship, British overseas territories citizenship, the status of a British national (Overseas) or British Overseas citizenship (Senior Courts Act 1981, s 31A(7)).

50.12 In circumstances where the third condition is not met (ie that there is no specification under a relevant Direction) but the other conditions are met, the High Court has a discretion to transfer a judicial review application to the Upper Tribunal where it is just and convenient to do so (Senior Courts Act 1981, s 31A(3)).

EFFECT OF TRANSFER OF CASES AS BETWEEN THE HIGH COURT AND THE UPPER TRIBUNAL

50.13 Where a judicial review application for permission has been transferred to the Upper Tribunal the effect of such transfer is that the Upper Tribunal has the function of deciding all subsequent applications and the substantive application even if the application falls outside the Direction requirement in TCEA 2007, s 18(6) (TCEA 2007, s 19(4)). The application is treated for all purposes as if it had been brought in the Upper Tribunal (see TCEA 2007, s 19(3))).

50.14 Where the Upper Tribunal lacks judicial review jurisdiction it is required to transfer the case to the High Court (TCEA 2007, s 18(3)). Where is does so, the application is treated for all purposes as if it had been made to the High Court (TCEA 2007, s 18(9)).

PROCEDURAL REQUIREMENTS

50.15 There are a number of procedural requirements for an application for judicial review in the Upper Tribunal including, most notably, a requirement to obtain permission to apply for judicial review and strict time limits for the bringing of such applications (see **Judicial review procedure in the Upper Tribunal**).

RELEVANT JUDICIAL REVIEW DIRECTIONS

50.16 To date, there has only been one relevant Direction affecting judicial review in the Upper Tribunal in England and Wales.

50.17 Lord Judge CJ made a Direction on 29 October 2008, with effect from 3 November 2008, transferring two classes of action for judicial review from the High Court to the Upper Tribunal: [2009] 1 WLR 327.

50.18 The two classes are:

- Any decision of the First-tier Tribunal on an appeal made in the exercise of a right conferred by the Criminal Injuries Compensation Scheme in compliance with the Criminal Injuries Compensation Act 1995, s 5(1) (appeals against decisions on review (see Criminal injuries compensation appeals); and
- Any decision of the First-tier Tribunal made under the Tribunal Procedure Rules or TCEA 2007, s 9 (review of decision of First-tier Tribunal by that Tribunal) where there is no right of appeal to the Upper Tribunal and that decision is not an excluded decision within paragraph (b) [any decision of the First-tier Tribunal on an appeal under the Data Protection Act 1998, s 28(4) or (6) (appeals against national security certificate)], (c) [any decision of the First-tier Tribunal on an appeal under the Freedom of Information Act 2000, s 60(1) or (4) (appeals against national security certificate)], or (f) [any decision of the First-tier Tribunal that is of a description specified in an order made by the Lord Chancellor] of TCEA 2007, s 11(5).

50.19 However, the Direction does not have effect where an application seeks (whether or not alone) a declaration of incompatibility under the Human Rights Act 1998, s 4.

50.20 Pursuant to the power conferred by TCEA 2007, s 11(5)(f), the Lord Chancellor has enacted the Appeals (Excluded Decisions) Order 2009, SI 2009/275 and the Tribunals, Courts and Enforcement Act 2007 (Miscellaneous Provisions) Order 2010, SI 2010/41 amending it. See **Excluded appeals** for the full list of further types of decision against which there is no appeal to the Upper Tribunal, and which now fall under the judicial review jurisdiction instead.

50.21 The Lord President of the Court of Session has made the Act of Sederunt (Transfer of Judicial Review Applications from the Court of Session) 2008, Scottish SI 2008/357 which specifies, from 10 November 2008, an application which challenges a procedural decision or a procedural ruling of the First-tier Tribunal as being the relevant class of case in which a transfer to the Upper Tribunal must be made from the Court of Session.

ABSENCE OF RIGHT OF APPEAL FROM DECISIONS OF FIRST-TIER TRIBUNAL

50.22 In the light of the above, the most common form of judicial review in the Upper Tribunal at present are those cases where the First-tier Tribunal has reached a decision against which there is no specified right of appeal (see **First-tier Tribunals**).

50.23 The absence of such right of appeal means that, in practice, the Upper Tribunal will still have jurisdiction to correct errors of law made by the First-tier Tribunal under its judicial review jurisdiction. The Upper Tribunal has, in a number of decisions, noted that where an appeal is lodged against a decision which is excluded, it will be treated as an application for judicial review instead. This was, for example, made clear in the ruling of a three judge panel of the Administrative Appeals Chamber of the Upper Tribunal in *Dorset Healthcare NHS Foundation Trust v MH* [2009] UKUT 4 (AAC); [2009] PTSR 1112.

50.24 In that case there was a dispute as to the Tribunal's jurisdiction to hear an appeal brought against an interlocutory decision of the Health, Education and Social Care Chamber directing disclosure of a detained patient's medical records and a subsequent decision refusing internal review of that decision.

50.25 At paragraph 8 of its judgment the Upper Tribunal said this:

> 'In the circumstances of this case, this issue could not entirely deprive us of jurisdiction in any event because, if there is no right of appeal, we could treat the appeal as an application for permission to apply for judicial review and waive the requirement to serve the First-tier Tribunal (such challenges by way of judicial review having been transferred from the Administrative Court to this tribunal: Lord Chief Justice's Practice Direction: Classes of Cases Specified under Section 18(6) of the Tribunals, Courts and Enforcement Act 2007, 31 October 2008).'

50.26 A Practice Statement has been issued by the First-tier Tribunal in relation to criminal injuries compensation decisions of the Social Entitlement Chamber where it is pointed out that save in respect of specified decisions where there is a right of appeal, the sole legal remedy is judicial review on the basis that the decision in question was erroneous in law: Practice and Guidance Statement (CI-6), Appeals on error of law against final decision of the Tribunal, 14 May 2009.

GROUNDS FOR SEEKING JUDICIAL REVIEW

50.27 The grounds for seeking judicial review in the Upper Tribunal are the same as for any judicial review application in the High Court (see **Judicial review grounds and principles**). The Upper Tribunal will apply judicial review principles with the same intensity that the Administrative Court would. In *British Sky Broadcasting Group plc v The Competition Commission* [2010] EWCA Civ 2 the context was the Competition Appeal Tribunal ('CAT') reviewing a decision of the Competition Commission, when it applied the same principles of judicial review as the High Court would (the Enterprise Act 2002, s 120). It was argued that the CAT should apply those principles with a greater intensity than an ordinary court would because the CAT is a specialist body. The Court of Appeal rejected that argument on the basis that it was contrary to the clear wording of the statute to apply the ordinary principles of judicial review, that it was contrary to authority (*Office of Fair Trading v IBA Health Ltd* [2004] EWCA Civ 142 at [90]–[100] per Carnwath LJ, under the same Act), and that it sought to engage the CAT in reassessing the weight accorded to the evidence and substituting its own judgment, contrary to the purpose of judicial review (see [32]–[41] per Lloyd LJ). Given that by TCEA 2007, s 15(4) the Tribunal 'must apply the principles that the High Court would apply in deciding whether to grant that relief on an application for judicial review' it seems highly improbable that any different approach to the Sky decision would be taken in respect of the Upper Tribunal's judicial review jurisdiction.

50.28 In the Administrative Appeals Chamber of the Upper Tribunal it is likely that a rather less formal approach to judicial review will be adopted than in conventional judicial review in the High Court. The Senior President Sir Robert Carnwath has suggested that the traditional court model of adjudicating on questions of law may be less suited to a tribunal with specialised expertise and that 'there is scope for it to develop a more extensive supervisory role, which may cross the traditional boundaries between law and fact as understood in the courts' ('Tribunal justice – a new start' [2009] PL 48, 58). In particular, the Senior President has suggested that there may be a special role for the Administrative Appeals Chamber in the area of giving general guidance and in developing general principles of proportionality (see **Guidance cases** and **Proportionality**).

51 Judicial Review Procedure in the Upper Tribunal

JUDICIAL REVIEW IN THE UPPER TRIBUNAL

51.1 The Upper Tribunal has a specific statutory power under the TCEA 2007, s 15 to conduct judicial review of certain decisions or actions. In practice this power is usually exercised by the Administrative Appeals Chamber of the Upper Tribunal ('AAC'), but some specific judicial review cases, primarily against financial decision-makers, are allocated to the Tax and Chancery Chamber ('TCC') (see **Administrative Appeals Chamber, Tax and Chancery Chamber** and **Upper Tribunal**).

51.2 The conditions under which the judicial review jurisdiction arises are tightly confined and are set out in detail in **Judicial review in the Upper Tribunal**.

51.3 Procedure in judicial review cases, in both the AAC and TCC, is governed by Part 4 of the Tribunal Procedure (Upper Tribunal) Rules 2008, SI 2008/2684 ('the UT Rules') as amended. All references to rules in this entry are to the UT Rules unless otherwise stated, and the usual UT Rules apply to all aspects of procedure with the exceptions set out below. The procedure very closely matches that in the Administrative Court under CPR Pt 54.

TYPES OF JUDICIAL REVIEW

51.4 For the purposes of the Rules, there are two main different types of judicial review case heard in the Upper Tribunal. First, there are applications directly to the Tribunal. Secondly, there are cases which began in the High Court but have been, either mandatorily or discretionarily, transferred to the Upper Tribunal.

TRANSFERRED CASES

51.5 In a case which has been transferred to the Upper Tribunal from the High Court (see **Transfer of judicial review applications**) Upper Tribunal Rules, r 27 applies. The Tribunal must notify each party to the proceedings in writing that the case has been transferred, and it must give directions as to the future conduct of proceedings (Upper Tribunal Rules, r 27(1)). Importantly, the directions may disapply or modify any procedural rule in Part 4 of the Rules (Upper Tribunal Rules, r 27(2)). This is necessary particularly because a case may have been transferred after the permission stage, in which case it would be inappropriate for the Tribunal to require the case to obtain permission again. Where it is an application for permission which is transferred by the High Court the ordinary rules, set out below, will ordinarily be applied. Equivalent provision is made for transfer from the Court of Session in Upper Tribunal Rules, r 27(3).

APPLICATIONS FOR PERMISSION

51.6 As in the High Court, an application for judicial review of a decision must be given permission by the Tribunal before it can proceed to a substantive hearing (TCEA 2007, s 16(2)).

Time limits

51.7 An application for permission must be made in writing to the Tribunal and must be made promptly and in any event received by the Tribunal within three months of the decision, act or omission to which the application relates (Upper Tribunal Rules, r 28(1), (2)). This replicates the time limit for bringing a judicial review claim in the Administrative Court and it will doubtless be construed in much the same way. Users should be warned that application of the promptness requirement can be difficult to predict. There will be cases in which the importance of acting quickly would ordinarily outweigh the importance of the courts considering the legality of a challenge and many examples in the case law bear this out. A challenge to the allocation of school places should be brought before the start of the new school year (*R v Rochdale Metropolitan Borough Council, ex p B* [2000] EdCR 117); challenges to planning decisions risk holding up important community developments (*R (Finn-Kelcey) v Milton Keynes Council* [2008] EWCA Civ 1067; [2009] EnvLR 17), particularly since it is possible to challenge both the planning resolution and the grant of permission (*R (Burkett) v Hammersmith and Fulham London Borough Council* [2002] UKHL 23; [2002] 1 WLR 1593); a system of rules may have been in place for some time with real practical problems if they were unravelled (*R v Secretary of State for Social Services, ex p Association of Metropolitan Authorities* [1986] 1 WLR 1); a challenge to the legality of disciplinary proceedings should be made before those proceedings start (*R v Chief Constable of Ministry of Defence Police, ex p Sweeney* [1999] COD 122); and in some cases simply waiting until the last day of the three month period when no further information was required will be sufficient for the promptness requirement to be invoked (*R (Crown Prosecution Service) v City of London Magistrates' Court* [2007] EWHC 1924 (Admin)). However, in cases where the claim is based upon European Union law there is now a very strong argument that it is contrary to EU law for the Tribunal to rely on the promptness requirement before the expiry of the three month limit: *Case C-406/08, Uniplex (UK) Ltd v NHS Business Services Authority*, judgment of 28 January 2010 (not yet reported) (on which see Knight, 'Procuring the End of the Promptness Requirement?' [2010] 29 CJQ 297).

51.8 Where the challenge is to a decision of the First-tier Tribunal, the relevant time limit is one month from the date on which the lower Tribunal sent written reasons for its decision, or a notification that an application to set aside was unsuccessful, even if that time is later than the three month limit in Upper Tribunal Rules, r 28(2) (Upper Tribunal Rules, r 28(3)).

Form of application

51.9 The application must provide (Upper Tribunal Rules, r 28(4), (6)):

- the name and address of the applicant, the respondent and any other person whom the applicant considers to be an interested party;
- the name and address of the applicant's representative (if any);
- an address where documents for the applicant may be sent or delivered;
- details of the decision challenged (including the date, the full reference and the identity of the decision maker);

- that the application is for permission to bring judicial review proceedings;
- the outcome that the applicant is seeking;
- the facts and grounds on which the applicant relies;
- a copy of any written record of the decision in the applicant's possession or control; and
- copies of any other documents in the applicant's possession or control on which the applicant intends to rely.

51.10 Any party to challenged proceedings not an applicant or respondent must be named as an interested party (Upper Tribunal Rules, r 28(5)).

51.11 Where an application is made out of time, it must include a request for an extension of time and the reason why the time limit has not been complied with. Unless the Tribunal extends the time period in the exercise of its case management powers it must not admit the application (Upper Tribunal Rules, r 28(7)).

51.12 When the Tribunal receives the application it must send a copy of the application and accompanying documents to any other party (Upper Tribunal Rules, r 28(8)).

Acknowledgement of service

51.13 Any party wishing to take part in the permission proceedings must, on receipt of the documents sent by the Tribunal under Upper Tribunal Rules, r 28(8), ensure that the Tribunal receives an acknowledgement of service within 21 days (Upper Tribunal Rules, r 29(1)). The acknowledgement of service must state whether permission is opposed or supported, the grounds for support or opposition, any other information which may assist the Tribunal, and the name and address of any person not named which the party considers may be an interested party to the proceedings (Upper Tribunal Rules, r 29(2)).

51.14 If a party decides not to take part in the permission proceedings it need not supply an acknowledgement of service and this does not bar it from taking part in the substantive hearing if permission is granted (Upper Tribunal Rules, r 29(3)).

THE PERMISSION DECISION

Standing

51.15 The Tribunal may not grant permission unless the applicant has a 'sufficient interest' in the matter (TCEA 2007, s 16(3)). This is the same test of standing as in ordinary judicial review claims. It has been interpreted broadly by the courts, and it is inconceivable that a party to a decision, appealed to the First-tier Tribunal, would not have a sufficient interest in the matter. In cases not covered by this paradigm – and the nature of judicial review does permit a broader category of involvement – the issue may be raised, but it has generally been accepted that a liberal approach to sufficient interest is appropriate, and that standing will be found where the court has concerns about the legality of the action challenged: *R v Inland Revenue Commissioners, ex p National Federation of Self-Employed and Small Businesses Ltd* [1982] AC 617, 641–644 per Lord Diplock.

Test

51.16 The test mandated TCEA 2007, s 16(4), (5) is that permission may be refused where the Tribunal considers that:

- there has been undue delay in making the application;
- granting the relief sought on the application would be likely to cause substantial hardship to, or substantially prejudice the rights of, any person or would be detrimental to good administration.

51.17 The former essentially replicates the promptness requirement in Upper Tribunal Rules, r 29(2), and it is the latter which really provides the permission test, which is essentially the same as the Senior Courts Act 1981, s 31(6) which governs judicial review in the High Court. What the permission involves has been the subject of some guidance from the Board of the Judicial Committee of the Privy Council in *Sharma v Brown-Antoine* [2006] UKPC 57; [2007] 1 WLR 780 at [14](4):

> 'The ordinary rule now is that the court will refuse leave to claim judicial review unless satisfied that there is an arguable ground for judicial review having a realistic prospect of success and not subject to a discretionary bar such as delay or an alternative remedy: *R v Legal Aid Board, Ex p Hughes* (1992) 5 Admin LR 623, 628; Fordham, *Judicial Review Handbook*, 4th ed (2004), p 426. But arguability cannot be judged without reference to the nature and gravity of the issue to be argued. It is a test which is flexible in its application. As the English Court of Appeal recently said with reference to the civil standard of proof in *R(N) v Mental Health Review Tribunal (Northern Region)* [2005] EWCA Civ 1605, [2006] QB 468, para 62, in a passage applicable mutatis mutandis to arguability:
>
> > "… the more serious the allegation or the more serious the consequences if the allegation is proved, the stronger must be the evidence before a court will find the allegation proved on the balance of probabilities. Thus the flexibility of the standard lies not in any adjustment to the degree of probability required for an allegation to be proved (such that a more serious allegation has to be proved to a higher degree of probability), but in the strength or quality of the evidence that will in practice be required for an allegation to be proved on the balance of probabilities."
>
> It is not enough that a case is potentially arguable: an applicant cannot plead potential arguability to "justify the grant of leave to issue proceedings upon a speculative basis which it is hoped the interlocutory processes of the court may strengthen": *Matalulu v Director of Public Prosecutions* [2003] 4 LRC 712, 733.'

51.18 The fact that TCEA 2007, s 16 does not expressly mention a test of arguability is not a strong argument for suggesting that there is not one, nor does it mean that a lower threshold will be applied than the Administrative Court which is governed by precisely the same test (both of these suggestions are hinted at by Mitchell, 'Judicial Review, But Not as we Know it: Judicial Review in the Upper Tribunal' [2010] JR 112 at [27]). Applicants in the Upper Tribunal will need to show that their claim is arguable, not vexatious, and that it will not prejudice the rights of other or good administration.

51.19 That arguability is part of the permission test is emphasised by Upper Tribunal Rules, r 8(3)(c), which gives the Tribunal power to strike out judicial review proceedings where the Tribunal considers that 'there is no reasonable prospect' of the applicant's case, or part of it, succeeding (see **Striking out**). This mirrors the test set out in *Sharma* above, although the terminology of striking out is not normally used in judicial review proceedings.

Procedure on permission decisions

51.20 The Tribunal must send to all parties a written notice of its decision on permission, and the reasons for any refusal of permission or conditions applied to the grant of permission (Upper Tribunal Rules, r 30(1)).

51.21 The decision may have been taken on the papers only (as it can be in the Administrative Court). If a decision on the papers is to refuse permission, or to grant permission only on conditions, the applicant may apply to have that decision reconsidered at a hearing. Such an application must be made in writing and received by the Tribunal within 14 days of the date on which its written reasons were sent to the applicant (Upper Tribunal Rules, r 30(3)–(5)).

FOLLOWING GRANT OF PERMISSION

51.22 Where permission has been granted, any party notified of the grant may provide detailed grounds in writing to the Tribunal for supporting or contesting the substantive application, and may raise additional grounds not considered at the permission stage (Upper Tribunal Rules, r 31(1)). Those submissions must be received by the Tribunal within 35 days of date on which the notice of permission was sent (Upper Tribunal Rules, r 31(2)). The successful applicant may not rely at the substantive hearing on grounds other than those put forward in support of permission unless the Tribunal has consented (Upper Tribunal Rules, r 32).

51.23 Each party (and any other person with the Tribunal's permission) may submit evidence, make representations at a hearing and make written representations where the case will be decided without a hearing (Upper Tribunal Rules, r 33).

51.24 Where any hearing is held (either on permission or substantively) the Tribunal must provide a minimum of two working days notice (Upper Tribunal Rules, r 36(2)(a)).

51.25 There is no requirement in relation to bundles of documents (cf CPR PD 54A paragraph 5.9).

RELIEF

51.26 TCEA 2007, s 15(1) provides that the Upper Tribunal may grant the following forms of relief in a judicial review application: (i) a mandatory order; (ii) a prohibiting order; (iii) a quashing order; (iv) a declaration; (v) an injunction. These are the same orders as the Administrative Court is empowered to make in judicial review cases before it. By TCEA 2007, s 15(3) such orders have the same effect as they would have if granted by the High Court and are enforceable in the same way as they would be if made by the High Court.

51.27 In deciding whether to make such orders, the Upper Tribunal is required by TCEA 2007, s 15(4), (5) to apply the same principles as the High Court would apply on an application for judicial review.

51.28 Where a quashing order is made, the Upper Tribunal may in addition, by TCEA 2007, s 17(1), remit the matter concerned to the court, tribunal or authority that made the decision which is the subject of the order, or it may substitute its own decision for the decision in question. However, a substituted decision may only be made (see TCEA 2007, s 17(2)) where: (i) the decision in question was made by a court or tribunal; (ii) on the basis of error of law; and (iii) without such error there would only have been one decision that the court or tribunal could have reached.

51.29 Relief in judicial review cases has always been at the discretion of the court. The Tribunal may refuse to grant the relief sought under TCEA 2007, s 16(4), (5) where the Tribunal considers that:

- there has been undue delay in making the application;
- granting the relief sought on the application would be likely to cause substantial hardship to, or substantially prejudice the rights of, any person or would be detrimental to good administration.

51.30 Although these provide some guidance as to when a remedy may be refused, it is quintessentially a matter of discretion for the Tribunal to be exercised based upon the conduct of the parties, the remedy sought, the nature of the unlawfulness and the circumstances of the case as a whole.

FEES, FUNDING AND COSTS

51.31 Unlike bringing a judicial review claim in the High Court, there is, at present, no fee to be paid in the Upper Tribunal. It may therefore be cost-effective for some claimants to go straight to the Tribunal.

51.32 Nor will bringing a claim in the Tribunal prevent the acquisition of legal aid. Public funding is available for judicial review claims on the same terms as in the Administrative Court under the Legal Services Commission Funding Code Guidance, 3C-227.1.

51.33 Judicial review proceedings in the Upper Tribunal are in a slightly different position in respect of costs to other Tribunal cases. Under Upper Tribunal Rules, r 10(3)(a) the Tribunal may make an award in respect of costs in judicial review proceedings. Individuals must still have their financial circumstances considered by the Tribunal (Upper Tribunal Rules, r 10(7)) and it is strongly hoped and expected by all that the general cost of bringing proceedings in the Tribunal will be less than in the High Court, but the Tribunal has a wide discretion.

51.34 The general approach of the Administrative Court under the CPR is that costs follow the event. This is particularly true where permission is refused (*R (Mount Cook Land Ltd) v Westminster City Council* [2003] EWCA Civ 1346; [2004] 1 PLR 29), but also following the substantive hearing (*R (Davey) v Aylesbury Vale District Council* [2007] EWCA Civ 1166; [2008] 1 WLR 878). However, there is a broad discretion for the court to take account of the role of third parties, the funding position of the applicant, whether the claim was brought in the public interest, and costs on an issue by issue basis. For a more detailed review of case law see Fordham, *Judicial Review Handbook* (2008, 5th edn), Ch 18.

52 Lands Chamber

INTRODUCTION

52.1 The Lands Chamber came into existence on 1 June 2009, becoming one of (currently) four Chambers of the Upper Tribunal. It replaces the pre-existing Lands Tribunal in England and Wales and maintains its jurisdiction (see below): Transfer of Tribunal Functions (Lands Tribunal and Miscellaneous Amendments) Order 2009, SI 2009/1307. Scotland retains a Lands Tribunal under the Lands Tribunal Act 1949. Under the First-tier Tribunal and Upper Tribunal (Chambers) Order 2008, SI 2008/2684, art 9 (as amended), the Lands Chamber is allocated the following functions:

- all functions relating to—
  - compensation and other remedies for measures taken which affect the ownership, value, enjoyment or use of land or water, or of rights over or property on land or water;
  - appeals from decisions of leasehold valuation tribunals, residential property tribunals and valuation tribunals;
  - appeals on questions of the value of land or interests in land arising in tax proceedings; and
  - proceedings in respect of restrictive covenants, blight notices or the obstruction of light;
- the Upper Tribunal's function as arbitrator under section 1(5) of the Lands Tribunal Act 1949; and
- any other functions transferred to the Upper Tribunal by the Transfer of Tribunal Functions (Lands Tribunal and Miscellaneous Amendments) Order 2009.

52.2 The Lands Chamber is based in Bedford Square in London but may sit anywhere in England and Wales if necessary.

52.3 Unlike the overwhelming majority of the TCEA 2007 structure, the Lands Chamber does not primarily cater for citizen-State disputes. While some aspects of its jurisdiction, particularly in relation to compensation references, are State-based, much of its work revolves around resolution of land and property disputes between private citizens. Even in that context, the importance of having speedy, specialist, efficient and cost-effective dispute resolution is obvious.

52.4 The Lands Chamber does not hear appeals from any First-tier Tribunal. Its cases are direct references against the decision-maker, or appeals from other tribunals not currently within the TCEA 2007 structure. It is expected that in the future a Land, Property and Housing Chamber of the First-tier Tribunal will be created with appeals to the Lands Chamber, but there is currently no timetable for this.

PROCEDURAL RULES

52.5 Unlike the other Chambers of the Upper Tribunal, the Lands Chamber is not governed by the Upper Tribunal Rules. It has its own rules, which are markedly different to the standard form rules produced by the Tribunal Procedure Committee (see **Tribunal Procedure Committee**), and they have been retained, with some amendments, from the Lands Tribunal. At the time of writing, a consultation process was ongoing in respect of changes to the rules, and it is likely that in due course the existing rules will be replaced with ones which more closely match the form and content of the other Chambers.

52.6 The procedural rules of the Lands Chamber are found in the Lands Tribunal Rules 1996, SI 1996/1022, as subsequently amended by SI 1997/1965, SI 1998/22, SI 2003/2945, SI 2006/880 and, in particular, the Transfer of Tribunal Functions (Lands Tribunal and Miscellaneous Amendments) Order 2009, SI 2009/1307. For ease of common reference with the rules of the other Chambers they are referred to in this Handbook as the Lands Chamber Rules. For details **see Lands Chamber procedural rules**.

JURISDICTION

52.7 As set out above, the Lands Chamber has jurisdiction over a number of different land and property related types of case, as did the Lands Tribunal. The legislative basis for these different jurisdictions will now be set out.

Blight notice references

52.8 Land which is affected by a local authority planning proposal may be blighted. Under the Town and Country Planning Act 1990, s 150 the owner or interest-holder in the blighted land may issue a notice to the authority requiring it to purchase blighted land. The local authority may serve a counter-notice refusing to purchase the land on specific grounds set out in s 151(4). The owner may then refer the counter-notice to the Lands Chamber under s 153(1) (and s 153(2) applying a two month time limit has been omitted by the 2009 Transfer Order), which will determine whether or not the counter-notice is valid.

Compensation references

52.9 The Lands Chamber has jurisdiction to determine the level of compensation paid where land is acquired compulsorily. The principles and rules of compensation are found in the Land Compensation Act 1961, the Land Compensation Act 1973, the Acquisition of Land Act 1981, and the Planning and Compensation Act 1991. Legislation under which compensation claims may arise include:

- Railways Clauses Consolidation Act 1845, s 78;
- Improvement of Land Act 1864, s 73;
- Coast Protection Act 1949, s 24;
- Opencast Coal Act 1958, s 40 and Sch 3, para 1;
- Pipe-lines Act 1962, s 48;
- Gas Act 1965, s 23;
- various provisions of the Compulsory Purchase Act 1965;
- City of London (Various Powers) Act 1967, s 16;

- Greater London Council (General Powers) Act 1969, 21;
- Reservoirs Act 1975, s 18;
- Ancient Monuments and Archaeological Areas Act 1979, ss 8, 47;
- Highways Act 1980, s 307;
- Telecommunications Act 1984, Sch 2, para 4;
- Housing Act 1985, s 550;
- various provisions of the Town and Country Planning Act 1990;
- various provisions of the Coal Mining Subsidence Act 1991;
- various provisions of the Water Resources Act 1991; and
- Planning Act 2008, ss 152, 219.

Land taxation appeals

52.10 In relation to certain decisions and assessments of HMRC in respect of the valuation of land, the Lands Chamber has jurisdiction to determine the valuation dispute under the Taxes Management Act 1970, s 46D. The listed decisions (in s 46D(2)) are:

- an appeal against an amendment of a self-assessment under s 9C of the 1970 Act or paragraph 30 of Schedule 18 to the Finance Act 1998;
- an appeal against an amendment of a return under paragraph 34(2) of Schedule 18 to the Finance Act 1998;
- an appeal against a conclusion stated or amendment made by a closure notice under ss 28A or 28B of the 1970 Act;
- an appeal against an amendment of a partnership return under s 30B(1) of the 1970 Act;
- an appeal against an assessment to tax which is not a self-assessment;
- an appeal against a conclusion stated or amendment made by a closure notice under paragraph 7(2) of Schedule 1A to the 1970 Act relating to a claim or election made otherwise than by being included in a return; and
- an appeal against a decision contained in a closure notice under paragraph 7(3) of Schedule 1A to the 1970 Act disallowing in whole or in part a claim or election made otherwise than by being included in a return.

Leasehold Valuation Tribunal appeals

52.11 Under the Commonhold and Leasehold Reform Act 2002, s 175, the Lands Chamber may hear appeals from the Leasehold Valuation Tribunal ('LVT'). These appeals require permission to have been granted either by the LVT or the Lands Chamber itself (s 175(2)). The LVT deals with a number of different types of case, including:

- under the Leasehold Reform Act 1967 to determine the price to be paid by the tenant for the acquisition of the freehold of his/her house, and if required, the terms to be contained in the conveyance; the ground rent to be paid by the tenant for a 50-year extension to the lease of his/her house, and if required, the terms to be contained in that lease; the amount of the landlord's reasonable costs incurred in dealing with an application to acquire a freehold or extend a lease.

- under the Leasehold Reform, Housing and Urban Development Act 1993 to determine the price to be paid by the Nominee Purchaser, on behalf of the qualifying tenants, to acquire collectively the freehold of their block of flats; any amounts due to the landlord by any tenants under the terms of their leases or collateral agreements, at the time of the conveyance of the freehold to the Nominee Purchaser; the premium to be paid by a tenant to acquire a new lease to run for 90 years beyond the expiry of the current lease, in substitution for the existing lease; and the amount of the landlord's reasonable costs incurred in dealing with an application to acquire a freehold or a new lease.
- under Part 1 of the Landlord and Tenant Act 1987 to determine various matters arising from the disposal of a landlord's interest in a block of fats where the qualifying tenants wish to exercise their right to first refusal.
- applications about service charges payable by a tenant to a landlord under the Landlord and Tenant Act 1987, s 27A, and about dispensation from the service charge consultation requirements under the Landlord and Tenant Act 1987, s 20ZA.
- applications about administration charges levied on tenants for or in connection with the grant of approvals or applications; for approvals; for or in connection with the provision of information or documents; in respect of a failure by the tenant to make a payment by the due date; and in connection with a breach (or alleged breach) of a covenant or condition in the lease, under Sch 11 to the Commonhold and Leasehold Reform Act 2002.
- applications about estate charges levied under the Leasehold Reform Act 1967, s 19 or Chapter 4 of Part I and the Leasehold Reform, Housing and Urban Development Act 1993, s 94(6). Estate charges can be variable or fixed. Applications to the LVT are made under the Commonhold and Leasehold Reform Act 2002, s 159.
- applications to vary long (21 years) leases on the grounds set out in Part IV of the Landlord and Tenant Act 1987.
- applications about the right to manage or the taking over the management of a property from the landlord (without the need for fault) on the grounds in Chapter 1 of Part 2 of the Commonhold and Leasehold Reform Act 2002.
- applications to appoint a manager under the Landlord and Tenant Act 1987, s 24, where it is usually necessary to prove that there is fault with the management of the property, for example a failure to carry out obligations under a lease or charging unreasonable service charges.
- an application of a landlord for determination of whether there has been a breach of a covenant or condition in the lease which can lead to forfeiture, made under the Commonhold and Leasehold Reform Act 2002, s 168(4).

- applications about insurance where a lease requires that a tenant insures a property with an insurer nominated or approved by the landlord, the LVT may determine whether the insurance provided is unsatisfactory in any respect and/or whether the premiums payable are excessive; and where insurance is payable as part of a service charge, then the LVT can decide on its recoverability under the lease and its reasonableness.

Ratings appeals

52.12 Under the Local Government Finance Act 1988, Sch 11, paras 11 and 14 the Lands Chamber has jurisdiction to hear certain types of appeal from the Valuation Tribunal ('VT'). Not all VT cases are appealable to the Lands Chamber; some still go to the High Court. However, in the following cases – all of which involve non-domestic properties and council rates applied to those properties under the 1988 Act – an appeal, which does not require permission, may be made to the Lands Chamber:

- *non-domestic rating.* The non-domestic rateable list is the list of all non-domestic properties in a billing authority's area which gives their rateable value and other relevant information. Valuation Officers determine a rateable value for every non-domestic property in the country. This is used as the basis for the amount of rates that a ratepayer must pay. The rateable value is based on an estimate of the annual rent for the property, that it might reasonably be expected to let for, on the open market, on the antecedent valuation date, subject to various assumptions. The rating allocated may be appealed to the VT.
- *non-domestic invalidity.* If, when the Valuation Office Agency receives a proposal from a council rate payer that they do not consider meets the legal requirements for such a proposal to be made, they can reject it and serve an invalidity notice. That may be appealed to the VT, which determines its validity.
- *non-domestic completion notice decisions.* This notice is served by a council for a new property, or a property that has been undergoing major changes. It gives the date at which the property is deemed to be complete or to have been completed for the purposes of becoming liable to council rates.
- *transitional certification.* Where there has been an alteration to a non-domestic property, which occurred before a revaluation, but which had not been taken into account in the rateable value in the previous rating list the valuation officer will, when requested, certify what its rateable value would have been by issuing a certificate. This allows for the correct application of the transitional arrangements and may be appealed to the VT.

References by consent

52.13 The Lands Chamber may act as an arbitrator under the Lands Tribunal Act 1949, s 1(5). This will arise where parties have contractually agreed to use the Lands Chamber as a form of dispute resolution, and those disputes will usually involve valuation of land, but not necessarily so. The Lands Chamber must agree to accept the reference. The Lands Chamber Rules apply certain provisions of the Arbitration Act 1996 to these proceedings, namely ss 8–10, 12, 23, 57 and 60 (Lands Chamber Rules, r 26).

Residential Property Tribunal appeals

52.14 Under the Housing Act 2004, s 231, the Lands Chamber may hear appeals from the Residential Property Tribunal ('RPT'). These appeals require permission to have been granted either by the RPT or the Lands Chamber itself (Housing Act 2004, s 231(2)(a)). The RPT deals with matters under the Rent Act 1977 and the Housing Act 2004 and encompasses 49 different jurisdictions. In particular, these include:

- appeals by a tenant from a decision by a Local Housing Authority or Housing Association to deny the right to buy their home on the grounds that the property is particularly suitable for occupation by elderly persons (under the Housing Act 1985, Sch 5, para 11). The RPT has no jurisdiction if the right to buy has been denied on any other grounds;
- applications made by a Local Housing Authority (LHA) for Empty Dwelling Management Orders (EDMOs);
- appeals against Empty Dwelling Management Orders (EDMOs);
- appeals against Improvement Notices;
- appeals against Prohibition Notices served by the LHA;
- appeals against Emergency Remedial Notices and Emergency Prohibition Orders;
- appeals/applications for demolition and closing orders.

Restrictive covenants

52.15 A person with an interest in freehold land (and, in leasehold land in certain circumstances: Law of Property Act 1925, s 84(12)) may, under the Law of Property Act 1925, s 84 apply to have a restrictive covenant which applies to the land discharged or modified. The Lands Chamber may make such an order where certain conditions are satisfied (Law of Property Act 1925, s 84(1), (1A)):

(a) that by reason of changes in the character of the property or the neighbourhood or other circumstances of the case which the Lands Tribunal may deem material, the restriction ought to be deemed obsolete, or

(aa) that, where the restriction does not secure to persons entitled to the benefit of it any practical benefits of substantial value or advantage to them or is contrary to the public interest and that money will be an adequate compensation, the continued existence of the restriction would impede some reasonable user of the land for public or private purposes or, as the case may be, would unless modified so impede such user; or

(b) that the persons of full age and capacity for the time being or from time to time entitled to the benefit of the restriction, whether in respect of estates in fee simple or any lesser estates or interests in the property to which the benefit of the restriction is annexed, have agreed, either expressly or by implication, by their acts or omissions, to the same being discharged or modified; or

(c) that the proposed discharge or modification will not injure the persons entitled to the benefit of the restriction.

52.16 The Lands Chamber may order the payment of compensation to make up for any loss or disadvantage suffered in consequence of the discharge or modification or for any effect which the restriction had, at the time when it was imposed, in reducing the consideration then received for the land affected by it (Law of Property Act 1925, s 84(1)).

52.17 The discharge of restrictive covenants is a complex area of case law, and also has detailed procedural provisions in the Rules in respect of notice and how the application is to be dealt with (see **Lands Chamber procedural rules**).

Rights of light applications

52.18 The owner of a building may acquire a prescriptive right to light across adjacent land if light is enjoyed for 20 years without interruption of a year or more. To prevent the acquisition of these rights, the owner of the adjacent land may apply to the relevant local authority under the Rights of Light Act 1959, s 2 for the registration of a notice which is the equivalent of an obstruction. The application must be accompanied by a certificate from the Lands Chamber that adequate notice was given to persons who may be affected by the application. It is for the Lands Chamber to determine the form of notice to be given and whether the applicant has complied with its directions (Lands Chamber Rules, r 22). In cases of exceptional urgency the Lands Chamber may issue a temporary certificate lasting no longer than six months, which must then be replaced with a definitive certificate providing the applicant has complied with the requirements (Lands Chamber Rules, rr 23, 24).

FEES

52.19 Almost unique amongst the other Chambers (with the exception of the First-tier Tribunal (Gambling)), the Lands Chamber charges fees to applicants and appellants using it. The fees are set out in the Schedule to The Upper Tribunal (Lands Chamber) Fees Order 2009, SI No 2009/1114 and range from £40 to a maximum of £5000. Users should contact the Lands Chamber if concerned about the level of fee they may be liable to pay.

53 Lands Chamber Procedural Rules

See **Lands Chamber**.

STATUTORY INSTRUMENT

53.1 The Lands Chamber of the Upper Tribunal is currently the only part of the Upper Tribunal (see **Upper Tribunal**) which has its own procedural rules. Instead of the standard Upper Tribunal Rules, the Lands Chamber procedure is governed by the Lands Chamber Rules, (subsequently amended by SI 1997/1965, SI 1998/22, SI 2003/2945, SI 2006/880 and, in particular, the Transfer of Tribunal Functions (Lands Tribunal and Miscellaneous Amendments) Order 2009, SI 2009/1307). They are an amended form of the original Lands Tribunal Rules and their structure is consequently rather different to Rules produced by the Tribunal Procedure Committee (see **Tribunal Procedure Committee**). For regularity of reference, they are referred to in this Handbook as the Lands Chamber Rules. All references in this entry are to the Lands Chamber Rules unless otherwise stated.

53.2 A consultation process is, at the time of writing, underway on amending the Rules further and it is expected that a set of Rules which more closely match the structure of the other Chambers' will be adopted.

53.3 More detail of the different procedural provision in the Lands Chamber for particular elements of the legal process are set out in individual entries.

PRACTICE DIRECTION

53.4 The Senior President of Tribunals has issued Interim Practice Directions and Guidance for the Lands Chamber (13 May 2009). This document is important, adding significant details to the Rules, and practitioners and users of the Lands Chamber must refer to it. Paragraph references to relevant passages from this document will be made alongside the Rule to which they relate.

53.5 Although there is no reference to either in the Lands Chamber Rules, both the overriding objective and the importance of mediation (and other forms of alternative dispute resolution) are stressed in the Interim Practice Direction (paragraphs 2–4).

ALLOCATION OF CASES TO PROCEDURES

53.6 In a manner reminiscent of proceedings in the Tax Chamber of the First-tier Tribunal (see **Tax Chamber**), the Interim Practice Direction – without any specific provision in the Rules for this – directs that the registrar or Tribunal will allocate every case to one of four procedures (paragraph 5.1):

- The standard procedure;
- The special procedure;
- The simplified procedure; or
- The written representations procedure.

53.7 Any party may express a preference as to the procedure to be adopted, and should do so in the application, notice of appeal, reference notice, or response as applicable (paragraph 5.8).

Standard procedure

53.8 The standard procedure applies to all cases not designated anything else. The case will follow the normal provisions of the Rules set out below, although the registrars and Tribunal will look to use pre-trial reviews where possible to narrow the scope of the final hearing. A standard procedure case can be transferred into another procedure at any time (paragraph 5.6).

Special procedure

53.9 Cases of particular complexity, amount in issue, or of wider importance are appropriate for the special procedure. Once allocated, a pre-trial review will be held under the Lands Chamber Rules, r 39 to ensure all appropriate directions are given for the fair, expeditious and economical conduct of the proceedings. Before the pre-trial review the parties will be asked to the extent that they are able to do so at that stage, to identify the issues in the case, and to state the areas of expertise of each expert witness that they propose to rely on and the general scope of their evidence. Parties should request any other orders they wish to be made in time for it to be considered at the pre-trial review (paragraph 5.2).

Simplified procedure

53.10 With the consent of the appellant, applicant or person bringing the reference, the Tribunal may order that a simplified procedure apply under the Lands Chamber Rules, r 28. Any objection must be made in writing within seven days (Lands Chamber Rules, r 28(2)). The purpose of this procedure is to provide for the speedy and economical determination of cases in which no substantial issue of law or valuation practice, or substantial conflict of fact, is likely to arise. It will often be suitable where the amount at stake is small (paragraph 5.3).

53.11 The need for a statement of case under Lands Chamber Rules, r 8 can be dispensed with (Lands Chamber Rules, r 28(5)). Directions will be made in respect of filing a statement of claim, and the parties must be given at least 21 days' notice of the hearing of the proceedings (Lands Chamber Rules, r 28(6)). Each party must send copies of all relevant documents to be relied upon to the other parties 14 days before the hearing, and any expert report seven days before (Lands Chamber Rules, r 28(7)).

53.12 The hearing shall be informal and the Lands Chamber can adopt any procedure it thinks is fair (Lands Chamber Rules, r 28(9)). Strict rules of evidence do not apply and evidence is not taken on oath (Lands Chamber Rules, r 28(10)). In most cases costs will not be awarded, except in exceptional circumstances or where a settlement offer has been rejected inappropriately (Lands Chamber Rules, r 28(11)). The Tribunal may end the application of the simplified procedure at any time (Lands Chamber Rules, r 28(12)).

Written representations procedure

53.13 The Lands Chamber may, with the consent of the parties to the proceedings, determine the case without an oral hearing. This procedure will only be adopted where the Tribunal considers that oral evidence and argument can properly be dispensed with having regard to costs and the issues in the case. Written representations may then be lodged with the Tribunal, including in respect of witness evidence. The Lands Chamber will make such directions as is necessary for a timetable. It may, on its own initiative or by application, reinstate an oral hearing at any time (Lands Chamber Rules, r 27; paragraph 5.5).

COMMENCING PROCEEDINGS IN THE LANDS CHAMBER

53.14 The jurisdiction of the Lands Chamber is wide and varied. There are consequently a number of different ways in which proceedings are begun in the Lands Chamber, depending on the type of case. See **Lands Chamber** for the different jurisdictions dealt with by the Lands Chamber.

Notices of appeal

53.15 In all cases not governed by specific rules (see below), a written notice of appeal to the Lands Chamber should be made within 28 days of the date on which the decision appealed against was notified to the appellant (unless a statute provides some other period), or from the date of permission to appeal given by the Leasehold Valuation Tribunal ('LVT') or the Residential Property Tribunal ('RPT') (Lands Chamber Rules, r 6(1), (1A)). The Tribunal may direct that a shorter period apply if it considers that it is in the interests of justice to do so in respect of cases where permission was granted by the LVT or RPT (Lands Chamber Rules, r 6(1B)).

53.16 The notice of appeal shall include (Lands Chamber Rules, r 6(3), (4)):

- the name and address of the appellant;
- the date and any reference number of the disputed decision and the name and address of the Authority;
- the grounds of appeal;
- where the appellant is represented, the name, address and profession of the representative;
- the signature of the appellant or his representative and the date the notice was signed;
- a copy of the disputed decision; and
- where the appeal is made following grant of permission to appeal by the authority, a copy of the decision granting permission to appeal;
- where the appeal relates to a rating appeal, a copy of the proposal or determination that was the subject of the proceedings which led to the disputed decision; and
- sufficient copies of the notice of appeal to be distributed by the Tribunal to the respondents.

53.17 A respondent may give written notice of his intention to oppose the appeal, providing his name and address for service, the grounds on which he relies and whether he opposes the appeal jointly or separately. The respondent has 28 days in which to respond, except that the Lands Chamber may direct a shorter period in the interests of justice where permission to appeal was granted by the LVT/RPT (Lands Chamber Rules, r 7).

53.18 Within 28 days of service of a notice of intention to respond, the appellant must send to the respondent a statement of case, including the full particulars of the appeal (fact and law) which will be relied upon. The respondent has a further 28 days from that to serve a respondent's statement of case (Lands Chamber Rules, r 8(2), (3)). A copy must also be sent to the registrar, along with a confirmation that the relevant time limit was observed (Lands Chamber Rules, r 8(5)). Where permission to appeal was granted by the LVT/RPT, the Lands Chamber may direct a shorter period in the interests of justice (Lands Chamber Rules, r 8(4B)).

53.19 Any valuation which is proposed to be used in evidence (including all the computations and comparisons), and the full references to any comparable property which will be relied upon (or a statement that there are no comparable properties) must be served with the statement of case (Lands Chamber Rules, r 8(6)). If evidence is adduced at the hearing which was not served with the statement the Lands Chamber may adjourn the hearing with costs penalties (Lands Chamber Rules, r 8(7)).

References

53.20 Where a reference is made to the Lands Chamber (as opposed to an appeal against a decision), the notice of reference shall contain (Lands Chamber Rules, r 10(3), (4)):

- the name and address of the person lodging the reference and, if he is represented, the name, address and profession of the representative;
- the name and address of every other person with an interest in the land to which the reference relates ('the land');
- the address or description of the land;
- the nature of the interest in the land of the person lodging the reference;
- the statutory provision under which the reference is made;
- the signature of the person lodging the reference or his representative and the date the reference was signed;
- where the matter relates to compensation payable on the compulsory acquisition of land –
    - a copy of the notice to treat if one has been served;
    - a copy of the notice of entry if one has been served; and
    - any notice of claim and amendments of it delivered to the acquiring authority in pursuance of section 4 of the 1961 Act; and
- in any other case, a copy of the order or other document in consequence of which proceedings for the determination of the reference are

instituted including a copy of any agreement conferring jurisdiction on the Tribunal.

53.21 Where the reference relates to compensation for compulsory purchase, no reference should be made before 28 days from the notice to treat or the notice of claim (Lands Chamber Rules, r 10(5)). In a reference under the Town and Country Planning Act 1990, s 153(1), the notice of reference must be given to the Tribunal within two months of the date of service of the counter-notice (Lands Chamber Rules, r 10(6). In a reference under the Town and Country Planning (Compensation and Certificates) Regulations 1974, SI 1974/1242, regs 7(1) or 12(3), the notice of reference must be given to the Tribunal within 30 days of the issue of notice of the decision or findings to which the dispute relates (Lands Chamber Rules, r 10(7)). In proceedings under reg 15 of the same Regulations the time limit is 30 days from the Secretary of State's determination and the reference should specify which ground in reg 14(4) is relied upon (Lands Chamber Rules, r 10(8)).

53.22 The registrar will send a copy of the reference to all other parties (Lands Chamber Rules, r 11).

Appeals from the Leasehold Valuation Tribunal and the Residential Property Tribunal

53.23 Where a party wishes to appeal against a decision of the LVT (under the Commonhold and Leasehold Reform Act 2002, s 175) or the RPT (under the Housing Act 2004, s 231), permission to appeal must have been granted by either the LVT/RPT or the Lands Chamber.

53.24 An applicant for permission to appeal must first apply to the lower tribunal (Lands Chamber Rules, r 5C(1)). If permission is refused, the applicant has 14 days from the date the letter was sent refusing permission to apply for permission from the Lands Chamber (Lands Chamber Rules, r 5C(2)). The notice of appeal must include (Lands Chamber Rules, r 5C(3)–(5)):

- the name and address of the applicant;
- the name and address of every respondent;
- the grounds of appeal against the decision in respect of which permission to appeal is sought;
- where the applicant is represented, the name, address and profession of the representative;
- the signature of the applicant or his representative and the date the application was signed;
- a copy of the decision against which permission to appeal is being sought;
- a copy of the decision of the first instance tribunal refusing leave to appeal;
- the fee payable to the Tribunal in respect of the proposed appeal; and
- sufficient copies for each respondent.

53.25 Applicants must specify whether the LVT/RPT wrongly interpreted or applied the relevant law; wrongly applied or misinterpreted relevant valuation principle or practice (LVT only); took account of an irrelevant consideration, failed to take account of a relevant one, or was procedurally flawed; and/or whether the points are of wide implication (paragraphs 6.7, 7.7). The applicant should also specify whether the appeal seeks a rehearing, a review which may lead to a rehearing, or a review (which will be taken to be the choice if no other is specified) (paragraphs 6.8, 7.8).

53.26 The Tribunal will grant permission to appeal only where it appears that there are reasonable grounds for concluding that the LVT or RPT may have been wrong for one or more of the reasons above. In considering whether to grant permission on such grounds, the importance of the point both to the decision itself and in terms of its wider implications will be a factor to be taken into consideration in determining the proportionality and expedience of permitting an appeal to proceed. Where a successful appeal by review will necessitate a re-hearing, the Tribunal will have regard to the scope of such re-hearing in considering the proportionality of granting permission (paragraph 6.9, 7.9).

53.27 The Lands Chamber will inform each respondent of any time limit within which any objections must be lodged (Lands Chamber Rules, r 5C(7)).

53.28 The Tribunal will ordinarily determine the application without a hearing (Lands Chamber Rules, r 5D). If permission is refused, the applicant's fee will be refunded (Lands Chamber Rules, r 5E). Permission may be granted on such conditions as the Tribunal sees fit (Lands Chamber Rules, r 5F(1)). The appeal then proceeds under the ordinary rules, except that a notice of appeal is not required and the respondent responds to the application notice (Lands Chamber Rules, r 5G).

Applications in restrictive covenants cases

53.29 An application may be made to the Lands Chamber in respect of restrictive covenants under the Law of Property Act 1925, s 84. An application shall contain (Lands Chamber Rules, r 13(1),(2)):

- the name and address of the person making the application and, if he is represented, the name, address and profession of the representative;
- the address or description of the land to which the application relates;
- the address or description of the land which is subject to the restriction;
- the address or description of the land which, and the identity of any person (if known) who, has the benefit of the restriction or any person whom the applicant believes may have such benefit and the reasons for that belief;
- the ground or grounds in section 84 on which the applicant relies and the reason he considers that that ground or those grounds apply;
- a statement as to whether the applicant is applying to discharge the restriction wholly or for its modification, and if the latter the extent of the modification;
- a statement as to whether any planning permission has been applied for, granted or refused within the five years preceding the application in respect of the land the subject of the application;

- the signature of the person making the application or his representative and the date of the signature;
- a copy of the instrument imposing the restriction or, if this is not available, documentary evidence of the restriction; and
- a plan identifying the land to which the application relates and, so far as practicable, all the land which is subject to the restriction and the land which has the benefit of the restriction.

53.30 The registrar will determine what publicity needs to be given, and in what form, to persons who have or may have an interest in the relevant dominant building. The registrar may require further documentation. The applicant must notify the Lands Chamber in writing of all steps taken in compliance with the registrar's determinations (Lands Chamber Rules, r 14). The notices shall require persons claiming to be entitled to the benefit of the restriction, to send to the registrar and to the applicant notice of any objections they may have and of the amount of compensation they claim (if any) (Lands Chamber Rules, r 14(3)). Additional notice may be directed if it appears that a person who ought to have had notice of the proceedings has not had such notice (Lands Chamber Rules, r 18).

53.31 Any notice of objection must be sent to the registrar within 28 days of the date of the publication of the notices and shall include: his name and address and if he is represented the name, address and profession of the representative; the basis upon which he claims to be entitled to the benefit of the restriction; any ground of objection; and his signature or that of his representative and the date the statement was signed (Lands Chamber Rules, r 15).

53.32 Any party, or the Tribunal on its own initiative, may suspend the proceedings pending any reference in the High Court on the matter (Lands Chamber Rules, r 16). A case may be adjourned by the Tribunal pending enquiries of the relevant local authority (Lands Chamber Rules, r 19).

53.33 Where there are no objections within the time limit permitted, or they have been subsequently withdrawn, the Lands Chamber may decide the matter without a hearing, if the applicant consents. The same applies if the Tribunal finds an objection inadmissible (Lands Chamber Rules, r 17(2), (3)). The Tribunal may strike out, with reasons, any application it deems not to have been made by a person other than the proper person (Lands Chamber Rules, r 17(1)).

53.34 Where a discharge or modification is subject to the payment of compensation, the order shall take effect only when the registrar certifies that the compensation has been paid. If a time limit for payment was not met then the order may cease (Lands Chamber Rules, r 20).

Applications in right of light cases

53.35 Where an application is made in a right of light case under the Rights of Light Act 1959, s 2, the prescribed form must be used and two additional copies of the application which is intended to be made to the relevant local authority should be provided (Lands Chamber Rules, r 21).

53.36 The registrar will determine what publicity needs to be given, and in what form, to persons who have or may have an interest in the relevant dominant building. The registrar may require further documentation. The applicant must notify the Lands Chamber in writing of all steps taken in compliance with the registrar's determinations (Lands Chamber Rules, r 22). Once satisfied that all the required steps have been taken, a definitive certificate that notice has been complied with will be issued (Lands Chamber Rules, r 24).

53.37 A temporary certificate of notice may be issued, for no more than six months, where the Lands Chamber is satisfied of the need for exceptional urgency (Lands Chamber Rules, r 23).

Arbitral reference cases

53.38 Where a matter is referred to the Lands Chamber as arbitrator by consent under the Lands Tribunal Act 1949, s 1(5), the following provisions of the Arbitration Act 1996 shall apply: s 8 (whether agreement discharged by death of a party); s 9 (stay of legal proceedings); s 10 (reference of interpleader issue to arbitration); s 12 (power of court to extend time for beginning arbitral proceedings, etc); s 23 (revocation of arbitrator's authority); s 57 (correction of award or additional award) in so far as it relates to costs and so that the reference to 'award' shall include a reference to any decision of the Tribunal; and s 60 (agreement to pay costs in any event) (Lands Chamber Rules, r 26). Any person making a reference to the Lands Chamber shall supply the relevant agreement containing the arbitration clause (Lands Chamber Rules, r 26A).

HEARINGS

53.39 All hearings in the Lands Chamber are to be in public unless the Tribunal is sitting as an arbitrator under the Lands Tribunal Act 1949, s 1(5), or it is satisfied that because of confidentiality or national security it is just and reasonable for the hearing (or part thereof) to be held in private. There is no exception in compulsory purchase cases (Lands Chamber Rules, r 5).

53.40 The Tribunal will notify the parties of the hearing date as soon as is reasonably practicable after the commencement of proceedings. It will also send that information to any person who indicates an intention to respond (Lands Chamber Rules, r 4).

53.41 A trial bundle should be filed with the Tribunal not less than 14 days prior to the hearing containing all experts reports, witness statements, other documents and a statement of agreed facts and issues. Skeleton arguments should be lodged seven days prior to the hearing (paragraphs 15.1–2).

53.42 The Lands Chamber may order a pre-trial review to be held, notifying the parties of any such decision. Unless the parties agree otherwise it shall not be held within 14 days of the decision to hold it (Lands Chamber Rules, r 39(1), (2)). Any direction may be made which appears to be necessary or desirable for securing the just, expeditious and economical disposal of the proceedings, including the encouragement of all admissions possible (Lands Chamber Rules, r 39(3)). Failure to appear at the pre-trial review permits the registrar or Tribunal to make such order as necessary to dispose of or expedite proceedings (Lands Chamber Rules, r 39(7)). Pre-trial reviews will invariably be held in special procedure cases, but may be held in standard procedure cases as well.

GENERAL CASE MANAGEMENT POWERS

53.43 The Rules give the Lands Chamber broad case management powers, including the power to:

- Make a site inspection of the land which is the subject of proceedings, or comparable property, on notice to the parties in the case (Lands Chamber Rules, r 29).
- Consolidate proceedings where proceedings raise the same issues, or are about the same land or are about different interests in the same land (Lands Chamber Rules, r 30).
- Select a test case on a particular issue, binding the stayed cases, with the consent of all the parties to all the relevant proceedings (Lands Chamber Rules, r 31).
- Order that evidence be given orally and on oath or affirmation, and that a witness attend for cross-examination (Lands Chamber Rules, r 33(1), (2)).
- Make the following types of order in respect of disclosure of documents (Lands Chamber Rules, r 34(1)), imposing a time limit for compliance of not less than 14 days (Lands Chamber Rules, r 34(2)):
  - to deliver to the registrar any document or information which the Tribunal may require and which it is in the power of the party to deliver;
  - to afford to every other party to the proceedings an opportunity to inspect those documents (or copies of them) and to take copies;
  - to deliver to the registrar an affidavit or make a list stating whether any document or class of document specified or described in the order or application is, or has at any time been in his possession, custody or power and stating when he parted with it;
  - to deliver to the registrar a statement in the form of a pleading setting out further and better particulars of the grounds on which he intends to rely and any relevant facts or contentions;
  - to answer interrogatories on affidavit relating to any matter at issue between the applicant and the other party;
  - to deliver to the registrar a statement of agreed facts, facts in dispute and the issue, or issues to be tried by the Tribunal; or
  - to deliver to the registrar witness statements or proofs of evidence.
- On application to the registrar, extend any time limit (even if the application is made outside the relevant time limit) (Lands Chamber Rules, r 35). In certain types of case, notably restrictive covenant applications and leasehold enfranchisement appeals, delay may have substantial adverse consequences for one of the parties and the Tribunal will seek to enforce strictly any time limits laid down if such consequences are likely to occur (paragraph 11.1).
- Shorten any time limit by making an urgency direction, by application or on its own initiative, providing it is done either by consent or with

the opportunity for all parties to make representations (Lands Chamber Rules, r 35A).

- Permit an appellant to put forward additional grounds on such terms as it thinks fit, including costs (Lands Chamber Rules, r 36).
- On the application of any party, order that an issue be determined as a preliminary issue (Lands Chamber Rules, r 43), which may be of law or fact, and may finally dispose of the proceedings, or reduce the issues in the case and thereby cost and delay (paragraph 10.2). Parties applying for the use of the r 43 power should specify precisely the point of law to be determined and how its determination will enable expedition and less expense (paragraph 10.3). It should not be used in restrictive covenant cases (paragraph 10.5).
- On application, dismiss the proceedings if it thinks fit (Lands Chamber Rules, r 45(2)).
- Where a party has failed to comply with an order or a provision of the Rules, the Lands Chamber may direct that the document be sent; adjourn proceedings; make costs orders; order the proceedings to a hearing; dismiss the proceedings or disbar the offending party; or make any other order which expedites or disposes of the proceedings (Lands Chamber Rules, r 46(2)).
- Make directions as to the procedure at the hearing (Lands Chamber Rules, r 48), which will normally follow the procedure adopted in the High Court or county court, especially in respect of turns of speaking and the rules of evidence (paragraph 19.1).
- Dismiss or otherwise determine the proceedings in the absence of any party at a hearing, providing that the absent party may apply for the order to be set aside within seven days (Lands Chamber Rules, r 49).

53.44 A failure to comply with the Lands Chamber Rules does not render proceedings invalid (Lands Chamber Rules, r 47).

53.45 An application for an interlocutory direction is made to the registrar, in writing giving the grounds on which the application is sought. If all parties consent then that should be recorded; if not, all parties must be served with the application and any objections must be made within seven days. The registrar may order an oral hearing, and must consider the convenience of all the parties and the desirability of limiting so far as practicable the costs of the proceedings. The registrar shall inform the parties in writing of his decision. An appeal to the Lands Chamber itself may be made within seven days of the decision of the registrar (Lands Chamber Rules, r 38).

DECISION

53.46 All decisions of the Lands Chamber shall be writing and with reasons. However, if satisfied that it would not be unjust or inconvenient the Tribunal may deliver its decision orally (Lands Chamber Rules, r 50(1), (2)), although this will not normally be appropriate (paragraph 21.1). It may, and on application shall, issue an order incorporating its decision (Lands Chamber Rules, r 50(3)). The Tribunal shall serve a copy of its decision or order on every party and other interested persons (such as a valuation officer or relevant authority) (Lands Chamber Rules, r 50(5)).

53.47 Where a value is reached but is dependent upon a decision on the law the Tribunal must state what the value would have been had its decision on the law been different (Lands Chamber Rules, r 50(4)).

APPEALS FROM THE LANDS CHAMBER

53.48 An appeal from the Lands Chamber is to the Court of Appeal, and permission to appeal must first be sought from the Lands Chamber (Lands Chamber Rules, r 58(1)). An application must be made within 28 days of the date on which the Lands Chamber sent the decision appealed against to the applicant for permission (Lands Chamber Rules, r 58(2)). If the application is out of time, it must include a request for an extension of time and the reason why it was not made within time. If there is no such request, the Tribunal must refuse the application (Lands Chamber Rules, r 58(3)). The application must identify the decision, the alleged error(s) of law in the decision, and state the result sought (Lands Chamber Rules, r 58(4)).

53.49 Where there is an application for permission to appeal, the Lands Chamber may, in certain circumstances, review its own decision and must notify the parties of its decision on any review. If a decision is taken without a party having had the opportunity to make representations the notification must state that that party can apply to have the reviewed decision set aside (Lands Chamber Rules, r 60).

53.50 The Lands Chamber may only review its own decision where it overlooked a legislative provision or a binding authority which would have had a material effect upon its decision, or, if, since the Tribunal's decision, a court has made a decision binding upon the Tribunal which would have had a material effect upon its decision (Lands Chamber Rules, r 59(1)).

53.51 If the Tribunal decides not to review its decision, or on review decides to make no change, it must consider whether to give permission to appeal (Lands Chamber Rules, r 59(2)). It must send a record of its decisions as soon as practicable (Lands Chamber Rules, r 59(3)). If permission to appeal is refused the Tribunal must send its reasons and a notification of the right to apply to the Court of Appeal and the time in which to do so (Lands Chamber Rules, r 59(4)). Permission may be given on limited grounds (Lands Chamber Rules, r 59(5)).

COSTS

53.52 There is a broad discretion as to costs, permitting the registrar to make any order as to costs, as can the Lands Chamber on appeal from registrar (Lands Chamber Rules, r 52(2), (3)). Assessment of costs shall be done as though proceedings were in the High Court or county court by the registrar, which may be appealed to the Tribunal (after a review by the registrar) within 10 days (Lands Chamber Rules, r 52(4)–(7)). Detailed costs guidance is provided in the Interim Practice Direction:

> 'The general rule is that the successful party ought to receive their costs. On a claim for compensation for compulsory acquisition of land, the costs incurred by a claimant in establishing the amount of disputed compensation are properly to be seen as part of the expense

that is imposed on the claimant by the acquisition. The Tribunal will, therefore, normally make an order for costs in favour of a claimant who receives an award of compensation unless there are special reasons for not doing so. Particular rules, however, apply by virtue of s.4 of the Land Compensation Act 1961. Under this provision, where an acquiring authority has made an unconditional offer in writing of compensation and the sum awarded does not exceed the sum offered, the Tribunal must, in the absence of special reasons, order the claimant to bear their own costs thereafter and to pay the post-offer costs of the acquiring authority. However, claimants will not be entitled to their costs if they have failed to deliver to the authority, in time to enable the authority to make a proper offer, a notice of claim containing the particulars set out in s.4(2). Where claimants have delivered a claim containing the required details and have made an unconditional offer in writing to accept a particular sum, if the Tribunal's award is equal to or exceeds that sum the Tribunal must, in the absence of special reasons, order the authority to bear their costs and to pay the claimants' post-offer costs.' (paragraph 23.3)

53.53 The general rule as to costs does not apply to restrictive covenant proceedings (except when an applicant disputes an objector's claimed entitlement to the benefit of the restriction) because under the Law of Property Act 1925, s 84 the applicant is seeking to have removed from the objector particular property rights that the objector has. Unless they have acted unreasonably, unsuccessful objectors will not normally have to pay any of the applicant's costs and successful objectors will normally get their costs (paragraph 23.4).

53.54 By virtue of the Commonhold and Leasehold Reform Act 2002, s 175 (6) and (7), in the case of appeals from the LVT a costs order may only be made where the losing party has, in the opinion of the Tribunal, acted frivolously, vexatiously, abusively, disruptively or otherwise unreasonably in connection with the appeal, and in any event not more than the LVT could have awarded (currently £500) (paragraph 23.5).

53.55 In a simple case or on an interlocutory hearing the Tribunal may assess the costs summarily. The Tribunal will normally award costs on the standard basis. On this basis, costs will only be allowed to the extent that they are reasonable and proportionate to the matters in issue, and any doubt as to whether costs were reasonably incurred or reasonable and proportionate in amount will be resolved in favour of the paying party. Exceptionally the Tribunal may award costs on the indemnity basis. On this basis, the receiving party will receive all his costs except for those which have been unreasonably incurred or which are unreasonable in amount; and any doubt as to whether the costs were reasonably incurred or are reasonable in amount will be resolved in favour of the receiving party (paragraph 23.8).

53.56 'Where proceedings are determined in accordance with the simplified procedure under rule 28, costs will only be awarded where an offer to settle has been made and the Tribunal considers it appropriate to have regard to this offer, or the circumstances are exceptional.' (paragraph 23.9).

54 Local Authority Standards Cases

See also **General Regulatory Chamber; General Regulatory Chamber procedural rules**

SUMMARY OF THE JURISDICTION

54.1 From 18 January 2010 and the coming into force of the Transfer of Tribunal Functions Order 2010, SI 2010/22, the GRC has had jurisdiction over local authority standards cases (see **General Regulatory Chamber**). This jurisdiction was formerly exercised by the Adjudication Panel for England ('APE'), which was an independent Tribunal, established by the Local Government Act 2000, s 75(1).

54.2 The principal functions of the APE were:

- as an appeal tribunal hearing appeals made by councillors against the decision of a local authority standards committee;
- as a case tribunal hearing references from an Ethical Standards Officer ('ESO') of the Standards Board for England or from a local authority standards committee that a member of an authority has failed to comply with the authority's Code of Conduct.

54.3 These functions have now been absorbed into the GRC's jurisdiction. Accordingly, all proceedings in local authority standards cases will be governed by the GRC Rules (see **General Regulatory Chamber procedural rules**). The APE had previously operated without any formal procedural rules. Accordingly, as a result of transfer into the GRC, local authority standards cases are now governed by more explicit powers of direction and the powers of the Tribunal have been expanded and, for example, include the power to summon witnesses. To aid users and the Tribunal specific guidance has been adopted by the Tribunals Service which supplements the GRC Rules.

APPEALS AGAINST DECISIONS OF A LOCAL AUTHORITY STANDARDS COMMITTEE

54.4 Where a standards committee makes a finding under the Standards Committee (England) Regulations 2008, SI 2008/1085 ('the Standards Regulations'), reg 19(1)(b) or (c) that the member of the authority subject to the decision failed to comply with the Code of Conduct, a right of appeal lies to the GRC under the Standards Regulations, reg 21.

54.5 The right of appeal may only be exercised with the permission of the First-tier Tribunal (the Standards Regulations, reg 21(4)).

Procedure for applications for permission to appeal

54.6 The procedure for appealing to the First-tier Tribunal is governed by the Standards Regulations and the GRC Rules. The general procedure for bring such an appeal is set out elsewhere in this Handbook (see **General Regulatory Chamber procedural rules** and **Bringing proceedings in the First-tier Tribunal**).

54.7 The time limit for appealing to the GRC against a decision of a standards committee is 28 days following the date on which the notice of the decision was sent to the appellant.

54.8 Applications for permission to appeal must be made in writing and must specify:

- the grounds of the appeal;
- whether any application for suspension of any sanction imposed under the Standards Regulations, reg 19(3)(b)–(k) pending determination of the appeal (the Standards Regulations, reg 21(1)(b)); and
- whether or not the member consents to the appeal being determined by way of written representations.

(Guidance: Tribunal Procedures for dealing with Appeals from decisions of Standards Committees, January 2010 (the 'Appeals Cases Guidance'), paragraph 6).

54.9 In determining whether or not permission to appeal should be granted, the GRC must have regard to whether there is a reasonable prospect of success on appeal (the Standards Regulations, reg 21(4)). The Standards Regulations do not specify that this is an absolute test in that an appeal with no reasonable prospect of success must not be permitted to proceed (only that regard must be had to this). However, the Standards Regulations also do not provide a second limb for permission to be granted for some other compelling reason (as is the case with appeals to the Court of Appeal under CPR Part 52). It is not possible to determine from the previous practice of the APE as to whether a lower or more flexible test was being applied as the number of appeal cases heard by APE is small. For example, in 2007/2008, 15 applications for permission to appeal were made of which 11 were allowed to proceed and of the eight cases ultimately determined by the appeal tribunal, three were successful (see APE Annual Report 2007/8)). It is suggested that the First-tier Tribunal will, in practice, also take into account the degree and impact of any sanction imposed upon a member by the sanctions committee.

54.10 Permission to appeal or suspension of the sanction may be granted in respect only of a particular specified part of the finding or sanction (the Standards Regulations, reg 21(5)).

54.11 If permission to appeal is refused, the notice of decision will provide the GRC's reasons (Appeals Cases Guidance, paragraph 10). If permission is granted, no further application is needed, and the GRC will regard the application for permission as constituting the notice of appeal (Appeals Cases Guidance, paragraph 11).

Procedure following the grant of permission

54.12 Appeals against the decisions of standards committees follow the standard timetable for non-charities cases under Chapter II of the GRC Rules. Further guidance can be found in the Appeals Cases Guidance, at paragraphs 12–20. The guidance does not deviate from the standard GRC procedure.

54.13 Appellant parties should note that, subject to the decision of the GRC as to relevance, the appellant may apply for permission to introduce before the

Tribunal evidence which was not before the standards committee (Appeal Cases Guidance, paragraph 34).

Determination of an appeal without an oral hearing

54.14 The GRC may determine an appeal without an oral hearing if the parties consent and the GRC considers that it can properly do so (GRC Rules, r 32; Appeal Cases Guidance, paragraph 15). The parties will be notified if the Tribunal intends to resolve the matter without a hearing, at which point the parties will have a further chance to insist upon an oral hearing.

54.15 Where an appeal has been scheduled to be determined without an oral hearing, the GRC may nonetheless refer the matter to an oral hearing if it considers it inappropriate to dispose of the proceedings on the written evidence available (Appeals Cases Guidance, paragraph 16).

Determination of an appeal at an oral hearing

54.16 The format of hearings before the GRC is considered elsewhere in the Handbook (see **General Regulatory Chamber procedural rules** and **Hearings**). It suffices to note that the GRC is free to determine its own procedure in accordance with the circumstances of each individual appeal. Its standard practice however is that unless there are matters of fact in dispute, no oral evidence will be heard (Appeal Cases Guidance, paragraph 28).

54.17 If relevant facts are in dispute, the GRC will first hear submissions and evidence concerning the disputed facts, and will form a view on how to resolve the matters in dispute. Once this has been done the Tribunal will turn to consider whether, on the facts as now found, there has or has not been a failure to comply with the relevant local authority Code of Conduct (Appeal Cases Guidance, paragraph 31).

54.18 Where an appellant alleges that there has been bias or that he or she has been disadvantaged by a procedural defect in the standards committee's hearing, the GRC will typically treat the appeal as a fresh determination on the merits if it considers that there may be substance in the appellant's procedural complaints (Appeal Cases Guidance, paragraph 35).

Outcome of appeals

54.19 The decision will usually (save for appeals determined by written representations) be announced on the day of the hearing. The written decision will set out the reasons for the Tribunal's decision and will be sent as soon as practicable (usually within 14 days) of the hearing and then posted on the Tribunal's website (Appeal Cases Guidance, paragraphs 36, 37).

54.20 The GRC may only uphold or reject the finding of the standards committee (the Standards Regulations, reg 25(1)).

54.21 Where a finding is upheld, the GRC may confirm or vary any sanction imposed and may impose any other sanction that was available to the standards committee (the Standards Regulations, reg 25(3), (4); Appeal Cases Guidance, paragraph 39).

54.22 Where the GRC rejects a finding of the standards committee, the committee's decision and sanction shall cease to have effect from the date of the Tribunal's decision (the Standards Regulations, reg 25(2); Appeal Cases Guidance, paragraph 40).

54.23 Any sanction imposed, varied or continued by the GRC will take effect immediately upon its decision, unless the GRC directs that any sanction imposed will take effect from a later date which must be no later than six months after its decision (the Standards Regulations, reg 25(6)).

Appealing against a decision of the GRC as an Appeals Tribunal

54.24 Previously, there was no right of appeal against a decision of the APE as an Appeals Tribunal (though the APE was a public body and its decisions were subject to judicial review). Disappointed parties in local authority standards cases now have a right to appeal to the Upper Tribunal where the lower Tribunal made an error of law (see **General Regulatory Chamber procedural rules; Appeals from the First-tier Tribunal** and **Appeals and References to the Upper Tribunal**).

REFERENCES FROM AN ESO OR STANDARDS COMMITTEE

54.25 Following a complaint to a local authority or the Standards Board for England that a relevant Code of Conduct has not been followed, an ESO or standards committee may decide that the matter should be referred to the GRC for determination (see the Standards Regulations, reg 17; the Local Government Act 2000, ss 59(4), 64, 65 and 66A).

54.26 Discussion of the circumstances in which the GRC will accept a reference from standards committee under the Standards Regulations, reg 17 is outside the scope of this Handbook. Standards committees should however have regard to the guidance set down by the Tribunals Service: Guidance on the circumstances in which the Tribunal would consider accepting a reference from a Standards Committee under Regulation 17 of the Standards Committee (England) Regulations 2008 (January 2010). This provides guidance on when a standards committee might consider that the action which it could itself take would be insufficient in the event that it reached a finding that there had been a failure to follow the provisions of the relevant Code. The GRC has also indicated a willingness to provide a preliminary view as to whether it would be willing to accept a reference. The committee should provide a copy of its report or an outline of the material facts and state why it is or might be of the view that a greater sanction would be appropriate than it is able to impose (see Tribunal Services guidance: Tribunal Procedures (references from an ESO/SC) (January 2010) (the 'References Guidance'), paragraph 7).

Procedure for referring a matter to the GRC

54.27 References are started by the filing of a notice of appeal. In the case of a reference from an ESO, this must be within 28 days of the completion of the final or interim report produced made in accordance with the Local Government Act 2000, ss 64(3) and 65(4) (GRC Rules, r 22(6)(d) (the version of the Rules currently in force appears incorrectly to cite the provision as s 63(3)(b)).

54.28 In the case of a reference from a standards committee, the notice of appeal must be filed within 28 days of the meeting at which the committee decided to make such a reference (GRC Rules, r 22(6)(e)).

54.29 In addition to the matters set out in the GRC Rules, r 26, all appeal notices should include:

- the name of the ESO's or standard committee's representative;
- the name of the original complainant (if applicable);
- the ESO's or Investigating Officer's recital of the facts that gave rise to the reference; and
- the ESO's or Investigating Officer's reasons as to why those facts constitute or might constitute a failure to comply with the relevant Code of Conduct.

(References Guidance, paragraph 8)

54.30 Following the receipt of the application notice, reference cases follow the standard timetable for non-charities cases under Chapter II of the GRC Rules. Further guidance can be found in the References Guidance, at paragraphs 9–20. The guidance does not however deviate from the standard GRC procedure.

Procedure at the hearing

54.31 References from an ESO or standards committee will be considered at an oral hearing. A party who does not intend to be present or represented at the hearing may submit written representations to the GRC, three working days before the date of the hearing, copying the same to the other parties (References Guidance, paragraph 23).

54.32 The Tribunal is free to set its own procedure. However, detailed guidance has been set down as to the usual procedure to be followed (References Guidance, paragraphs 27–30).

54.33 Typically, the GRC will begin by seeking to determine any disputes of fact that have been identified prior to the hearing.

- First, the appellant ESO or standards committee will produce evidence and make submissions on the disputed facts. If witnesses are called, all parties and the Tribunal will have the opportunity to question those witnesses.
- The respondent will then be afforded an opportunity to produce his or her own evidence and to make submissions. Again, if witnesses are called, all parties and the Tribunal will have an opportunity to question them.
- The Tribunal will then adjourn to deliberate on the submissions and evidence and will then announce its decision on the disputed facts.

54.34 The GRC then seeks to establish whether the facts lead to the conclusion that there has been a failure to comply with the relevant Code of Conduct.

- The respondent usually makes his submissions first on why, on the basis of the facts as found, there has been no failure to comply with the Code of Conduct.

- The appellant then responds.
- The Tribunal will then, after a further adjournment, announce its decision on whether there has been a failure to comply with the Code of Conduct.

54.35 If the Tribunal finds a failure to comply with of the Code of Conduct has occurred, the appellant and respondent will be invited to make submissions as to what action the Tribunal should take.

54.36 Following a further adjournment, the Tribunal may announce its decision or reserve it until a later date.

Procedure following the hearing

54.37 A signed and dated notice of the Tribunal's decision will be distributed to the parties either at the hearing or as soon thereafter as practicable. The notice will be published in a newspaper circulating within the area of the local authority concerned within 28 days of the hearing (References Guidance, paragraph 35).

54.38 The Tribunal will within 14 days of the hearing send a copy of the written reasons for the decision to the respondent, the standards committee of the relevant authority, Standards for England, and the person who made the original allegation (if known).

Appealing against a decision of the GRC

54.39 Disappointed parties in local authority standards cases now have a right to appeal to the Upper Tribunal against an error of law (see **General Regulatory Chamber procedural rules; Appeals from the First-tier Tribunal** and **Appeals and References to the Upper Tribunal**).

55 Mental Health Cases

LEGISLATIVE BACKGROUND

55.1 Although it is unusual for a Tribunal – rather than a court – to decide issues of personal liberty, the Mental Health Review Tribunal ('MHRT'), which could do so, was first established under the Mental Health Act 1959. An MHRT is comprised of a legally qualified chair, a medical member who is or has been a consultant psychiatrist, and another member with experience of social and mental health care (see **Constitution and composition of the First-tier Tribunal**).

55.2 The current jurisdiction in respect of mental health cases is regulated by Part V of the Mental Health Act 1983 ('the 1983 Act'), as amended in parts by the Mental Health Act 2007. All legislative references here are to the 1983 Act unless otherwise stated.

55.3 Mental health law is extremely complex, with the statutory framework being convoluted and difficult to penetrate. No attempt will be made here to set out or explain the details of substantive mental health law, or the principles underpinning it. The user is instead referred to some of the admirable works on the subject: Hale, *Mental Health Law* (2010, 5th edn, Sweet & Maxwell); and the annually updated Jones, *Mental Health Act Manual* (2010, 13th edn, Sweet & Maxwell).

55.4 Cases come before the Tribunal as either an application by or on behalf of a patient by his nearest relative, or in the form of a reference from the responsible authority (which may be the hospital, the local authority responsible for a patient under a guardianship order, or the Secretary of State). Applications to the Tribunal may be made in the following circumstances:

- Patients admitted for assessment under s 2 may apply within 14 days (s 66(1)(a) and (2)(a));
- Patients admitted for treatment under s 3 may apply within six months (s 66(1)(b) and (2)(b));
- Patients received into guardianship under ss 7–10 may apply within six months (s 66(1)(c) and (2)(c));
- Patients made subject to a community treatment order ('CTO') under s 17A may apply within six months (s 66(1)(ca) and (2)(ca));
- Patients whose CTO is revoked and who are recalled to hospital under s 17F may apply within six months (s 66(1)(cb) and (2)(cb));
- Patients who are transferred from guardianship to hospital under s 19 may apply within six months (s 66(1)(e) and (2)(e));
- Patient placed under guardianship by a court may apply within six months (s 69(1)(b));
- Patients found unfit to plead or not guilty by reason of insanity and admitted under the Criminal Procedure (Insanity) Act 1964, s 5(1) may apply within six months (s 69(2));
- Patients transferred to hospital from prison (with or without restrictions) by the Secretary of State under ss 47, 48 may apply within six months (s 69(2));

- Patients transferred from other parts of the UK under Part VI may apply within six months (s 69(2));
- Patients who became ordinary hospital order patients when their restriction order ceased under s 41(5) may apply within six months (s 69(2));
- Patients hospitalised in the long term without restriction may apply in each subsequent period of detention, CTO or guardianship (ie, the second six months, and every year thereafter) (s 66(1)(f), (fza), (faa) and (2)(f), (fza));
- Restricted patients may apply in each subsequent period of detention (ie, the second six months, and every year thereafter) (ss 70 and 79(1));
- Conditionally discharged restricted patients may apply within the second 12 months after discharge, and in every two years after that (s 75(2));
- The patient's nearest relative may apply within 28 days of the responsible clinician blocking discharge on the basis that the patient would be likely to act in 'a manner dangerous to other persons or to himself' (ss 66(1)(g) and (2)(d));
- The patient's nearest relative may apply within 12 months (and once in every subsequent 12 months) of an order being made replacing him as the nearest relative (s 66(1)(h) and (2)(g)):
- Foreign patients held under the Repatriation of Prisoners Act 1984, in addition to any right of application above, may apply within six months of provisions relating to him taking effect (paragraph 5(2) of the Schedule to the 1984 Act).

55.5 Not all patients will, for a number of reasons, be able or willing to apply to the Tribunal to review their cases and their treatment. In order to comply with Article 5 of the European Convention on Human Rights (protection against arbitrary detention) the authorities which detain patients are required to refer cases to the Tribunal to ensure periodic reviews of the progress of the patient. References must or may be made in following circumstances:

- By the hospital manager for patients admitted for assessment six months after the admission (s 68(1)(a) and (2));
- By the hospital manager for patients admitted for treatment six months after the admission (s 68(1)(b) and (2));
- By the hospital manager for patients subject to a CTO six months after the admission (s 68(1)(c) and (2));
- By the hospital manager for patients whose CTO has been revoked six months after the admission (s 68(1)(d) and (2)). A reference should be made as soon as possible after the patient is recalled to hospital and the CTO revoked (s 68(7)) (see guidance below);
- By the hospital manager for patients who have been transferred from guardianship to hospital six months after the transfer (s 68(1)(e) and (2));
- By the hospital manager for every patient aged over 18 whose case has not been considered within the last three years (s 68(6));

- By the hospital manager for every patient aged under 18 whose case has not been considered within the last 12 months (s 68(6));
- By the Secretary of State for any patient detained, at any time (s 67(1));
- By the Secretary of State for any patient subject to a guardianship order, at any time (s 67(1));
- By the Secretary of State for any patient under a CTO, at any time (s 67(1));
- By the Secretary of State for any restricted patient (including one who has been conditionally discharged), at any time (s 71(1));
- By the Secretary of State for restricted patients (including one who has been conditionally discharged) whose case has not been considered within the last three years (s 71(2));
- By the Secretary of State for any conditionally discharged restricted patient who is recalled to hospital, within 1 month of the date of arrival back in hospital (s 75(1)(a)).

55.6 The Upper Tribunal has held, in the context of patients admitted under the 1983 Act, ss 2 and 3, that a referral will generally survive changes in status because, periodically, a patient is entitled to an independent review of their circumstances under the 1983 Act and these periodic reviews should not be derailed by changes in status: *KF, MO and FF v Birmingham and Solihull NHS Mental Health Foundation Trust* [2010] UKUT 185 (AAC).

55.7 The Tribunal is not concerned with the procedural aspect of admission, which must be challenged by way of judicial review (*Re Waldron* [1986] QB 824). The circumstances in which the Tribunal may order the discharge of an unrestricted patient are set out in s 72, which also includes powers to order discharge on a future date, or recommend the transfer of the patient to another hospital or into guardianship, or to be granted a leave of absence (s 72(3)). It may also recommend the consideration of imposing a CTO (s 72(3A)). Powers of the Tribunal in cases concerning restricted patients are set out in the 1983 Act, ss 73 and 74.

TRANSFER OF JURISDICTION

55.8 From 3 November 2008 the MHRT's functions have been subsumed by the Health, Education and Social Care Chamber of the First-tier Tribunal ('HESCC'): Schedule 1 to the Transfer of Tribunal Functions Order 2008, SI 2008/2833 ('the 2008 Order'). Judges and other members of the MHRT have been transferred in as judges and other members of the HESCC.

55.9 There was no right of appeal from the MHRT, and parties who considered that the MHRT had committed an error of law had to judicially review the MHRT in the High Court. Now, like almost all divisions of the First-tier Tribunal, appeals from the HESCC go the Administrative Appeals Chamber of the Upper Tribunal on a point of law. Judicial review is not needed, unless the subject-matter of the appeal is an excluded decision (see **Excluded appeals**) (for an example see *R (RB) v First-tier Tribunal (Review)* [2010] UKUT 160 (AAC)).

55.10 Procedure in mental health cases is now governed by the Tribunal Procedure (First–tier Tribunal) (Health, Education and Social Care Chamber) Rules 2008, SI 2008/2699 as amended ('HESCC Rules'). The HESCC Rules are reproduced at Appendix 2. See **Health, Education and Social Care Chamber procedural rules** for details of the provisions.

55.11 The First-tier Tribunal (Mental health) is based in London and Preston but can and does sit at any venue in England as necessary.

55.12 The Mental Health Review Tribunal for Wales was established under the Mental Health Act 1983, s 65 has not been incorporated into the HESCC, but appeals from it go to the Administrative Appeals Chamber of the Upper Tribunal directly: the 2008 Order, art 6(2)(a), and the 1983 Act, s 78A (as amended). The MHRT (Wales) is not governed by the HESCC Rules, although its own rules are extremely similar. They are contained in the Mental Health Review Tribunal for Wales Rules 2008, SI 2008/2705 and are not discussed in further detail here.

References made under s 68(7) of the 1983 Act

55.13 The Deputy Chamber President has issued guidance (dated 1 August 2010, amended slightly on 22 September 2010) on how the Tribunal will approach references under the 1983 Act, s 68(7) made by hospital managers in respect of patients whose CTO has been revoked and who have been recalled to hospital. If, following the making of a reference, the patient is placed on a new CTO the Tribunal must be notified and the existing reference will be treated as having lapsed. This does not prevent the patient making an application if they wish to contest the CTO, and it does not apply to other references arising under s 68 which do not lapse (and if more than one reference was made, the surviving reference will not lapse). The *KF* decision (discussed above at paragraph 55.6) did not consider s 68(7) references and the guidance considers them to be different because they are not triggered by the passage of time.

PROCEDURE IN MENTAL HEALTH CASES

55.14 The HESCC Rules make specific provision for mental health cases, particularly in respect to the pre-hearing, hearing and decision stages of the process. The general rules are also adapted for the mental health context.

General powers of the Tribunal

55.15 If a party has failed to comply with a provision of the Rules, or an order of the Tribunal the Tribunal may not restrict that party's participation in the proceedings (HESCC Rules, r 7(2)(e)).

The Tribunal is not permitted to strike out a mental health case (HESCC Rules, r 8(1)), except that it is required to do so where the Tribunal does not have jurisdiction over the case and is not able to transfer the case to the appropriate venue (HESCC Rules, r 8(3)).

A costs award may only be made in a mental health case in respect of wasted costs (HESCC Rules, r 10(1), (2)). Parties should be aware that the presence on the Tribunal of medical expertise, particularly in psychiatry, reduces the need for the parties to each have their own expert evidence. Any experts used must, in accordance with the overriding objective, be made available to comply with Tribunal directions: *MD v Nottinghamshire Health Care NHS Trust* [2010] UKUT 59 (AAC) at [46]–[47].

55.16 Information about patients in mental health cases, including names of parties, must not be disclosed unless the Tribunal makes an order to the contrary (HESCC Rules, r 14(7)). It is important to note the requirement on the Tribunal not to disclose documentation if it is satisfied that the disclosure would cause serious harm and that is in the interests of justice and proportionate to refuse disclosure (HESCC Rules, r 14(2)). The AAC considered HESCC Rules, r 14(2) in *RM v St Andrew's Healthcare* [2010] UKUT 119 (AAC), which involved a patient admitted for treatment under the 1983 Act, s 3 who was being covertly medicated through his food. He applied for discharge and the HESCC prohibited disclosure to the patient of medical reports revealing the covert medication on the basis that it was a proportionate interference and that his solicitor could still conduct the case without specific instructions on this point. The AAC allowed the appeal and ordered disclosure on the basis that 'they would exclude the claimant completely from knowing of the real process that was being followed and allow him to participate only in a pretence of a process. They would severely hamper his legal team in participating effectively in that process' (at [32]) despite the short-term consequences involving risk to the patient. Relying on the decision in *Secretary of State for the Home Department v AF (No 3)* [2009] UKHL 28; [2009] 3 WLR 74 on special advocates in control order cases, the AAC considered that it showed 'how highly a fair hearing is rated in the balance with non-disclosure' (at [31]). The analysis of the balancing exercise is contained in the judgment at [27]–[30].

55.17 A party which makes a reference to the Tribunal under the Mental Health Act 1983, ss 68, 71(2) or 75(1) may not withdraw its case (HESCC Rules, r 17(3)). However, the Tribunal does not need to consent to the withdrawal of a reference under the 1983 Act, ss 67 or 71(1) (HESCC Rules, r 17(2)(b)). Following an amendment to the 1983 Act, s 77(2) (by the Transfer of Tribunal Functions (Lands Tribunal and Miscellaneous Amendments) Order 2009, SI 2009/1307, paragraph 161) an application to the Tribunal which is withdrawn does not prevent the patient from making another application to the Tribunal within the same period.

55.18 If a patient has not appointed a representative the Tribunal itself may appoint a legal representative where: the patient has stated that they do not wish to conduct their own case or that they wish to be represented; or the patient lacks the capacity to appoint a representative but the Tribunal believes that it is in the patient's best interests for the patient to be represented (HESCC Rules, r 11(7)). A patient may not appoint, or be represented by, a person liable to be detained or subject to guardianship or after-care under supervision, or who is a community patient, under the Mental Health Act 1983; or a person receiving treatment for mental disorder at the same hospital as the patient (HESCC Rules, r 11(8)).

55.19 Guidance has recently been given the Administrative Appeals Chamber of the Upper Tribunal on the role of the representative under HESCC Rules, r 11(7). In *AA v Cheshire and Wirral Partnership NHS Foundation Trust* [2009] UKUT 195 (AAC) it was suggested at [18]–[20] that:

'rule 11(7)(b) plainly contemplates the possibility of a solicitor being appointed to represent a patient who does not have the capacity to give any instructions at all.In such a case, the rule must, as the Law Society's guidance plainly expects, anticipate that the solicitor will ascertain any relevant wishes that the patient may be able to express, will inform the tribunal of such wishes, make such points in support of them as can properly be made and generally ensure that the tribunal has all the relevant material before it and does not overlook any statutory provision. However, in the absence of the patient's capacity to give valid instructions, the rule must, in my view, also anticipate that the solicitor will exercise his or her judgment and advance any argument that he or she considers to be in the patient's "best interests", which, as the Law Society's guidance recognises, will not necessarily involve arguing for the patient's discharge. In those circumstances, it seems to me that the solicitor has the same freedom of action as a litigation friend in the courts.

What, then, is the position if the patient does have the capacity to give instructions on some matters but not others? The Law Society's guidance is unequivocal: a solicitor is bound to act in accordance with the instructions that have been given. Therefore, the more a patient has the capacity to give detailed instructions, the less the solicitor has complete freedom of action.

However, even where a patient has full capacity, a solicitor may be entitled, and in some circumstances may be under a duty, to draw a tribunal's attention to significant matters – particularly points of law – that appear to be in the patient's best interests despite his or her instructions and which it appears the tribunal might otherwise overlook. A solicitor has a duty not just to his or her client but also to the tribunal or, perhaps more accurately, to the administration of justice. A distinction is to be drawn between merely drawing a matter to a tribunal's attention and fully arguing it.'

(See also **Representation**).

Application and reference procedure

See **Bringing proceedings in the First-tier Tribunal**

55.20 In mental health cases, proceedings are commenced by application or reference in the HESCC. An application or reference must be (HESCC Rules, r 32(1)):

- made in writing;
- signed (in the case of an application, by the applicant or any person authorised by the applicant to do so); and
- sent or delivered to the Tribunal so that it is received within the time specified in the Mental Health Act 1983 or the Repatriation of Prisoners Act 1984.

55.21 If possible (see HESCC Rules, r 32(2)) an application must include:

- the name and address of the patient;

- if the application is made by the patient's nearest relative, the name, address and relationship to the patient of the patient's nearest relative;
- the provision under which the patient is detained, liable to be detained, subject to guardianship, a community patient or subject to after-care under supervision;
- whether the person making the application has appointed a representative or intends to do so, and the name and address of any representative appointed;
- the name and address of the responsible authority in relation to the patient.

55.22 Subject to the power in HESCC Rules, r 14(2) to withhold evidence likely to cause harm, when the Tribunal receives a document from any party it must send a copy of that document to each other party (HESCC Rules, r32(3)).

55.23 If the patient is a conditionally discharged patient (as defined in the 1983 Act) the Secretary of State must send or deliver a statement containing the information and documents required by Practice Direction (see below) to the Tribunal so that it is received by the Tribunal as soon as practicable and in any event within six weeks after the Secretary of State received a copy of the application or a request from the Tribunal (HESCC Rules, r 32(4)).

55.24 In proceedings under the 1983 Act, s 66(1)(a), on the earlier of receipt of the copy of the application or a request from the Tribunal, the responsible authority must (HESCC Rules, r 32(6)) send or deliver to the Tribunal:

(a) the application for admission;

(b) the medical recommendations on which the application is founded;

(c) such of the information specified in the relevant practice direction as is within the knowledge of the responsible authority and can reasonably be provided in the time available; and

(d) such of the documents specified in the relevant practice direction as can reasonably be provided in the time available.

55.25 Otherwise (HESCC Rules, r 32(6)), the responsible authority must send or deliver a statement containing the information and documents required by the Practice Direction (see below) to the Tribunal so that it is received by the Tribunal as soon as practicable and in any event within three weeks after the responsible authority received a copy of the application or reference. If the patient is a restricted patient the responsible authority must (HESCC Rules, r 32(7)) also send the statement to the Secretary of State, and the Secretary of State must send a statement of any further relevant information to the Tribunal as soon as practicable and in any event:

- in proceedings under the 1983 Act, s 75(1), within two weeks after the Secretary of State received the relevant authority's statement; or
- otherwise, within three weeks after the Secretary of State received the relevant authority's statement.

55.26 By HESCC Rules, r 32(8) if the Secretary of State wishes to seek the approval of the Tribunal under the 1983 Act, s 86(3), the Secretary of State must refer the patient's case to the Tribunal and the provisions of the HESCC Rules applicable to references under the 1983 Act apply to such proceedings.

55.27 When the Tribunal receives the stipulated information the Tribunal must give notice of the proceedings (HESCC Rules, r 33):

- where the patient is subject to the guardianship of a private guardian, to the guardian;
- where there is an extant order of the Court of Protection, to that court;
- subject to a patient with capacity to do so requesting otherwise, where any person other than the applicant is named by the authority as exercising the functions of the nearest relative, to that person;
- where a health authority, Primary Care Trust, National Health Service Trust or NHS Foundation Trust has a right to discharge the patient under the provisions of the Mental Health Act 1983, s 23(3), to that authority or trust; and
- to any other person who, in the opinion of the Tribunal, should have an opportunity of being heard.

55.28 The information and reports required by the Rules from the responsible authority and/or Secretary of State are set out in the Practice Direction – First-tier Tribunal: Mental Health Cases of 30 October 2008 which, because of the level of detail and the number of different types of report, is set out in full below as an Annexe to this entry.

55.29 Before the hearing there must be a medical examination of the patient conducted by the appropriate member of the Tribunal (see **Constitution and Composition of the First-tier Tribunal**) which takes the steps necessary to form an opinion of the patient's medical condition (HESCC Rules, r 34(1)). For the purposes of the examination the Tribunal member may examine the patient in private, examine records relating to the patient's detention, treatment and after-care, and take notes and copies for use in the proceedings (HESCC Rules, r 34(2)). The parties should be made aware of any new facts or arguments adduced by the medical member of the Tribunal in order to have an opportunity of dealing with them, and the medical member should be careful to retain an open mind about the patient, especially where other expert evidence will be adduced (*R v Mental Health Review Tribunal, ex p Clatworthy* [1985] 3 All ER 699; *R (S) v Mental Health Review Tribunal* [2002] EWHC 2522 (Admin); [2003] MHLR 118).

Hearings

See **Hearings**.

55.30 All mental health cases must only be disposed of after an oral hearing (HESCC Rules, r 35), although that does not apply to a decision on review, setting aside or permission to appeal. The general rule is that each party is entitled to attend the hearing, and make written and oral representations to the Tribunal (HESCC Rules, r 36).

55.31 The Tribunal must give reasonable notice of the time and place of the hearing to the parties and any notified person (HESCC Rules, r 37(3)). That notice must ordinarily be at least 14 days unless the parties consent, or there are urgent or exceptional circumstances (HESCC Rules, r 37(4)(b)), or in a case under the 1983 Act, s 66(1)(a) where a period of three working days applies (HESCC Rules, r 37(4)(a)). In a s 66(1)(a) case the hearing must take place within seven days of the Tribunal receiving the application (HESCC Rules, r 37(1)); and in a case under the 1983 Act, s 75(1) the hearing must take place at least five weeks, but less than eight weeks, after the Tribunal received the reference (HESCC Rules, r 37(2)).

55.32 In mental health cases, the Tribunal may not proceed with a hearing in the absence of the patient unless there has been a medical examination of the patient by the Tribunal in accordance with the HESCC Rules, r 34 and the Tribunal is satisfied that patient has either chosen not to attend or is unable to attend for reasons of ill health (HESCC Rules, r 39). The Tribunal may proceed in the absence of a party other than the patient if the normal conditions – notification and interests of justice – are met (HESCC Rules, r 39(1)).

55.33 The default position in mental health cases before the HESCC is that hearings will be held in private (HESCC Rules, r 38(1)). The Tribunal has a discretion in the interests of justice to permit mental health cases to be heard in public. In determining whether to hold a hearing in a mental health case in public, the Tribunal must consider the patient's safety and the potential impact on the patient's condition of the hearing being held in public. In this regard, the extent to which reporting can be controlled is important. If the patient applies for the hearing to be in public, the Tribunal must evaluate the patient's understanding of the request as well as the wider public interest (see *R (Mersey Care NHS Trust) v Mental Health Review Tribunal* [2004] EWHC 1749 (Admin); [2005] 1 WLR 2469).

55.34 Detailed guidance was given by a three-judge panel of the AAC (including the Senior President) on the correct approach to mental health hearings in public or private in *AH v West London Mental Health Review Tribunal and the Secretary of State for Justice* [2010] UKUT 264 (AAC). The AAC confirmed that it had jurisdiction to hear an appeal against a decision of the HESCC refusing an application to hold the hearing in public (at [14]–[15]). The AAC considered the jurisprudence on the right to a public hearing, and noted that applications for public hearings in mental health cases are very rare (at [24]). The issues for the HESCC to consider when dealing with an application are (at [29]):

- Is it consistent with the subjective and informed wishes of the applicant (assuming he is competent to make an informed choice)?
- Will it have an adverse effect on his mental health in the short or long term, taking account of the views of those treating him and any other expert views?
- Are there any other special factors for or against a public hearing?
- Can practical arrangements be made for an open hearing without disproportionate burden on the authority?

55.35 The HESCC was criticised by the AAC for failing to recognise that a public hearing is the starting-point, and any exception to that must be justified in the circumstances of the case (at [41]–[43]). The AAC adjourned its own final decision in order to receive evidence on the potential use of the patient appearing via video-link at a public hearing off-site, how regular a problem public hearings are in mental health cases, and how other jurisdictions deal with similar problems (at [50]–[52]).

55.36 The Tribunal has the power to make a payment in respect of travelling expenses, subsistence and loss of earnings to any person who attended a hearing as an applicant, witness, a patient who is neither the applicant nor a witness, or a (non-legal) representative of an applicant (HESCC Rules, r 40).

Decisions

See **Decisions**.

55.37 The Tribunal may give its decision orally at the hearing (HESCC Rules, r 41(1)), but as soon as is reasonably practicable after a decision which finally disposes of the proceedings the Tribunal must provide to the parties (HESCC Rules, r 41(2)):

- A decision notice;
- Written reasons for the decision (see **Reasons**); and
- Notification of any right of appeal against the decision and the time within which, and the manner in which, such right of appeal may be exercised.

55.38 The notice and reasons must be provided (HESCC Rules, r 41(3)):

- in respect of proceedings under the 1983 Act, s 66(1)(a), either at the hearing or within three working days after the hearing; and
- in all other mental health cases, either at the hearing or within seven days after the hearing.

55.39 Rule 42 of the HESCC Rules deals with provisional decisions and provides that a decision with recommendations under the 1983 Act, ss 72(3)(a) or (3A)(a) or a deferred direction for conditional discharge under s 73(7) is a decision which is to be taken as finally disposing of proceedings. Such a decision is thus one in respect of which the Tribunal is under an obligation to give written reasons within the time limits in HESCC Rules, r 41.

Appeals

55.40 Appeals from the HESCC on a point of law go to the Administrative Appeals Chamber of the Upper Tribunal (see **Administrative Appeals Chamber**). The ordinary HESCC Rules on review, setting aside, and permission to appeal apply to mental health cases (see **Review, correction and setting aside of Tribunal decisions** and **Appeals from the First-tier Tribunal**). If the AAC refuses permission to appeal, or grants permission only on limited grounds or on terms, an appellant against a decision of the HESCC (or the Mental Health Review Tribunal for Wales) may apply for the decision to be reconsidered at an oral hearing, and such application must be made within 14 days of the date on which the AAC sent written notice to the appellant (Tribunal Procedure (Upper Tribunal) Rules 2008 ('Upper Tribunal Rules'), r 22(3)–(5)).

55.41 On appeal in the AAC the Upper Tribunal Rules apply to the proceedings. Those Rules contain the same general powers as in the HESCC Rules so that party is under no procedural disadvantage on appeal that he would not have suffered before the HESCC.

55.42 However, the Upper Tribunal Rules do not make specific provision for mental health cases – and do not replicate the provisions of the HESCC Rules – in respect of the permission notice, the notice of appeal (if one is necessary), the hearing of the appeal, and the decision of the AAC. In many circumstances, particularly the conduct of the hearing, the AAC will have a discretion as to how to regulate its own procedure and can ordinarily be expected to follow the procedure of the HESCC unless thought unnecessary. But the requirements of the permission application and notice of appeal, for instance, must be complied with by the parties. The appeal is on a point of law only, and the procedural protections required for vulnerable parties are consequently considered less necessary for replication in the Rules.

56 New Chambers

See **Chambers**.

LEGISLATIVE MACHINERY FOR THE DIVISION OF TRIBUNALS AND CREATION OF NEW CHAMBERS

56.1 The division of jurisdictions within the two-tier Tribunals system is intended to be flexible, so that changes can be made to the boundaries as the workload of the Tribunals changes, while also allowing similar jurisdictions to be grouped together to facilitate judicial deployment and build on judicial expertise (Explanatory Notes to TCEA, paragraphs 78 and 80).

56.2 Accordingly, the TCEA 2007 makes provision for both tiers to be reorganised and for Chambers to be added, removed and merged. TCEA 2007, s 7(1) gives the Lord Chancellor the power, exercised with the concurrence of the Senior President (see **Senior President**), to make provision for the organisation of each of the First-tier and Upper Tribunal into a number of Chambers. TCEA 2007, s 7(9) enables the Senior President and the Lord Chancellor together to vary by order the distribution of functions between the chambers in either the First-tier Tribunal or the Upper Tribunal, whether on a functional or geographical basis, or a combination of the two.

56.3 Paragraph 84 of the Explanatory Notes to the TCEA sets out some of the main factors that are expected to drive the establishment of new Chambers, addition of jurisdictions to existing Chambers and transfer of functions and/or jurisdictions between Chambers, namely:

- the transfer of functions of other Tribunals to the First-tier or Upper Tribunals;
- changes in original decisions;
- the creation of new areas of appeal;
- the prevalence of a particular jurisdiction at a point in time; and
- other business and user needs.

NEW CHAMBERS ESTABLISHED TO DATE

56.4 Since the Tribunals Service was created on 3 April 2006, there have been seven main phases of implementation.

56.5 In the first, which came into effect on 3 November 2008, the main jurisdictions of the original three First-tier Chambers, the Health Education and Social Care Chamber; the Social Entitlement Chamber and the War Pensions and Armed Forces Compensation Chamber were brought within the system, along with the creation of the Administrative Appeals Chamber of the Upper Tribunal. See **Health Education and Social Care Chamber; Social Entitlement Chamber; War Pensions and Armed Forces Compensation Chamber** and **Administrative Appeals Chamber**.

56.6 In the second, on 1 April 2009, the Tax Chamber in the First-tier Tribunal and the Tax and Chancery Chamber of the Upper Tribunal (originally named Finance and Tax) came into existence. See **Tax and Chancery Chamber** and **Tax Chamber**.

56.7 In the third phase, on 1 June 2009, the Lands Chamber of the Upper Tribunal came into existence. See **Lands Chamber**.

56.8 In the fourth phase, on 1 September 2009, the General Regulatory Chamber came into existence. See **General Regulatory Chamber**. In October 2009, the new Chamber acquired the jurisdictions of the Charity Tribunal, the Consumer Credit Appeal Tribunal, the Estate Agents Appeal Panel, and the Transport Tribunal.

56.9 In January 2010, the fifth phase, the GRC acquired a number of new jurisdictions from the former Gambling Appeals Tribunal, Claims Management Services Tribunal, Information Tribunal, Immigration Services Tribunal, and the Adjudication Panel for England.

56.10 In one of the most important phases, on 15 February 2010 the old Asylum and Immigration Tribunal was abolished and its functions adopted by a new Immigration and Asylum Chamber at both First-tier and Upper Tribunal level. See **Immigration and Asylum Chamber (First-tier Tribunal)** and **Immigration and Asylum Chamber (Upper Tribunal)**.

56.11 In the seventh phase, on 6 April 2010, the Financial Services and Markets Tribunal and the Pensions Regulator Tribunal were transferred into the Tax and Chancery Chamber of the Upper Tribunal, and a new environment jurisdiction was created within the General Regulatory Chamber.

56.12 It is highly likely that additional jurisdictions will be added as the system settles down.

57 Overriding Objective

THE PRINCIPLES TO BE FOLLOWED BY THE TRIBUNAL PROCEDURE COMMITTEE

57.1 The TCEA 2007, s 22, supplemented by TCEA 2007, Sch 5, provides for the making of Tribunal Procedure Rules by the Tribunal Procedure Committee (see **Tribunal procedure committee**). Section 22(4) requires the Tribunal Procedure Committee must exercise its rule-making power with a view to ensuring that certain fundamental principles are observed, namely that:

- in proceedings before the First-tier and Upper Tribunals, justice is done;
- the tribunal system is accessible and fair;
- proceedings before the First-tier and Upper Tribunals are handled quickly and efficiently;
- the rules are both simple and simply expressed; and
- that the rules where appropriate confer on members of the First-tier or Upper Tribunals responsibility for ensuring that proceedings are handled quickly and efficiently.

57.2 As paragraph 140 of the Explanatory Notes to the TCEA explains, these fundamental principles indicate the overriding objective to be followed by the Tribunal Procedure Committee in making procedural rules.

HOW THE OVERRIDING OBJECTIVE IS REFLECTED IN TRIBUNAL PROCEDURE RULES

57.3 The structure and content of the procedural rules of the Upper Tribunal and the various chambers of the First-tier Tribunal reflect the overriding objective in several significant respects. Five particular such respects are singled out below.

57.4 First, the various sets of procedural rules are drafted simply and follow a common structure.

57.5 Second, for each set of procedural rules, the first substantive rule (r 2) is entitled, 'Overriding objective and parties' obligation to co-operate with the Tribunal'. (For the Upper Tribunal, substitute in the title and in the text below 'Upper Tribunal' for 'Tribunal'). The Rules of the Immigration and Asylum Chamber do contain an overriding objective (r 4), but it is not set out in the same way, providing simply: 'The overriding objective of these Rules is to secure that proceedings before the Tribunal are handled as fairly, quickly and efficiently as possible; and, where appropriate, that members of the Tribunal have responsibility for ensuring this, in the interests of the parties to the proceedings and in the wider public interest.' The Lands Chamber Rules do not contain an overriding objective, although it is difficult to imagine that the Tribunal will not be seeking to deal with cases fairly and justly in any event. The Practice Direction accompanying the Lands Chamber Rules does apply the overriding objective to proceedings in the Lands Chamber (paragraph 2) (see **Lands Chamber procedural rules**).

57.6 Rule 2 explains both what the overriding objective includes and what it entails for the tribunal and the parties:

> '(1) The overriding objective of these Rules is to enable the Tribunal to deal with cases fairly and justly.
>
> (2) Dealing with a case fairly and justly includes—
>
> (a) dealing with the case in ways which are proportionate to the importance of the case, the complexity of the issues, the anticipated costs and the resources of the parties;
>
> (b) avoiding unnecessary formality and seeking flexibility in the proceedings;
>
> (c) ensuring, so far as practicable, that the parties are able to participate fully in the proceedings;
>
> (d) using any special expertise of the Tribunal effectively; and
>
> (e) avoiding delay, so far as compatible with proper consideration of the issues.
>
> (3) The Tribunal must seek to give effect to the overriding objective when it—
>
> (a) exercises any power under these Rules; or
>
> (b) interprets any rule or practice direction.
>
> (4) Parties must—
>
> (a) help the Tribunal to further the overriding objective; and
>
> (b) co-operate with the Tribunal generally.'

57.7 Third, rule 3 encourages the Tribunal/Upper Tribunal to seek, where appropriate, to bring the availability of any appropriate alternative dispute resolution procedures to the attention of the parties and, if the parties wish and if it is compatible with the overriding objective, to facilitate the use of such procedures. This emphasis on the use of alternative dispute resolution methods is consistent with the requirements of efficiency, flexibility and proportionality (see **Alternative dispute resolution**).

57.8 Fourth, rule 4 of the various sets of procedural rules empowers, with the approval of the Senior President, the delegation of functions of a judicial nature to staff, provided that there is scope for the parties to request reconsideration by a judge. This, too, reflects the requirements of efficiency and proportionality, and enables the specialist expertise of Tribunal judges to be deployed effectively.

57.9 Fifth, rule 5 of the procedural rules confers on the Tribunal/Upper Tribunal a general power, subject to the TCEA 2007 and other enactments, to regulate its own procedure (r 5(1)), supplemented by wide powers of case management.

57.10 It will doubtless take some time for the Tribunals to become used to the existence of the overriding objective, and for parties to stop seeing the overriding objective as a panacea for all procedural ills. There will be much useful material to be gained from the jurisprudence of the courts concerning the overriding objective of the CPR. The existence of the overriding objective provides an important policy statement on the part of the Tribunals Service and system generally, but it will rarely provide a direct answer to a practical problem.

57.11 In the context of an appeal against a decision which had encompassed a refusal to adjourn, the Administrative Appeals Chamber of the Upper Tribunal made some useful comments in *MA v Secretary of State for Work and Pensions* [2009] UKUT 211 (AAC) about the role of the overriding objective. The judge held (at [11]) that:

> 'It is unlikely that these principles will dictate the decision for the tribunal. In the majority of cases, there will be factors pointing both for and against a proposed adjournment. The nature of the decision is likely to require the tribunal to undertake a balancing exercise between competing considerations. And it is the nature of such an exercise that different tribunals might properly make different assessments of the factors. On appeal, the Upper Tribunal will not find an error of law simply because it would have made a different assessment. That is in accordance with the approach taken by the courts to appeals on issues of judgment (*Bellenden v Satterthwaite* [1948] 1 All ER 343 at 345) and on the exercise of case management powers (*Grupo Torras SA v Al Sabah (No 2)* reported in The Times on 17 April 1997).'

57.12 The judge went on to find that there had been no error of law in refusing the adjournment (at [24]):

> 'I can find no significant error in the tribunal's approach to the case. It took account of the grounds for the application and made an assessment of the likely value that would be obtained by an adjournment. That was the key consideration. Its analysis is rational. It took advantage of the tribunal's flexibility in using its members' combined special expertise to avoid delay and to allow the claimant full and effective participation in the proceedings. All of those factors are within the scope of the overriding objective. By using its expertise, it reconciled fairness and efficiency with making the proceedings accessible to a claimant whose evidence was not complete.'

58 Parties

58.1 All proceedings before the Tribunals must have parties to those proceedings, even if one or more of those parties does not appear at a hearing, or make any submissions to the Tribunal.

58.2 The two main sources of information in the Tribunal rules about parties are the definitions adopted of who is meant by 'appellant', 'applicant' and 'respondent'; and the rules on adding, substituting and removing parties.

DEFINITIONS

General Regulatory Chamber ('GRC')

58.3 In the GRC, 'party' is defined as a person who is an appellant or a respondent; or if the proceedings have been concluded, a person who was an appellant or a respondent when the Tribunal finally disposed of all issues in the proceedings.

58.4 'appellant' means a person who:

- commences Tribunal proceedings, whether by making an appeal, an application, a claim, a complaint, a reference or otherwise; or
- is added or substituted as an appellant under r 9 (see below).

58.5 'respondent' means a person who:

- in proceedings appealing against or challenging a decision, direction or order, the person who made the decision, direction or order appealed against or challenged;
- a person against whom an appellant otherwise brings proceedings; or
- a person added or substituted as a respondent under r 9 (see below). (GRC Rules, r 1(3)).

Health, Education and Social Care Chamber

58.6 In the HESCC 'party' is defined as:

- in a mental health case, the patient, the responsible authority, the Secretary of State (if the patient is a restricted patient or in a reference under HESCC Rules, r 32(8) (seeking approval under the Mental Health Act 1983, s 86)), and any other person who starts a mental health case by making an application;
- in any other case, a person who is an applicant or respondent in proceedings before the Tribunal or, if the proceedings have been concluded, a person who was an applicant or respondent when the Tribunal finally disposed of all issues in the proceedings.

58.7 'applicant' means a person who:

- starts Tribunal proceedings, whether by making an application, an appeal, a claim or a reference;

- makes an application to the Tribunal for leave to start such proceedings; or
- is substituted as an applicant under r 9(1) (see below).

58.8 'patient' means the person who is the subject of a mental health case. A 'restricted patient' has the meaning set out in the Mental Health Act 1983, s 79(1).

58.9 'respondent' means:

- in an appeal against an order made by a justice of the peace under the Children Act 1989, s 79K, the Care Standards Act 2000, s 20 or the Childcare Act 2006, s 72, the person who applied to the justice of the peace for the order;
- in an appeal against any other decision, the person who made the decision;
- in proceedings on a claim under the Disability Discrimination Act 1995, s 28I, the body responsible for the school as determined in accordance with paragraph 1 of Schedule 4A to that Act or, if the claim concerns the residual duties of a local education authority under s 28F of that Act, that local education authority;
- in proceedings on an application under the Protection of Children Act 1999, s 4(2) or the Care Standards Act 2000, s 86(2), the Secretary of State; or
- a person substituted or added as a respondent under r 9 (see below).

58.10 'responsible authority' means:

- in relation to a patient detained under the Mental Health Act 1983 in a hospital within the meaning of Part 2 of that Act, the managers (as defined in s 145 of that Act);
- in relation to a patient subject to guardianship, the responsible local social services authority (as defined in the Mental Health Act 1983, s 34(3));
- in relation to a community patient, the managers of the responsible hospital (as defined in the Mental Health Act 1983, s 145); or
- in relation to a patient subject to after-care under supervision, the Primary Care Trust or Local Health Board which has the duty to provide after-care for the patient. (Tribunal Procedure (First-tier Tribunal) (Health, Education and Social Care Chamber) Rules 2008 ('HESCC Rules'), r 1(3))

Immigration and Asylum Chamber

58.11 In the Immigration and Asylum Chamber of the First-tier Tribunal 'appellant' is defined as a person who has given a notice of appeal against a relevant decision in accordance with the Rules; 'respondent' means the decision maker specified in the notice of decision against which a notice of appeal has been given (Asylum and Immigration Tribunal (Procedure) Rules 2005 ('IAC Rules'), r 2).

Social Entitlement Chamber

58.12 In the Social Entitlement Chamber ('SEC') 'party' is defined as:

- a person who is an appellant or respondent in proceedings before the Tribunal;
- a person who makes a reference to the Tribunal under the Child Support Act 1991, s 28D;
- a person who starts proceedings before the Tribunal under paragraph 3 of Schedule 2 to the Tax Credits Act 2002; or
- if the proceedings have been concluded, a person who was a party under paragraph (a), (b) or (c) when the Tribunal finally disposed of all issues in the proceedings.

58.13 'appellant' means a person who makes an appeal to the Tribunal, or a person substituted as an appellant under r 9(1) (see below).

58.14 'respondent' means:

- in an appeal against a decision, the decision maker and any person other than the appellant who had a right of appeal against the decision;
- in a reference under the Child Support Act 1991, s 28D—
  - the absent parent or non-resident parent;
  - the person with care; and
  - in Scotland, the child if the child made the application for a departure direction or a variation;
- in proceedings under paragraph 3 of Schedule 2 to the Tax Credits Act 2002, a person on whom it is proposed that a penalty be imposed; or
- a person substituted or added as a respondent under r 9 (see below). (Tribunal Procedure (First-tier Tribunal) (Social Entitlement Chamber) Procedural Rules 2008 ('SEC Rules'), r 1(3))

Tax Chamber

58.15 In the Tax Chamber ('TC'), 'party' is defined as a person who is (or was at the time that the Tribunal disposed of the proceedings) an appellant or respondent in proceedings before the Tribunal.

58.16 'appellant' means:

- the person who starts proceedings (whether by bringing or notifying an appeal, by making an originating application, by a reference, or otherwise);
- in proceedings started jointly by more than one person, such persons acting jointly or each such person, as the context requires;
- a person substituted as an appellant under r 9 (see below).

58.17 'respondent' means:

- HMRC, where the appellant (or one of them) is not HMRC;
- in proceedings brought by HMRC alone, a person against whom the proceedings are brought or to whom the proceedings relate;

- a person substituted or added as a respondent under r 9 (see below). (Tribunal Procedure (First-tier Tribunal) (Tax Chamber) Rules 2009 ('TC Rules'), r 1(3))

War Pensions and Armed Forces Compensation Chamber

58.18 In the War Pensions and Armer Forces Compensation Chamber ('WPAFCC'), 'party' is defined as a person who is an appellant or respondent in proceedings before the Tribunal or, if the proceedings have been concluded, a person who was an appellant or respondent when the Tribunal finally disposed of all issues in the proceedings.

58.19 'appellant' means a person who makes an appeal to the Tribunal, or a person substituted as an appellant under r 9(1) (see below).

58.20 'respondent' means:

- in an appeal against a decision, the decision maker and any person other than the appellant who had a right of appeal against the decision; or
- a person substituted or added as a respondent under r 9 (see below). (Tribunal Procedure (First-tier Tribunal) (War Pensions and Armed Forces Compensation Chamber) Rules 2008 ('WPAFCC Rules'), r 1(3))

Upper Tribunal

58.21 In the Upper Tribunal, 'party' is defined as a person who is an appellant, an applicant, a respondent or an interested party in proceedings before the Upper Tribunal, a person who has referred a question or matter to the Upper Tribunal or, if the proceedings have been concluded, a person who was an appellant, an applicant, a respondent or an interested party when the Tribunal finally disposed of all issues in the proceedings.

58.22 'appellant' means:

- a person who makes an appeal, or applies for permission to appeal, to the Upper Tribunal;
- in proceedings transferred or referred to the Upper Tribunal from the First-tier Tribunal, a person who started the proceedings in the First-tier Tribunal; or
- a person substituted as an appellant under r 9(1) (see below).

58.23 'applicant' means:

- a person who applies for permission to bring, or does bring, judicial review proceedings before the Upper Tribunal and, in judicial review proceedings transferred to the Upper Tribunal from a court, includes a person who was a claimant or petitioner in the proceedings immediately before they were transferred; or
- a person who refers a financial services case to the Upper Tribunal.

58.24 'interested party' means:

- a person who is directly affected by the outcome sought in judicial review proceedings, and has been named as an interested party under Upper

Tribunal Rules, rr 28 or 29 (judicial review), or has been substituted or added as an interested party under r 9 (see below);

- in judicial review proceedings transferred to the Upper Tribunal under the Judicature (Northern Ireland) Act 1978, s 25A(2) or (3) or the Senior Courts Act 1981, s 31A(2) or (3), a person who was an interested party in the proceedings immediately before they were transferred to the Upper Tribunal; and
- in a financial services case, any person other than the applicant who could have referred the case to the Upper Tribunal and who has been added or substituted as an interested party under r 9 (see below).

58.25 'respondent' means:

- in an appeal, or application for permission to appeal, against a decision of another tribunal, any person other than the appellant who—
  - was a party before that other tribunal; or [(ii) has been repealed]
  - otherwise has a right of appeal against the decision of the other tribunal and has given notice to the Upper Tribunal that they wish to be a party to the appeal;
- in an appeal against any other decision except a decision of a traffic commissioner, the person who made the decision;
- in judicial review proceedings—
  - in proceedings started in the Upper Tribunal, the person named by the applicant as the respondent;
  - in proceedings transferred to the Upper Tribunal under the Judicature (Northern Ireland) Act 1978, s 25A(2) or (3) or the Senior Courts Act 1981, s 31A(2) or (3), a person who was a defendant in the proceedings immediately before they were transferred;
  - in proceedings transferred to the Upper Tribunal under the Tribunals,Courts and Enforcement Act 2007 ('TCEA 2007'), s 20(1), a person to whom intimation of the petition was made before the proceedings were transferred, or to whom the Upper Tribunal has required intimation to be made.
- in proceedings transferred or referred to the Upper Tribunal from the First-tier Tribunal, person who was a respondent in the proceedings in the First-tier Tribunal;
- in a reference under the Forfeiture Act 1982, the person whose eligibility for a benefit or advantage is in issue;
- in a financial services case, the maker of the decision in respect of which a reference has been made; or
- a person substituted or added as a respondent under r 9 (see below). (Tribunal Procedure (Upper Tribunal) Rules 2008 ('UT Rules'), r 1(3))

Lands Chamber

58.26 In the Lands Chamber of the Upper Tribunal 'party' is defined as 'in relation to an appeal, means the appellant, the authority and any person who has served notice of intention to respond in accordance with r 7' (Lands Tribunal Rules 1996 ('Lands Chamber Rules'), r 2(1)).

ADDITION, SUBSTITUTION AND REMOVAL OF PARTIES

58.27 Provision for adding, substituting or removing a party to the proceedings is made (with the exception of the Immigration and Asylum Chamber of the First-tier Tribunal and the Lands Chamber of the Upper Tribunal) in rule 9 of the various procedural rules.

58.28 The rules tend to take two forms. The first is that there is a general provision that the tribunal may give a direction adding, substituting or removing a party as an appellant, respondent or (in the Upper Tribunal only) an interested party (GRC Rules, Upper Tribunal Rules, r 9(1)), followed by a power to give any appropriate consequential directions (GRC Rules, Upper Tribunal Rules, r 9(2)). Any person not already a party may apply to the Tribunal to be added or substituted as a party (GRC Rules, Upper Tribunal Rules, r 9(3)). If a person who is entitled to be a party to proceedings by virtue of another enactment applies to be added as a party, and any conditions applicable to that entitlement have been satisfied, the tribunal must give a direction adding that person as a respondent or, if appropriate, as an appellant (GRC Rules, Upper Tribunal Rules, r 9(4)).

58.29 The second form is more restrictive. The tribunal may only permit the substitution of a party where the wrong person has been named as a party, or if the substitution becomes necessary because of a change of circumstances since proceedings began (HESCC Rules, SEC Rules, TC Rules, WPAFCC Rules, r 9(1)). There are no restrictions on the circumstances in which the tribunal may direct the addition of a party, except that they may only be a respondent to the proceedings (HESCC Rules, SEC Rules, TC Rules, WPAFCC Rules, r 9(2)), and there is a power to give any appropriate consequential directions when a party is added or substituted (HESCC Rules, SEC Rules, WPAFCC Rules, r 9(3); TC Rules, r 9(5)). In the Tax Chamber only may a person apply to be added as a party, and if the application is refused the TC should nonetheless consider whether to permit that person to provide submissions or evidence – a form of quasi-interested party (TC Rules, r 9(3), (4)).

58.30 In the FTTIAC there is no provision equivalent to r 9. However, in an asylum case, the United Kingdom Representative of the United Nations High Commissioner for Refugees may give notice that he wishes to participate, and where such notice has been given he may attend the hearing, he must be sent copies of all documents in the proceedings and he may make representations at the hearing. The Tribunal may make directions to this effect (IAC Rules, r 49). In an asylum appeal in the Upper Tribunal the same rules apply (UT Rules, r 9(5), (6)).

58.31 There is no equivalent provision in the Lands Chamber. The nature of the respondent may be wider than in other proceedings, because a number of persons may provide to the Tribunal a notice of intention to respond upon seeing a notice of appeal, or an application notice (for example, to remove a restrictive covenant) (Lands Chamber Rules, rr 7,10,15), but those opposing the appeal or application are generally known as respondents (see Lands Chamber Rules, r 8(1)).

59 Primary Health Lists Cases

LEGISLATIVE BACKGROUND

59.1 Primary Care Trusts in England and Wales are obliged to maintain lists of medical, dental and ophthalmic performers in their locality under the National Health Service (Performers Lists) Regulations 2004, SI 2004/585. The 2004 Regulations are now to be treated as made under the National Health Service Act 2006 (see the National Health Service (Wales) Act 2006 for Wales). Applications to join the list may be refused, or already listed performers may be de-listed, by reason of (for example) criminal conviction, professional disqualification, if inclusion would be prejudicial to the efficient running of the relevant services, involvement in a fraud case or other unsuitability for inclusion (see the 2004 Regulations, reg 10).

59.2 The 2004 Regulations provide for a right of appeal against a relevant decision of a PCT (reg 15). The appealable decisions are:

- Refusal of admission onto the performers list;
- Imposition of a condition for admission, or the variation of any condition;
- On a review, any conditional inclusion;
- Removal of a listed performer;
- Imposition of a condition for continued listing, or the variation of any condition;
- On a review, any contingent removal.

59.3 The PCT may also suspend performers if it considers that it is necessary to protect the public pending the outcome of appeals and other relevant decisions (2004 Regulations, reg 13). All appealable decisions and suspension action taken by PCTs are required to be notified to the NHS Litigation Authority (2004 Regulations, reg 16).

59.4 Appeals were heard by the Family Health Services Appeal Authority (the 'FHSAA'), which came into existence on 1 December 2001. Its executive functions were provided by the NHS Litigation Authority. The FHSAA procedure was governed by the Family Health Services Appeal Authority (Procedure) Rules 2001, SI 2001/3570) as amended by SI 2002/1921.

OTHER JURISDICTIONS OF THE FSHAA

59.5 Aside from performers lists, the FHSAA's jurisdiction encompassed appeals against decisions in relation to persons listed (or denied inclusion in the list) as authorised to provide pharmaceutical services under Part 7 of the 2006 Act and the National Health Service (Pharmaceutical Services) Regulations 2005, SI 2005/641 as amended by the National Health Service (Miscellaneous Amendments Relating to Community Pharmaceutical Services and Optometrist Prescribing) Regulations 2009, SI 2009/2205.

59.6 The FHSAA also dealt with PCT contractual disputes with service providers of general dental services, general medical services, general ophthalmic services, personal dental services agreements, and personal medical services agreements. These are now governed by the National Health Service (Functions of the First-tier Tribunal relating to Primary Medical, Dental and Ophthalmic Services) Regulations 2010, SI 2010/76.

Transfer of jurisdiction

59.7 As of 18 January 2010 the FHSAA's functions have been subsumed by the Health, Education and Social Care Chamber of the First-tier Tribunal: The Transfer of Tribunal Functions Order 2010, SI 2010/22, art 2(1)(e). Judges and other members of the FHSAA have been transferred in as judges and other members of the HESCC.

59.8 Procedure in primary health list cases is now governed by the Tribunal Procedure (First–tier Tribunal) (Health, Education and Social Care Chamber) Rules 2008, SI 2008/2699 as amended ('HESCC Rules'). The HESCC Rules are reproduced at Appendix 2. See **Health, Education and Social Care Chamber procedural rules** for details of the provisions.

59.9 The FHSAA Rules are not drastically different from the HESCC Rules, but users are recommended to consult the various relevant sections of this Handbook to ensure that time limits and other procedural requirements are met. The Primary Health Lists Tribunal of the HESCC is based in Darlington but can sit at any venue in England and Wales as necessary.

60 Procedural Rules

STATUTORY INSTRUMENTS CONTAINING PROCEDURAL RULES

60.1 The statutory instruments containing the procedural rules of the various Chambers are to be found in Appendices 1–9. In the interests of completeness, they are set out below (in chronological order of the jurisdictions joining the TCEA structure, with subsequent amendments shown):

- The Tribunal Procedure (First–tier Tribunal) (Social Entitlement Chamber) Rules 2008, SI 2008/2685, subsequently amended by SI 2009/274 and SI 2009/1975
- The Tribunal Procedure (First–tier Tribunal) (War Pensions and Armed Forces Compensation Chamber) Rules 2008, SI 2008/2686, subsequently amended by SI 2009/1975
- The Tribunal Procedure (Upper Tribunal) Rules 2008, SI 2008/2698,subsequently amended by SI 2009/274, SI 2009/1975, SI 2010/43, SI 2010/44 and SI 2010/747
- The Tribunal Procedure (First–tier Tribunal) (Health, Education and Social Care Chamber) Rules 2008, SI 2008/2699, subsequently amended by SI 2009/1975
- The Tribunal Procedure (First–tier Tribunal) (Tax Chamber) Rules 2009, SI 2009/273, subsequently amended by SI 2010/43
- The Tribunal Procedure (First–tier Tribunal) (General Regulatory Chamber) Rules 2009, SI 2009/1976, subsequently amended by SI 2010/43
- The Lands Tribunal Rules 1996, SI 1996/1022, subsequently amended by SI 1997/1965, SI 1998/22, SI 2003/2945, SI 2006/880 and, in particular, the Transfer of Tribunal Functions (Lands Tribunal and Miscellaneous Amendments) Order 2009, SI 2009/1307 (referred to here as the Lands Chamber Rules)
- Asylum and Immigration Tribunal (Procedure) Rules 2005, SI 2005/230, subsequently amended by SI 2005/569, SI 2006/1003, SI 2006/2788, SI 2007/835, SI 2007/3170, SI 2008/1088, SI 2008/2683, and, in particular, the Transfer of Functions of the Asylum and Immigration Tribunal Order 2010, SI 2010/21, and the Tribunal Procedure (Amendment No 2) Rules 2010, SI 2010/44 (referred to here as the Immigration and Asylum Chamber Rules)
- Asylum and Immigration Tribunal (Fast Track Procedure) Rules 2005, SI 2005/560, subsequently amended by SI 2006/2789, SI 2008/1089, and, in particular, the Transfer of Functions of the Asylum and Immigration Tribunal Order 2010, SI 2010/21, and the Tribunal Procedure (Amendment No 2) Rules 2010, SI 2010/44 (referred to here as the Immigration and Asylum Chamber (Fast Track) Rules)

Consolidated versions of the procedural rules are to be found on the Tribunals Service website, on the 'Tribunal Procedure Committee;

webpage (**http://www.tribunals.gov.uk/Tribunals/Rules/tribunal procedurecommittee.htm**).

Other statutory instruments under TCEA 2007

60.2 With the exception of the TCEA 2007, which put in place a new structure allowing tribunals currently outside the tribunals system to be transferred into the system, the majority of the changes required to create the new, unified structure have been implemented by way of statutory instrument and the majority of procedural rules are contained in statutory instruments.

60.3 An up-to-date list of the relevant statutory instruments can be found on the website of the Tribunals Service, on the 'Rules & Legislation' webpage (**http://www.tribunals.gov.uk/Tribunals/Rules/rules.htm**).

STATUTORY INSTRUMENTS CONCERNING THE ESTABLISHMENT AND FUNCTIONING OF THE NEW TRIBUNALS SYSTEM

60.4 The most important statutory instruments, other than those containing procedural rules (which are set out in the following section), are discussed below.

60.5 There have been several commencement orders under the TCEA, the most important of which are the Tribunals, Courts and Enforcement Act 2007 (Commencement No 1) Order, SI 2007/2709 and the Tribunals, Courts and Enforcement Act 2007 (Commencement No 6 and Transitional Provisions) Order 2008, SI 2008/2696. The former brought into force the initial structure into force in September 2007 and then the latter brought most of Part 1 of the TCEA 2007 into force in November 2008 and the Tax Chamber provisions and enforcement of awards provisions in April 2009.

60.6 The Tribunals, Courts and Enforcement Act 2007 (Transitional and Consequential Provisions) Order 2008, SI 2008/2683 made, in its Schedules, consequential amendments to and revocations of secondary legislation for those Tribunal functions which transferred to the First-tier Tribunal and Upper Tribunal in November 2008.

60.6 The organisation and functional allocation between the chambers of the First-tier Tribunal and Upper Tribunal was set out in the First–tier Tribunal and Upper Tribunal (Chambers) Order 2008, SI 2008/2684, which has since been amended on a number of occasions to take account of new Chambers. The composition of the Tribunals, in terms of numbers of members and the judicial/non-judicial split, was set out in the First-tier Tribunal and Upper Tribunal (Composition of Tribunal) Order 2008, SI 2008/2835, while the qualifications or experience required to be eligible for appointment as a non-judicial Tribunal member were prescribed by the Qualifications for Appointment of Members to the First–tier Tribunal and Upper Tribunal Order 2008, SI 2008/2692.

60.7 The actual transfer of existing Tribunals into the new structure was largely effected by the Transfer of Tribunal Functions Order 2008, SI 2008/2833, which also transferred the members of the Tribunals and made various other minor and consequential amendments. Since the initial Functions Order a number of new Chambers have been created and new jurisdictions have been added to existing Chambers. Those have been done through separate Transfer of Functions Orders, which are available on the Tribunals Service website.

60.8 In relation to appellate jurisdiction over tribunal decisions, the Appeals (Excluded Decisions) Order 2008, SI 2008/2707 set out the initial categories of decision from which there was no appeal on a point of law from the First-tier Tribunal to the Upper Tribunal, but this has been revoked and replaced by the Appeals (Excluded Decisions) Order 2009, SI 2009/275, which has itself had additional categories added to it by the The Tribunals Courts and Enforcement Act 2007 (Miscellaneous Provisions) Order 2010, SI 2010/41.

60.9 The Appeals from the Upper Tribunal to the Court of Appeal Order 2008, SI 2008/2834 sets out the grounds on which permission (or leave) to appeal from the Upper Tribunal to the Court of Appeal might be granted (namely, (i) the proposed appeal would raise some important point of principle or practice, or (ii) there is some other compelling reason for the relevant appellate court to hear the appeal).

61 Proportionality

INTRODUCTION

61.1 Not all interferences with a right are unlawful. Much administrative conduct involves limiting or in some way impinging upon the rights of affected citizens. In general, where that infringement is proportionate, it is permissible.

61.2 Proportionality is the standard of review which the tribunal will apply in a case under the Human Rights Act 1998 ('HRA') where it is alleged that a public authority has not acted compatibly with a right in the European Convention on Human Rights ('ECHR') which has been incorporated into English law by Sch 1 to the HRA, contrary to HRA, s 6. A claim for breach of an ECHR right will ordinarily be brought under s 6, but ECHR rights may arise in other cases as interpretative aids or a factor to be taken into account.

61.3 Proportionality is also the standard of review which must be applied in any judicial review challenge based upon European Union law, although the focus here will be on proportionality under the HRA.

61.4 For the cause of action under HRA, s 6, and for the general approach of the Upper Tribunal to judicial review applications, see **Judicial review grounds and principles** and **Judicial review in the Upper Tribunal**. This entry will concentrate only on proportionality.

PROPORTIONALITY AND REASONABLENESS

61.5 Using the HRA allows a claimant to challenge the substance of a decision, but proportionality is not the same as *Wednesbury* unreasonableness. It requires a structured analysis by the Tribunal of decision challenged and the justification of the decision-maker for that challenge. The standard of review under a s 6 claim for an infringement of an ECHR right is proportionality (*R v Secretary of State for the Home Department, ex p Daly* [2001] UKHL 26; [2001] 2 AC 532 at [27] per Lord Steyn). Even anxious scrutiny *Wednesbury* review is insufficiently intensive (*Smith & Grady v UK* (1999) 29 EHRR 493). In many cases, the outcome under *Wednesbury* and proportionality will be the same, but not in all. Proportionality requires the court to take additional steps and engage with the challenged decision in much greater depth.

61.6 Lord Steyn famously set out the difference between the two tests in *Daly* at [27]–[28]:

> 'The starting point is that there is an overlap between the traditional grounds of review and the approach of proportionality. Most cases would be decided in the same way whichever approach is adopted. But the intensity of review is somewhat greater under the proportionality approach. Making due allowance for important structural differences between various convention rights, which I do not propose to discuss, a few generalisations are perhaps permissible. I would mention three concrete differences without suggesting that my statement is exhaustive. First, the doctrine of proportionality may require the reviewing court to assess the balance which the decision maker has struck, not merely whether it is within the range of rational or reasonable decisions. Secondly, the proportionality test may go further than the traditional

grounds of review inasmuch as it may require attention to be directed to the relative weight accorded to interests and considerations. Thirdly, even the heightened scrutiny test developed in *R v Ministry of Defence ex p Smith* [1996] QB 517, 554 is not necessarily appropriate to the protection of human rights... In other words, the intensity of the review, in similar cases, is guaranteed by the twin requirements that the limitation of the right was necessary in a democratic society, in the sense of meeting a pressing social need, and the question whether the interference was really proportionate to the legitimate aim being pursued. The differences in approach between the traditional grounds of review and the proportionality approach may therefore sometimes yield different results. It is therefore important that cases involving convention rights must be analysed in the correct way.'

61.7 It is quite possible that in time proportionality will be recognised as a ground of judicial review, or as the standard of review in substantive challenges, in purely domestic judicial review cases which have no connection to either the HRA or EU law. Substantive legitimate expectation cases support that move. However, at the moment, proportionality is not fully a part of domestic judicial review and it has not supplanted *Wednesbury*.

THE PROPORTIONALITY TEMPLATE

61.8 The proportionality test adopted by the English courts under the HRA has been set out by the Privy Council in *de Freitas v Permanent Secretary of Ministry of Agriculture, Fisheries, Lands and Housing* [1999] 1 AC 69, 80 as a carefully structured analysis. The court must ask three questions, namely whether:

(1) the legislative objective is sufficiently important to justify limiting a fundamental right;

(2) the measures designed to meet the legislative objective are rationally connected to it; and

(3) the means used to impair the right or freedom are no more than is necessary to accomplish the objective.

61.9 The House of Lords in *Huang v Secretary of State for the Home Department* [2007] UKHL 11; [2007] 2 AC 167 at [19] added the following fourth step, that the analysis must:

> 'always involve the striking of a fair balance between the rights of the individual and the interests of the community which is inherent in the whole of the Convention. The severity and consequences of the interference will call for careful assessment at this stage.'

61.10 In truth, the fourth step rolls back into the third, but it broadens the scope of the exercise under step three. That broader third step is the balancing test, where the Tribunal must assess whether a fair balance has been struck between the factors which the parties rely on. The addition from *Huang* makes clear that the third step is not simply to ask whether a less restrictive approach was possible, although that is relevant to consider, but whether the decision as a whole has struck a fair balance, taking into account the importance of the right and any other possible methods of achieving the legitimate aim.

61.11 What proportionality adds to unreasonableness, beyond the sense of fair balance, is a need for structured justification. Once the claimant has shown that there is an interference with a right (that the facts fall within the scope of an ECHR right), it will be for the claimant to prove that there is no legitimate aim, and that there is no rational connection. These first two stages will invariably be difficult to prove and are rarely met. But it is for the public authority to prove the key third stage (and fourth, following *Huang*) that the impairment of the right has been no more than necessary. The bulk of the work of proportionality is done at the third stage, and the burden being on the public authority requires the Tribunal to closely engage with the justifications put forward by the authority.

CONDUCTING THE ANALYSIS

61.12 It is important that the proportionality analysis be conducted properly and in a structured manner in each case in which it is raised. In certain types of case lower courts and tribunals have learnt from long experience that particular arguments are often run but that they will almost never succeed under the existing law. There is a consequent, and understandable, tendency on the part of those courts and tribunals to simply apply a test of 'exceptionality': does this case have something about it which takes it out of the ordinary?

61.13 Such an approach is not permitted. The proportionality analysis must always be gone through carefully and cautiously. It may in fact be only in exceptional cases that the infringement of the right will be disproportionate (for example, Article 8 rights overcoming deportation of those with no right to be in the UK), but this cannot be converted into a legal test, and the wording of 'exceptionality' is best avoided altogether. The House of Lords and the Supreme Court have stressed repeatedly, in a variety of contexts, that there can be no test of exceptionality: *Huang* at [20]; *Norris v Government of the USA* [2010] UKSC 9; [2010] 2 WLR 572; *Re W (Children)* [2010] UKSC 12; [2010] 1 WLR 701 at [30]. Exceptionality can be the outcome of the test but must not be the threshold.

DIFFERENT RIGHTS – DIFFERENT APPROACHES

61.14 It is important to recognise that different ECHR rights use different language under which proportionality may be employed. The standard template set out above is primarily applied under the rights which entitle the courts to enquire into the justification for acting by using the formula 'necessary in a democratic society'. These rights are Articles 8–11 (private and family life; thought, conscience and religion; expression; and assembly and association).

61.15 Article 1 of Protocol 1 (right to property) is more widely drafted, permitting an infringement of the right 'in the public interest'. It is well-established that this permits the public authority significantly more leeway than the standard proportionality test: *R (Countryside Alliance) v Attorney General* [2007] UKHL 52; [2008] 1 AC 719 at [47] per Lord Bingham, [121] and [129] per Baroness Hale, [155]–[156] per Lord Brown.

61.16 There are rights to trial or hearing within 'a reasonable time' in Articles 5(3) and 6(1), which have not been interpreted as applying proportionality, but a lighter-touch reasonableness assessment: *Porter v Magill* [2001] UKHL 67; [2002] 2 AC 357 at [108] per Lord Hope.

61.17 A stricter test than ordinary proportionality is adopted in Article 2(2) (deprivation of life in certain circumstances) ('absolutely necessary'), Article 5(1)(c) (detention to prevent commission of offence) ('reasonably considered necessary'), and Article 6(1) (exclusion of public from hearings) ('strictly necessary'). (See also Article 15 and the right to derogate from the ECHR insofar as is 'strictly required). The European Court of Human Rights has made clear that a stricter proportionality test is to be applied, requiring careful scrutiny and the least drastic solution: *McCann v UK* (1996) 21 EHRR 97 at [147]; *James v UK* (1986) 8 EHRR 123 at [51].

61.18 Other rights, such as Articles 3 (torture), 4 (slavery), 7 (no punishment without law) and aspects of 5 (liberty) and 6 (fair trial), are framed in absolute terms. It is not, for example, possible to assess whether a decision to deport a person is proportionate, balancing the rights of the individual and the need to protect national security where deportation presents a real risk that the deportee will be tortured (*Chahal v UK* (1997) 23 EHRR 413). That does not mean that no control mechanisms are exercised by the courts in the context of absolute rights: the definitions and scope of the rights will be interpreted to avoid unsatisfactory results. But the proportionality template itself cannot apply to an allegation of infringement.

DEFERENCE

61.19 Much judicial and academic ink has been spilled on the subject of margins of appreciation for, discretionary areas of judgment for and deference to the decision-maker. This involves the tribunal in some way recognising that the decision-maker's justifications and reasoning may have advantages over the legal process. These advantages, as acknowledged in the case law, may be constitutional – in the sense that the decision-maker has been specifically allocated its function by Parliament, or where primary legislation is challenged under the HRA the decision-maker may be Parliament itself – or it may be institutional – in the sense that the decision-maker is best placed to undertake the balancing exercise because it has particular expertise in the area. It is undoubtedly the case that, despite considerable academic debate, the courts have always been willing to afford the decision-maker a degree of latitude in the choices made, in a similar manner to the European Court of Human Rights affording a margin of appreciation to individual states.

61.20 In *Huang* the House of Lords, in a single opinion, took the whole debate back to basics and held that:

> '[14] Much argument was directed on the hearing of these appeals, and much authority cited, on the appellate immigration authority's proper approach to its task, due deference, discretionary areas of judgment, the margin of appreciation, democratic accountability, relative institutional competence, a distinction drawn by the Court of Appeal between decisions based on policy and decisions not so based, and so on. We think, with respect, that there has been a tendency, both in the arguments addressed to the courts and in the judgments of the courts, to complicate and mystify what is not, in principle, a hard task to define, however difficult the task is, in practice, to perform...

> [16] ...The giving of weight to factors such as these is not, in our opinion, aptly described as deference: it is performance of the ordinary judicial task of weighing up the competing considerations on each side and according appropriate weight to the judgment of a person with responsibility for a given subject matter and access to special sources of knowledge and advice. That is how any rational judicial decision-maker is likely to proceed.'

61.21 This should be the approach of the Upper Tribunal. Some guidance may be provided in the existing case law where deference or latitude has been shown to specific decision-makers in specific contexts, but it will be unhelpful to the Tribunal to be weighed down by every precedent on deference, discretionary areas of judgment and margins of appreciation in every proportionality case. Proportionality is ultimately, like all legal tests, a matter for the court.

ROLE OF THE COURT AND THE DECISION-MAKER

61.22 When an infringement of a Convention right is alleged it is for the court to make the determination. The House of Lords in *R (SB) v Governors of Denbigh High School* [2006] UKHL 15; [2007] 1 AC 100 stressed that '[w]hat matters is the result': per Lord Hoffmann at [68]. The fact that the decision-maker has taken into account Convention rights in reaching its conclusion will not save that decision if the court finds it to be disproportionate. Equally, as in *Denbigh* itself, where no apparent balancing exercise has taken place this will not prove to be a ground of illegality under HRA, s 6 unless the decision in substance infringes a Convention right. The decision-maker 'cannot be expected to make such decisions with textbooks on human rights law at their elbows': per Lord Hoffmann at [68].

61.23 In *Belfast City Council v Miss Behavin' Ltd* [2007] UKHL 19; [2007] 1 WLR 1420 Lord Rodger held that there was no HRA, s 6 unlawful action by the decision-maker simply because they had not overtly conducted a rights balance (at [23]). However, his Lordship did note that where the balancing exercise had been undertaken it would be accorded 'due weight' (at [26]). Precisely what is meant by 'due weight' is unclear. In *Miss Behavin'* itself there was no such exercise conducted, and so 'the court had to go about its task without that particular kind of assistance' (at [27]). There is an immediately obvious issue with this approach. If a 'good' rights balance made by the decision-maker is relevant to the court's adjudication, why is a 'bad' or a non-existent one not relevant too? Surely if conducting their own proportionality exercise is to be accorded some weight in deciding that the decision actually was proportionate, the fact that the decision-maker has not conducted that exercise should logically be accorded at least some weight towards the decision itself not actually being proportionate.

61.24 It is suggested here that no consideration should ordinarily be given to the decision-making process when evaluating whether a Convention right has been infringed. It is, for the purposes of the court, irrelevant. It may be useful for the decision-maker to consider the matter in a judicial manner, but only instrumentally insofar as it may increase the likelihood of his reaching the same answer as the court will. However, the two are separate factors. The court must be entirely unconcerned with whether the decision-maker has 'talked the rights talk'. It is the job of the court to assess whether the decision-maker has 'walked the rights walk'. To the extent that members of the House of Lords in *Miss Behavin'* take a different approach, it should be rejected.

61.25 However, a case which falls into an area where the courts would ordinarily show a certain degree of deference to the primary decision-maker may be treated differently. Where they would do so, it may be relevant in reaching a judgment on whether the decision-maker has 'walked the rights walk' to take into account whether it has persuasively 'talked the rights talk'. It is relevant in this type of case because the court is already concerned with what the decision-maker is saying, as well as what they are doing. Thus in *Denbigh* and *Miss Behavin'* if the school or the City Council had balanced the rights themselves that would have been a relevant factor to consider, providing one accepts that some deference is due in the areas of uniform policy and free speech restrictions in cases of pornography. (See Knight, 'Proportionality, the Decison-Maker and the House of Lords' [2007] JR 221).

THE ROLE OF THE UPPER TRIBUNAL

61.26 The Senior President of Tribunals, Carnwath LJ, has expressed the view that the Upper Tribunal will be well-placed to understand the practical implications of their judgments on proportionality ('Tribunal justice – a new start' [2009] PL 48, 67). In his words:

> 'It is their role to provide guidance on issues of fact or law relevant to the exercise of the specialist jurisdiction. In doing so they are able to draw on the practical experience of their fellow tribunal judges and expert members. Questions of proportionality, like those of reasonableness in employment law, are well suited to the development of working guidelines through such a collaborative process.'

61.27 The importance of the Tribunal conducting the proportionality analysis carefully can be emphasised by the suggestions in the case law that the appellate courts will be slow to interfere with the striking of the balance undertaken by the Tribunal, and especially the weight given to particular factors: see *EB (Kosovo) v Secretary of State for the Home Department* [2008] UKHL 41; [2009] 1 AC 1159 at [16] and [21] per Lord Bingham. This does not mean that proportionality is a question of fact immune from appeal (*A v Secretary of State for the Home Department* [2004] UKHL 56; [2005] 2 AC 68 at [44] per Lord Bingham), but it will not be easy to supplant the conclusions on proportionality of the Tribunal.

62 Reasons

REQUIREMENT TO GIVE REASONS IN THE FIRST-TIER TRIBUNAL

62.1 The Procedural Rules of the different Chambers impose some obligations to give reasons.

62.2 In the First-tier Tribunal, the tribunals are under an obligation to give written reasons:

- for a decision which finally resolves all the issues in the proceedings – which does not include a decision whether or not to review the decision – (GRC Rules, r 38(2); HESCC Rules, rr 30(2), 41(2) (mental health cases); SEC Rules, r 34(1) (asylum support cases); TC Rules, r 35(3) (unless the parties agree reasons are unnecessary)); and
- when refusing permission to appeal (GRC Rules, r 43(4); HESCC Rules, r 47(4); SEC Rules, r 39(4); TC Rules, r 40(4); Tribunal Procedure (First-tier Tribunal) (War Pensions and Armed Forces Compensation Chamber) Rules 2008 ('WPAFCC Rules'), r 37(4)).

62.3 In the Social Entitlement Chamber of the First-tier Tribunal ('SEC') and War Pensions and Armed Forces Compensation Chamber ('WPAFCC') the Tribunal has a discretion to provide reasons for decisions which finally dispose of all the issues in the proceedings, but where the Tribunal does not do so the parties may apply to the Tribunal for those reasons, which it must ordinarily disclose (SEC Rules, r 34(2)–(4); WPAFCC Rules, r 32(1)–(3)).

62.4 Certain tribunals have a power to give written reasons for any other decision which they reach (GRC Rules, r 38(3); HESCC Rules, rr 30(4), 41(4) (mental health cases)). Where the power is not expressly granted under the Rules it can nonetheless be implied at common law (see, for example, in the Social Security Commissioner's case of CH 2553/05 at [24]).

62.5 In every case in the Immigration and Asylum Chamber of the First-tier Tribunal ('FTTIAC') the Tribunal must serve a written determination containing its decision and the reasons for that decision (Asylum and Immigration Tribunal (Procedure) Rules 2005 ('IAC Rules'), r 22(1)). Where bail is refused the notice must include reasons for the decision (IAC Rules, r 39(5)).

REQUIREMENT TO GIVE REASONS IN THE UPPER TRIBUNAL

62.6 The Upper Tribunal is under an obligation to give written reasons for:

- a decision which finally resolves all the issues in the proceedings – which does not include a decision whether or not to review the decision – unless the decision is one reached by consent, or the parties consent to written reasons not being provided (Tribunal Procedure (Upper Tribunal) Rules 2008 ('UT Rules'), r 40(3)); and
- when it refuses permission to appeal (UT Rules, r 45(4)).

62.7 Special rules on the provision of the notice of an asylum decision in the Upper Tribunal are set out in UT Rules, r 40A, but they do not depart from the position on reasons.

62.8 The Upper Tribunal has the power to give written reasons for any other decision which it reaches (UT Rules, r 40(4)).

62.9 In the Lands Chamber of the Upper Tribunal, the decision of the Tribunal on an appeal, reference or application shall be given in writing, and shall state the reasons for the decision (Lands Tribunal Rules ('Lands Chamber Rules'), r 50(1)). Reasons must be given where the Tribunal refuses permission to appeal (Lands Chamber Rules, r 59(4)). An order made without a hearing dismissing the application must be accompanied by reasons (Lands Chamber Rules, r 17(1)). A decision by the registrar on the taxation of costs shall be accompanied by written reasons for that decision (Lands Chamber Rules, r 52(6)).

ADEQUACY OF THE REASONS

62.10 One area of tribunal practice and procedure which has quickly given rise to appellate tribunal guidance is the provision of reasons by the First-tier Tribunals.

62.11 In *BB v South London & Maudsley NHS Trust* [2009] UKUT 157 (AAC) a three-judge panel of the AAC found that the First-tier HESCC Tribunal had inadequately explained why it preferred the reasoning of the responsible clinician to the reasoning of the independent psychiatric expert. This amounted to an error of law. The AAC held at [6] that:

> 'The legal test when determining the adequacy of reasons is not in doubt. It is fully discussed in the decision of the Court of Appeal in *R (H) v Mental Health Review Tribunal for North and East London Region* [2001] EWCA Civ 415; [2002] QB 1. Adopting what was said in *English v Emery Reimbold & Strick Limited* [2002] EWCA Civ 605; [2002] 1 WLR 2409, the essential requirement is that what the tribunal says should enable the parties and any appellate tribunal readily to analyse the reasoning that was essential to the decision. The tribunal should provide an explanation as to why it has accepted the evidence of one expert and rejected that of another. As these cases make clear, the test is the same regardless of subject matter. Accordingly if tribunals are unsure about what is required when giving reasons they may find assistance from cases outside the specific area of law that they are dealing with.'

62.12 These considerations will apply equally to cases in which the tribunal is called upon to assess the evidence of lay witness of fact. The tribunal should give adequate reasons as to why it preferred the evidence of one over the other. This is particularly so in cases which turn on the evidence of a particular witness (see *Southwark LBC v Kofi-Adu* [2006] EWCA Civ 281; [2006] HLR 33, at [138]–[141] per Jonathan Parker LJ).

62.13 The AAC provided guidance on the need to give reasons as to why it accepted the evidence of a particular expert in *Hampshire County Council v JP* [2009] UKUT 239 (AAC) at [37] and [39]:

> 'The fact that an expert has given an opinion is not in itself an adequate reason for a tribunal to adopt that opinion unless the opinion is unchallenged. In the event of a conflict of opinions, it is necessary for a tribunal to give a reason for preferring one opinion rather than the other. Where an opinion is fully reasoned, a tribunal accepting the opinion may be taken to have adopted the reasoning and in those cases merely referring to the opinion may be sufficient provided that the expert has given adequate reasons for disagreeing with any opposing view... where there is a crucial disagreement between experts and "the dispute involves something in the nature of an intellectual exchange, with reasons and analysis advanced on either side, the judge must enter into the issues canvassed before him and explain why he prefers one case over the other" (*Flannery v Halifax Estate Agencies Limited* [2001] 1 WLR 377 (CA)).'

62.14 For examples of appeals against the reasoning of the First-tier Tribunal in which the Upper Tribunal was mildly critical of the reasoning but found no error of law see: *DC v London Borough of Ealing* [2010] UKUT 10 (AAC); and *RH v South London & Maudsley NHS Trust* [2010] UKUT 32 (AAC).

62.15 More general guidance, given prior to the Tribunals, Courts and Enforcement Act 2007 ('TCEA 2007') but worded in a particularly clear way, can be found in the judgment of James Goudie QC (sitting as a Deputy High Court Judge) in *F Primary School v Mr & Mrs T and SENDIST* [2006] EWHC 1250 (Admin); [2006] ELR 465 at [15]:

> 'The decision of a Tribunal is not required to be an elaborate, formalistic product of refined legal draftsmanship. It must contain an outline of the story which has given rise to the complaint, a summary of the Tribunal's basic factual conclusions, and a statement of the reasons which have led them to reach the conclusion which they do on those basic facts. The parties are entitled to be told why they have won or lost. There should be a sufficient account of the facts and of the reasoning to enable an appeal court to see whether any question of law arises. A Tribunal's reasons are not, however, intended to include a comprehensive and detailed analysis of the case, either in terms of fact or in law. Their purpose remains what it has always been, which is to tell the parties in broad terms why they lose or (as the case may be) win. These reasons should not be subjected to a detailed analysis. That is to misuse the purpose for which the reasons are given.'

62.16 See also *W v Leeds City Council and SENDIST* [2005] EWCA Civ 988; [2006] ELR 617 at [53]–[54] per Wall LJ; and *H v East Sussex County Council* [2009] EWCA Civ 249; [2009] ELR 161 at [14]–[19] per Waller LJ.

62.17 An appeal based upon the reasoning – or lack thereof – of the lower tribunal should clarify as much as possible in what way the reasoning is deficient and how it amounts to an error of law.

FORM OF DECISION

62.18 It is vitally important for tribunals to produce their written reasons in a manner which is clear, structured, precise and not unduly long or verbose.

62.19 Reasons

Many tribunal users will be unrepresented, and the desire to make tribunal proceedings accessible to the ordinary lay litigant ought to be carried through into the decision-writing process. Detailed guidance will not be set out here, but those writing tribunal decisions or are interested in how to do so are referred to Jacobs, *Tribunal Practice and Procedure* (2009) at 14.199–14.240.

62.19 The Senior President issued a Practice Statement: Form of Decisions and Neutral Citation, First-tier Tribunal and Upper Tribunal on or after 3 November 2008, 31 October 2008. Little express guidance is given on form, but it is said that 'First-tier Tribunal and Upper Tribunal decisions must be prepared for delivery, or issued as approved decisions, with paragraph numbering' (paragraph 2).

63 Representation

GENERAL MATTERS

63.1 There are a number of different types of person who may be present at tribunal hearings accompanying a party to the proceedings. There may be representatives in the formal legal sense who are lawyers and are specifically briefed to present the case. There may be representatives who are not lawyers, but are there to present the case because they are experts in the area (such as trade union representatives in Employment Tribunals). There may be accompanying persons who are simply there for support and who do not make any express contribution in the hearing. There may be assistants, who aid the party by supplying documents and prompts but who do not present the case. Generally, the tribunals do not distinguish between these different types of representatives.

63.2 Any representative who is notified to the tribunal (see below) is under the same duty to co-operate with the tribunal as is a party to the proceedings. This includes drawing to the attention of the tribunal any error that it is making which might otherwise be appealable (and which, in any case, should be caught by the reviewing process). A party and a representative must act fairly. See *Bache v Essex County Council* [2000] ICR 313, 323 per Mummery LJ (in the context of the Employment Tribunal):

> 'Just as the tribunal is under a duty to behave fairly, so are the parties and their representatives. The tribunal is accordingly entitled to require the parties and their representatives to act in a fair and reasonable way in the presentation of their evidence, in challenging the other side's evidence and in making submissions. The rulings of the tribunal on what is and is not relevant and on what is the fair and appropriate procedure ought to be respected even by a party and his representative who do not agree with a ruling.'

63.3 The ruling in *Bache* that the Employment Tribunal could not stop a representative acting for a party and addressing them, does not address the power of the First-tier Tribunals and the Upper Tribunal to exclude from the hearing a person whose presence is disrupting the hearing (see **Hearings**). However, such a power should be exercised only in the face of flagrant misconduct or disruption by a representative, especially where the representative is legally qualified.

63.4 A legal or other representative may be liable for a wasted costs order in the TCEA 2007, s 29(4), (6)).

REPRESENTATIVES IN THE FIRST-TIER TRIBUNAL

63.5 The procedural governance of representatives is found, for the most part, in rule 11 of the various procedural rules. References to separate Chambers' rules will only be made where there are differences. The IAC will be dealt with distinctly below.

63.6 A party may appoint a representative to represent that party in the proceedings. That representative need not be a legal representative (r 11(1)).

63.7 Representation

A 'legal representative' is defined as a person who, for the purposes of the Legal Services Act 2007, is an authorised person in relation to an activity which constitutes the exercise of a right of audience or the conduct of litigation within the meaning of that Act (r 1(3), except that it is r 11(7) in the TC Rules).

63.7 Where a representative is appointed, the party must notify the Tribunal and all other parties (except in the Social Entitlement Chamber of the First-tier Tribunal ('SEC') where there is no reference to other parties and the duty is on the tribunal to send on the details: Tribunal Procedure (First-tier Tribunal) (Social Entitlement Chamber) Procedural Rules 2008 ('SEC Rules'), r 11(4)) in writing the representative's name and address. If the representative is a legal one, the duty is on the representative and not the party (r 11(2)). This duty does not apply where the representative's details have already been provided to the respondent in an application notice or other correspondence served on the respondent (r 11(3) SEC Rules and Tribunal Procedure (First-tier Tribunal) (War Pensions and Armed Forces Compensation Chamber) Rules 2008 ('WPAFCC Rules') only).

63.8 In the GRC, no mention is made in the opening provisions of a legal representative. The representative may be 'legally qualified or not', and the duty to inform the Tribunal of the representative's details is always on the party (GRC Rules, r 11(1), (2)), save in the case of a legal representative as defined above who may send the notice to the Tribunal (GRC Rules, r 11(3)(b)). This slight variation in the framing of the rules perhaps arises out of the width of the GRC jurisdiction, which provides more scope for representation which is quasi-legal but which does not fall within the definition set out above.

63.9 Anything done or permitted to be done under the Rules, a practice direction or a direction may be done by the representative of the party, except signing a witness statement (GRC Rules, HESCC Rules, TC Rules, r 11(3); WPAFCC Rules, r 11(4); SEC Rules, r 11(5)). However, HESCC Rules, r 11(3)(b) specify that a representative who is not a legal representative may not sign an application notice.

63.10 Having been notified of the representation, any other party and the Tribunal need only provide documents in the proceedings to the representative and not the represented party directly. Parties are entitled to assume that the representative remains authorised until receipt of written notification to the contrary (GRC Rules, HESCC Rules, TC Rules, r 11(4); WPAFCC Rules, r 11(5); SEC Rules, r 11(6)).

63.11 In recognition of the different types of person who may accompany a party, a party may, at a hearing, be accompanied by a person not notified as a representative but who, with the permission of the Tribunal, may act as a representative or otherwise assist in presenting the party's case at the hearing (GRC Rules, HESCC Rules, TC Rules, r 11(5); WPAFCC Rules, r 11(6); SEC Rules, r 11(7)).

63.12 Special provisions apply in the HESCC in respect of mental health cases. If a patient has not appointed a representative, the Tribunal itself may appoint a legal representative where:

- the patient has stated that they do not wish to conduct their own case or that they wish to be represented; or

- the patient lacks the capacity to appoint a representative but the Tribunal believes that it is in the patient's best interests for the patient to be represented (HESCC Rules, r 11(7)).

63.13 A patient may not appoint, or be represented by:

- a person liable to be detained or subject to guardianship or after-care under supervision, or who is a community patient, under the Mental Health Act 1983; or
- a person receiving treatment for mental disorder at the same hospital as the patient (r 11(8)).

63.14 Guidance has recently been given the Administrative Appeals Chamber of the Upper Tribunal on the role of the representative under r 11(7). In *AA v Cheshire and Wirral Partnership NHS Foundation Trust* [2009] UKUT 195 (AAC) it was suggested at [18]–[20] that:

> 'rule 11(7)(b) plainly contemplates the possibility of a solicitor being appointed to represent a patient who does not have the capacity to give any instructions at all. In such a case, the rule must, as the Law Society's guidance plainly expects, anticipate that the solicitor will ascertain any relevant wishes that the patient may be able to express, will inform the tribunal of such wishes, make such points in support of them as can properly be made and generally ensure that the tribunal has all the relevant material before it and does not overlook any statutory provision. However, in the absence of the patient's capacity to give valid instructions, the rule must, in my view, also anticipate that the solicitor will exercise his or her judgment and advance any argument that he or she considers to be in the patient's "best interests", which, as the Law Society's guidance recognises, will not necessarily involve arguing for the patient's discharge. In those circumstances, it seems to me that the solicitor has the same freedom of action as a litigation friend in the courts.
>
> What, then, is the position if the patient does have the capacity to give instructions on some matters but not others? The Law Society's guidance is unequivocal: a solicitor is bound to act in accordance with the instructions that have been given. Therefore, the more a patient has the capacity to give detailed instructions, the less the solicitor has complete freedom of action.
>
> However, even where a patient has full capacity, a solicitor may be entitled, and in some circumstances may be under a duty, to draw a tribunal's attention to significant matters – particularly points of law – that appear to be in the patient's best interests despite his or her instructions and which it appears the tribunal might otherwise overlook. A solicitor has a duty not just to his or her client but also to the tribunal or, perhaps more accurately, to the administration of justice. A distinction is to be drawn between merely drawing a matter to a tribunal's attention and fully arguing it.'

63.15 In the FTTIAC, representation is governed by IAC Rules, r 48. An appellant (or applicant for bail) under the IAC Rules may be represented by any person not prohibited under the Immigration and Asylum Act 1999, s 84 (see **Immigration services cases**) from doing so, although if they are prohibited that will not prevent the validity of any decision (IAC Rules, r 48(1), (3)). The Secretary of State may be represented by anyone authorised to do so (IAC Rules, r 48(2)).

63.16 Any representative must immediately notify the Tribunal and the other party of the fact of his representation, filing a written notice. That notification may be deemed where the representative has signed the notice of appeal (IAC Rules, r 48(4)–(4B)). Notification need not be given in writing where the representation only begins on the day of the hearing, where it may made orally (IAC Rules, r 48(8)).

63.17 A representative may do anything the Rules require or permit the party to do (IAC Rules, r 48(5)). The party is under a duty to maintain contact with the representative and notify him of any change of address (IAC Rules, r 48(6)).

63.18 Where a representative ceases to act for a party, he must notify in writing the Tribunal and other party of that fact and of the name and address of the new representative if known (IAC Rules, r 48(7)). Until the Tribunal is notified of a change, all documents served on a representative are deemed properly served (IAC Rules, r 48(9)).

REPRESENTATIVES IN THE UPPER TRIBUNAL

63.19 The Tribunal Procedure (Upper Tribunal) Rules 2008 ('Upper Tribunal Rules') preserve precisely the same provisions in respect of representatives as are found in the First-tier Tribunal. Again, this is done in r 11, except that the format of the rule differs slightly from the First-tier rules because the Upper Tribunal Rules must take account of all the variations between the Chambers, particularly in respect of mental health and immigration and asylum cases.

63.20 There is also specific provision in the Upper Tribunal Rules for parties to have the right to submit evidence (except in an application for permission), make oral representations at a hearing they are entitled to attend, and to make written representations where there is to be no hearing (Upper Tribunal Rules, r 33). It is in the discretion of the Upper Tribunal to permit 'any other person' the same right, so any person attending a hearing as a representative in any sense has the ability to request to address the tribunal. This flexibility is an important aspect of tribunal justice (see **Tribunal justice**).

63.21 Where a party has obtained funding from the Legal Services Commission for representation in the Upper Tribunal it must, as soon as is practicable, send a copy of the funding notice to the Tribunal and notify any other party in writing (Upper Tribunal Rules, r 18).

63.22 In the Lands Chamber, the rules are less detailed. Any party may appear in person (except a valuation officer, who requires permission to do so), or may be represented by a solicitor or counsel. If a party wishes to represented by any other person they need the leave of the Tribunal or the registrar depending on whom the hearing is before (Lands Tribunal Rules 1996 ('Lands Chamber Rules'), r 37).

63.23 Where a party to proceedings is represented by a person other than a solicitor, written authorisation for the representative to act must be sent to the registrar. If the representative changes, the registrar must be notified of the change along with the details of and authorisation for any new representative (Lands Chamber Rules, r 54(2)).

63.24 Where a solicitor responds to communications to a party from the Tribunal, that solicitor shall be on the record as acting for that party. A solicitor may be appointed as representative at any time, notifying the Tribunal and the other parties. A solicitor on the record shall be presumed to be the representative of a party until the Tribunal and other parties are notified otherwise. A solicitor on the record is responsible for the payment of fees owed by a party (Lands Chamber Rules, r 53).

64 Responses

INTRODUCTION

64.1 In almost all types of appeal, application or reference to the First-tier and Upper Tribunals, provision is made for the party defending the claim (usually the public authority decision-maker) to put forward a notice of response setting out the reasons why the tribunal should dismiss the case and uphold the original decision.

64.2 The requirements of the notices of appeal are set out in detail elsewhere in the Handbook, particularly in entries for the individual Chambers' procedural rules, categories of case and, especially, Bringing proceedings in the First-tier Tribunal. The focus of this entry will be to collect together the requirements applicable to the response. Generally speaking these closely follow the same model in the different Chambers, but there are occasional differences of which the user should be aware. The rules will be addressed Chamber by Chamber.

RESPONSES IN THE FIRST-TIER TRIBUNAL

General Regulatory Chamber

64.3 In proceedings other than charities cases (see **Charities cases**), each respondent to an appeal must put in a response to the notice of appeal within 28 days of the date on which the respondent receives the notice of appeal (GRC Rules, r 23(1)(b)). The time for responding to a notice of appeal in a transport case is 14 days (GRC Rules, r 23(1)(a)) (see **Transport cases**).

64.4 The response must include (GRC Rules, r 23(2)–(4)):

- the name and address of the respondent;
- the name and address of the respondent's representative (if any);
- an address where documents for the respondent may be sent or delivered;
- any further information or documents required by a practice direction or direction;
- whether the respondent would be content for the case to be dealt with or without a hearing if the Tribunal considers it appropriate;
- a statement as to whether the respondent opposes the appellant's case and the grounds for that opposition;
- any copy or written record of any decision which is being challenged and any statement of reasons for the decision which the appellant has not provided and which the respondent has or can reasonably obtain.

64.5 If the response is made out of time, the response must include a request for an extension of time together with the reasons why the response was not provided in time (GRC Rules, r 23(5)) (see **Extensions of time**).

64.6 The respondent must send the response and any accompanying documents to each other party at the same time as it sends the response to the GRC (save in transport cases, where the GRC sends the copy to the other parties) (GRC Rules, r 23(6), (7)).

64.7 In charities cases, the respondent party must send or deliver to the GRC a response to the notice of appeal within 28 days after the date on which the respondent received the notice of appeal (GRC Rules, r 27(1)).

64.8 The response must include or enclose (GRC Rules, r 27(2)–(5)):

- the name and address of the respondent;
- the name and address of the respondent's representative (if any);
- an address where documents for the respondent may be sent or delivered;
- a statement as to whether the respondent opposes the appellant's case and, if so, any grounds for such opposition which are not contained in another document provided with the response;
- a statement as to whether the respondent would be content for the case to be dealt with or without a hearing if the GRC considers it appropriate;
- a copy of any written record of the decision being challenged, and any statement of reasons for that decision, that the appellant did not provide with the notice of appeal and the respondent has or can reasonably obtain;
- the documents relied upon by the respondent when reaching the decision;
- any other documents which the respondent considers could adversely affect its case or support the appellant's case. Respondent parties should note that this is a more extensive disclosure obligation than that which pertains under non-charities cases before the GRC (see GRC Rules, r 23). Respondents in charities cases should be astute to the need to satisfy this duty and to consider carefully whether there are documents in its possession or control that are helpful to the appellant.

64.9 If the respondent provides the response to the GRC out of time, the response must include a request for an extension of time and the reason why the response was not provided in time (GRC Rules, r 27(6)) (see **Extensions of time**).

64.10 The respondent must send or deliver a copy of the response and any accompanying documents to each other party at the same time as it provides the response to the GRC (GRC Rules, r 27(7)).

Health, Education and Social Care Chamber

64.11 In proceedings other than mental health cases, each respondent to an appeal must put in a response to the notice of appeal within 21 days of the date on which the respondent receives the notice of appeal, or such other time as is set out in the Schedule to the Tribunal Procedure (First-tier Tribunal) (Health, Education and Social Care Chamber) Rules 2008 ('HESCC Rules') (HESCC Rules, r 21(1)).

64.12 The response must include (HESCC Rules, r 21(2)):

- the name and address of the respondent;
- the name and address of the respondent's representative (if any);
- an address where documents for the respondent may be sent or delivered;
- a statement as to whether the respondent opposes the appellant's case and the grounds for that opposition which are not contained in another document provided with the response;
- in a special educational needs case, the views of the child about the issues raised by the proceedings, or the reason why the respondent has not ascertained those views.
- any further information or documents required by a practice direction or direction;
- the response may include a statement whether the respondent would be content for the case to be dealt with or without a hearing if the Tribunal considers it appropriate (HESCC Rules, r 21(3));

64.13 If the response is made out of time, the response must include a request for an extension of time together with the reasons why the response was not provided in time (HESCC Rules, r 21(4)) (see **Extensions of time**).

64.14 The respondent must send the response and any accompanying documents to each other party at the same time as it sends the response to the HESCC (HESCC Rules, r 21(5)).

64.15 In mental health cases, there is no equivalent to a response, although the public authority is under a number of procedural obligations when an application to the Tribunal is made (see **Mental health cases**).

Immigration and Asylum Chamber

64.16 As in other respects, the Asylum and Immigration Tribunal (Procedure) Rules 2005 ('IAC Rules') do not yet follow the same model as those used in the other Chambers of the First-tier Tribunal.

64.17 Unless the Tribunal gives other directions, as soon as is reasonably practicable after the filing of the notice of appeal with the decision-maker and in any event not later than 2.00pm on the business day before the earliest date appointed for any hearing of or in relation to the appeal (IAC Rules, r 13(2)), the respondent must file with the Immigration and Asylum Chamber of the First-tier Tribunal ('FTTIAC') (IAC Rules, r 13(1)):

- the notice of decision to which the appeal relates and any other document served on the appellant giving reasons for the decision;
- any statement of evidence form and record of an interview with the appellant in relation to the appealed decision;
- any other document referred to elsewhere which is not publicly available and is referred to in the notice of decision or other document giving reasons for the decision or relied upon by the respondent;

- the notice of any other immigration decision made in relation to the appellant in respect of which he has a right of appeal.

64.18 The respondent must send the response and any accompanying documents to the appellant at the same time as it sends the response to the FTTIAC, except for any documents it has already sent to the appellant (IAC Rules, r 13(4)).

64.19 Any objections to bail being granted must be filed by the respondent not later than 2.00pm on the business day before the hearing, or if he was served with notice of the hearing less than 24 hours before that time, as soon as reasonably practicable (IAC Rules, r 39(2)).

64.20 In proceedings governed by the Asylum and Immigration Tribunal (Fast Track Procedure) Rules 2005 ('IAC (Fast Track) Rules'), the respondent must file the documents listed above not later than two days after the day on which the Tribunal serves the respondent with the notice of appeal (IAC (Fast Track) Rules, r 10).

Social Entitlement Chamber

64.21 The decision-maker which is a respondent to an appeal must put in a response to the notice of appeal as soon as is reasonably practicable after the date on which the respondent receives the notice of appeal (Tribunal Procedure (First-tier Tribunal) (Social Entitlement Chamber) Procedural Rules 2008 ('SEC Rules'), r 24(1)(b)). The time for responding to a notice of appeal in an asylum support case is three days (SEC Rules, r 24(1)(a)) (see **Asylum support cases**).

64.22 The response must include (SEC Rules, r 24(2), (4)):

- the name and address of the respondent;
- the name and address of the respondent's representative (if any);
- an address where documents for the respondent may be sent or delivered;
- the names and addresses of any other respondents and their representatives (if any);
- any further information or documents required by a practice direction or direction;

The response may include a submission as to (SEC Rules, r 2.4(3)):

- whether it would be appropriate for the case to be disposed of with or without a hearing;
- a statement as to whether the respondent opposes the appellant's case and the grounds for that opposition which are not contained in another document provided with the response;
- a copy of any written record of any decision which is being challenged and any statement of reasons for the decision if they were not sent with the notice of appeal;
- copies of all documents relevant to the case in the decision maker's possession, unless a practice direction or direction states otherwise; and

- in cases to which rule 23 (cases in which the notice of appeal is to be sent to the decision maker) applies, a copy of the notice of appeal, any documents provided by the appellant with the notice of appeal and (if they have not otherwise been provided to the Tribunal) the name and address of the appellant's representative (if any).

64.23 The respondent must send the response and any accompanying documents to each other party at the same time as it sends the response to the SEC (SEC Rules, r 24(5)).

64.24 In a case under the Child Support Act 1991, s 28D and paragraph 3 of Schedule 2 to the Tax Credits Act 2002 each respondent may send or deliver to the Tribunal a written submission and any further relevant documents within one month of the date on which the person starting proceedings sent a copy of the written reference or the information in writing to that respondent (SEC Rules, r 26(7)).

Tax Chamber

64.25 A different structure applies in the Tax Chamber because of the categorisation of types of case within that Chamber. Instead of a response, the respondent (HMRC) is required to supply a respondent's statement of case except in basic cases. In default paper cases the statement must be supplied within 42 days after the Tribunal sent the notice of the appeal or a copy of the application notice or notice of reference, and in standard or complex cases it must be supplied within 60 days (Tribunal Procedure (First-tier Tribunal) (Tax Chamber) Rules 2009 ('TC Rules'), r 25(1)).

64.26 A statement of case must state the legislative provision under which the decision appealed was made, and the respondent's position in relation to the case. The respondent may include a request that the matter be determined with or without a hearing if the Tribunal considers it appropriate (TC Rules, r 25(2),(3)).

64.27 If the response is made out of time, the response must include a request for an extension of time together with the reasons why the response was not provided in time (TC Rules, r 25(4)) (see **Extensions of time**).

War Pensions and Armed Forces Compensation Chamber

64.28 The decision-maker which is a respondent to an appeal must put in a response to the notice of appeal as soon as is reasonably practicable after the date on which the respondent receives the notice of appeal (Tribunal Procedure (First-tier Tribunal) (War Pensions and Armed Forces Compensation Chamber) Rules 2008 ('WPAFCC Rules'), r 23(1)).

64.29 The response must include (WPAFCC Rules, r 23(2)–(4)):

- the name and address of the respondent;
- the name and address of the respondent's representative (if any);
- an address where documents for the respondent may be sent or delivered;
- the names and addresses of any other respondents and their representatives (if any);

- any further information or documents required by a practice direction or direction;
- a statement as to whether the respondent opposes the appellant's case and the grounds for that opposition;
- a copy of any written record of any decision which is being challenged and any statement of reasons for the decision;
- copies of all documents relevant to the case in the decision maker's possession, unless a practice direction or direction states otherwise; and
- a copy of the notice of appeal, any documents provided by the appellant with the notice of appeal and unless stated in the notice of appeal, the name and address of the appellant's representative (if any).

The response may include a submission as to whether it would be appropriate for the case to be dealt with without a hearing (see WPAFCC Rules, r 23(3)).

64.30 The respondent must send the response and any accompanying documents to each other party at the same time as it sends the response to the WPAFCC (WPAFCC Rules, r 23(5)).

RESPONSES IN THE UPPER TRIBUNAL

Administrative Appeals Chamber, Immigration and Asylum Chamber & Tax and Chancery Chamber

64.31 A respondent will usually have the right to respond to the notice of appeal, unless the Upper Tribunal directs otherwise (Tribunal Procedure (Upper Tribunal) Rules 2008 ('UT Rules'), r 24(1A)). Any response must be in writing and received by the Upper Tribunal no later than one month after the respondent has received a copy of the notice of appeal from the Upper Tribunal or, if the Upper Tribunal directs that the application for permission stands as the notice of appeal, no later than one month after the date on which the Upper Tribunal sent notice to the respondent that it had granted permission to appeal (UT Rules, r 24(2)). In a fast track immigration and asylum case, the response must be received one day before the hearing of the appeal (UT Rules, r 24(2)(aa)).

64.32 The response must state (UT Rules, r 24(3)):

- the name and address of the respondent;
- the name and address of the respondent's representative (if any);
- an address where documents for the respondent may be sent or delivered;
- whether the respondent opposes the appeal;
- the grounds on which the respondent relies, including (in the case of an appeal against the decision of another Tribunal) any grounds on which the respondent was unsuccessful in the proceedings which are the subject of the appeal, but intends to rely in the appeal; and
- whether the respondent wants the case to be dealt with at a hearing.

64.33 As with applications for permission to appeal (see above), if the respondent provides its written response to the Upper Tribunal outside of the one month time limit (or any extended time limit prescribed by the Upper Tribunal under the UT Rules, r 5(3)(a)), the notice of appeal must include a request for an extension of time and state the reasons why the response was not provided in time (UT Rules, r 24(4)). Unlike applications for permission to appeal and notices of appeal received out of time, it does not appear that the Upper Tribunal is obliged to refuse to accept a response to a notice of appeal received out of time unless it extends time.

64.34 When the Upper Tribunal receives a written response to the notice of appeal it must send a copy of the response and any accompanying documents to the appellant and each other party (UT Rules, r 24(5)).

64.35 In an appeal against the decision of a traffic commissioner (see **Transport cases**), Schedule 1 to the UT Rules applies in place of r 24 (UT Rules, r 24(1)). On receipt of a copy of a notice of appeal under UT Rules, r 23(6)(b), the traffic commissioner must send to the Upper Tribunal a copy (and, on request, further copies) of:

- a written record of the decision appealed against and reasons for the decision;
- all documents produced to the traffic commissioner in connection with the decision;
- if a public inquiry was held, the transcript of the inquiry or, if no such transcript was produced, the traffic commissioner's note of the inquiry; and
- in an appeal under the Public Passenger Vehicles Act 1981, s 50 or the Goods Vehicles (Licensing of Operators) Act 1995, s 37, a list of the names and addresses of objectors and representors (Upper Tribunal Rules, Sch 1, para 3).

64.36 In a financial services case (see **Financial services cases**), Sch 3 to the UT Rules applies in place of r 24 (UT Rules, r 26B). The respondent must send or deliver a statement of case in support of the referred action so that it is received by the Upper Tribunal no later than 28 days after the day on which the respondent received the reference notice from the Tribunal. The statement of case must set out:

- the statutory provisions providing for the referred action;
- the reasons for the referred action;
- all the matters and facts upon which the respondent relies to support the referred action;
- a list of any documents on which the respondent relies in support of the referred action; and
- a list of any further material which in the opinion of the respondent might undermine the decision to take that action.

64.37 The respondent must send the statement of case and any additional documents to the referring party at the same time as it sends them to the Tribunal (UT Rules, Sch 3, para 4).

In a national security certificate case transferred from the GRC to the Upper Tribunal, the relevant minister must provide a response to the notice of appeal (Upper Tribunal Rules, Sch 2, para 3). For details of what the response should include, see **Information Rights Cases**.

64.38 For responses in judicial review cases in the Upper Tribunal see **Judicial review procedure in the Upper Tribunal**.

Lands Chamber

64.39 In case begun by a notice of appeal (for instance, from the Leasehold Valuation Tribunal ('LVT') and the Residential Property Tribunal ('RPT')), a respondent may give written notice of his intention to oppose the appeal, providing his name and address for service, the grounds on which he relies and whether he opposes the appeal jointly or separately. The respondent has 28 days in which to serve the notice of intention to respond, except that the Lands Chamber may direct a shorter period in the interests of justice where permission to appeal was granted by the LVT/RPT (Lands Chamber Rules, r 7). Following the service of the appellant's statement of case, the respondent who has filed a notice of intention, may also serve a statement of case, including the full particulars of the appeal (fact and law) which will be relied upon (Lands Chamber Rules, r 8(2), (3)). Any valuation which is proposed to be used in evidence (including all the computations and comparisons), and the full references to any comparable property which will be relied upon (or a statement that there are no comparable properties) must be served with the statement of case (Lands Chamber Rules, r 8(6)).

64.40 Where an application is made under the Law of Property Act 1925, s 84 in respect of restrictive covenants, any notice of objection must be sent to the registrar within 28 days of the date of the publication of the notices and shall include: his name and address and if he is represented the name, address and profession of the representative; the basis upon which he claims to be entitled to the benefit of the restriction; any ground of objection; and his signature or that of his representative and the date the statement was signed (Lands Chamber Rules, r 15).

65 Review, Correction and Setting Aside of Tribunal Decisions

See also **Decisions**.

REVIEW

Limitations on the power of review at common law

65.1 Statutory tribunals generally have no inherent power to rescind or review their own decisions: see *Akewushola v Secretary of State for the Home Department* [2000] 1 WLR 2295, 2301 per Sedley LJ. It has been suggested that the Upper Tribunal may have more inherent powers by virtue of the TCEA 2007, s 25, which confers on the Upper Tribunal, in relation to certain specified matters, the same rights, powers, privileges and authority as the High Court in England and Wales or the Court of Session in Scotland: see Jacobs, *Tribunal Practice and Procedure* (2009), paragraph 15.8. This conclusion cannot be correct. The list of matters in respect of which the Upper Tribunal is so empowered (and the empowerment is limited solely to those matters enumerated in TCEA 2007, s 25(2)) does not expressly include any power of review. It is limited to:

- the attendance and examination of witnesses;
- the production and inspection of documents; and
- all other matters incidental to the Upper Tribunal's functions.

65.2 Exceptionally, an appellate court may decide to reconsider its own final decision: see *Taylor v Lawrence* [2002] EWCA Civ 90; [2003] QB 528. However, the Employment Appeal Tribunal declined to follow this example in *Asda Stores Ltd v Thompson & Ors* [2004] IRLR 598, with Burton J remarking, at [45](1), 'We are not by any stretch of the imagination the final Court of Appeal.'

The power of review under TCEA 2007

65.3 TCEA 2007, ss 9 and 10 confer on the First-tier and Upper Tribunals, respectively, the power to review their own decisions on a matter in a case. This power is exercisable either of the tribunal's own initiative or on application by a person who has a right of appeal in respect of the decision in question (TCEA 2007, ss 9(2) and 10(2)).

65.4 Where the First-tier Tribunal has reviewed a decision it may, in the light of the review:

- correct accidental errors in the decision or in a record of the decision;
- amend reasons given for the decision; or
- set the decision aside (TCEA 2007, s 9(4)).

If it chooses the last of these options, the Tribunal must either re-decide the matter itself (TCEA 2007, s 9(5)(a)) or refer it to the Upper Tribunal (TCEA 2007, s 9(5)(b)), which, on such reference, must re-decide the matter with all of the powers that would be open to the First-tier Tribunal (TCEA 2007, s 9(6)–(8)).

65.5 Where the Upper Tribunal has reviewed a decision, it has the same powers save that, if it sets aside the decision, it must re-decide the matter itself (TCEA 2007, s 10(5)).

65.6 In either case, the re-decision is not subject to the right of appeal applicable to the original decision as an excluded matter (TCEA 2007, ss 11(5)(d) and 13(8)(d)) but is, rather, a new decision which generates a fresh power of review and right of appeal (TCEA 2007, ss 9(11) and 10(9)).

The power of review as implemented in the procedural rules

65.7 The power in TCEA 2007, ss 9 and 10 is reflected in the last part of the procedural rules of the various Chambers.

65.8 In the Chambers of the First-tier Tribunal, the power of review may only be exercised on an application for permission to appeal to the Upper Tribunal and if the Tribunal is satisfied that there was an error of law in the decision: Tribunal Procedure (GRC Rules, r 44(1); HESCC Rules, r 49(1)(a); SEC Rules, r 40(2); TC Rules, r 41(1); WPAFCC Rules, r 38(1); and IAC Rules, r 26(1). There is an exception in the Health, Education and Social Care Chamber of the First-tier Tribunal ('HESCC') for special educational needs decisions, which may be reviewed, on application, if circumstances relevant to the decision have changed since the decision was made (HESCC Rules, rr 48 and 49(1)(b)).

65.9 The First-tier Tribunal should notify the parties in writing of the outcome of the review. In most of the Chambers, if the Tribunal takes any action following a review without first giving every party an opportunity to make representations, the notification must state that any party who did not have an opportunity to make representations may apply for such action to be set aside and for a re-review: GRC Rules, r 44(3); HESCC Rules, r 49(3); SEC Rules, r 40(4); WPAFCC Rules, r 38(3); and IAC Rules, r 26(3). However, in the Tax Chamber, the Tribunal cannot take any action with first giving every party an opportunity to make representations: TC Rules, r 41(3).

65.10 The Upper Tribunal may exercise the power of review on an application for permission to appeal to the Court of Appeal but only if:

- when making the decision, the Upper Tribunal overlooked a legislative provision or binding authority which could have had a material effect on its decision; or
- since the decision, a court has made a decision which is binding on the Upper Tribunal and which, had it been made in time, could have had a material effect on the decision (Tribunal Procedure (Upper Tribunal) Rules 2008 ('UT Rules'), r 45(1); Lands Tribunal Rules 1996 ('Lands Chamber Rules'), rr 59(1) and 60(1)).

65.11 The Upper Tribunal may also review decisions in proceedings under the Forfeiture Act 1982 if:

- there was an error of law;
- the decision was made in ignorance of, or based on a mistake as to, a material fact; or
- there has been a relevant change in circumstances since the decision was made (UT Rules, rr 46(1)(b) and 47(2)).

65.12 If the Upper Tribunal decides not to review the decision or, on review, decides to take no action, it must consider whether to give permission to appeal (UT Rules, r 45(2); Lands Chamber Rules, r 59(2)). The Upper Tribunal must notify the parties in writing of the outcome of any review and of any rights of review or appeal in relation to that outcome (UT Rules, r 46(2); Lands Chamber Rules, r 60(2)). Like most Chambers of the First-tier Tribunal, the Upper Tribunal can decide to take an action in relation to a decision, on review, without first giving every party an opportunity to make representations but must give an opportunity to apply for the action to be set aside in the notice of the decision (UT Rules, r 46(3); Lands Chamber Rules, r 60(3)).

The approach to the exercise of the power of review

65.13 The power of review conferred on the First-tier and Upper Tribunals by TCEA 2007, ss 9 and 10 is clearly not the same as a complete power of rehearing. This can be seen from the limited circumstances in which the power may be used and from the language of the statutory provisions: the Tribunal is not empowered to re-take the decision but merely to 're-decide the matter concerned'.

65.14 In this regard, Jacobs (paragraph 15.53) cites *DK (Serbia) v Secretary of State for the Home Department* [2006] EWCA Civ 1747; [2007] 2 All ER 483, in which Latham LJ indicated (at [22]), in the context of an Asylum and Immigration Tribunal reconsideration, that 'any body asked to reconsider a decision on the grounds of an identified error of law will approach its reconsideration on the basis that any factual findings and conclusions or judgments arising from those findings which are unaffected by the error of law need not be revisited. It is not a rehearing'.

65.15 That having been said, Cane has observed ('Judicial review in the age of tribunals' [2009] PL 479) that the power conferred on the Upper Tribunal, in the event that the First-tier Tribunal sets aside a decision and refers it, to 'make any decision which the First-tier Tribunal could make if the First-tier Tribunal were re-deciding the matter' (TCEA 2007, s 9(7)) seems to enable the Upper Tribunal, procedurally, to act as a merits reviewer of the First-tier Tribunal's decisions.

65.16 On balance, it is suggested that – in view of the limited language of the relevant statutory and rule provisions and the existence of a power of appeal (more on which below) – the power of review is likely to be exercised cautiously, in cases of obvious error, and is unlikely to be used to engage in wider review exercises analogous to a full 'merits review' of the original decision. Support for this conclusion can be drawn from the Senior President's Practice Statements, Immigration and Asylum Chambers of the First-tier Tribunal and the Upper Tribunal (10 February 2010) at paragraph 4.2, where it is said that:

> 'Following such a review, the First-tier Tribunal may (subject to section 9(10)) set the decision aside under section 9(4)(c) and re-decide the matter concerned under section 9(5)(a). The First-tier Tribunal is, however, likely to adopt this course only if it is satisfied that:-
>
> (a) the effect of any error of law has been to deprive a party before the First-tier Tribunal of a fair hearing or other opportunity for that party's case to be put to and considered by the First-tier Tribunal; or

(b) there are highly compelling reasons why the matter should be re-decided by the First-tier Tribunal. (Such reasons are likely to be rare.)'

65.17 Although there is particular pressure on resources in the FTTIAC context, it is highly likely that a similar approach to reviews will pervade all parts of the Tribunals Service.

65.18 Some guidance on the First-tier Tribunal power of review has recently been provided by a three-judge panel of the Administrative Appeals Chamber of the Upper Tribunal ('AAC') (including the Senior President, Carnwath LJ and the Chamber President, Walker J) in *R (RB) v First-tier Tribunal* [2010] UKUT 160 (AAC). The case was a judicial review of the HESCC judge's reviewing of a decision to review (which the judge had no jurisdiction to do, the proper course being to set aside, and from which it is not possible to appeal), and involved consideration of the interaction of reviews and permission to appeal. The AAC held, at [24]–[27]:

> 'It cannot have been intended that the power of review should enable the First-tier Tribunal to usurp the Upper Tribunal's function of determining appeals on contentious points of law. Nor can it have been intended to enable a later First-tier Tribunal judge or panel, or the original First-tier Tribunal judge or panel on a later occasion, to take a different view of the law from that previously reached, when both views are tenable. Both these considerations demonstrate that if a power of review is to be exercised to set aside the original decision because of perceived error of law, this should only be done in clear cases.
>
> There are, of course, degrees of clarity and there are practical reasons for taking a flexible approach. An important consideration may be the likelihood of the party in whose favour the original decision was made objecting to the review. In the event of an objection, the review may well cause delay rather then reducing it.
>
> Rule 49(3) enables the First-tier Tribunal to take a robust approach when it first receives an application for permission to appeal for it enables it to take a decision without calling for representations by the other side, on the basis that if the other side objects there can be an application to set aside. However, if the tribunal receives an application to set aside the action it has taken following a review, it must consider afresh whether that action was appropriate, in the knowledge that it is contentious. Moreover the tribunal is not obliged to take the robust approach permitted by rule 49(3) and in many cases it will be preferable to invite representations before concluding that an original decision should be set aside.
>
> We agree with [counsel] that consideration whether or not to review a decision involves a large element of judgment or discretion. Indeed, even if the First-tier Tribunal is satisfied that there is a clear error of law, it may decide not to review a decision but instead to give permission to appeal. The error may be a common one and, for that or other reasons, it may be helpful to have an authoritative decision of the Upper Tribunal on the point.'

The interaction of the power of review and appeals

65.19 The explanatory notes to the TCEA 2007 indicate that the power of review complements the appeal procedure by filtering out at an early stage decisions that are clearly erroneous: '[it] is intended to capture decisions that are clearly wrong, so avoiding the need for an appeal. The power has been provided in the form of a discretionary power for the tribunal so that only appropriate decisions are reviewed. This contrasts with cases where an appeal on a point of law is made, because, for instance, it is important to have an authoritative ruling.' (paragraph 100).

65.20 This filter for clear errors is consistent with the objectives of efficiency and proportionality. As Jacobs has put it ('Something old, something new: the new tribunal system' [2009] ILJ 417), the tribunals are able to take responsibility for their own quality control and leave the Upper Tribunal and appellate courts to focus on cases that raise issues of more general importance.

CORRECTION

The power of correction at common law

65.21 It was the view of Sedley LJ in *Akewushola v Immigration Officer, Heathrow* [2000] 1 WLR 2295, CA that statutory tribunals have an inherent jurisdiction to correct slips.

The power of correction under TCEA 2007

65.22 As well as this inherent power and TCEA 2007, ss 9(4)(a) and 10(4)(a), which provide for a power to correct accidental errors in a decision or in the record thereof, the power to correct also arises from the TCEA 2007, Sch 5, para 15. This explicitly allows the procedural rules to allow for the correction of accidental errors in a decision or record thereof.

The power of correction as implemented in the procedural rules

65.23 Consistent with the TCEA 2007 provisions, the procedural rules in the various Tribunal Chambers allow the tribunal to correct at any time any clerical mistake or other accidental slip or omission in any decision, direction or document by sending notification of the amendment, or a copy of the amended document to all parties, and making any necessary amendment to any information published in relation to the decision, direction or document: GRC Rules, r 40; HESCC Rules, r 44; SEC Rules, r 36; TC Rules, r 37; WPAFCC Rules, r 34; (in different terms) IAC Rules, r 60(1); and (in slightly different terms but to similar effect) UT Rules, r 42. There is no equivalent provision in the Lands Chamber Rules; the Lands Chamber will accordingly have to fall back on inherent powers.

The approach to the exercise of the power of correction

65.24 It is expected that, save in exceptional circumstances that would render it inequitable, where a tribunal had made an accidental mistake it would be appropriate to exercise the power of correction.

SETTING ASIDE

Limitations on the power to set aside at common law

65.25 Statutory Tribunals do not have an inherent power to set aside their own decisions at common law: see Sedley LJ in *Akewushola*. Insofar as limited exceptions appear to have evolved (for example, the jurisdiction claimed by the Social Security Commissioners to set aside decisions that were made in procedural error: see Jacobs at paragraph 15.11), they have generally been limited in scope and arise from tribunals' power to control their procedures and to promulgate their decisions.

The power to set aside under TCEA

65.26 As with the power of correction, as well as TCEA 2007, ss 9(4)(c) and 10(4)(c), which provide for a power to set aside decisions, there is also explicit provision in the TCEA 2007, Sch 5, para 15 for the power to set aside to be included in the procedural rules.

The power to set aside as implemented in the procedural rules

65.27 The procedural rules in the various tribunal Chambers appear not to allow the Tribunal to set aside a decision of its own initiative but only on an application, to be made (with some, unexplained, exceptions) within 28 days of the receipt of the notice of the decision: GRC Rules, r 41(3); HESCC Rules, r 45(3); SEC Rules, r 37(3) (one month); TC Rules, r 38(3); WPAFCC Rules, r 35(1) (one month); and UT Rules, r 43(3) (one month). The power to set aside in the FTTIAC is available on application by the parties or at the initiative of the Tribunal where there is considered to have been an administrative error on the part of the Tribunal or its staff (IAC Rules, r 60(1A)). The time limit for making such an application is 10 days if within the UK, or 28 days if outside the UK (IAC Rules, r 60(1B)). Where the Upper Tribunal has considered an immigration or asylum appeal the time limit for applying to set aside a decision is 12 days from the date of sending the notice to the applicant if in the UK, or 38 days if outside the UK (UT Rules, r 43(4)). If service is electronic or personal those time limits are reduced to ten working days (UT Rules, r 43(5)). There is no equivalent provision in the Lands Chamber Rules.

65.28 The Tribunal may set aside the decision if it considers that it is in the interests of justice to do so, and at least one of the following four conditions is satisfied:

- a document relating to the proceedings was not sent to, or was not received at an appropriate time by, a party or a party's representative;
- a document relating to the proceedings was not sent to the Tribunal at an appropriate time;
- a party, or a party's representative, was not present at a hearing related to the proceedings; or
- there has been some other procedural irregularity in the proceedings.

See GRC Rules, r 41(2); HESCC Rules, r 45(2); SEC Rules, r 37(2); TC Rules, r 38(2); WPAFCC Rules, r 35(2); and UT Rules, r 43(2).

65.29 Thus, in essence, the power is limited to procedural errors, as was the power previously exercised by the Social Security Commissioners.

The approach to the exercise of the power to set aside

65.30 The default position at common law was that a party who has been deprived of an oral hearing by some procedural mishap is entitled to have the decision set aside so that a hearing can be held: see *Grimshaw v Dunbar* [1953] 1 QB 408. It is expected that, consistent with the emphasis in the overriding objective on dealing with cases fairly and justly, the same will apply in the tribunals. However, it will be appropriate to take into account all the individual circumstances of the case, including the reason for non-attendance and any subsequent events.

65.31 It has been accepted by the Administrative Appeals Chamber of the Upper Tribunal that an appeal can lie against a decision to refuse to set aside: *Patterson v Secretary of State for Work and Pensions* [2010] UKUT 103 (AAC) at [17]–[18].

Other powers to set aside

65.32 The TCEA 2007, Sch 15, para 15(3) also preserves any other previously extant powers to set aside decisions. This would include, of course, the power to set aside a decision obtained by fraud of a party: see *Taylor v Lawrence* [2002] EWCA Civ 90; [2003] QB 528 at [26].

66 Schools Registration Cases

See also **Care standards cases; Health, Education and Social Care Chamber** and **Health, Education and Social Care Chamber procedural rules.**

HEALTH, EDUCATION AND SOCIAL CARE CHAMBER

66.1 The First-tier Tribunal (Care Standards), which is within the HESCC, hears appeals against decisions concerning the registration of independent schools (see **Health, Education and Social Care Chamber**).

66.2 Proceedings before the HESCC are governed by the HESCC Rules. The HESCC Rules are reproduced at Appendix 2. See also **Health, Education and Social Care Chamber procedural rules.**

DECISIONS COVERED

The role of the Secretary of State for Education and Skills in the registration of independent schools

66.3 The Education Act 2002 ('EA 2002') requires the Secretary of State for Education and Skills to maintain a register of independent schools in England (and the National Assembly for Wales to maintain a register for Wales): see EA 2002, s 158. All independent schools must be on this register: running an unregistered school is an offence (EA 2002, s 159). Material changes to registered schools must be approved by the Secretary of State (EA 2002, s 162).

66.4 If the Secretary of State is satisfied, in respect of a particular independent school, that that school is not meeting one or more of the prescribed standards for independent schools then EA 2002, s 165 requires him to undertake certain steps:

- If he considers that there is a risk of serious harm to the welfare of pupils at the school, identifying the standard or standards not being met, he may determine that it shall be removed from the register (EA 2002, s 165(2)).
- If he does not make such a determination, he must serve notice on the proprietor of the school and require the proprietor to submit an action plan (EA 2002, s 165(3)).
- If the action plan is not submitted, is rejected or is not complied with, he may then either make a determination to deregister or make an order requiring the proprietor of the school to do one or more of the following specified actions:
  - to cease using any part of the school premises for all purposes or purposes specified in the order;
  - to close any part of the school's operation; or

  - to cease to admit any new pupils, or new pupils of a description specified in the order (EA 2002, s 165(8)).

- If the Secretary of State makes an order under EA 2002, s 165(8), the proprietor of the independent school in question may apply to the Secretary of State for the order in question to be varied or revoked (EA 2002, s 165(10)).

The decisions which may be appealed

66.5 Under EA 2002, s 166(1), the proprietor of a registered school may appeal against:

- a refusal under s 162 to approve a material change;
- a determination under s 165 to remove the school from the register;
- an order under s 165(8) requiring the taking of specified action; or
- a refusal under s 165(10) to vary or revoke such an order.

66.6 The appeal used to lie to the Tribunal established under the Protection of Children Act 1999 ('PCA 1999'), s 9 but now, by virtue of the First-tier Tribunal and Upper Tribunal (Chambers) Order 2008, SI 2008/2684, para 5(g) lies to the HESCC.

APPEALING TO THE FIRST-TIER TRIBUNAL

See **Bringing proceedings in the First-tier Tribunals** and **Health, Education and Social Care Chamber**.

66.7 Unlike other proceedings before the First-tier Tribunal (Care Standards), which cannot be brought without leave (see HESCC Rules, r 19), appeals in schools registration cases in respect of the decisions set out above lie as of right.

Time for making an appeal

66.8 Under EA 2002, s 166(2), an appeal in a schools case must be made within 28 days of the day on which notice of the refusal, determination or order was served on the proprietor of the independent school: see also r 20(1)(a) and Schedule to the HESCC Rules.

66.9 The application notice is sent to the Tribunal (HESCC Rules, r 20). If the applicant provides the notice late then it must include a request for an extension of time and the reason why the application was out of time (HESCC Rules, r 20(4)(a)). The Tribunal must not admit the notice unless it extends time (HESCC Rules, r 20(4)(b)).

Application notice

66.10 An application notice in a schools case must be signed by the applicant and must include (HESCC Rules, r 20(2)):

- the name and address of the applicant;
- the name and address of the applicant's representative (if any);

- an address where documents for the applicant may be sent or delivered;
- the name and address of any respondent;
- details of the decision or act, or failure to decide or act, to which the proceedings relate;
- the result the applicant is seeking;
- the grounds on which the applicant relies; and
- any further information or documents required by an applicable practice direction.

The applicant must send with the application notice a copy of any written record of any decision under challenge, and any statement of reasons for that decision (HESCC Rules, r 20(3)).

66.11 In practice, there is a specific form (Appeal Form IS) for use in schools cases. This is available on the website of the First-tier Tribunal (Care Standards).

Response by the Secretary of State

66.12 Once the Tribunal receives an Appeal Form IS, it must send a copy of this and any accompanying documents to the Secretary of State. When the Secretary of State receives a copy of the relevant documents, he has 20 working days in which to respond (r 21(1)(a) and Schedule to the HESCC Rules).

66.13 The response must include (HESCC Rules, r 21(2)):

- the name and address of the respondent;
- the name and address of the respondent's representative (if any);
- an address where documents for the respondent may be sent or delivered;
- a statement as to whether the respondent opposes the applicant's case and, if so, any grounds for such opposition which are not contained in another document provided with the response; and
- any further information or documents required by an applicable practice direction or direction.

The response may include a statement as to whether the respondent would be content for the case to be dealt with without a hearing if the Tribunal considers it appropriate (HESCC Rules, r 21(3)).

Order that a school be regarded as not registered pending determination of an appeal

66.14 By virtue of EA 2002, s 166(3), if an appeal is made against a deregistration determination, in general the effect of making an appeal is to suspend the effect of the determination until the appeal is withdrawn or disposed of. But under EA 2002, s 166(5), if at any time the Tribunal considers there is a risk of serious harm occurring to the welfare of pupils before an appeal is determined, it may by order provide that the school is to be regarded as not registered for the purposes of EA 2002, s 159 until the Tribunal determines the appeal. Provision is made in HESCC Rules, r 22 for the use of this power.

66.15 Pursuant to HESCC Rules, r 22(3), the Secretary of State must make any application for an order under EA 2002, s 166(5) in writing and this application must be received within 28 days of the date on which he received a copy of the application notice. An application for an order under s 166(5) must (HESCC Rules, r 22(4)):

- be signed by the respondent and dated;
- state the grounds for the application;
- state the nature of the evidence that will be provided in support of the application and the names of the witnesses who will give that evidence;
- specify any working days in the following 30 days when the respondent or a witness named under sub-paragraph (c) would not be available to attend a hearing, and provide reasons why they would not be available; and
- include, so far as practicable, any documentary evidence (including witness statements) that the respondent intends to rely on.

66.16 The applicant must give a written response to the application, to be received within 16 days of the date on which the respondent sent the application (HESCC Rules, r 22(5)). Failure to provide this response disentitles the applicant from having any further say in relation to the application (HESCC Rules, r 22(7)). The applicant's response must (HESCC Rules, r 22(6)):

- acknowledge receipt of the application and any documentary evidence included with it;
- state whether the applicant requests that the application be decided at a hearing, and if so:
- state the nature of the evidence that will be provided in support of the applicant's case and the names of the witnesses who will give that evidence; and
- specify any working days in the following 16 days when the applicant or a witness named under sub-paragraph (b)(i) would not be available to attend a hearing, and provide reasons why they would not be available; and
- include, so far as practicable, any documentary evidence (including witness statements) that the applicant intends to rely on.

66.17 If the applicant sends a response in time and requests a hearing to determine the application, the Tribunal must hold a hearing (HESCC Rules, r 22(8)) and do so as soon as reasonably practicable. At the latest, the hearing must be held by the earlier of 14 days after the date when the Tribunal received the response or 30 days after the date on which the application was originally sent (HESCC Rules, r 22(9)).

66.18 Although the Tribunal is empowered to make an order under EA 2002, r 166(5) on its own initiative, it may not do so without giving the applicant an opportunity to make representations at a hearing and must give directions for the parties to provide documents or evidence (HESCC Rules, r 22(10)).

HEARINGS IN SCHOOLS CASES

66.19 The First-tier Tribunal must hold a hearing (see **Hearings**) before making a decision which disposes of proceedings unless all parties consent to the matter being decided without a hearing and the Tribunal considers that it is able to decide the matter without a hearing (HESCC Rules, r 23(1)). Unless the Tribunal directs otherwise, the hearing will be held in public (HESCC Rules, r 26(1)).

APPEALS IN SCHOOLS REGISTRATION CASES

66.20 Appeals lie to the Administrative Appeals Chamber of the Upper Tribunal (see **Administrative Appeals Chamber and Upper Tribunal**). See **Appeals from the First-tier Tribunal** and **Health, Education and Social Care Chamber procedural rules** for relevant details.

67 Senior President of Tribunals

OFFICE

67.1 The Senior President of Tribunals ('Senior President') is the judicial head of the Tribunals Service. The office of Senior President was created by the TCEA 2007, s 2. More detailed provisions concerning his selection, appointment and term of office are to be found in TCEA 2007, Sch 1.

67.2 The Senior President may be recommended either: (i) following consultation by the Lord Chancellor and agreement between him, the Lord Chief Justice of England and Wales, the Lord President of the Court of Session and the Lord Chief Justice of Northern Ireland (TCEA 2007, Sch 1, paras 2(2)–(4)); or (ii) following selection by a panel of the Judicial Appointments Commission (TCEA 2007, Sch 1, Part 2, and the Constitutional Reform Act 2005, ss 75A–75G as amended). If the former route to a recommendation is used, the Senior President must be a Lord Justice of Appeal in England and Wales or of Northern Ireland, or a judge of the Court of Session who is a member of the First or Second Division of the Inner House (TCEA 2007, Sch 1, para 2(2)(b)).

67.3 As is consistent with the independence of the Tribunals Service and its judiciary, the Senior President is independent of both the Government and the Chief Justices. Once appointed, by whichever route, the Senior President cannot be removed until the end of his fixed term or the statutory retirement age under the Judicial Pensions and Retirement Act 1993 (whichever is earlier) save by the Queen on an address by both Houses of Parliament (TCEA 2007, Sch 1, para 6(2)).

FUNCTIONS

Duties

67.4 Under TCEA 2007, s 2(3), the Senior President must, in carrying out the functions of that office, have regard to:

- the need for tribunals to be accessible,
- the need for proceedings before tribunals—
  - to be fair, and
  - to be handled quickly and efficiently,
- the need for members of tribunals to be experts in the subject-matter of, or the law to be applied in, cases in which they decide matters, and
- the need to develop innovative methods of resolving disputes that are of a type that may be brought before tribunals.

67.5 He is also, by virtue of TCEA 2007, s 47, under a duty of mutual co–operation with the Chief Justices in relation to their responsibilities for the training, welfare and guidance of the tribunal judiciary.

General roles

67.6 The Senior President presides over and is a member of the First–tier and Upper Tribunals (TCEA 2007, ss 3(4), 5(1)(a) and 4(1)(c)). He is empowered to delegate any function to a judge or other member of either tribunal or to staff (TCEA 2007, s 8), save for his functions under TCEA 2007, s 57(9) (as to which see para 67.9 below).

67.7 The Senior President has the power to lay before Parliament written representations on matters relating to tribunal members or the administration of justice by tribunals (TCEA 2007, Sch 1, para 13) and is responsible for representing the views of tribunal members to Parliament, the Lord Chancellor and the Ministers of the Government (TCEA 2007, Sch 1, para 14).

67.8 The Senior President is also obliged to report each year to the Lord Chancellor on cases which he wishes to bring to the attention of the Lord Chancellor and cases which the Lord Chancellor has asked him to cover (TCEA 2007, s 43(1)). The Lord Chancellor, for his part, is required to publish the report (TCEA 2007, s 43(2)).

Tribunals and Chambers

67.9 The Lord Chancellor may by order make provision for the organisation of each of the First-tier Tribunal and the Upper Tribunal into a number of Chambers with the concurrence of the Senior President (TCEA 2007, s 7(1)). Each of the Lord Chancellor and the Senior President may, with the concurrence of the other, allocate by order the functions of the First-tier Tribunal or the Upper Tribunal between their respective Chambers (TCEA 2007, s 7(9)). See further **Chambers, First-tier Tribunal** and **Upper Tribunal**.

67.10 As well as having functions relating to the allocation of functions across the tribunals, the Senior President also has responsibilities in relation to the tribunals' procedural rules. He may, with the approval of the Lord Chancellor, give directions as to the practice and procedure of the First-tier Tribunal and the Upper Tribunal (TCEA 2007, s 23(1) and (4)). If a Chamber President wishes to give directions as to the practice and procedure of his Chamber, the Senior President's approval (as well as that of the Lord Chancellor) is required (TCEA 2007, s 23(2) and (5)).

67.11 The Senior President must either sit on the Tribunal Procedure Committee or nominate someone to do so (TCEA 2007, Sch 5, para 20). Indeed, it is expected that he or his nominee will chair the Committee. See **Tribunal Procedure Committee**.

Appointments and Tribunal membership

67.12 Under TCEA 2007, Sch 4, para 2(1), the Lord Chancellor is required to consult the Senior President before appointing a member of the judiciary as a Chamber President under TCEA 2007, s 7(7). The Lord Chancellor is also required to consult the Senior President as to whether a Deputy Chamber President is required before deciding that one is necessary (TCEA 2007, Sch 4, para 5(3)).

67.13 If no one is appointed under TCEA 2007, s 7 to act as Chamber President of a First-tier Tribunal or Upper Tribunal chamber, the Senior President may appoint an Acting Chamber President (TCEA 2007, Sch 4, para 6(1) and (2)). He may also appoint a person who is a Chamber President to preside instead, or also, over another chamber (TCEA 2007, s 7(6)) and do the same in respect of Deputy Chamber Presidents (TCEA 2007, Sch 4, para 5(2)).

67.14 So far as other members of the First-tier Tribunal and Upper Tribunal are concerned:

- The concurrence of the Senior President is required in respect of the orders made by the Lord Chancellor prescribing the qualifications for non-judicial members of the First-tier and Upper Tribunals (TCEA 2007, Sch 2, para 2(2) and Sch 3, para 2(2)).
- The Senior President may request court judges to act as judges of the First–tier and Upper Tribunals (TCEA 2007, Sch 2, para 6(2) and TCEA 2007, Sch 3, para 6(2)).
- The Senior President must maintain appropriate arrangements for training, guidance and welfare of judges and other members of the First–tier and Upper Tribunals (TCEA 2007, Sch 2, para 8 and Sch 3, para 9).
- The Senior President may take oaths of allegiance and judicial oaths (or nominate someone to do so) from judges and other members of the First–tier and Upper Tribunals (TCEA 2007, Sch 2, para 9 and Sch 3, para 10) and from Chamber Presidents, Deputy Chamber Presidents and Acting Chamber Presidents (TCEA 2007, Sch 4, para 8).

Case allocation

67.15 The Senior President has the power to assign judges and other members to Chambers (TCEA 2007, Sch 4, para 9), subject to a policy to be published following agreement with the Lord Chancellor (TCEA 2007, Sch 4, para 13). He may choose members to decide cases (TCEA 2007, Sch 4, para 14) and, where the Lord Chancellor provides for it to be determined by the Senior President, may also determine the number of tribunal members who are to decide a matter that falls to be decided by the First–tier or Upper Tribunal (TCEA 2007, Sch 4, para 15).

Employment Tribunal and Employment Appeal Tribunal

67.16 The Employment Tribunal ('ET') and Employment Appeal Tribunal ('EAT') are outside the scope of this work because they do fall within the scope of the two-tier Tribunal system administered under the TCEA 2007. Nor are there any current plans to bring them within that scope. However, the Senior President has, in relation to these Tribunals, the following further powers and functions:

- a duty to maintain appropriate arrangements for the training, guidance and welfare of members of panels of members of employment tribunals (Employment Tribunals Act 1996, s 5A);
- the power to take the oath of allegiance and judicial oath from the Presidents and members of panels (Employment Tribunals Act 1996, s 5C);

- the power to nominate a relevant tribunal judge or a relevant judge to act as a member of a panel of members of the ET, with the consent of the President of ETs (for England and Wales or Scotland as appropriate), the relevant judge and the relevant chief justice as appropriate (Employment Tribunals Act 1996, s 5D(2)(a));
- the power to give Practice Directions about the procedure of ET and the EAT, with the approval of the Lord Chancellor (Employment Tribunals Act 1996, ss 7A(A1) and 29A(1)(a));
- the power to approve Practice Directions given by the Presidents of the ETs and EAT (Employment Tribunals Act 1996, ss 7A(2C)(a), 29A(4)(a) and 29A(6)(a)) with the Lord Chancellor;
- a duty to maintain appropriate arrangements for the training, guidance and welfare of members of panels of judges and other members of the EAT (Employment Tribunals Act 1996, s 24A); and
- the power to take the oath of allegiance and judicial oath from relevant appointees (Employment Tribunals Act 1996, s 24B).

INCUMBENT OFFICE HOLDER

67.17 The current Senior President and first holder of the office is Sir Robert Carnwath CVO. He has been a Lord Justice of Appeal since September 2001 and divides his time between the two roles. He was previously a judge of the High Court, Chancery Division, from 1994 and has been a Privy Counsellor since July 2004.

67.18 As at the time of publication, Lord Justice Carnwath has published three Implementation Reviews in his capacity as Senior President, in June 2008, October 2008 and July 2009. He has also published an Annual Report in February 2010 on the Tribunals Service and system more generally. (It is not the s 43 report. No s 43 report has yet been made or requested and the Senior President indicated in his Annual Report that the case law of the Tribunals was not yet in a state which enabled reporting on it).

68 Social Care Cases

See also **Care standards cases; Health, Education and Social Care Chamber** and **Health, Education and Social Care Chamber procedural rules.**

HEALTH, EDUCATION AND SOCIAL CARE CHAMBER

68.1 'Social care' is defined in the Health and Social Care Act 2008 ('HSCA 2008'), s 9 (3) as 'all forms of personal care and other practical assistance provided for individuals who by reason of age, illness, disability, pregnancy, childbirth, dependence on alcohol or drugs, or any other similar circumstances, are in need of such care or other assistance'. A 'social care case' is defined herein as one concerning a provider of social care (ie not cases concerning the registration of individual social workers and social care workers).

68.2 The First-tier Tribunal (Care Standards), which is within the HESCC, has jurisdiction to hear almost all care standards cases, namely, appeals against decisions to restrict or bar an individual from working with children or vulnerable adults and decisions to cancel, vary or refuse registration of certain health, childcare and social care provision (see **Care standards cases** and **Health, Education and Social Care Chamber**). As is readily apparent, the phrase 'care standards cases' encompasses social care cases.

68.3 Proceedings before the HESCC are governed by the HESCC Rules. The HESCC Rules are reproduced at Appendix 2. See also **Health, Education and Social Care Chamber procedural rules.**

DECISIONS COVERED

The system for the registration of establishments and agencies and the role of the Care Quality Commission

68.4 The Care Standards Act 2000 ('CSA 2000') provided for a new regulatory system for social care and private and voluntary healthcare services (collectively, 'care services'). The CSA 2000 established a register of all establishments and agencies (a wide definition, encompassing children's homes, care homes, nursing agencies, fostering and adoption agencies and healthcare providers) and, by CSA 2000, s 11(1), required all such establishments or agencies to be registered. The relevant registration authorities were the newly-created National Care Standards Commission ('NCSC') in England and the National Assembly for Wales.

68.5 Under CSA 2000, s 12, all applications for registration had to be made to the registration authority, which could decide to grant them (conditionally or unconditionally) or refuse them under s 13. The same applied, pursuant to s 15, to applications to remove or vary conditions of registration or to cancel a registration. A right to appeal against decisions of registration authorities was provided by CSA 2000, s 21.

68.6 The Health and Social Care (Community Health and Standards) Act 2003 transferred the functions of the NCSC to the Commission for Healthcare

Audit and Inspection ('CHAI', commonly known as the 'Healthcare Commission') and the Commission for Social Care Inspection ('CSCI'). The former took over the NCSC's functions relating to independent hospitals, independent clinics and independent medical agencies. The latter took over its functions in respect of children's homes; care homes; residential family centres; domiciliary care agencies; nurses agencies; fostering agencies; voluntary adoption agencies; and adoption support agencies.

68.7 As of 31 March 2009, both bodies and the Mental Health Act Commission have been replaced by a single integrated regulator for health and adult social care, namely, the Care Quality Commission ('CQC'). This transfer was effected by the Health and Social Care Act 2008. Under HSCA 2008, s 10, any person who carries on a 'regulated activity' (defined in s 8(2)(a) as an activity which 'involves, or is connected with, the provision of health or social care in, or in relation to, England') must be registered, with applications for registration being made to the CQC.

68.8 HSCA 2008, s 32 provided for a right of appeal in respect of decisions of the CQC relating to registration, or the conditions of registration (or cancellation decisions made by a justice of the peace under the urgent cancellations procedure in s 30). It should be noted that the CQC's jurisdiction does not extend to certain education-related and childcare-related establishments and agencies, which are now regulated by the Office for Standards in Education, Children's Services and Skills.

The decisions which may be appealed

68.9 Thus any decision concerning the registration of a social care provider, the cancellation of such registration or the conditions of registration may be appealed, pursuant to CSA 2000, s 21 and, more recently, HSCA 2008, s 32.

68.10 The appeal used to lie to the Tribunal established under the Protection of Children Act 1999 ('PCA 1999'), s 9 but now, by virtue of the First-tier Tribunal and Upper Tribunal (Chambers) Order 2008, SI 2008/2684, para 5(d)–(dd) lies to the HESCC.

APPEALING TO THE FIRST-TIER TRIBUNAL

See **Bringing proceedings in the First-tier Tribunals** and **Health, Education and Social Care Chamber**.

68.11 Unlike other proceedings before the First-tier Tribunal (Care Standards), which cannot be brought without leave (see HESCC Rules, r 19), appeals in respect of the decisions set out above lie as of right. It should be noted that appeals by individual workers under CSA 2000, s 86 against their inclusion in the list of individuals who are considered unsuitable to work with vulnerable adults (CSA 2000, s 81) are, by contrast to decisions in respect of social care providers, subject to leave.

Time for making an appeal

68.12 Under CSA 2000, s 21(2) and HSCA 2008, s 32(2), an appeal in a social care case must be made within 28 days of the day on which notice of the act or decision was sent to the applicant: see also r 20(1)(a) and Schedule to the HESCC Rules.

68.13 The notice of appeal is sent to the Tribunal (HESCC Rules, r 20(1)). If the applicant provides the notice late then it must include a request for an extension of time and the reason why the application was out of time (HESCC Rules, r 20(4)(a)). The Tribunal must not admit the notice unless it extends time (HESCC Rules, r 20(4)(b)).

Notice of appeal

68.14 An application notice in a social care case must be signed by the applicant and must include (HESCC Rules, r 20(2)):

- the name and address of the applicant;
- the name and address of the applicant's representative (if any);
- an address where documents for the applicant may be sent or delivered;
- the name and address of any respondent;
- details of the decision or act, or failure to decide or act, to which the proceedings relate;
- the result the applicant is seeking;
- the grounds on which the applicant relies; and
- any further information or documents required by an applicable practice direction.

The applicant must send with the application notice a copy of any written record of any decision under challenge, and any statement of reasons for that decision (HESCC Rules, r 20(3)).

68.15 In practice, the general Appeal Form A, available on the website of the First-tier Tribunal (Care Standards), is to be used in social care and other care standards cases.

Response by the Secretary of State

68.16 Once the Tribunal receives an Appeal Form A, it must send a copy of this and any accompanying documents to the respondent. When the respondent receives a copy of the relevant documents, it has 20 working days in which to respond (HESCC Rules, r 21(1)(a), Sch).

68.17 The response must include (HESCC Rules, r 21(2)):

- the name and address of the respondent;
- the name and address of the respondent's representative (if any);
- an address where documents for the respondent may be sent or delivered;
- a statement as to whether the respondent opposes the applicant's case and, if so, any grounds for such opposition which are not contained in another document provided with the response; and
- any further information or documents required by an applicable practice direction or direction.

The response may include a statement as to whether the respondent would be content for the case to be dealt with without a hearing if the Tribunal considers it appropriate (HESCC Rules, r 21(3)).

HEARINGS IN SOCIAL CARE CASES

68.18 The First-tier Tribunal must hold a hearing (see **Hearings**) before making a decision which disposes of proceedings unless all parties consent to the matter being decided without a hearing and the Tribunal considers that it is able to decide the matter without a hearing (HESCC Rules, r 23(1)). Unless the Tribunal directs otherwise, the hearing will be held in public (HESCC Rules, r 26(1)).

APPEALS IN SOCIAL CARE CASES

68.19 Appeals lie to the Administrative Appeals Chamber of the Upper Tribunal (see **Administrative Appeals Chamber** and **Upper Tribunal**). See **Appeals from the First-tier Tribunal** and **Health, Education and Social Care Chamber procedural rules** for relevant details.

69 Social Entitlement Chamber

COMPOSITION AND LOCATION

69.1 The SEC is one of six Chambers that collectively comprise the First-tier Tribunals (see **First-tier Tribunals** and **Chambers**).

69.2 The SEC is, like the Upper Tribunal and other Chambers of the First-tier Tribunals, presided over by the Senior President. The SEC itself has a Chamber President and comprises judges and other members, in accordance with the TCEA 2007, s 4. The SEC came into existence on 3 November 2008 with the core of its jurisdiction, and subsequent additions to that jurisdiction have occurred with effect from April, June and September 2009, and January 2010.

69.3 Each of the three separate tribunals that comprise the SEC (the Asylum Support Tribunal, the Criminal Injuries Compensation Tribunal and the Social Security and Child Support Tribunal) has its own judicial staff, including a Principal Judge.

69.4 The SEC has a network of hearing venues throughout the United Kingdom.

Procedural rules

69.5 Proceedings before the SEC are governed by the Tribunal Procedure (First–tier Tribunal) (Social Entitlement Chamber) Rules 2008, SI 2008/2685 as amended ('SEC Rules'). The SEC Rules are reproduced at Appendix 5. See **Social Entitlement Chamber procedural rules** for details on their content.

APPELLATE JURISDICTION AND POWERS

69.6 The SEC has, by the First-tier Tribunal and Upper Tribunal (Chambers) Order 2008, SI 2008/2684, art 3 (as amended), been assigned all functions relating to appeals:

(a) in cases regarding support for asylum seekers, failed asylum seekers, persons designated under section 130 of the Criminal Justice and Immigration Act 2008, or the dependants of any such persons;

(b) in criminal injuries compensation cases;

(c) regarding entitlement to, payments of, or recovery or recoupment of payments of, social security benefits, child support, vaccine damage payment, health in pregnancy grant, and tax credits, with the exception of—

(ai) appeals under section 11 of the Social Security Contributions (Transfer of Functions, etc) Act 1999 (appeals against decisions of Her Majesty's Revenue and Customs);

(i) appeals in respect of employer penalties or employer information penalties (as defined in section 63(11) and (12) of the Tax Credits Act 2002);

(ii) appeals under regulation 28(3) of the Child Trust Funds Regulations 2004;

(ca) regarding saving gateway accounts with the exception of appeals against requirements to account for an amount under regulations made under section 14 of the Saving Gateway Accounts Act 2009;

(cb) regarding child trust funds with the exception of appeals against requirements to account for an amount under regulations made under section 22(4) Child Trust Funds Act 2004 in relation to section 13 of that Act;

(d) regarding payments in consequence of diffuse mesothelioma;

(e) regarding a certificate or waiver decision in relation to NHS charges;

(f) regarding entitlement to be credited with earnings or contributions;

(g) against a decision as to whether an accident was an industrial accident.

69.7 The three sub-divisions of the SEC are asylum support (see **Asylum support appeals**), criminal injuries compensation (see **Criminal injuries compensation cases**) and social security and child support, which is by far the biggest (see **Social security and child support**).

69.8 The SEC may hear appeals on both fact and law.

69.9 The SEC does not deal with asylum claims or any other immigration matters. Its Asylum Support Tribunal only considers appeals against a refusal or termination of support made by the UK Borders Agency ('UKBA').

69.10 Appeals from the SEC go to the Administrative Appeals Chamber of the Upper Tribunal (see **Administrative Appeals Chamber**).

70 Social Entitlement Chamber Procedural Rules

See also **Procedural rules.**

STATUTORY INSTRUMENT

70.1 Proceedings before the SEC are governed by the SEC Rules. The SEC Rules are reproduced at Appendix 5. See also **Social Entitlement Chamber**.

STRUCTURE

70.2 The SEC Rules are similar in structure to the rules of four of the other Chambers of the First-tier Tribunals (the Immigration and Asylum Chamber of the First-tier Tribunal ('FTTIAC') having different rules), comprising the standard four parts ('Introduction', 'General powers and provisions', 'Proceedings before the Tribunal' and 'Correcting, setting aside, reviewing and appealing Tribunal decisions').

APPEALING TO THE SEC

See **Bringing proceedings in the First-tier Tribunals.**

70.3 As explained above, the SEC comprises three types of tribunals for hearing three types of proceedings. The procedure for bringing each type is set out in the specific entry for that type. See, respectively, **Asylum support appeals, Criminal injuries compensation appeals** and **Social security and child support cases**. What follows below is a general overview in which the similarities and differences between the three types of proceeding are noted.

Time for making an appeal

See **Time limits** and **Extensions of time.**

70.4 A wide variety of time limits applies in the SEC. For example:

- in asylum support cases, the appellant has three days from the date on which he received written notice of the decision being challenged (SEC Rules, r 22(2)(a));
- in criminal injuries compensation cases, the appellant has 90 days (SEC Rules, r 22(2)(b)); and
- in most social security and child support cases (SEC Rules, Sch 1), the appellant has one month from the date on which notice of the decision, or failure to revise the decision (as the case may be), or longer if a written statement of reasons is requested.

70.5 For asylum support and criminal injuries compensation cases, if the notice of appeal to the First-tier Tribunal is provided late, it must include a request for an extension of time and the reason why it was provided out of time (SEC Rules, r 22(6)(a)). In such a case the First-tier Tribunal must not admit the notice unless it extends time (SEC Rules, r 22(6)(b)). There is no long-stop date in the SEC Rules after which no appeal may be made for asylum support and criminal injuries compensation cases.

70.6 By contrast, for social security and child support cases (except references under the Child Support Act 1991 and proceedings under the Tax Credits Act 2002, Sch 2, para 3), in which the notice of appeal is sent to the decision maker, if the appellant provides the notice late then, while he must include the reason (SEC Rules, r 23(3)), the appeal will be treated as having been made in time if the decision maker does not object (SEC Rules, r 23(4)). However, no appeal may be made more than 12 months after the relevant time limit in Sch 1 (SEC Rules, r 23(5)).The Tribunal has no power to extend that 12 month time limit (SEC Rules, r 23(8)).

70.7 Schedule 1 sets out other time limits for specific types of case in a table:

Cases other than those listed below	The latest of— (a) one month after the date on which notice of the decision being challenged was sent to the appellant; (b) if a written statement of reasons for the decision is requested, 14 days after the later of (i) the date on which the period at (a) expires; and (ii) the date on which the written statement of reasons was provided; or (c) where the appellant made an application for revision of the decision under— (i) regulation 17(1)(a) of the Child Support (Maintenance Assessment Procedure) Regulations 1992; (ii) regulation 3(1) or (3) or 3A(1) of the Social Security and Child Support (Decision & Appeals) Regulations 1999; or (iii) regulation 4 of the Housing Benefit and Council Tax Benefit (Decisions and Appeals) Regulations 2001 and that application was unsuccessful, one month of the date on which notice that the decision would not be revised was sent to the appellant.

Appeal against a certificate of NHS charges under section 157(1) of the Health and Social Care (Community Health and Standards) Act 2003	(a) 3 months after the latest of— (i) the date on the certificate; (ii) the date on which the compensation payment was made; (iii) if the certificate has been reviewed, the date the certificate was confirmed or a fresh certificate was issued; or (iv) the date of any agreement to treat an earlier compensation payment as having been made in final discharge of a claim made by or in respect of an injured person and arising out of the injury or death; or (b) if the person to whom the certificate has been issued makes an application under section 157(4) of the Health and Social Care (Community Health and Standards) Act 2003, one month after— (i) the date of the decision on that application; or (ii) if the person appeals against that decision under section 157(6) of that Act, the date on which the appeal is decided or withdrawn.
Appeal against a waiver decision under section 157(6) of the Health and Social Care (Community Health and Standards) Act 2003	One month after the date of the decision.
Appeal against a certificate of NHS charges under section 7 of the Road Traffic (NHS Charges) Act 1999	3 months after the latest of— (a) the date on which the liability under section 1(2) of the Road Traffic (NHS Charges) Act 1999 was discharged; (b) if the certificate has been reviewed, the date the certificate was confirmed or a fresh certificate was issued; or (c) the date of any agreement to treat an earlier compensation payment as having been made in final discharge of a claim made by or in respect of a traffic casualty and arising out of the injury or death.

Appeal against a certificate of recoverable benefits under section 11 of the Social Security (Recovery of Benefits) Act 1997	One month after the latest of— (a) the date on which any payment to the Secretary of State required under section 6 of the Social Security (Recovery of Benefits) Act 1997 was made; (b) if the certificate has been reviewed, the date the certificate was confirmed or a fresh certificate was issued; or (c) the date of any agreement to treat an earlier compensation payment as having been made in final discharge of a claim made by or in respect of an injured person and arising out of the accident, injury or disease.
Appeal under the Vaccine Damage Payments Act 1979	No time limit.
Appeal under the Tax Credits Act 2002 or under the Child Trust Funds Act 2004	As set out in the Tax Credits Act 2002 or the Child Trust Funds Act 2004.

Notice

70.8 The usual requirements apply to a notice of appeal in SEC cases: it must be in writing, in English or Welsh, signed by the appellant and containing the standard set of information (SEC Rules, rr 22(3) and 23(6)). These are:

- the name and address of the appellant;
- the name and address of the appellant's representative (if any);
- an address where documents for the appellant may be sent or delivered;
- details of the decision being appealed; and
- the grounds on which the appellant relies.

70.9 In asylum support and criminal injuries compensation cases, the notice must also state the name and address of any respondent (SEC Rules, r 22(3)(d)). In such cases, the appellant must provide with the notice of appeal (SEC Rules, r 22(4)):

- a copy of any written record of the decision being challenged;
- any statement of reasons for that decision that the appellant has or can reasonably obtain;
- any documents in support of the appellant's case which have not been supplied to the respondent; and
- any further information or documents required by an applicable practice direction.

70.10 For asylum support cases only, the notice must also state whether the appellant will require an interpreter at any hearing and whether he intends to attend or be represented at any hearing (SEC Rules, r 22(5)).

70.11 For proceedings under the Child Support Act 1991, s 28D and the Tax Credits Act 2002, Sch 2, para 3, the person starting proceedings must send or deliver a written reference or information to the First-tier Tribunal (SEC Rules, r 26(2), (3)). That information or reference must include (SEC Rules, r 26(4)):

- an address where documents for the person starting proceedings may be sent or delivered;
- the names and addresses of the respondents and their representatives (if any); and
- a submission on the issues that arise for determination by the First-tier Tribunal.

70.12 Subject to confidentiality, the appellant must send the reference or information and any accompanying documents to the respondent (SEC Rules, r 26(6)).

Response by the decision-maker

70.13 For social security and child support cases (except references under the Child Support Act 1991 and proceedings under the Tax Credits Act 2002, Sch 2, para 3), the decision maker must refer the case to the First-tier Tribunal immediately if the appeal has been made out of time and the decision-maker objects to treating it as having been made in time or if he considers that the appeal is more than 12 months out of time (SEC Rules, r 23(7)).

70.14 Otherwise, the decision maker must send or deliver a response to the Tribunal (SEC Rules, r 24(1):

- in asylum support cases, so that it is received within three days after the date on which the Tribunal received the notice of appeal; and
- in other cases, as soon as reasonably practicable after the decision maker received the notice of appeal.

70.15 The response must include (SEC Rules, r 24(2), (4)):

- the name and address of the decision maker;
- the name and address of the decision maker's representative (if any);
- an address where documents for the decision maker may be sent or delivered;
- the names and addresses of any other respondents and their representatives (if any);
- whether the decision maker opposes the appellant's case and, if so, any grounds for such opposition which are not set out in any documents which are before the Tribunal; and
- any further information or documents required by a practice direction or direction;

- a copy of any written record of the decision under challenge, and any statement of reasons for that decision, if they were not sent with the notice of appeal;
- copies of all documents relevant to the case in the decision maker's possession, unless a practice direction or direction states otherwise; and
- in cases to which SEC Rules, r 23 (cases in which the notice of appeal is to be sent to the decision maker) applies, a copy of the notice of appeal, any documents provided by the appellant with the notice of appeal and (if they have not otherwise been provided to the Tribunal) the name and address of the appellant's representative (if any).

The response may include a submission as to whether it would be appropriate for the case to be disposed of without a hearing (SEC Rules, r 24(3)).

70.16 Under the Child Support Act 1991, s 281 and proceedings under the Tax Credits Act 2002, Sch 2, para 3, respondents have one month from the date of the appeal having been sent to send or deliver to the Tribunal a written submission and any further relevant documents (SEC Rules, r 26(7)).

Reply

70.17 The appellant is entitled to reply to the response, but must do so within one month; the Tribunal must send the reply to the other parties (SEC Rules, r 24(6), (7)).

HEARINGS IN THE SEC

See **Hearings**.

70.18 The First-tier Tribunal must hold a hearing before making a substantive decision which disposes of proceedings unless all parties consent to, or do not object to, the matter being decided without a hearing and the Tribunal considers that it is able to decide the matter without a hearing (SEC Rules, r 27(1)).

70.19 The Tribunal may dispose of criminal injuries compensation cases without a hearing (SEC Rules, r 27(4)(a)) but if it does so, any party may make a written application to the Tribunal for the decision to be reconsidered at a hearing (SEC Rules, r 27(4)(b)).

70.20 For appeals under the Social Security Act 1998, s 12, if there is a hearing then SEC Rules, r 25 empowers an appropriate member of the Tribunal to carry out a physical examination of the appellant in certain circumstances (SEC Rules, r 25(2)) or to refer him to a healthcare professional approved by the Secretary of State for such examination where the issue is one listed in Sch 2 to the Rules (SEC Rules, r 25(3)) save that the Tribunal may not require a peson to undergo a physical test for the purpose of determining whether he or she is unable, or virtually unable, to walk (SEC Rules, r 25(4)).

70.21 The Tribunal must give the parties reasonable notice of the hearing date, which must be at least 14 days unless the parties consent to less, there are urgent or exceptional circumstance, or in an asylum support case the period must not be less than one day and not more than five days (SEC Rules, r 29).

APPEALS FROM THE SEC

70.22 Appeals from the SEC lie to the Administrative Appeals Chamber of the Upper Tribunal (see **Administrative Appeals Chamber** and **Upper Tribunal**). There are no appeals in respect of asylum support or criminal injuries compensation cases (SEC Rules, r 38(1)); in these cases, the only further application is by way of judicial review in the AAC. The rest of this section therefore applies only to social security and child support cases.

Time for making an appeal

70.23 An application for permission to appeal must be made in writing to the First-tier Tribunal (SEC Rules, r 38(2)) within one month of the latest of the dates that the Tribunal sends (as applicable):

- written reasons for its decisions;
- notification of amended reasons for, or correction of, the decision following a review; or
- notification that an application to set aside the decision was unsuccessful (SEC Rules, r 38(3)).

70.24 If the party seeking to appeal sends or delivers the application out of time or by any extension of time, the application must include a request for an extension of time and the reason why the application notice was not provided in time and the Tribunal must not admit the application unless it extends time (SEC Rules, r 38(5)).

Application for permission

70.25 An application for permission to appeal must (SEC Rules, r 38(6)):

- identify the decision of the First-tier Tribunal to which it relates;
- identify the alleged error or errors of law in the decision; and
- state the result the party making the application is seeking.

Consideration by the First-tier Tribunal

70.26 On receiving an application for permission to appeal, the Tribunal must first consider whether to review its own decision (SEC Rules, r 39(1)). If the Tribunal decides not to review the decision, or reviews the decision and decides to take no action in relation to it, the Tribunal must then consider whether to give permission to appeal (SEC Rules, r 39(2)).

70.27 The Tribunal must send a record of its decision to the parties as soon as practicable (SEC Rules, r 39(3)). If permission is refused, the Tribunal must send with the record of its decision: (i) a statement of its reasons and (ii) notification of the right to apply to the Upper Tribunal and the procedure and time limits for making such an application (SEC Rules, r 39(4)). This also applies in respect of any grounds on which permission was refused, if permission was granted on limited grounds only (SEC Rules, r 39(5)).

70.28 In relation to renewing the application for permission before the Upper Tribunal, see **Appeals and references to the Upper Tribunal**.

71 Social Security and Child Support Cases

SOCIAL ENTITLEMENT CHAMBER

71.1 Appeals in social security and child support cases are allocated to the SEC (see **Social Entitlement Chamber**).

71.2 Proceedings before the SEC are governed by the SEC Rules as amended. The SEC Rules are reproduced at Appendix 5. See also **Social Entitlement Chamber procedural rules**.

DECISIONS COVERED

71.3 The phrase 'social security and child support cases' encompasses appeals against a wide range of decisions made by different administrative bodies. These include:

- decisions of the Secretary of State for Work and Pensions concerning entitlement to and amount of benefits, including income support, jobseekers allowance, incapacity benefit, employment and support allowance, disability living allowance, attendance allowance and retirement pension;
- decisions of the Child Maintenance and Enforcement Commission (formerly called the Child Support Agency) concerning child support maintenance;
- decisions by Her Majesty's Revenue and Customs ('HMRC') concerning tax credits; and
- decisions by local authorities concerning housing benefit and council tax benefit.

71.4 The SEC has, by the First-tier Tribunal and Upper Tribunal (Chambers) Order 2008, SI 2008/2684, art 3 been assigned all functions relating to appeals against all of the above types of decision. More specifically, art 3(c) lists the following categories of case and certain exceptions which do and do not fall within the jurisdiction of the SEC:

> '(c) regarding entitlement to, payments of, or recovery or recoupment of payments of, social security benefits, child support, vaccine damage payment, health in pregnancy grant,and tax credits, with the exception of--
>
> (ai) appeals under section 11 of the Social Security Contributions (Transfer of Functions, etc) Act 1999 (appeals against decisions of Her Majesty's Revenue and Customs);
>
> (i) appeals in respect of employer penalties or employer information penalties (as defined in section 63(11) and (12) of the Tax Credits Act 2002);
>
> (ii) appeals under regulation 28(3) of the Child Trust Funds Regulations 2004;

71.5 In respect of many of the decisions listed above, there is a right to apply for the original decision to be revised before having to appeal to the SEC. Parties should consult the relevant underlying legislation.

71.6 The procedure in respect of relevant decisions by the Secretary of State and the Child Maintenance and Enforcement Commission is to be found in the Social Security and Child Support (Decisions and Appeals) Regulations 1999, SI 1999/991 and the Child Support (Maintenance Assessment Procedure) Regulations 1992, SI 1992/1813. These regulations cover, for example, decisions made under the Social Security Act 1998, ss 8 and 10 and under the Child Support Act 1991, ss 11 and 12.

71.7 The procedure in respect of relevant decisions by local authorities is to be found in the Housing Benefit and Council Tax Benefit (Decisions and Appeals) Regulations 2001, SI 2001/1002. These regulations cover decisions by authorities administering housing benefit or council tax benefit in relation to claims for housing benefit or council tax benefit.

71.8 In general, applications for revisions of decisions should be made within one month of the date of notification of the original decision (see the Social Security and Child Support (Decisions and Appeals) Regulations 1999, SI 1999/991, reg 3(1)(a) and the Housing Benefit and Council Tax Benefit (Decisions and Appeals) Regulations 2001, SI 2001/1002, reg 4(1)(a)(i)).

APPEALING TO THE SEC

See **Bringing proceedings in the First-tier Tribunals, Social Entitlement Chamber procedural rules** and **Social Entitlement Chamber**.

71.9 An applicant who is dissatisfied with either his original decision or the outcome of a review of that decision can appeal to the SEC. Unlike in criminal injuries compensation cases, a right of appeal lies even if there has been no prior application for review. Social security and child support cases are the main type of proceedings in the SEC. The procedural rules governing social security and child support cases are set out in detail in **Social Entitlement Chamber procedural rules**.

Venues

71.10 The large volume of work undertaken by the social security and child support branch of the SEC requires a substantial network of venues to be available for use by the Tribunal across the country. Currently, 129 venues are used by the Tribunal, falling into seven areas: Birmingham, Cardiff, Glasgow, Leeds, Liverpool, Newcastle and Sutton (which includes London). Details of the nearest venue are available through the Tribunal's website (http://www.appeals-service.gov.uk/Venues/venues.htm).

72 Special Educational Needs and Disability Cases

LEGISLATIVE BACKGROUND

72.1 Under its most recent form, the Special Educational Needs and Disability Tribunal ('SENDIST') heard appeals under the Education Act 1996 and the Disability Discrimination Act 1995. SENDIST's procedure was regulated by the Special Educational Needs Tribunal Regulations 2001, SI 2001/600 and the Special Educational Needs and Disability Tribunal (General Provisions and Disability Claims Procedure) Regulations 2002, SI 2002/1985.

72.2 Under the primary legislation, a local educational authority ('LEA') has various duties to children with special educational needs. An alleged failure to comply with those duties gives rise to a right to appeal, formerly to the SENDIST. In particular, under the 1996 Act, s 324 the LEA is under a duty to create a statement of special educational needs for children assessed to have such needs. The statement must give details of the assessment of the child's needs; specify the special educational provision to be made for the purpose of meeting those needs; specify the type of school or other institution which the LEA consider would be appropriate for the child, and in some cases, the name of the school; and specify any provision for the child outside of school which they consider should be specified in the statement.

72.3 The jurisdiction of the SENDIST in special education needs cases encompassed:

- LEA determinations not to comply with requests for assessments of the educational needs of a child in respect of whom a statement of special educational needs is maintained (Education Act 1996, s 328(3)(b));
- LEA determinations not to comply with parental requests for assessments of the educational needs of a child in respect of whom no statement is maintained (Education Act 1996, s 329(2)(b);
- LEA determinations not to comply with requests for assessments of the educational needs of children made by the responsible body of a maintained school, a maintained nursery school, a pupil referral unit, an independent school, or an approved school (Education Act 1996, s 329A(8)(b));
- LEA determinations not to comply with requests to change the name of a school or institution specified in a statement of special educational needs (Education Act 1996, Sch 27, para 8(3)(b));
- LEA decisions not to make statements of special educational needs (Education Act 1996, s 325(2));
- The content of statements of special educational needs, including Part 2 (needs), Part 3 (provision) and Part 4 (placement) (Education Act 1996, s 326(1), (1A); and
- LEA determinations to cease to maintain a statement of special educational needs (Education Act 1996, Sch 27, para 11(2)(b)).

72.4 Claims used to be made to SENDIST under the 1995 Act for disability discrimination in schools. It was unlawful for a school to discriminate against a disabled pupil, or a disabled person who might be admitted to the school as a pupil, in the arrangements it made for determining admission as a pupil; in the terms on which it offered admission as a pupil; by refusing or deliberately omitting to accept an application for admission as a pupil; in the education or associated services provided for, or offered to, at the school; or by excluding a disabled pupil from school (Disability Discrimination Act, s 28A). It was also unlawful for an LEA, in the discharge of its functions, to discriminate against a disabled pupil, or a disabled person who might be admitted to the school as a pupil (Disability Discrimination Act, s 28F).

72.5 The Disability Discrimination Act 1995, s 28I, provided for a claim for discrimination to be made by the parent of a disabled child to the appropriate tribunal. However, the 1995 Act provided for alternative routes of appeal in respect of admissions and exclusions decisions (ss 28K and 28L), so the bulk of SENDIST's work in disability cases comprised temporary exclusions and other educational provision.

72.6 As of 1 October 2010, the relevant provisions of the Disability Discrimination Act 1995 have been replaced by the Equality Act 2010. Section 85 of the 2010 Act (which is found in Chapter 1 of Part 6 of the Act) prohibits, among other things, discrimination by a school against a person in its admissions, its provision of education and other benefits, facilities or services and its exclusions. Schedule 17 provides for the enforcement of these prohibitions in respect of disabled pupils. Equality Act 2010, Sch 17, para 3 provides that a claim that responsible body has contravened Chapter 1, Part 6 of the Act because of a person's disability may be made to the First-tier Tribunal (or its Welsh or Scottish counterpart). Sch 17, para 5 empowers the First-tier Tribunal to make such order as it thinks fit in the event that it finds the contravention has occurred. This power does not extend to ordering the payment of compensation but 'may, in particular, be exercised with a view to obviating or reducing the adverse effect on the person of any matter to which the claim relates'. The First-tier Tribunal is therefore empowered to make a wide range of orders – including, for example, staff training, guidance, letters of apology or the provision of activities or tuition to make up for time or experiences missed.

TRANSFER OF JURISDICTION

72.7 As of 3 November 2008 the SENDIST's functions have been subsumed by the Health, Education and Social Care Chamber of the First-tier Tribunal: the Transfer of Tribunal Functions Order 2008, SI 2008/2833, Sch 1. Judges and other members of the SENDIST have been transferred in as judges and other members of the HESCC.

72.8 The Special Educational Needs Tribunal for Wales established under the Education Act 1996, s 336ZA has not been incorporated into the HESCC, but appeals from it go to the Administrative Appeals Chamber of the Upper Tribunal directly: the 2008 Order, art 6(2)(b). Appeals from the HESCC also go the Administrative Appeals Chamber, and not to the High Court as was the case for the SENDIST.

72.9 Procedure in special educational needs and disability cases is now governed by the Tribunal Procedure (First–tier Tribunal) (Health, Education and Social

Care Chamber) Rules 2008, SI 2008/2699 as amended ('HESCC Rules'). The HESCC Rules are reproduced at Appendix 2. See **Health, Education and Social Care Chamber procedural rules** for details of the provisions.

72.10 The procedural rules of the SENDIST were not drastically different from the HESCC Rules, but users are recommended to consult the various relevant sections of this Handbook to ensure that time limits and other procedural requirements are met. However, users should note that there are no longer parallel case submissions, and the HESCC procedure is now that the applicant first puts in his/her case and the response then follows. The duty to co-operate with the Tribunal is new, and a joint expert will not be ordered against the wishes of the parties and will only be appointed if both parties agree, are agreed on who that person should be and have agreed how that person will be funded. The process of review prior to consideration of permission to appeal also did not happen in the SENDIST.

72.11 The First-tier Tribunal (Special Educational Needs and Disability) is based in Darlington but can and does sit at any venue in England as necessary.

SPECIAL PROCEDURAL PROVISIONS

72.12 Certain special provisions are contained in the HESCC Rules in respect of special educational needs and disability cases, particularly to take account of school closures and the vulnerable nature of the child. In HESCC Rules, r 12(3) if the time for starting proceedings by providing the application notice to the Tribunal ends on a day from 25th December to 1st January inclusive, or on any day in August, the application notice is provided in time if it is provided on the first working day after 1st January or 31st August, as appropriate. The days from 25th December to 1st January inclusive and any day in August must not be counted when calculating the time by which any other act must be done, unless the Tribunal directs otherwise (HESCC Rules, r 12(4)).

72.13 Under HESCC Rules, r 15(4) the Tribunal may require that the child be made available for assessment by a suitably qualified person, either in the school or at home. The Tribunal may consider a failure by a party to comply with a requirement made, in the absence of any good reason for such failure, as a failure to co-operate with the Tribunal, which could lead to a result which is adverse to that party's case (HESCC Rules, r 15(5)).

72.14 The respondent LEA is reminded in HESCC Rules, r 21(2)(e) to ensure that the response includes the views of the child about the issues raised by the proceedings, or the reason why the respondent has not ascertained those views. For clarification, HESCC Rules, r 24(b) entitles the child in a special educational needs or disability case to attend the hearing, to give evidence and to address the Tribunal. However, hearings will be held in private unless the Tribunal considers that it is in the interests of justice for the hearing to be held in public (HESCC Rules, r 26(2)) and the Tribunal may exclude the child from any hearing if it considers that it would be adverse to their interests to be present (HESCC Rules, r 26(5)(e)).

72.15 Rule 48 makes special provision for the Tribunal to review its own decision in special educational needs and disability cases, entitling a party to apply for a review on the basis that circumstances have changed since the decision, but before 28 days from the date the decision was sent (the time limit for such a review) (HESCC Rules, r 48(2), (3)). This provision is wider than the ordinary review principles, but is still restrictive in terms of time, and parties concerned will need to act swiftly. If the application for review is made out of time, it must acknowledge that fact, give reasons for it, and apply for an extension of time or the Tribunal will be obliged not to accept the application (HESCC Rules, r 48(4)). This does not prevent a party applying for permission to appeal under HESCC Rules, r 46 because the decision discloses an error of law, and the Tribunal conducting a review on that basis under HESCC Rules, rr 47 and 49.

72.16 The Schedule to the HESCC Rules sets out time limits for applying to the Tribunal in non-standard cases. These include an appeal under the Disability Discrimination Act 1995, s 28I (disability discrimination in the education of a child), the time limit for which is six months after the decision or act complained of, with a response time limit of 30 working days after the respondent received the application notice. The Schedule also includes an appeal under Part 4 of and Schedule 27 to the Education Act 1996 (provision of education to a child with special educational needs), the time limit for which is two months after the decision or act complained of, with a response time limit of 30 working days after the respondent received the application notice.

FURTHER PROVISION IN THE PRACTICE DIRECTION

72.17 The Senior President issued a Practice Direction, Special Educational Needs or Disability Discrimination in Schools Cases, 30 October 2008 (at [2009] PTSR 318) to supplement the HESCC Rules in certain respects. Some of the directions are most helpfully quoted in full.

Application notices

72.18 In a special educational needs case, the application notice should, as well as the information set out in HESCC Rules, r 20(2), (3), also include (paragraph 5):

- The name and date of birth of the child;
- If possible, the names and addresses of all persons or bodies who have or share parental responsibility for the child or have care of the child;
- The name of the LEA and the date upon which the applicant was notified of the decision in relation to which the application is made;
- A list of documents included in or provided with the application notice;
- If the applicant seeks an order that a child's statement shall be amended, details as to which part or parts of the statement the application relates as well as details of the changes sought;
- If the applicant seeks an order that a different school from that already named in the child's statement be named in it either; the name and address of that preferred school, or a sufficient description of the type and nature of the school which the applicant considers would constitute an appropriate placement for the child; and if available, in the case of an independent or non-maintained school, written confirmation that there is a place available for the child (provision of place) and, if the school is an independent school and not registered to take a pupil with the

special educational needs of the child, confirmation from the Secretary of State that he consents to the child attending that school (enabling consent);

- Where the application is made under s 326 of or paragraphs 8 or 11 of Schedule 27 to the Education Act 1996, a copy of the child's statement together with all appendices and supporting documentation provided by the LEA to the parent, if available; and
- Where the application notice states the name of a preferred school, written confirmation that the applicant has informed the school that they proposed to request that it be named in the child's statement in proceedings before the Tribunal.

72.19 In a disability discrimination case, the application notice should, as well as the information set out in HESCC Rules, r 20(2), (3), also include (paragraph 6):

- The name and date of birth of the child;
- The names and addresses of all persons or bodies who have or share parental responsibility for the child or have care of the child;
- Where it is alleged that a school has discriminated against a child, the name and address of the school;
- Where it is alleged that a local authority has discriminated against a child or where the school named is maintained by a local authority, the name of the local authority;
- A description of the child's disability, including evidence of a medical or other professional diagnosis, if available;
- Details of the alleged discrimination, including the date or dates on which it is alleged to have taken place; and
- If there is a statement of special educational needs in relation to the child, a copy of that statement and appendices, if available.

72.20 Where an application is struck out for want of jurisdiction the respondent is not sent the application unless it has requested to be sent such cases (paragraph 8).

The response

72.21 In addition to the information required in the response notice by HESCC Rules, r 21(2), in a special educational needs case the respondent must also include (paragraph 10):

- Where the application relates to the contents of the child's statement and the LEA states it does not resist the application or that it withdraws its opposition to the application, a final amended statement incorporating the amendments (if any) to the child's statement which it agrees to make;
- A copy of the child's statement, appendices and supporting documents where these were not submitted by the applicant with the notice of application;
- Any supplemental evidence and professional reports currently available to the LEA and upon which it intends to rely, and

- Detailed grounds setting out what parts of the application are admitted, detailed grounds setting out what parts of the application are resisted, and details of any legal points that will be relied on at a final hearing.

72.22 In a disability discrimination case the respondent must also include (paragraph 11) detailed grounds setting out what parts of the application are admitted, detailed grounds setting out what parts of the application are resisted, and details of any legal points that will be relied on at a final hearing.

Information for the hearing

72.23 The parties must provide the following information to the Tribunal prior to the hearing, within the time directed by the Tribunal (paragraph 15):

- Details of what the party believes to be the issues in the proceedings;
- Details of what evidence, in addition to that filed with the notice of application or response, the party intends to rely on at the final hearing;
- If they were not available by the time of sending the response to the Tribunal, the views of the child about the issues raised by the proceedings;
- Any field in which a party wishes to rely on expert evidence; and where practicable the expert in that field on whose evidence the party wishes to rely; and whether the party wishes the evidence to be provided in the form of an expert report only or whether the party also wishes the expert to attend the hearing as a witness;
- The name, address and occupation (or other description that shows their relevance to the proceedings) of any other witnesses the party wishes to attend the final hearing and the name, address and occupation (or other description that shows their relevance to proceedings) of any other person the party wishes to attend the final hearing (but not give evidence) where it is to be held in private;
- Confirmation of whether the party wishes to attend and/or be represented at the final hearing;
- If a party does wish to attend or be represented, confirmation of whether any proposed hearing date is convenient to the party and, if not, details of their availability;
- Whether the party or any witness will require the assistance of an interpreter or signer at the final hearing and, if so, details of the language, dialect or type of signing skill required; and
- Whether the party has any disabilities that may require adjustments to be made.

72.24 Any application for a witness summons must be made at least 14 days prior to the hearing unless there is good reason (paragraph 16). Where evidence is in audio or visual form, five copies must be supplied within the directed time (paragraph 17).

Hearing

72.25 Where the hearing takes place in private, the following persons are ordinarily permitted to attend (paragraph 18):

- The party's representative and witnesses;
- Any other person the party has informed the Tribunal they wish to attend the hearing unless the Tribunal determines that any such person should not attend the hearing and has notified that party accordingly;
- A parent of the child who is not a party to the application;
- The Chamber President and any judge or other member of the First-tier Tribunal (when not sitting as a member of the Tribunal);
- A person undergoing training as a judge or other member of the First-tier Tribunal or as a member of staff;
- A person acting under the supervision of the Chamber President in the training or supervision of a member of staff;
- An interpreter.

Extensions of time

72.26 Where the application notice is not provided within the specified time limit and an extension of time is requested, the Tribunal may have regard to any failure on the part of the LEA to comply with the requirements of the Education (Special Educational Needs) (England) (Consolidation) Regulations 2001, SI 2001/3455 to notify parents of their right of appeal and the time limit within which it must be pursued (paragraphs 13–14).

73 Striking Out

THE PROCEDURAL RULE

73.1 The provisions relating to the striking out of proceedings are to be found in r 8 of the procedural rules for the Upper Tribunal and the Chambers of the First-tier Tribunal. These rules are to be found in the Appendices. See also the entries on the various different Chambers.

73.2 The IAC Rules contain no power to strike-out an appeal.

73.3 The Lands Chamber Rules contain no specific power, but permit a party to make an interlocutory application under r 38 which could be used to apply for a strike-out. This entry will not consider the position of the Lands Chamber further (see **Lands Chamber**).

73.4 As explained below, there are three circumstances in which the question of strike-out arises, namely:

- circumstances in which strike-out takes place automatically;
- circumstances in which the Tribunal in question is obliged to strike proceedings out; and
- circumstances in which the Tribunal has discretionary power of strike-out.

73.5 In all three circumstances, r 8 provides for either the whole proceedings or part of them to be struck out, as appropriate. The rule also applies equally to respondents (or an interested party in the Upper Tribunal) except that instead of the case being struck out the respondent is simply barred from taking further part in the proceedings and the Tribunal need not consider any response or submission by the respondent (r 8(7) (8) of all procedural rules, except that it is HESCC Rules, r 8(8), (9)).

AUTOMATIC STRIKE-OUT

73.6 The proceedings, or the appropriate part of them, will automatically be struck out if: (i) the appellant/applicant (as appropriate) has failed to comply with a direction and (ii) that direction stated that a failure to comply with it would lead to the striking out of the proceedings (or that part of them) (r 8(1) of all procedural rules, except that it is Tribunal Procedure (First-tier Tribunal) (Health, Education and Social Care Chamber) Rules 2008 ('HESCC Rules'), r 8(2)).

73.7 If proceedings are struck out automatically, the appellant/applicant may apply for the proceedings or relevant part of them to be reinstated (r 8(5) of all procedural rules and HESCC Rules, r 8(6)), such application to be made in writing and received within a month of the notification of striking out having been sent (SEC Rules and Upper Tribunal Rules, r 8(6)). The relevant time period is 28 days in the GRC, the TC and the HESCC (except that it is HESCC Rules, r 8(7)) and 42 days in the WPAFCC.

There is no automatic strike out in mental health cases in the First-tier Tribunal or in asylum or immigration cases in the Upper Tribunal (HESCC Rules, r 8(1); Upper Tribunal Rules, r 8(119)).

MANDATORY STRIKE-OUT

73.8 The Tribunal in question must strike out proceedings, or the appropriate part of them, if it does not have jurisdiction in relation to the proceedings/part in question and it does not exercise its power to transfer the proceedings/part to another court or Tribunal (r 8(2) of all procedural rules, except that it is HESCC Rules, r 8(3)).

73.9 Although the appellant/applicant has no right to apply for reinstatement, the Tribunal should not make an order striking out the appellant/applicant's case should not be ordered without first giving the appellant/applicant an opportunity to make representations (r 8(4) of all procedural rules with this exception of the HESCC Rules where the relevant provision is HESCC Rules, r 8(5)).

73.10 Mental health and immigration or asylum cases can be struck out in cases in which the Tribunal has no jurisdiction or in cases of non-transfer (HESCC Rules, r 8(1); Upper Tribunal Rules, r 8(1A)).

DISCRETIONARY STRIKE-OUT

73.11 The Tribunal in question has a power to strike out proceedings, or part of them, if: (i) the appellant/applicant has failed to comply with a direction and (ii) that direction stated that a failure to comply with it could lead to the striking out of the proceedings (or that part of them) (r 8(3)(a) of all procedural rules, except that it is HESCC Rules, r 8(4)(a)).

73.12 If proceedings are struck out on this basis, the appellant/applicant may apply for the proceedings or relevant part of them to be reinstated (r 8(5) of all procedural rules, except that it is HESCC Rules, r8(5), (6)), such application to be made in writing and received within a month of the notification of striking out having been sent (r 8(3)(b) of all procedural rules, except that it is HESCC Rules, r 8(6)).

73.13 The Tribunal also has a power to strike out proceedings, or part of them if the appellant/applicant has failed to cooperate with the Tribunal to such an extent that the Tribunal cannot deal with the proceedings fairly and justly (r 8(3)(b) of all procedural rules, except that it is HESCC Rules, rr 8(3)(c)).

73.14 Finally the Tribunal may strike-out a case or part of a case where it considers there is no reasonable prospect of the appellant/applicant's case (or the relevant part of it) succeeding (r 8(3)(c) of all procedural rules, except that it is HESCC Rules, r 8(4)(c)). (The latter of these does not apply in the Upper Tribunal to proceedings which are an appeal from the decision of another Tribunal or judicial review proceedings, because if there were no reasonable prospect of success the case would not have got permission.)

73.15 Because of the greater guidance in the procedural rules as to the circumstances in which a strike-out is, or may be, applicable than is given under the Civil Procedure Rules it is unnecessary here to repeat the large amount of case law the CPR has produced on the issue. A discretionary strike-out should, of course, be a remedy of last resort for the Tribunal which is exercised sparingly. Some guidance may be drawn from the CPR case law on when a case has a reasonable prospect of success. The test was expounded by Lord Woolf MR in the leading authority *Swain v Hillman* [2001] 1 All ER 91. Lord

Woolf MR outlined what was meant by the CPR test of 'no real prospect of success' at [7]:

> 'the court now has a very salutary power, both to be exercised in a claimant's favour or, where appropriate, in a defendant's favour. It enables the court to dispose summarily of both claims or defences which have no real prospect of being successful. The words "no real prospect of being successful or succeeding" do not need any amplification, they speak for themselves. The word "real" distinguishes fanciful prospects of success or, as Mr Bidder submits, they direct the court to the need to see whether there is a "realistic" as opposed to a "fanciful" prospect of success'.

73.16 The proceedings/part may not be struck out on the basis of failure to cooperate with the Tribunal or no reasonable chance of success without first giving the appellant/applicant an opportunity to make representations (r 8(4) of all procedural rules, except that it is HESCC Rules, r 8(5)). If the proceedings are struck out, the appellant/applicant has no right to apply for reinstatement.

73.17 Some guidance on reinstatement was given by the Administrative Appeals Chamber of the Upper Tribunal in *Synergy Child Services Ltd v Ofstead* [2009] UKUT 125 (AAC) at [13]:

> 'When considering whether an appeal should be reinstated under rule 8(6), a Tribunal should have regard to the broad justice of the case, in the light of all the circumstances obtaining at the time the application for reinstatement is being considered.'

73.18 In *Synergy* itself the AAC held that a refusal to reinstate proceedings after being struck out was a 'decision' which could be appealed to the Upper Tribunal under the Tribunals, Courts and Enforcement Act 2007 ('TCEA 2007'), s 11 because it is a substantive decision which is not an 'excluded decision' under s 11(5): at [5].

73.19 The same approach was taken in *AW v Essex County Council (SEN)* [2010] UKUT 74 (AAC); [2010] ELR 349 which agreed that a decision which brought proceedings to an end was an appealable decision under TCEA 2007, s 11: at [8]–[10]. At [15] the judge opined that 'There is a distinction between: (i) a tribunal having no jurisdiction; and (ii) a case having no reasonable prospect of success. Rule 8(3) makes provision for (i); rule 8(4)(c) makes provision for (ii). In the case of (i), the test is whether the tribunal had authority to decide an issue. In the case of (ii), the test is what decision the tribunal is entitled to give on an issue. It may be that a tribunal has jurisdiction over an issue, but can only properly give one decision on the evidence. That case is covered by (ii), not (i).' (Incidentally, on the issue of substance as to whether special educational needs duties extend to a person aged 19, the decision in AW has been strongly criticised by the High Court in *R (B) v Islington Borough Council* [2010] All ER (D) 97 (Aug)).

74 Submissions

74.1 The procedural rules for the Chambers of the First-tier and Upper Tribunals do not contain any prescriptive requirements as to the content of submissions, the format (eg, whether skeleton arguments are required or expected) and the timing. This is consistent with the tribunal system's aims of procedural efficiency and accessibility to all users, and the emphasis in the overriding objective of dealing with cases in a manner that is expeditious, proportionate and avoids unnecessary formality. (See **Tribunal justice** and **Overriding objective**).

74.2 That having been said, the parties are not entirely free to make their submissions however and whenever they wish. As well as the general case management powers in r 5 of the procedural rules for most of the various Chambers (except the Lands Chamber and the IAC of the First-tier Tribunal), a tribunal also has, by r 15(1) (again, of the procedural rules save for the two Chambers referred to), the power to give directions as to: the issues on which it requires submissions; the nature of the submissions it requires; the manner in which any submissions are to be provided (which may include a direction for them to be given orally or in writing); and the time at which they are to be provided.

74.3 Thus the parties have considerable flexibility as to how they present their submissions, when and on what issues, but always subject to the case management powers of the Tribunal.

74.4 In relatively simple cases with an oral hearing, especially in the First-tier Tribunal, oral submissions are often sufficient. By contrast, in cases involving more complex issues (eg, cases in the TC that are designated as Complex), and judicial review and appeal hearings in the Upper Tribunal, written submissions may be helpful to amplify the basic grounds given in the appeal notice/application and response.

74.5 The procedural rules for the various Chambers generally provide that, where there is an oral hearing, each party is entitled to attend (subject to certain limited exclusions). In the Upper Tribunal Rules, r 33 further confers on each party a right to make representations, which includes the right to make representations at any hearing which he or she is entitled to attend and the right to make written representations in relation to a decision to be made without a hearing.

75 Tax and Chancery Chamber

JURISDICTION OF THE TAX AND CHANCERY CHAMBER

75.1 The Tax and Chancery Chamber ('TCC') of the Upper Tribunal is presided over by a Chamber President and is under the ultimate supervision of the Senior President (see **Senior President**). It has four main types of jurisdiction:

- It hears appeals against decisions of the TC;
- It hears appeals against decisions of the GRC in charities cases only (see **Charities cases**);
- It hears certain types of appeal against the decision-maker directly (such as finance cases: see **Financial services cases**); and
- It hears certain categories of judicial review application.

75.2 The first two categories, appeals, are straightforward and encompass proceedings which the First-tier Tribunal decides to refer to the Upper Tribunal because of its complexity, either of law or of fact. This is particularly likely to happen in tax cases which are categorised as Complex (see **Tax Chamber**).

75.3 The jurisdiction of the TCC is governed by the First-tier Tribunal and Upper Tribunal (Chambers) Order 2008, SI 2008/2684 (as amended), art 8.

DIRECT APPEALS IN THE TCC

75.4 The 2008 Order allocated, in art 8(1)(aa), appeals against decisions of the Financial Services Authority, the Bank of England and compensation and consideration assessors under the Banking (Special Provisions) Act 2008, and, in art 8(1)(ab), appeals against decisions of the Pensions Regulator, to the TCC. This transfer of functions took effect on 6 April 2010, when the Financial Markets and Services Tribunal and the Pensions Regulator Tribunal (except for Northern Ireland) were abolished: see the Transfer of Tribunal Functions Order 2010, SI 2010/22 (see **Financial services cases**). The TCC also hears cases directly against the imposition of a penalty by HMRC under the Finance Act 2008, Sch 36, para 39 for failure to comply with an information notice or obstruction of an HMRC investigation where HMRC contend that an additional penalty should be imposed: Finance Act 2008, Sch 36, para 50(1)(d).

JUDICIAL REVIEW IN THE TCC

75.5 Ordinarily, it will be the Administrative Appeals Chamber of the Upper Tribunal which exercises the judicial review functions of the Upper Tribunal, but in certain categories of case which particularly suit the expertise of the TCC it is the TCC which has jurisdiction. Those categories are (art 8(1)(e) of the 2008 Order):

- a decision of the Tax Chamber of the First-tier Tribunal or a charities case in the General Regulatory Chamber;

- a function of the Commissioners for Her Majesty's Revenue and Customs or an officer of Revenue and Customs, with the exception of any function in respect of which an appeal would be allocated to the Social Entitlement Chamber;
- the exercise by the Serious Organised Crime Agency of general Revenue functions or Revenue inheritance tax functions (as defined in the Proceeds of Crime Act 2002, s 323), with the exception of any function in relation to which an appeal would be allocated to the Social Entitlement Chamber;
- a function of the Charity Commission, the Financial Services Authority, the Bank of England, a person assessing compensation or consideration under the Banking (Special Provisions) Act 2008, or the Pensions Regulator.

75.6 For details on how judicial review proceeds in the Upper Tribunal see **Judicial review in the Upper Tribunal, Judicial review procedure in the Upper Tribunal** and **Judicial review grounds and principles.**

VENUE

75.7 The TCC is based in London but can hear cases in venues around the country if necessary.

PROCEDURE

75.8 The TCC is governed by the ordinary Upper Tribunal rules of procedure. These are the Tribunal Procedure (Upper Tribunal) Rules 2008, SI 2008/2684 (as amended) (see 'Upper Tribunal Rules'). Certain special rules have been included in respect of some TCC cases (see **Financial services cases**).

76 Tax Chamber

COMPOSITION AND LOCATION

76.1 The TC is one of six Chambers that collectively comprise the First-tier Tribunal (see **First-tier Tribunals and Chambers**). The TC was established on 1 April 2009. It replaces the four former separate Tax Tribunals, namely:

- the General Commissioners;
- the Special Commissioners;
- Value Added Tax ('VAT') and Duties Tribunals;
- Tribunals appointed under the Income and Corporation Taxes Act 1988, s 706; and
- Tribunals appointed under the Income Tax Act 2007, s 704.

76.2 More generally, the First-tier Tribunal and Upper Tribunal (Chambers) Order 2008, SI 2008/2684 (as amended) provides for the following jurisdiction of the TC (art 5A):

> 'To the Tax Chamber are assigned all functions, except those functions assigned to the Social Entitlement Chamber by article 3 or to the Tax and Chancery Chamber by article 8, relating to–
>
> (a) an appeal, application, reference or other proceeding in respect of a function of the Commissioners for Her Majesty's Revenue and Customs or an officer of Revenue and Customs;
>
> (b) an appeal in respect of the exercise by the Serious Organised Crime Agency of general Revenue functions or Revenue inheritance tax functions (as defined in section 323 of the Proceeds of Crime Act 2002).'

76.3 The TC is, like the Upper Tribunal and other Chambers of the First-tier Tribunal, presided over by the Senior President and has its own Chamber President. The TC comprises judges and other members, in accordance with the TCEA 2007, s 4.

76.4 Under the Transfer of Tribunal Functions and Revenue and Customs Appeals Order 2009, SI 2009/56, persons who, immediately before 1 April 2009, were office-holders in the following roles became transferred-in judges or other members of the First-tier Tribunal (as appropriate) (art 5):

- Deputy Commissioners for the special purposes of the Income Tax Acts appointed under s 4A of the Taxes Management Act 1970;
- persons appointed to a panel of chairmen of a VAT and duties tribunal under paragraph 7 of Schedule 12 to the Value Added Tax Act 1994;
- persons appointed to a panel of other members of a VAT and duties tribunal under paragraph 7 of Schedule 12 to the Value Added Tax Act 1994;
- non-chairman members of the tribunal appointed under s 706(1)(b) of the Income and Corporation Taxes Act 1988; and
- non-chairman members of the tribunal appointed under s 704(1)(b) of the Income Taxes Act 2007.

76.5 The TC has a network of hearing venues throughout the United Kingdom using tribunals service venues.

APPELLATE JURISDICTION AND POWERS

76.6 The TC has, by the Transfer of Tribunal Functions and Revenue and Customs Appeals Order 2009, SI 2009/56, art 3 and Schs 1 and 2, been transferred all of the functions of the four Tax Tribunals set out at the start of this entry. Thus it hears appeals from decisions relating to tax made by Her Majesty's Revenue and Customs ('HMRC'). These include, but are not limited to, appeals relating to:

- income tax
- corporation tax
- capital gains tax
- inheritance tax
- petroleum revenue tax
- student loans
- stamp duty land tax
- tax collected under Pay As You Earn ('PAYE') and PAYE coding notices
- tax collected under the Construction Industry Scheme
- national insurance contributions
- statutory payments
- VAT
- custom duties
- excise duties (including aggregates duties levy, air passenger duty, alcoholic liquor duties, bingo duty, climate change levy, gaming duty, general betting duty, hydrocarbon oils duties, insurance premium tax, landfill tax, lottery duty, money laundering decisions, pool betting duty, remote gaming duty and tobacco products duty).

76.7 The appeal may be against the amount of tax or duty to be paid, penalties imposed upon the appellant and certain other tax-related decisions by HMRC. The TC may hear appeals on both fact and law.

76.8 The TC does not hear appeals against HMRC decisions in relation to tax credits, child benefit or child trust funds. These are social security and child support cases, which fall within the jurisdiction of the Social Entitlement Chamber. See **Social security and child support cases** and **Social Entitlement Chamber**.

PROCEDURAL RULES

76.9 Proceedings before the TC are governed by the TC Rules as amended. The TC Rules are reproduced at Appendix 6. See **Tax Chamber procedural rules**.

77 Tax Chamber Procedural Rules

STATUTORY INSTRUMENT

77.1 Proceedings before the TC are governed by the TC Rules as amended. The TC Rules are reproduced at Appendix 6. For the jurisdiction of the TC see **Tax Chamber**.

STRUCTURE

77.2 The TC Rules are similar in structure to the standard rules of the other Chambers of the First-tier Tribunals, comprising the usual four parts ('Introduction', 'General powers and provisions', 'Procedure before the Tribunal' (which contains more sub-divisions than are usually found) and 'Correcting, setting aside, reviewing and appealing Tribunal decisions').

APPEALING TO THE TC

See **Bringing proceedings in the First-tier Tribunals.**

Time for making an appeal

77.3 Certain appeals to the TC are required by enactment to be started with a notice of appeal (TC Rules, r 20). Others require the appellant to make an originating application or reference to the First-tier Tribunal (TC Rules, r 21). Whichever the enactment provides for, the TC has a standardised 'Notice of Appeal form' to be used in all cases.

77.4 An appellant must send or deliver a notice of appeal, application notice or notice of reference (as appropriate) to the Tribunal within the time limit imposed by the appropriate enactment (TC Rules, rr 20(1) and 21(1)). (The generic description 'notice' is hereafter used in this section.) The normal time limit is 30 days. If the appellant makes use of HMRC's review process, the 30 days begin from the date HMRC sends the appellant the outcome.

77.5 If the appellant provides the notice to the decision maker outside of the prescribed time limit, the notice must include a request for an extension of time and the reason why the notice was not provided in time (TC Rules, rr 20(4)(a) and 21(3)(a)). The Tribunal must not admit the notice unless it extends time (TC Rules, rr 20(4)(b) and 21(3)(b)).

Notice

77.6 A notice in TC cases must include (TC Rules, rr 20(2) and 21(2)):

- the name and address of the appellant;
- the name and address of the appellant's representative (if any);
- an address where documents for the appellant may be sent or delivered;
- the result the appellant is seeking; and
- the grounds for making the appeal.

77.7 For proceedings for which the relevant enactment requires a notice of appeal, the appellant must also provide details of the decision appealed against (TC Rules, r 20(2)(d)) a copy of any written record of any decision appealed against, and any statement of reasons for that decision, that he has or can reasonably obtain (TC Rules, r 20(3)).

77.8 For proceedings for which the relevant enactment requires an application notice or notice of reference, the notice must also include the name and address of each respondent (if any) and the facts relevant to the application or reference (TC Rules, r 21(2)(d), (e)).

77.9 When the Tribunal receives the notice, it must send a copy of the notice to any respondent (TC Rules, rr 20(5) and 21(4)).

Hardship applications

77.10 Where an enactment provides, in any terms, that an appeal may not proceed if the liability to pay the amount in dispute is outstanding without the consent of HMRC or the Tribunal, the appellant must include in or with the notice (TC Rules, r 22(2)):

(a) a statement as to whether the appellant has paid the amount in dispute;

(b) if the appellant has not paid the amount in dispute, a statement as to the status or outcome of any application to HMRC for consent to the appeal proceeding; and

(c) if HMRC have refused such an application, an application to the tribunal for consent to the appeal proceeding.

77.11 An application to the Tribunal must include the reasons for the application and a list of any documents the appellant intends to produce or rely upon in support of it (TC Rules, r 22(3)). If consent is needed, the Tribunal must stay the proceedings until any applications to HMRC or the Tribunal have been determined (TC Rules, r 22(4)).

CATEGORISATION OF CASES AND HEARINGS IN THE TC

See **Hearings**.

77.12 Cases in the TC must be allocated to one of four categories once the notice has been received (TC Rules, r 23):

(a) Default Paper cases, which will usually be disposed of without a hearing;

(b) Basic cases, which will usually be disposed of after a hearing, with minimal exchange of documents before the hearing;

(c) Standard cases, which will usually be subject to more detailed case management and be disposed of after a hearing; and

(d) Complex cases, which are subject to different costs rules and which may, with the parties' consent, be referred to the Chamber President with a request for a transfer to the Finance and Tax Chamber of the Upper Tribunal (TC Rules, rr 10(1)(c), 23(5) and 28). A Complex case is one which requires a lengthy or complex hearing, involves important or complex issues or points of principle, or involves a large sum of money (TC Rules, r 23(4)).

77.13 Statements of case are not required in Basic cases (TC Rules, r 24(2)) and are generally dealt with at informal hearings, with the decision being provided at the end of the hearing. If the respondent has grounds of response which the appellant is not already aware of those should be provided to the appellant as soon as is reasonably practicable (TC Rules, r 24(4)).

77.14 For Default Paper cases, the Tribunal must determine the case without a hearing once it has received the respondent's statement of case (which is to be filed within 42 days of the Tribunal sending the notice of appeal: TC Rules, r 25(1)(a)) and the appellant's reply (or once the time for the appellant's reply has elapsed, the time being 30 days: TC Rules, r 26(2)) (TC Rules, r 26(6)) but a hearing will be held if either party requests one in writing (TC Rules, r 26(7)).

77.15 In a Standard or Complex case the respondent must send the Tribunal its statement of case within 60 days from the date the notice of appeal was sent to it (TC Rules, r 25(1)(b)). Within 42 days of that date all parties must send to the Tribunal a list of documents that that party has or controls and upon which it intends to rely at the hearing. Those documents may then be inspected by any other party unless privileged (TC Rules, r 27(2), (3)).

77.16 Subject to TC Rules, r 26(6) (and striking out decisions under r 8), the Tribunal must hold a hearing to dispose of the proceedings unless all parties consent to the matter being decided without a hearing and the Tribunal considers that it is able to decide the matter without a hearing (TC Rules, r 29(1)). The Tribunal must give parties reasonable notice of any hearing, and if the hearing will involve the disposal of the appeal that time must be at least 14 days unless the parties consent otherwise or there are urgent or exceptional circumstances (TC Rules, r 31). Hearings will be held in public unless the Tribunal directs otherwise under TC Rules, r 32. A hearing can proceed in the absence of a party if the Tribunal is satisfied that the party was informed or reasonable attempts to inform were made, and it is in the interests of justice (TC Rules, r 33).

77.17 Unlike in other Chambers of the First-tier Tribunal (eg, the Social Entitlement Chamber), if the TC makes a decision which disposes of proceedings without a hearing, the rules do not provide for an entitlement for the First-tier Tribunal to reconsider the decision at a hearing.

Categorisation of types of appeal

77.18 Under a Practice Direction issued by the Senior President, Categorisation of Cases in the Tax Chamber (27 July 2010), certain types of cases have been designated as Default Paper and Basic cases unless the Tribunal considers there is a reason why it would be appropriate not to designate that particular case.

77.19 Default Paper cases are to include:

(a) Appeals against the following types of fixed penalties:

i. penalties for late income tax and corporation tax self assessment returns (including penalties under sections 93(2) and 93(4) of the Taxes Management Act 1970 and paragraph 17(2) and (3) of Schedule 18 to the Finance Act 1998);

ii. penalties for late employer end of year returns under section 98A(2)(a) of the Taxes Management Act 1970;

iii. penalties for late construction industry returns under section 98A(2)(a) of the Taxes Management Act 1970; and

iv. penalties for late Class 2 national insurance contribution notifications under section 98A(2)(a) of the Taxes Management Act 1970 and paragraph 7 of Schedule 1 to the Social Security Contributions & Benefits Act 1992.

v. penalties for late submission of land transaction returns under s76 of the Finance Act 2003 or for late submission of further returns under section 81 of that Act.

vi. penalties for late submission of notice of charge to stamp duty reserve tax under regulations made under section 98 of Finance Act 1986.

vii. penalties for failure to make payment of stamp duty land tax under section 86 (1) or (2) of Finance Act 2003.

viii. penalties for failure to deliver a document or provide information, or to make a document available for inspection, for the purposes of stamp duty land tax under section 93(3) or (4) of Finance Act 2003

ix. penalties for late Pension Scheme Return under S257(1)-(2) Finance Act 2004

x. penalties for late Accounting for Tax Return under S260(1)-(2) Finance Act 2004

(b) Appeals against fixed percentage surcharges for late payment of income tax under section 59C of the Taxes Management Act 1970.

(c) Applications for penalties under section 93(3) of the Taxes Management Act 1970.

(d) Appeals against late filing penalties in respect of land transaction returns or further returns within paragraphs 3, 4 and 8 of Schedule 17A Finance Act 2003 (in accordance with Schedule 10).

(e) Appeals against late filing penalties in respect of land transaction returns or further returns under section 81A Finance Act 2003 (in accordance with Schedule 10).

(f) Appeals against late filing penalties in respect of returns or further returns under paragraph 24 Stamp Duty Land Tax (Administration) Regulations 2003 (SI No 2003/2837) (in accordance with Schedule 10 Finance Act 2003).

77.20 Basic cases are to include:

(a) Appeals:

(i) against penalties for late filing and late payment, including daily penalties;

(ii) against penalties for incorrect returns under paragraph 15 of Schedule 24 to the Finance Act 2007, except appeals against penalties for deliberate action (whether concealed or not) and cases where an appeal is also brought against the assessment of the tax to which the return relates;

(iii) seeking the mitigation or reduction of, or appeals on the basis of reasonable excuse against, penalties in relation to indirect taxes;

(iv) against decisions in relation to Construction Industry Scheme gross payment status under regulation 25(5) of the Income Tax (Construction Industry Scheme) Regulations 2005;

(v) against information notices; and

(vi) against Pay As You Earn (PAYE) coding under Regulation 18(3) of the Income Tax (PAYE) Regulations 2003 (SI No 2003/2682).

(b) Applications:

(i) for permission to make a late appeal;

(ii) for the postponement of the payment of tax pending an appeal (including applications under section 55(3)(b) and 55(4) of the Taxes Management Act 1970), paragraph 39(1)(b) and (4) of Schedule 10 to the Finance Act 2003 and Regulation 22(1)(b) and (3) of the Stamp Duty Land Tax (Administration) Regulations 2003); and

(iii) for a direction that HMRC close an enquiry (including applications under section 28A(4) and paragraph 7(5) of Schedule 1A to the Taxes Management Act 1970, paragraph 33 of Schedule 18 to the Finance Act 1998 and paragraph 24 of Schedule 10 and paragraph 12 of Schedule 11A to the Finance Act 2003).

APPEALS FROM THE TC

77.21 Appeals from the TC lie to the Tax and Chancery Chamber of the Upper Tribunal (see **Tax and Chancery Chamber** and **Upper Tribunal**).

Time for making an appeal

77.22 An application for permission to appeal must be made in writing to the First-tier Tribunal (TC Rules, r 39(1)) within 56 days of the latest of the dates that the Tribunal sends (as applicable): (i) written reasons for its decisions; (ii) notification of amended reasons for, or correction of, the decision following a review; or (iii) notification that an application to set aside the decision was unsuccessful (TC Rules, r 39(2)).

77.23 If the party seeking to appeal sends or delivers the application out of time or by any extension of time, the application must include a request for an extension of time and the reason why the application notice was not provided in time and the Tribunal must not admit the application unless it extends time (TC Rules, r 39(4)).

Application for permission

77.24 An application for permission to appeal must (TC Rules, r 39(5)):

- identify the decision of the First-tier Tribunal to which it relates;

- identify the alleged error or errors of law in the decision; and
- state the result the party making the application is seeking.

Consideration by the First-tier Tribunal

77.25 On receiving an application for permission to appeal, the First-tier Tribunal must first consider whether to review its own decision (TC Rules, r 40(1)). If the Tribunal decides not to review the decision, or reviews the decision and decides to take no action in relation to it, the Tribunal must then consider whether to give permission to appeal (TC Rules, r 40(2)).

77.26 The First-tier Tribunal must send a record of its decision to the parties as soon as practicable (TC Rules, r 40(3)). If permission is refused, the Tribunal must send with the record of its decision: (i) a statement of its reasons; and (ii) notification of the right to apply to the Upper Tribunal and the procedure and time limits for making such an application (TC Rules, r 40(4)). This also applies in respect of any grounds on which permission was refused, if permission was granted on limited grounds only (TC Rules, r 40(5)).

77.27 In relation to renewing the application for permission before the Upper Tribunal, see **Appeals from the First-tier Tribunal** and **Appeals and references to the Upper Tribunal**.

78 Time Limits

GENERAL

78.1 The relevant time limits for taking steps in the Chambers of the First-tier and Upper Tribunals are to be found in the procedural rules of those tribunals. The time limits differ from Chamber to Chamber, so it is important to check the specific rules for the relevant Chamber. Below are some general guidelines on the time limits for certain important steps in proceedings.

Time limits for bringing proceedings in the First-tier Tribunal

78.2 The time limits for bringing an appeal to the First-tier Tribunal vary widely depending on the decision appealed against. For example, in asylum support cases, which are heard in the Social Entitlement Chamber of the First-tier Tribunal, the appellant has three days from the date on which he received written notice of the decision being challenged (SEC Rules, r 22(2)(a)). By contrast, for an appeal against a criminal injuries compensation decision, which is also heard in the Social Entitlement Chamber, the appellant has 90 days from the date of the decision challenged (SEC Rules, r 22(2)(b)). In a fast track immigration or asylum case an appellant has just two days from the service of the notice of the immigration decision to file a notice of appeal with the Immigration and Asylum Chamber of the First-tier Tribunal (IAC (Fast Track) Rules, r 8(1).

Time limits for responding to proceedings brought in the First-tier Tribunal

78.3 In the majority of cases brought in the First-tier Tribunal, the decision-maker or public authority whose decision is under challenge is required to respond to the notice of appeal or application. Like the time limits for bringing proceedings, the time limits for responding vary widely. In asylum support cases, the response must be received within three days after the date on which the Tribunal received the notice of appeal (SEC Rules, r 24(1)(a)); in proceedings before the War Pensions and Armed Forces Compensation Chamber, the respondent is not even set a time limit, only having to act as speedily as is reasonably practicable Tribunal Procedure (First-tier Tribunal) (WPAFCC Rules, r 23(1). In a fast track immigration or asylum case a respondent has just two days from the service of the notice of appeal on it by the Tribunal to file a response (IAC (Fast Track) Rules, r 10).

Time limits for seeking permission to appeal to the Upper Tribunal

78.4 A person seeking to appeal from a decision of the First-tier Tribunal to the Upper Tribunal must make a written application for permission to the Tribunal. The time limit for doing so is 28 days for appeals from the General Regulatory Chamber or Health, Education and Social Care Chamber (Tribunal Procedure (First-tier Tribunal) (GRC Rules, r 42(2); HESCC Rules, r 46(2)); one month for appeals from the (SEC Rules, r 38(3)), 42 days for appeals from the (WPAFCC Rules, r 36(2)) and 56 days for appeals from the TC Rules, r 39(2)). It is two days for a fast track appeal in the IAC (IAC, r 17(1)), and for ordinary proceedings in the FTTIAC it is five days for an 'in country' appeal or 28 days where the appellant is outside of the UK (IAC Rules, r 24(2), (3)).

Time limits for applying for permission to the Upper Tribunal

78.5 An application for permission to appeal to the Upper Tribunal must be made by the appellant in writing and received by the Upper Tribunal no later than one month after the date on which the Tribunal that made the decision the appellant wishes to appeal sent notice of its refusal of permission to appeal or refusal to admit the application for permission to appeal to the appellant (Upper Tribunal Rules, r 21(3)(b)).

78.6 The time limit for an application for permission to appeal a decision under the Safeguarding Vulnerable Groups Act 2006, s 4 must be made received by the Upper Tribunal no later than three months after the date on which written notice of the decision being challenged was sent to the appellant (Upper Tribunal Rules, r 21(3)(a)).

78.7 Immigration and asylum cases have different time limits on appeals. Any appeal must be made no later than seven working days after the date on which written notice of the decision being challenged was sent to the appellant, or four working days if it is a fast track case where the appellant is in the UK (Upper Tribunal Rules, r 21(3)(aa)). The time limit is 56 days if the appellant is outside the UK (r 21(3)(ab)). Those time limits are shortened to five working days, two working days and 28 days respectively if notice is sent electronically or served personally (r 21(3A)).

78.8 In the Lands Chamber of the Upper Tribunal the appellant must send the Tribunal a written notice of appeal so that it is received within 28 days of the date the decision appealed against was sent (unless legislation provides a shorter date), or within 28 days of a lower tribunal having granted permission to appeal (Lands Tribunal Rules 1996 ('Lands Chamber Rules'), r 6(1)). Where there is a lower tribunal, permission must have been sought from that tribunal, and if it is refused the appellant has 14 days from the sending of the decision to refuse to apply to the Lands Chamber (Lands Chamber Rules, r 5C(1)).

78.9 The appellant must provide a notice of appeal to the Upper Tribunal within one month of receiving notice from the tribunal granting permission to appeal (whether this is the Upper Tribunal or the tribunal making the decision being appealed), or from the decision to which the appeal which does not require permission relates (Upper Tribunal Rules, r 23(2)).

CALCULATION OF TIME

78.10 Most of the procedural rules of the Chambers of the First-tier and Upper Tribunals contain in r 12 details as to the calculation of time periods. Rule 12 provides that if an act is to be done on or by a particular day, it must be done by 5pm on that day (r 12(1)) except in asylum support cases (in which acts may be done by any time on a given day) (SEC Rules, r 12(1)) and no equivalent provision appears in the IAC Rules. If the time for doing any act ends on a day other than a working day, the act is done in time if it is done on the next working day (r 12(2)). See also IAC Rules, r 57(2)).

78.11 The standard procedural rules provide in r 12(3) that 'working day' excludes weekends, Christmas Day, Good Friday and bank holidays. The HESCC Rules replicate the definition of 'working day' in the interpretation section and provide that for special educational needs and disability discrimination in schools cases no time limit shall expire if it falls in the period between 25 December and 1 January, or on any date in August (HESCC Rules, r 12(3)). The IAC Rules also defines 'business day' as not including 25–31 December (1 January being included as a bank holiday) in its the interpretation section, while the IAC (Fast Track) Rules additionally include in the definition of 'business day' Maundy Thursday and the Tuesday after the last Monday in May. The Upper Tribunal Rules replicate the same definitions in r 12(3), (3A), although in both the Upper Tribunal and the HESCC a direction can be made to do something on or by a date specified in r 12(3) (or (3A)).

78.12 The IAC Rules additionally provide that the calculation of time does not include the date on which the period begins, and that for a time limit which is less than 10 days, a business day is to be excluded from the calculation of time (IAC Rules, r 57(1)).

78.13 There does not appear to be any calculation of time provision in the Lands Chamber Rules. Parties are advised to follow the usual rule 12 (see eg the GRC Rules, r 12).

78.14 Users of the Tribunals are warned to be very careful when considering the time limits which apply to their type of case. The different rules often use different starting points for time beginning to run, the reason for which is often not easily explicable. It is important to be sure whether time runs from the date of receipt of a decision or notice, or from the date that the decision or notice was sent to the party, or from the date of the decision or notice itself. Generally, in communications with the Tribunal time stops when the communication is received, but not uniformly.

DISCRETION TO EXTEND TIME

78.15 All of the Chambers of the First-tier Tribunal and the Upper Tribunal have a general case management power, embodied in r 5(3)(a) of their respective procedural rules, to extend or shorten time limits for complying with any rule, practice direction or direction (save, in some cases, for where this would conflict with a statutory provision). An extension power is also found in Lands Chamber Rules, r 35 and IAC Rules, r 45(4).

78.16 The procedural rules generally require the party seeking to take a procedural step out of time to include a request for an extension of time and the reason why the relevant step was not taken in time. The rules also generally then go on to state that unless the tribunal in question extends time under its power in r 5(3)(a), it must not admit the notice, application or response in question (see, for example, TC Rules, r 39(4) concerning applications for permission to appeal).

78.17 It is therefore clear that the onus is on the party seeking to take a step out of time to explain his or her tardiness and justify the tribunal exercising its discretion.

78.18 See **Extensions of time** for further details in relation to the discretion to extend time limits.

79 Transfer of Judicial Review Applications

JUDICIAL REVIEW JURISDICTION

See **Judicial review in the Upper Tribunal** and **Upper Tribunal**.

79.1 The judicial review jurisdiction of the Upper Tribunal arises in respect of:

- applications which fall within categories specified by the Lord Chief Justice, which should be issued in the Upper Tribunal (below);
- applications for judicial review which are mandatorily transferred by the High Court (Administrative Court); and
- applications which are discretionarily transferred by the High Court (Administrative Court).

79.2 In addition to the Direction of the Lord Chief Justice, the First-tier Tribunal and Upper Tribunal (Chambers) Order 2008, SI 2008/2684 (as amended) specifies the following allocation of particular types of judicial review case which applies to an application which is started in the Upper Tribunal, or which is transferred to the Upper Tribunal from the High Court:

- In the Administrative Appeals Chamber (paragraph 7(b) of the 2008 Order):
  - to grant the relief mentioned in s 15(1) TCEA (Upper Tribunal's "judicial review" jurisdiction);
  - to exercise the powers of review under s 21(2) TCEA (Upper Tribunal's "judicial review" jurisdiction: Scotland);
  - except an application assigned to the Tax and Chancery Chamber.
- In the Tax and Chancery Chamber (paragraph 8(e) of the 2008 Order):
  - a decision of the Tax Chamber of the First-tier Tribunal or a charities case in the General Regulatory Chamber;
  - a function of the Commissioners for Her Majesty's Revenue and Customs or an officer of Revenue and Customs, with the exception of any function in respect of which an appeal would be allocated to the Social Entitlement Chamber;
  - the exercise by the Serious Organised Crime Agency of general Revenue functions or Revenue inheritance tax functions (as defined in section 323 of the Proceeds of Crime Act 2002), with the exception of any function in relation to which an appeal would be allocated to the Social Entitlement Chamber;
  - a function of the Charity Commission, the Financial Services Authority, the Bank of England, a person assessing compensation or consideration under the Banking (Special Provisions) Act 2008, or the Pensions Regulator.

79.3 The Administrative Appeals Chamber is therefore the primary home of the Upper Tribunal's judicial review jurisdiction, but with certain exceptions for cases in which the subject matter will be most obviously within the expertise of the Tax and Chancery Chamber judges.

79.4 The Lord Chief Justice has, since 3 November 2008, directed that the following types of application be commenced in the Upper Tribunal, or mandatorily transferred to the Upper Tribunal (see **Judicial review in the Upper Tribunal**):

- where there is a procedural decision of a First-tier Tribunal against which there is no right of appeal; and
- in Criminal Injuries Compensation Appeals decided by the Social Entitlement Chamber of the First–tier Tribunal.

THE CONDITIONS FOR THE TRANSFER OF CASES FROM THE HIGH COURT

79.5 By the TCEA 2007, s 19, a new s 31A was inserted into the Supreme Court Act 1981 (the name of which changed on 1 October 2009 to the Senior Courts Act 1981) setting out four conditions for the transfer of judicial review applications from the High Court to the Upper Tribunal, namely that:

- the application does not seek anything other than:
  - relief under s 31(1)(a) and (b) Senior Courts Act 1981 (which encompasses a mandatory order, a prohibiting order, a quashing order, a declaration, and an injunction);
  - permission to apply for relief under s 31(1)(a) and (b);
  - an award under s 31(4) (damages or restitution);
  - interest; and/or
  - costs.
- the application does not call into question anything done by the Crown Court.;
- the application falls within a category of case specified by a Practice Direction made by the Lord Chief Justice (or person nominated by the Lord Chief Justice) under Part 1 of Schedule 2 to the Constitutional Reform Act 2005;
- the application does not call into question any decision made under:
  - the Immigration Acts;
  - the British Nationality Act 1981;
  - any instrument having effect under the enactments in (a) and (b); or
  - any other provision of law for the time being in force which determines British citizenship, British overseas territories citizenship, the status of a British National (Overseas) or British Overseas citizenship.

(So far as Condition (3) is concerned, to date the only categories are the two set out above, namely (i) procedural decisions of the First-tier Tribunal against which there is no right of appeal and (ii) decisions of the First-tier Tribunal on criminal injuries compensation appeals.)

79.6 TCEA 2007, s 19 also inserts an analogous new power of transfer in the Judicature (Northern Ireland) Act 1978, s 25A.

79.7 If all four of the Conditions are met, the application must be transferred to the Upper Tribunal.

79.8 If Condition (1), Condition (2) and Condition (4) are met but not Condition (3) (ie, if the case is not in one of the two specified categories), Senior Courts Act 1981, s 31A(3) provides that High Court may by order transfer the application to the Upper Tribunal if it appears to the High Court to be just and convenient to do so. It is expected that the High Court will be willing to consider transferring cases which require detailed consideration of specific and specialised statutory schemes (such as tax or social security) because of the particular expertise of the Tribunal judges, and that the High Court will be less willing to transfer where the judicial review raises public law issues of general principle more commonly within the experience of an Administrative Court judge.

79.9 A recent example of transfer was *R (Reed Personnel Services plc) v HM Revenue & Customs* [2009] EWHC 2250 (Admin), a case in which there were issues of legitimate expectation arising out of HMRC conduct, the construction of tax legislation, and possible consequent issues of factual determination. It was held by Charles J that the appropriate course would be to transfer the judicial review application to the Upper Tribunal for case management purposes to ensure that existing First-tier Tribunal hearings and the judicial review were dealt with sensibly. He contemplated that the Tribunal may wish to transfer the case back to the Administrative Court, although neither the TCEA 2007 nor the Upper Tribunal Rules specifically deal with such a power. Incidentally, it would probably be permissible because the Tribunal would only have the power to decide a case not caught by the Lord Chief Justice's Direction because of the transfer (TCEA 2007, s 19(3), (4), below), so the Upper Tribunal cannot be mandated to determine an application transferred to it. In *Reed* itself Charles J was willing to transfer despite the case having to be heard in the Administrative Appeals Chamber because at the time that was the only Upper Tribunal Chamber with a judicial review jurisdiction. The case would now be transferred to the Tax and Chancery Chamber where the benefits of transfer are even clearer.

THE EFFECT OF TRANSFERRING CASES FROM THE HIGH COURT

79.10 Once an application has been transferred, the Upper Tribunal has the function of deciding it, whatever the category of application.

79.11 Under TCEA 2007, s 19(3), where an application is transferred to the Upper Tribunal under the mandatory or discretionary route above, it is to be treated for all purposes as if it had been the same application, for the same relief, made to the Upper Tribunal.

79.12 Any steps taken, permission given, leave given or orders made by the High Court in relation to the application are to be treated as taken, given or made by the Upper Tribunal.

79.13 Where the application in question is a permission application and the Upper Tribunal grants permission, the Upper Tribunal has the function of deciding any subsequent application brought under the permission, even if the subsequent application is not in a category specifically reserved to the Upper Tribunal by Direction of the Lord Chief Justice: TCEA 2007, s 19(4).

80 Transport Cases

TRANSPORT TRIBUNAL

80.1 Under the Transfer of Functions (Transport Tribunal and Appeal Panel) Order 2009, SI 2009/1885, almost all of the functions of the Transport Tribunal were transferred, as of 1 September 2009, to the First-tier Tribunal (Transport) and the Administrative Appeals Chamber of the Upper Tribunal.

80.2 The Transport Tribunal was not abolished by the 2009 Order. It retains jurisdiction to deal with appeals in relation to the Transport (Scotland) Act 2001. However, appeals under the Transport (Scotland) Act 2007 can be made alongside appeals to the Upper Tribunal, using the same appeal forms.

80.3 Appeals to the Transport Tribunal under the Transport (Scotland) Act 2001 are governed by the procedural rules in the Transport Tribunal Rules 2000, SI 2000/3226, the Transport Tribunal (Amendment) Rules 2001, SI 2001/4041, the Transport Tribunal (Amendment) Rules 2002, SI 2002/643 and the Transport Tribunal (Amendment) Rules 2008, SI 2008/2142.

TRANSPORT CASES IN THE FIRST-TIER TRIBUNAL

Jurisdiction

80.4 On 1 September 2009, most of the functions of the Transport Tribunal were transferred to the First-tier Tribunal (Transport), which falls within the GRC. See **First-tier Tribunal, General Regulatory Chamber** and **Chambers**.

80.5 The First-tier Tribunal (Transport) hears and decides appeals relating to:

- decisions of the Registrar of Approved Driving Instructors (the 'Registrar'), in relation to approved driving instructors and training provider appeals under the Road Traffic Act 1988, the Road Traffic Offenders Act 1988, the Transport Act 2000, the Motor Cars (Driving Instruction) Regulations 2005, SI 2005/1902, the Vehicle Drivers (Certificates of Professional Competence) Regulations 2007, SI 2007/605 and the European Communities (Recognition of Professional Qualifications) Regulations 2007, SI 2007/2781;
- decisions of Transport for London in London Service Permit appeals under the Greater London Authority Act 1999; and
- disputes between postal service providers and carriers, arising from the Postal Services Act 2000, s 94.

80.6 It is expected that the majority of the Tribunal's workload will fall within the first category – ie, that they will be appeals concerning approved driving instructors, trainee driving instructors and training providers. A right of appeal arises if the Registrar refuses to enter the name of a driving instructor on the register; refuses to maintain a name on the register; removes a name from the register; or refuses to grant or revokes a trainee driving instructor's licence.

Venue

80.7 The Tribunal's offices are in London. Hearings usually take place in London or Glasgow for Scottish cases.

Procedural rules

80.8 Proceedings before the First-tier Tribunal (Transport) are governed by the GRC Rules. These are reproduced at Appendix 1. See also **General Regulatory Chamber** and **General Regulatory Chamber procedural rules.**

Appealing to the First-tier Tribunal (Transport)

See **Bringing proceedings in the First-tier Tribunals.**

80.9 Unlike charities cases, there are no special procedural rules of the General Regulatory Chamber that apply to transport cases. The usual application notice, time limit, hearings and appeals provisions of the General Regulatory Chamber therefore apply.

80.10 There is, however, one notable difference, namely that the time limit for appealing against a decision of the Registrar refusing or revoking a licence to give driving instruction is 14 days instead of the usual 28 days (GRC Rules, r 22(1)(a)). The respondent in a transport case also has 14 days rather than 28 from receipt of the notice of appeal to lodge his response with the Tribunal. The Tribunal itself is under an obligation to send the response to the appellant, rather than the respondent (GRC Rules, r 23(1)(a) and (6)). If the appellant makes a reply to the response, it is for the Tribunal to send that reply to the other parties (GRC Rules, r 24(4)).

80.11 Appeals against decisions of the General Regulatory Chamber go to the Administrative Appeals Chamber of the Upper Tribunal under the usual rules (see **Appeals and references to the Upper Tribunal**).

ADMINISTRATIVE APPEALS CHAMBER (UPPER TRIBUNAL)

Jurisdiction

See **Administrative Appeals Chamber** and **Upper Tribunal.**

80.12 On 1 September 2009, one function of the Transport Tribunal was transferred directly to the Administrative Appeals Chamber of the Upper Tribunal, namely, appeals against decisions of the Traffic Commissioners.

80.13 Decisions against which a right of appeal lies to the Upper Tribunal include:

- a refusal to grant a licence;
- a refusal to vary an existing licence;
- the attaching of conditions to a licence;
- the granting of a licence which allows fewer vehicles than the number applied for;
- in public service vehicles cases, a determination that registered local bus services have not been operated properly (and the imposition of financial penalties);

- a revocation, suspension or curtailment of an existing licence; and
- the disqualification of an individual or a company.

80.14 The Administrative Appeals Chamber also hears transport-related appeals against decisions of the First-tier Tribunal (Transport).

Procedural rules

80.15 Proceedings in transport cases before the Upper Tribunal are governed by the ('Upper Tribunal Rules'). The Upper Tribunal Rules are reproduced at Appendix 8. See also **Upper Tribunal**.

Appealing to the Administrative Appeals Chamber (Upper Tribunal)

80.16 For the most part, the ordinary Upper Tribunal Rules apply to appeals against the Traffic Commissioners. However, there are certain differences and the response to the notice of appeal in particular is governed by special procedural rules set out as Sch 1 to the Upper Tribunal Rules. The notice of appeal itself is governed by the ordinary rules, and has a time limit of one month from the sending of the notice of the decision (Upper Tribunal Rules, r 23). The Tribunal must then send a copy of the notice of appeal to the Traffic Commissioner, the appropriate national authority and the authorised person if the case concerns the detention of a vehicle (Upper Tribunal Rules, r 23(6)(b)).

80.17 Following receipt of the notice of appeal, the Commissioner must send to the Tribunal (Upper Tribunal Rules, Sch 1, para 3):

(a) a written record of the decision appealed against and reasons for the decision;

(b) all documents produced to the traffic commissioner in connection with the decision;

(c) if a public inquiry was held, the transcript of the inquiry or, if no such transcript was produced, the traffic commissioner's note of the inquiry; and

(d) in an appeal under section 50 of the Public Passenger Vehicles Act 1981 or section 37 of the Goods Vehicles (Licensing of Operators) Act 1995, a list of the names and addresses of objectors and representors.

80.18 Persons listed in (d) are entitled to receive a copy of the notice of appeal from the Tribunal, who must send it to them (Upper Tribunal Rules, Sch 1, para 4). Any national authority sent the notice of appeal under r 23(6)(b)(ii) may apply to be added as a respondent to the proceedings, providing that the application is made within 14 days (Upper Tribunal Rules, Sch 1, paras 5–6). If the national authority, or a person falling within paragraph 4, applies to be joined the Tribunal must add them as a respondent, notifying any other party of the application and decision (Upper Tribunal Rules, Sch 1, paras 7–9). Any party to the proceedings may request copies of the documents provided by the Commissioner, which the Tribunal must provide unless it is considered unreasonable giving reasons why it so considers (Upper Tribunal Rules, Sch 1, paras 10, 11).

80.19 Special rules are also provided in respect of a party wishing to apply for a stay of the Commissioner's decision pending the appeal. If such an application is made under r 20A the applicant must notify the Commissioner, who has seven days from notification to send to the applicant and Tribunal reasons for refusing or withdrawing the stay (Upper Tribunal Rules, r 20A(3)).

81 Tribunal Justice

KEY CHARACTERISTICS

81.1 In the report of Sir Andrew Leggatt, 'Tribunals for Users — One System, One Service', which was published in August 2001, the main advantages of tribunals were described in the following terms at paragraph 1.2:

> 'Choosing a tribunal to decide disputes should bring two distinctive advantages for users. First, tribunal decisions are often made jointly by a panel of people who pool legal and other expert knowledge, and are the better for that range of skills. Secondly, tribunals' procedures and approach to overseeing the preparation of cases and their hearing can be simpler and more informal than the courts, even after the civil justice reforms. Most users ought therefore to be capable of preparing and presenting their cases to the tribunal themselves, providing they have the right kind of help. Enabling that kind of direct participation is an important justification for establishing tribunals at all.'

This passage indicates the three characteristics which are regarded as key advantages of tribunal justice: expert membership (including non-lawyers), procedural efficiency and accessibility.

81.2 In a decision of the House of Lords (*Gillies v Secretary of State for Work and Pensions* [2006] UKHL 2; [2006] 1 WLR 781) concerning a bias challenge to a medical member of the-then Disability Appeals Tribunal (now within the remit of the Social Entitlement Chamber), Baroness Hale, a former member of the Council on Tribunals, made some comments about tribunal justice:

> 'The relevant facts of tribunal life include the great advantage, both to its users and to its decision-making, of being able to call upon the people with the greatest expertise in the subject matter of the claim...The greatest expertise in assessing the claimant's condition and applying the statutory criteria to it is likely to be held by those doctors who are experienced in making these assessments at the point of claim. To have such expertise available on the tribunal can only be an advantage to it.
>
> It is also a fact of tribunal life that they are presided over by lawyers whose role is not only to conduct the hearing in a fair and user-friendly fashion, to understand the relevant law, and to explain it to their colleagues. It is also to assist those colleagues to address the relevant issues in a reasonable and fair-minded way and then write the reasons for their decision.' (at [40] and [46])

81.3 But it is important to remember the warning of the current Senior President, Sir Robert Carnwath CVO in 'Tribunal justice – a new start' [2009] PL 48, 53:

> 'When talking about tribunals, generalisations are dangerous. Tribunals vary greatly in the complexity of the cases before them, their financial significance, and the degree of procedural formality appropriate to them. Gillies was concerned with the role of the medical member of a social security tribunal in assessing disability benefit. In such cases, no doubt, cheapness, accessibility and freedom from technicality are desirable and achievable objectives. But there is no obvious parallel

with, for example, a major case before the Special Commissioners of Tax or the Lands Tribunal. The sums there involved may be as great as in any case in the High Court, and the legal and factual issues equally complex. A degree of procedural formality is unavoidable if justice is to be done, and the specialist expertise of the tribunal is unlikely to be an adequate substitute for expert representation of the parties. There may be little in reality to distinguish such a "tribunal" case from a case before a specialist "court", such as the Technology and Construction Court.'

TRIBUNAL MEMBERSHIP

81.4 TCEA 2007, s 2(3)(c) places the Senior President under a duty to have regard to 'the need for members of tribunals to be experts in the subject-matter of, or the law to be applied in, cases in which they decide matters'.

81.5 This duty is reflected in the use of appropriately qualified non-judicial members in the Chambers of both the First-tier and Upper Tribunals. Under the Qualifications for Appointment of Members to the First-tier tribunal and Upper Tribunal Order 2008, SI 2008/2692, reg 2, a wide range of non-lawyers with relevant expertise are eligible for appointment to tribunal membership, including (to give three examples) medics, accountants and those with substantial experience of service in the armed forces. The various Practice Statements made by the Senior President on the composition of tribunals indicates how much thought has gone into the need to balance legal and contextual expertise: see **Constitution and composition of the First-tier Tribunal** and **Constitution and composition of the Upper Tribunal**.

PROCEDURAL EFFICIENCY

Speed

81.6 TCEA 2007, s 2(3)(b)(ii) requires the Senior President to have regard to the need for proceedings before tribunals to be handled quickly and efficiently. TCEA 2007, s 22(4) also requires the Tribunal Procedure Committee to exercise its rule-making power with this objective in mind.

81.7 Thus the importance of speed is reflected in the procedural rules of the various Chambers. For example, neither the First-tier nor the Upper Tribunal rules require formal pleading and disclosure stages and (in many cases) provide for the case to be decided on the papers, with the parties' agreement.

Flexibility

81.8 The importance of flexibility is reflected in the procedural rules of the various Chambers of the First-tier and Upper Tribunals. Rule 2(2), which explains the overriding objective, states that, 'Dealing with a case fairly and justly includes ... (b) avoiding unnecessary formality and seeking flexibility in the proceedings'.

Innovation

81.9 TCEA 2007, s 2(3)(d) requires the Senior President to have regard to 'the need to develop innovative methods of resolving disputes that are of a type that may be brought before tribunals'. It is notable in this regard that TCEA 2007, s 24 allows practice directions to provide for tribunal members to act as mediators in relation to disputed matters in cases that are the subject of proceedings, thus showing a willingness to encourage methods of alternative dispute resolution.

Accessibility

81.10 TCEA 2007, s 2(3)(a) places the Senior President under a duty to have regard to the need for tribunals to be accessible. This is a particularly important aspect of the new two-tier tribunals system. Below are some of the main respects in which this aspect is translated into specific features of tribunal justice.

Encouragement of participation

81.11 Rule 2(2) of (most of) the Chambers' procedural rules provides that, 'Dealing with a case fairly and justly includes ... (c) ensuring, so far as practicable, that the parties are able to participate fully in the proceedings'. Accordingly, there are no limits on rights of audience and (in most cases) no limits on whom a party can choose to represent him or her.

81.12 The emphasis on participation is also furthered by the limited ability of parties to recover costs and expenses (which can act as a deterrent to bringing proceedings) and the caution with which the power in TCEA 2007, s 42 to impose fees for bringing proceedings has, to date, been exercised. The inability to obtain legal aid for most types of case before the First-tier Tribunal (although there are exceptions: immigration and mental health being two main ones) can be justified as an important reflection of the understanding that the tribunals are not imposing detailed and formalistic legal procedures, but aim to engage with parties – particularly individuals – to ensure that justice is done. In the Upper Tribunal, where appeals are on points of law, a greater degree of formalism and 'legalese' is inevitable and the provision of legal aid reflects that.

Simplicity

81.13 TCEA 2007, s 22(4)(c) requires the Tribunal Procedure Committee to exercise its rule-making power with a view to ensuring that the procedural rules are both simple and simply expressed. This is an essential aim if individual users of the new system are to navigate their way around what remains a complex and vast structure. The website of the Tribunals Service (www.tribunals.gov.uk) is to be commended for its provision of the procedurals rules and links to the legislation, as well as linking easily to the myriad of sub-level websites for each specialised division of the First-tier and Upper Tribunals.

Enabling and inquisitorial approach

81.14 Although there are no express legal requirements to this effect, tribunals are expected to approach cases – and, in particular, hearings – in two particular ways. Firstly, they are expected to be enabling, ie, to encourage individual participation. This is because it is important to ensure that tribunal users, many of whom are unrepresented and unfamiliar with judicial or quasi-judicial procedure, not only have a right of access and participation but are able to exercise that right effectively. This may require encouragement and assistance from the tribunal (see *R(I) 6/69* at [7]).

81.15 The Leggatt Report itself stressed the need for an enabling approach at paragraphs 7.4–7.5:

> '[I]n greater or lesser degrees, tribunals have developed different ways of assisting unrepresented parties, in particular when the encounter is between citizen and state, and departments are represented by an official or an advocate who is familiar with the law, the tribunal and its procedures. In these circumstances, tribunal chairmen may find it necessary to intervene in the proceedings more than might be thought proper in the courts in order to hold the balance between the parties, and enable citizens to present their cases. All the members of a tribunal must do all they can to understand the point of view, as well as the case, of the citizen. They must be alert for factual or legal aspects of the case which appellants may not bring out, adequately or at all, but which have a bearing on the possible outcomes. It may also be necessary on occasion to intervene to protect a witness or party, to avoid proceedings becoming too confrontational. The balance is a delicate one, and must not go so far on any side that the tribunal's impartiality appears to be endangered. An unrepresented citizen will naturally feel discomforted if he feels that the tribunal is favouring the Government side. This may need particular care when the role of the state's representatives is often geared to assisting the tribunal to understand considerable legal and factual complexities. In party and party tribunals, where the adversarial model is stronger, one party may feel that the other is getting too much help.
>
> We are convinced that the tribunal approach must be an enabling one: supporting the parties in ways which give them confidence in their own abilities to participate in the process, and in the tribunal's capacity to compensate for the appellants' lack of skills or knowledge.'

81.16 Second, and closely related, tribunals are expected to be inquisitorial, ie, to be proactive in identifying issues, examining evidence, requesting further evidence, etc. Unlike the approach of a court in many cases between professionally represented parties, it cannot be assumed that the applicant has identified the right issues, formulated correctly his or her own case or marshalled the evidence needed to support that case. If the right to be heard is to be effective, not only must the applicant be encouraged to have his or her say but the Tribunal must also ensure that the correct issues are addressed in the light of the appropriate evidence. In many cases, it will be for the Tribunal itself to take the lead. Although the TCEA 2007 does not prescribe an inquisitorial approach specifically it has been recognised for some time in case law that Tribunal adjudication can be 'inquisitorial rather than adversarial', a 'co-operative process of investigation': *Kerr v Department for Social Development (Northern Ireland)* [2004] UKHL 23; [2004] 1 WLR 1372 at [60]–[61] per Baroness Hale. Of course, this will be context dependent, so that if the individual is in fact legally represented the Tribunal will ordinarily step back and assume that the necessary issues and evidence are being dealt with: see *Jeleniewicz v Secretary of State for Work and Pensions* [2008] EWCA Civ 1163 at [13] per Mummery LJ and *Chandra v Care Standards Tribunal*

[2008] EWHC 2833 (Admin) at [17] per Tim Corner QC (sitting as a Deputy High Court Judge).

81.17 These two requirements of approach are reflected in, for example, the lack of formal rules of evidence and the fact that tribunal hearings generally do not involve the testing by each party of the other's case by way of cross-examination but rather more general questioning by the Tribunal. It is also reflected in the informal approach taken at hearings and the emphasis on making tribunals user-friendly, especially for the unrepresented party.

81.18 There are, of course, limits to the degree of informality which is permitted and the extent to which it is appropriate for the members of the tribunal to be pro-active in raising matters or reformulating a party's case. But the nature of the issues before tribunals and the users of the tribunal system will often make a greater degree of informality and pro-activity on the part of the tribunal necessary and acceptable than would be the case at a court hearing. As was said in the report of Sir Andrew Leggatt at paragraph 1.25:

> 'However informal the atmosphere, and however sympathetic the chairmen and members are to the user, the experience of a tribunal hearing is extremely stressful for most users. They value the option of presenting their case personally, and in general they feel that they are given a fair hearing. But the issue, whether it is their tax bill or the level of their social security benefits, the schooling of their child or the level of their rent, matters personally to them, and the hearing is an important and possibly daunting occasion. Perhaps the biggest challenge for tribunals is to enable users who feel that they have been unfairly treated to come to the tribunal without undue apprehension, and to leave feeling that they have been given a fair opportunity to put their case.'

82 Tribunal Procedure Committee

82.1 The Tribunal Procedure Committee is the advisory body which makes the Tribunal Procedural Rules. It is a non-departmental public body.

STATUTORY BASIS

82.2 The TCEA 2007 provides, in s 22(2) for Tribunal Procedure Rules to be made by the Tribunal Procedure Committee. The detailed legislative provisions concerning the Tribunal Procedure Committee are to be found in TCEA 2007, Part 2, Sch 5.

MEMBERSHIP

82.3 TCEA 2007, para 20, Part 2, Sch 5 provides that the Tribunal Procedure Committee is to consist of:

- the Senior President of Tribunals or a person nominated by him;
- the persons currently appointed by the Lord Chancellor;
- the persons currently appointed by the Lord Chief Justice;
- the person currently appointed by the Lord President of the Court of Session; and
- any person currently appointed at the request of the Senior President of Tribunals.

82.4 The Lord Chancellor has three appointees (TCEA 2007, para 21, Part 2, Sch 5); the Lord Chief Justice, also three (one judge of the First-tier Tribunal, one judge of the Upper Tribunal and one non-judge member of either) (para 22); the Lord President of the Court of Session, one appointee with experience in and knowledge of the Scottish legal system (para 23); and the Senior President of Tribunals can request the appointment of up to four people with experience or knowledge of a particular area (para 24).

OBJECTIVE IN MAKING RULES

82.5 The Tribunal Procedure Committee exercises its power to make rules with a view to ensuring, by TCEA 2007, s 22(4), that:

- justice is done in proceedings in the First-tier and Upper Tribunals;
- the tribunal system is accessible and fair;
- proceedings in the first-tier and Upper Tribunals are handled quickly and efficiently;
- the rules are simple and simply expressed; and
- the rules, where appropriate, confer on tribunal members responsibility for ensuring that proceedings before the tribunal are handled quickly and efficiently.

PROCESS FOR MAKING RULES

82.6 TCEA 2007, para 28(1), Part 3, Sch 5 provides that the Tribunal Procedure Committee must consult appropriate persons (including the relevant Chamber President) before making rules (and, specifically, that the Committee must consult the Lord President of the Court of Session if the Rules contain provision relating to proceedings in Scotland) and also meet, unless it is not expedient to do so. In practice, the Committee meets up to nine times a year.

82.7 TCEA 2007, para 28(2), Part 3, Sch 5 requires rules made by the Committee to be signed by a majority of its members and submitted to the Lord Chancellor. The Lord Chancellor may choose to disallow a rule but, where he does so, he must give written reasons (TCEA 2007, para 28(3) and (4), Part 3, Sch 5). The Lord Chancellor may also, under TCEA 2007, para 29, Part 3, Sch 5, require certain Tribunal Procedure Rules to be made if he considers it expedient.

82.8 When the Tribunal Procedure Committee draws up new proposed rules, they are ordinarily published on the Committee's website (http://www.tribunals.gov.uk/Tribunals/Rules/tribunalprocedurecommittee.htm) for consultation. The Committee usually then publishes its response to the consultation process and then the Rules made as a result of the consultation process are published there in the final version.

82.9 One body having the function of drafting rules in a manner which encourages consistency is, as Professor Craig has said, 'to be welcomed' ('Perspectives on process: common law, statutory and political' [2010] PL 275, 290). Hickinbottom J has said, extra-judicially, that the Committee 'is one of the great success stories of the reform programme' ('Tribunal reform: a new coherent system' [2010] JR 103 at [10]).

OTHER FUNCTIONS

82.10 In addition to making the Tribunal Procedure Rules, the Tribunal Procedure Committee is also consulted on Practice Directions received from the Senior President or Chamber Presidents.

83 Tribunals, Courts and Enforcement Act 2007

SUMMARY

83.1 Part 1 of the TCEA 2007 established two new, generic Tribunals: a First-tier Tribunal and Upper Tribunal, into which previously existing tribunal jurisdictions could be transferred. The Act thereby created a new, flexible framework for the unification of the Tribunal system and judiciary, under the unified control of the Senior President.

83.2 Provision was made for the membership of the new tribunals, their jurisdiction, the transfer of functions to them and appeals to and from them. The Lord Chancellor was empowered to transfer to himself certain statutory powers and duties relating to the provision of administrative support for the new Tribunals.

83.3 Part 1 of the TCEA 2007 also provided for the replacement of the Council on Tribunals, the supervisory body for tribunals, with the Administrative Justice and Tribunals Council, which has a broader remit.

83.4 The other Parts of the TCEA 2007 do not relate to the new tribunals system, They concern, respectively, judicial appointments (Part 2), enforcement by taking control of goods (Part 3), enforcement of judgments and orders (Part 4), debt management and relief (Part 5), protection of cultural objects on loan (Part 6) and various other matters such as appeals in relation to design rights (Part 7). For obvious reasons, these are not covered in this Handbook.

83.5 The preamble to the Act is in the following terms:

> 'An Act to make provision about tribunals and inquiries; to establish an Administrative Justice and Tribunals Council; to amend the law relating to judicial appointments and appointments to the Law Commission; to amend the law relating to the enforcement of judgments and debts; to make further provision about the management and relief of debt; to make provision protecting cultural objects from seizure or forfeiture in certain circumstances; to amend the law relating to the taking of possession of land affected by compulsory purchase; to alter the powers of the High Court in judicial review applications; and for connected purposes.'

COMMENCEMENT

83.6 The TCEA 2007 received Royal Assent on 19 July 2007.

83.7 Parts of the Act (for example, s 7(1), which empowers the Lord Chancellor to make provision for the organisation of the First-tier Tribunal and Upper Tribunal into Chambers) came into force on 18 September 2007, pursuant to the Tribunals, Courts and Enforcement Act 2007 (Commencement No 1) Order 2007, SI 2007/2709.

83.8 Most of Part 1 of the TCEA 2007, actually creating the First-tier and Upper Tribunals and their jurisdictions, was brought into force on 3 November 2008 by the Tribunals, Courts and Enforcement Act 2007 (Commencement No 6 and Transitional Provisions) Order 2008, SI 2008/2696.

83.9 The same Order brought the enforcement provisions in s 27 and the Tax Chamber provisions into force on 1 April 2009.

STRUCTURE OF PART 1

Chapter 1: Tribunal judiciary, independence and Senior President

83.10 Section 1 amends the definition of 'judiciary' in the Constitutional Reform Act 2005, s 3 to ensure that the duty imposed on the Lord Chancellor and other Ministers of the Crown under the Constitutional Reform Act 2005 to uphold the continued independence of the judiciary, extends to all of the tribunal judges.

83.11 Section 2 creates the new statutory judicial post of Senior President of Tribunals, to provide unified leadership of the tribunal judiciary. See **Senior President** for further details. Further details as to the eligibility, selection and appointment of the Senior President are to be found in Sch 1.

Chapter 2: First-tier Tribunal and Upper Tribunal

83.12 Section 3 provides for the creation of a First-tier Tribunal and an Upper Tribunal, each consisting of judges and other non-judicial members and presided over by the Senior President.

83.13 Section 4 and Sch 2 contain provisions relating to the judges and other members of the First-tier Tribunal, while s 5 and Sch 3 contain analogous provisions for the Upper Tribunal. Section 6 lists which judges are to be considered as members of both the First-tier Tribunal and the Upper Tribunal within England, Wales, Scotland and Northern Ireland by virtue of their judicial office in the courts. Temporary office holders or deputies are not included within the list. Section 7 and Sch 4 make provision for the organisation of the First-tier and Upper Tribunals into different Chambers, with Chamber Presidents. Section 8 enables the Senior President to delegate any of his functions to any judge or member of the First-tier or Upper Tribunal or any member of staff, with the exception of his function under s 7(9) of allocating Tribunal functions between the Chambers of the tribunals by order made with the concurrence of the Lord Chancellor.

83.14 Moving on to the review of decisions and appeals, ss 9 and 10 empower the First-tier and Upper Tribunals to review their own decisions and, where the tribunal concludes that an error was made, to re-decide the matter. This discretionary power, which is exercisable without the need for a full onward appeal, is intended to capture decisions that are clearly wrong and thereby avoiding the need for appeals. Section 11 provides for a general right of appeal on a point of law from the First-tier Tribunal to the Upper Tribunal, for all but 'excluded' decisions. Where such an appeal is made and upheld, s 12 sets out the Upper Tribunal's powers. Section 13 provides for a power to appeal to the Court of Appeal on any point of law, with permission either from the Upper Tribunal or from the relevant appellate court (and subject to the Lord Chancellor's power in s 13(6) to restrict appeals to the Court of Appeal to cases where the court or the Upper Tribunal considers that the proposed appeal would raise some important point of principle or practice or that there is some other compelling reason for the appeal to be heard). Section 14 sets out the powers of the Court of Appeal if it concludes that there has been an error of law.

83.15 Sections 15 to 21 create a statutory regime which enables the Upper Tribunal to exercise judicial review powers in appropriate cases. Section 15 confers power on the Upper Tribunal to grant certain forms of relief in the same way as the High Court on an application for judicial review. Sections 16 and 18 set out the circumstances in which the Upper Tribunal has this judicial review jurisdiction, while s 17 makes further provision as to the powers of the Upper Tribunal if it decides to grant a quashing order. Section 19 amends the Senior Courts Act 1981 and the Judicature (Northern Ireland) Act 1978 to allow for the transfer of certain High Court cases to the Upper Tribunal. Sections 20 and 21 concern the Upper Tribunal's powers of judicial review in Scotland and the transfer of applications from the Court of Session.

83.16 Section 22 and Sch 5 create and make provision for the contents of Tribunal Procedure Rules, and endowing the Tribunal Procedure Committee with rule-making responsibility. Section 23 gives the Senior President the statutory authority to supplement Tribunal Procedure Rules with practice directions. Section 24 provides the statutory basis for the use of mediation with the Tribunals system. In particular, s 24(2) provides that practice directions may provide for Tribunal members to act as mediators in relation to disputed matters in a case that is the subject of proceedings. Section 25 provides the Upper Tribunal with the powers of the High Court or Court of Session to require the attendance and examination of witnesses and the production and inspection of documents, and all other matters incidental to the Upper Tribunal's functions, while s 26 allows both the First-tier and the Upper Tribunals to sit anywhere in the UK irrespective of the law of a case. Section 27 concerns the enforcement of Tribunal awards. Subsections (1) to (3) ensure that monetary awards made by the First-tier and Upper Tribunals are enforceable through the courts. These provisions do not alter the methods of enforcement by the courts. Subsection (4) separates out from these provisions enforcement of awards made by the Upper Tribunal exercising its judicial review powers under ss 16(6) and 21(1). Section 28 empowers the First-tier Tribunal or the Upper Tribunal to appoint an assessor to assist where it is dealing with matters that require a special expertise that the Tribunal would otherwise not have available to it. Section 29 gives the Tribunals the power to order costs and expenses in the same way as courts (subject to the Tribunal Procedure Rules).

Chapter 3: Transfer of Tribunal functions

83.17 Section 30 empowers the Lord Chancellor to provide for the transfer of the functions of Tribunals listed in the relevant parts of Sch 6 to the First-tier or Upper Tribunal, an Employment Tribunal or the Employment Appeal Tribunal. Thus jurisdictions can be consolidated into the new tribunals and the Employment Tribunals and Employment Appeal Tribunal. Section 31 confers on the Lord Chancellor the necessary supplementary powers to effect the transfers in s 30 (eg abolishing the Tribunals the functions of which have already been transferred). Sections 32–34 deal, respectively, with the power in Wales, Scotland and Northern Ireland to provide for a right of appeal to the Upper Tribunal in circumstances where the equivalent tribunal jurisdiction in England (or in England and Wales) has been transferred to the First-tier Tribunal under s30 but the relevant Welsh, Scottish or Northern Irish Tribunal jurisdiction has not been. Thus the Lord Chancellor can prevent there being different onward routes of appeal from different tribunals in the UK.

Section 35 makes it possible to transfer to the Lord Chancellor administrative functions of other ministers (and functions of the Commissioners for Her Majesty's Revenue and Customs) in relation to tribunals listed in Sch 6. Sections 36 and 37 enable the Lord Chancellor to, respectively, transfer power to make procedural rules for certain tribunals to himself or to the Tribunal Procedure Committee and amend the lists of tribunals in Sch 6 to the TCEA 2007. Finally, s 38 provides for power to amend, repeal or revoke enactments in connection with orders under ss 30–36.

Chapter 4: Administrative matters in respect of certain tribunals

83.18 Section 39 places the Lord Chancellor under a general duty to ensure that there is an efficient and effective system of administration in respect of the First-tier and Upper Tribunals, the Employment Tribunal, the Employment Appeal Tribunal. Sections 40 and 41 (modelled on the Courts Act 2003, ss 2 and 3) give the Lord Chancellor similar powers to provide staff, services and accommodation for tribunals. Section 40 allows him to employ civil servants as Tribunal staff, so that he can discharge his duty of administering the tribunals and providing support services. Section 42 provides for the possibility of tribunals charging a fee. Finally, s 43 requires the Senior President to give the Lord Chancellor a report on the cases that have come before the First-tier Tribunal, the Upper Tribunal, the Employment Tribunals and the Employment Appeal Tribunal each year.

Chapter 5: Oversight of administrative justice system, Tribunals and inquiries

83.19 Section 44 and Sch 7 establish an Administrative Justice and Tribunals Council, to replace the previous Council on Tribunals, which s 45 abolishes.

Chapter 6: Supplementary

83.20 Section 46 enables the Lord Chief Justice to nominate a judicial office holder (as defined in the Constitutional Reform Act 2005, s 109(4)) to exercise any of the listed functions given to him under the Act. These functions primarily concern the nomination and removal of judges from the First-tier and Upper Tribunals and the appointment of members to the Tribunal Procedure Committee. Section 47 establishes a duty of co-operation between the offices of the Senior President of Tribunals, the Lord Chief Justices and the Lord President in relation to judicial guidance, training and welfare. Section 48 gives effect to Schs 8 and 9, which contain consequential and other amendments and transitional provisions, while s 49 sets out the procedure to be followed in respect of the various types of order which can be made under Part 1 (mainly by the Lord Chancellor).

84 Tribunals Service

ROLE

84.1 The Tribunals Service was created on 3 April 2006. It is an executive agency of what was the Department for Constitutional Affairs and is now the Ministry of Justice ('MoJ'). The Tribunals Service is the counterpart, for tribunals, of Her Majesty's Courts Service. It provides administrative support to most of the Tribunals which are the responsibility of central Government, including those which are presently outside the scope of the new two-tier tribunals structure (in particular, the Employment Tribunals and the Employment Appeal Tribunal).

84.2 The primary tasks of the Tribunals Service, as described in its most recent Annual Report (2009–2010), are to:

- provide a responsive and efficient Tribunals administration;
- promote and protect the independence of the judiciary;
- contribute to the improvement of the quality of original decision-making across government; and
- reform the tribunals' justice system for the benefit of customers and the wider public.

84.3 Tribunals not within the two-tier structure but within the responsibility of the Tribunals Service are:

- Employment Tribunals
- Employment Appeal Tribunal
- Adjudicator to HM Land Registry
- Gender Recognition Panel
- Pathogen Access Appeal Commission
- Proscribed Organisations Appeal Commission
- Special Immigration Appeals Commission
- Reserve Forces Appeal Tribunal
- Reinstatement Committees and Umpires

HISTORY

84.4 The origins of the Tribunals Service lie in the report of Sir Andrew Leggatt, 'Tribunals for Users – One System, One Service', which was published in August 2001. Sir Andrew recommended that the disparate tribunals in existence at the time should be brought together in a single system, separate from their sponsoring governmental departments. Sir Andrew recommended that such a system be administered by a single Tribunals Service, in what was then the Lord Chancellor's Department.

84.5 The Government accepted Sir Andrew's recommendation in its White Paper 'Transforming Public Services: Complaints, Redress and Tribunals' (Cm 6243), published in July 2004.

84.6 The Tribunals Service was created by machinery of government changes. Legislation was not required.

COMPOSITION AND FUNCTIONS

84.7 According to its Annual Report 2009–2010 the Tribunals Service employs 2,922 staff and deals with almost 650,000 cases a year.

84.8 As well as administering the system of tribunals, the Tribunals Service also works closely with other bodies involved in the wider administration of justice. It is part of the 'Access to Justice Group', which was set up in April 2008 to deliver more effective and integrated working between the Courts Service, the Tribunals Service and other entities such as the Legal Services Commission.

84.9 The tribunals system as a whole, including the Tribunals Service, is overseen by the Administrative Justice and Tribunals Council ('AJTC'). The AJTC was created by the TCEA 2007, s 44 and came into existence on 1 November 2007. The AJTC replaced the Council on Tribunals (see **Administrative Justice** and **Tribunals Council**).

85 Upper Tribunal

PERSONNEL AND LOCATION

85.1 The Senior President of Tribunals ('Senior President') presides over the Upper Tribunal. The office of Senior President was created by the TCEA 2007, s 2 (see **Senior President of Tribunals**). The judges of the Upper Tribunal may be drawn from the High Court, the Court of Appeal, the Court of Session or may be a circuit or district judge: TCEA 2007, s 6.

APPELLATE JURISDICTION AND POWERS

85.2 The Upper Tribunal is divided into four Chambers:

- The Administrative Appeals Chamber (see **Administrative Appeals Chamber**) dealing (in summary) with onward appeals from all the First–tier Tribunals (except the TC, the IAC and charities cases from the GRC); appeals from the Mental Health Review Tribunal (Wales); and Special Educational Needs Tribunal (Wales); appeals from the Pensions Appeal Tribunal (Scotland); appeals under the Pensions Appeal Tribunals Act 1943, s 5 from the Pensions Appeal Tribunal (Northern Ireland); appeals under the Safeguarding Vulnerable Groups Act 2006, s 4; references under the Forfeiture Act 1982; appeals from the Traffic Commissioners and most judicial review matters;
- The Tax and Chancery Chamber (see **Tax and Chancery Chamber**) dealing with onward appeals from the First-tier Tax Chamber Tribunal and the charities cases from the General Regulatory Chamber; appeals from the Financial Services Authority; appeals from the Pensions Regulator; and some judicial review matters.
- The Lands Chamber (see **Lands Chamber**) dealing with certain disputes concerning land, particularly the valuation of land adopting the jurisdiction of the old Lands Tribunal;
- The IAC (see **Immigration and Asylum Chamber (Upper Tribunal)**) dealing with onward appeals from the Immigration and Asylum Chamber of the First-tier Tribunal on immigration and asylum matters.

85.3 Most appeals are on points of law alone (TCEA 2007, s 11), although the existing appeal jurisdiction of other tribunals on both fact and law is also preserved. Certain types of appeal are excluded by order (see **Excluded appeals**).

85.4 Where an appeal is brought before the Upper Tribunal it has the power to substitute its own decision on the facts and to make any necessary findings of fact if it sets aside the decision of the First-tier Tribunal (TCEA 2007, s 12). It has been said in one case that it would not be appropriate for a single judge sitting on an appeal in the Upper Tribunal to substitute a decision in a case where the First-tier Tribunal would have had the benefit of specialist expertise: *MW v Halton Borough Council* [2010] UKUT 34 (AAC) at [32].

85.5 It was also held in *MW* that the principle of deference to expert tribunals adopted by the appellate courts (see, for example, *AH (Sudan) v Secretary of State for the Home Department* [2007] UKHL 49; [2008] 1 AC 678 at [30] per Baroness Hale and other cases cited in Appeals from the Upper Tribunal) did not apply to the Upper Tribunal in respect of the First-tier Tribunals because the structure of the TCEA 2007 already imposed restraint through permitting an appeal on a point of law only: *MW* at [43].

VENUES

85.6 The different Chambers of the Upper Tribunal have different venues. The Lands Chamber and Tax and Chancery Chamber are based in London but can hear cases in other venues if necessary.

85.7 The Administrative Appeals Chamber has hearing centres in Belfast, Cardiff, Edinburgh, Leeds, London and Manchester. It can also sit in other hearing centres if necessary.

85.8 The Immigration and Asylum Chamber currently sits in 11 different hearing centres: Belfast, Birmingham, Bradford, Glasgow, Harmondsworth, London (Field House), Manchester, Newport, North Shields, Stoke-on-Trent and Yarl's Wood.

JUDICIAL REVIEW IN THE UPPER TRIBUNAL

85.9 Where so empowered, the Upper Tribunal also possesses a judicial review jurisdiction comparable to that of the Administrative Court (see **Judicial review in the Upper Tribunal**). This jurisdiction arises where public law cases are transferred to the Upper Tribunal from the High Court by arrangement with the Lord Chief Justice (see **Directions and Transfer of judicial review applications**) or as otherwise set out by Order. In addition to the Direction of the Lord Chief Justice, the First-tier Tribunal and Upper Tribunal (Chambers) Order 2008, SI 2008/2684 (as amended) specifies the following allocation of particular types of judicial review case:

– In the Administrative Appeals Chamber (paragraph 7(b) of the 2008 Order):
  - to grant the relief mentioned in s 15(1) TCEA (Upper Tribunal's "judicial review" jurisdiction);
  - to exercise the powers of review under s 21(2) TCEA (Upper Tribunal's "judicial review" jurisdiction: Scotland);
  - except an application assigned to the Tax and Chancery Chamber.

– In the Tax and Chancery Chamber (paragraph 8(e) of the 2008 Order):
  - a decision of the Tax Chamber of the First-tier Tribunal or a charities case in the General Regulatory Chamber;
  - a function of the Commissioners for Her Majesty's Revenue and Customs or an officer of Revenue and Customs, with the exception of any function in respect of which an appeal would be allocated to the Social Entitlement Chamber;

- the exercise by the Serious Organised Crime Agency of general Revenue functions or Revenue inheritance tax functions (as defined in section 323 of the Proceeds of Crime Act 2002), with the exception of any function in relation to which an appeal would be allocated to the Social Entitlement Chamber;
- a function of the Charity Commission, the Financial Services Authority, the Bank of England, a person assessing compensation or consideration under the Banking (Special Provisions) Act 2008, or the Pensions Regulator.

85.10 The Administrative Appeals Chamber is therefore the primary home of the Upper Tribunal's judicial review jurisdiction, but with certain exceptions for cases in which the subject matter will be most obviously within the expertise of the Tax and Chancery Chamber judges.

PROCEDURE

85.11 The Upper Tribunal has its own rules of procedure. These are the Upper Tribunal Rules (see **Upper Tribunal procedure rules**).

APPEALS FROM THE UPPER TRIBUNAL

85.12 Appeals from the Upper Tribunal lie to the Court of Appeal but only on a point of law (see **Appeals from the Upper Tribunal**).

SUPERIOR COURT OF RECORD

85.13 The Upper Tribunal has been designated a superior court of record (TCEA 2007, s 3(5)).As a superior court of record decisions of the Upper Tribunal will be binding on inferior courts and lower tier tribunals. Decisions of the Upper Tribunal will be persuasive for courts of equal jurisdiction and will not be departed from unless 'plainly wrong' (*R v Greater Manchester Coroner, ex p Tal* [1985] QB 67). Certainly, the Upper Tribunal is likely to follow its own consistent line of authority, particularly where the decision on a point of law was handed down by a panel of more than a single judge, but it is not absolutely bound to do so: *Dorset Healthcare NHS Trust v MH* [2009] UKUT 4 (AAC); [2009] PTSR 1112 at [38]. However, it is unlikely in practice that the High Court will consider itself bound by a decision of the Upper Tribunal, even where it is a decision exercising the Tribunal's judicial review jurisdiction. Indeed, it appears from *Aggio v Howard de Walden Estates Ltd* [2007] EWCA Civ 499; [2008] Ch 26 at [86]–[95] that where the High Court and a lower court (in that case, the county court) exercised a shared statutory jurisdiction the 'Chancery Division of the High Court does not cease to be a higher court than the county court when it exercises the same first instance jurisdiction as has been conferred on the county court by the Leasehold Reform Acts. The fact that both the High Court and the county court are courts of first instance exercising the same statutory jurisdiction does not justify the creation of an exception to the general rule of stare decisis' (at [94]). The case was overturned on appeal to the House of Lords but not on the precedent point, and it is difficult to see how, superior court of record or not, the High Court will not see the Upper Tribunal as anything other than a lower court and bound by the High Court (and not vice versa) where there is shared jurisdiction.

85.14 It has been assumed by commentators that because the Upper Tribunal has been designated a superior court of record it has consequent powers to punish for contempt of court and is immune from judicial review (see, eg, Jacobs, *Tribunal Practice and Procedure* (2009), paragraph 1.119; Gething et al, 'Transformation of the Tax Tribunal' [2009] British Tax Review 250, 251; Woolf, Jowell & Le Sueur, *de Smith on Judical Review* (2007, 6th edn), paragraph 1-093). As to contempt, the assumption is probably correct because the Contempt of Court Act 1981 expressly recognises a distinction between 'superior' and 'inferior' courts: see ss 14 and 19. However, the judicial reviewability of the Upper Tribunal is not nearly so straightforward and has been the subject of important case law.

85.15 There can be little real doubt that the designation of the Upper Tribunal as a superior court of record, and the choice of those particular words, was at least in part designed to avoid the Tribunal being judicially reviewed. This was the assumption of the Leggatt Report (Tribunals for Users – One System, One Service (2001), paragraphs 6.31–6.34), high dicta supported it – see *Re Racal Communications Ltd* [1981] AC 374, 384 per Lord Diplock; *R v Manchester Crown Court, ex p DPP* [1993] 1 WLR 1524, HL, 1528 per Lord Browne-Wilkinson – and it was very clear in the debates on the Anti-Terrorism, Crime and Security Bill in 2001 that the designation of the Special Immigration Appeals Commission ('SIAC') as a superior court of record was expected to have that effect: see, for example, the intervention of Lord Goodhart that the 'effect of being a superior court of record, as opposed to a mere court of record, is a little more significant. The law recognises the principle that one superior court of record cannot review the acts of another. By making SIAC a superior court of record, the powers of the High Court to review its activities are necessarily excluded' (Hansard, HL Vol. 629, col.1438 (December 13, 2001)). The Attorney General, Lord Goldsmith, did not dissent from this objection.

85.16 *Cart* (Divisional Court)

The point arose for decision in an attempted judicial review of both SIAC and the Upper Tribunal in *R (Cart) v Upper Tribunal* [2009] EWHC 3052 (Admin); [2010] 2 WLR 1012. Mr Cart had been the subject of a direction varying upwards his liability to pay child maintenance and sought to challenge it in (now) the Social Entitlement Chamber on a number of bases, not least that he had not had notice of the application by his ex-wife to vary the amount. His appeal was dismissed and he sought permission to appeal to the Upper Tribunal, who granted him permission on three of his four grounds and refused permission on the notice point. A permission to appeal decision of the Upper Tribunal is an excluded matter for the purposes of an appeal to the Court of Appeal by TCEA 2007, s 13(8)(c) (see **Excluded appeals**) and so Mr Cart sought to judicially review the refusal in the High Court.

85.17 In the Divisional Court, Laws LJ undertook a detailed consideration of the impact and importance of the term 'superior court of record'. The court held that the proposition that 'judicial review will have been excluded by the application of a formula – "shall be a superior court of record"' – which

(a) says nothing on its face about judicial review, so that the exclusion is only implicit, and (b) is in the nature of a deeming provision' (at [29]) was a 'constitutional solecism' (at [31]) and that the TCEA 2007 could not be construed as impliedly 'excluding the judicial review jurisdiction from SIAC and UT respectively, whatever the historic scope of the expression "superior court of record"' (at [33]). The reason for finding was, according to Laws LJ, that legislation needs an authoritative determinator:

> 'If the meaning of statutory text is not controlled by such a judicial authority, it would at length be degraded to nothing more than a matter of opinion. Its scope and content would become muddied and unclear. Public bodies would not, by means of the judicial review jurisdiction, be kept within the confines of their powers prescribed by statute. The very effectiveness of statute law, Parliament's law, requires that none of these things happen. Accordingly, as it seems to me, the need for such an authoritative judicial source cannot be dispensed with by Parliament. This is not a denial of legislative sovereignty, but an affirmation of it: as is the old rule that Parliament cannot bind itself. The old rule means that successive Parliaments are always free to make what laws they choose; that is one condition of Parliament's sovereignty. The requirement of an authoritative judicial source for the interpretation of law means that Parliament's statutes are always effective; that is another.' (at [38])

85.18 As a consequence of this holding it was unnecessary for the Divisional Court to deal with the historical evolution and various meanings of the term 'superior court of record', although much of the material is set out at [43]–[75]. This aspect of Laws LJ's judgment was not reconsidered by the Court of Appeal, which focussed instead on the Upper Tribunal itself. It would appear that the primary finding of the Divisional Court that the term 'superior court of record' cannot by itself exclude judicial review remains good law in England. Although the reasoning of Laws LJ is, on this point, imaginative, the basic point must be correct. If Parliament wishes to exclude judicial review of a decision-making body then it must attempt to do so expressly rather than by relying on an ancient and ambiguous form of words (especially where the form of words has no meaning in Scottish law, as system to which the wording applies under the TCEA 2007 just as in English law).

85.19 However, Laws LJ went on to hold, at [94], that the Upper Tribunal is:

> 'an alter ego of the High Court. It therefore satisfies the material principle of the rule of law: it constitutes an authoritative, impartial and independent judicial source for the interpretation and application of the relevant statutory texts. It is not amenable to judicial review for excess of jurisdiction in the second sense: the case where, albeit acting within the field ascribed to it, the court perpetrates a legal mistake. It is a court possessing the final power to interpret for itself the law it must apply. Mr Drabble's elegant argument has not persuaded me to the contrary. UT's role at the apex of a new and comprehensive judicial structure ought to be respected and given effect. Its judicial review function is highly material to that role's status and authority. And it must, I think, be obvious that judicial review decisions of UT could not themselves be the subject of judicial review by the High Court; but I cannot see that UT might be reviewable when acting under TCEA ss.11 – 12 but not when acting under ss.15 – 21.'

85.20 His Lordship did, however, accept that in the 'grossly improbable event that UT were to embark upon a case that was frankly beyond the four corners of its statutory remit – the first sense of excess of jurisdiction – I see no reason why the High Court should not correct it' (at [99]), stating that this might include some forms of unfair hearing but that the possible exceptional review could not help Mr Cart.

85.21 *Eba* (Outer House, Court of Session)

Shortly after the decision in *Cart*, the Outer House of the Court of Session heard precisely the same issue in *Eba (Petitioner) v Upper Tribunal* [2010] CSOH 45; 2010 SLT 547. The Advocate General took the decision in *Cart* to be correct in that judicial review of the Upper Tribunal was available only in exceptional circumstances – excess of jurisdiction – and argued that a refusal to grant leave to appeal was not such a circumstance. Lord Glennie noted that the historical context of judicial review was very different in Scotland, and much of Laws LJ's analysis in Cart had little application there (at [71]–[74]). At its heart, the question was the same: whether the Upper Tribunal enjoyed a status equivalent to that of the Court of Session. Lord Glennie adopted the reasoning of the court in *Cart*, holding that the Upper Tribunal did have such a status (at [76]).

85.22 However, Lord Glennie had one major point of concern given that he was deciding the case after the Immigration and Asylum Chambers had begun their work. It had previously been accepted that the AIT was susceptible to judicial review in cases which were not covered by statutory review: *R (G) v Immigration Appeal Tribunal* [2004] EWCA Civ 1731; [2005] 1 WLR 1445 at [27]. In the light of this structural development he held that there was not one answer for all Upper Tribunals. Instead the courts should consider '(a) the nature of the tribunal, (b) the mechanisms for review and appeals in the new tribunals structure created by the Act, (c) the legislative intention (in so far as this is a separate point), (d) the need to balance the requirement for finality and the desire to achieve the right result – all of which, to my mind, point in favour of restricting the grounds of challenge – but also having regard to (e) the "generic nature of the issues involved"' (at [86]). Lord Glennie had no difficulty in holding that the decision of the Upper Tribunal refusing leave to appeal from the Social Entitlement Chamber was, as in *Cart*, not amenable to judicial review, which was available only 'in exceptional circumstances, ie on pre-Anisminic grounds (excess of jurisdiction in the narrow sense) or because there has been a breakdown of fair procedure' (at [90]).

85.23 It is important that the same approach be taken by the courts in both England and Scotland in relation to the TCEA 2007 regime, and it is interesting to see that the decision in *Eba* is very similar to that of the Court of Appeal in *Cart* (below). One suspects that it will be for the Supreme Court to ensure a harmonised answer in a joined appeal with both cases being considered so that there be no nuances of distinction which would give rise to Tribunal venue forum shopping.

85.24 *Cart* (Court of Appeal)

An appeal by Mr Cart to the Court of Appeal ([2010] EWCA Civ 859: Sedley, Richards LJJ & Sir Scott Baker) was unanimously dismissed. The court accepted that the TCEA 2007 could not impliedly exclude judicial review by the use of the 'superior court of record' formula, and that 'the name "superior court of record" is not a reliable guide, let alone a definiens, of courts which are so immune' (Laws LJ at [56]): at [17]. However, the Secretary of State accepted on the appeal that the Upper Tribunal was not the alter ego of the High Court, not least because it stands in the shoes of the old tribunals, arguing instead that Parliament took a policy decision to place the Tribunal wholly beyond judicial review: at [19]. The Court did not accept that, as Laws LJ had not. The Upper Tribunal has had to be given certain powers akin to those of the High Court precisely because it is not co-ordinate with the High Court: at [20]. The remaining issue for the court was when judicial review of the Upper Tribunal could lie.

85.25 The scope of judicial review is, in the eyes of the Court of Appeal, a matter of law. It was correct of the Court of Appeal in *R (Sivasubramaniam) v Wandsworth County Court* [2002] EWCA Civ 1738; [2003] 1 WLR 475 at [56] to permit judicial review of a lower court against a refusal of permission 'on the ground of jurisdictional error in the narrow, pre-*Anisminic* sense, or procedural irregularity of such a kind as to constitute a denial of the applicant's right to a fair hearing.' The court in *Cart* approved that statement (at [26]) in the following way:

> 'The rightness of this reservation is not in question. To permit a lower court or tribunal to embark on an adjudication which Parliament had given it no authority to embark on would be a dereliction of the High Court's duty. So would standing by in the face of evidence that it had denied a party the fair hearing to which everyone is entitled, whether because of actual or ostensible bias or because of some fundamentally unfair procedural step: forms of challenge to which judicial review is in fact peculiarly well suited since, unlike appeal, it is able to investigate and establish the relevant facts.'

85.26 The core of the reasoning of the Court of Appeal is seen at [35]–[37]:

> '35. Judicial policy in this context can and should correspond with legal principle. It seems to us that there are two principles which need to be reconciled in order to arrive at a proper judicial policy. One is the relative autonomy with which Parliament has invested the tribunals as a whole and the UT in particular. The other is the constitutional role of the High Court as the guardian of standards of legality and due process from which the UT, for reasons we have given, is not exempt. Although central government has opposed this appeal, its interest in ensuring that departures from legality and due process do not occur is at least as great as that of private individuals.
>
> 36. It seems to us that there is a true jurisprudential difference between an error of law made in the course of an adjudication which a tribunal is authorised to conduct and the conducting of an adjudication without lawful authority. Both are justiciable before the UT if committed by the FTT, but if committed by the UT will go uncorrected unless judicial review lies. The same of course is true of errors of law within jurisdiction; but these, in our judgment, reside within the principle that a system of law, while it can guarantee to be fair, cannot guarantee to be infallible. Outright excess of jurisdiction by the UT and denial by it of fundamental justice, should they ever occur, are in a different class: they represent the doing by the UT of something that Parliament cannot possibly have authorised it to do.

37. Thus if for some reason the UT made an order giving a money judgment which it had no power to give, with the possibility of enforcement under its s.25 powers, it would be inimical to the rule of law if the High Court could not step in, should the appellate system for some reason not do so. Similarly if a member of the UT were to sit when ineligible or disqualified by a pecuniary interest, or if the UT conducted a hearing so unfairly as to render its decision a nullity, the High Court ought to be able to quash the determination. We do not mean this list to be exhaustive but to be illustrative of the kind of error, rare as it will be, which would take the UT outside the range of its decision-making authority. Such a division is, we consider, one of legal principle which can properly form the basis of judicial policy. It applies only to the UT, since it is the role of the UT itself to correct errors of every kind, including outright excesses of jurisdiction and fundamental denials of justice, in the FTT.'

85.27 The court moved away from the suggestion of Dyson LJ in *Wiles v Social Security Commissioner* [2010] EWCA Civ 258 that judicial review of the Commissioners should extend beyond the narrow *Sivasubramaniam* categories and include issues of general public importance (see at [48]) because the new TCEA 2007 structure provided an internal appeal system with recourse on second appeal principles to the higher appellate courts. Mr Cart's pleaded error of law did not fall within the exceptional categories and so the appeal failed.

85.28 *Eba* (Inner House)

The judgment of the Inner House of the Court of Session in *Eba* was handed down on 10 September 2010: [2010] CSIH 78. The timing of this Handbook has meant that only a cursory summary can be made here, but the judgment is an important one. In the eyes of Scottish law, the Inner House held that the Upper Tribunal was a Tribunal and not a court (at [47]) and that any suggestion that the Court of Session was automatically excluded from reviewing the Upper Tribunal was to be rejected (at [54]).

85.29 The decision of Lord Glennie in the Outer House had been that judicial review was available in certain exceptional circumstances only. The Inner House overturned that approach and declined to take significant guidance from the intricacies of the English case on jurisdiction, which it considered to be 'a delimitation by the English courts on policy grounds of the circumstances in which the High Court will entertain judicial review' (at [60]). It commented that if 'Parliament wishes to exclude or restrict the supervisory jurisdiction of the Court of Session in particular circumstances, then it should legislate expressly to that effect' (at [60]). Noting the concerns of Lord Glennie about immigration and asylum cases the Inner House held that distinguishing between different Chambers of the Upper Tribunal was inappropriate and that they were 'not satisfied that, for the purposes of the availability or not of judicial review, any such distinction can properly be made' (at [61]). The concerns of the Outer House were an argument in themselves that judicial review should run against all Upper Tribunal decisions.

85.30 The Inner House decision is closely anchored to Scottish case law and the historical evolution of judicial review in the Court of Session. However, in declining to apply some sort of artificial distinction between types of error of law – and accepting the applicability and correctness of *Anisminic* in Scottish law (at [45] and see *Brown v Hamilton District Court* 1983 SC (HL) 1, 42 per Lord Fraser) – the Inner House has provided a useful stand of principle to be compared with that of the Court of Appeal in *Cart*.

85.31 *Comment*

The decision of the Court of Appeal in *Cart* is extremely practically important. It significantly restricts the ability of individuals unhappy with a decision of the Upper Tribunal to do anything about it, and the narrow second appeal criteria imposed for appeals to the Court of Appeal will often not be sufficient where, for example, the Upper Tribunal is said to have applied an established principle incorrectly. The court itself was evidently aware of the potential for injustice in particularly sensitive cases, and its judgment is notably hesitant and cavilled, strongly hinting that the point may be revisited in future cases (at [21] and [45]). It does not take much reading between the lines to see that the concern is primarily about precisely the same type of case that concerned Lord Glennie in *Eba*: immigration and asylum cases (see the reference to preserving judicial review in asylum cases in *Sivasubramaniam* at [52] cited in *Cart* at [25]). But as Dyson LJ pointed out in *Wiles*, social security involves fundamental rights too and it will be deeply unsatisfactory if different parts of the Tribunal structure are dealt with in different ways.

85.32 The distinction drawn in all three of the judgments addressed above between 'ordinary' judicial review and judicial review in exceptional circumstances only is undoubtedly based on some authority. *Sivasubramaniam*, *Wiles*, *R v Cripps, ex p Muldoon* [1984] QB 68, 87 per Goff LJ and *R (Sinclair Gardens Investments (Kensington) Ltd) v Lands Tribunal* [2005] EWCA Civ 1305; [2006] 3 All ER 650 at [56]-[57] per Neuberger LJ all support, and possibly bound, the Court of Appeal in *Cart*, although some cases (such as *R v Secretary of State for Social Services, ex p Connolly* [1986] 1 WLR 421) appear to permit much wider judicial review.

85.33 However, the approach taken in these cases is, with respect, fundamentally flawed. The courts have – and one sees it quite openly in the Court of Appeal in *Cart* – resurrected a distinction between different types of error of law that every law student thinks was buried in *Anisminic Ltd v Foreign Compensation Commission* [1969] 2 AC 147. That case established that there was no such thing, in relation to a decision-maker, between errors of law within jurisdiction and errors of law going to jurisdiction. All errors of law could be corrected by judicial review. True, *Anisminic* itself purported to be maintaining the distinction, but it was clarified by Lord Diplock in *Re Racal Communications Ltd* [1981] AC 374 and *O'Reilly v Mackman* [1983] 2 AC 237 and confirmed in *R v Hull University Visitor, ex p Page* [1993] AC 682 by Lord Browne-Wilkinson (although in *Page* itself the position of the University Visitor was considered to be so well-established in case law that there was no review for error within jurisdiction). *Anisminic* of course directly concerned a tribunal, and the position of inferior courts has always been unclear. A distinction might be drawn: Parliament intended by the overall mechanism of the TCEA 2007 for the Upper Tribunal to finally determine issues of law, subject to limited appeal rights, whereas a tribunal which is primarily a fact-finder cannot be expected to be the final arbiter of the law. The appellate structure of the Upper Tribunal is important. The personnel staffing the Upper Tribunal is, with respect, much less convincing a factor; High Court judges may sit on some Upper Tribunal hearings, including most of the judicial review cases (probably), but it is not necessarily so and the vast majority of Upper Tribunal judges are not of that seniority.

85.34 The re-emergence of pre-*Anisminic* error is both unjustified and undesirable, as the Inner House has recognised. It is a recipe for confusion in a system which is designed to bring clarity. The principle of *Anisminic* is vital. Judicial review should lie for all errors of law, be it procedural unfairness, irrationality, or simple illegality, or it should lie for none. Removing the right of judicial review completely is not a positive outcome – Tribunal justice will have the perhaps unfair image of being a little 'cheap and easy', and without the ability of correction injustice may follow – although the Supreme Court has been willing to take a pro-tribunal and anti-High Court approach where the legislation is clear enough: see *R (A) v B* [2009] UKSC 12; [2010] 2 WLR 1 (upholding the Investigatory Powers Tribunal as the sole arena for redress under the Human Rights Act 1998 in cases against the intelligence services, despite the case not being about investigatory powers). It would be preferable for judicial review to remain available, and not just against the UTIAC, with the consequential control mechanism that appeals ought to have been pursued where available before review and that the High Court ought to be more willing to refuse permission in a borderline case than where the review was of an administrative body. The greater likelihood of refusal of permission – and consequent costs orders which will usually flow from that under *Mount Cook Land Ltd v Westminster City Council* [2003] EWCA Civ 1346; [2004] 2 P&CR 22; [2004] 2 Costs LR 211 – ought to be sufficient deterrence against undermining the Tribunal structure. One must accept that some control mechanisms, such as the need for permission, do not apply in Scotland, but this has not generally led the Court of Session to be overwhelmed with judicial review cases.

85.35 The House of Lords has spent the 40 years since *Anisminic* strongly approving it as the guiding principle of public law jurisdiction. It is strongly to be hoped that permission will be granted, along with an appeal in *Eba*, by the Supreme Court so that the whole TCEA 2007 regime can receive clear guidance in both jurisdictions, and that *Anisminic's* destruction of unhelpful and distracting distinctions can be reaffirmed once again.

86 Upper Tribunal Procedural Rules

See also **Procedural rules.**

STATUTORY INSTRUMENT

86.1 Proceedings before the Upper Tribunal are governed by the Upper Tribunal Rules. The Upper Tribunal Rules are reproduced at Appendix 8. See also **Upper Tribunal**. The Upper Tribunal Rules do not cover proceedings in the Lands Chamber (see **Lands Chamber**).

STRUCTURE

86.2 The Upper Tribunal Rules are broadly similar in structure to the model rules of the First-tier Tribunal Chambers (ie, other than the Immigration and Asylum Chamber). However, a number of modifications and amendments have been made, particularly to deal with appeals from the Immigration and Asylum Chamber. The Upper Tribunal Rules are split into seven parts: Part 1 ('Introduction'), Part 2 ('General powers and provisions'), Part 3 ('Procedure for cases in the Upper Tribunal'), Part 4 ('Judicial review proceedings in the Upper Tribunal'), Part 5 ('Hearings'), Part 6 ('Decisions') and Part 7 ('Correcting, setting aside, reviewing and appealing decisions of the Upper Tribunal'), as well as three Schedules with additional procedural rules for specific types of case.

CONTENT

86.3 Parts 1 and 2 of the Upper Tribunal Rules are similar in content to those of the Chambers of the First-tier Tribunal. The additions are: Upper Tribunal Rules, r 18, which covers legal aid (which is not ordinarily available for hearings before First-tier Tribunals, because it is thought that users can generally represent themselves before a Tribunal which will question the user to get the relevant information (although immigration and mental health cases are obvious exceptions were representation is thought desirable); Upper Tribunal Rules, r 19, which covers confidentiality in child support or child trust fund cases and is similar in content to SEC Rules, r 19; and Upper Tribunal Rules, r 20, which concerns the power to pay expenses and allowances in certain cases. The Upper Tribunal also has the power to stay or suspend a decision which is being appealed to it, pending the appeal, where the existing primary legislation provides in any terms for such a right. The procedure to be followed in such a case, with specific mention of transport cases (see **Transport cases**), is set out in Upper Tribunal Rules, r 20A.

86.4 Under Upper Tribunal Rules, r 10, the Upper Tribunal may make costs orders:

- to the extent and in the circumstances that the tribunal from which the proceedings were transferred or referred by or are on appeal from had the power to make an order in respect of costs (Upper Tribunal Rules, r 10(1)(b));

- in proceedings transferred by or on appeal from the Tax Chamber of the First-tier Tribunal (Upper Tribunal Rules, r 10(1)(a));
- in judicial review proceedings (Upper Tribunal Rules, r 10(3)(a));
- if it considers that a wasted costs order under the TCEA 2007, s 29(4) is appropriate (see below) (Upper Tribunal Rules, r 10(3)(c));
- if it considers that a party or its representative has acted unreasonably in bringing, defending or conducting the proceedings (Upper Tribunal Rules, r 10(3)(d));
- if, in a financial services case, it considers that the decision in respect of which the reference was made was unreasonable (Upper Tribunal Rules, r 10(3)(e));
- in a national security appeal, if it considers a wasted costs order is appropriate, or there has been unreasonable conduct; if, where there has been a certificate it may order costs against the Minister when the certificate has been quashed or withdrawn; and if where the case is an application for a certificate a costs order may be made against any party losing the appeal to the Upper Tribunal in whole or in part (see Upper Tribunal Rules, r 10(1)(aa) and (1A)).

86.5 Part 3 concerns the pre-hearing procedural steps for appeals and references to the Upper Tribunal (see **Appeals and references to the Upper Tribunal**). Upper Tribunal Rules, r 21 sets out the circumstances in which an application may be made to the Upper Tribunal for permission to appeal, the timing of the application and its form and content. The Upper Tribunal's obligations in deciding the application are contained in Upper Tribunal Rules, r 22. Upper Tribunal Rules, r 23 prescribes the form, content and timing of the notice of appeal, which is provided to the Upper Tribunal after permission to appeal has been received, while Upper Tribunal Rules, r 24 concerns the response to the notice and r 25 provides for the appellant's reply. Upper Tribunal Rules, r 26 deals with the procedure for references under the Forfeiture Act 1982, s 4. Upper Tribunal Rules, r 26A makes provision for proceedings transferred to the Upper Tribunal, and cases begun directly in the Upper Tribunal.

86.6 Part 4 concerns judicial review proceedings in the Upper Tribunal (see **Judicial review in the Upper Tribunal** and **Judicial review procedure in the Upper Tribunal**). Upper Tribunal Rules, r 27 clarifies that Part 4 applies to judicial review proceedings transferred from a court. Thereafter, the content of this part is broadly similar to the analogous procedural rules in the High Court in CPR Part 54: Upper Tribunal Rules, r 28 governs applications to the Upper Tribunal for permission to bring judicial review proceedings; Upper Tribunal Rules, r 29 provides for acknowledgment of service; Upper Tribunal Rules, r 30 provides for decisions on permission or summary dismissal and reconsideration; Upper Tribunal Rules, r 31 concerns responses; Upper Tribunal Rules, r 32 stipulates that applicants may not rely on additional grounds to those at the permission stage without the Upper Tribunal's consent; and Upper Tribunal Rules, r 33 empowers each party (and, with the Upper Tribunal's permission, any other party) to make representations.

86.7 Part 5 ('Hearings') and Part 6 ('Decisions') mirror very closely the equivalent provisions in the First-tier Tribunal rules of procedure, with additional provisions for immigration and asylum cases.

86.8 Part 7 ('Correcting, setting aside, reviewing and appealing Tribunal decisions') (see **Appeals from the Upper Tribunal**) is similar in content to Part 4 of the procedural rules of the first-tier tribunal, save that there is no rule providing for a power to treat an application under this part as a different type of application and there is a separate rule (Upper Tribunal Rules, r 47) providing for review of questions referred under Upper Tribunal Rules, r 26 (ie, references under the Forfeiture Act 1982, s 4). The time limit for applying for permission to appeal is ordinarily one month from the decision of the Upper Tribunal, but different time limits apply in a number of types of case.

87 War Pensions and Armed Forces Compensation Chamber

COMPOSITION AND LOCATION

87.1 The WPAFCC is, like the Upper Tribunal and other Chambers of the First-tier Tribunals, presided over by the Senior President. The WPAFCC itself has a Chamber President. The WPAFCC comprises judges and other members, in accordance with the TCEA 2007, s 4.

87.2 The WPAFCC has hearing centres in Birmingham, Cardiff, Leeds, London, Manchester, North Shields, Plymouth and Taunton.

JURISDICTION AND POWERS

87.3 The WPAFCC is one of the Chambers that collectively comprise the First-tier Tribunal (see **First-tier Tribunal** and **Chambers**).

87.4 The WPAFCC has, by the First-tier Tribunal and Upper Tribunal (Chambers) Order 2008, SI 2008/2684, art 4 been assigned all functions relating to appeals under the War Pensions (Administrative Provisions) Act 1919 and the Pensions Appeal Tribunals Act 1943. Thus the WPAFCC hears appeals from decisions of the Service Personnel and Veterans Agency ('SPVA') in relation to the War Pensions Scheme and the Armed Forces Compensation Scheme.

87.5 The WPAFCC may hear appeals on both fact and law. Matters appealed to the WPAFCC include: entitlement to a war pension or an award under the Armed Forces Compensation Scheme; the assessment of the percentage of disablement awarded; the assessment of eligibility for a supplementary allowance and the rate awarded for a supplementary allowance; and various other decisions made by SPVA such as the commencing date of awards, changes in rates, withholding of pension or recoveries of pension, etc.

PROCEDURAL RULES

87.6 Proceedings before the WPAFCC are governed by the Tribunal Procedure (First–tier Tribunal) (War Pensions and Armed Forces Compensation Chamber) Rules 2008, SI 2008/2686 ('WPAFCC Rules') as amended. The WPAFCC Rules are reproduced at Appendix 6. See **War Pensions and Armed Forces Compensation Chamber procedural rules**.

88 War Pensions and Armed Forces Compensation Chamber Procedural Rules

See also **Procedural rules**.

STATUTORY INSTRUMENT

88.1 Proceedings before the WPAFCC are governed by the WPAFCC Rules. The WPAFCC Rules are reproduced at Appendix 7. For the jurisdiction of the WPAFCC see **War Pensions and Armed Forces Compensation Chamber**.

STRUCTURE

88.2 The WPAFCC Rules are similar in structure and content to the rules of the other Chambers of the First-tier Tribunal, comprising the usual four parts ('Introduction', 'General powers and provisions', 'Proceedings before the Tribunal' and 'Correcting, setting aside, reviewing and appealing Tribunal decisions').

APPEALING TO THE WPAFCC

See **Bringing proceedings in the First-tier Tribunal**.

Time for making an appeal

88.3 An appellant must start proceedings by sending or delivering a notice of appeal to the maker of the decision against which he wishes to appeal, so that it is received by the decision-maker within three months after the date on which written notice of the decision was sent to the appellant (for proceedings under the Pensions Appeal Tribunals Act 1943, s 5(1)) or within six months after the same date (for other cases under the Pensions Appeal Tribunals Act 1943) (WPAFCC Rules, r 21(1)). The Pensions Appeal Tribunals Act 1943, s 5(1) concerns appeals against interim assessments of the extent of disablement.

88.4 If the appellant provides the notice of appeal to the decision maker outside of the prescribed time limit, the notice of appeal may include reasons why the notice of appeal was not provided in time (WPAFCC Rules, r 21(2)). If an appeal is not made within time, it will be treated as in time if the respondent decision maker does not object (WPAFCC Rules, r 21(3)). No appeal may be made more than 12 months out of time (WPAFCC Rules, r 21(4)) and the Tribunal has no power to extend time where it is more than 12 months late (WPAFCC Rules, r 21(7)).

Notice of appeal

88.5 A notice of appeal in WPAFCC cases must be in writing, in English or Welsh and must be signed by the appellant and must state (WPAFCC Rules, r 21(5)):

- the name and address of the appellant;

- the name and address of the appellant's representative (if any);
- an address where documents for the appellant may be sent or delivered;
- details (including the full reference) of the decision being appealed; and
- the grounds on which the appellant intends to rely.

Referral, review and response by the decision-maker

88.6 The decision-maker must refer the case to the Tribunal immediately if the appeal has been made out of time and the decision-maker objects to treating it as having been made in time or if he considers that the appeal is more than 12 months out of time (WPAFCC Rules, r 21(6)). The purpose of referring a 12 months out of time case to the Tribunal is somewhat limited, given the complete bar on the Tribunal of extending time. The Tribunal will be able to assess whether or not time was correctly calculated, but more usually it will be simply rubber-stamping that nothing can be done, which is a rather procedurally long-winded way of achieving nothing very much.

88.7 The decision-maker may revise his decision and the proceedings will continue against the revised decision if the appellant makes representations to the Tribunal within 42 days of receipt of the revised decision (WPAFCC Rules, r 22(1)). The proceedings will lapse if the appellant, having received the revised decision, informs the Tribunal that he no longer wishes to proceed or fails to make any representations within the 42 day time limit (unless the appellant has no representations to make and informs the Tribunal accordingly) (WPAFCC Rules, r 22(2), (3)).

88.8 The decision-maker must send a response to the proceedings to the Tribunal as soon as is reasonably practicable after the date of the receipt of the notice of appeal (WPAFCC Rules, r 23(1)).

88.9 A response must state (WPAFCC Rules, r 23(2)):

- the name and address of the decision-maker;
- the name and address of the decision-maker's representative (if any);
- an address where documents for the decision-maker may be sent or delivered;
- the names and addresses of any other respondents and their representatives (if any);
- whether the decision-maker opposes the appellant's case and, if so, any grounds for such opposition; and
- any further information or documents required by a practice direction or direction.

88.10 The decision-maker may include in the response a submission as to whether it would be appropriate for the case to be dealt with without a hearing (WPAFCC Rules, r 23(3)).

88.11 The decision-maker must provide with the response (WPAFCC Rules, r 23(4)):

- a copy of any written record of the decision under challenge and any statement of reasons for that decision;

- copies of all documents relevant to the case in the decision-maker's possession, unless a practice direction or direction states otherwise; and
- a copy of the notice of appeal, any documents provided by the appellant with the notice of appeal and (if they have not otherwise been provided to the First-tier Tribunal) the name and address of the appellant's representative (if any).

88.12 The decision-maker must provide a copy of the response and any accompanying documents to each other party at the same time as it provides the response to the First-tier Tribunal (WPAFCC Rules, r 23(5)). The appellant and any other respondent may make written submissions and supply further documents in reply to the response (WPAFCC Rules, r 23(6)) within one month after the date on which the decision-maker sent them the response (WPAFCC Rules, r 23(7)).

HEARINGS IN THE WPAFCC

See **Hearings**.

88.13 The First-tier Tribunal must hold a hearing before making a decision which disposes of proceedings unless all parties consent to, or do not object to, the matter being decided without a hearing and the Tribunal considers that it is able to decide the matter without a hearing (WPAFCC Rules, r 25(1)).

88.14 Unlike in other Chambers of the First-tier Tribunal (eg, the Social Entitlement Chamber), if the WPAFCC makes a decision which disposes of proceedings without a hearing, the rules do not provide for an entitlement for the Tribunal to reconsider the decision at a hearing. Rule 25 does not apply to the Tribunal reviewing its decision following an application for permission to appeal (WPAFCC Rules, r 25(2)).

88.15 The Tribunal must give the parties at least 14 days' notice of the hearing, unless the parties consent to a shorter period or the case is urgent or exceptional (WPAFCC Rules, r 27(2)).

88.16 All hearings must be held in public unless the Tribunal directs otherwise (WPAFCC Rules, r 28).

88.17 The Tribunal may proceed with a hearing in the absence of a party if it is satisfied that the party was notified, or reasonable steps to notify were taken, and that it is in the interests of justice to proceed (WPAFCC Rules, r 29).

APPEALS FROM THE WPAFCC

88.18 Appeals from the WPAFCC lie to the Administrative Appeals Chamber of the Upper Tribunal (see **Administrative Appeals Chamber** and **Upper Tribunal**).

Time for making an appeal

88.19 An application for permission to appeal must be made in writing to the First-tier Tribunal (WPAFCC Rules, r 36(1)) within 42 days of the latest of the dates that the First-tier Tribunal sends (as applicable): (i) written reasons for its decisions; (ii) notification of amended reasons for, or correction of, the decision following a review; or (iii) notification that an application to set aside the decision was unsuccessful (WPAFCC Rules, r 36(2)).

88.20 If the party seeking to appeal sends or delivers the application out of time or by any extension of time, the application must include a request for an extension of time and the reason why the application notice was not provided in time and the Tribunal must not admit the application unless it extends time (WPAFCC Rules, r 36(4)).

Application for permission

88.21 An application for permission to appeal must (WPAFCC Rules, r 36(5)):

- identify the decision of the First-tier Tribunal to which it relates;
- identify the alleged error or errors of law in the decision; and
- state the result the party making the application is seeking.

88.22 If an application is made when the Tribunal has not given a written statement of reasons for its decision (WPAFCC Rules, r 36(6)):

- if no application for a written statement of reasons has been made to the Tribunal, the application for permission must be treated as such an application;
- unless the Tribunal decides to give permission, the application is not to be treated as an application for permission to appeal; and
- if an application for a written statement of reasons has been, or is, refused because of a delay in making the application, the Tribunal must only admit the application for permission if the Tribunal considers that it is in the interests of justice to do so.

Consideration by the First-tier Tribunal

(see **Review, correction and setting aside of Tribunal decisions**).

88.23 On receiving an application for permission to appeal, the First-tier Tribunal must first consider whether to review its own decision (WPAFCC Rules, r 37(1)), taking into account the overriding objective (see **Overriding objective**). If the Tribunal decides not to review the decision, or reviews the decision and decides to take no action in relation to it, the Tribunal must then consider whether to give permission to appeal (WPAFCC Rules, r 37(2)).

88.24 The First-tier Tribunal must send a record of its decision to the parties as soon as practicable (WPAFCC Rules, r 37(3)). If permission is refused, the First-tier Tribunal must send with the record of its decision: (i) a statement of its reasons; and (ii) notification of the right to apply to the Upper Tribunal and the procedure and time limits for making such an application (WPAFCC Rules, r 37(4)). This also applies in respect of any grounds on which permission was refused, if permission was granted on limited grounds only (WPAFCC Rules, r 37(5)).

88.25 In relation to renewing the application for permission before the Upper Tribunal, see **Appeals from the First-tier Tribunal** and **Appeals and references to the Upper Tribunal**.

89 Withdrawal of Proceedings

89.1 Withdrawal of proceedings is dealt with usually dealt with by r 17 of the Chamber's procedural rules. Reinstatement of withdrawn proceedings is dealt with below.

89.2 Parties should be aware that unreasonable conduct which later results in a case being withdrawn may be penalised in costs (see **Costs**).

WITHDRAWING PROCEEDINGS IN THE FIRST-TIER TRIBUNAL

Withdrawing proceedings in the GRC

89.3 The procedural requirements for withdrawing proceedings in the GRC are the same as those that apply in the other Chambers. A party wishing to withdraw proceedings started in the GRC may do so by giving notice to the Tribunal. Such notice may be given either at any time before a hearing to consider a disposal of the proceedings (or, if the Tribunal disposes of the proceedings without a hearing, before that disposal) or orally at a hearing (Tribunal Procedure (First-tier Tribunal) (General Regulatory Chamber) Rules 2009 ('GRC Rules'), r 17(1)). If the former, the party must send to the Tribunal a written notice of withdrawal (GRC Rules, r 17(1)(a)). Notice of withdrawal will not take effect until the Tribunal consents to the withdrawal (GRC Rules, r 17(2)). The Tribunal must notify each party in writing of a withdrawal under TC Rules, r 17 (GRC Rules, r 17(5)).

89.4 In the case of the withdrawal of a reference from an ethical standards officer (see **Local authority standards cases**) the provisions of the Case Tribunals (England) Regulations 2008, SI 2008/2938, reg 5 apply instead (GRC Rules, r 17(1)). That regulation provides as follows:

> (1) Subject to any provision in Tribunal Procedure Rules relating to the withdrawal of proceedings, an ethical standards officer who has referred a matter to the president of the First-tier Tribunal under section 64(3)(b) or 65(4) of the Act may withdraw that reference if—
>
> (a) the circumstances are as mentioned in any of sub-paragraphs (a) to (c) of paragraph (2); and
>
> (b) the requirements of paragraph (3) of this regulation are satisfied.
>
> (2) (a) A sentence of imprisonment (whether suspended or not) for a period of not less than three months, without the option of a fine, has been passed on the respondent.
>
> (b) The ethical standards officer is satisfied—
>
> (i) that the matter is materially less serious than appeared to be the case when it was referred to the president of the First-tier Tribunal and that as a consequence is not sufficiently serious to be determined by the First-tier Tribunal or a standards committee; or

(ii) that the pursuit of the matter would not be in the public interest.

(c) The First-tier Tribunal invites the ethical standards officer to withdraw the reference.

(3) Except in a case where the president or deputy president of the First-tier Tribunal agrees to dispense with the requirement in this paragraph, the ethical standards officer—

(a) has given 28 days notice in writing to— .

(i) the person who made the written allegation under section 57A of the Act which gave rise to the investigation;

(ii) the respondent;

(iii) the standards committee of any relevant authority concerned; and

(iv) the monitoring officer of any relevant authority concerned, that a request is to be made to the president of the First-tier Tribunal to withdraw the reference, and

(b) has considered any representations received from any person in that regard.

(5) The First-tier Tribunal shall give reasons in writing for the giving of an invitation under paragraph (2)(c).

(6) Where a reference to the president of the First-tier Tribunal is withdrawn under this regulation, the ethical standards officer shall give to each person or body to whom notice was given under paragraph (3)(a)—

(a) written notice of the withdrawal; and

(b) any written reasons given by the First-tier Tribunal in relation to the withdrawal, including any written reasons given under paragraph (5)

Withdrawing proceedings in the HESCC

89.5 A party wishing to withdraw proceedings started in the HESCC must give notice to the Tribunal. Such notice may be given either at any time before a hearing to consider a disposal of the proceedings (or, if the Tribunal disposes of the proceedings without a hearing, before that disposal) or orally at a hearing (HESCC Rules, r 17(1)). If the former, the party must send to the Tribunal a written notice of withdrawal (HESCC Rules, r 17(1)(a)). The notice will not take effect (ie, the withdrawal will not be effective) unless the Tribunal consents, except: (a) in proceedings concerning the suitability of a person to work with children or vulnerable adults; or (b) in proceedings started by a reference under the Mental Health Act 1983, ss 67 or 71(1) (HESCC Rules, r 17(2)). The Tribunal must notify each party in writing of a withdrawal under HESCC Rules, r 17 (HESCC Rules, r 17(6)).

89.6 A party which started a mental health case by making a reference to the Tribunal under the Mental Health Act 1983, ss 68,71(2) or 75(1) may not withdraw its case (HESCC Rules, r 17(3)). See **Mental health cases**.

Withdrawing proceedings in the FTTIAC

89.7 The appellant may withdraw an appeal to the FTTIAC at any time in writing to the Tribunal, or orally at a hearing. No consent is needed on the part of the IAC Rules, r 17(1)). An appeal will be treated as withdrawn if the respondent notifies the Tribunal that the decision or decisions to which the appeal relates have been withdrawn (IAC Rules, r 17(2)). The Tribunal must notify each party in writing of a withdrawal under r 17 (IAC Rules, r 17(3)). If the appellant dies before the appeal is heard the Tribunal will consider the appeal withdrawn unless the Tribunal considers it necessary that the personal representative of the appellant continue with the proceedings (IAC Rules, r 17(2A)).

89.8 Proceedings may also be treated as abandoned if the conditions in ss 104(4)–(4C) and (5) of the Nationality, Immigration and Asylum Act 2002 are met. For detailed guidance in these cases see IAC Rules, r 18.

Withdrawing proceedings in the SEC

89.9 The procedural requirements for withdrawing proceedings in the SEC are the same as those that apply in the HESCC. A party wishing to withdraw proceedings started in the SEC must give notice to the Tribunal. Such notice may be given either at any time before a hearing to consider a disposal of the proceedings (or, if the Tribunal disposes of the proceedings without a hearing, before that disposal) or orally at a hearing (SEC Rules, r 17(1)). If the former, the party must send to the Tribunal a written notice of withdrawal (SEC Rules, r 17(1)(a)).

89.10 Unlike in the HESCC, the Tribunal's consent is only required for the notice to take effect in two circumstances:

- in a criminal injuries compensation case (see Criminal injury compensation appeals); or
- when notice of withdrawal is given orally at a hearing (SEC Rules, r 17(2),(3)).

89.11 The Tribunal must notify each party in writing of a withdrawal under SEC Rules, r 17 (SEC Rules, r 17(6)).

Withdrawing proceedings in the WPAFCC

89.12 The procedural requirements for withdrawing proceedings in the WPAFCC are almost the same as those that apply in the HESCC and the SEC. A party wishing to withdraw proceedings started in the WPAFCC must give notice to the Tribunal. Such notice may be given either at any time before a hearing to consider a disposal of the proceedings (or, if the Tribunal disposes of the proceedings without a hearing, before that disposal) or orally at a hearing (Tribunal Procedure (First-tier Tribunal) (War Pensions and Armed Forces Compensation Chamber) Rules 2008 ('WPAFCC Rules'), r 17(1)). If the former, the party must send to the Tribunal a written notice of withdrawal (WPAFCC Rules, r 17(1)(a)). If the latter (ie, if the notice is given orally at a hearing), the notice will not take effect unless the Tribunal consents (WPAFCC Rules, r 17(2)).

Withdrawing proceedings in the TC

89.13 The procedural requirements for withdrawing proceedings in the TC are the same as those that apply in the HESCC, SEC and WPAFCC. Subject to any provision in an enactment relating to withdrawal or settlement of particular proceedings, a party wishing to withdraw proceedings started in the TC may do so by giving notice to the Tribunal. Such notice may be given either at any time before a hearing to consider a disposal of the proceedings (or, if the Tribunal disposes of the proceedings without a hearing, before that disposal) or orally at a hearing (TC Rules, r 17(1)). If the former, the party must send to the Tribunal a written notice of withdrawal (TC Rules, r 17(1)(a)). There are no requirements for the Tribunal to consent for the notice to take effect. The Tribunal must notify each party in writing of a withdrawal under TC Rules, r 17 (TC Rules, r 17(2)).

WITHDRAWING PROCEEDINGS IN THE UPPER TRIBUNAL

89.14 A party wishing to withdraw proceedings in the Upper Tribunal must give notice to the Tribunal. Such notice may be given either at any time before a hearing to consider a disposal of the proceedings (or, if the Tribunal disposes of the proceedings without a hearing, before that disposal) or orally at a hearing (Upper Tribunal Rules, r 17(1)). If the former, the party must send to the Upper Tribunal a written notice of withdrawal (Upper Tribunal Rules, r 17(1)(a)). Unless the notice relates to an application for permission to appeal, it will not take effect unless the Upper Tribunal consents to the withdrawal (Upper Tribunal Rules, r 17(2)). The Upper Tribunal must notify each party in writing of a withdrawal under r 17 (Upper Tribunal Rules, r 17(5)). There is no automatic withdrawal of the case if the respondent withdraws the relevant decision in an immigration or asylum case, despite the position in the First-tier Tribunal, although an appeal will ordinarily be statutorily withdrawn under the Nationality, Immigration and Asylum Act 2002, s 104(4A) if leave to remain is granted (see the exceptions in the 2002 Act, s 104(4B)).

89.15 A party to an asylum case or an immigration case before the Upper Tribunal must notify the Tribunal if they are aware (Upper Tribunal Rules, r 17A(1)) that:

> '(a) the appellant has left the United Kingdom;
>
> (b) the appellant has been granted leave to enter or remain in the United Kingdom;
>
> (c) a deportation order has been made against the appellant; or
>
> (d) a document listed in paragraph 4(2) of Schedule 2 to the Immigration (European Economic Area) Regulations 2006 has been issued to the appellant.'

89.16 These categories amount to the provisions of the Nationality, Immigration and Asylum Act 2002 (as amended), ss 104(4)–(4C) and (5). The Tribunal must inform the parties that the appeal is treated as abandoned or finally determined, but if the case is one under s 104(4A) the appellant has 30 days (28 if served electronically or in person) in which to inform the Tribunal that they wish to pursue the appeal. The time limits cannot be extended (Upper Tribunal Rules, r 17A(2)–(5)).

89.17 In the Lands Chamber of the Upper Tribunal, proceedings on an appeal, reference or application may only be withdrawn where all parties sign a written notice of withdrawal received by the registrar (Lands Chamber Rules, r 45(1)).

REINSTATING PROCEEDINGS

89.18 A party which has withdrawn its case from a First-tier Tribunal or the Upper Tribunal may apply to the relevant Tribunal or Upper Tribunal (as appropriate) for the case to be reinstated (HESCC Rules, r 17(4); SEC Rules, r 17(4); WPAFCC Rules, r 17(3); TC Rules, r 17(3); Upper Tribunal Rules, r 17(3)). The application for reinstatement must be made in writing and be received by the Tribunal or Upper Tribunal (as appropriate) within 28 days (one month in the SEC or the Upper Tribunal) of:

- the date that the Tribunal received the notice of withdrawal (where the notice was given in writing); or
- the date of the hearing at which the case was withdrawn orally (where the notice was given orally at the hearing) (HESCC Rules, r 17(5); SEC Rules, r 17(5); WPAFCC Rules, r 17(4); TC Rules, r 17(4); Upper Tribunal Rules, r 17(4)).

89.19 Reinstatement in the Upper Tribunal does not apply to financial services cases (see **Financial services cases**) unless it is a reference against a penalty (Upper Tribunal Rules, r 17(6)).

See above and **Time limits**.

90 Witnesses

See also **Evidence** and **Hearings** generally.

GENERAL DISCRETION OF THE TRIBUNALS AS TO WHETHER TO ADMIT EVIDENCE

90.1 Both the First-tier Tribunal and the Upper Tribunal have a broad discretion in relation to witness evidence. They can admit evidence whether or not: (i) the evidence would be admissible in a civil trial in England and Wales; or (ii) the evidence was available to a previous decision maker (Upper Tribunal Rules; GRC Rules; HESCC Rules; SEC Rules; TC Rules and WPAFCC Rules, r 15(2)(a). See also Asylum and Immigration Tribunal (Procedure) Rules 2005 ('IAC Rules'), r 51(1)). Conversely, they can exclude evidence that would otherwise be admissible where: (i) the evidence was not provided within the time allowed by a direction or a practice direction; (ii) the evidence was otherwise provided in a manner that did not comply with a direction or a practice direction; or (iii) it would otherwise be unfair to admit the evidence (r 15(2)(b)). They may also consent to a witness giving, or require any witness to give, evidence on oath, and may administer an oath for that purpose (r 15(3) and see also IAC Rules, r 51(3)).

90.2 In the Upper Tribunal in an immigration or asylum case, if a party wishes the Tribunal to consider evidence which was not before the First-tier Tribunal it must notify the Tribunal and any other party indicating the nature of the evidence and an explaining why it had not been produced below. The Tribunal will consider whether there has been unreasonable delay in deciding whether or not to admit the evidence (Upper Tribunal Rules, r 15(2A)).

90.3 In the Health, Education and Social Care Chamber of the First-tier Tribunal ('HESCC') in a special educational needs case, the Tribunal may (HESCC Rules, r 15(4)) require:

- the parents of the child, or any other person with care of the child or parental responsibility for the child (as defined in the Children Act 1989, s 3), to make the child available for examination or assessment by a suitably qualified professional person; or
- the person responsible for a school or educational setting to allow a suitably qualified professional person to have access to the school or educational setting for the purpose of assessing the child or the provision made, or to be made, for the child.

90.4 Furthermore, the Tribunal may consider a failure by a party to comply with a requirement made under the forgoing rule, in the absence of a good reason for the failure, as a failure of co-operation leading to a result adverse to the party's case (HESCC Rules, r 15(5)).

90.5 In the Lands Chamber of the Upper Tribunal evidence may be given orally and on oath or affirmation, or if the Tribunal orders or the parties consent, by affidavit. The Tribunal may require the personal attendance of any witness for examination or cross-examination (Lands Chamber Rules, r 33(1), (2)).

DIRECTIONS THE TRIBUNALS MAY GIVE IN RELATION TO EVIDENCE

90.6 Without restriction on their general powers of case management (see **Case management powers**), a First-tier Tribunal or Upper Tribunal may (Upper Tribunal Rules, GRC Rules, HESCC Rules, SEC Rules, TC Rules and WPAFCC Rules, r 15(1)) give directions as to:

- issues on which it requires evidence or submissions;
- the nature of the evidence or submissions it requires;
- whether the parties are permitted or required to provide expert evidence, and if so
- whether the parties must jointly appoint a single expert to provide such evidence (the latter sub-clause not being present in the SEC Rules);
- any limit on the number of witnesses whose evidence a party may put forward, whether in relation to a particular issue or generally;
- the manner in which any evidence or submissions are to be provided, which may include a direction for them to be given—
  - orally at a hearing; or
  - by written submissions or witness statement; and
  - the time at which any evidence or submissions are to be provided.

90.7 In the General Regulatory Chamber of the First-tier Tribunal ('GRC') the Tribunal may also give directions as to the exchange between parties of lists of documents which are relevant to the appeal, or relevant to particular issues, and the inspection of such documents; and the provision by parties of statements of agreed matters (GRC Rules, r 15(1)(a), (b)).

90.8 See IAC Rules, r 45(4) for directions which may be given in the FTTIAC.

POWERS OF THE TRIBUNALS TO SUMMON WITNESSES

90.9 A First-tier Tribunal or Upper Tribunal may, either on the application of a party or on its own initiative, (i) by summons require any person to attend as a witness at a hearing at the time and place specified or (ii) order any person to answer any questions or produce any documents in that person's possession or control which relate to any issue in the proceedings (Upper Tribunal Rules, GRC Rules, HESCC Rules, SEC Rules, TC Rules and WPAFCC Rules, r 16(1). See also IAC Rules, r 50(1)). However, the Tribunals cannot compel any person to give any evidence or produce any document that the person could not be compelled to give or produce on a trial of an action in a court of law (r 16(3) and see also IAC Rules, r 51(2)).

90.10 A summons or order made under r 16 must:

- state that the person on whom the requirement is placed may apply to the tribunal in question to vary or set aside the summons or order, if they have not had an opportunity to object to it; and
- state the consequences of failure to comply with the summons or order (r 16(4)) (except that this is r 16(6) in the Upper Tribunal Rules and the TC Rules).

90.11 The Upper Tribunal and TC Rules specifically provide a right for a person summonsed to apply to the Tribunal for it to be varied or set aside if they did not have an opportunity to object to it before it was made or issued. Any such application must be made as soon as is reasonably practicable after receiving notice of the summons (Upper Tribunal Rules and TC Rules, r 16(4), (5)).

90.12 Furthermore, to be valid, a summons requiring attendance at a hearing must, under r 16(2):

- give the person required to attend 14 days' notice of the hearing, or such shorter period as the tribunal may direct; and
- where the person is not a party, make provision for the person's necessary expenses of attendance to be paid, and state who is to pay them.

90.13 The same rule as r 16(2) is applicable by IAC Rules, r 50(2), except that no minimum notice period is required and that if a party requests the attendance of a witness that party shall remunerate the expenses of the witness.

90.14 The Tribunals, Courts and Enforcement Act 2007 ('TCEA 2007'), s 25 provides the Upper Tribunal with the powers of the High Court or Court of Session to require the attendance and examination of witnesses and the production and inspection of documents, and all other matters incidental to the Upper Tribunal's functions.

CHILD, VULNERABLE ADULT AND SENSITIVE WITNESSES

90.15 The Senior President has made a Practice Direction (First-tier and Upper Tribunal, Child, Vulnerable Adult and Sensitive Witnesses, 30 October 2008), with the agreement of the Lord Chancellor, concerning the giving of evidence in the First-tier Tribunal and Upper Tribunal by witnesses who are children, vulnerable adults (within the meaning of the Safeguarding Vulnerable Groups Act 2006) and adult witnesses the quality of whose evidence is likely to be diminished by reason of fear or distress on the witness's part in connection with giving evidence in the case ('sensitive witnesses').

90.16 A child, vulnerable adult or sensitive witness will only be required to attend as a witness and give evidence at a hearing where the tribunal in question determines that the evidence is necessary to enable the fair hearing of the case and the prospective witness's welfare would not be prejudiced by doing so (paragraph 2).

90.17 In determining whether the prospective witness's evidence is necessary, the tribunal should have regard to all the available evidence and any representations made by the parties. In determining whether the prospective witness's welfare would be prejudiced it may be appropriate for the Tribunal to invite submissions from interested persons, such as a child's parents (paragraphs 3, 4).

90.18 The tribunal may decline to issue a witness summons under its procedure rules or to permit a child, vulnerable adult or sensitive witness to give evidence where it is satisfied that the evidence is not necessary to enable the fair hearing of the case and must decline to do so where the prospective witness's welfare would be prejudiced by him or her giving evidence (paragraph 5).

90.19 Witnesses

90.19 If the tribunal does decide to issue a witness summons or to permit a child, vulnerable adult or sensitive witness to give evidence, the tribunal must consider how to facilitate the giving of any evidence by that witness. It may be appropriate for the tribunal to direct that the evidence should be given by telephone, video link or other means directed by the tribunal, or to direct that a person be appointed for the purpose of the hearing who has the appropriate skills or experience in facilitating the giving of evidence by a child, vulnerable adult or sensitive witness (paragraphs 7, 8).

Appendices

Appendix 1

SI 2009 No 1976 (L 20)

TRIBUNALS AND INQUIRIES

The Tribunal Procedure (First-tier Tribunal) (General Regulatory Chamber) Rules 2009

Version in force from 18th January 2010, showing amendments made by SI 2010/43. This document has been produced in order to assist users but its accuracy is not guaranteed and should not be relied upon. For a definitive version of the Rules, users should refer to the original statutory instruments.

Made	*16th July 2009*
Laid before Parliament	*21st July 2009*
Coming into force	*1st September 2009*

CONTENTS

PART 3

Proceedings before the Tribunal

CHAPTER 1

Before the hearing – cases other than charities cases

CHAPTER 2

Before the hearing – charities cases

CHAPTER 3

Hearings

CHAPTER 4

Decisions

PART 4

Correcting, setting aside, reviewing and appealing Tribunal decisions

After consulting in accordance with paragraph 28(1) of Schedule 5 to the Tribunals, Courts and Enforcement Act 2007(**a**), the Tribunal Procedure Committee has made the following Rules in

---

(**a**) 2007 c.15.

exercise of the power conferred by sections 9(3), 22 and 29(3) and (4) of, and Schedule 5 to, that Act.

The Lord Chancellor has allowed the Rules in accordance with paragraph 28(3) of Schedule 5 to the Tribunals, Courts and Enforcement Act 2007.

PART 1
Introduction

Citation, commencement, application and interpretation

1.—(1) These Rules may be cited as the Tribunal Procedure (First-tier Tribunal) (General Regulatory Chamber) Rules 2009 and come into force on 1st September 2009.

(2) These Rules apply to proceedings before the Tribunal which have been allocated to the General Regulatory Chamber by the First-tier Tribunal and Upper Tribunal (Chambers) Order 2008(**a**).

(3) In these Rules—

"the 2007 Act" means the Tribunals, Courts and Enforcement Act 2007;

"appellant" means a person who—

(a) commences Tribunal proceedings, whether by making an appeal, an application, a claim, a complaint, a reference or otherwise; or

(b) is added or substituted as an appellant under rule 9 (addition, substitution and removal of parties);

"charities case" means an appeal or application in respect of a decision, order or direction of the Charity Commission, or a reference under Schedule 1D of the Charities Act 1993;

"document" means anything in which information is recorded in any form, and an obligation under these Rules or any practice direction or direction to provide or allow access to a document or a copy of a document for any purpose means, unless the Tribunal directs otherwise, an obligation to provide or allow access to such document or copy in a legible form or in a form which can be readily made into a legible form;

"General Regulatory Chamber" means the General Regulatory Chamber of the First-tier Tribunal established by the First-tier Tribunal and Upper Tribunal (Chambers) Order 2008;

"hearing" means an oral hearing and includes a hearing conducted in whole or in part by video link, telephone or other means of instantaneous two-way electronic communication;

"notice of appeal" means a document which starts proceedings;

"party" means—

(a) a person who is an appellant or a respondent;

(b) if the proceedings have been concluded, a person who was an appellant or a respondent when the Tribunal finally disposed of all issues in the proceedings;

"practice direction" means a direction given under section 23 of the 2007 Act;

"respondent" means—

(a) in proceedings appealing against or challenging a decision, direction or order, the person who made the decision, direction or order appealed against or challenged;

(b) a person against whom an appellant otherwise brings proceedings; or

---

(**a**) SI 2008/2684. Article 5B was inserted by the First-tier Tribunal and Upper Tribunal (Chambers) (Amendment No.3) Order 2009 (SI 2009/1590).

(c) a person added or substituted as a respondent under rule 9 (addition, substitution and removal of parties);

"transport case" means proceedings under the Road Traffic Act 1988(**a**), the Road Traffic Offenders Act 1988(**b**), the Greater London Authority Act 1999(**c**), the Postal Services Act 2000(**d**), the Vehicle Drivers (Certificates of Professional Competence) Regulations 2007(**e**) and the European Communities (Recognition of Professional Qualifications) Regulations 2007(**f**);

"Tribunal" means the First-tier Tribunal.

Overriding objective and parties' obligation to co-operate with the tribunal

2.—(1) The overriding objective of these Rules is to enable the Tribunal to deal with cases fairly and justly.

(2) Dealing with a case fairly and justly includes—

(a) dealing with the case in ways which are proportionate to the importance of the case, the complexity of the issues, the anticipated costs and the resources of the parties;

(b) avoiding unnecessary formality and seeking flexibility in the proceedings;

(c) ensuring, so far as practicable, that the parties are able to participate fully in the proceedings;

(d) using any special expertise of the Tribunal effectively; and

(e) avoiding delay, so far as compatible with proper consideration of the issues.

(3) The Tribunal must seek to give effect to the overriding objective when it 2014

(a) exercises any power under these Rules; or

(b) interprets any rule or practice direction.

(4) Parties must—

(a) help the Tribunal to further the overriding objective; and

(b) co-operate with the Tribunal generally.

Alternative dispute resolution and arbitration

3.—(1) The Tribunal should seek, where appropriate—

(a) to bring to the attention of the parties the availability of any appropriate alternative procedure for the resolution of the dispute; and

(b) if the parties wish, and provided that it is compatible with the overriding objective, to facilitate the use of the procedure.

(2) Part 1 of the Arbitration Act 1996(**g**) does not apply to proceedings before the Tribunal.

(**a**) 1988 c. 52.
(**b**) 1988 c. 53.
(**c**) 1999 c. 29.
(**d**) 2000 c. 26.
(**e**) SI 2007/605.
(**f**) SI 2007/2781.
(**g**) 1996 c.23.

PART 2

General powers and provisions

Delegation to staff

4.—(1) Staff appointed under section 40(1) of the 2007 Act (tribunal staff and services) may, with the approval of the Senior President of Tribunals, carry out functions of a judicial nature permitted or required to be done by the Tribunal.

(2) The approval referred to at paragraph (1) may apply generally to the carrying out of specified functions by members of staff of a specified description in specified circumstances.

(3) Within 14 days after the date that the Tribunal sends notice of a decision made by a member of staff pursuant to an approval under paragraph (1) to a party, that party may apply in writing to the Tribunal for that decision to be considered afresh by a judge.

Case management powers

5.—(1) Subject to the provisions of the 2007 Act and any other enactment, the Tribunal may regulate its own procedure.

(2) The Tribunal may give a direction in relation to the conduct or disposal of proceedings at any time, including a direction amending, suspending or setting aside an earlier direction.

(3) In particular, and without restricting the general powers in paragraphs (1) and (2), the Tribunal may—

- (a) extend or shorten the time for complying with any rule, practice direction or direction, unless such extension or shortening would conflict with a provision of another enactment containing a time limit;
- (b) consolidate or hear together two or more sets of proceedings or parts of proceedings raising common issues, or treat a case as a lead case (whether under rule 18 or otherwise);
- (c) permit or require a party to amend a document;
- (d) permit or require a party or another person to provide documents, information or submissions to the Tribunal or a party;
- (e) deal with an issue in the proceedings as a preliminary issue;
- (f) hold a hearing to consider any matter, including a case management issue;
- (g) decide the form of any hearing;
- (h) adjourn or postpone a hearing;
- (i) require a party to produce a bundle for a hearing;
- (j) stay (or, in Scotland, sist) proceedings;
- (k) transfer proceedings to another court or tribunal if that other court or tribunal has jurisdiction in relation to the proceedings and—
    - (i) because of a change of circumstances since the proceedings were started, the Tribunal no longer has jurisdiction in relation to the proceedings; or
    - (ii) the Tribunal considers that the other court or tribunal is a more appropriate forum for the determination of the case;
- (l) suspend the effect of its own decision pending the determination by the Tribunal or the Upper Tribunal of an application for permission to appeal against, and any appeal or review of, that decision.

Procedure for applying for and giving directions

6.—(1) The Tribunal may give a direction on the application of one or more of the parties or on its own initiative.

(2) An application for a direction may be made—

(a) by sending or delivering a written application to the Tribunal; or

(b) orally during the course of a hearing.

(3) An application for a direction must include the reason for making that application.

(4) Unless the Tribunal considers that there is good reason not to do so, the Tribunal must send written notice of any direction to every party and to any other person affected by the direction.

(5) If a party or any other person sent notice of the direction under paragraph (4) wishes to challenge a direction which the Tribunal has given, they may do so by applying for another direction which amends, suspends or sets aside the first direction.

Failure to comply with rules, practice directions or tribunal directions

7.—(1) An irregularity resulting from a failure to comply with any provision of these Rules, a practice direction or a direction does not of itself render void the proceedings or any step taken in the proceedings.

(2) If a party has failed to comply with a requirement in these Rules, a practice direction or a direction, the Tribunal may take such action as the Tribunal considers just, which may include—

(a) waiving the requirement;

(b) requiring the failure to be remedied;

(c) exercising its power under rule 8 (striking out a party's case);

(d) exercising its power under paragraph (3); or

(e) barring or restricting a party's participation in the proceedings.

(3) The Tribunal may refer to the Upper Tribunal, and ask the Upper Tribunal to exercise its power under section 25 of the 2007 Act in relation to, any failure by a person to comply with a requirement imposed by the Tribunal—

(a) to attend at any place for the purpose of giving evidence;

(b) otherwise to make themselves available to give evidence;

(c) to swear an oath in connection with the giving of evidence;

(d) to give evidence as a witness;

(e) to produce a document; or

(f) to facilitate the inspection of a document or any other thing (including any premises).

Striking out a party's case

8.—(1) The proceedings, or the appropriate part of them, will automatically be struck out if the appellant has failed to comply with a direction that stated that failure by the appellant to comply with the direction would lead to the striking out of the proceedings or that part of them.

(2) The Tribunal must strike out the whole or a part of the proceedings if the Tribunal—

(a) does not have jurisdiction in relation to the proceedings or that part of them; and

(b) does not exercise its power under rule 5(3)(k)(i) (transfer to another court or tribunal) in relation to the proceedings or that part of them.

(3) The Tribunal may strike out the whole or a part of the proceedings if—

(a) the appellant has failed to comply with a direction which stated that failure by the appellant to comply with the direction could lead to the striking out of the proceedings or part of them;

(b) the appellant has failed to co-operate with the Tribunal to such an extent that the Tribunal cannot deal with the proceedings fairly and justly; or

(c) the Tribunal considers there is no reasonable prospect of the appellant's case, or part of it, succeeding.

(4) The Tribunal may not strike out the whole or a part of the proceedings under paragraph (2) or (3)(b) or (c) without first giving the appellant an opportunity to make representations in relation to the proposed striking out.

(5) If the proceedings, or part of them, have been struck out under paragraph (1) or (3)(a), the appellant may apply for the proceedings, or part of them, to be reinstated.

(6) An application under paragraph (5) must be made in writing and received by the Tribunal within 28 days after the date on which the Tribunal sent notification of the striking out to that party.

(7) This rule applies to a respondent as it applies to an appellant except that—

(a) a reference to the striking out of the proceedings is to be read as a reference to the barring of the respondent from taking further part in the proceedings; and

(b) a reference to an application for the reinstatement of proceedings which have been struck out is to be read as a reference to an application for the lifting of the bar on the respondent from taking further part in the proceedings.

(8) If a respondent has been barred from taking further part in proceedings under this rule and that bar has not been lifted, the Tribunal need not consider any response or other submission made by that respondent, and may summarily determine any or all issues against that respondent.

Addition, substitution and removal of parties

9.—(1) The Tribunal may give a direction adding, substituting or removing a party as an appellant or a respondent.

(2) If the Tribunal gives a direction under paragraph (1) it may give such consequential directions as it considers appropriate.

(3) Any person who is not a party may apply to the Tribunal to be added or substituted as a party.

(4) If a person who is entitled to be a party to proceedings by virtue of another enactment applies to be added as a party, and any conditions applicable to that entitlement have been satisfied, the Tribunal must give a direction adding that person as a respondent or, if appropriate, as an appellant.

Orders for costs

10.—(1) The Tribunal may make an order in respect of costs (or, in Scotland, expenses) only—

(a) under section 29(4) of the 2007 Act (wasted costs);

(b) if the Tribunal considers that a party has acted unreasonably in bringing, defending or conducting the proceedings; or

(c) where the Charity Commission [or the Information Commissioner] is the respondent and a decision, direction or order of the Charity Commission [or the Information Commissioner] is the subject of the proceedings, if the Tribunal considers that the decision, direction or order was unreasonable.

(2) The Tribunal may make an order under paragraph (1) on an application or on its own initiative.

(3) A person making an application for an order under this rule must—

(a) send or deliver a written application to the Tribunal and to the person against whom it is proposed that the order be made; and

(b) send or deliver a schedule of the costs or expenses claimed with the application.

(4) An application for an order under paragraph (1) may be made at any time during the proceedings but may not be made later than 14 days after the date on which the Tribunal sends

to the person making the application the decision notice recording the decision which finally disposes of all issues in the proceedings.

(5) The Tribunal may not make an order under paragraph (1) against a person ("the paying person") without first—

(a) giving that person an opportunity to make representations; and

(b) if the paying person is an individual, considering that person's financial means.

(6) The amount of costs or expenses to be paid under an order under paragraph (1) may be ascertained by—

(a) summary assessment by the Tribunal;

(b) agreement of a specified sum by the paying person and the person entitled to receive the costs or expenses ("the receiving person"); or

(c) assessment of the whole or a specified part of the costs or expenses incurred by the receiving person, if not agreed.

(7) Following an order under paragraph (6)(c) a party may apply—

(a) in England and Wales, to the county court for a detailed assessment of costs in accordance with the Civil Procedure Rules 1998(**a**)(**a**) on the standard basis or, if specified in the order, on the indemnity basis;

(b) in Scotland, to the Auditor of the Court of Session for the taxation of the expenses according to the fees payable in the Court of Session; or

(c) in Northern Ireland, to the county court for the costs to be taxed.

Representatives

11.—(1) A party may appoint a representative (whether legally qualified or not) to represent that party in the proceedings.

(2) If a party appoints a representative, that party must send or deliver to the Tribunal and to each other party written notice of the representative's name and address.

(3) Anything permitted or required to be done by or provided to a party under these Rules, a practice direction or a direction may be done by or provided to the representative of that party except—

(a) signing a witness statement; or

(b) sending or delivering a notice under paragraph (2), if the representative is not [a person who, for the purposes of the Legal Services Act 2007, is an authorised person in relation to an activity which constitutes the exercise of a right of audience or the conduct of litigation within the meaning of that Act(**b**)], an advocate or solicitor in Scotland or a barrister or solicitor in Northern Ireland.

(4) A person who receives due notice of the appointment of a representative—

(a) must provide to the representative any document which is required to be sent to the represented party, and need not provide that document to the represented party; and

(b) may assume that the representative is and remains authorised until receiving written notification to the contrary from the representative or the represented party.

(5) At a hearing a party may be accompanied by another person whose name and address has not been notified under paragraph (2) but who, with the permission of the Tribunal, may act as a representative or otherwise assist in presenting the party's case at the hearing.

(6) Paragraphs (2) to (4) do not apply to a person who accompanies a party under paragraph (5).

(**a**) SI 1998/3132.
[(**b**) 2007 c.29.]

Calculating time

12.—(1) An act required by these Rules, a practice direction or a direction to be done on or by a particular day must be done before 5pm on that day.

(2) If the time specified by these Rules, a practice direction or a direction for doing any act ends on a day other than a working day, the act is done in time if it is done on the next working day.

(3) In this rule "working day" means any day except a Saturday or Sunday, Christmas Day, Good Friday or a bank holiday under section 1 of the Banking and Financial Dealings Act 1971**(a)**.

Sending and delivery of documents

13.—(1) Any document to be provided to the Tribunal under these Rules, a practice direction or a direction must be—

(a) sent by prepaid post or by document exchange, or delivered by hand to the address specified for the proceedings;

(b) sent by fax to the number specified for the proceedings; or

(c) sent or delivered by such other method as the Tribunal may permit or direct.

(2) Subject to paragraph (3), if a party provides a fax number, email address or other details for the electronic transmission of documents to them, that party must accept delivery of documents by that method.

(3) If a party informs the Tribunal and all other parties that a particular form of communication, other than pre-paid post or delivery by hand, should not be used to provide documents to that party, that form of communication must not be so used.

(4) If the Tribunal or a party sends a document to a party or the Tribunal by email or any other electronic means of communication, the recipient may request that the sender provide a hard copy of the document to the recipient. The recipient must make such a request as soon as reasonably practicable after receiving the document electronically.

(5) The Tribunal and each party may assume that the address provided by a party or its representative is and remains the address to which documents should be sent or delivered until receiving written notification to the contrary.

Prevention of disclosure or publication of documents and information

14.—(1) The Tribunal may make an order prohibiting the disclosure or publication of—

(a) specified documents or information relating to the proceedings; or

(b) any matter likely to lead members of the public to identify any person whom the Tribunal considers should not be identified.

(2) The Tribunal may give a direction prohibiting the disclosure of a document or information to a person if—

(a) the Tribunal is satisfied that such disclosure would be likely to cause that person or some other person serious harm; and

(b) the Tribunal is satisfied, having regard to the interests of justice, that it is proportionate to give such a direction.

(3) If a party ("the first party") considers that the Tribunal should give a direction under paragraph (2) prohibiting the disclosure of a document or information to another party ("the second party"), the first party must—

(a) exclude the relevant document or information from any documents that will be provided to the second party; and

---

(a) 1971 c.80.

(b) provide to the Tribunal the excluded document or information, and the reason for its exclusion, so that the Tribunal may decide whether the document or information should be disclosed to the second party or should be the subject of a direction under paragraph (2).

(4) If the Tribunal gives a direction under paragraph (2) which prevents disclosure to a party who has appointed a representative, the Tribunal may give a direction that the documents or information be disclosed to that representative if the Tribunal is satisfied that—

(a) disclosure to the representative would be in the interests of the party; and

(b) the representative will act in accordance with paragraph (5).

(5) Documents or information disclosed to a representative in accordance with a direction under paragraph (4) must not be disclosed either directly or indirectly to any other person without the Tribunal's consent.

(6) The Tribunal may give a direction that certain documents or information must or may be disclosed to the Tribunal on the basis that the Tribunal will not disclose such documents or information to other persons, or specified other persons.

(7) A party making an application for a direction under paragraph (6) may withhold the relevant documents or information from other parties until the Tribunal has granted or refused the application.

(8) Unless the Tribunal considers that there is good reason not to do so, the Tribunal must send notice that a party has made an application for a direction under paragraph (6) to each other party.

(9) In a case involving matters relating to national security, the Tribunal must ensure that information is not disclosed contrary to the interests of national security.

(10) The Tribunal must conduct proceedings and record its decision and reasons appropriately so as not to undermine the effect of an order made under paragraph (1), a direction given under paragraph (2) or (6) or the duty imposed by paragraph (9).

Disclosure, evidence and submissions

15.—(1) Without restriction on the general powers in rule 5(1) and (2) (case management powers), the Tribunal may give directions as to—

(a) the exchange between parties of lists of documents which are relevant to the appeal, or relevant to particular issues, and the inspection of such documents;

(b) the provision by parties of statements of agreed matters;

(c) issues on which it requires evidence or submissions;

(d) the nature of the evidence or submissions it requires;

(e) whether the parties are permitted or required to provide expert evidence, and if so whether the parties must jointly appoint a single expert to provide such evidence;

(f) any limit on the number of witnesses whose evidence a party may put forward, whether in relation to a particular issue or generally;

(g) the manner in which any evidence or submissions are to be provided, which may include a direction for them to be given—

(i) orally at a hearing; or

(ii) by written submissions or witness statement; and

(h) the time at which any evidence or submissions are to be provided.

(2) The Tribunal may—

(a) admit evidence whether or not—

(i) the evidence would be admissible in a civil trial in [the United Kingdom]; or

(ii) the evidence was available to a previous decision maker; or

(b) exclude evidence that would otherwise be admissible where—

(i) the evidence was not provided within the time allowed by a direction or a practice direction;

(ii) the evidence was otherwise provided in a manner that did not comply with a direction or a practice direction; or

(iii) it would otherwise be unfair to admit the evidence.

(3) The Tribunal may consent to a witness giving, or require any witness to give, evidence on oath, and may administer an oath for that purpose.

Summoning or citation of witnesses and orders to answer questions or produce documents

16.—(1) On the application of a party or on its own initiative, the Tribunal may—

(a) by summons (or, in Scotland, citation) require any person to attend as a witness at a hearing at the time and place specified in the summons or citation; or

(b) order any person to answer any questions or produce any documents in that person's possession or control which relate to any issue in the proceedings.

(2) A summons or citation under paragraph (1)(a) must—

(a) give the person required to attend 14 days' notice of the hearing or such shorter period as the Tribunal may direct; and

(b) where the person is not a party, make provision for the person's necessary expenses of attendance to be paid, and state who is to pay them.

(3) No person may be compelled to give any evidence or produce any document that the person could not be compelled to give or produce on a trial of an action in a court of law in the part of the United Kingdom where the proceedings are due to be determined.

(4) A summons, citation or order under this rule must—

(a) state that the person on whom the requirement is imposed may apply to the Tribunal to vary or set aside the summons, citation or order, if they have not had an opportunity to object to it; and

(b) state the consequences of failure to comply with the summons, citation or order.

Withdrawal

17.—(1) Subject to paragraph (2)[, and, in the case of a withdrawal of a reference from an ethical standards officer, to the provisions of regulation 5 of the Case Tribunals (England) Regulations 2008(**a**)], a party may give notice of the withdrawal of its case, or any part of it

(a) at any time before a hearing to consider the disposal of the proceedings (or, if the Tribunal disposes of the proceedings without a hearing, before that disposal), by sending or delivering to the Tribunal a written notice of withdrawal; or

(b) orally at a hearing.

(2) Notice of withdrawal will not take effect unless the Tribunal consents to the withdrawal.

(3) A party who has withdrawn their case may apply to the Tribunal for the case to be reinstated.

(4) An application under paragraph (3) must be made in writing and be received by the Tribunal within 28 days after—

[(**a**) SI 2008/2938.]

(a) the date on which the Tribunal received the notice under paragraph (1)(a); or

(b) the date of the hearing at which the case was withdrawn orally under paragraph (1)(b).

(5) The Tribunal must notify each party in writing of a withdrawal under this rule.

Lead cases

18.—(1) This rule applies if—

(a) two or more cases have been started before the Tribunal;

(b) in each such case the Tribunal has not made a decision disposing of the proceedings; and

(c) the cases give rise to common or related issues of fact or law.

(2) The Tribunal may give a direction—

(a) specifying one or more cases falling under paragraph (1) as a lead case or lead cases; and

(b) staying (or, in Scotland, sisting) the other cases falling under paragraph (1) ("the related cases").

(3) When the Tribunal makes a decision in respect of the common or related issues—

(a) the Tribunal must send a copy of that decision to each party in each of the related cases; and

(b) subject to paragraph (4), that decision shall be binding on each of those parties.

(4) Within 28 days after the date on which the Tribunal sent a copy of the decision to a party under paragraph (3)(a), that party may apply in writing for a direction that the decision does not apply to, and is not binding on the parties to, a particular related case.

(5) The Tribunal must give directions in respect of cases which are stayed [(or, in Scotland, sisted)] under paragraph (2)(b), providing for the disposal of or further directions in those cases.

(6) If the lead case or cases lapse or are withdrawn before the Tribunal makes a decision in respect of the common or related issues, the Tribunal must give directions as to—

(a) whether another case or other cases are to be specified as a lead case or lead cases; and

(b) whether any direction affecting the related cases should be set aside or amended.

[Entry directions

18A.—(1) This rule applies to an appeal against a decision of, or notice issued by, the Information Commissioner.

(2) The Tribunal may give a direction ("an entry direction") requiring the occupier of any premises ("the occupier"), including a party, to permit entry to specified persons in order to allow such persons to—

(a) inspect, examine, operate or test relevant equipment;

(b) inspect, examine or test relevant materials.

(3) In paragraph (2)—

"relevant equipment" means equipment on the premises used or intended to be used in connection with the processing of personal data, or the storage, recording or deletion of other information; and

"relevant materials" means any documents and other materials on the premises connected with the processing of personal data, or the storage, recording or deletion of other information.

(4) A direction under paragraph (2) may not require a person to permit the inspection, examination or testing of any document or other materials which a person could not be compelled to produce in the trial of an action in a court of law in the part of the United Kingdom where the proceedings are due to be determined.

(5) A direction under paragraph (2) must specify the date and time at which the entry is to take place.

(6) The Tribunal must send a copy of the direction to the occupier so that it is received at least 7 days before the date specified for the entry.]

Transfer of cases to the Upper Tribunal

19.—(1) This rule applies to charities cases [and proceedings under the Data Protection Act 1998(**a**) and the Freedom of Information Act 2000(**b**) (including those Acts as applied and modified by the Privacy and Electronic Communications (EC Directive) Regulations 2003(**c**) and the Environmental Information Regulations 2004)(**d**)].

[(1A) On receiving a notice of appeal in an appeal under section 28 of the Data Protection Act 1998 or section 60 of the Freedom of Information Act 2000 (including that section as applied and modified by regulation 18 of the Environmental Information Regulations 2004) (appeals in relation to national security certificates) the Tribunal must transfer the case to the Upper Tribunal without taking further action in relation to the appeal.]

(2) [In any other case] The Tribunal may refer a case or a preliminary issue to the President of the General Regulatory Chamber with a request that the case or issue be considered for transfer to the Upper Tribunal.

(3) If a case or issue has been referred by the Tribunal under paragraph (2), the President of the General Regulatory Chamber may, with the concurrence of the President of the appropriate Chamber of the Upper Tribunal, direct that the case or issue be transferred to and determined by the Upper Tribunal.

[Power to stay or sist decision pending an appeal to, or decision by, the Tribunal

19A.—(1) The Tribunal may suspend the effect of a decision of the Gambling Commission (whether or not the decision has already taken effect) while an appeal against that decision—

(a) could be brought within the time required by these Rules; or

(b) has been brought and has not yet been finally determined or withdrawn.

(2) In an appeal against a decision of the Immigration Services Commissioner, the Tribunal may direct that while the appeal is being dealt with the decision appealed against shall have—

(a) no effect; or

(b) only such limited effect as is specified in the direction.

(3) If the Tribunal makes a direction under paragraph (2), the Tribunal must consider any application by the Immigration Services Commissioner for the cancellation or variation of the direction.

(4) The Tribunal may vary or cancel a direction made under paragraph 9(3) of Schedule 5 to the Immigration and Asylum Act 1999 (interim directions pending the decision of the Tribunal).]

Procedure for applying for a stay of a decision pending an appeal

20.—(1) This rule applies where [rule 19A or] another enactment provides in any terms for the Tribunal to stay [(or, in Scotland, sist)] or suspend, or to lift a stay [(or, in Scotland, sist)]

(**a**) 1998 c.29.
(**b**) 2000 c.36.
(**c**) SI 2003/2426.
(**d**) SI 2004/3391.

or suspension of, a decision which is or may be the subject of an appeal to the Tribunal ("the substantive decision") pending such appeal, including an enactment which provides for—

(a) an appeal to the Tribunal against a decision not to stay the effect of the substantive decision pending an appeal; or

(b) an application to the Tribunal for an order that the substantive decision shall take effect immediately.

(2) A person who wishes the Tribunal to decide whether the substantive decision should be stayed [(or, in Scotland, sisted)] suspended must make a written application to the Tribunal which must include—

(a) the name and address of the person making the application;

(b) the name and address of any representative of that person;

(c) the address to which documents for that person should be sent or delivered;

(d) the name and address of any person who will be a respondent to the appeal;

(e) details of the substantive decision and any decision as to when that decision is to take effect, and copies of any written record of, or reasons for, those decisions; and

(f) the grounds on which the person making the application relies.

(3) In the case of an appeal against a refusal by the registrar to stay [(or, in Scotland, sist)] a decision to refuse an application for registration as a driving instructor, an application under paragraph (2) must be sent or delivered to the Tribunal so that it is received within 10 days after the date on which the registrar sent notice of the refusal to the person making the application.

(4) If the Tribunal grants a stay [(or, in Scotland, sist)] or suspension following an application under this rule—

(a) the Tribunal may give directions as to the conduct of the appeal of the substantive decision; and

(b) the Tribunal may, where appropriate, grant the stay [(or, in Scotland, sist)] or suspension subject to conditions.

(5) Unless the Tribunal considers that there is good reason not to do so, the Tribunal must send written notice of any decision made under this rule to each party.

PART 3

Proceedings before the Tribunal

CHAPTER 1

Before the hearing – cases other than charities cases

Application of this Chapter

21. This Chapter applies to cases other than charities cases.

The notice of appeal

22.—(1) An appellant must start proceedings before the Tribunal by sending or delivering to the Tribunal a notice of appeal so that it is received—

(a) [if a time for providing the notice of appeal is set out in paragraph (6), within that time];

(b) otherwise, within 28 days of the date on which notice of the act or decision to which the proceedings relate was sent to the appellant.

(2) The notice of appeal must include—

(a) the name and address of the appellant;

(b) the name and address of the appellant's representative (if any);

(c) an address where documents for the appellant may be sent or delivered;

(d) the name and address of any respondent;

(e) details of the decision or act, or failure to decide or act, to which the proceedings relate;

(f) the result the appellant is seeking;

(g) the grounds on which the appellant relies; and

(h) any further information or documents required by a practice direction.

(3) If the proceedings challenge a decision, the appellant must provide with the notice of appeal a copy of any written record of that decision, and any statement of reasons for that decision that the appellant has or can reasonably obtain.

(4) If the appellant provides the notice of appeal to the Tribunal later than the time required by paragraph (1) or by any extension of time under rule 5(3)(a) (power to extend time)—

(a) the notice of appeal must include a request for an extension of time and the reason why the notice of appeal was not provided in time; and

(b) unless the Tribunal extends time for the notice of appeal under rule 5(3)(a) (power to extend time) the Tribunal must not admit the notice of appeal.

(5) When the Tribunal receives the notice of appeal [, subject to rule 19(2)(national security appeals),] it must send a copy of the notice of appeal and any accompanying documents to each respondent.

[(6) The time for providing the notice of appeal referred to in paragraph (1)(a) is as follows—

(a) in an appeal against a refusal or revocation of a licence to give driving instruction, within 14 days of the date on which notice of the decision was sent to the appellant;

(b) in an appeal under section 28(4) of the Data Protection Act 1998 or section 60(1) of the Freedom of Information Act 2000 (including that subsection as applied and modified by regulation 18 of the Environmental Information Regulations 2004), at any time during the currency of the disputed certificate to which it relates;

(c) in an appeal under section 28(6) of the Data Protection Act 1998 or section 60(4) of the Freedom of Information Act 2000 (including that subsection as applied and modified by regulation 18 of the Environmental Information Regulations 2004), within 28 days of the date on which the claim was made that the certificate applies to the information or data in question;

(d) in the case of a reference from an ethical standards officer made in accordance with sections 63(3)(b) or section 65(4) of the Local Government Act 2000(**a**), within 28 days of the completion of the report made in accordance with sections 63(3)(a) and 65(1) of that Act; or

(e) in the case of a reference from a Standards Committee under the Local Government Act 2000 within 28 days of the meeting which decided to make such a reference.]

The response

23.—(1) Each respondent must send or deliver to the Tribunal a response to the notice of appeal so that it is received—

(a) in a transport case, within 14 days after the date on which the respondent received the notice of appeal;

(b) otherwise, within 28 days after the date on which the respondent received the notice of appeal.

(2) The response must include—

(a) the name and address of the respondent;

(b) the name and address of the respondent's representative (if any);

(c) an address where documents for the respondent may be sent or delivered;

(d) any further information or documents required by a practice direction or direction; and

(e) whether the respondent would be content for the case to be dealt with without a hearing if the Tribunal considers it appropriate.

(3) The response must include a statement as to whether the respondent opposes the appellant's case and, if so, any grounds for such opposition which are not contained in another document provided with the response.

(4) If the proceedings challenge a decision, the respondent must provide with the response a copy of any written record of that decision, and any statement of reasons for that decision, that the appellant did not provide with the notice of appeal and the respondent has or can reasonably obtain.

(5) If the respondent provides the response to the Tribunal later than the time required by paragraph (1) or by any extension of time under rule 5(3)(a) (power to extend time), the response must include a request for an extension of time and the reason why the response was not provided in time.

(6) In a transport case, the Tribunal must send a copy of the response and any accompanying documents to each other party.

(7) In any other case, the respondent must send or deliver a copy of the response and any accompanying documents to each other party at the same time as it provides the response to the Tribunal.

Appellant's reply

24.—(1) The appellant may make a written submission and provide further documents in reply to a response.

(2) Any reply and accompanying documents provided under paragraph (1) must be sent or delivered to the Tribunal within 14 days after the date on which the respondent or the Tribunal sent the response to the appellant.

(3) If the appellant provides the reply to the Tribunal later than the time required by paragraph (2) or by any extension of time under rule 5(3)(a) (power to extend time) the reply must include a request for an extension of time and the reason why the reply was not provided in time.

(4) In a transport case, the Tribunal must send a copy of any reply and any accompanying documents to each other party.

(5) In any other case, the appellant must send or deliver a copy of any reply and any accompanying documents to each other party at the same time as it provides the reply to the Tribunal.

CHAPTER 2

Before the hearing – charities cases

Application of this Chapter

25. This Chapter applies to charities cases.

The notice of appeal

26.—(1) An appellant must start proceedings before the Tribunal by sending or delivering to the Tribunal a notice of appeal so that it is received—

(a) if the appellant was the subject of the decision to which the proceedings relate, within 42 days of the date on which notice of the decision was sent to the appellant; or

(b) if the appellant was not the subject of the decision to which the proceedings relate, within 42 days of the date on which the decision was published.

(2) The notice of appeal must include—

(a) the name and address of the appellant;

(b) the name and address of the appellant's representative (if any);

(c) an address where documents for the appellant may be sent or delivered;

(d) the basis on which the appellant has standing to start proceedings before the Tribunal;

(e) the name and address of any respondent;

(f) details of the decision or act, or failure to decide or act, to which the proceedings relate;

(g) the result the appellant is seeking;

(h) the grounds on which the appellant relies; and

(i) any further information or documents required by a practice direction.

(3) If the proceedings challenge a decision, the appellant must provide with the notice of appeal a copy of any written record of that decision, and any statement of reasons for that decision that the appellant has or can reasonably obtain.

(4) If the notice of appeal relates to a reference under Schedule 1D of the Charities Act 1993—

(a) if the appellant is the Charity Commission, it must send evidence of the Attorney General's consent to the reference with the notice of appeal; and

(b) on receiving the notice of appeal the Tribunal must publish details of the reference and information as to how a person likely to be affected by the reference can apply to be added as a party to the proceedings.

(5) If the appellant provides the notice of appeal to the Tribunal later than the time required by paragraph (1) or by any extension of time under rule 5(3)(a) (power to extend time)—

(a) the notice of appeal must include a request for an extension of time and the reason why the notice of appeal was not provided in time; and

(b) unless the Tribunal extends time for the notice of appeal under rule 5(3)(a) (power to extend time) the Tribunal must not admit the notice of appeal.

(6) The appellant must send or deliver a copy of the notice of appeal and any accompanying documents to the respondent at the same time as it provides the notice of appeal to the Tribunal.

The response

27.—(1) The respondent must send or deliver to the Tribunal a response to the notice of appeal so that it is received within 28 days after the date on which the respondent received the notice of appeal.

(2) The response must include—

(a) the name and address of the respondent;

(b) the name and address of the respondent's representative (if any);

(c) an address where documents for the respondent may be sent or delivered;

(d) any further information or documents required by a practice direction or direction; and

(e) whether the respondent would be content for the case to be dealt with without a hearing if the Tribunal considers it appropriate.

(3) The response must include a statement as to whether the respondent opposes the appellant's case and, if so, any grounds for such opposition which are not contained in another document provided with the response.

(4) If the proceedings challenge a decision, the respondent must provide with the response a copy of any written record of that decision, and any statement of reasons for that decision, that the appellant did not provide with the notice of appeal and the respondent has or can reasonably obtain.

(5) If the proceedings challenge a decision, the respondent must provide with the response a list of—

(a) the documents relied upon by the respondent when reaching the decision; and

(b) any other documents which the respondent considers could adversely affect its case or support the appellant's case.

(6) If the respondent provides the response to the Tribunal later than the time required by paragraph (1) or by any extension of time under rule 5(3)(a) (power to extend time), the response must include a request for an extension of time and the reason why the response was not provided in time.

(7) The respondent must send or deliver a copy of the response and any accompanying documents to each other party at the same time as it provides the response to the Tribunal.

Appellant's reply

28.—(1) The appellant may send or deliver to the Tribunal a reply to the respondent's response and any additional documents relied upon by the appellant.

(2) Any reply must be sent or delivered to the Tribunal so that it is received within 28 days after the date on which the respondent sent the response to the appellant.

(3) If the appellant provides a reply to the Tribunal later than the time required by paragraph (2) or by any extension of time under rule 5(3)(a) (power to extend time) the reply must include a request for an extension of time and the reason why the reply was not provided in time.

(4) The appellant may provide with the reply a list of documents on which the appellant relies in support of the appeal or application, and which—

(a) the appellant did not provide with the notice of appeal; and

(b) the respondent did not include in any list of documents provided under rule 27(5).

(5) The appellant must send or deliver a copy of any reply and any accompanying documents to each respondent at the same time as it provides the reply to the Tribunal.

Secondary disclosure by the respondent

29.—(1) If the appellant provides a reply under rule 28, the respondent must send or deliver to the Tribunal, so that it is received within 14 days after the date on which the respondent received the appellant's reply, a list of any further material which—

(a) might reasonably be expected to assist that appellant's case as disclosed by that appellant's reply; and.

(b) was not included in a list of documents provided by the respondent with the response.

(2) If the respondent provides the list to the Tribunal later than the time required by paragraph (1) or by any extension of time under rule 5(3)(a) (power to extend time), the response must include a request for an extension of time and the reason why the response was not provided in time.

(3) The respondent must send or deliver a copy of the list to each other party at the same time as it provides the response to the Tribunal.

Provision of copy documents

30.—(1) If a party has provided a list of documents under rule 27, 28 or 29, that party must within 7 days of receiving a request from another party—

(a) provide that other party with a copy of any document specified in the list; or

(b) make such document available to that party to read or copy.

Involvement of the Attorney General under section 2D of the Charities Act 1993

31.—(1) If the Tribunal directs that all the necessary papers in proceedings be sent to the Attorney General under section 2D(2) and (3) of the Charities Act 1993, the Attorney General must notify the Tribunal whether the Attorney General intends to intervene in the proceedings within 28 days of receiving the papers.

(2) The Attorney General may at any time notify the Tribunal that the Attorney General intends to intervene in the proceedings on the Attorney General's own initiative.

(3) If the Tribunal requests that the Attorney General argue a question in relation to the proceedings under section 2D(4)(b) of the Charities Act 1993, the Tribunal must provide to the Attorney General—

(a) a statement of the question;

(b) an account of the proceedings to date;

(c) the reasons the Tribunal considers it necessary to have the question fully argued; and

(d) copies of the documents the Tribunal considers necessary to enable the Attorney General to decide whether it is appropriate to argue the question.

(4) If the Attorney General notifies the Tribunal that the Attorney General intends to intervene in, or to argue a question in relation to, proceedings under section 2D(4) of the Charities Act 1993, the Tribunal must hold a case management hearing.

CHAPTER 3

Hearings

Decision with or without a hearing

32.—(1) Subject to paragraphs (2) and (3), the Tribunal must hold a hearing before making a decision which disposes of proceedings unless—

(a) each party has consented to the matter being determined without a hearing; and

(b) the Tribunal is satisfied that it can properly determine the issues without a hearing.

(2) This rule does not apply to a decision under Part 4 (correcting, setting aside, reviewing and appealing Tribunal decisions).

(3) The Tribunal may in any event dispose of proceedings without a hearing under rule 8 (striking out a party's case).

(4) Notwithstanding any other provision in these Rules, if the Tribunal holds a hearing to consider a preliminary issue, and following the disposal of that preliminary issue no further issue remains to be determined, the Tribunal may dispose of the proceedings without holding any further hearing.

Entitlement to attend and take part in a hearing

33.—(1) Subject to rule 35(4) (exclusion of a person from a hearing) each party is entitled to—

(a) attend any hearing that is held; and

(b) send written representations to the Tribunal and each other party prior to the hearing.

(2) The Tribunal may give a direction permitting or requesting any person to—

(a) attend and take part in a hearing to such extent as the Tribunal considers proper; or

(b) make written submissions in relation to a particular issue.

Notice of hearings

34.—(1) The Tribunal must give each person entitled, permitted or requested to attend a hearing (including any adjourned or postponed hearing) reasonable notice of the time and place of the hearing and any changes to the time and place of the hearing.

(2) The period of notice under paragraph (1) in relation to a hearing to consider disposal of the proceedings must be at least 14 days, except that the Tribunal may give shorter notice—

(a) with the parties' consent; or

(b) in urgent or exceptional circumstances.

Public and private hearings

35.—(1) Subject to the following paragraphs, all hearings must be held in public.

(2) The Tribunal may give a direction that a hearing, or part of it, is to be held in private.

(3) Where a hearing, or part of it, is to be held in private, the Tribunal may determine who is permitted to attend the hearing or part of it.

(4) The Tribunal may give a direction excluding from any hearing, or part of it—

(a) any person whose conduct the Tribunal considers is disrupting or is likely to disrupt the hearing;

(b) any person whose presence the Tribunal considers is likely to prevent another person from giving evidence or making submissions freely;

(c) any person who the Tribunal considers should be excluded in order to give effect to the requirement at rule 14(10) (prevention of disclosure or publication of documents and information); or

(d) any person where the purpose of the hearing would be defeated by the attendance of that person.

(5) The Tribunal may give a direction excluding a witness from a hearing until that witness gives evidence.

Hearings in a party's absence

36. If a party fails to attend a hearing the Tribunal may proceed with the hearing if the Tribunal—

(a) is satisfied that the party has been notified of the hearing or that reasonable steps have been taken to notify the party of the hearing; and

(b) considers that it is in the interests of justice to proceed with the hearing.

CHAPTER 4

Decisions

Consent orders

37.—(1) The Tribunal may, at the request of the parties but only if it considers it appropriate, make a consent order disposing of the proceedings and making such other appropriate provision as the parties have agreed.

(2) Notwithstanding any other provision of these Rules, the Tribunal need not hold a hearing before making an order under paragraph (1), or provide reasons for the order.

Decisions

38.—(1) The Tribunal may give a decision orally at a hearing.

(2) Subject to rule 14(10) (prevention of disclosure or publication of documents and information), the Tribunal must provide to each party as soon as reasonably practicable after making a decision which finally disposes of all issues in the proceedings (except a decision under Part 4)—

(a) a decision notice stating the Tribunal's decision;

(b) written reasons for the decision; and

(c) notification of any right of appeal against the decision and the time within which, and manner in which, such right of appeal may be exercised.

(3) The Tribunal may provide written reasons for any decision to which paragraph (2) does not apply.

PART 4

Correcting, setting aside, reviewing and appealing Tribunal decisions

Interpretation

39. In this Part—

"appeal" means the exercise of a right of appeal on a point of law under section 11 of the 2007 Act [or by any other enactment]; and

"review" means the review of a decision by the Tribunal under section 9 of the 2007 Act.

Clerical mistakes and accidental slips or omissions

40. The Tribunal may at any time correct any clerical mistake or other accidental slip or omission in a decision, direction or any document produced by it, by—

(a) sending notification of the amended decision or direction, or a copy of the amended document, to each party; and

(b) making any necessary amendment to any information published in relation to the decision, direction or document.

Setting aside a decision which disposes of proceedings

41.—(1) The Tribunal may set aside a decision which disposes of proceedings, or part of such a decision, and re-make the decision or the relevant part of it, if—

(a) the Tribunal considers that it is in the interests of justice to do so; and

(b) one or more of the conditions in paragraph (2) are satisfied.

(2) The conditions are—

(a) a document relating to the proceedings was not sent to, or was not received at an appropriate time by, a party or a party's representative;

(b) a document relating to the proceedings was not sent to the Tribunal at an appropriate time;

(c) a party, or a party's representative, was not present at a hearing related to the proceedings; or

(d) there has been some other procedural irregularity in the proceedings.

(3) A party applying for a decision, or part of a decision, to be set aside under paragraph (1) must make a written application to the Tribunal so that it is received no later than 28 days after the date on which the Tribunal sent notice of the decision to the party.

Application for permission to appeal

42.—(1) A person seeking permission to appeal must make a written application to the Tribunal for permission to appeal.

(2) An application under paragraph (1) must be sent or delivered to the Tribunal so that it is received no later than 28 days after the latest of the dates that the Tribunal sends to the person making the application—

(a) written reasons for the decision;

(b) notification of amended reasons for, or correction of, the decision following a review; or

(c) notification that an application for the decision to be set aside has been unsuccessful.

(3) The date in paragraph (2)(c) applies only if the application for the decision to be set aside was made within the time stipulated in rule 41 (setting aside a decision which disposes of proceedings) or any extension of that time granted by the Tribunal.

(4) If the person seeking permission to appeal sends or delivers the application to the Tribunal later than the time required by paragraph (2) or by any extension of time under rule 5(3)(a) (power to extend time)—

(d) the application must include a request for an extension of time and the reason why the application was not provided in time; and

(e) unless the Tribunal extends time for the application under rule 5(3)(a) (power to extend time) the Tribunal must not admit the application.

(5) An application under paragraph (1) must—

(f) identify the decision of the Tribunal to which it relates;

(g) identify the alleged error or errors of law in the decision; and

(h) state the result the party making the application is seeking.

Tribunal's consideration of application for permission to appeal

43.—(1) On receiving an application for permission to appeal the Tribunal must first consider, taking into account the overriding objective in rule 2, whether to review the decision in accordance with rule 44 (review of a decision).

(2) If the Tribunal decides not to review the decision, or reviews the decision and decides to take no action in relation to the decision, or part of it, the Tribunal must consider whether to give permission to appeal in relation to the decision or that part of it.

(3) The Tribunal must send a record of its decision to the parties as soon as practicable.

(4) If the Tribunal refuses permission to appeal it must send with the record of its decision—

(a) a statement of its reasons for such refusal; and

(b) notification of the right to make an application to the Upper Tribunal for permission to appeal and the time within which, and the method by which, such application must be made.

(5) The Tribunal may give permission to appeal on limited grounds, but must comply with paragraph (4) in relation to any grounds on which it has refused permission.

Review of a decision

44.—(1) The Tribunal may only undertake a review of a decision—

(a) pursuant to rule 43(1) (review on an application for permission to appeal); and

(b) if it is satisfied that there was an error of law in the decision.

(2) The Tribunal must notify the parties in writing of the outcome of any review, and of any right of appeal in relation to the outcome.

(3) If the Tribunal takes any action in relation to a decision following a review without first giving every party an opportunity to make representations, the notice under paragraph (2) must state that any party that did not have an opportunity to make representations may apply for such action to be set aside and for the decision to be reviewed again.

Power to treat an application as a different type of application

45. The Tribunal may treat an application for a decision to be corrected, set aside or reviewed, or for permission to appeal against a decision, as an application for any other one of those things.

Patrick Elias
Phillip Brook Smith Q.C.
Lesley Clare
Carolyn Kirby
Peter Lane
Douglas J. May
Bronwyn McKenna
M.J. Reed
Mark Rowland
Nicholas Warren

I allow these Rules

Signed by authority of the Lord Chancellor

Bridget Prentice
Parliamentary Under Secretary of State
Ministry of Justice

16th July 2009

EXPLANATORY NOTE

(This note is not part of the Rules)

Part 1 of the Tribunals, Courts and Enforcement Act 2007 (c.15) establishes a new tribunal structure comprising the First-tier Tribunal and the Upper Tribunal. Appeal functions of existing tribunals are being transferred to this structure and assigned to chambers within the new tribunals. These Rules govern the practice and procedure to be followed in the First-tier Tribunal in proceedings which have been allocated to the General Regulatory Chamber by the First-tier Tribunal and Upper Tribunal (Chambers) Order 2008(**a**).

Part 1 contains provisions for interpreting and applying the Rules and sets out the overriding objective of the Rules.

Part 2 contains general powers and provisions including the Tribunal's case management powers, the giving of directions, the power to strike out a party's case, the service of documents and rules about representatives, evidence, submissions, witnesses and costs.

Part 3 contains provisions relating to starting proceedings and procedure up to and including the making and notification of Tribunal decisions.

Part 4 deals with correcting, setting aside, reviewing and appealing Tribunal decisions.

(a) SI 2008/2684. Article 5B was inserted by the First-tier Tribunal and Upper Tribunal (Chambers) (Amendment No.3) Order 2009 (SI 2009/1590).

Appendix 2

SI 2008 No 2699 (L 16)

The Tribunal Procedure (First-tier Tribunal) (Health, Education and Social Care Chamber) Rules 2008

Version in force from 18th January 2010, showing amendments made by S.I. 2009/1975 and S.I. 2010/43. This document has been produced in order to assist users but its accuracy is not guaranteed and should not be relied upon. For a definitive version of the Rules, users should refer to the original statutory instruments.

Made	*9th October 2008*
Laid before Parliament	*15th October 2008*
Coming into force	*3rd November 2008*

CONTENTS

PART 3

Proceedings before the Tribunal other than in mental health cases

CHAPTER 1

Before the hearing

18. Application of Part 3
19. Application for leave
20. The application notice
21. The response
22. Order that a school be regarded as not registered pending determination of an appeal

CHAPTER 2

Hearings

23. Decision with or without a hearing
24. Entitlement to attend a hearing
25. Notice of hearings
26. Public and private hearings
27. Hearings in a party's absence
28. Power to pay allowances

CHAPTER 3

Decisions

29. Consent orders
30. Decisions

PART 4

Proceedings before the Tribunal in mental health cases

CHAPTER 1

Before the hearing

31. Application of Part 4
32. Procedure in mental health cases
33. Notice of proceedings to interested persons
34. Medical examination of the patient

CHAPTER 2

Hearings

35. No disposal of proceedings without a hearing
36. Entitlement to attend a hearing
37. Time and place of hearings
38. Public and private hearings
39. Hearings in a party's absence
40. Power to pay allowances

CHAPTER 3

Decisions

PART 5

Correcting, setting aside, reviewing and appealing Tribunal decisions

After consulting in accordance with paragraph 28(1) of the Tribunals, Courts and Enforcement Act 2007(a), the Tribunal Procedure Committee has made the following Rules in exercise of the power conferred by sections 9(3), 22 and 29(3) and (4) of, and Schedule 5 to, that Act.

The Lord Chancellor has allowed the Rules in accordance with paragraph 28(3) of Schedule 5 to the Tribunals, Courts and Enforcement Act 2007.

PART 1

Introduction

Citation, commencement, application and interpretation

1.—(1) These Rules may be cited as the Tribunal Procedure (First-tier Tribunal) (Health, Education and Social Care Chamber) Rules 2008 and come into force on 3rd November 2008.

(2) These Rules apply to proceedings before the Tribunal which have been assigned to the Health, Education and Social Care Chamber by the First-tier Tribunal and Upper Tribunal (Chambers) Order 2008(b).

(3) In these Rules—

"the 2007 Act" means the Tribunals, Courts and Enforcement Act 2007;

"applicant" means a person who—

(a) starts Tribunal proceedings, whether by making an application, an appeal, a claim or a reference;

(b) makes an application to the Tribunal for leave to start such proceedings; or

(c) is substituted as an applicant under rule 9(1) (substitution and addition of parties);

(a) 2007 c.15.
(b) S.I. 2008/2684.

"childcare provider" means a person who is a childminder or provides day care as defined in section 79A of the Children Act 1989(**a**), or a person who provides childcare as defined in section 18 of the Childcare Act 2006(**b**);

"disability discrimination in schools case" means proceedings concerning disability discrimination in the education of a child or related matters;

"dispose of proceedings" includes, unless indicated otherwise, disposing of a part of the proceedings;

"document" means anything in which information is recorded in any form, and an obligation under these Rules or any practice direction or direction to provide or allow access to a document or a copy of a document for any purpose means, unless the Tribunal directs otherwise, an obligation to provide or allow access to such document or copy in a legible form or in a form which can be readily made into a legible form;

"Health, Education and Social Care Chamber" means the Health, Education and Social Care Chamber of the First-tier Tribunal established by the First-tier Tribunal and Upper Tribunal (Chambers) Order 2008;

"hearing" means an oral hearing and includes a hearing conducted in whole or in part by video link, telephone or other means of instantaneous two-way electronic communication;

"legal representative" means [a person who, for the purposes of the Legal Services Act 2007(**c**), is an authorised person in relation to an activity which constitutes the exercise of a right of audience or the conduct of litigation within the meaning of that Act];

"mental health case" means proceedings brought under the Mental Health Act 1983(**d**) or paragraph 5(2) of the Schedule to the Repatriation of Prisoners Act 1984(**e**);

"nearest relative" has the meaning set out in section 26 of the Mental Health Act 1983;

"party" means—

(a) in a mental health case, the patient, the responsible authority, the Secretary of State (if the patient is a restricted patient or in a reference under rule 32(8) (seeking approval under section 86 of the Mental Health Act 1983)), and any other person who starts a mental health case by making an application;

(b) in any other case, a person who is an applicant or respondent in proceedings before the Tribunal or, if the proceedings have been concluded, a person who was an applicant or respondent when the Tribunal finally disposed of all issues in the proceedings;

"patient" means the person who is the subject of a mental health case;

"practice direction" means a direction given under section 23 of the 2007 Act;

"respondent" means—

(a) in an appeal against an order made by a justice of the peace under section 79K of the Children Act 1989(**f**), section 20 of the Care Standards Act 2000(**g**) or section 72 of the Childcare Act 2006, the person who applied to the justice of the peace for the order;

(b) in an appeal against any other decision, the person who made the decision;

(**a**) 1989 c.41. Section 79A was inserted by section 79(1) of the Care Standards Act 2000 (c.14).
(**b**) 2006 c.21.
(**c**) 2007 c.29.
(**d**) 1983 c.20.
(**e**) 1984 c.47.
(**f**) 1989 c.41. Section 79K was inserted by section 79(1) of the Care Standards Act 2000 (c.14).
(**g**) 2000 c.14.

(c) in proceedings on a claim under section 28I of the Disability Discrimination Act 1995(**a**), the body responsible for the school as determined in accordance with paragraph 1 of Schedule 4A to that Act or, if the claim concerns the residual duties of a local education authority under section 28F of that Act, that local education authority;

(d) in proceedings on an application under section 4(2) of the Protection of Children Act 1999(**b**) or section 86(2) of the Care Standards Act 2000, the Secretary of State; or

(e) a person substituted or added as a respondent under rule 9 (substitution and addition of parties);

"responsible authority" means—

(a) in relation to a patient detained under the Mental Health Act 1983 in a hospital within the meaning of Part 2 of that Act, the managers (as defined in section 145 of that Act);

(b) in relation to a patient subject to guardianship, the responsible local social services authority (as defined in section 34(3) of the Mental Health Act 1983);

(c) in relation to a community patient, the managers of the responsible hospital (as defined in section 145 of the Mental Health Act 1983);

(d) in relation to a patient subject to after-care under supervision, the Primary Care Trust or Local Health Board which has the duty to provide after-care for the patient.

"restricted patient" has the meaning set out in section 79(1) of the Mental Health Act 1983;

"special educational needs case" means proceedings concerning the education of a child who has or may have special educational needs;

"Suspension Regulations" means regulations which provide for a right of appeal against a decision to suspend, or not to lift the suspension of, a person's registration as a childcare provider;

"Tribunal" means the First-tier Tribunal;

"working day" means any day except a Saturday or Sunday, Christmas Day, Good Friday or a bank holiday under section 1 of the Banking and Financial Dealings Act 1971(**c**).

Overriding objective and parties' obligation to co-operate with the Tribunal

2.—(1) The overriding objective of these Rules is to enable the Tribunal to deal with cases fairly and justly.

(2) Dealing with a case fairly and justly includes—

(a) dealing with the case in ways which are proportionate to the importance of the case, the complexity of the issues, the anticipated costs and the resources of the parties;

(b) avoiding unnecessary formality and seeking flexibility in the proceedings;

(c) ensuring, so far as practicable, that the parties are able to participate fully in the proceedings;

(d) using any special expertise of the Tribunal effectively; and

(e) avoiding delay, so far as compatible with proper consideration of the issues.

(**a**) 1995 c.50. Section 28F was inserted by section 16 of the Special Educational Needs and Disability Act 2001 (c.10), section 28I was inserted by section 18 of that Act, and Schedule 4A was inserted by section 11(2) of, and Schedule 2 to, that Act.

(**b**) 1999 c.14.

(**c**) 1971 c.80.

(3) The Tribunal must seek to give effect to the overriding objective when it—

(a) exercises any power under these Rules; or

(b) interprets any rule or practice direction.

(4) Parties must—

(a) help the Tribunal to further the overriding objective; and

(b) co-operate with the Tribunal generally.

Alternative dispute resolution and arbitration

3.—(1) The Tribunal should seek, where appropriate—

(a) to bring to the attention of the parties the availability of any appropriate alternative procedure for the resolution of the dispute; and

(b) if the parties wish and provided that it is compatible with the overriding objective, to facilitate the use of the procedure.

(2) Part 1 of the Arbitration Act 1996(a) does not apply to proceedings before the Tribunal.

PART 2

General powers and provisions

Delegation to staff

4.—(1) Staff appointed under section 40(1) of the 2007 Act (tribunal staff and services) may, with the approval of the Senior President of Tribunals, carry out functions of a judicial nature permitted or required to be done by the Tribunal.

(2) The approval referred to at paragraph (1) may apply generally to the carrying out of specified functions by members of staff of a specified description in specified circumstances.

(3) Within 14 days after the date on which the Tribunal sends notice of a decision made by a member of staff under paragraph (1) to a party, that party may apply in writing to the Tribunal for that decision to be considered afresh by a judge.

Case management powers

5.—(1) Subject to the provisions of the 2007 Act and any other enactment, the Tribunal may regulate its own procedure.

(2) The Tribunal may give a direction in relation to the conduct or disposal of proceedings at any time, including a direction amending, suspending or setting aside an earlier direction.

(3) In particular, and without restricting the general powers in paragraphs (1) and (2), the Tribunal may—

(a) extend or shorten the time for complying with any rule, practice direction or direction, unless such extension or shortening would conflict with a provision of another enactment containing a time limit(b);

(a) 1996 c.23.

(b) Provisions in primary legislation which contain time limits include: sections 66(1) and (2), 68(2) (subject to any order made under section 68A), 69(1), (2) and (4), 70, 71(2) (subject to any order made under section 71(3)) and 75(1) and (2) of the Mental Health Act 1983; sections 21(2) and 86(5) of the Care Standards Act 2000; section 166(2) of the Education Act 2002 (c.32); and section 32(2) of the Health and Social Care Act 2008 (c.14).

(b) consolidate or hear together two or more sets of proceedings or parts of proceedings raising common issues, or treat a case as a lead case;

(c) permit or require a party to amend a document;

(d) permit or require a party or another person to provide documents, information or submissions to the Tribunal or a party;

(e) deal with an issue in the proceedings as a preliminary issue;

(f) hold a hearing to consider any matter, including a case management issue;

(g) decide the form of any hearing;

(h) adjourn or postpone a hearing;

(i) require a party to produce a bundle for a hearing;

(j) stay proceedings;

(k) transfer proceedings to another court or tribunal if that other court or tribunal has jurisdiction in relation to the proceedings and—

 (i) because of a change of circumstances since the proceedings were started, the Tribunal no longer has jurisdiction in relation to the proceedings; or

 (ii) the Tribunal considers that the other court or tribunal is a more appropriate forum for the determination of the case; or

(l) suspend the effect of its own decision pending the determination by the Tribunal or the Upper Tribunal of an application for permission to appeal against, and any appeal or review of, that decision.

Procedure for applying for and giving directions

6.—(1) The Tribunal may give a direction on the application of one or more of the parties or on its own initiative.

(2) An application for a direction may be made—

(a) by sending or delivering a written application to the Tribunal; or

(b) orally during the course of a hearing.

(3) An application for a direction must include the reason for making that application.

(4) Unless the Tribunal considers that there is good reason not to do so, the Tribunal must send written notice of any direction to every party and to any other person affected by the direction.

(5) If a party, or any other person given notice of the direction under paragraph (4), wishes to challenge a direction which the Tribunal has given, they may do so by applying for another direction which amends, suspends or sets aside the first direction.

Failure to comply with rules etc.

7.—(1) An irregularity resulting from a failure to comply with any requirement in these Rules, a practice direction or a direction, does not of itself render void the proceedings or any step taken in the proceedings.

(2) If a party has failed to comply with a requirement in these Rules, a practice direction or a direction, the Tribunal may take such action as it considers just, which may include—

(a) waiving the requirement;

(b) requiring the failure to be remedied;

(c) exercising its power under rule 8 (striking out a party's case);

(d) exercising its power under paragraph (3); or

(e) except in mental health cases, restricting a party's participation in the proceedings.

(3) The Tribunal may refer to the Upper Tribunal, and ask the Upper Tribunal to exercise its power under section 25 of the 2007 Act in relation to, any failure by a person to comply with a requirement imposed by the Tribunal—

(a) to attend at any place for the purpose of giving evidence;

(b) otherwise to make themselves available to give evidence;

(c) to swear an oath in connection with the giving of evidence;

(d) to give evidence as a witness;

(e) to produce a document; or

(f) to facilitate the inspection of a document or any other thing (including any premises).

Striking out a party's case

8.—(1) With the exception of paragraph (3), this rule does not apply to mental health cases.

(2) The proceedings, or the appropriate part of them, will automatically be struck out if the applicant has failed to comply with a direction that stated that failure by the applicant to comply with the direction would lead to the striking out of the proceedings or that part of them.

(3) The Tribunal must strike out the whole or a part of the proceedings if the Tribunal—

(a) does not have jurisdiction in relation to the proceedings or that part of them; and

(b) does not exercise its power under rule 5(3)(k)(i) (transfer to another court or tribunal) in relation to the proceedings or that part of them.

(4) The Tribunal may strike out the whole or a part of the proceedings if—

(a) the applicant has failed to comply with a direction which stated that failure by the applicant to comply with the direction could lead to the striking out of the proceedings or part of them;

(b) the applicant has failed to co-operate with the Tribunal to such an extent that the Tribunal cannot deal with the proceedings fairly and justly; or

(c) the Tribunal considers there is no reasonable prospect of the applicant's case, or part of it, succeeding.

(5) The Tribunal may not strike out the whole or a part of the proceedings under paragraph (3) or (4)(b) or (c) without first giving the applicant an opportunity to make representations in relation to the proposed striking out.

(6) If the proceedings, or part of them, have been struck out under paragraph (2) or (4)(a), the applicant may apply for the proceedings, or part of them, to be reinstated.

(7) An application under paragraph (6) must be made in writing and received by the Tribunal within 28 days after the date on which the Tribunal sent notification of the striking out to that party.

(8) This rule applies to a respondent as it applies to an applicant except that—

(a) a reference to the striking out of the proceedings is to be read as a reference to the barring of the respondent from taking further part in the proceedings; and

(b) a reference to an application for the reinstatement of proceedings which have been struck out is to be read as a reference to an application for the lifting of the bar on the respondent from taking further part in the proceedings.

(9) If a respondent has been barred from taking further part in proceedings under this rule and that bar has not been lifted, the Tribunal need not consider any response or other submission made by that respondent.

Substitution and addition of parties

9.—(1) The Tribunal may give a direction substituting a party if—

(a) the wrong person has been named as a party; or

(b) the substitution has become necessary because of a change in circumstances since the start of proceedings.

(2) The Tribunal may give a direction adding a person to the proceedings as a respondent.

(3) If the Tribunal gives a direction under paragraph (1) or (2) it may give such consequential directions as it considers appropriate.

Orders for costs

10.—(1) Subject to paragraph (2), the Tribunal may make an order in respect of costs only—

(a) under section 29(4) of the 2007 Act (wasted costs); or

(b) if the Tribunal considers that a party or its representative has acted unreasonably in bringing, defending or conducting the proceedings.

(2) The Tribunal may not make an order under paragraph (1)(b) in mental health cases.

(3) The Tribunal may make an order in respect of costs on an application or on its own initiative.

(4) A person making an application for an order under this rule must—

(a) send or deliver a written application to the Tribunal and to the person against whom it is proposed that the order be made; and

(b) send or deliver a schedule of the costs claimed with the application.

(5) An application for an order under paragraph (1) may be made at any time during the proceedings but may not be made later than 14 days after the date on which the Tribunal sends the decision notice recording the decision which finally disposes of all issues in the proceedings.

(6) The Tribunal may not make an order under paragraph (1) against a person (the "paying person") without first—

(a) giving that person an opportunity to make representations; and

(b) if the paying person is an individual, considering that person's financial means.

(7) The amount of costs to be paid under an order under paragraph (1) may be ascertained by—

(a) summary assessment by the Tribunal;

(b) agreement of a specified sum by the paying person and the person entitled to receive the costs ("the receiving person"); or

(c) assessment of the whole or a specified part of the costs incurred by the receiving person, if not agreed.

(8) Following an order for assessment under paragraph (7)(c), the paying person or the receiving person may apply to a county court for a detailed assessment of costs in accordance with the Civil Procedure Rules 1998(a) on the standard basis or, if specified in the order, on the indemnity basis.

Representatives

11.—(1) A party may appoint a representative (whether a legal representative or not) to represent that party in the proceedings.

(a) (a) S.I. 1998/3132.

(2) If a party appoints a representative, that party (or the representative if the representative is a legal representative) must send or deliver to the Tribunal and to each other party written notice of the representative's name and address.

(3) Anything permitted or required to be done by a party under these Rules, a practice direction or a direction may be done by the representative of that party, except—

(a) signing a witness statement; or

(b) signing an application notice under rule 20 (the application notice) if the representative is not a legal representative.

(4) A person who receives due notice of the appointment of a representative—

(a) must provide to the representative any document which is required to be provided to the represented party, and need not provide that document to the represented party; and

(b) may assume that the representative is and remains authorised as such until they receive written notification that this is not so from the representative or the represented party.

(5) At a hearing a party may be accompanied by another person whose name and address has not been notified under paragraph (2) but who, subject to paragraph (8) and with the permission of the Tribunal, may act as a representative or otherwise assist in presenting the party's case at the hearing.

(6) Paragraphs (2) to (4) do not apply to a person who accompanies a party under paragraph (5).

(7) In a mental health case, if the patient has not appointed a representative, the Tribunal may appoint a legal representative for the patient where—

(a) the patient has stated that they do not wish to conduct their own case or that they wish to be represented; or

(b) the patient lacks the capacity to appoint a representative but the Tribunal believes that it is in the patient's best interests for the patient to be represented.

(8) In a mental health case a party may not appoint as a representative, or be represented or assisted at a hearing by—

(a) a person liable to be detained or subject to guardianship or after-care under supervision, or who is a community patient, under the Mental Health Act 1983; or

(b) a person receiving treatment for mental disorder at the same hospital as the patient.

Calculating time

12.—(1) An act required by these Rules, a practice direction or a direction to be done on or by a particular day must be done by 5pm on that day.

(2) If the time specified by these Rules, a practice direction or a direction for doing any act ends on a day other than a working day, the act is done in time if it is done on the next working day.

(3) In a special educational needs case or a disability discrimination in schools case—

(a) if the time for starting proceedings by providing the application notice to the Tribunal under rule 20 (the application notice) ends on a day from 25th December to 1st January inclusive, or on any day in August, the application notice is provided in time if it is provided to the Tribunal on the first working day after 1st January or 31st August, as appropriate; and

(b) the days from 25th December to 1st January inclusive and any day in August must not be counted when calculating the time by which any other act must be done.

(4) Paragraph (3)(b) does not apply where the Tribunal directs that an act must be done by or on a specified date.

Sending and delivery of documents

13.—(1) Any document to be provided to the Tribunal under these Rules, a practice direction or a direction must be—

(a) sent by pre-paid post or delivered by hand to the address specified for the proceedings;

(b) sent by fax to the number specified for the proceedings; or

(c) sent or delivered by such other method as the Tribunal may permit or direct.

(2) Subject to paragraph (3), if a party provides a fax number, email address or other details for the electronic transmission of documents to them, that party must accept delivery of documents by that method.

(3) If a party informs the Tribunal and all other parties that a particular form of communication, other than pre-paid post or delivery by hand, should not be used to provide documents to that party, that form of communication must not be so used.

(4) If the Tribunal or a party sends a document to a party or the Tribunal by email or any other electronic means of communication, the recipient may request that the sender provide a hard copy of the document to the recipient. The recipient must make such a request as soon as reasonably practicable after receiving the document electronically.

(5) The Tribunal and each party may assume that the address provided by a party or its representative is and remains the address to which documents should be sent or delivered until receiving written notification to the contrary.

Use of documents and information

14.—(1) The Tribunal may make an order prohibiting the disclosure or publication of—

(a) specified documents or information relating to the proceedings; or

(b) any matter likely to lead members of the public to identify any person whom the Tribunal considers should not be identified.

(2) The Tribunal may give a direction prohibiting the disclosure of a document or information to a person if—

(a) the Tribunal is satisfied that such disclosure would be likely to cause that person or some other person serious harm; and

(b) the Tribunal is satisfied, having regard to the interests of justice, that it is proportionate to give such a direction.

(3) If a party ("the first party") considers that the Tribunal should give a direction under paragraph (2) prohibiting the disclosure of a document or information to another party ("the second party"), the first party must—

(a) exclude the relevant document or information from any documents that will be provided to the second party; and

(b) provide to the Tribunal the excluded document or information, and the reason for its exclusion, so that the Tribunal may decide whether the document or information should be disclosed to the second party or should be the subject of a direction under paragraph (2).

(4) The Tribunal must conduct proceedings as appropriate in order to give effect to a direction given under paragraph (2).

(5) If the Tribunal gives a direction under paragraph (2) which prevents disclosure to a party who has appointed a representative, the Tribunal may give a direction that the documents or information be disclosed to that representative if the Tribunal is satisfied that—

(a) disclosure to the representative would be in the interests of the party; and

(b) the representative will act in accordance with paragraph (6).

(6) Documents or information disclosed to a representative in accordance with a direction under paragraph (5) must not be disclosed either directly or indirectly to any other person without the Tribunal's consent.

(7) Unless the Tribunal gives a direction to the contrary, information about mental health cases and the names of any persons concerned in such cases must not be made public.

Evidence and submissions

15.—(1) Without restriction on the general powers in rule 5(1) and (2) (case management powers), the Tribunal may give directions as to—

(a) issues on which it requires evidence or submissions;

(b) the nature of the evidence or submissions it requires;

(c) whether the parties are permitted or required to provide expert evidence, and if so whether the parties must jointly appoint a single expert to provide such evidence;

(d) any limit on the number of witnesses whose evidence a party may put forward, whether in relation to a particular issue or generally;

(e) the manner in which any evidence or submissions are to be provided, which may include a direction for them to be given—

(i) orally at a hearing; or

(ii) by written submissions or witness statement; and

(f) the time at which any evidence or submissions are to be provided.

(2) The Tribunal may—

(a) admit evidence whether or not—

(i) the evidence would be admissible in a civil trial in England and Wales; or

(ii) the evidence was available to a previous decision maker; or

(b) exclude evidence that would otherwise be admissible where—

(i) the evidence was not provided within the time allowed by a direction or a practice direction;

(ii) the evidence was otherwise provided in a manner that did not comply with a direction or a practice direction; or

(iii) it would otherwise be unfair to admit the evidence.

(3) The Tribunal may consent to a witness giving, or require any witness to give, evidence on oath, and may administer an oath for that purpose.

(4) In a special educational needs case the Tribunal may require—

(a) the parents of the child, or any other person with care of the child or parental responsibility for the child (as defined in section 3 of the Children Act 1989), to make the child available for examination or assessment by a suitably qualified professional person; or

(b) the person responsible for a school or educational setting to allow a suitably qualified professional person to have access to the school or educational setting for the purpose of assessing the child or the provision made, or to be made, for the child.

(5) The Tribunal may consider a failure by a party to comply with a requirement made under paragraph (4), in the absence of any good reason for such failure, as a failure to co-operate with the Tribunal, which could lead to a result which is adverse to that party's case.

Summoning of witnesses and orders to answer questions or produce documents

16.—(1) On the application of a party or on its own initiative, the Tribunal may—

(a) by summons require any person to attend as a witness at a hearing at the time and place specified in the summons; or

(b) order any person to answer any questions or produce any documents in that person's possession or control which relate to any issue in the proceedings.

(2) A summons under paragraph (1)(a) must—

(a) give the person required to attend 14 days' notice of the hearing, or such shorter period as the Tribunal may direct; and

(b) where the person is not a party, make provision for the person's necessary expenses of attendance to be paid, and state who is to pay them.

(3) No person may be compelled to give any evidence or produce any document that the person could not be compelled to give or produce on a trial of an action in a court of law.

(4) A summons or order under this rule must—

(a) state that the person on whom the requirement is imposed may apply to the Tribunal to vary or set aside the summons or order, if they have not had an opportunity to object to it; and

(b) state the consequences of failure to comply with the summons or order.

Withdrawal

17.—(1) Subject to paragraphs (2) and (3), a party may give notice of the withdrawal of its case, or any part of it—

(a) at any time before a hearing to consider the disposal of the proceedings (or, if the Tribunal disposes of the proceedings without a hearing, before that disposal), by sending or delivering to the Tribunal a written notice of withdrawal; or

(b) orally at a hearing.

(2) Notice of withdrawal will not take effect unless the Tribunal consents to the withdrawal except—

(a) in proceedings concerning the suitability of a person to work with children or vulnerable adults; or

(b) in proceedings started by a reference under section 67 or 71(1) of the Mental Health Act 1983.

(3) A party which started a mental health case by making a reference to the Tribunal under section 68, 71(2) or 75(1) of the Mental Health Act 1983 may not withdraw its case.

(4) A party which has withdrawn its case may apply to the Tribunal for the case to be reinstated.

(5) An application under paragraph (4) must be made in writing and be received by the Tribunal within 28 days after—

(a) the date on which the Tribunal received the notice under paragraph (1)(a); or

(b) the date of the hearing at which the case was withdrawn orally under paragraph (1)(b).

(6) The Tribunal must notify each party in writing of a withdrawal under this rule.

PART 3

Proceedings before the Tribunal other than in mental health cases

CHAPTER 1

Before the hearing

Application of Part 3

18. This Part does not apply to mental health cases.

Application for leave

19.—(1) This rule applies to applications for leave to bring proceedings under—

(a) section 4(1)(b) of the Protection of Children Act 1999(a) (appeal against a decision not to remove the applicant from the list kept under section 1 of that Act);

(b) section 4(2) of the Protection of Children Act 1999 (application to have the issue of the applicant's inclusion in the list kept under section 1 of that Act determined by the Tribunal);

(c) section 86(1)(b) of the Care Standards Act 2000(b) (appeal against a decision not to remove the applicant from the list kept under section 81 of that Act);

(d) section 86(2) of the Care Standards Act 2000 (application to have the issue of the applicant's inclusion in the list kept under section 81 of that Act determined by the Tribunal); and

(e) section 32 of the Criminal Justice and Court Services Act 2000(c) (application to have the issue of the continuation of a disqualification order determined by the Tribunal).

(2) An application to the Tribunal for leave must—

(a) give full reasons why the applicant considers that the Tribunal should give leave; and

(b) comply with paragraphs (1) to (4) of rule 20 (the application notice) as if the application for leave were an application notice.

(3) The Tribunal may make any directions it considers appropriate before determining the application for leave.

(4) The Tribunal must—

(a) notify the applicant of its decision in relation to the application for leave; and

(b) if it gives leave, give directions as to the future conduct of the proceedings.

The application notice

20.—(1) If rule 19 (application for leave) does not apply, an applicant must start proceedings before the Tribunal by sending or delivering an application notice to the Tribunal so that it is received—

(a) if a time for providing the application notice is specified in the Schedule to these Rules (time limits for providing application notices and responses), within that time; or

(b) otherwise, within 28 days after notice of the act or decision to which the proceedings relate was sent to the applicant.

(a) 1999 c.14.
(b) 2000 c.14.
(c) 2000 c.43.

(2) The application notice must be signed by the applicant and must include—

(a) the name and address of the applicant;

(b) the name and address of the applicant's representative (if any);

(c) an address where documents for the applicant may be sent or delivered;

(d) the name and address of any respondent;

(e) details of the decision or act, or failure to decide or act, to which the proceedings relate;

(f) the result the applicant is seeking;

(g) the grounds on which the applicant relies; and

(h) any further information or documents required by an applicable practice direction.

(3) The applicant must send with the application notice a copy of any written record of any decision under challenge, and any statement of reasons for that decision that the applicant has or can reasonably obtain.

(4) If the applicant provides the application notice to the Tribunal later than the time required by paragraph (1) or by any extension of time under rule 5(3)(a) (power to extend time)—

(a) the application notice must include a request for an extension of time and the reason why the application notice was not provided in time; and

(b) unless the Tribunal extends time for the application notice under rule 5(3)(a) (power to extend time) the Tribunal must not admit the application notice.

(5) In proceedings under Suspension Regulations, the applicant must send or deliver a copy of the application notice and any accompanying documents to the respondent at the same time as it provides the application notice to the Tribunal.

(6) In proceedings other than proceedings under paragraph (5), when the Tribunal receives the application notice it must send a copy of the application notice and any accompanying documents to each other party.

The response

21.—(1) When a respondent receives a copy of the application notice, the respondent must send or deliver to the Tribunal a response so that it is received—

(a) if a time for providing the response is specified in the Schedule to these Rules (time limits for providing application notices and responses), within that time;

(b) otherwise, within 21 days after the date on which the respondent received the application notice.

(2) The response must include—

(a) the name and address of the respondent;

(b) the name and address of the respondent's representative (if any);

(c) an address where documents for the respondent may be sent or delivered;

(d) a statement as to whether the respondent opposes the applicant's case and, if so, any grounds for such opposition which are not contained in another document provided with the response;

(e) in a special educational needs case, the views of the child about the issues raised by the proceedings, or the reason why the respondent has not ascertained those views; and

(f) any further information or documents required by an applicable practice direction or direction.

(3) The response may include a statement as to whether the respondent would be content for the case to be dealt with without a hearing if the Tribunal considers it appropriate.

(4) If the respondent provides the response to the Tribunal later than the time required by paragraph (1) or by any extension of time under rule 5(3)(a) (power to extend time), the response must include a request for an extension of time and the reason why the response was not provided in time.

(5) The respondent must send or deliver a copy of the response and any accompanying documents to each other party at the same time as it provides the response to the Tribunal.

Order that a school be regarded as not registered pending determination of an appeal

22.—(1) This rule sets out the procedure for the making of an order under section 166(5) of the Education Act 2002(a) that a school is to be regarded as not registered for the purposes of section 159 of that Act until the Tribunal determines an appeal under section 165(2) of that Act (decision to remove an independent school from the register).

(2) In this rule—

(a) "the applicant" means the applicant bringing the appeal under section 165(2) of the Education Act 2002; and

(b) "the respondent" means the respondent to that appeal.

(3) The respondent must make any application for an order under this rule in writing and must send or deliver it to the Tribunal and the applicant so that it is received within 28 days after the date on which the respondent received a copy of the application notice starting the appeal.

(4) An application under paragraph (3) must—

(a) be signed by the respondent and dated;

(b) state the grounds for the application;

(c) state the nature of the evidence that will be provided in support of the application and the names of the witnesses who will give that evidence;

(d) specify any working days in the following 30 days when the respondent or a witness named under sub-paragraph (c) would not be available to attend a hearing, and provide reasons why they would not be available; and

(e) include, so far as practicable, any documentary evidence (including witness statements) that the respondent intends to rely on.

(5) The applicant must send or deliver a written response to the application under paragraph (3) to the Tribunal and the respondent so that it is received within 16 days after the date on which the respondent sent that application to the applicant under paragraph (3).

(6) The response must—

(a) acknowledge receipt of the application and any documentary evidence included with it;

(b) state whether the applicant requests that the application be decided at a hearing, and if so—

(i) state the nature of the evidence that will be provided in support of the applicant's case and the names of the witnesses who will give that evidence; and

(ii) specify any working days in the following 16 days when the applicant or a witness named under sub-paragraph (b)(i) would not be available to attend a hearing, and provide reasons why they would not be available; and

---

(a) 2002 c.32.

(c) include, so far as practicable, any documentary evidence (including witness statements) that the applicant intends to rely on.

(7) If the applicant fails to comply with paragraph (5) the applicant will not be entitled to take any further part in the proceedings in relation to the application.

(8) If the applicant complies with paragraph (5) and requests that the application be decided at a hearing, the Tribunal must hold a hearing to consider the application.

(9) Any hearing to consider the making of an order must be held as soon as reasonably practicable, and if the respondent has applied for such an order any such hearing must be held no later than the earlier of—

(a) 14 days after the date on which the Tribunal received the applicant's response to the application; or

(b) 30 days after the date on which the respondent sent the application to the applicant.

(10) If the Tribunal is considering whether to make an order on its own initiative, the Tribunal—

(a) may not do so without giving the applicant an opportunity to make representations at a hearing in relation to the making of the order;

(b) must give directions as to the provision to the Tribunal by the parties of documents or evidence that the parties wish to be taken into account.

CHAPTER 2

Hearings

Decision with or without a hearing

23.—(1) Subject to paragraphs (2) and (3), the Tribunal must hold a hearing before making a decision which disposes of proceedings unless—

(a) each party has consented to the matter being decided without a hearing; and

(b) the Tribunal considers that it is able to decide the matter without the hearing.

(2) This rule does not apply to a decision under Part 5.

(3) The Tribunal may dispose of proceedings without a hearing under rule 8 (striking out a party's case).

Entitlement to attend a hearing

24. Subject to rules 22(7) (exclusion of applicant from proceedings to consider an order under section 166(5) of the Education Act 2002) and 26(5) (exclusion of a person from a hearing)—

(a) each party is entitled to attend a hearing; and

(b) in a special educational needs case, or a disability discrimination in schools case, the child is entitled to attend a hearing, and the Tribunal may permit the child to give evidence and to address the Tribunal.

Notice of hearings

25.—(1) The Tribunal must give each party entitled to attend a hearing reasonable notice of the time and place of the hearing (including any adjourned or postponed hearing) and any changes to the time and place of the hearing.

(2) The period of notice under paragraph (1) must be at least 14 days, except that—

(a) in proceedings under Suspension Regulations the period of notice must be at least 3 working days;

(b) the period of notice in respect of a hearing to consider the making of an order under section 166(5) of the Education Act 2002 must be at least 7 days; and

(c) the Tribunal may give shorter notice—

(i) with the parties' consent; or

(ii) in urgent or exceptional circumstances.

Public and private hearings

26.—(1) Subject to the following paragraphs, all hearings must be held in public.

(2) Hearings in special educational needs cases and disability discrimination in schools cases must be held in private unless the Tribunal considers that it is in the interests of justice for a hearing to be held in public.

(3) Subject to paragraph (2), the Tribunal may give a direction that a hearing, or part of it, is to be held in private.

(4) Where a hearing, or part of it, is to be held in private, the Tribunal may determine who is permitted to attend the hearing or part of it.

(5) The Tribunal may give a direction excluding from any hearing, or part of it—

(a) any person whose conduct the Tribunal considers is disrupting or is likely to disrupt the hearing;

(b) any person whose presence the Tribunal considers is likely to prevent another person from giving evidence or making submissions freely;

(c) any person who the Tribunal considers should be excluded in order to give effect to a direction under rule 14(2) (withholding information likely to cause harm);

(d) any person where the purpose of the hearing would be defeated by the attendance of that person; or

(e) in a special educational needs case or a disability discrimination in schools case, the child, if the Tribunal considers that the child's presence at the hearing would be adverse to the child's interests.

(6) The Tribunal may give a direction excluding a witness from a hearing until that witness gives evidence.

Hearings in a party's absence

27. If a party fails to attend a hearing the Tribunal may proceed with the hearing if the Tribunal—

(a) is satisfied that the party has been notified of the hearing or that reasonable steps have been taken to notify the party of the hearing; and

(b) considers that it is in the interests of justice to proceed with the hearing.

Power to pay allowances

28. The Secretary of State may pay such allowances for the purpose of or in connection with the attendance of persons at hearings as the Secretary of State may determine.

CHAPTER 3

Decisions

Consent orders

29.—(1) The Tribunal may, at the request of the parties but only if it considers it appropriate, make a consent order disposing of the proceedings and making such other appropriate provision as the parties have agreed.

(2) Notwithstanding any other provision of these Rules, the Tribunal need not hold a hearing before making an order under paragraph (1), or provide reasons for the order.

Decisions

30.—(1) The Tribunal may give a decision orally at a hearing.

(2) Subject to rule 14(2) (withholding information likely to cause harm), the Tribunal must provide to each party as soon as reasonably practicable after making a decision which finally disposes of all issues in the proceedings (except a decision under Part 5)—

(a) a decision notice stating the Tribunal's decision;

(b) written reasons for the decision; and

(c) notification of any rights of review or appeal against the decision and the time within which, and the manner in which, such rights of review or appeal may be exercised.

(3) In proceedings under Suspension Regulations, the documents and information referred to in paragraph (2) must be provided at the hearing or sent within 3 working days after the hearing.

(4) The Tribunal may provide written reasons for any decision to which paragraph (2) does not apply.

PART 4

Proceedings before the Tribunal in mental health cases

CHAPTER 1

Before the hearing

Application of Part 4

31. This Part applies only to mental health cases.

Procedure in mental health cases

32.—(1) An application or reference must be—

(a) made in writing;

(b) signed (in the case of an application, by the applicant or any person authorised by the applicant to do so); and

(c) sent or delivered to the Tribunal so that it is received within the time specified in the Mental Health Act 1983 or the Repatriation of Prisoners Act 1984.

(2) An application must, if possible, include—

(a) the name and address of the patient;

(b) if the application is made by the patient's nearest relative, the name, address and relationship to the patient of the patient's nearest relative;

(c) the provision under which the patient is detained, liable to be detained, subject to guardianship, a community patient or subject to after-care under supervision;

(d) whether the person making the application has appointed a representative or intends to do so, and the name and address of any representative appointed;

(e) the name and address of the responsible authority in relation to the patient.

(3) Subject to rule 14(2) (withholding evidence likely to cause harm), when the Tribunal receives a document from any party it must send a copy of that document to each other party.

(4) If the patient is a conditionally discharged patient (as defined in the Mental Health Act 1983) the Secretary of State must send or deliver a statement containing the information and documents required by the relevant practice direction to the Tribunal so that it is received by the Tribunal as soon as practicable and in any event within 6 weeks after the Secretary of State received a copy of the application or a request from the Tribunal.

(5) In proceedings under section 66(1)(a) of the Mental Health Act 1983 (application for admission for assessment), on the earlier of receipt of the copy of the application or a request from the Tribunal, the responsible authority must send or deliver to the Tribunal—

(a) the application for admission;

(b) the medical recommendations on which the application is founded;

(c) such of the information specified in the relevant practice direction as is within the knowledge of the responsible authority and can reasonably be provided in the time available; and

(d) such of the documents specified in the relevant practice direction as can reasonably be provided in the time available.

(6) If paragraph (4) or (5) does not apply, the responsible authority must send or deliver a statement containing the information and documents required by the relevant practice direction to the Tribunal so that it is received by the Tribunal as soon as practicable and in any event within 3 weeks after the responsible authority received a copy of the application or reference.

(7) If the patient is a restricted patient the responsible authority must also send the statement under paragraph (6) to the Secretary of State, and the Secretary of State must send a statement of any further relevant information to the Tribunal as soon as practicable and in any event—

(a) in proceedings under section 75(1) of the Mental Health Act 1983, within 2 weeks after the Secretary of State received the relevant authority's statement; or

(b) otherwise, within 3 weeks after the Secretary of State received the relevant authority's statement.

(8) If the Secretary of State wishes to seek the approval of the Tribunal under section 86(3) of the Mental Health Act 1983, the Secretary of State must refer the patient's case to the Tribunal and the provisions of these Rules applicable to references under that Act apply to the proceedings.

Notice of proceedings to interested persons

33. When the Tribunal receives the information required by rule 32(4), (5) or (6) (procedure in mental health cases) the Tribunal must give notice of the proceedings—

(a) where the patient is subject to the guardianship of a private guardian, to the guardian;

(b) where there is an extant order of the Court of Protection, to that court;

(c) subject to a patient with capacity to do so requesting otherwise, where any person other than the applicant is named by the authority as exercising the functions of the nearest relative, to that person;

(d) where a health authority, Primary Care Trust, National Health Service trust or NHS foundation trust has a right to discharge the patient under the provisions of section 23(3) of the Mental Health Act 1983, to that authority or trust; and

(e) to any other person who, in the opinion of the Tribunal, should have an opportunity of being heard.

Medical examination of the patient

34.—(1) Before a hearing to consider the disposal of a mental health case, an appropriate member of the Tribunal must, so far as practicable—

(a) examine the patient; and

(b) take such other steps as that member considers necessary to form an opinion of the patient's mental condition.

(2) For the purposes of paragraph (1) that member may—

(a) examine the patient in private;

(b) examine records relating to the detention or treatment of the patient and any after-care services;

(c) take notes and copies of records for use in connection with the proceedings.

CHAPTER 2

Hearings

No disposal of proceedings without a hearing

35.—(1) The Tribunal must not dispose of proceedings without a hearing.

(2) This rule does not apply to a decision under Part 5.

Entitlement to attend a hearing

36.—(1) Subject to rule 38(4) (exclusion of a person from a hearing), each party to proceedings is entitled to attend a hearing.

(2) Any person notified of the proceedings under rule 33 (notice of proceedings to interested persons) may—

(a) attend and take part in a hearing to such extent as the Tribunal considers proper; or

(b) provide written submissions to the Tribunal.

Time and place of hearings

37.—(1) In proceedings under section 66(1)(a) of the Mental Health Act 1983 the hearing of the case must start within 7 days after the date on which the Tribunal received the application notice.

(2) In proceedings under section 75(1) of that Act, the hearing of the case must start at least 5 weeks but no more than 8 weeks after the date on which the Tribunal received the reference.

(3) The Tribunal must give reasonable notice of the time and place of the hearing (including any adjourned or postponed hearing), and any changes to the time and place of the hearing, to—

(a) each party entitled to attend a hearing; and

(b) any person who has been notified of the proceedings under rule 33 (notice of proceedings to interested persons).

(4) The period of notice under paragraph (3) must be at least 14 days, except that—

(a) in proceedings under section 66(1)(a) of the Mental Health Act 1983 the period must be at least 3 working days; and

(b) the Tribunal may give shorter notice—

(i) with the parties' consent; or

(ii) in urgent or exceptional circumstances.

Public and private hearings

38.—(1) All hearings must be held in private unless the Tribunal considers that it is in the interests of justice for the hearing to be held in public.

(2) If a hearing is held in public, the Tribunal may give a direction that part of the hearing is to be held in private.

(3) Where a hearing, or part of it, is to be held in private, the Tribunal may determine who is permitted to attend the hearing or part of it.

(4) The Tribunal may give a direction excluding from any hearing, or part of it—

(a) any person whose conduct the Tribunal considers is disrupting or is likely to disrupt the hearing;

(b) any person whose presence the Tribunal considers is likely to prevent another person from giving evidence or making submissions freely;

(c) any person who the Tribunal considers should be excluded in order to give effect to a direction under rule 14(2) (withholding information likely to cause harm); or

(d) any person where the purpose of the hearing would be defeated by the attendance of that person.

(5) The Tribunal may give a direction excluding a witness from a hearing until that witness gives evidence.

Hearings in a party's absence

39.—(1) Subject to paragraph (2), if a party fails to attend a hearing the Tribunal may proceed with the hearing if the Tribunal—

(a) is satisfied that the party has been notified of the hearing or that reasonable steps have been taken to notify the party of the hearing; and

(b) considers that it is in the interests of justice to proceed with the hearing.

(2) The Tribunal may not proceed with a hearing in the absence of the patient unless—

(a) the requirements of rule 34 (medical examination of the patient) have been satisfied; and

(b) the Tribunal is satisfied that—

(i) the patient has decided not to attend the hearing; or

(ii) the patient is unable to attend the hearing for reasons of ill health.

Power to pay allowances

40. The Tribunal may pay allowances in respect of travelling expenses, subsistence and loss of earnings to—

(a) any person who attends a hearing as an applicant or a witness;

(b) a patient who attends a hearing otherwise than as the applicant or a witness; and

(c) any person (other than a legal representative) who attends as the representative of an applicant.

CHAPTER 3

Decisions

Decisions

41.—(1) The Tribunal may give a decision orally at a hearing.

(2) Subject to rule 14(2) (withholding information likely to cause harm), the Tribunal must provide to each party as soon as reasonably practicable after making a decision which finally disposes of all issues in the proceedings (except a decision under Part 5)—

(a) a decision notice stating the Tribunal's decision;

(b) written reasons for the decision; and

(c) notification of any right of appeal against the decision and the time within which, and the manner in which, such right of appeal may be exercised.

(3) The documents and information referred to in paragraph (2) must—

(a) in proceedings under section 66(1)(a) of the Mental Health Act 1983, be provided at the hearing or sent within 3 working days after the hearing; and

(b) in other cases, be provided at the hearing or sent within 7 days after the hearing.

(4) The Tribunal may provide written reasons for any decision to which paragraph (2) does not apply.

Provisional decisions

42. For the purposes of this Part and Parts 1, 2 and 5, a decision with recommendations under section 72(3)(a) or (3A)(a) of the Mental Health Act 1983(a) or a deferred direction for conditional discharge under section 73(7) of that Act is a decision which disposes of the proceedings.

PART 5

Correcting, setting aside, reviewing and appealing Tribunal decisions

Interpretation

43. In this Part—

"appeal" means the exercise of a right of appeal on a point of law under section 11 of the 2007 Act; and

"review" means the review of a decision by the Tribunal under section 9 of the 2007 Act.

Clerical mistakes and accidental slips or omissions

44. The Tribunal may at any time correct any clerical mistake or other accidental slip or omission in a decision, direction or any document produced by it, by—

(a) sending notification of the amended decision or direction, or a copy of the amended document, to all parties; and

(b) making any necessary amendment to any information published in relation to the decision, direction or document.

Setting aside a decision which disposes of proceedings

45.—(1) The Tribunal may set aside a decision which disposes of proceedings, or part of such a decision, and re-make the decision or the relevant part of it, if—

(a) the Tribunal considers that it is in the interests of justice to do so; and

(b) one or more of the conditions in paragraph (2) are satisfied.

(2) The conditions are—

(a) a document relating to the proceedings was not sent to, or was not received at an appropriate time by, a party or a party's representative;

(b) a document relating to the proceedings was not sent to the Tribunal at an appropriate time;

(a) 1983 c.20. Section 72(3A) was inserted by section 1(2) to, and paragraph 10(1) and (2) of Schedule 1 to, the Mental Health (Patients in the Community) Act 1995 (c.52), and is substituted by section 32(4) of, and paragraphs 1 and 21(1) and (4) of Schedule 3 to, the Mental Health Act 2007 (c.12).

(c) a party, or a party's representative, was not present at a hearing related to the proceedings; or

(d) there has been some other procedural irregularity in the proceedings.

(3) A party applying for a decision, or part of a decision, to be set aside under paragraph (1) must make a written application to the Tribunal so that it is received no later than 28 days after the date on which the Tribunal sent notice of the decision to the party.

Application for permission to appeal

46.—(1) A person seeking permission to appeal must make a written application to the Tribunal for permission to appeal.

(2) An application under paragraph (1) must be sent or delivered to the Tribunal so that it is received no later than 28 days after the latest of the dates that the Tribunal sends to the person making the application—

(a) written reasons for the decision;

(b) notification of amended reasons for, or correction of, the decision following a review; or

(c) notification that an application for the decision to be set aside has been unsuccessful.

(3) The date in paragraph (2)(c) applies only if the application for the decision to be set aside was made within the time stipulated in rule 45 (setting aside a decision which disposes of proceedings) or any extension of that time granted by the Tribunal.

(4) If the person seeking permission to appeal sends or delivers the application to the Tribunal later than the time required by paragraph (2) or by any extension of time under rule 5(3)(a) (power to extend time)—

(a) the application must include a request for an extension of time and the reason why the application was not provided in time; and

(b) unless the Tribunal extends time for the application under rule 5(3)(a) (power to extend time) the Tribunal must not admit the application.

(5) An application under paragraph (1) must—

(a) identify the decision of the Tribunal to which it relates;

(b) identify the alleged error or errors of law in the decision; and

(c) state the result the party making the application is seeking.

Tribunal's consideration of application for permission to appeal

47.—(1) On receiving an application for permission to appeal the Tribunal must first consider, taking into account the overriding objective in rule 2, whether to review the decision in accordance with rule 49 (review of a decision).

(2) If the Tribunal decides not to review the decision, or reviews the decision and decides to take no action in relation to the decision, or part of it, the Tribunal must consider whether to give permission to appeal in relation to the decision or that part of it.

(3) The Tribunal must send a record of its decision to the parties as soon as practicable.

(4) If the Tribunal refuses permission to appeal it must send with the record of its decision—

(a) a statement of its reasons for such refusal; and

(b) notification of the right to make an application to the Upper Tribunal for permission to appeal and the time within which, and the method by which, such application must be made.

(5) The Tribunal may give permission to appeal on limited grounds, but must comply with paragraph (4) in relation to any grounds on which it has refused permission.

Application for review in special educational needs cases

48.—(1) This rule applies to decisions which dispose of proceedings in special educational needs cases, but not to decisions under this Part.

(2) A party may make a written application to the Tribunal for a review of a decision if circumstances relevant to the decision have changed since the decision was made.

(3) An application under paragraph (2) must be sent or delivered to the Tribunal so that it is received within 28 days after the date on which the Tribunal sent the decision notice recording the Tribunal's decision to the party making the application.

(4) If a party sends or delivers an application to the Tribunal later than the time required by paragraph (3) or by any extension of time under rule 5(3)(a) (power to extend time)—

- (a) the application must include a request for an extension of time and the reason why the application was not provided in time; and
- (b) unless the Tribunal extends time for the application under rule 5(3)(a) (power to extend time) the Tribunal must not admit the application.

Review of a decision

49.—(1) The Tribunal may only undertake a review of a decision—

- (a) pursuant to rule 47(1) (review on an application for permission to appeal) if it is satisfied that there was an error of law in the decision; or
- (b) pursuant to rule 48 (application for review in special educational needs cases).

(2) The Tribunal must notify the parties in writing of the outcome of any review, and of any right of appeal in relation to the outcome.

(3) If the Tribunal takes any action in relation to a decision following a review without first giving every party an opportunity to make representations, the notice under paragraph (2) must state that any party that did not have an opportunity to make representations may apply for such action to be set aside and for the decision to be reviewed again.

Power to treat an application as a different type of application

50. The Tribunal may treat an application for a decision to be corrected, set aside or reviewed, or for permission to appeal against a decision, as an application for any other one of those things.

Patrick Elias
Phillip Brook Smith Q.C. Lesley Clare
Douglas J. May Q.C.
Newton of Braintree
M.J. Reed Mark Rowland
Nicholas Warren

I allow these Rules
Signed by authority of the Lord Chancellor

Bridget Prentice
Parliamentary Under Secretary of State
Ministry of Justice

9th October 2008

SCHEDULE(**a**) Rules 20(1)(a) and 21(1)(a)

Time limits for providing application notices and responses

Type of proceedings	*Time for application notice*	*Time for response*
Under Suspension Regulations (suspension of registration as a childcare provider)	10 working days after written notice of the decision was sent to the applicant	3 working days after the respondent received the application notice
Under section 79M of the Children Act 1989(**b**), except against a notice under section 79L(1)(a) of that Act (notice of intention to refuse an application for registration for childminding or providing day care) Under paragraph 10 of Schedule 26 to the School Standards and Framework Act 1998(**c**) (appeal against a decision of the Chief Inspector for Wales) Under section 68 of the Care Standards Act 2000 (appeal against a decision of the Council) except an appeal against a refusal under section 58 of that Act (refusal of an application to be included on a register of social workers) Under section 74(1)(b) to (e) and (2) of the Childcare Act 2006 (appeal against steps taken by the Chief Inspector except refusal of application for registration or against a prescribed determination)	28 days after written notice of the decision was sent to the applicant	20 working days after the respondent received the application notice
Under section 21 of the Care Standards Act 2000 (refusal or cancellation of registration, or variation of conditions of registration, by registration authority or by order of a justice of the peace) Under section 32 of the Health and Social Care Act 2008(**d**) (appeal against a decision of the Care Quality Commission or an order of a justice of the peace cancelling registration) Health and Social Care Act 2008 Under section 166 of the Education Act 2002 (appeal against steps taken by the registration authority) [Under section 124 of the Education and Skills Act 2008(**e**) (appeal against removal of a registered independent educational institution from the register)]	28 day time limits are set out in section 21(2) of the Care Standards Act 2000, section 166(2) of the Education Act 2002[, section 32(2) of the Health and Social Care Act 2008 and section 124 of the Education and Skills Act 2008]	20 working days after the respondent received the application notice

(a) The wording in square brackets in the third row of the table was inserted by S.I. 2009/1975.
(b) 1989 c.41. Sections 79L and 79M were inserted by section 79(1) of the Care Standards Act 2000 (c.14).
(c) 1998 c.31.
(d) 2008 c.14.
(e) 2008 c. 25.

Type of proceedings	*Time for application notice*	*Time for response*
Under section 65A of the Children Act 1989(**a**) (refusal to give consent for a person who is disqualified from fostering a child privately to carry on, be otherwise concerned in the management of, have any financial interest in, or be employed in, a children's home)	3 months after written notice of the decision was sent to the applicant	20 days after the respondent received the application notice
Under section 79M of the Children Act 1989 against a notice under 79L(1)(a) of that Act (notice of intention to refuse an application for registration for childminding or for providing day care)		
Under section 4 of the Protection of Children Act 1999 (inclusion of a person on a list of individuals who are considered unsuitable to work with children, a refusal to remove a person from such list, or determination of inclusion on the list where a person has been provisionally included on the list for more than 9 months)		
Under section 68 of the Care Standards Act 2000 where the appeal is against a refusal under section 58 of that Act (refusal of an application to be included on a register of social workers)		
Under section 86 of the Care Standards Act 2000 (inclusion of a person on a list of individuals who are considered unsuitable to work with vulnerable adults, a refusal to remove a person from such list, or determination of inclusion on the list where a person has been provisionally included on the list for more than 9 months)		
Under the Education (Prohibition from Teaching or Working with Children) Regulations 2003(**b**) (decision to give a direction, or a refusal to revoke a direction, prohibiting or restricting a person from working in education or in a job which brings them regularly into contact with children)		
Under section 74(1)(a) of the Childcare Act 2006 (refusal of registration as a childcare provider)		

(**a**) 1989 c.41. Section 65A was inserted by section 116 of, and paragraph 14(1) and (14) of Schedule 4 to, the Care Standards Act 2000 (c.14).

(**b**) S.I. 2003/1184.

Appendix 2

Type of proceedings	*Time for application notice*	*Time for response*
Under regulations made under section 28X of the National Health Service Act 1977**(a)** (decision contingently to remove a person from a list maintained by a Primary Care Trust or Local Health Board of persons authorised to perform primary medical, dental or ophthalmic services, or local pharmaceutical services)	(a) for the first application in relation to a decision, 3 months after the decision was made; (b) for any further application in respect of the same decision, 6 months after the Tribunal made its last determination in relation to that decision; (c) for any further application in respect of the same decision where the parties apply jointly to the Tribunal with a view to seeking— (i) the same variation of conditions, (ii) the same imposition of different conditions, or (iii) for the contingent removal to be revoked, 1 month after the Tribunal made its last determination in relation to that decision.	21 days after the respondent received the application notice
Under Part 4 of and Schedule 27 to the Education Act 1996**(b)** (provision of education to a child with special educational needs)	2 months after written notice of the decision was sent to the applicant	30 working days after the respondent received the application notice
Under section 28I of the Disability Discrimination Act 1995**(c)** (disability discrimination in the education of a child)	6 months after the decision or act complained of	30 working days after the respondent received the application notice

(a) 1977 c.49. Section 28X was inserted by section 179(1) of the Health and Social Care (Community Health and Standards) Act 2003 (c.43). It was repealed by section 6 of, and Schedule 4 to, the National Health Service (Consequential Provisions) Act 2006 (c.43) subject to savings provisions in paragraph 1 of Schedule 2 to that Act.

(b) 1996 c.56.

(c) 1995 c.50. Section 28I was inserted by section 18 of the Special Educational Needs and Disability Act 2001 (c.10).

EXPLANATORY NOTE

(This note is not part of the Rules)

Part 1 of the Tribunals, Courts and Enforcement Act 2007 (c.15) establishes a new tribunal structure comprising a First-tier Tribunal and an Upper Tribunal. Appeal functions of existing tribunals are being transferred to this structure and assigned to chambers within the new tribunals. These Rules govern the practice and procedure to be followed in the First-tier Tribunal in proceedings which have been allocated to the Health, Education and Social Care Chamber by the First-tier Tribunal and Upper Tribunal (Chambers) Order 2008(a).

Part 1 contains provisions for interpreting and applying the Rules and sets out the overriding objective of the Rules.

Part 2 contains general powers and provisions including the Tribunal's general case management powers, the giving of directions, the power to strike out a party's case, the service of documents and rules about evidence, submissions and witnesses.

Part 3 contains provisions on starting proceedings and on responses and replies in cases other than mental health cases. It also makes provision for hearings and for decisions made by the Tribunal in those cases.

Part 4 contains provisions on starting proceedings and on statements by authorities in mental health cases. It also makes provision for hearings and for decisions made by the Tribunal in those cases.

Part 5 deals with correcting, setting aside, reviewing and appealing against Tribunal decisions.

(a) S.I. 2008/2684.

Appendix 3

SI 2005 No 230

The Asylum and Immigration Tribunal (Procedure) Rules 2005

Version in force from 15th February 2010. This document has been produced in order to assist users but its accuracy is not guaranteed and should not be relied upon. For a definitive version of the Rules, users should refer to the original statutory instruments.

PART 1

Introduction

1 Citation and commencement

These Rules may be cited as the Asylum and Immigration Tribunal (Procedure) Rules 2005 and shall come into force on 4th April 2005.

2 Interpretation

In these Rules—

"the 2002 Act" means the Nationality, Immigration and Asylum Act 2002;

"the 2004 Act" means the Asylum and Immigration (Treatment of Claimants, etc) Act 2004;

"appeal to the Upper Tribunal" means the exercise of a right of appeal on a point of law under section 11 of the Tribunals, Courts and Enforcement Act 2007;

"appellant" means a person who has given a notice of appeal to the Tribunal against a relevant decision in accordance with these Rules;

"asylum claim" has the meaning given in section 113(1) of the 2002 Act;

"business day" means any day other than a Saturday or Sunday, a bank holiday, 25th to 31st December or Good Friday;

"determination", in relation to an appeal, means a decision by the Tribunal in writing to allow or dismiss the appeal, and does not include a procedural, ancillary or preliminary decision;

"the Immigration Acts" means the Acts referred to in section 44(1) of the 2004 Act;

"Immigration and Asylum Chamber" means the Immigration and Asylum Chamber of the First-tier Tribunal established by the First-tier Tribunal and Upper Tribunal (Chambers) Order 2008((1));

"immigration decision" means a decision of a kind listed in section 82(2) of the 2002 Act;

"immigration rules" means the rules referred to in section 1(4) of the Immigration Act 1971;

---

(1) S.I. 2008/2684 was amended by the First-tier Tribunal and Upper Tribunal (Chambers) (Amendment) Order 2009 (S.I. 2009/196 and the First-tier Tribunal and Upper Tribunal (Chambers) (Amendment No. 2) Order 2009 (S.I. 2009/1021) and the First-tier Tribunal and Upper Tribunal (Chambers) (Amendment No. 3) Order 2009 (S.I. 2009/1590).

"relevant decision" means a decision against which there is an exercisable right of appeal to the Tribunal;

"respondent" means the decision maker specified in the notice of decision against which a notice of appeal has been given;

"Tribunal" means the First-tier Tribunal;

"United Kingdom Representative" means the United Kingdom Representative of the United Nations High Commissioner for Refugees.

3 Scope of these Rules

These Rules apply to proceedings before the Tribunal which have been allocated to the Immigration and Asylum Chamber by the First-tier Tribunal and Upper Tribunal (Chambers) Order 2008.

4 Overriding objective

The overriding objective of these Rules is to secure that proceedings before the Tribunal are handled as fairly, quickly and efficiently as possible; and, where appropriate, that members of the Tribunal have responsibility for ensuring this, in the interests of the parties to the proceedings and in the wider public interest.

PART 2

Appeals to the Tribunal

5 Scope of this Part

This Part applies to appeals to the Tribunal.

6 Giving notice of appeal

(1) An appeal to the Tribunal may only be instituted by giving notice of appeal against a relevant decision in accordance with these Rules.

(2) Subject to paragraphs (3) and (4), notice of appeal must be given by filing it with the Tribunal in accordance with rule 55(1).

(3) A person who is in detention under the Immigration Acts may give notice of appeal either—

(a) in accordance with paragraph (2); or

(b) by serving it on the person having custody of him.

(4) A person who is outside the United Kingdom and wishes to appeal against a decision of an entry clearance officer may give notice of appeal either—

(a) in accordance with paragraph (2); or

(b) by serving it on the entry clearance officer.

(5) Where a notice of appeal is served on a custodian under paragraph (3)(b), that person must—

(a) endorse on the notice the date that it is served on him; and

(b) forward it to the Tribunal within 2 days.

(6) Where a notice of appeal is served on an entry clearance officer under paragraph (4)(b), the officer must—

(a) endorse on the notice the date that it is served on him;

(b) forward it to the Tribunal as soon as reasonably practicable, and in any event within 10 days; and

(c) if it is practicable to do so within the time limit in sub-paragraph (b), send to the Tribunal with the notice of appeal a copy of the documents listed in rule 13(1).

7 Time limit for appeal

(1) A notice of appeal by a person who is in the United Kingdom must be given—

(a) if the person is in detention under the Immigration Acts when he is served with notice of the decision against which he is appealing, not later than 5 days after he is served with that notice; and

(b) in any other case, not later than 10 days after he is served with notice of the decision.

(2) A notice of appeal by a person who is outside the United Kingdom must be given—

(a) if the person—

(i) was in the United Kingdom when the decision against which he is appealing was made; and

(ii) may not appeal while he is the United Kingdom by reason of a provision of the 2002 Act,

not later than 28 days after his departure from the United Kingdom; or

(b) in any other case, not later than 28 days after he is served with notice of the decision.

(3) Where a person—

(a) is served with notice of a decision to reject an asylum claim; and

(b) on the date of being served with that notice does not satisfy the condition in section 83(1)(b) of the 2002 Act, but later satisfies that condition,

paragraphs (1) and (2)(b) apply with the modification that the time for giving notice of appeal under section 83(2) runs from the date on which the person is served with notice of the decision to grant him leave to enter or remain in the United Kingdom by which he satisfies the condition in section 83(1)(b).

8 Form and contents of notice of appeal

(1) The notice of appeal must be made on a form approved for the purpose by the Senior President and must—

(a) state the name and address of the appellant; and

(b) state whether the appellant has authorised a representative to act for him in the appeal and, if so, give the representative's name and address;

(c) set out the grounds for the appeal;

(d) give reasons in support of those grounds; and

(e) so far as reasonably practicable, list any documents which the appellant intends to rely upon as evidence in support of the appeal.

(2) The notice of appeal must be accompanied by—

(a) the notice of decision against which the appellant is appealing; or

(b) if it is not practicable to include the notice of decision, the reasons why it is not practicable.

(3) The notice of appeal must be signed by the appellant or his representative, and dated.

(4) If a notice of appeal is signed by the appellant's representative, the representative must certify in the notice of appeal that he has completed it in accordance with the appellant's instructions.

9 Where the Tribunal may not accept a notice of appeal

(1) Where a person has given a notice of appeal to the Tribunal and the circumstances in paragraph (1A) apply, the Tribunal may not accept the notice of appeal.

(1A) The circumstances referred to in paragraph (1) are that—

(a) there is no relevant decision; or

(b) the notice of appeal concerns the refusal of an application for entry clearance which was not made for a purpose falling within section 88A(1)(a) or (b) of the 2002 Act, and the notice of appeal does not rely on either of the grounds specified in section 88A(3)(a) of the 2002 Act.

(2) Where the Tribunal does not accept a notice of appeal, it must—

(a) notify the person giving the notice of appeal and the respondent; and

(b) take no further action.

10 Late notice of appeal

(1) If a notice of appeal is given outside the applicable time limit, it must include an application for an extension of time for appealing, which must—

(a) include a statement of the reasons for failing to give the notice within that period; and

(b) be accompanied by any written evidence relied upon in support of those reasons.

(2) If a notice of appeal appears to the Tribunal to have been given outside the applicable time limit but does not include an application for an extension of time, unless the Tribunal extends the time for appealing of its own initiative, it must notify the person giving notice of appeal in writing that it proposes to treat the notice of appeal as being out of time.

(3) Where the Tribunal gives notification under paragraph (2), if the person giving notice of appeal contends that—

(a) the notice of appeal was given in time, or

(b) there were special circumstances for failing to give the notice of appeal in time which could not reasonably have been stated in the notice of appeal,

he may file with the Tribunal written evidence in support of that contention.

(4) Written evidence under paragraph (3) must be filed

(a) if the person giving notice of appeal is in the United Kingdom, not later than 3 days; or

(b) if the person giving notice of appeal is outside the United Kingdom, not later than 10 days,

after notification is given under paragraph (2).

(5) Where the notice of appeal was given out of time, the Tribunal may extend the time for appealing if satisfied that by reason of special circumstances it would be unjust not to do so.

(6) The Tribunal must decide any issue as to whether a notice of appeal was given in time, or whether to extend the time for appealing, as a preliminary decision without a hearing, and in doing so may only take account of—

(a) the matters stated in the notice of appeal;

(b) any evidence filed by the person giving notice of appeal in accordance with paragraph (1) or (3); and

(c) any other relevant matters of fact within the knowledge of the Tribunal.

(6A) Where the Tribunal makes a decision under this rule it must give written notice of its decision, including its reasons which may be in summary form.

(7) Subject to paragraphs (8) and (9), the Tribunal must serve the written notice given under paragraph (6A) on the parties.

(8) Where—

(a) a notice of appeal under section 82 of the 2002 Act which relates in whole or in part to an asylum claim was given out of time;

(b) the person giving notice of appeal is in the United Kingdom; and

(c) the Tribunal refuses to extend the time for appealing,

the Tribunal must serve written notice of its decision on the respondent, which must—

(i) serve the notice of decision on the person giving notice of appeal not later than 28 days after receiving it from the Tribunal; and

(ii) as soon as practicable after serving the notice of decision, notify the Tribunal on what date and by what means it was served.

(9) Where paragraph (8) applies, if the respondent does not give the Tribunal notification under sub-paragraph (ii) within 29 days after the Tribunal serves the notice of decision on it, the Tribunal must serve the notice of decision on the person giving notice of appeal as soon as reasonably practicable thereafter.

11 Special provisions for imminent removal cases

(1) This rule applies in any case in which the respondent notifies the Tribunal that removal directions have been issued against a person who has given notice of appeal, pursuant to which it is proposed to remove him from the United Kingdom within 5 calendar days of the date on which the notice of appeal was given.

(2) The Tribunal must, if reasonably practicable, make any preliminary decision under rule 10 before the date and time proposed for his removal.

(3) Rule 10 shall apply subject to the modifications that the Tribunal may—

(a) give notification under rule 10(2) orally, which may include giving it by telephone;

(b) shorten the time for giving evidence under rule 10(3); and

(c) direct that any evidence under rule 10(3) is to be given orally, which may include requiring the evidence to be given by telephone, and hold a hearing or telephone hearing for the purpose of receiving such evidence.

12 Service of notice of appeal on respondent

(1) Subject to paragraph (2), when the Tribunal receives a notice of appeal it shall serve a copy upon the respondent as soon as reasonably practicable.

(2) Paragraph (1) does not apply where the notice of appeal was served on an entry clearance officer under rule 6(4)(b).

13 Filing of documents by respondent

(1) When the respondent is served with a copy of a notice of appeal, it must (unless it has already done so) file with the Tribunal a copy of—

(a) the notice of the decision to which the notice of appeal relates, and any other document served on the appellant giving reasons for that decision;

(b) any—

(i) statement of evidence form completed by the appellant; and

(ii) record of an interview with the appellant,

in relation to the decision being appealed;

(c) any other unpublished document which is referred to in a document mentioned in sub-paragraph (a) or relied upon by the respondent; and

(d) the notice of any other immigration decision made in relation to the appellant in respect of which he has a right of appeal under section 82 of the 2002 Act.

(2) Subject to paragraph (3), the respondent must file the documents listed in paragraph (1)—

(a) in accordance with any directions given by the Tribunal; and

(b) if no such directions are given, as soon as reasonably practicable and in any event not later than 2.00 pm on the business day before the earliest date appointed for any hearing of or in relation to the appeal.

(3) If the Tribunal considers the timeliness of a notice of appeal as a preliminary issue under rule 10, the respondent must file the documents listed in paragraph (1) as soon as reasonably practicable after being served with a decision of the Tribunal allowing the appeal to proceed, and in any event not later than 2.00 pm on the business day before the earliest date appointed for any hearing of or in relation to the appeal following that decision.

(4) The respondent must, at the same time as filing them, serve on the appellant a copy of all the documents listed in paragraph (1), except for documents which the respondent has already sent to the appellant.

14 Variation of grounds of appeal

Subject to section 85(2) of the 2002 Act, the appellant may vary his grounds of appeal only with the permission of the Tribunal.

15 Method of determining appeal

(1) Every appeal must be considered by the Tribunal at a hearing, except where—

(a) the appeal—

(i) lapses pursuant to section 99 of the 2002 Act;

(ii) is treated as abandoned pursuant to section 104(4) of the 2002 Act;

(iii) is treated as finally determined pursuant to section 104(5) of the 2002 Act; or

(iv) is withdrawn by the appellant or treated as withdrawn in accordance with rule 17;

(b) paragraph (2) of this rule applies; or

(c) any other provision of these Rules or of any other enactment permits or requires the Tribunal to dispose of an appeal without a hearing.

(2) The Tribunal may determine an appeal without a hearing if—

(a) all the parties to the appeal consent;

(b) the appellant is outside the United Kingdom or it is impracticable to give him notice of a hearing and, in either case, he is unrepresented;

(ba) the appellant is outside the United Kingdom and his representative's address for service is outside the United Kingdom;

(c) a party has failed to comply with a provision of these Rules or a direction of the Tribunal, or to provide a satisfactory explanation under rule 8(2)(b), and the Tribunal is satisfied that in all the circumstances, including the extent of the failure and any reasons for it, it is appropriate to determine the appeal without a hearing; or

(d) subject to paragraph (3), the Tribunal is satisfied, having regard to the material before it and the nature of the issues raised, that the appeal can be justly determined without a hearing.

(3) Where paragraph (2)(d) applies, the Tribunal must not determine the appeal without a hearing without first giving the parties notice of its intention to do so, and an opportunity to make written representations as to whether there should be a hearing.

16 Certification of pending appeal

(1) If the Secretary of State or an immigration officer issues a certificate under section 97 or 98 of the 2002 Act which relates to a pending appeal, he must file notice of the certification with the Tribunal.

(2) Where a notice of certification is filed under paragraph (1), the Tribunal must—

(a) notify the parties; and

(b) take no further action in relation to the appeal.

17 Withdrawal of appeal

(1) An appellant may withdraw an appeal—

(a) orally, at a hearing; or

(b) at any time, by filing written notice with the Tribunal.

(2) An appeal shall be treated as withdrawn if the respondent notifies the Tribunal that the decision (or, where the appeal relates to more than one decision, all of the decisions) to which the appeal relates has been withdrawn.

(2A) Where an appellant dies before his appeal has been determined by the Tribunal, the Tribunal may direct that—

(a) the appeal shall be treated as withdrawn; or

(b) where the Tribunal considers it necessary, the personal representative of the appellant may continue the proceedings in the place of the appellant.

(3) If an appeal is withdrawn or treated as withdrawn, the Tribunal must serve on the parties a notice that the appeal has been recorded as having been withdrawn.

18 Abandonment of appeal

(1) Any party to a pending appeal must notify the Tribunal if they are aware that an event specified in—

(a) section 104(4)[, (4A)] or (5) of the 2002 Act; or

(b) regulation 33(1A) of the Immigration (European Economic Area) Regulations 2000 ("the 2000 Regulations") [or, on or after 30th April 2006, paragraph 4(2) of Schedule 2 to the Immigration (European Economic Area) Regulations 2006 ("the 2006 Regulations")],

has taken place.

(1A) Where section 104(4A) of the 2002 Act applies and the appellant wishes to pursue his appeal, the appellant must file a notice with the Tribunal—

(a) where section 104(4B) of the 2002 Act applies, within 28 days of the date on which the appellant received notice of the grant of leave to enter or remain in the United Kingdom for a period exceeding 12 months; or

(b) where section 104(4C) of the 2002 Act applies, within 28 days of the date on which the appellant received notice of the grant of leave to enter or remain in the United Kingdom.

(1B) Where the appellant does not comply with the time limits specified in paragraph (1A) the appeal will be treated as abandoned in accordance with section 104(4) of the 2002 Act.

(1C) At the same time as filing the notice under paragraph (1A), the appellant must serve a copy of the notice on the respondent.

(1D) Where section 104(4B) of the 2002 Act applies, the notice filed under paragraph (1A) must state—

(a) the appellant's full name and date of birth;

(b) the Tribunal's reference number;

(c) the Home Office reference number, if applicable;

(d) the Foreign and Commonwealth Office reference number, if applicable;

(e) the date on which the appellant was granted leave to enter or remain in the United Kingdom for a period exceeding 12 months; and

(f) that the appellant wishes to pursue the appeal in so far as it is brought on the ground specified in section 84(1)(g) of the 2002 Act which relates to the Refugee Convention.

(1E) Where section 104(4C) of the 2002 Act applies, the notice filed under paragraph (1A) must state—

(a) the appellant's full name and date of birth;

(b) the Tribunal's reference number;

(c) the Home Office reference number, if applicable;

(d) the Foreign and Commonwealth Office reference number, if applicable;

(e) the date on which the appellant was granted leave to enter or remain in the United Kingdom; and

(f) that the appellant wishes to pursue the appeal in so far as it is brought on the ground specified in section 84(1)(b) of the 2002 Act which relates to section 19B of the Race Relations Act 1976.

(1F) Where an appellant has filed a notice under paragraph (1A) the Tribunal will notify the appellant of the date on which it received the notice.

(1G) The Tribunal will send a copy of the notice issued under paragraph (1F) to the respondent.

(2) Where an appeal is treated as abandoned pursuant to section 104(4) [or (4A)] of the 2002 Act or regulation 33(1A) of the 2000 Regulations [or paragraph 4(2) of Schedule 2 to the 2006 Regulations], or finally determined pursuant to section 104(5) of the 2002 Act, the Tribunal must—

(a) serve on the parties a notice informing them that the appeal is being treated as abandoned or finally determined; and

(b) take no further action in relation to the appeal.

19 Hearing appeal in absence of a party

(1) The Tribunal may hear an appeal in the absence of a party or his representative, if satisfied that—

(a) [the party or his representative] has been given notice of the date, time and place of the hearing, and

(b) there is no good reason for such absence.

(2) Where paragraph (1) does not apply, the Tribunal may hear an appeal in the absence of a party if satisfied that—

(a) a representative of the party is present at the hearing;

(b) the party is outside the United Kingdom;

(c) the party is suffering from a communicable disease or there is a risk of him behaving in a violent or disorderly manner;

(d) the party is unable to attend the hearing because of illness, accident or some other good reason;

(e) the party is unrepresented and it is impracticable to give him notice of the hearing; or

(f) the party has notified the Tribunal that he does not wish to attend the hearing.

20 Hearing two or more appeals together

Where two or more appeals are pending at the same time, the Tribunal may direct them to be heard together if it appears that—

(a) some common question of law or fact arises in each of them;

(b) they relate to decisions or action taken in respect of persons who are members of the same family; or

(c) for some other reason it is desirable for the appeals to be heard together.

21 Adjournment of appeals

(1) Where a party applies for an adjournment of a hearing of an appeal, he must—

(a) if practicable, notify all other parties of the application;

(b) show good reason why an adjournment is necessary; and

(c) produce evidence of any fact or matter relied upon in support of the application.

(2) The Tribunal must not adjourn a hearing of an appeal on the application of a party, unless satisfied that the appeal cannot otherwise be justly determined.

(3) The Tribunal must not, in particular, adjourn a hearing on the application of a party in order to allow the party more time to produce evidence, unless satisfied that—

(a) the evidence relates to a matter in dispute in the appeal;

(b) it would be unjust to determine the appeal without permitting the party a further opportunity to produce the evidence; and

(c) where the party has failed to comply with directions for the production of the evidence, he has provided a satisfactory explanation for that failure.

(4) Where the hearing of an appeal is adjourned, the Tribunal will fix a new hearing date which—

(a) shall be not more than 28 days after the original hearing date, unless the Tribunal is satisfied that because of exceptional circumstances the appeal cannot justly be heard within that time; and

(b) shall in any event be not later than is strictly required by the circumstances necessitating the adjournment.

22 Giving of determination

(1) Except in cases to which rule 23 applies, where the Tribunal determines an appeal it must serve on every party a written determination containing its decision and the reasons for it.

(2) The Tribunal must send its determination—

(a) if the appeal is considered at a hearing, not later than 10 days after the hearing finishes; or

(b) if the appeal is determined without a hearing, not later than 10 days after it is determined.

23 Special procedures and time limits in asylum appeals

(1) This rule applies to appeals under section 82 of the 2002 Act where—

(a) the appellant is in the United Kingdom; and

(b) the appeal relates, in whole or in part, to an asylum claim.

(2) Subject to paragraph (3)—

(a) where an appeal is to be considered by the Tribunal at a hearing, the hearing must be fixed for a date not more than [35] days after the later of—

(i) the date on which the Tribunal receives the notice of appeal; or

(ii) if the Tribunal makes a preliminary decision under rule 10 (late notice of appeal), the date on which notice of that decision is served on the appellant; and

(b) where an appeal is to be determined without a hearing, the Tribunal must determine it not more than [35] days after the later of those dates.

(3) If the respondent does not file the documents specified in rule 13(1) within the time specified in rule 13 or directions given under that rule—

(a) paragraph (2) does not apply; and

(b) the Tribunal may vary any hearing date that it has already fixed in accordance with paragraph (2)(a), if it is satisfied that it would be unfair to the appellant to proceed with the hearing on the date fixed.

(4) The Tribunal must serve its determination on the respondent—

(a) if the appeal is considered at a hearing, by sending it not later than 10 days after the hearing finishes; or

(b) if the appeal is determined without a hearing, by sending it not later than 10 days after it is determined.

(5) The respondent must—

(a) serve the determination on the appellant—

(i) if the respondent makes an application for permission to appeal against a decision of the Tribunal, by sending, delivering or personally serving the determination not later than the date on which the respondent makes that application; and

(ii) otherwise, not later than 28 days after receiving the determination from the Tribunal; and

(b) as soon as practicable after serving the determination, notify the Tribunal on what date and by what means it was served.

(6) If the respondent does not give the Tribunal notification under paragraph (5)(b) within 29 days after the Tribunal serves the determination on it, the Tribunal must serve the determination on the appellant as soon as reasonably practicable thereafter.

(7) In paragraph (2) of this rule, references to a hearing do not include a case management review hearing or other preliminary hearing.

No power to award costs

23A The Tribunal may not make any order in respect of costs (or, in Scotland, expenses) pursuant to section 29 of the Tribunals, Courts and Enforcement Act 2007 (power to award costs).

PART 3

Appeals to the Upper Tribunal

Application for permission to appeal to the Upper Tribunal

24.—(1) A party seeking permission to appeal to the Upper Tribunal must make a written application to the Tribunal for permission to appeal.

(2) Subject to paragraph (3), an application under paragraph (1) must be sent or delivered to the Tribunal so that it is received no later than 5 days after the date on which the party making the application is deemed to have been served with written reasons for the decision

(3) Where an appellant is outside the UK, the time limit for that person sending or delivering an application under paragraph (1) is 28 days.

(4) If a person makes an application under paragraph (1) later than the time required by paragraph (2)—

- (a) the Tribunal may extend the time for appealing if satisfied that by reason of special circumstances it would be unjust not to do so; and
- (b) unless the Tribunal extends time under sub-paragraph (a), the Tribunal must not admit the application.

(5) An application under paragraph (1) must—

- (a) identify the decision of the Tribunal to which it relates;
- (b) identify the alleged error or errors of law in the decision; and
- (c) state the result the party making the application is seeking.

Tribunal's consideration of an application for permission to appeal to the Upper Tribunal

25.—(1) On receiving an application for permission to appeal the Tribunal must first consider whether to review the decision in accordance with rule 26.

(2) If the Tribunal decides not to review the decision, or reviews the decision and decides to take no action in relation to the decision, or part of it, the Tribunal must consider whether to give permission to appeal in relation to the decision or that part of it.

(3) The Tribunal must make a decision under paragraph (1) and, where relevant, paragraph (2), no later than 10 days after receiving the application.

(4) Subject to rule 27, the Tribunal must send to the parties—

- (a) written reasons for a decision under this rule; and
- (b) if the application is refused, notification of the right to make an application to the Upper Tribunal for permission to appeal and the time within which, and the method by which, such application must be made.

(5) The Tribunal may give permission to appeal on limited grounds, but must comply with paragraph (4) in relation to any grounds on which it has refused permission.

Review of a decision

26.—(1) The Tribunal may only undertake a review of a decision pursuant to rule 25(2) if it is satisfied that there was an error of law in the decision.

(2) Subject to rule 27, the Tribunal must notify the parties in writing of the outcome of any review, and of any right of appeal in relation to the outcome.

(3) If the Tribunal takes any action in relation to a decision following a review without first giving every party an opportunity to make representations, the notice under paragraph (2) must

state that any party that did not have an opportunity to make representations may apply for such action to be set aside and for the decision to be reviewed again.

Special procedure for providing notice of a decision relating to an asylum case

27.—(1) This Rule applies to an application to the Tribunal for permission to appeal to the Upper Tribunal where—

(a) the appellant is in the United Kingdom at the time the application is made; and

(b) the appeal relates, in whole or in part, to an asylum claim.

(2) In cases to which this paragraph applies—

(a) the Tribunal must send the documents mentioned in rule 25(4), or, where appropriate, rule 26(2), to the Secretary of State for the Home Department;

(b) the Secretary of State for the Home Department must serve those documents on the appellant not later than 28 days after receiving them from the Tribunal;

(c) the Secretary of State for the Home Department must, as soon as practicable after serving the documents mentioned in sub-paragraph (b), notify the Tribunal on what date and by what means they were served; and

(d) if the Secretary of State for the Home Department does not give the Tribunal notification under sub-paragraph (c) within 29 days after the Tribunal sends the documents mentioned in rule 25(4), or, where appropriate, rule 26(2) on it, the Tribunal must serve those documents on the appellant as soon as reasonably practicable thereafter.

PART 4

Bail

37 Scope of this Part and interpretation

(1) This Part applies to applications under the Immigration Acts to the Tribunal, by persons detained under those Acts, to be released on bail.

(2) In this Part, "applicant" means a person applying to the Tribunal to be released on bail.

(3) The parties to a bail application are the applicant and the Secretary of State.

38 Applications for bail

(1) An application to be released on bail must be made by filing with the Tribunal an application notice in a form approved for the purpose by the Senior President.

(2) The application notice must contain the following details—

(a) the applicant's—

(i) full name;

(ii) date of birth; and

(iii) date of arrival in the United Kingdom;

(b) the address of the place where the applicant is detained;

(c) whether an appeal by the applicant to the Tribunal is pending;

(d) the address where the applicant will reside if his application for bail is granted, or, if he is unable to give such an address, the reason why an address is not given;

(e) where the applicant is aged 18 or over, whether he will, if required, agree as a condition of bail to co-operate with electronic monitoring under section 36 of the 2004 Act;

(f) the amount of the recognizance in which he will agree to be bound;

(g) the full names, addresses, occupations and dates of birth of any persons who have agreed to act as sureties for the applicant if bail is granted, and the amounts of the recognizances in which they will agree to be bound;

(h) the grounds on which the application is made and, where a previous application has been refused, full details of any change in circumstances which has occurred since the refusal; and

(i) whether an interpreter will be required at the hearing, and in respect of what language or dialect.

(3) The application must be signed by the applicant or his representative or, in the case of an applicant who is a child or is for any other reason incapable of acting, by a person acting on his behalf.

39 Bail hearing

(1) Where an application for bail is filed, the Tribunal must—

(a) as soon as reasonably practicable, serve a copy of the application on the Secretary of State; and

(b) fix a hearing.

(2) If the Secretary of State wishes to contest the application, he must file with the Tribunal and serve on the applicant a written statement of his reasons for doing so—

(a) not later than 2.00 pm on the business day before the hearing; or

(b) if he was served with notice of the hearing less than 24 hours before that time, as soon as reasonably practicable.

(3) The Tribunal must serve written notice of its decision on—

(a) the parties; and

(b) the person having custody of the applicant.

(4) Where bail is granted, the notice must include—

(a) the conditions of bail; and

(b) the amount in which the applicant and any sureties are to be bound.

(5) Where bail is refused, the notice must include reasons for the refusal.

40 Recognizances

(1) The recognizance of an applicant or a surety must be in writing and must state—

(a) the amount in which he agrees to be bound; and

(b) that he has read and understood the bail decision and that he agrees to pay that amount of money if the applicant fails to comply with the conditions set out in the bail decision.

(2) The recognizance must be—

(a) signed by the applicant or surety; and

(b) filed with the Tribunal.

41 Release of applicant

The person having custody of the applicant must release him upon—

(a) being served with a copy of the decision to grant bail; and

(b) being satisfied that any recognizances required as a condition of that decision have been entered into.

42 Application of this Part to Scotland

This Part applies to Scotland with the following modifications—

(a) in rule 38, for paragraph (2)(f) and (g) substitute—

"(f) the amount, if any, to be deposited if bail is granted;

(g) the full names, addresses and occupations of any persons offering to act as cautioners if the application for bail is granted;";

(b) in rule 39, for paragraph (4)(b) substitute—

"(b) the amount (if any) to be deposited by the applicant and any cautioners.";

(c) rule 40 does not apply; and

(d) in rule 41, for sub-paragraph (b) substitute—

"(b) being satisfied that the amount to be deposited, if any, has been deposited.".

PART 5

General Provisions

43 Conduct of appeals and applications

(1) The Tribunal may, subject to these Rules, decide the procedure to be followed in relation to any appeal or application.

(2) Anything of a formal or administrative nature which is required or permitted to be done by the Tribunal under these Rules may be done by a member of the Tribunal's staff.

45 Directions

(1) The Tribunal may give directions to the parties relating to the conduct of any appeal or application.

(2) The power to give directions is to be exercised subject to any specific provision of these Rules.

(3) Directions must be given orally or in writing to every party.

(4) Directions of the Tribunal may, in particular—

(a) relate to any matter concerning the preparation for a hearing;

(b) specify the length of time allowed for anything to be done;

(c) vary any time limit in these Rules or in directions previously given by the Tribunal for anything to be done by a party [(including, where the Tribunal considers that there are exceptional reasons for doing so, extending a time limit which has expired)];

(d) provide for—

(i) a particular matter to be dealt with as a preliminary issue;

(ii) a case management review hearing to be held;

(iii) a party to provide further details of his case, or any other information which appears to be necessary for the determination of the appeal;

(iv) the witnesses, if any, to be heard;

(v) the manner in which any evidence is to be given (for example, by directing that witness statements are to stand as evidence in chief);

(e) require any party to file and serve—

(i) statements of the evidence which will be called at the hearing;

(ii) a paginated and indexed bundle of all the documents which will be relied on at the hearing;

(iii) a skeleton argument which summarises succinctly the submissions which will be made at the hearing and cites all the authorities which will be relied on, identifying any particular passages to be relied on;

(iv) a time estimate for the hearing;

(v) a list of witnesses whom any party wishes to call to give evidence;

(vi) a chronology of events; and

(vii) details of whether an interpreter will be required at the hearing, and in respect of what language and dialect;

(f) limit—

(i) the number or length of documents upon which a party may rely at a hearing;

(ii) the length of oral submissions;

(iii) the time allowed for the examination and cross-examination of witnesses; and

(iv) the issues which are to be addressed at a hearing; and

(g) require the parties to take any steps to enable two or more appeals to be heard together under rule 20.

(h) provide for a hearing to be conducted or evidence given or representations made by video link or by other electronic means; and

(i) make provision to secure the anonymity of a party or a witness.

(5) The Tribunal must not direct an unrepresented party to do something unless it is satisfied that he is able to comply with the direction.

(6) The Tribunal may direct that, in individual cases or in such classes of case as he shall specify, any time period in these Rules for the Tribunal to do anything shall be extended by such period as he shall specify.

46 Notification of hearings

(1) When the Tribunal fixes a hearing it must serve notice of the date, time and place of the hearing on every party.

(2) The Tribunal may vary the date of a hearing, but must serve notice of the new date, time and place of the hearing on every party.

47 Adjournment

Subject to any provision of these Rules, the Tribunal may adjourn any hearing.

48 Representation

(1) An appellant or applicant for bail may act in person or be represented by any person not prohibited from representing him by section 84 of the Immigration and Asylum Act 1999.

(2) A respondent to an appeal, the Secretary of State or the United Kingdom Representative may be represented by any person authorised to act on his behalf.

(3) If a party to whom paragraph (1) applies is represented by a person not permitted by that paragraph to represent him, any determination given or other step taken by the Tribunal in the proceedings shall nevertheless be valid.

(4) Where a representative begins to act for a party, he must immediately notify the Tribunal and the other party of that fact.

[(4A) Where a notice of appeal, or an application for bail under rule 38, is signed by a representative, the representative will be deemed to have notified the Tribunal and the other party that he is acting for a party in accordance with paragraph (4).

(4B) Where a notice of appeal, or an application for bail under rule 38, is not signed by a representative, the representative must file a separate notice with the Tribunal and serve it on the other party to comply with his obligations under paragraph (4).]

(5) Where a representative is acting for a party, he may on behalf of that party do anything that these Rules require or permit that party to do.

(6) Where a representative is acting for an appellant, the appellant is under a duty—

- (a) to maintain contact with his representative until the appeal is finally determined; and
- (b) to notify the representative of any change of address.

(7) Where a representative ceases to act for a party, the representative and the party must immediately notify the Tribunal and the other party [in writing] of that fact, and of the name and address of any new representative (if known).

(8) Notification under paragraph (4) . . .—

- (a) [where a representative is appointed to act for a party on the day of a hearing,] may be given orally at [that] hearing to the Tribunal and to any other party present at that hearing; but
- (b) must otherwise be given in writing.

(9) Until the Tribunal is notified that a representative has ceased to act for a party, any document served on that representative shall be deemed to be properly served on the party he was representing.

49 United Kingdom Representative

(1) The United Kingdom Representative may give notice to the Tribunal that he wishes to participate in any proceedings where the appellant has made an asylum claim.

(2) Where the United Kingdom Representative has given notice under paragraph (1)—

- (a) rules 54(6) and 55(7) shall apply; and
- (b) the Tribunal must permit him to make representations in the proceedings if he wishes to do so, and may give directions for that purpose.

49A Interpreters

An appellant is entitled to the services of an interpreter—

- (a) when giving evidence; and
- (b) in such other circumstances as the Tribunal considers necessary.

50 Summoning of witnesses

(1) The Tribunal may, by issuing a summons ("a witness summons"), require any person in the United Kingdom—

- (a) to attend as a witness at the hearing of an appeal; and
- (b) subject to rule 51(2), at the hearing to answer any questions or produce any documents in his custody or under his control which relate to any matter in issue in the appeal.

(2) A person is not required to attend a hearing in obedience to a witness summons unless—

- (a) the summons is served on him; and
- (b) the necessary expenses of his attendance are paid or tendered to him.

(3) If a witness summons is issued at the request of a party, that party must pay or tender the expenses referred to in paragraph (2)(b).

51 Evidence

(1) The Tribunal may allow oral, documentary or other evidence to be given of any fact which appears to be relevant to an appeal or an application for bail, even if that evidence would be inadmissible in a court of law.

(2) The Tribunal may not compel a party or witness to give any evidence or produce any document which he could not be compelled to give or produce at the trial of a civil claim in the part of the United Kingdom in which the hearing is taking place.

(3) The Tribunal may require the oral evidence of a witness to be given on oath or affirmation.

(4) Where the Tribunal has given directions setting time limits for the filing and serving of written evidence, it must not consider any written evidence which is not filed or served in accordance with those directions unless satisfied that there are good reasons to do so.

(5) Where a party seeks to rely upon a copy of a document as evidence, the Tribunal may require the original document to be produced.

(6) In an appeal to which section 85(5) of the 2002 Act applies, the Tribunal must only consider evidence relating to matters which it is not prevented by that section from considering.

(7) Subject to section 108 of the 2002 Act, the Tribunal must not take account of any evidence that has not been made available to all the parties.

52 Language of documents

(1) Subject to paragraph (2)—

(a) any notice of appeal or application notice filed with the Tribunal must be completed in English; and

(b) any other document filed with the Tribunal must be in English, or accompanied by a translation into English signed by the translator to certify that the translation is accurate.

(2) In proceedings in or having a connection with Wales, a document may be filed with the Tribunal in Welsh.

(3) The Tribunal shall be under no duty to consider a document which is not in English (or, where paragraph (2) applies, in Welsh), or accompanied by a certified translation.

53 Burden of proof

(1) If an appellant asserts that a relevant decision ought not to have been taken against him on the ground that the statutory provision under which that decision was taken does not apply to him, it is for that party to prove that the provision does not apply to him.

(2) If—

(a) an appellant asserts any fact; and

(b) by virtue of an Act, statutory instrument or immigration rules, if he had made such an assertion to the Secretary of State, an immigration officer or an entry clearance officer, it would have been for him to satisfy the Secretary of State or officer that the assertion was true,

it is for the appellant to prove that the fact asserted is true.

54 Admission of public to hearings

(1) Subject to the following provisions of this rule, every hearing before the Tribunal must be held in public.

(2) Where the Tribunal is considering an allegation referred to in section 108 of the 2002 Act—

(a) all members of the public must be excluded from the hearing, and

(b) any party or representative of a party may be excluded from the hearing.

(3) The Tribunal may exclude any or all members of the public from any hearing or part of a hearing if it is necessary—

(a) in the interests of public order or national security; or

(b) to protect the private life of a party or the interests of a minor.

(4) The Tribunal may also, in exceptional circumstances, exclude any or all members of the public from any hearing or part of a hearing to ensure that publicity does not prejudice the interests of justice, but only if and to the extent that it is strictly necessary to do so.

(5) . . .

(6) The United Kingdom Representative, where he has given notice to the Tribunal under rule 49, is entitled to attend any hearing except where paragraph (2) applies, and may not be excluded pursuant to paragraph (3) or (4) of this rule.

55 Filing and service of documents

(1) Any document which is required or permitted by these Rules or by a direction of the Tribunal to be filed with the Tribunal, or served on any person may be—

(a) delivered, or sent by post, to an address;

(b) sent via a document exchange to a document exchange number or address;

(c) sent by fax to a fax number; or

(d) sent by e-mail to an e-mail address,

specified for that purpose by the Tribunal or person to whom the document is directed.

(2) A document to be served on an individual may be served personally by leaving it with that individual.

(3) Where a person has notified the Tribunal that he is acting as the representative of an appellant and has given an address for service, if a document is served on the appellant, a copy must also at the same time be sent to the appellant's representative.

(4) If any document is served on a person who has notified the Tribunal that he is acting as the representative of a party, it shall be deemed to have been served on that party.

(5) Subject to paragraph (6), any document that is served on a person in accordance with this rule shall, unless the contrary is proved, be deemed to be served—

(a) where the document is sent by post or document exchange from and to a place within the United Kingdom, on the second day after it was sent;

(b) where the document is sent by post or document exchange from or to a place outside the United Kingdom, on the twenty-eighth day after it was sent; and

(c) in any other case, on the day on which the document was sent or delivered to, or left with, that person.

(6) Any notice of appeal which is served on a person under rule 6(3)(b) or 6(4)(b) shall be treated as being served on the day on which it is received by that person.

(7) Where the United Kingdom Representative has given notice to the Tribunal under rule 49 in relation to any proceedings, any document which is required by these Rules or by a direction of the Tribunal to be served on a party in those proceedings must also be served on the United Kingdom Representative.

56 Address for service

(1) Every party, and any person representing a party, must notify the Tribunal in writing of a postal address at which documents may be served on him and of any changes to that address.

(2) Until a party or representative notifies the Tribunal of a change of address, any document served on him at the most recent address which he has notified to the Tribunal shall be deemed to have been properly served on him.

(3) If the respondent knows that the appellant has changed the address referred to in paragraph (1), he must notify the Tribunal in writing of that fact and, if he is aware of it, the new address.

57 Calculation of time

(1) Where a period of time for doing any act is specified by these Rules or by a direction of the Tribunal, that period is to be calculated—

(a) excluding the day on which the period begins; and

(b) where the period is 10 days or less, excluding any day which is not a business day (unless the period is expressed as a period of calendar days).

(2) Where the time specified by these Rules or by a direction of the Tribunal for doing any act ends on a day which is not a business day, that act is done in time if it is done on the next business day.

58 Signature of documents

Any requirement in these Rules for a document to be signed by a party or his representative shall be satisfied, in the case of a document which is filed or served electronically in accordance with these rules, by the person who is required to sign the document typing his name or producing it by computer or other mechanical means.

59 Errors of procedure

(1) Where, before the Tribunal has determined an appeal or application, there has been an error of procedure such as a failure to comply with a rule—

(a) subject to these Rules, the error does not invalidate any step taken in the proceedings, unless the Tribunal so orders; and

(b) the Tribunal may make any order, or take any other step, that it considers appropriate to remedy the error.

(2) In particular, any determination made in an appeal or application under these Rules shall be valid notwithstanding that—

(a) a hearing did not take place; or

(b) the determination was not made or served,

within a time period specified in these Rules.

60 Correction of orders and determinations

(1) The Tribunal may at any time amend an order, notice of decision or determination to correct a clerical error or other accidental slip or omission.

(1A) The Tribunal may, either of its own motion or on application, review any order, notice of decision or determination made by the Tribunal and, after consulting all the parties to the appeal, may set it aside and direct that the relevant proceedings be dealt with again by the Tribunal, on the ground that it was wrongly made as the result of an administrative error on the part of the Tribunal or its staff.

(1B) An application under paragraph (1A) must be filed—

(a) if the party making the application is in the United Kingdom, within 10 days; or

(b) if the party making the application is outside the United Kingdom, within 28 days,

of the date on which the party is served with the order, notice of decision or determination.

(1C) At the same time as filing an application under paragraph (1A), the party making the application must serve a copy on the other party to the appeal.

(2) Where an order, notice of decision or determination is amended under this rule—

(a) the Tribunal must serve an amended version on the party or parties on whom it served the original; and

(b) if rule 10(8) and (9) or rule 23(5) and (6) applied in relation to the service of the original, it shall also apply in relation to the service of the amended version.

(3) The time within which a party may apply for permission to appeal against, or for a review of, an amended determination runs from the date on which the party is served with the amended determination.

Appendix 4

SI 2005 No 560

The Asylum and Immigration Tribunal (Fast Track Procedure) Rules 2005

Version in force from 15th February 2010. This document has been produced in order to assist users but its accuracy is not guaranteed and should not be relied upon. For a definitive version of the Rules, users should refer to the original statutory instruments.

PART 1

Introduction

1 Citation and commencement

These Rules may be cited as the Asylum and Immigration Tribunal (Fast Track Procedure) Rules 2005 and shall come into force on 4th April 2005.

2 Interpretation

(1) In these Rules, "the Principal Rules" means the Asylum and Immigration Tribunal (Procedure) Rules 2005.

(2) Subject to paragraph (3), words and expressions used in these Rules which are defined in rule 2 of the Principal Rules have the same meaning in these Rules as in the Principal Rules.

(3) In these Rules, and in any provision of the Principal Rules which applies by virtue of these Rules, "business day" means any day other than a Saturday or Sunday, a bank holiday, 24th to 31st December, Maundy Thursday, Good Friday or the Tuesday after the last Monday in May.

(5) Where a provision of the Principal Rules applies by virtue of these Rules—

(a) any reference in that provision to the Principal Rules is to be interpreted as including a reference to these Rules; and

(b) any reference in that provision to a specific Part or rule in the Principal Rules is to be interpreted as including a reference to any equivalent Part or rule in these Rules.

3 Scope of these Rules

(1) Part 2 of these Rules applies to appeals to the Tribunal in the circumstances specified in rule 5.

(2) Part 3 applies to applications to appeal to the Upper Tribunal in the circumstances specified in rule 15.

(3) Part 4 applies to proceedings before the Tribunal to which Part 2 or 3 applies.

(4) Part 5 applies to proceedings before the Tribunal to which Part 2 or 3 applies or has applied.

(5) For the purpose of rules 5 and 15, a party does not cease to satisfy a condition that he must have been continuously in detention under the Immigration Acts at a place or places specified in Schedule 2 to these Rules by reason only of—

(a) being transported from one place of detention specified in that Schedule to another place which is so specified; or

(b) leaving and returning to such a place of detention for any purpose between the hours of 6am and 10pm.

4 Application of the Principal Rules

(1) Rule 4 of the Principal Rules (Overriding objective) applies to these Rules.

(2) Where Part 2 or 3 of these Rules applies to proceedings before the Tribunal, the Principal Rules also apply to the extent specified in rules 6 and 27 of these Rules.

PART 2

Appeals to the Tribunal

5 Scope of this Part

(1) This Part applies to an appeal to the Tribunal where the person giving notice of appeal—

(a) was in detention under the Immigration Acts at a place specified in Schedule 2 when he was served with notice of the immigration decision against which he is appealing; and

(b) has been continuously in detention under the Immigration Acts at a place or places specified in Schedule 2 since that notice was served on him.

(2) This Part shall cease to apply if the Tribunal makes an order under rule 30(1).

6 Application of Part 2 of the Principal Rules

Where this Part applies to an appeal, the following provisions of Part 2 of the Principal Rules apply—

(a) rule 6(1) to (3), omitting the reference to rule 6(4) in rule 6(2);

(b) rule 8;

(c) rule 10(1);

(d) rule 13(1) and (4);

(e) rule 14;

(f) rules 17 to 19;

(g) rule 20, provided that this Part applies to all of the appeals proposed to be heard together; and

(h) rule 23A.

7 Giving notice of appeal

Where a notice of appeal is served on a custodian under rule 6(3)(b) of the Principal Rules, the custodian must—

(a) endorse on the notice the date that it is served on him; and

(b) forward it to the Tribunal immediately.

8 Time limit

(1) A person who wishes to appeal must give a notice of appeal not later than 2 days after the day on which he is served with notice of the immigration decision against which he is appealing.

(2) Where a notice of appeal is given outside the time limit in paragraph (1), the Tribunal must not extend the time for appealing unless it is satisfied that, because of circumstances outside the control of the person giving notice of appeal or his representative, it was not practicable for the notice of appeal to be given within that time limit.

9 Service of notice of appeal on respondent

When the Tribunal receives a notice of appeal it shall immediately serve a copy upon the respondent.

10 Filing of documents by respondent

The respondent must file the documents listed in rule 13(1) of the Principal Rules not later than 2 days after the day on which the Tribunal serves the respondent with the notice of appeal.

11 Listing

(1) The Tribunal shall fix a hearing date which is—

- (a) not later than 2 days after the day on which the respondent files the documents under rule 10; or
- (b) if the Tribunal is unable to arrange a hearing within that time, as soon as practicable thereafter.

(2) The Tribunal must serve notice of the date, time and place of the hearing on every party as soon as practicable, and in any event not later than noon on the business day before the hearing.

12 Deciding timeliness issues

(1) The Tribunal shall consider any issue as to—

- (a) whether a notice of appeal was given outside the applicable time limit; and
- (b) whether to extend the time for appealing where the notice of appeal was given outside that time limit,

as a preliminary issue at the hearing fixed under rule 11, subject to paragraph (2) of this rule.

(2) Rule 13 applies to the consideration and decision of such an issue as it applies to the consideration and determination of an appeal.

(3) Where the notice of appeal was given outside the applicable time limit and the Tribunal does not grant an extension of time, the Tribunal must take no further action in relation to the notice of appeal, except that it must serve on every party written notice of its decision under this rule, including its reasons which may be in summary form, not later than 1 day after the day on which that decision is made.

13 Method of determining appeal

(1) The Tribunal must consider the appeal at the hearing fixed under rule 11 except where—

- (a) the appeal—
  - (i) lapses pursuant to section 99 of the 2002 Act;
  - (ii) is treated as abandoned pursuant to section 104(4) or (4A) of the 2002 Act;
  - (iii) is treated as finally determined pursuant to section 104(5) of the 2002 Act; or
  - (iv) is withdrawn by the appellant or treated as withdrawn in accordance with rule 17 of the Principal Rules;
- (b) the Tribunal adjourns the hearing under rule 28 or 30(2)(a) of these Rules; or
- (c) all of the parties to the appeal consent to the Tribunal determining the appeal without a hearing.

(2) The Tribunal may consider an appeal without a hearing where—

(a) the person giving notice of appeal fails to comply with rule 8(2) of the Principal Rules; or

(b) the Tribunal does not consider that the reasons given under rule 8(2)(b) of those Rules are satisfactory.

14 Giving of determination

(1) Where the Tribunal determines an appeal, it must give a written determination containing its decision and the reasons for it.

(2) The Tribunal must serve its determination on every party to the appeal—

(a) if the appeal is considered at a hearing, not later than 2 days after the day on which the hearing of the appeal finishes; or

(b) if the appeal is determined without a hearing, not later than 2 days after the day on which it is determined.

PART 3

Appeals to the Upper Tribunal

Scope of this Part

15.—(1) This Part applies to applications for permission to appeal to the Upper Tribunal made pursuant to rule 25 of the Principal Rules, where—

(a) Part 2 of these Rules applied at all times to the appeal to the Tribunal; and

(b) the appellant has been continuously in detention under the Immigration Acts at a place or places specified in Schedule 2 to these Rules since being served with notice of the immigration decision that is the subject of the appeal.

(2) This Part shall cease to apply if the Tribunal makes an order under rule 30(1).

Application of the Principal Rules to this Part

16. The following provisions of the Principal Rules apply to proceedings to which this Part applies—

(a) rule 24 except paragraphs (2) and (4); and

(b) rule 25 except for paragraph (1).

Time limits for making an application for permission to appeal

17.—(1) An application under rule 24(1) of the Principal Rules must be sent or delivered to the Tribunal so that it is received no later than 2 days after the date on which the party is served with written reasons for the decision.

(2) If a person makes an application under rule 24(1) of the Principal Rules later than the time required by paragraph (1)—

(a) the Tribunal may extend the time for appealing if satisfied that by reason of special circumstances it would be unjust not to do so; and

(b) unless the Tribunal extends time under sub-paragraph (a), the Tribunal must not admit the application.

Service of permission application decision

18. The Tribunal must send to the parties written reasons for its decision in relation to an application for permission to appeal not later than 1 business day after the application was received by the Tribunal.

PART 4

General Provisions

27 Application of Part 5 of the Principal Rules

Where this Part applies, Part 5 of the Principal Rules applies, except that—

(a) rule 47 applies subject to rule 28 of these Rules; and

(b) rule 60(2) does not apply.

28 Adjournment

The Tribunal may only adjourn a hearing where—

(a) it is necessary to do so because there is insufficient time to hear the appeal or application which is before the Tribunal;

(b) a party has not been served with notice of the hearing in accordance with these Rules;

(c) the Tribunal is satisfied by evidence filed or given by or on behalf of a party that—

  (i) the appeal or application cannot be justly determined on the date on which it is listed for hearing; and

  (ii) there is an identifiable future date, not more than 10 days after the date on which the appeal or application is listed for hearing, by which it can be justly determined; or

(d) the Tribunal makes an order under rule 30.

29 Correction of orders and determinations

Where an order, notice of decision or determination is amended under rule 60(1) of the Principal Rules, the Tribunal must, not later than 1 day after making the amendment, serve an amended version on every party on whom it served the original.

29A Correction of administrative errors

Where an order, notice of decision or determination is set aside and the Tribunal orders that the relevant proceedings be dealt with again by the Tribunal under rule 60(1A) of the Principal Rules, the Tribunal must, not later than 1 day after making the order, notify every party of its decision.

PART 5

Removal of Pending Proceedings from Fast Track

30 Transfer out of fast track procedure

(1) Where Part 2 or 3 of these Rules applies to an appeal or application, the Tribunal must order that that Part shall cease to apply—

(a) if all the parties consent;

(b) if it is satisfied by evidence filed or given by or on behalf of a party that there are exceptional circumstances which mean that the appeal or application cannot otherwise be justly determined; or

(c) if—

  (i) the respondent to the appeal has failed to comply with a provision of these Rules, or the Principal Rules as applied by these Rules, or a direction of the Tribunal; and

(ii) the Tribunal is satisfied that the appellant would be prejudiced by that failure if the appeal or application were determined in accordance with these Rules.

(2) When making an order under paragraph (1), the Tribunal may—

(a) adjourn any hearing of the appeal or application; and

(b) give directions relating to the further conduct of the appeal or application.

(3) Where the Tribunal adjourns a hearing under paragraph (2)(a)—

(a) it must fix a new date, time and place for the hearing; and

(b) in the case of an adjournment of an appeal, rule 21(4) of the Principal Rules shall apply.

31 Application of the Principal Rules on transfer out of fast track

(1) This rule applies where Part 2 or 3 of these Rules ceases to apply to an appeal or application because—

(a) the conditions in rule 5 or 15 cease to apply; or

(b) the Tribunal makes an order under rule 30(1).

(2) Subject to paragraph (3), the Principal Rules shall apply to the appeal or application from the date on which these Rules cease to apply.

(3) Where—

(a) a period of time for doing something has started to run under a provision of these Rules; and

(b) that provision ceases to apply,

if the Principal Rules contain a time limit for doing the same thing, the time limit in the Principal Rules shall apply, and the relevant period of time shall be treated as running from the date on which the period of time under these Rules started to run.

SCHEDULE 2

Specified Places of Detention

Rules 5 and 15

Campsfield House Immigration Removal Centre, Kidlington, Oxfordshire

Colnbrook House Immigration Removal Centre, Harmondsworth, Middlesex

Harmondsworth Immigration Removal Centre, Harmondsworth, Middlesex

Oakington Reception Centre, Longstanton, Cambridgeshire

Yarls Wood Immigration Removal Centre, Clapham, Bedfordshire

Appendix 5

SI 2008 No 2685 (L 13)

The Tribunal Procedure (First-tier Tribunal) (Social Entitlement Chamber) Rules 2008

Version in force from 18th January 2010, showing amendments made by S.I. 2009/274, S.I. 2009/1975 and S.I. 2010/43. This document has been produced in order to assist users but its accuracy is not guaranteed and should not be relied upon. For a definitive version of the Rules, users should refer to the original statutory instruments.

Made	*9th October 2008*
Laid before Parliament	*15th October 2008*
Coming into force	*3rd November 2008*

CONTENTS

PART 3

Proceedings before the Tribunal

CHAPTER 1

Before the hearing

CHAPTER 2

Hearings

CHAPTER 3

Decisions

PART 4

Correcting, setting aside, reviewing and appealing Tribunal decisions

After consulting in accordance with paragraph 28(1) of Schedule 5 to, the Tribunals, Courts and Enforcement Act 2007(a), the Tribunal Procedure Committee has made the following Rules in exercise of the powers conferred by sections 20(2) and (3) of the Social Security Act 1998(b)

(a) 2007 c.15.
(b) 1998 c.14.

and sections 9(3), 22 and 29(3) of, and Schedule 5 to, the Tribunals, Courts and Enforcement Act 2007.

The Lord Chancellor has allowed the Rules in accordance with paragraph 28(3) of Schedule 5 to the Tribunals, Courts and Enforcement Act 2007.

PART 1

Introduction

Citation, commencement, application and interpretation(a)

1.—(1) These Rules may be cited as the Tribunal Procedure (First-tier Tribunal) (Social Entitlement Chamber) Rules 2008 and come into force on 3rd November 2008.

(2) These Rules apply to proceedings before the Tribunal which have been assigned to the Social Entitlement Chamber by the First-tier Tribunal and Upper Tribunal (Chambers) Order 2008(b).

(3) In these Rules—

"the 2007 Act" means the Tribunals, Courts and Enforcement Act 2007;

"appeal" includes an application under section 19(9) of the Tax Credits Act 2002(**c**);

"appellant" means a person who makes an appeal to the Tribunal, or a person substituted as an appellant under rule 9(1) (substitution of parties);

"asylum support case" means proceedings concerning the provision of support for an asylum seeker[, a failed asylum seeker or a person designated under section 130 of the Criminal Justice and Immigration Act 2008(**d**) (designation), or the dependents of any such person];

"criminal injuries compensation case" means proceedings concerning the payment of compensation under a scheme made under the Criminal Injuries Compensation Act 1995(**e**);

"decision maker" means the maker of a decision against which an appeal has been brought;

"dispose of proceedings" includes, unless indicated otherwise, disposing of a part of the proceedings;

"document" means anything in which information is recorded in any form, and an obligation under these Rules to provide or allow access to a document or a copy of a document for any purpose means, unless the Tribunal directs otherwise, an obligation to provide or allow access to such document or copy in a legible form or in a form which can be readily made into a legible form;

"hearing" means an oral hearing and includes a hearing conducted in whole or in part by video link, telephone or other means of instantaneous two-way electronic communication;

"legal representative" means [a person who, for the purposes of the Legal Services Act 2007(**f**), is an authorised person in relation to an activity which constitutes the exercise of a right of audience or the conduct of litigation within the meaning of that Act], an advocate or solicitor in Scotland or a barrister or solicitor in Northern Ireland;

"party" means—

(a) a person who is an appellant or respondent in proceedings before the Tribunal;

(**a**) In rule 1(3), the words in square brackets in the definition of "asylum support case" were substituted by S.I. 2009/274.
(**b**) S.I. 2008/2684.
(**c**) 2002 c.21.
(**d**) 2008 c. 4.
(**e**) 1995 c.53.
(**f**) 2007 c.29.

(b) a person who makes a reference to the Tribunal under section 28D of the Child Support Act 1991(**a**);

(c) a person who starts proceedings before the Tribunal under paragraph 3 of Schedule 2 to the Tax Credits Act 2002; or

(d) if the proceedings have been concluded, a person who was a party under paragraph (a), (b) or (c) when the Tribunal finally disposed of all issues in the proceedings;

"practice direction" means a direction given under section 23 of the 2007 Act;

"respondent" means—

(a) in an appeal against a decision, the decision maker and any person other than the appellant who had a right of appeal against the decision;

(b) in a reference under section 28D of the Child Support Act 1991—

(i) the absent parent or non-resident parent;

(ii) the person with care; and

(iii) in Scotland, the child if the child made the application for a departure direction or a variation;

(c) in proceedings under paragraph 3 of Schedule 2 to the Tax Credits Act 2002, a person on whom it is proposed that a penalty be imposed; or

(d) a person substituted or added as a respondent under rule 9 (substitution and addition of parties);

"Social Entitlement Chamber" means the Social Entitlement Chamber of the First-tier Tribunal established by the First-tier Tribunal and Upper Tribunal (Chambers) Order 2008;

"social security and child support case" means any case allocated to the Social Entitlement Chamber except an asylum support case or a criminal injuries compensation case;

"Tribunal" means the First-tier Tribunal.

Overriding objective and parties' obligation to co-operate with the Tribunal

2.—(1) The overriding objective of these Rules is to enable the Tribunal to deal with cases fairly and justly.

(2) Dealing with a case fairly and justly includes—

(a) dealing with the case in ways which are proportionate to the importance of the case, the complexity of the issues, the anticipated costs and the resources of the parties;

(b) avoiding unnecessary formality and seeking flexibility in the proceedings;

(c) ensuring, so far as practicable, that the parties are able to participate fully in the proceedings;

(d) using any special expertise of the Tribunal effectively; and

(e) avoiding delay, so far as compatible with proper consideration of the issues.

(3) The Tribunal must seek to give effect to the overriding objective when it—

(a) exercises any power under these Rules; or

(b) interprets any rule or practice direction.

(4) Parties must—

(a) help the Tribunal to further the overriding objective; and

---

(**a**) 1991 c.48. Section 28D was inserted by section 4 of the Child Support Act 1995 (c.34).

(b) co-operate with the Tribunal generally.

Alternative dispute resolution and arbitration

3.—(1) The Tribunal should seek, where appropriate—

(a) to bring to the attention of the parties the availability of any appropriate alternative procedure for the resolution of the dispute; and

(b) if the parties wish and provided that it is compatible with the overriding objective, to facilitate the use of the procedure.

(2) Part 1 of the Arbitration Act 1996(a) does not apply to proceedings before the Tribunal.

PART 2

General powers and provisions

Delegation to staff

4.—(1) Staff appointed under section 40(1) of the 2007 Act (tribunal staff and services) may, with the approval of the Senior President of Tribunals, carry out functions of a judicial nature permitted or required to be done by the Tribunal.

(2) The approval referred to at paragraph (1) may apply generally to the carrying out of specified functions by members of staff of a specified description in specified circumstances.

(3) Within 14 days after the date on which the Tribunal sends notice of a decision made by a member of staff under paragraph (1) to a party, that party may apply in writing to the Tribunal for that decision to be considered afresh by a judge.

Case management powers

5.—(1) Subject to the provisions of the 2007 Act and any other enactment, the Tribunal may regulate its own procedure.

(2) The Tribunal may give a direction in relation to the conduct or disposal of proceedings at any time, including a direction amending, suspending or setting aside an earlier direction.

(3) In particular, and without restricting the general powers in paragraphs (1) and (2), the Tribunal may—

(a) extend or shorten the time for complying with any rule, practice direction or direction;

(b) consolidate or hear together two or more sets of proceedings or parts of proceedings raising common issues, or treat a case as a lead case (whether in accordance with rule 18 (lead cases) or otherwise);

(c) permit or require a party to amend a document;

(d) permit or require a party or another person to provide documents, information, evidence or submissions to the Tribunal or a party;

(e) deal with an issue in the proceedings as a preliminary issue;

(f) hold a hearing to consider any matter, including a case management issue;

(g) decide the form of any hearing;

(h) adjourn or postpone a hearing;

(i) require a party to produce a bundle for a hearing;

(a) 1996 c.23.

(j) stay (or, in Scotland, sist) proceedings;

(k) transfer proceedings to another court or tribunal if that other court or tribunal has jurisdiction in relation to the proceedings and—

(i) because of a change of circumstances since the proceedings were started, the Tribunal no longer has jurisdiction in relation to the proceedings; or

(ii) the Tribunal considers that the other court or tribunal is a more appropriate forum for the determination of the case; or

(l) suspend the effect of its own decision pending the determination by the Tribunal or the Upper Tribunal of an application for permission to appeal against, and any appeal or review of, that decision.

Procedure for applying for and giving directions

6.—(1) The Tribunal may give a direction on the application of one or more of the parties or on its own initiative.

(2) An application for a direction may be made—

(a) by sending or delivering a written application to the Tribunal; or

(b) orally during the course of a hearing.

(3) An application for a direction must include the reason for making that application.

(4) Unless the Tribunal considers that there is good reason not to do so, the Tribunal must send written notice of any direction to every party and to any other person affected by the direction.

(5) If a party or any other person sent notice of the direction under paragraph (4) wishes to challenge a direction which the Tribunal has given, they may do so by applying for another direction which amends, suspends or sets aside the first direction.

Failure to comply with rules etc.

7.—(1) An irregularity resulting from a failure to comply with any requirement in these Rules, a practice direction or a direction, does not of itself render void the proceedings or any step taken in the proceedings.

(2) If a party has failed to comply with a requirement in these Rules, a practice direction or a direction, the Tribunal may take such action as it considers just, which may include—

(a) waiving the requirement;

(b) requiring the failure to be remedied;

(c) exercising its power under rule 8 (striking out a party's case); or

(d) exercising its power under paragraph (3).

(3) The Tribunal may refer to the Upper Tribunal, and ask the Upper Tribunal to exercise its power under section 25 of the 2007 Act in relation to, any failure by a person to comply with a requirement imposed by the Tribunal—

(a) to attend at any place for the purpose of giving evidence;

(b) otherwise to make themselves available to give evidence;

(c) to swear an oath in connection with the giving of evidence;

(d) to give evidence as a witness;

(e) to produce a document; or

(f) to facilitate the inspection of a document or any other thing (including any premises).

Striking out a party's case

8.—(1) The proceedings, or the appropriate part of them, will automatically be struck out if the appellant has failed to comply with a direction that stated that failure by a party to comply with the direction would lead to the striking out of the proceedings or that part of them.

(2) The Tribunal must strike out the whole or a part of the proceedings if the Tribunal—

(a) does not have jurisdiction in relation to the proceedings or that part of them; and

(b) does not exercise its power under rule 5(3)(k)(i) (transfer to another court or tribunal) in relation to the proceedings or that part of them.

(3) The Tribunal may strike out the whole or a part of the proceedings if—

(a) the appellant has failed to comply with a direction which stated that failure by the appellant to comply with the direction could lead to the striking out of the proceedings or part of them;

(b) the appellant has failed to co-operate with the Tribunal to such an extent that the Tribunal cannot deal with the proceedings fairly and justly; or

(c) the Tribunal considers there is no reasonable prospect of the appellant's case, or part of it, succeeding.

(4) The Tribunal may not strike out the whole or a part of the proceedings under paragraph (2) or (3)(b) or (c) without first giving the appellant an opportunity to make representations in relation to the proposed striking out.

(5) If the proceedings, or part of them, have been struck out under paragraph (1) or (3)(a), the appellant may apply for the proceedings, or part of them, to be reinstated.

(6) An application under paragraph (5) must be made in writing and received by the Tribunal within 1 month after the date on which the Tribunal sent notification of the striking out to the appellant.

(7) This rule applies to a respondent as it applies to an appellant except that—

(a) a reference to the striking out of the proceedings is to be read as a reference to the barring of the respondent from taking further part in the proceedings; and

(b) a reference to an application for the reinstatement of proceedings which have been struck out is to be read as a reference to an application for the lifting of the bar on the respondent from taking further part in the proceedings.

(8) If a respondent has been barred from taking further part in proceedings under this rule and that bar has not been lifted, the Tribunal need not consider any response or other submission made by that respondent.

Substitution and addition of parties

9.—(1) The Tribunal may give a direction substituting a party if—

(a) the wrong person has been named as a party; or

(b) the substitution has become necessary because of a change in circumstances since the start of proceedings.

(2) The Tribunal may give a direction adding a person to the proceedings as a respondent.

(3) If the Tribunal gives a direction under paragraph (1) or (2) it may give such consequential directions as it considers appropriate.

No power to award costs

10. The Tribunal may not make any order in respect of costs (or, in Scotland, expenses).

Representatives

11.—(1) A party may appoint a representative (whether a legal representative or not) to represent that party in the proceedings.

(2) Subject to paragraph (3), if a party appoints a representative, that party (or the representative if the representative is a legal representative) must send or deliver to the Tribunal written notice of the representative's name and address.

(3) In a case to which rule 23 (cases in which the notice of appeal is to be sent to the decision maker) applies, if the appellant (or the appellant's representative if the representative is a legal representative) provides written notification of the appellant's representative's name and address to the decision maker before the decision maker provides its response to the Tribunal, the appellant need not take any further steps in order to comply with paragraph (2).

(4) If the Tribunal receives notice that a party has appointed a representative under paragraph (2), it must send a copy of that notice to each other party.

(5) Anything permitted or required to be done by a party under these Rules, a practice direction or a direction may be done by the representative of that party, except signing a witness statement.

(6) A person who receives due notice of the appointment of a representative—

- (a) must provide to the representative any document which is required to be provided to the represented party, and need not provide that document to the represented party; and
- (b) may assume that the representative is and remains authorised as such until they receive written notification that this is not so from the representative or the represented party.

(7) At a hearing a party may be accompanied by another person whose name and address has not been notified under paragraph (2) or (3) but who, with the permission of the Tribunal, may act as a representative or otherwise assist in presenting the party's case at the hearing.

(8) Paragraphs (2) to (6) do not apply to a person who accompanies a party under paragraph (7).

Calculating time

12.—(1) Except in asylum support cases, an act required by these Rules, a practice direction or a direction to be done on or by a particular day must be done by 5pm on that day.

(2) If the time specified by these Rules, a practice direction or a direction for doing any act ends on a day other than a working day, the act is done in time if it is done on the next working day.

(3) In this rule "working day" means any day except a Saturday or Sunday, Christmas Day, Good Friday or a bank holiday under section 1 of the Banking and Financial Dealings Act 1971(a).

Sending and delivery of documents

13.—(1) Any document to be provided to the Tribunal under these Rules, a practice direction or a direction must be—

- (a) sent by pre-paid post or delivered by hand to the address specified for the proceedings;
- (b) sent by fax to the number specified for the proceedings; or
- (c) sent or delivered by such other method as the Tribunal may permit or direct.

(2) Subject to paragraph (3), if a party provides a fax number, email address or other details for the electronic transmission of documents to them, that party must accept delivery of documents by that method.

(a) 1971 c.80.

(3) If a party informs the Tribunal and all other parties that a particular form of communication (other than pre-paid post or delivery by hand) should not be used to provide documents to that party, that form of communication must not be so used.

(4) If the Tribunal or a party sends a document to a party or the Tribunal by email or any other electronic means of communication, the recipient may request that the sender provide a hard copy of the document to the recipient. The recipient must make such a request as soon as reasonably practicable after receiving the document electronically.

(5) The Tribunal and each party may assume that the address provided by a party or its representative is and remains the address to which documents should be sent or delivered until receiving written notification to the contrary.

Use of documents and information

14.—(1) The Tribunal may make an order prohibiting the disclosure or publication of—

(a) specified documents or information relating to the proceedings; or

(b) any matter likely to lead members of the public to identify any person whom the Tribunal considers should not be identified.

(2) The Tribunal may give a direction prohibiting the disclosure of a document or information to a person if—

(a) the Tribunal is satisfied that such disclosure would be likely to cause that person or some other person serious harm; and

(b) the Tribunal is satisfied, having regard to the interests of justice, that it is proportionate to give such a direction.

(3) If a party ("the first party") considers that the Tribunal should give a direction under paragraph (2) prohibiting the disclosure of a document or information to another party ("the second party"), the first party must—

(a) exclude the relevant document or information from any documents that will be provided to the second party; and

(b) provide to the Tribunal the excluded document or information, and the reason for its exclusion, so that the Tribunal may decide whether the document or information should be disclosed to the second party or should be the subject of a direction under paragraph (2).

(4) The Tribunal must conduct proceedings as appropriate in order to give effect to a direction given under paragraph (2).

(5) If the Tribunal gives a direction under paragraph (2) which prevents disclosure to a party who has appointed a representative, the Tribunal may give a direction that the documents or information be disclosed to that representative if the Tribunal is satisfied that—

(a) disclosure to the representative would be in the interests of the party; and

(b) the representative will act in accordance with paragraph (6).

(6) Documents or information disclosed to a representative in accordance with a direction under paragraph (5) must not be disclosed either directly or indirectly to any other person without the Tribunal's consent.

Evidence and submissions

15.—(1) Without restriction on the general powers in rule 5(1) and (2) (case management powers), the Tribunal may give directions as to—

(a) issues on which it requires evidence or submissions;

(b) the nature of the evidence or submissions it requires;

(c) whether the parties are permitted or required to provide expert evidence;

(d) any limit on the number of witnesses whose evidence a party may put forward, whether in relation to a particular issue or generally;

(e) the manner in which any evidence or submissions are to be provided, which may include a direction for them to be given—

(i) orally at a hearing; or

(ii) by written submissions or witness statement; and

(f) the time at which any evidence or submissions are to be provided.

(2) The Tribunal may—

(a) admit evidence whether or not—

(i) the evidence would be admissible in a civil trial in the United Kingdom; or

(ii) the evidence was available to a previous decision maker; or

(b) exclude evidence that would otherwise be admissible where—

(i) the evidence was not provided within the time allowed by a direction or a practice direction;

(ii) the evidence was otherwise provided in a manner that did not comply with a direction or a practice direction; or

(iii) it would otherwise be unfair to admit the evidence.

(3) The Tribunal may consent to a witness giving, or require any witness to give, evidence on oath, and may administer an oath for that purpose.

Summoning or citation of witnesses and orders to answer questions or produce documents

16.—(1) On the application of a party or on its own initiative, the Tribunal may—

(a) by summons (or, in Scotland, citation) require any person to attend as a witness at a hearing at the time and place specified in the summons or citation; or

(b) order any person to answer any questions or produce any documents in that person's possession or control which relate to any issue in the proceedings.

(2) A summons or citation under paragraph (1)(a) must—

(a) give the person required to attend 14 days' notice of the hearing or such shorter period as the Tribunal may direct; and

(b) where the person is not a party, make provision for the person's necessary expenses of attendance to be paid, and state who is to pay them.

(3) No person may be compelled to give any evidence or produce any document that the person could not be compelled to give or produce on a trial of an action in a court of law in the part of the United Kingdom where the proceedings are due to be determined.

(4) A summons, citation or order under this rule must—

(a) state that the person on whom the requirement is imposed may apply to the Tribunal to vary or set aside the summons, citation or order, if they have not had an opportunity to object to it; and

(b) state the consequences of failure to comply with the summons, citation or order.

Withdrawal

17.—(1) Subject to paragraph (2), a party may give notice of the withdrawal of its case, or any part of it—

(a) at any time before a hearing to consider the disposal of the proceedings (or, if the Tribunal disposes of the proceedings without a hearing, before that disposal), by sending or delivering to the Tribunal a written notice of withdrawal; or

(b) orally at a hearing.

(2) In the circumstances described in paragraph (3), a notice of withdrawal will not take effect unless the Tribunal consents to the withdrawal.

(3) The circumstances referred to in paragraph (2) are where a party gives notice of withdrawal—

(a) under paragraph (1)(a) in a criminal injuries compensation case; or

(b) under paragraph (1)(b).

(4) A party who has withdrawn their case may apply to the Tribunal for the case to be reinstated.

(5) An application under paragraph (4) must be made in writing and be received by the Tribunal within 1 month after—

(a) the date on which the Tribunal received the notice under paragraph (1)(a); or

(b) the date of the hearing at which the case was withdrawn orally under paragraph (1)(b).

(6) The Tribunal must notify each party in writing of an withdrawal under this rule.

Lead cases

18.—(1) This rule applies if—

(a) two or more cases have been started before the Tribunal;

(b) in each such case the Tribunal has not made a decision disposing of the proceedings; and

(c) the cases give rise to common or related issues of fact or law.

(2) The Tribunal may give a direction—

(a) specifying one or more cases falling under paragraph (1) as a lead case or lead cases; and

(b) staying (or, in Scotland, sisting) the other cases falling under paragraph (1) ("the related cases").

(3) When the Tribunal makes a decision in respect of the common or related issues—

(a) the Tribunal must send a copy of that decision to each party in each of the related cases; and

(b) subject to paragraph (4), that decision shall be binding on each of those parties.

(4) Within 1 month after the date on which the Tribunal sent a copy of the decision to a party under paragraph (3)(a), that party may apply in writing for a direction that the decision does not apply to, and is not binding on the parties to, a particular related case.

(5) The Tribunal must give directions in respect of cases which are stayed or sisted under paragraph (2)(b), providing for the disposal of or further directions in those cases.

(6) If the lead case or cases lapse or are withdrawn before the Tribunal makes a decision in respect of the common or related issues, the Tribunal must give directions as to—

(a) whether another case or other cases are to be specified as a lead case or lead cases; and

(b) whether any direction affecting the related cases should be set aside or amended.

Confidentiality in child support or child trust fund cases

19.—(1) Paragraph (3) applies to proceedings under the Child Support Act 1991 in the circumstances described in paragraph (2), other than an appeal against a reduced benefit decision (as defined in section 46(10)(b) of the Child Support Act 1991, as that section had effect prior to the commencement of section 15(b) of the Child Maintenance and Other Payments Act 2008(a)).

(2) The circumstances referred to in paragraph (1) are that the absent parent, non-resident parent or person with care would like their address or the address of the child to be kept confidential and has given notice to that effect—

(a) to the Secretary of State or the Child Maintenance and Enforcement Commission in the notice of appeal or when notifying any subsequent change of address;

(b) to the Secretary of State or the Child Maintenance and Enforcement Commission, whichever has made the enquiry, within 14 days after an enquiry is made; or

(c) to the Tribunal when notifying any change of address.

(3) Where this paragraph applies, the Secretary of State, the Child Maintenance and Enforcement Commission and the Tribunal must take appropriate steps to secure the confidentiality of the address, and of any information which could reasonably be expected to enable a person to identify the address, to the extent that the address or that information is not already known to each other party.

(4) Paragraph (6) applies to proceedings under the Child Trust Funds Act 2004(b) in the circumstances described in paragraph (5).

(5) The circumstances referred to in paragraph (4) are that a relevant person would like their address or the address of the eligible child to be kept confidential and has given notice to that effect, or a local authority with parental responsibility in relation to the eligible child would like the address of the eligible child to be kept confidential and has given notice to that effect—

(a) to HMRC in the notice of appeal or when notifying any subsequent change of address;

(b) to HMRC within 14 days after an enquiry by HMRC; or

(c) to the Tribunal when notifying any change of address.

(6) Where this paragraph applies, HMRC and the Tribunal must take appropriate steps to secure the confidentiality of the address, and of any information which could reasonably be expected to enable a person to identify the address, to the extent that the address or that information is not already known to each other party.

(7) In this rule—

"eligible child" has the meaning set out in section 2 of the Child Trust Funds Act 2004;

"HMRC" means Her Majesty's Revenue and Customs;

"non-resident parent" and "parent with care" have the meanings set out in section 54 of the Child Support Act 1991;

"parental responsibility" has the meaning set out in section 3(9) of the Child Trust Funds Act 2004; and

"relevant person" has the meaning set out in section 22(3) of the Child Trust Funds Act 2004.

Expenses in criminal injuries compensation cases

20.—(1) This rule applies only to criminal injuries compensation cases.

(2) The Tribunal may meet reasonable expenses—

(a) incurred by the appellant, or any person who attends a hearing to give evidence, in attending the hearing; or

---

(a) 2008 c.6.
(b) 2004 c.6.

(b) incurred by the appellant in connection with any arrangements made by the Tribunal for the inspection of the appellant's injury.

Expenses in social security and child support cases

21.—(1) This rule applies only to social security and child support cases.

(2) The Secretary of State may pay such travelling and other allowances (including compensation for loss of remunerative time) as the Secretary of State may determine to any person required to attend a hearing in proceedings under section 20 of the Child Support Act 1991, section 12 of the Social Security Act 1998 or paragraph 6 of Schedule 7 to the Child Support, Pensions and Social Security Act 2000(a).

PART 3

Proceedings before the Tribunal

CHAPTER 1

Before the hearing

Cases in which the notice of appeal is to be sent to the Tribunal

22.—(1) This rule applies to asylum support cases and criminal injuries compensation cases.

(2) An appellant must start proceedings by sending or delivering a notice of appeal to the Tribunal so that it is received—

(a) in asylum support cases, within 3 days after the date on which the appellant received written notice of the decision being challenged;

(b) in criminal injuries compensation cases, within 90 days after the date of the decision being challenged.

(3) The notice of appeal must be in English or Welsh, must be signed by the appellant and must state—

(a) the name and address of the appellant;

(b) the name and address of the appellant's representative (if any);

(c) an address where documents for the appellant may be sent or delivered;

(d) the name and address of any respondent;

(e) details (including the full reference) of the decision being appealed; and

(f) the grounds on which the appellant relies.

(4) The appellant must provide with the notice of appeal—

(a) a copy of any written record of the decision being challenged;

(b) any statement of reasons for that decision that the appellant has or can reasonably obtain;

(c) any documents in support of the appellant's case which have not been supplied to the respondent; and

(d) any further information or documents required by an applicable practice direction.

(5) In asylum support cases the notice of appeal must also—

(a) 2000 c.19.

(a) state whether the appellant will require an interpreter at any hearing, and if so for which language or dialect; and

(b) state whether the appellant intends to attend or be represented at any hearing.

(6) If the appellant provides the notice of appeal to the Tribunal later than the time required by paragraph (2) or by an extension of time allowed under rule 5(3)(a) (power to extend time)—

(a) the notice of appeal must include a request for an extension of time and the reason why the notice of appeal was not provided in time; and

(b) unless the Tribunal extends time for the notice of appeal under rule 5(3)(a) (power to extend time) the Tribunal must not admit the notice of appeal.

(7) The Tribunal must send a copy of the notice of appeal and any accompanying documents to each other party—

(a) in asylum support cases, on the day that the Tribunal receives the notice of appeal, or (if that is not reasonably practicable) as soon as reasonably practicable on the following day;

(b) in criminal injuries compensation cases, as soon as reasonably practicable after the Tribunal receives the notice of appeal.

Cases in which the notice of appeal is to be sent to the decision maker(a)

23.—(1) This rule applies to social security and child support cases (except references under the Child Support Act 1991 and proceedings under paragraph 3 of Schedule 2 to the Tax Credits Act 2002).

(2) An appellant must start proceedings by sending or delivering a notice of appeal to the decision maker so that it is received within the time specified in Schedule 1 to these Rules (time limits for providing notices of appeal to the decision maker).

(3) If the appellant provides the notice of appeal to the decision maker later than the time required by paragraph (2) the notice of appeal must include the reason why the notice of appeal was not provided in time.

(4) Subject to paragraph (5), where an appeal is not made within the time specified in Schedule 1, it will be treated as having been made in time if the decision maker does not object.

(5) No appeal may be made more than 12 months after the time specified in Schedule 1.

(6) The notice of appeal must be in English or Welsh, must be signed by the appellant and must state—

(a) the name and address of the appellant;

(b) the name and address of the appellant's representative (if any);

(c) an address where documents for the appellant may be sent or delivered;

(d) details of the decision being appealed; and

(e) the grounds on which the appellant relies.

(7) The decision maker must refer the case to the Tribunal immediately if—

(a) the appeal has been made after the time specified in Schedule 1 and the decision maker objects to it being treated as having been made in time; or

(b) the decision maker considers that the appeal has been made more than 12 months after the time specified in Schedule 1.

(8) [Notwithstanding rule 5(3)(a) (case management powers) and rule 7(2) (failure to comply with rules etc.), the Tribunal must not extend the time limit in paragraph (5).]

(a) Rule 23(8) was inserted by S.I. 2009/1975.

Responses and replies

24.—(1) When a decision maker receives the notice of appeal or a copy of it, the decision maker must send or deliver a response to the Tribunal—

(a) in asylum support cases, so that it is received within 3 days after the date on which the Tribunal received the notice of appeal; and

(b) in other cases, as soon as reasonably practicable after the decision maker received the notice of appeal.

(2) The response must state—

(a) the name and address of the decision maker;

(b) the name and address of the decision maker's representative (if any);

(c) an address where documents for the decision maker may be sent or delivered;

(d) the names and addresses of any other respondents and their representatives (if any);

(e) whether the decision maker opposes the appellant's case and, if so, any grounds for such opposition which are not set out in any documents which are before the Tribunal; and

(f) any further information or documents required by a practice direction or direction.

(3) The response may include a submission as to whether it would be appropriate for the case to be disposed of without a hearing.

(4) The decision maker must provide with the response—

(a) a copy of any written record of the decision under challenge, and any statement of reasons for that decision, if they were not sent with the notice of appeal;

(b) copies of all documents relevant to the case in the decision maker's possession, unless a practice direction or direction states otherwise; and

(c) in cases to which rule 23 (cases in which the notice of appeal is to be sent to the decision maker) applies, a copy of the notice of appeal, any documents provided by the appellant with the notice of appeal and (if they have not otherwise been provided to the Tribunal) the name and address of the appellant's representative (if any).

(5) The decision maker must provide a copy of the response and any accompanying documents to each other party at the same time as it provides the response to the Tribunal.

(6) The appellant and any other respondent may make a written submission and supply further documents in reply to the decision maker's response.

(7) Any submission or further documents under paragraph (6) must be provided to the Tribunal within 1 month after the date on which the decision maker sent the response to the party providing the reply, and the Tribunal must send a copy to each other party.

Medical and physical examination in appeals under section 12 of the Social Security Act 1998

25.—(1) This rule applies only to appeals under section 12 of the Social Security Act 1998.

(2) At a hearing an appropriate member of the Tribunal may carry out a physical examination of a person if the case relates to—

(a) the extent of that person's disablement and its assessment in accordance with section 68(6) of and Schedule 6 to, or section 103 of, the Social Security Contributions and Benefits Act 1992(a); or

(b) diseases or injuries prescribed for the purpose of section 108 of that Act.

(a) 1992 c.4.

(3) If an issue which falls within Schedule 2 to these Rules (issues in relation to which the Tribunal may refer a person for medical examination) is raised in an appeal, the Tribunal may exercise its power under section 20 of the Social Security Act 1998 to refer a person to a health care professional approved by the Secretary of State for—

(a) the examination of that person; and

(b) the production of a report on the condition of that person.

(4) Neither paragraph (2) nor paragraph (3) entitles the Tribunal to require a person to undergo a physical test for the purpose of determining whether that person is unable to walk or virtually unable to do so.

Social security and child support cases started by reference or information in writing

26.—(1) This rule applies to proceedings under section 28D of the Child Support Act 1991 and paragraph 3 of Schedule 2 to the Tax Credits Act 2002.

(2) A person starting proceedings under section 28D of the Child Support Act 1991 must send or deliver a written reference to the Tribunal.

(3) A person starting proceedings under paragraph 3 of Schedule 2 to the Tax Credits Act 2002 must send or deliver an information in writing to the Tribunal.

(4) The reference or the information in writing must include—

(a) an address where documents for the person starting proceedings may be sent or delivered;

(b) the names and addresses of the respondents and their representatives (if any); and

(c) a submission on the issues that arise for determination by the Tribunal.

(5) Unless a practice direction or direction states otherwise, the person starting proceedings must also provide a copy of each document in their possession which is relevant to the proceedings.

(6) Subject to any obligation under rule 19(3) (confidentiality in child support cases), the person starting proceedings must provide a copy of the written reference or the information in writing and any accompanying documents to each respondent at the same time as they provide the written reference or the information in writing to the Tribunal.

(7) Each respondent may send or deliver to the Tribunal a written submission and any further relevant documents within one month of the date on which the person starting proceedings sent a copy of the written reference or the information in writing to that respondent.

CHAPTER 2

Hearings

Decision with or without a hearing

27.—(1) Subject to the following paragraphs, the Tribunal must hold a hearing before making a decision which disposes of proceedings unless—

(a) each party has consented to, or has not objected to, the matter being decided without a hearing; and

(b) the Tribunal considers that it is able to decide the matter without a hearing.

(2) This rule does not apply to decisions under Part 4.

(3) The Tribunal may in any event dispose of proceedings without a hearing under rule 8 (striking out a party's case).

(4) In a criminal injuries compensation case—

(a) the Tribunal may make a decision which disposes of proceedings without a hearing; and

(b) subject to paragraph (5), if the Tribunal makes a decision which disposes of proceedings without a hearing, any party may make a written application to the Tribunal for the decision to be reconsidered at a hearing.

(5) An application under paragraph (4)(b) may not be made in relation to a decision—

(a) not to extend a time limit;

(b) not to set aside a previous decision;

(c) not to allow an appeal against a decision not to extend a time limit; or

(d) not to allow an appeal against a decision not to reopen a case.

(6) An application under paragraph (4)(b) must be received within 1 month after the date on which the Tribunal sent notice of the decision to the party making the application.

Entitlement to attend a hearing

28. Subject to rule 30(5) (exclusion of a person from a hearing), each party to proceedings is entitled to attend a hearing.

Notice of hearings

29.—(1) The Tribunal must give each party entitled to attend a hearing reasonable notice of the time and place of the hearing (including any adjourned or postponed hearing) and any changes to the time and place of the hearing.

(2) The period of notice under paragraph (1) must be at least 14 days except that—

(a) in an asylum support case the Tribunal must give at least 1 day's and not more than 5 days' notice; and

(b) the Tribunal may give shorter notice—

(i) with the parties' consent; or

(ii) in urgent or exceptional circumstances.

Public and private hearings

30.—(1) Subject to the following paragraphs, all hearings must be held in public.

(2) A hearing in a criminal injuries compensation case must be held in private unless—

(a) the appellant has consented to the hearing being held in public; and

(b) the Tribunal considers that it is in the interests of justice for the hearing to be held in public.

(3) The Tribunal may give a direction that a hearing, or part of it, is to be held in private.

(4) Where a hearing, or part of it, is to be held in private, the Tribunal may determine who is permitted to attend the hearing or part of it.

(5) The Tribunal may give a direction excluding from any hearing, or part of it—

(a) any person whose conduct the Tribunal considers is disrupting or is likely to disrupt the hearing;

(b) any person whose presence the Tribunal considers is likely to prevent another person from giving evidence or making submissions freely;

(c) any person who the Tribunal considers should be excluded in order to give effect to a direction under rule 14(2) (withholding information likely to cause harm); or

(d) any person where the purpose of the hearing would be defeated by the attendance of that person.

(6) The Tribunal may give a direction excluding a witness from a hearing until that witness gives evidence.

Hearings in a party's absence

31. If a party fails to attend a hearing the Tribunal may proceed with the hearing if the Tribunal—

(a) is satisfied that the party has been notified of the hearing or that reasonable steps have been taken to notify the party of the hearing; and

(b) considers that it is in the interests of justice to proceed with the hearing.

CHAPTER 3

Decisions

Consent orders

32.—(1) The Tribunal may, at the request of the parties but only if it considers it appropriate, make a consent order disposing of the proceedings and making such other appropriate provision as the parties have agreed.

(2) Notwithstanding any other provision of these Rules, the Tribunal need not hold a hearing before making an order under paragraph (1), or provide reasons for the order.

Notice of decisions

33.—(1) The Tribunal may give a decision orally at a hearing.

(2) Subject to rule 14(2) (withholding information likely to cause harm), the Tribunal must provide to each party as soon as reasonably practicable after making a decision which finally disposes of all issues in the proceedings (except a decision under Part 4)—

(a) a decision notice stating the Tribunal's decision;

(b) where appropriate, notification of the right to apply for a written statement of reasons under rule 34(3); and

(c) notification of any right of appeal against the decision and the time within which, and the manner in which, such right of appeal may be exercised.

(3) In asylum support cases the notice and notifications required by paragraph (2) must be provided at the hearing or sent on the day that the decision is made.

Reasons for decisions

34.—(1) In asylum support cases the Tribunal must send a written statement of reasons for a decision which disposes of proceedings (except a decision under Part 4) to each party—

(a) if the case is decided at a hearing, within 3 days after the hearing; or

(b) if the case is decided without a hearing, on the day that the decision is made.

(2) In all other cases the Tribunal may give reasons for a decision which disposes of proceedings (except a decision under Part 4)—

(a) orally at a hearing; or

(b) in a written statement of reasons to each party.

(3) Unless the Tribunal has already provided a written statement of reasons under paragraph (2)(b), a party may make a written application to the Tribunal for such statement following a decision which finally disposes of all issues in the proceedings.

(4) An application under paragraph (3) must be received within 1 month of the date on which the Tribunal sent or otherwise provided to the party a decision notice relating to the decision which finally disposes of all issues in the proceedings.

(5) If a party makes an application in accordance with paragraphs (3) and (4) the Tribunal must, subject to rule 14(2) (withholding information likely to cause harm), send a written statement of reasons to each party within 1 month of the date on which it received the application or as soon as reasonably practicable after the end of that period.

PART 4

Correcting, setting aside, reviewing and appealing Tribunal decisions

Interpretation

35. In this Part—

"appeal" means the exercise of a right of appeal—

(a) under paragraph 2(2) or 4(1) of Schedule 2 to the Tax Credits Act 2002(**a**);

(b) under section 21(10) of the Child Trust Funds Act 2004(**b**); or

(c) on a point of law under section 11 of the 2007 Act; and

"review" means the review of a decision by the Tribunal under section 9 of the 2007 Act.

Clerical mistakes and accidental slips or omissions

36. The Tribunal may at any time correct any clerical mistake or other accidental slip or omission in a decision, direction or any document produced by it, by—

(a) sending notification of the amended decision or direction, or a copy of the amended document, to all parties; and

(b) making any necessary amendment to any information published in relation to the decision, direction or document.

Setting aside a decision which disposes of proceedings

37.—(1) The Tribunal may set aside a decision which disposes of proceedings, or part of such a decision, and re-make the decision, or the relevant part of it, if—

(a) the Tribunal considers that it is in the interests of justice to do so; and

(b) one or more of the conditions in paragraph (2) are satisfied.

(2) The conditions are—

(a) a document relating to the proceedings was not sent to, or was not received at an appropriate time by, a party or a party's representative;

(b) a document relating to the proceedings was not sent to the Tribunal at an appropriate time;

(c) a party, or a party's representative, was not present at a hearing related to the proceedings; or

(d) there has been some other procedural irregularity in the proceedings.

(**a**) 2002 c.21. Paragraphs 2(2) and 4(1) of Schedule 2 are modified by section 63(6) and (7) of the same Act.
(**b**) 2004 c.6. Section 21(10) is modified by section 24(1) and (2) of the same Act.

(3) A party applying for a decision, or part of a decision, to be set aside under paragraph (1) must make a written application to the Tribunal so that it is received no later than 1 month after the date on which the Tribunal sent notice of the decision to the party.

Application for permission to appeal

38.—(1) This rule does not apply to asylum support cases or criminal injuries compensation cases.

(2) A person seeking permission to appeal must make a written application to the Tribunal for permission to appeal.

(3) An application under paragraph (2) must be sent or delivered to the Tribunal so that it is received no later than 1 month after the latest of the dates that the Tribunal sends to the person making the application—

(a) written reasons for the decision;

(b) notification of amended reasons for, or correction of, the decision following a review; or

(c) notification that an application for the decision to be set aside has been unsuccessful.

(4) The date in paragraph (3)(c) applies only if the application for the decision to be set aside was made within the time stipulated in rule 37 (setting aside a decision which disposes of proceedings) or any extension of that time granted by the Tribunal.

(5) If the person seeking permission to appeal sends or delivers the application to the Tribunal later than the time required by paragraph (3) or by any extension of time under rule 5(3)(a) (power to extend time)—

(a) the application must include a request for an extension of time and the reason why the application was not provided in time; and

(b) unless the Tribunal extends time for the application under rule 5(3)(a) (power to extend time) the Tribunal must not admit the application.

(6) An application under paragraph (2) must—

(a) identify the decision of the Tribunal to which it relates;

(b) identify the alleged error or errors of law in the decision; and

(c) state the result the party making the application is seeking.

(7) If a person makes an application under paragraph (2) when the Tribunal has not given a written statement of reasons for its decision—

(a) if no application for a written statement of reasons has been made to the Tribunal, the application for permission must be treated as such an application;

(b) unless the Tribunal decides to give permission and directs that this sub-paragraph does not apply, the application is not to be treated as an application for permission to appeal; and

(c) if an application for a written statement of reasons has been, or is, refused because of a delay in making the application, the Tribunal must only admit the application for permission if the Tribunal considers that it is in the interests of justice to do so.

Tribunal's consideration of application for permission to appeal

39.—(1) On receiving an application for permission to appeal the Tribunal must first consider, taking into account the overriding objective in rule 2, whether to review the decision in accordance with rule 40 (review of a decision).

(2) If the Tribunal decides not to review the decision, or reviews the decision and decides to take no action in relation to the decision, or part of it, the Tribunal must consider whether to give permission to appeal in relation to the decision or that part of it.

(3) The Tribunal must send a record of its decision to the parties as soon as practicable.

(4) If the Tribunal refuses permission to appeal it must send with the record of its decision—

(a) a statement of its reasons for such refusal; and

(b) notification of the right to make an application to the Upper Tribunal for permission to appeal and the time within which, and the method by which, such application must be made.

(5) The Tribunal may give permission to appeal on limited grounds, but must comply with paragraph (4) in relation to any grounds on which it has refused permission.

Review of a decision

40.—(1) This rule does not apply to asylum support cases or criminal injuries compensation cases.

(2) The Tribunal may only undertake a review of a decision—

(a) pursuant to rule 39(1) (review on an application for permission to appeal); and

(b) if it is satisfied that there was an error of law in the decision.

(3) The Tribunal must notify the parties in writing of the outcome of any review, and of any right of appeal in relation to the outcome.

(4) If the Tribunal takes any action in relation to a decision following a review without first giving every party an opportunity to make representations, the notice under paragraph (3) must state that any party that did not have an opportunity to make representations may apply for such action to be set aside and for the decision to be reviewed again.

Power to treat an application as a different type of application

41. The Tribunal may treat an application for a decision to be corrected, set aside or reviewed, or for permission to appeal against a decision, as an application for any other one of those things.

Patrick Elias
Phillip Brook Smith Q.C. Lesley Clare
Douglas J. May Q.C.
Newton of Braintree
M.J. Reed Mark Rowland
Nicholas Warren

I allow these Rules

Signed by authority of the Lord Chancellor

Bridget Prentice
Parliamentary Under Secretary of State
Ministry of Justice

9th October 2008

SCHEDULE 1(a) RULE 23

Time limits for providing notices of appeal to the decision maker

Type of proceedings	*Time for providing notice of appeal*
cases other than those listed below	the latest of— (a) one month after the date on which notice of the decision being challenged was sent to the appellant; (b) if a written statement of reasons for the decision is requested, 14 days after the later of (i) the date on which the period at (a) expires; and (ii) the date on which the written statement of reasons was provided; or [(c) where the appellant made an application for revision of the decision under— (i) regulation 17(1)(a) of the Child Support (Maintenance Assessment Procedure) Regulations 1992(**b**); (ii) regulation 3(1) or (3) or 3A(1) of the Social Security and Child Support (Decision & Appeals) Regulations 1999(**c**); or (iii) regulation 4 of the Housing Benefit and Council Tax Benefit (Decisions and Appeals) Regulations 2001(**d**) and that application was unsuccessful, one month of the date on which notice that the decision would not be revised was sent to the appellant]
appeal against a certificate of NHS charges under section 157(1) of the Health and Social Care (Community Health and Standards) Act 2003(**e**)	(a) 3 months after the latest of— (i) the date on the certificate; (ii) the date on which the compensation payment was made; (iii) if the certificate has been reviewed, the date the certificate was confirmed or a fresh certificate was issued; or (iv) the date of any agreement to treat an earlier compensation payment as having been made in final discharge of a claim made by or in respect of an injured person and arising out of the injury or death; or (b) if the person to whom the certificate has been issued makes an application under section 157(1) of the Health and Social Care (Community Health and Standards) Act 2003, one month after— (i) the date of the decision on that application; or (ii) if the person appeals against that decision under section 157(6) of that Act, the date on which the appeal is decided or withdrawn
appeal against a waiver decision under section 157(6) of the Health and Social Care (Community Health and Standards) Act 2003	one month after the date of the decision

(**a**) In the first entry in the table, paragraph (c) was substituted by S.I. 2009/1975.

(**b**) S.I. 1992/1813.

(**c**) S.I. 1999/991. Regulation 3A was inserted by regulation 5 of the Child Support (Decision & Appeals) (Amendment) Regulations 2000 (S.I. 2000/3185).

(**d**) S.I. 2001/1002.

(**e**) 2003 c.43.

Type of proceedings	*Time for providing notice of appeal*
appeal against a certificate of NHS charges under section 7 of the Road Traffic (NHS Charges) Act 1999(**a**)	3 months after the latest of— (a) the date on which the liability under section 1(2) of the Road Traffic (NHS Charges) Act 1999 was discharged; (b) if the certificate has been reviewed, the date the certificate was confirmed or a fresh certificate was issued; or (c) the date of any agreement to treat an earlier compensation payment as having been made in final discharge of a claim made by or in respect of a traffic casualty and arising out of the injury or death
appeal against a certificate of recoverable benefits under section 11 of the Social Security (Recovery of Benefits) Act 1997(**b**)	one month after the latest of— (a) the date on which any payment to the Secretary of State required under section 6 of the Social Security (Recovery of Benefits) Act 1997 was made; (b) if the certificate has been reviewed, the date the certificate was confirmed or a fresh certificate was issued; or (c) the date of any agreement to treat an earlier compensation payment as having been made in final discharge of a claim made by or in respect of an injured person and arising out of the accident, injury or disease
appeal under the Vaccine Damage Payments Act 1979(**c**)	no time limit
appeal under the Tax Credits Act 2002(**d**)	as set out in the Tax Credits Act 2002
appeal under the Child Trust Funds Act 2004(**e**)	as set out in the Child Trust Funds Act 2004
appeal against a decision in respect of a claim for child benefit or guardian's allowance under section 12 of the Social Security Act 1998(**f**)	as set out in regulation 28 of the Child Benefit and Guardian's Allowance (Decisions and Appeals) Regulations 2003(**g**)

(a) 1999 c.3.
(b) 1997 c.27.
(c) 1979 c.17.
(d) 2002 c.21.
(e) 2004 c.6.
(f) 1998 c.14.
(g) S.I. 2003/916.

SCHEDULE 2 RULE 25(3)

Issues in relation to which the Tribunal may refer a person for medical examination under section 20(2) of the Social Security Act 1998

An issue falls within this Schedule if the issue—

(a) is whether the claimant satisfies the conditions for entitlement to—

(i) an attendance allowance specified in section 64 and 65(1) of the Social Security Contributions and Benefits Act 1992(**a**);

(ii) severe disablement allowance under section 68 of that Act;

(iii) the care component of a disability living allowance specified in section 72(1) and (2) of that Act;

(iv) the mobility component of a disability living allowance specified in section 73(1), (8) and (9) of that Act; or

(v) a disabled person's tax credit specified in section 129(1)(b) of that Act.

(b) relates to the period throughout which the claimant is likely to satisfy the conditions for entitlement to an attendance allowance or a disability living allowance;

(c) is the rate at which an attendance allowance is payable;

(d) is the rate at which the care component or the mobility component of a disability living allowance is payable;

(e) is whether a person is incapable of work for the purposes of the Social Security Contributions and Benefits Act 1992;

(f) relates to the extent of a person's disablement and its assessment in accordance with Schedule 6 to the Social Security Contributions and Benefits Act 1992;

(g) is whether the claimant suffers a loss of physical or mental faculty as a result of the relevant accident for the purposes of section 103 of the Social Security Contributions and Benefits Act 1992;

(h) relates to any payment arising under, or by virtue of a scheme having effect under, section 111 of, and Schedule 8 to, the Social Security Contributions and Benefits Act 1992 (workmen's compensation);

(i) is whether a person has limited capability for work or work-related activity for the purposes of the Welfare Reform Act 2007(**b**).

(**a**) 1992 c.4.
(**b**) 2007 c.5.

EXPLANATORY NOTE

(This note is not part of the Rules)

Part 1 of the Tribunals, Courts and Enforcement Act 2007 (c.15) establishes a new tribunal structure comprising a First-tier Tribunal and an Upper Tribunal. Appeal functions of existing tribunals are being transferred to this structure and assigned to chambers within the new tribunals. These Rules govern the practice and procedure to be followed in the First-tier Tribunal in proceedings which have been allocated to the Social Entitlement Chamber by the First-tier Tribunal and Upper Tribunal (Chambers) Order 2008(**a**).

Part 1 contains provisions for interpreting and applying the Rules and sets out the overriding objective of the Rules.

Part 2 contains general powers and provisions including the Tribunal's general case management powers, the giving of directions, the power to strike out a party's case, the service of documents and rules about evidence, submissions and witnesses.

Part 3 contains provisions on the notice of appeals and on responses and replies. It also makes provision for hearings and for decisions made by the Tribunal.

Part 4 deals with correcting, setting aside, reviewing and appealing against Tribunal decisions.

(**a**) S.I. 2008/2684.

Appendix 6

SI 2009 No 273 (L 1)

The Tribunal Procedure (First-tier Tribunal) (Tax Chamber) Rules 2009

Version in force from 18th January 2010, showing amendments made by S.I. 2010/43. This document has been produced in order to assist users but its accuracy is not guaranteed and should not be relied upon. For a definitive version of the Rules, users should refer to the original statutory instruments.

Made	*5th February 2009*
Laid before Parliamen	*13th February 2009*
Coming into force	*1st April 2009*

CONTENTS

PART 3

Procedure before the Tribunal

CHAPTER 1

Starting proceedings and allocation of cases to categories

CHAPTER 2

Procedure after allocation of cases to categories

CHAPTER 3

Hearings

CHAPTER 4

Decisions

PART 4

Correcting, setting aside, reviewing and appealing Tribunal decisions

After consulting in accordance with paragraph 28(1) of Schedule 5 to the Tribunals, Courts and Enforcement Act 2007(**a**), the Tribunal Procedure Committee has made the following Rules in exercise of the power conferred by sections 9(3), 22 and 29(3) of, and Schedule 5 to, that Act.

(**a**) 2007 c.15.

The Lord Chancellor has allowed the Rules in accordance with paragraph 28(3) of Schedule 5 to the Tribunals, Courts and Enforcement Act 2007.

PART 1

Introduction

Citation, commencement, application and interpretation

1.—(1) These Rules may be cited as the Tribunal Procedure (First-tier Tribunal) (Tax Chamber) Rules 2009 and come into force on 1st April 2009.

(2) These Rules apply to proceedings before the Tribunal which have been allocated to the Tax Chamber by the First-tier Tribunal and Upper Tribunal (Chambers) Order 2008(**a**).

(3) In these Rules—

"the 2007 Act" means the Tribunals, Courts and Enforcement Act 2007;

"appellant" means—

(a) the person who starts proceedings (whether by bringing or notifying an appeal, by making an originating application, by a reference, or otherwise);

(b) in proceedings started jointly by more than one person, such persons acting jointly or each such person, as the context requires;

(c) a person substituted as an appellant under rule 9 (substitution and addition of parties);

"Basic case" means a case allocated to the Basic category under rule 23 (allocation of cases to categories);

"Complex case" means a case allocated to the Complex category under rule 23 (allocation of cases to categories);

"Default Paper case" means a case allocated to the Default Paper category under rule 23 (allocation of cases to categories);

"document" means anything in which information is recorded in any form, and an obligation under these Rules to provide or allow access to a document or a copy of a document for any purpose means, unless the Tribunal directs otherwise, an obligation to provide or allow access to such document or copy in a legible form or in a form which can be readily made into a legible form;

"hearing" means an oral hearing and includes a hearing conducted in whole or in part by video link, telephone or other means of instantaneous two-way electronic communication;

"HMRC" means Her Majesty's Revenue and Customs and includes the Serious Organised Crime Agency when carrying out functions under section 317 of the Proceeds of Crime Act 2002(**b**);

"party" means a person who is (or was at the time that the Tribunal disposed of the proceedings) an appellant or respondent in proceedings before the Tribunal;

"practice direction" means a direction given under section 23 of the 2007 Act;

"respondent" means—

(a) HMRC, where the appellant (or one of them) is not HMRC;

(**a**) S.I. 2008/2684. The Order is amended by the First-tier Tribunal and Upper Tribunal (Chambers) (Amendment) Order 2009 (S.I. 2009/196).

(**b**) 2002 c.29.

(b) in proceedings brought by HMRC alone, a person against whom the proceedings are brought or to whom the proceedings relate;

(c) a person substituted or added as a respondent under rule 9 (substitution and addition of parties);

"Standard case" means a case allocated to the Standard category under rule 23 (allocation of cases to categories);

"Tax Chamber" means the Tax Chamber of the First-tier Tribunal established by the First-tier Tribunal and Upper Tribunal (Chambers) Order 2008;

"Tribunal" means the First-tier Tribunal.

Overriding objective and parties' obligation to co-operate with the Tribunal

2.—(1) The overriding objective of these Rules is to enable the Tribunal to deal with cases fairly and justly.

(2) Dealing with a case fairly and justly includes—

(a) dealing with the case in ways which are proportionate to the importance of the case, the complexity of the issues, the anticipated costs and the resources of the parties;

(b) avoiding unnecessary formality and seeking flexibility in the proceedings;

(c) ensuring, so far as practicable, that the parties are able to participate fully in the proceedings;

(d) using any special expertise of the Tribunal effectively; and

(e) avoiding delay, so far as compatible with proper consideration of the issues.

(3) The Tribunal must seek to give effect to the overriding objective when it—

(a) exercises any power under these Rules; or

(b) interprets any rule or practice direction.

(4) Parties must—

(a) help the Tribunal to further the overriding objective; and

(b) co-operate with the Tribunal generally.

Alternative dispute resolution and arbitration

3.—(1) The Tribunal should seek, where appropriate—

(a) to bring to the attention of the parties the availability of any appropriate alternative procedure for the resolution of the dispute; and

(b) if the parties wish and provided that it is compatible with the overriding objective, to facilitate the use of the procedure.

(2) Part 1 of the Arbitration Act 1996(**a**) does not apply to proceedings before the Tribunal.

PART 2

General powers and provisions

Delegation to staff

4.—(1) Staff appointed under section 40(1) of the 2007 Act (tribunal staff and services) may, with the approval of the Senior President of Tribunals, carry out functions of a judicial nature permitted or required to be done by the Tribunal.

(a) 1996 c.23.

(2) The approval referred to at paragraph (1) may apply generally to the carrying out of specified functions by members of staff of a specified description in specified circumstances.

(3) Within 14 days after the date that the Tribunal sends notice of a decision made by a member of staff pursuant to an approval under paragraph (1) to a party, that party may make a written application to the Tribunal requiring that decision to be considered afresh by a judge.

Case management powers

5.—(1) Subject to the provisions of the 2007 Act and any other enactment, the Tribunal may regulate its own procedure.

(2) The Tribunal may give a direction in relation to the conduct or disposal of proceedings at any time, including a direction amending, suspending or setting aside an earlier direction.

(3) In particular, and without restricting the general powers in paragraphs (1) and (2), the Tribunal may by direction—

- (a) extend or shorten the time for complying with any rule, practice direction or direction, unless such extension or shortening would conflict with a provision of another enactment setting down a time limit;
- (b) consolidate or hear together two or more sets of proceedings or parts of proceedings raising common issues, or treat a case as a lead case (whether in accordance with rule 18 (lead cases) or otherwise);
- (c) permit or require a party to amend a document;
- (d) permit or require a party or another person to provide documents, information or submissions to the Tribunal or a party;
- (e) deal with an issue in the proceedings as a preliminary issue;
- (f) hold a hearing to consider any matter, including a case management hearing;
- (g) decide the form of any hearing;
- (h) adjourn or postpone a hearing;
- (i) require a party to produce a bundle for a hearing;
- (j) stay (or, in Scotland, sist) proceedings;
- (k) transfer proceedings to another tribunal if that other tribunal has jurisdiction in relation to the proceedings and, because of a change of circumstances since the proceedings were started—
    - (i) the Tribunal no longer has jurisdiction in relation to the proceedings; or
    - (ii) the Tribunal considers that the other tribunal is a more appropriate forum for the determination of the case;
- (l) suspend the effect of its own decision pending the determination by the Tribunal or the Upper Tribunal, as the case may be, of an application for permission to appeal, a review or an appeal.

Procedure for applying for and giving directions

6.—(1) The Tribunal may give a direction on the application of one or more of the parties or on its own initiative.

(2) An application for a direction may be made—

- (a) by sending or delivering a written application to the Tribunal; or
- (b) orally during the course of a hearing.

(3) An application for a direction must include the reasons for making that application.

(4) Unless the Tribunal considers that there is good reason not to do so, the Tribunal must send written notice of any direction to every party and to any other person affected by the direction.

(5) If a party or other person sent notice of the direction under paragraph (4) wishes to challenge a direction which the Tribunal has given, they may do so by applying for another direction which amends, suspends or sets aside the first direction.

Failure to comply with rules etc.

7.—(1) An irregularity resulting from a failure to comply with any requirement in these Rules, a practice direction or a direction does not of itself render void the proceedings or any step taken in the proceedings.

(2) If a party has failed to comply with a requirement in these Rules, a practice direction or a direction, the Tribunal may take such action as it considers just, which may include—

- (a) waiving the requirement;
- (b) requiring the failure to be remedied;
- (c) exercising its power under rule 8 (striking out a party's case);
- (d) restricting a party's participation in proceedings; or
- (e) exercising its power under paragraph (3).

(3) The Tribunal may refer to the Upper Tribunal, and ask the Upper Tribunal to exercise its power under section 25 of the 2007 Act (Upper Tribunal to have powers of High Court or Court of Session) in relation to, any failure by a person to comply with a requirement imposed by the Tribunal—

- (a) to attend at any place for the purpose of giving evidence;
- (b) otherwise to make themselves available to give evidence;
- (c) to swear an oath in connection with the giving of evidence;
- (d) to give evidence as a witness;
- (e) to produce a document; or
- (f) to facilitate the inspection of a document or any other thing (including any premises).

Striking out a party's case

8.—(1) The proceedings, or the appropriate part of them, will automatically be struck out if the appellant has failed to comply with a direction that stated that failure by a party to comply with the direction would lead to the striking out of the proceedings or that part of them.

(2) The Tribunal must strike out the whole or a part of the proceedings if the Tribunal—

- (a) does not have jurisdiction in relation to the proceedings or that part of them; and
- (b) does not exercise its power under rule 5(3)(k)(i) (transfer to another court or tribunal) in relation to the proceedings or that part of them.

(3) The Tribunal may strike out the whole or a part of the proceedings if—

- (a) the appellant has failed to comply with a direction which stated that failure by the appellant to comply with the direction could lead to the striking out of the proceedings or part of them;
- (b) the appellant has failed to co-operate with the Tribunal to such an extent that the Tribunal cannot deal with the proceedings fairly and justly; or
- (c) the Tribunal considers there is no reasonable prospect of the appellant's case, or part of it, succeeding.

(4) The Tribunal may not strike out the whole or a part of the proceedings under paragraphs (2) or (3)(b) or (c) without first giving the appellant an opportunity to make representations in relation to the proposed striking out.

(5) If the proceedings, or part of them, have been struck out under paragraphs (1) or (3)(a), the appellant may apply for the proceedings, or part of them, to be reinstated.

(6) An application under paragraph (5) must be made in writing and received by the Tribunal within 28 days after the date that the Tribunal sent notification of the striking out to the appellant.

(7) This rule applies to a respondent as it applies to an appellant except that—

(a) a reference to the striking out of the proceedings must be read as a reference to the barring of the respondent from taking further part in the proceedings; and

(b) a reference to an application for the reinstatement of proceedings which have been struck out must be read as a reference to an application for the lifting of the bar on the respondent taking further part in the proceedings.

(8) If a respondent has been barred from taking further part in proceedings under this rule and that bar has not been lifted, the Tribunal need not consider any response or other submissions made by that respondent, and may summarily determine any or all issues against that respondent.

Substitution and addition of parties

9.—(1) The Tribunal may give a direction substituting a party if—

(a) the wrong person has been named as a party; or

(b) the substitution has become necessary because of a change in circumstances since the start of proceedings.

(2) The Tribunal may give a direction adding a person to the proceedings as a respondent.

(3) A person who is not a party to proceedings may make an application to be added as a party under this rule.

(4) If the Tribunal refuses an application under paragraph (3) it must consider whether to permit the person who made the application to provide submissions or evidence to the Tribunal.

(5) If the Tribunal gives a direction under paragraph (1) or (2) it may give such consequential directions as it considers appropriate.

Orders for costs

10.—(1) The Tribunal may only make an order in respect of costs (or, in Scotland, expenses)—

(a) under section 29(4) of the 2007 Act (wasted costs);

(b) if the Tribunal considers that a party or their representative has acted unreasonably in bringing, defending or conducting the proceedings; or

(c) if—

(i) the proceedings have been allocated as a Complex case under rule 23 (allocation of cases to categories); and

(ii) the taxpayer (or, where more than one party is a taxpayer, one of them) has not sent or delivered a written request to the Tribunal, within 28 days of receiving notice that the case had been allocated as a Complex case, that the proceedings be excluded from potential liability for costs or expenses under this sub-paragraph.

(2) The Tribunal may make an order under paragraph (1) on an application or of its own initiative.

(3) A person making an application for an order under paragraph (1) must—

(a) send or deliver a written application to the Tribunal and to the person against whom it is proposed that the order be made; and

(b) send or deliver with the application a schedule of the costs or expenses claimed in sufficient detail to allow the Tribunal to undertake a summary assessment of such costs or expenses if it decides to do so.

(4) An application for an order under paragraph (1) may be made at any time during the proceedings but may not be made later than 28 days after the date on which the Tribunal sends—

(a) a decision notice recording the decision which finally disposes of all issues in the proceedings; or

(b) notice of a withdrawal under rule 17 (withdrawal) which ends the proceedings.

(5) The Tribunal may not make an order under paragraph (1) against a person (the "paying person") without first—

(a) giving that person an opportunity to make representations; and

(b) if the paying person is an individual, considering that person's financial means.

(6) The amount of costs (or, in Scotland, expenses) to be paid under an order under paragraph (1) may be ascertained by—

(a) summary assessment by the Tribunal;

(b) agreement of a specified sum by the paying person and the person entitled to receive the costs or expenses (the "receiving person"); or

(c) assessment of the whole or a specified part of the costs or expenses incurred by the receiving person, if not agreed.

(7) Following an order for assessment under paragraph (6)(c) the paying person or the receiving person may apply—

(a) in England and Wales, to a county court, the High Court or the Costs Office of the Supreme Court (as specified in the order) for a detailed assessment of the costs on the standard basis or, if specified in the order, on the indemnity basis; and the Civil Procedure Rules 1998**(a)** shall apply, with necessary modifications, to that application and assessment as if the proceedings in the tribunal had been proceedings in a court to which the Civil Procedure Rules 1998 apply;

(b) in Scotland, to the Auditor of the Sheriff Court or the Court of Session (as specified in the order) for the taxation of the expenses according to the fees payable in that court; or

(c) in Northern Ireland, to the Taxing Office of the High Court of Northern Ireland for taxation on the standard basis or, if specified in the order, on the indemnity basis.

(8) In this rule "taxpayer" means a party who is liable to pay, or has paid, the tax, duty, levy or penalty to which the proceedings relate or part of such tax, duty, levy or penalty, or whose liability to do so is in issue in the proceedings;

Representatives

11.—(1) A party may appoint a representative (whether a legal representative or not) to represent that party in the proceedings.

(2) If a party appoints a representative, that party (or the representative if the representative is a legal representative) must send or deliver to the Tribunal and to each other party to the proceedings written notice of the representative's name and address.

(a) S.I. 1998/3132.

(3) Anything permitted or required to be done by a party under these Rules, a practice direction or a direction may be done by the representative of that party, except signing a witness statement.

(4) A person who receives due notice of the appointment of a representative—

(a) must provide to the representative any document which is required to be provided to the represented party, and need not provide that document to the represented party; and

(b) may assume that the representative is and remains authorised as such until they receive written notification that this is not so from the representative or the represented party.

(5) At a hearing a party may be accompanied by another person who, with the permission of the Tribunal, may act as a representative or otherwise assist in presenting the party's case at the hearing.

(6) Paragraphs (2) to (4) do not apply to a person (other than an appointed representative) who accompanies a party in accordance with paragraph (5).

(7) In this rule "legal representative" means [a person who, for the purposes of the Legal Services Act 2007(**a**), is an authorised person in relation to an activity which constitutes the exercise of a right of audience or the conduct of litigation within the meaning of that Act], an advocate or solicitor in Scotland, or a barrister or solicitor in Northern Ireland.

Calculating time

12.—(1) An act required by these Rules, a practice direction or a direction to be done on or by a particular day must be done before 5pm on that day.

(2) If the time specified by these Rules, a practice direction or a direction for doing any act ends on a day other than a working day, the act is done in time if it is done on the next working day.

(3) In this rule "working day" means any day except a Saturday or Sunday, Christmas Day, Good Friday or a bank holiday under section 1 of the Banking and Financial Dealings Act 1971(**b**).

Sending and delivery of documents

13.—(1) Any document to be provided to the Tribunal under these Rules, a practice direction or a direction must be—

(a) sent by pre-paid post or document exchange, or delivered by hand, to the address specified for the proceedings; or

(b) sent or delivered by such other method as the Tribunal may permit or direct.

(2) Subject to paragraph (3), if a party or representative provides a fax number, email address or other details for the electronic transmission of documents to them, that party or representative must accept delivery of documents by that method.

(3) If a party informs the Tribunal and all other parties that a particular form of communication (other than pre-paid post or delivery by hand) should not be used to provide documents to that party, that form of communication must not be so used.

(4) If the Tribunal or a party sends a document to a party or the Tribunal by email or any other electronic means of communication, the recipient may request that the sender provide a hard copy of the document to the recipient. The recipient must make such a request as soon as reasonably practicable after receiving the document electronically.

(5) The Tribunal and each party may assume that the address provided by a party or its representative is and remains the address to which documents should be sent or delivered until receiving written notification to the contrary.

(**a**) 2007 c.29.
(**b**) 1971 c.80.

Use of documents and information

14. The Tribunal may make an order prohibiting the disclosure or publication of—

(a) specified documents or information relating to the proceedings; or

(b) any matter likely to lead members of the public to identify any person whom the Tribunal considers should not be identified.

Evidence and submissions

15.—(1) Without restriction on the general powers in rule 5(1) and (2) (case management powers), the Tribunal may give directions as to—

(a) issues on which it requires evidence or submissions;

(b) the nature of the evidence or submissions it requires;

(c) whether the parties are permitted or required to provide expert evidence, and if so whether the parties must jointly appoint a single expert to provide such evidence;

(d) any limit on the number of witnesses whose evidence a party may put forward, whether in relation to a particular issue or generally;

(e) the manner in which any evidence or submissions are to be provided, which may include a direction for them to be given—

(i) orally at a hearing; or

(ii) by written submissions or witness statement; and

(f) the time at which any evidence or submissions are to be provided.

(2) The Tribunal may—

(a) admit evidence whether or not the evidence would be admissible in a civil trial in the United Kingdom; or

(b) exclude evidence that would otherwise be admissible where—

(i) the evidence was not provided within the time allowed by a direction or a practice direction;

(ii) the evidence was otherwise provided in a manner that did not comply with a direction or a practice direction; or

(iii) it would otherwise be unfair to admit the evidence.

(3) The Tribunal may consent to a witness giving, or require any witness to give, evidence on oath, and may administer an oath for that purpose.

Summoning or citation of witnesses and orders to answer questions or produce documents

16.—(1) On the application of a party or on its own initiative, the Tribunal may—

(a) by summons (or, in Scotland, citation) require any person to attend as a witness at a hearing at the time and place specified in the summons or citation;

(b) order any person to answer any questions or produce any documents in that person's possession or control which relate to any issue in the proceedings.

(2) A summons or citation under paragraph (1)(a) must—

(a) give the person required to attend at least 14 days' notice of the hearing, or such shorter period as the Tribunal may direct; and

(b) where the person is not a party, make provision for the person's necessary expenses of attendance to be paid, and state who is to pay them.

(3) No person may be compelled to give any evidence or produce any document that the person could not be compelled to give or produce on a trial of an action in a court of law in the part of the United Kingdom where the proceedings are due to be determined.

(4) A person who receives a summons, citation or order may apply to the Tribunal for it to be varied or set aside if they did not have an opportunity to object to it before it was made or issued.

(5) A person making an application under paragraph (4) must do so as soon as reasonably practicable after receiving notice of the summons, citation or order.

(6) A summons, citation or order under this rule must—

(a) state that the person on whom the requirement is imposed may apply to the Tribunal to vary or set aside the summons, citation or order, if they did not have an opportunity to object to it before it was made or issued; and

(b) state the consequences of failure to comply with the summons, citation or order.

Withdrawal

17.—(1) Subject to any provision in an enactment relating to withdrawal or settlement of particular proceedings, a party may give notice to the Tribunal of the withdrawal of the case made by it in the Tribunal proceedings, or any part of that case—

(a) at any time before a hearing to consider the disposal of the proceedings (or, if the Tribunal disposes of the proceedings without a hearing, before that disposal), by sending or delivering to the Tribunal a written notice of withdrawal; or

(b) orally at a hearing.

(2) The Tribunal must notify each other party in writing of a withdrawal under this rule.

(3) A party who has withdrawn their case may apply to the Tribunal for the case to be reinstated.

(4) An application under paragraph (3) must be made in writing and be received by the Tribunal within 28 days after—

(a) the date that the Tribunal received the notice under paragraph (1)(a); or

(b) the date of the hearing at which the case was withdrawn orally under paragraph (1)(b).

Lead cases

18.—(1) This rule applies if—

(a) two or more cases have been started before the Tribunal;

(b) in each such case the Tribunal has not made a decision disposing of the proceedings; and

(c) the cases give rise to common or related issues of fact or law.

(2) The Tribunal may give a direction—

(a) specifying one or more cases falling under paragraph (1) as a lead case or lead cases; and

(b) staying (or, in Scotland, sisting) the other cases falling under paragraph (1) ("the related cases").

(3) When the Tribunal makes a decision in respect of the common or related issues—

(a) the Tribunal must send a copy of that decision to each party in each of the related cases; and

(b) subject to paragraph (4), that decision shall be binding on each of those parties.

(4) Within 28 days after the date that the Tribunal sent a copy of the decision to a party under paragraph (3)(a), that party may apply in writing for a direction that the decision does not apply to, and is not binding on the parties to, that case.

(5) The Tribunal must give directions in respect of cases which are stayed or sisted under paragraph (2)(b), providing for the disposal of or further steps in those cases.

(6) If the lead case or cases are withdrawn or disposed of before the Tribunal makes a decision in respect of the common or related issues, the Tribunal must give directions as to—

(a) whether another case or other cases are to be heard as a lead case or lead cases; and

(b) whether any direction affecting the related cases should be set aside or amended.

PART 3

Procedure before the Tribunal

CHAPTER 1

Starting proceedings and allocation of cases to categories

Proceedings without notice to a respondent

19. If a case or matter is to be determined without notice to or the involvement of a respondent—

(a) any provision in these Rules requiring a document to be provided by or to a respondent; and

(b) any other provision in these Rules permitting a respondent to participate in the proceedings

does not apply to that case or matter.

Starting appeal proceedings

20.—(1) Where an enactment provides for a person to make or notify an appeal to the Tribunal, the appellant must start proceedings by sending or delivering a notice of appeal to the Tribunal within any time limit imposed by that enactment.

(2) The notice of appeal must include—

(a) the name and address of the appellant;

(b) the name and address of the appellant's representative (if any);

(c) an address where documents for the appellant may be sent or delivered;

(d) details of the decision appealed against;

(e) the result the appellant is seeking; and

(f) the grounds for making the appeal.

(3) The appellant must provide with the notice of appeal a copy of any written record of any decision appealed against, and any statement of reasons for that decision, that the appellant has or can reasonably obtain.

(4) If the appellant provides the notice of appeal to the Tribunal later than the time required by paragraph (1) or by an extension of time allowed under rule 5(3)(a) (power to extend time)—

(a) the notice of appeal must include a request for an extension of time and the reason why the notice of appeal was not provided in time; and

(b) unless the Tribunal extends time for the notice of appeal under rule 5(3)(a) (power to extend time) the Tribunal must not admit the notice of appeal.

(5) When the Tribunal receives the notice of appeal it must give notice of the proceedings to the respondent.

Starting proceedings by originating application or reference

21.—(1) Where an enactment provides for a person or persons to make an originating application or reference to the Tribunal, the appellant must start proceedings by providing an application notice or notice of reference to the Tribunal within any time limit imposed by that enactment.

(2) The application notice or notice of reference must state—

(a) the name and address of the appellant;

(b) the name and address of the appellant's representative (if any);

(c) an address where documents for the appellant may be sent or delivered;

(d) the name and address of each respondent (if any);

(e) the facts relevant to the originating application or reference;

(f) the result the appellant is seeking (if any); and

(g) the grounds for making the originating application or reference.

(3) If the appellant provides the application notice or notice of reference to the Tribunal later than the time required by paragraph (1) or by any extension of time under rule 5(3)(a) (power to extend time)—

(a) the application notice or notice of reference must include a request for an extension of time and the reason why the application notice or notice of reference was not provided in time; and

(b) unless the Tribunal extends time for the application notice or notice of reference under rule 5(3)(a) (power to extend time) the Tribunal must not admit the application notice or notice of reference.

(4) When the Tribunal receives an application notice or a notice of reference it must send a copy of the notice and any accompanying document to any respondent.

Hardship applications

22.—(1) This rule applies where an enactment provides, in any terms, that an appeal may not proceed if the liability to pay the amount in dispute is outstanding unless HMRC or the Tribunal consent to the appeal proceeding.

(2) When starting proceedings, the appellant must include or provide the following in or with the notice of appeal—

(a) a statement as to whether the appellant has paid the amount in dispute;

(b) if the appellant has not paid the amount in dispute, a statement as to the status or outcome of any application to HMRC for consent to the appeal proceeding; and

(c) if HMRC have refused such an application, an application to the Tribunal for consent to the appeal proceeding.

(3) An application under paragraph (2)(c) must include the reasons for the application and a list of any documents the appellant intends to produce or rely upon in support of that application.

(4) If the appellant requires the consent of HMRC or the Tribunal before the appeal may proceed, the Tribunal must stay the proceedings until any applications to HMRC or the Tribunal in that respect have been determined.

Allocation of cases to categories

23.—(1) When the Tribunal receives a notice of appeal, application notice or notice of reference, the Tribunal must give a direction allocating the case to one of the categories set out in paragraph (2).

(2) The categories referred to in paragraph (1) are—

(a) Default Paper cases, which will usually be disposed of without a hearing;

(b) Basic cases, which will usually be disposed of after a hearing, with minimal exchange of documents before the hearing;

(c) Standard cases, which will usually be subject to more detailed case management and be disposed of after a hearing; and

(d) Complex cases, in respect of which see paragraphs (4) and (5) below.

(3) The Tribunal may give a further direction re-allocating a case to a different category at any time, either on the application of a party or on its own initiative.

(4) The Tribunal may allocate a case as a Complex case under paragraph (1) or (3) only if the Tribunal considers that the case—

(a) will require lengthy or complex evidence or a lengthy hearing;

(b) involves a complex or important principle or issue; or

(c) involves a large financial sum.

(5) If a case is allocated as a Complex case—

(a) rule 10(1)(c) (costs in Complex cases) applies to the case; and

(b) rule 28 (transfer of Complex cases to the Upper Tribunal) applies to the case.

CHAPTER 2

Procedure after allocation of cases to categories

Basic cases

24.—(1) This rule applies to Basic cases.

(2) Rule 25 (respondent's statement of case) does not apply and, subject to paragraph (3) and any direction given by the Tribunal, the case will proceed directly to a hearing.

(3) If the respondent intends to raise grounds for contesting the proceedings at the hearing which have not previously been communicated to the appellant, the respondent must notify the appellant of such grounds.

(4) If the respondent is required to notify the appellant of any grounds under paragraph (3), the respondent must do so—

(a) as soon as reasonably practicable after becoming aware that such is the case; and

(b) in sufficient detail to enable the appellant to respond to such grounds at the hearing.

Respondent's statement of case

25.—(1) A respondent must send or deliver a statement of case to the Tribunal, the appellant and any other respondent so that it is received—

(a) in a Default Paper case, within 42 days after the tribunal sent the notice of the appeal or a copy of the application notice or notice of reference; or

(b) in a Standard or Complex case, within 60 days after the tribunal sent the notice of the appeal or a copy of the application notice or notice of reference.

(2) A statement of case must—

(a) in an appeal, state the legislative provision under which the decision under appeal was made; and

(b) set out the respondent's position in relation to the case.

(3) A statement of case may also contain a request that the case be dealt with at a hearing or without a hearing.

(4) If a respondent provides a statement of case to the Tribunal later than the time required by paragraph (1) or by any extension allowed under rule 5(3)(a) (power to extend time), the statement of case must include a request for an extension of time and the reason why the statement of case was not provided in time.

Further steps in a Default Paper case

26.—(1) This rule applies to Default Paper cases.

(2) The appellant may send or deliver a written reply to the Tribunal so that it is received within 30 days after the date on which the respondent sent to the appellant the statement of case to which the reply relates.

(3) The appellant's reply may—

- (a) set out the appellant's response to the respondent's statement of case;
- (b) provide any further information (including, where appropriate, copies of the documents containing such information) which has not yet been provided to the Tribunal and is relevant to the case; and
- (c) contain a request that the case be dealt with at a hearing.

(4) The appellant must send or deliver a copy of any reply provided under paragraph (2) to each respondent at the same time as it is provided to the Tribunal.

(5) If the appellant provides a reply to the Tribunal later than the time required by paragraph (2) or by any extension allowed under rule 5(3)(a) (power to extend time), the reply must include a request for an extension of time and the reason why the reply was not provided in time.

(6) Following receipt of the appellant's reply, or the expiry of the time for the receipt of the appellant's reply then, unless it directs otherwise and subject in any event to paragraph (7), the Tribunal must proceed to determine the case without a hearing.

(7) If any party has made a written request to the Tribunal for a hearing, the Tribunal must hold a hearing before determining the case.

Further steps in a Standard or Complex case

27.—(1) This rule applies to Standard and Complex cases.

(2) Subject to any direction to the contrary, within 42 days after the date the respondent sent the statement of case (or, where there is more than one respondent, the date of the final statement of case) each party must send or deliver to the Tribunal and to each other party a list of documents—

- (a) of which the party providing the list has possession, the right to possession, or the right to take copies; and
- (b) which the party providing the list intends to rely upon or produce in the proceedings

(3) A party which has provided a list of documents under paragraph (2) must allow each other party to inspect or take copies of the documents on the list (except any documents which are privileged).

Transfer of Complex cases to the Upper Tribunal

28.—(1) If a case has been allocated as a Complex case the Tribunal may, with the consent of the parties, refer a case to the President of the Tax Chamber with a request that the case be considered for transfer to the Upper Tribunal.

(2) If a case has been referred by the Tribunal under paragraph (1), the President of the Tax Chamber may, with the concurrence of the President of the Finance and Tax Chamber of the Upper Tribunal (if that is a different person) direct that the case be transferred to and determined by the Upper Tribunal.

CHAPTER 3

Hearings

Determination with or without a hearing

29.—(1) Subject to rule 26(6) (determination of a Default Paper case without a hearing) and the following paragraphs in this rule, the Tribunal must hold a hearing before making a decision which disposes of proceedings, or a part of proceedings, unless—

(a) each party has consented to the matter being decided without a hearing; and

(b) the Tribunal considers that it is able to decide the matter without a hearing.

(2) This rule does not apply to decisions under Part 4 (correcting, setting aside, reviewing and appealing Tribunal decisions).

(3) The Tribunal may dispose of proceedings, or a part of proceedings, without a hearing under rule 8 (striking out a party's case).

Entitlement to attend a hearing

30. Subject to rules 19 (proceedings without notice to a respondent) and 32(4) (exclusion from a hearing), each party to proceedings is entitled to attend a hearing.

Notice of hearings

31.—(1) The Tribunal must give each party entitled to attend a hearing reasonable notice of the time and place of any hearing (including any adjourned or postponed hearing) and any changes to the time and place of any hearing.

(2) In relation to a hearing to consider the disposal of proceedings, the period of notice under paragraph (1) must be at least 14 days except that the Tribunal may give less than 14 days' notice—

(a) with the parties' consent; or

(b) in urgent or exceptional circumstances.

Public and private hearings

32.—(1) Subject to the following paragraphs, all hearings must be held in public.

(2) The Tribunal may give a direction that a hearing, or part of it, is to be held in private if the Tribunal considers that restricting access to the hearing is justified—

(a) in the interests of public order or national security;

(b) in order to protect a person's right to respect for their private and family life;

(c) in order to maintain the confidentiality of sensitive information;

(d) in order to avoid serious harm to the public interest; or

(e) because not to do so would prejudice the interests of justice.

(3) Where a hearing, or part of it, is to be held in private, the Tribunal may determine who is permitted to attend the hearing or part of it.

(4) The Tribunal may give a direction excluding from any hearing, or part of it—

(a) any person whose conduct the Tribunal considers is disrupting or is likely to disrupt the hearing;

(b) any person whose presence the Tribunal considers is likely to prevent another person from giving evidence or making submissions freely;

(c) any person where the purpose of the hearing would be defeated by the attendance of that person; or

(d) a person under the age of eighteen years.

(5) The Tribunal may give a direction excluding a witness from a hearing until that witness gives evidence.

(6) If the Tribunal publishes a report of a decision resulting from a hearing which was held wholly or partly in private, the Tribunal must, so far as practicable, ensure that the report does not disclose information which was referred to only in a part of the hearing that was held in private (including such information which enables the identification of any person whose affairs were dealt with in the part of the hearing that was held in private) if to do so would undermine the purpose of holding the hearing in private.

Hearings in a party's absence

33. If a party fails to attend a hearing the Tribunal may proceed with the hearing if the Tribunal—

(a) is satisfied that the party has been notified of the hearing or that reasonable steps have been taken to notify the party of the hearing; and

(b) considers that it is in the interests of justice to proceed with the hearing.

CHAPTER 4

Decisions

Consent orders

34.—(1) The Tribunal may, at the request of the parties but only if it considers it appropriate, make a consent order disposing of the proceedings and making such other appropriate provision as the parties have agreed.

(2) Notwithstanding any other provision of these Rules, the Tribunal need not hold a hearing before making an order under paragraph (1), or provide reasons for the order.

Notice of decisions and reasons

35.—(1) The Tribunal may give a decision orally at a hearing.

(2) The Tribunal must provide to each party within 28 days after making a decision which finally disposes of all issues in proceedings (except a decision under Part 4), or as soon as practicable thereafter, a decision notice which—

(a) states the Tribunal's decision; and

(b) notifies the party of any right of appeal against the decision and the time within which, and the manner in which, the right of appeal may be exercised.

(3) Unless each party agrees that it is unnecessary, the decision notice must—

(a) include a summary of the findings of fact and reasons for the decision; or

(b) be accompanied by full written findings of fact and reasons for the decision.

(4) If the Tribunal provides no findings and reasons, or summary findings and reasons only, in or with the decision notice, a party to the proceedings may apply for full written findings and reasons, and must do so before making an application for permission to appeal under rule 39 (application for permission to appeal).

(5) An application under paragraph (4) must be made in writing and be sent or delivered to the Tribunal so that it is received within 28 days after the date that the Tribunal sent or otherwise provided the decision notice under paragraph (2) to the party making the application.

(6) The Tribunal must send a full written statement of findings and reasons to each party within 28 days after receiving an application for full written reasons made in accordance with paragraphs (4) and (5), or as soon as practicable thereafter.

PART 4

Correcting, setting aside, reviewing and appealing Tribunal decisions

Interpretation

36. In this Part—

"appeal" means the exercise of a right of appeal against a decision of the Tribunal; and

"review" means the review of a decision by the Tribunal under section 9 of the 2007 Act.

Clerical mistakes and accidental slips or omissions

37. The Tribunal may at any time correct any clerical mistake or other accidental slip or omission in a decision, direction or any document produced by it, by—

(a) sending notification of the amended decision or direction, or a copy of the amended document, to all parties; and

(b) making any necessary amendment to any information published in relation to the decision, direction or document.

Setting aside a decision which disposes of proceedings

38.—(1) The Tribunal may set aside a decision which disposes of proceedings, or part of such a decision, and re-make the decision, or the relevant part of it, if—

(a) the Tribunal considers that it is in the interests of justice to do so; and

(b) one or more of the conditions in paragraph (2) is satisfied.

(2) The conditions are—

(a) a document relating to the proceedings was not sent to, or was not received at an appropriate time by, a party or a party's representative;

(b) a document relating to the proceedings was not sent to the Tribunal at an appropriate time;

(c) there has been some other procedural irregularity in the proceedings; or

(d) a party, or a party's representative, was not present at a hearing related to the proceedings.

(3) A party applying for a decision, or part of a decision, to be set aside under paragraph (1) must make a written application to the Tribunal so that it is received no later than 28 days after the date on which the Tribunal sent notice of the decision to the party.

(4) If the Tribunal sets aside a decision or part of a decision under this rule, the Tribunal must notify the parties in writing as soon as practicable.

Application for permission to appeal

39.—(1) A person seeking permission to appeal must make a written application to the Tribunal for permission to appeal.

(2) An application under paragraph (1) must be sent or delivered to the Tribunal so that it is received no later than 56 days after the latest of the dates that the Tribunal sends to the person making the application—

(a) full written reasons for the decision;

(b) notification of amended reasons for, or correction of, the decision following a review; or

(c) notification that an application for the decision to be set aside has been unsuccessful.

(3) The date in paragraph (2)(c) applies only if the application for the decision to be set aside was made within the time stipulated in rule 38 (setting aside a decision which disposes of proceedings), or any extension of that time granted by the Tribunal.

(4) If the person seeking permission to appeal sends or delivers the application to the Tribunal later than the time required by paragraph (2) or by any extension of time under rule 5(3)(a) (power to extend time)—

(a) the application must include a request for an extension of time and the reason why the application notice was not provided in time; and

(b) unless the Tribunal extends time for the application under rule 5(3)(a) (power to extend time) the Tribunal must not admit the application.

(5) An application under paragraph (1) must—

(a) identify the decision of the Tribunal to which it relates;

(b) identify the alleged error or errors in the decision; and

(c) state the result the party making the application is seeking.

Tribunal's consideration of application for permission to appeal

40.—(1) On receiving an application for permission to appeal the Tribunal must first consider, taking into account the overriding objective in rule 2, whether to review the decision in accordance with rule 41 (review of a decision).

(2) If the Tribunal decides not to review the decision, or reviews the decision and decides to take no action in relation to the decision, or a part of it, the Tribunal must consider whether to give permission to appeal in relation to the decision or that part of it.

(3) The Tribunal must send a record of its decision to the parties as soon as practicable.

(4) If the Tribunal refuses permission to appeal it must send with the record of its decision—

(a) a statement of its reasons for such refusal; and

(b) notification of the right to make an application to the Upper Tribunal for permission to appeal and the time within which, and the method by which, such application must be made.

(5) The Tribunal may give permission to appeal against part only of the decision or on limited grounds, but must comply with paragraph (4) in relation to any part of the decision or grounds on which it has refused permission.

Review of a decision

41.—(1) The Tribunal may only undertake a review of a decision—

(a) pursuant to rule 40(1) (review on an application for permission to appeal); and

(b) if it is satisfied that there was an error of law in the decision.

(2) The Tribunal must notify the parties in writing of the outcome of any review, unless the Tribunal decides to take no action following the review.

(3) The Tribunal may not take any action in relation to a decision following a review without first giving every party an opportunity to make representations in relation to the proposed action.

Power to treat an application as a different type of application

42. The Tribunal may treat an application for a decision to be corrected, set aside or reviewed, or for permission to appeal against a decision, as an application for any other one of those things.

Patrick Elias
Philip Brook Smith Q.C.
Carolyn Kirby
Nicholas Warren
Douglas J May
Newton of Braintree
Nuala Brice Mark Rowland
M J Reed

I allow these Rules

Signed by authority of the Lord Chancellor

Name
Parliamentary Under Secretary of State

Date Ministry of Justice

EXPLANATORY NOTE

(This note is not part of the Rules)

Part 1 of the Tribunals, Courts and Enforcement Act 2007 (c.15) establishes a new tribunal structure comprising a First-tier Tribunal and an Upper Tribunal. Appeal functions of existing tribunals are being transferred to this structure and assigned to chambers within the new tribunals. These Rules govern the practice and procedure to be followed in the First-tier Tribunal in proceedings which have been allocated to the Tax Chamber by the First-tier Tribunal and Upper Tribunal (Chambers) Order 2008(**a**).

Part 1 contains provisions for interpreting and applying the Rules and sets out the overriding objective of the Rules.

Part 2 contains general powers and provisions including the Tribunal's general case management powers, the giving of directions, the power to strike out a party's case, the service of documents and rules about evidence, submissions and witnesses.

Part 3 contains provisions relating to starting proceedings and procedure up to and including the making and notification of Tribunal decisions.

Part 4 deals with correcting, setting aside, reviewing and appealing against Tribunal decisions.

(a) S.I. 2008/2684. The Order is amended by the First-tier Tribunal and Upper Tribunal (Chambers) (Amendment) Order 2009 (S.I. 2009/196).

Appendix 7

SI 2008 No 2686 (L 14)

The Tribunal Procedure (First-tier Tribunal) (War Pensions and Armed Forces Compensation Chamber) Rules 2008

Version in force from 18th January 2010, showing amendment made by S.I. 2009/1975 and S.I. 2010/43. This document has been produced in order to assist users but its accuracy is not guaranteed and should not be relied upon. For a definitive version of the Rules, users should refer to the original statutory instruments.

Made - - - -	*9th October 2008*
Laid before Parliament	*15th October 2008*
Coming into force - -	*3rd November 2008*

CONTENTS

PART 3

Proceedings before the Tribunal

CHAPTER 1

Before the hearing

21. Notice of appeal
22. Lapse of cases
23. Responses and replies
24. Medical examinations and commissioning of medical evidence etc.

CHAPTER 2

Hearings

25. Decision with or without a hearing
26. Entitlement to attend a hearing
27. Notice of hearings
28. Public and private hearings
29. Hearings in a party's absence

CHAPTER 3

Decisions

30. Consent orders
31. Notice of decisions
32. Reasons for decisions

PART 4

Correcting, setting aside, reviewing and appealing Tribunal decisions

33. Interpretation
34. Clerical mistakes and accidental slips or omissions
35. Setting aside a decision which disposes of proceedings
36. Application for permission to appeal
37. Tribunal's consideration of application for permission to appeal
38. Review of a decision
39. Power to treat an application as a different type of application

After consulting in accordance with paragraph 28(1) of Schedule 5 to the Tribunals, Courts and Enforcement Act 2007(**a**), the Tribunal Procedure Committee has made the following Rules in exercise of the powers conferred by sections 9(3), 22 and 29(3) of, and Schedule 5 to, the Tribunals, Courts and Enforcement Act 2007.

The Lord Chancellor has allowed the Rules in accordance with paragraph 28(3) of Schedule 5 to the Tribunals, Courts and Enforcement Act 2007.

(a) 2007 c.15.

PART 1

Introduction

Citation, commencement, application and interpretation

1.—(1) These Rules may be cited as the Tribunal Procedure (War Pensions and Armed Forces Compensation Chamber) Rules 2008 and come into force on 3rd November 2008.

(2) These Rules apply to proceedings before the Tribunal which have been assigned to the War Pensions and Armed Forces Compensation Chamber by the First-tier Tribunal and Upper Tribunal (Chambers) Order 2008(**a**).

(3) In these Rules—

"the 2007 Act" means the Tribunals, Courts and Enforcement Act 2007;

"appellant" means a person who makes an appeal to the Tribunal, or a person substituted as an appellant under rule 9(1) (substitution of parties);

"decision maker" means the maker of a decision against which an appeal has been brought;

"dispose of proceedings" includes, unless indicated otherwise, disposing of a part of the proceedings;

"document" means anything in which information is recorded in any form, and an obligation under these Rules to provide or allow access to a document or a copy of a document for any purpose means, unless the Tribunal directs otherwise, an obligation to provide or allow access to such document or copy in a legible form or in a form which can be readily made into a legible form;

"hearing" means an oral hearing and includes a hearing conducted in whole or in part by video link, telephone or other means of instantaneous two-way electronic communication;

"legal representative" means [a person who, for the purposes of the Legal Services Act 2007(**b**), is an authorised person in relation to an activity which constitutes the exercise of a right of audience or the conduct of litigation within the meaning of that Act];

"party" means a person who is an appellant or respondent in proceedings before the Tribunal or, if the proceedings have been concluded, a person who was an appellant or respondent when the Tribunal finally disposed of all issues in the proceedings;

"practice direction" means a direction given under section 23 of the 2007 Act;

"respondent" means—

(a) in an appeal against a decision, the decision maker and any person other than the appellant who had a right of appeal against the decision; or

(b) a person substituted or added as a respondent under rule 9 (substitution and addition of parties);

"Tribunal" means the First-tier Tribunal.

Overriding objective and parties' obligation to co-operate with the Tribunal

2.—(1) The overriding objective of these Rules is to enable the Tribunal to deal with cases fairly and justly.

(2) Dealing with a case fairly and justly includes—

(a) dealing with the case in ways which are proportionate to the importance of the case, the complexity of the issues, the anticipated costs and the resources of the parties;

(**a**) S.I. 2008/2684.
(**b**) 2007 c.29.

(b) avoiding unnecessary formality and seeking flexibility in the proceedings;

(c) ensuring, so far as practicable, that the parties are able to participate fully in the proceedings;

(d) using any special expertise of the Tribunal effectively; and

(e) avoiding delay, so far as compatible with proper consideration of the issues.

(3) The Tribunal must seek to give effect to the overriding objective when it—

(a) exercises any power under these Rules; or

(b) interprets any rule or practice direction.

(4) Parties must—

(a) help the Tribunal to further the overriding objective; and

(b) co-operate with the Tribunal generally.

Alternative dispute resolution and arbitration

3.—(1) The Tribunal should seek, where appropriate,—

(a) to bring to the attention of the parties the availability of any appropriate alternative procedure for the resolution of the dispute; and

(b) if the parties wish and provided that it is compatible with the overriding objective, to facilitate the use of the procedure.

(2) Part 1 of the Arbitration Act 1996(**a**) does not apply to proceedings before the Tribunal.

PART 2

General powers and provisions

Delegation to staff

4.—(1) Staff appointed under section 40(1) of the 2007 Act (tribunal staff and services) may, with the approval of the Senior President of Tribunals, carry out functions of a judicial nature permitted or required to be done by the Tribunal.

(2) The approval referred to at paragraph (1) may apply generally to the carrying out of specified functions by members of staff of a specified description in specified circumstances.

(3) Within 14 days after the date on which the Tribunal sends notice of a decision made by a member of staff under paragraph (1) to a party, that party may apply in writing to the Tribunal for that decision to be considered afresh by a judge.

Case management powers

5.—(1) Subject to the provisions of the 2007 Act and any other enactment, the Tribunal may regulate its own procedure.

(2) The Tribunal may give a direction in relation to the conduct or disposal of proceedings at any time, including a direction amending, suspending or setting aside an earlier direction.

(3) In particular, and without restricting the general powers in paragraphs (1) and (2), the Tribunal may—

(**a**) 1996 c.23.

(a) extend or shorten the time for complying with any rule, practice direction or direction;

(b) consolidate or hear together two or more sets of proceedings or parts of proceedings raising common issues, or treat a case as a lead case (whether in accordance with rule 18 (lead cases) or otherwise);

(c) permit or require a party to amend a document;

(d) permit or require a party or another person to provide documents, information, evidence or submissions to the Tribunal or a party;

(e) deal with an issue in the proceedings as a preliminary issue;

(f) hold a hearing to consider any matter, including a case management issue;

(g) decide the form of any hearing;

(h) adjourn or postpone a hearing;

(i) require a party to produce a bundle for a hearing;

(j) stay proceedings;

(k) transfer proceedings to another court or tribunal if that other tribunal has jurisdiction in relation to the proceedings and—

  (i) because of a change of circumstances since the proceedings were started, the Tribunal no longer has jurisdiction in relation to the proceedings; or

  (ii) the Tribunal considers that the other court or tribunal is a more appropriate forum for the determination of the case; or

(l) suspend the effect of its own decision pending the determination by the Tribunal or the Upper Tribunal of an application for permission to appeal against, and any appeal or review of, that decision.

Procedure for applying for and giving directions

6.—(1) The Tribunal may give a direction on the application of one or more of the parties or on its own initiative.

(2) An application for a direction may be made—

(a) by sending or delivering a written application to the Tribunal; or

(b) orally during the course of a hearing.

(3) An application for a direction must include the reason for making that application.

(4) Unless the Tribunal considers that there is good reason not to do so, the Tribunal must send written notice of any direction to every party to the proceedings and to any other person affected by the direction.

(5) If a party or any other person sent notice of the direction under paragraph (4) wishes to challenge a direction which the Tribunal has given, they may do so by applying for another direction which amends, suspends or sets aside the first direction.

Failure to comply with rules etc.

7.—(1) An irregularity resulting from a failure to comply with any requirement in these Rules, a practice direction or a direction, does not of itself render void the proceedings or any step taken in the proceedings.

(2) If a party has failed to comply with a requirement in these Rules, a practice direction or a direction, the Tribunal may take such action as it considers just, which may include—

(a) waiving the requirement;

(b) requiring the failure to be remedied;

(c) exercising its power under rule 8 (striking out a party's case); or

(d) exercising its power under paragraph (3).

(3) The Tribunal may refer to the Upper Tribunal, and ask the Upper Tribunal to exercise its power under section 25 of the 2007 Act in relation to, any failure by a person to comply with a requirement imposed by the Tribunal—

(a) to attend at any place for the purpose of giving evidence;

(b) otherwise to make themselves available to give evidence;

(c) to swear an oath in connection with the giving of evidence;

(d) to give evidence as a witness;

(e) to produce a document; or

(f) to facilitate the inspection of a document or any other thing (including any premises).

Striking out a party's case

8.—(1) The proceedings, or the appropriate part of them, will automatically be struck out if the appellant has failed to comply with a direction that stated that failure by a party to comply with the direction would lead to the striking out of the proceedings or that part of them.

(2) The Tribunal must strike out the whole or a part of the proceedings if the Tribunal—

(a) does not have jurisdiction in relation to the proceedings or that part of them; and

(b) does not exercise its power under rule 5(3)(k)(i) (transfer to another court or tribunal) in relation to the proceedings or that part of them.

(3) The Tribunal may strike out the whole or a part of the proceedings if—

(a) the appellant has failed to comply with a direction which stated that failure by the appellant to comply with the direction could lead to the striking out of the proceedings or part of them;

(b) the appellant has failed to co-operate with the Tribunal to such an extent that the Tribunal cannot deal with the proceedings fairly and justly; or

(c) the Tribunal considers there is no reasonable prospect of the appellant's case, or part of it, succeeding.

(4) The Tribunal may not strike out the whole or a part of the proceedings under paragraph (2) or (3)(b) or (c) or without first giving the appellant an opportunity to make representations in relation to the proposed striking out.

(5) If the proceedings, or part of them, have been struck out under paragraph (1) or (3)(a), the appellant may apply for the proceedings, or part of them, to be reinstated.

(6) An application under paragraph (5) must be made in writing and received by the Tribunal within 42 days after the date on which the Tribunal sent notification of the striking out to the appellant.

(7) This rule applies to a respondent as it applies to an appellant except that—

(a) a reference to the striking out of the proceedings is to be read as a reference to the barring of the respondent from taking further part in the proceedings; and

(b) a reference to an application for the reinstatement of proceedings which have been struck out is to be read as a reference to an application for the lifting of the bar on the respondent from taking further part in the proceedings.

(8) If a respondent has been barred from taking further part in proceedings under this rule and that bar has not been lifted, the Tribunal need not consider any response or other submission made by that respondent.

Substitution and addition of parties

9.—(1) The Tribunal may give a direction substituting a party if—

(a) the wrong person has been named as a party; or

(b) the substitution has become necessary because of a change in circumstances since the start of proceedings.

(2) The Tribunal may give a direction adding a person to the proceedings as a respondent.

(3) If the Tribunal gives a direction under paragraph (1) or (2) it may give such consequential directions as it considers appropriate.

No power to award costs

10. The Tribunal may not make any order in respect of costs.

Representatives

11.—(1) A party may appoint a representative (whether a legal representative or not) to represent that party in the proceedings.

(2) Subject to paragraph (3), if a party appoints a representative, that party (or the representative if the representative is a legal representative) must send or deliver to the Tribunal and to each other party to the proceedings written notice of the representative's name and address.

(3) If the appellant (or the appellant's representative if the representative is a legal representative) provides written notification of the appellant's representative's name and address to the decision maker before the decision maker provides its response to the Tribunal, the appellant need not take any further steps in order to comply with paragraph (2).

(4) Anything permitted or required to be done by a party under these Rules, a practice direction or a direction may be done by the representative of that party, except signing a witness statement.

(5) A person who receives due notice of the appointment of a representative—

(a) must provide to the representative any document which is required to be provided to the represented party, and need not provide that document to the represented party; and

(b) may assume that the representative is and remains authorised as such until they receive written notification that this is not so from the representative or the represented party.

(6) At a hearing a party may be accompanied by another person whose name and address has not been notified under paragraph (2) or (3) but who, with the permission of the Tribunal, may act as a representative or otherwise assist in presenting the party's case at the hearing.

(7) Paragraphs (2) to (5) do not apply to a person who accompanies a party under paragraph (6).

Calculating time

12.—(1) An act required by these Rules, a practice direction or a direction to be done on or by a particular day must be done by 5pm on that day.

(2) If the time specified by these Rules, a practice direction or a direction for doing any act ends on a day other than a working day, the act is done in time if it is done on the next working day.

(3) In this rule "working day" means any day except a Saturday or Sunday, Christmas Day, Good Friday or a bank holiday under section 1 of the Banking and Financial Dealings Act 1971(**a**).

(**a**) 1971 c.80.

Sending and delivery of documents

13.—(1) Any document to be provided to the Tribunal under these Rules, a practice direction or a direction must be—

(a) sent by pre-paid post or delivered by hand to the address specified for the proceedings;

(b) sent by fax to the number specified for the proceedings; or

(c) sent or delivered by such other method as the Tribunal may permit or direct.

(2) Subject to paragraph (3), if a party provides a fax number, email address or other details for the electronic transmission of documents to them, that party must accept delivery of documents by that method.

(3) If a party informs the Tribunal and all other parties that a particular form of communication (other than pre-paid post or delivery by hand) should not be used to provide documents to that party, that form of communication must not be so used.

(4) If the Tribunal or a party sends a document to a party or the Tribunal by email or any other electronic means of communication, the recipient may request that the sender provide a hard copy of the document to the recipient. The recipient must make such a request as soon as reasonably practicable after receiving the document electronically.

(5) The Tribunal and each party may assume that the address provided by a party or its representative is and remains the address to which documents should be sent or delivered until receiving written notification to the contrary.

Use of documents and information

14.—(1) The Tribunal may make an order prohibiting the disclosure or publication of—

(a) specified documents or information relating to the proceedings; or

(b) any matter likely to lead members of the public to identify any person whom the Tribunal considers should not be identified.

(2) The Tribunal may give a direction prohibiting the disclosure of a document or information to a person if—

(a) the Tribunal is satisfied that such disclosure would be likely to cause that person or some other person serious harm; and

(b) the Tribunal is satisfied, having regard to the interests of justice, that it is proportionate to give such a direction.

(3) If a party ("the first party") considers that the Tribunal should give a direction under paragraph (2) prohibiting the disclosure of a document or information to another party ("the second party"), the first party must—

(a) exclude the relevant document or information from any documents that will be provided to the second party; and

(b) provide to the Tribunal the excluded document or information, and the reason for its exclusion, so that the Tribunal may decide whether the document or information should be disclosed to the second party or should be the subject of a direction under paragraph (2).

(4) The Tribunal must conduct proceedings as appropriate in order to give effect to a direction given under paragraph (2).

(5) If the Tribunal gives a direction under paragraph (2) which prevents disclosure to a party who has appointed a representative, the Tribunal may give a direction that the documents or information be disclosed to that representative if the Tribunal is satisfied that—

(a) disclosure to the representative would be in the interests of the party; and

(b) the representative will act in accordance with paragraph (6).

(6) Documents or information disclosed to a representative in accordance with a direction under paragraph (5) must not be disclosed either directly or indirectly to any other person without the Tribunal's consent.

Evidence and submissions

15.—(1) Without restriction on the general powers in rule 5(1) and (2) (case management powers), the Tribunal may give directions as to—

(a) issues on which it requires evidence or submissions;

(b) the nature of the evidence or submissions it requires;

(c) whether the parties are permitted or required to provide expert evidence, and if so whether the parties must jointly appoint a single expert to provide such evidence;

(d) any limit on the number of witnesses whose evidence a party may put forward, whether in relation to a particular issue or generally;

(e) the manner in which any evidence or submissions are to be provided, which may include a direction for them to be given—

(i) orally at a hearing; or

(ii) by written submissions or witness statement; and

(f) the time at which any evidence or submissions are to be provided.

(2) The Tribunal may—

(a) admit evidence whether or not—

(i) the evidence would be admissible in a civil trial in England and Wales; or

(ii) the evidence was available to a previous decision maker; or

(b) exclude evidence that would otherwise be admissible where—

(i) the evidence was not provided within the time allowed by a direction or a practice direction;

(ii) the evidence was otherwise provided in a manner that did not comply with a direction or a practice direction; or

(iii) it would otherwise be unfair to admit the evidence.

(3) The Tribunal may consent to a witness giving, or require any witness to give, evidence on oath, and may administer an oath for that purpose.

Summoning of witnesses and orders to answer questions or produce documents

16.—(1) On the application of a party or on its own initiative, the Tribunal may—

(a) by summons require any person to attend as a witness at a hearing at the time and place specified in the summons; or

(b) order any person to answer any questions or produce any documents in that person's possession or control which relate to any issue in the proceedings.

(2) A summons under paragraph (1)(a) must—

(a) give the person required to attend 14 days' notice of the hearing or such shorter period as the Tribunal may direct; and

(b) where the person is not a party, make provision for the person's necessary expenses of attendance to be paid, and state who is to pay them.

(3) No person may be compelled to give any evidence or produce any document that the person could not be compelled to give or produce on a trial of an action in a court of law.

(4) A summons or order under this rule must—

(a) state that the person on whom the requirement is imposed may apply to the Tribunal to vary or set aside the summons or order, if they have not had an opportunity to object to it; and

(b) state the consequences of failure to comply with the summons or order.

Withdrawal

17.—(1) Subject to paragraph (2), a party may give notice of withdrawal of its case, or any part of it—

(a) at any time before a hearing to consider the disposal of the proceedings (or, if the Tribunal disposes of the proceedings without a hearing, before that disposal), by sending or delivering to the Tribunal a written notice of withdrawal; or

(b) orally at a hearing.

(2) Notice of withdrawal given under paragraph (1)(b) will not take effect unless the Tribunal consents to the withdrawal.

(3) A party which has withdrawn its case may apply to the Tribunal for the case to be reinstated.

(4) An application under paragraph (3) must be made in writing and be received by the Tribunal within 28 days after—

(a) the date on which the Tribunal received the notice under paragraph (1)(a); or

(b) the date of the hearing at which the case was withdrawn orally under paragraph (1)(b).

(5) The Tribunal must notify each party in writing of a withdrawal under this rule.

Lead cases

18.—(1) This rule applies if—

(a) two or more cases have been started before the Tribunal;

(b) in each such case the Tribunal has not made a decision disposing of the proceedings; and

(c) the cases give rise to common or related issues of fact or law.

(2) The Tribunal may give a direction—

(a) specifying one or more cases falling under paragraph (1) as a lead case or lead cases; and

(b) staying the other cases falling under paragraph (1) ("the related cases").

(3) When the Tribunal makes a decision in respect of the common or related issues—

(a) the Tribunal must send a copy of that decision to each party in each of the related cases; and

(b) subject to paragraph (4), that decision shall be binding on each of those parties.

(4) Within 28 days after the date on which the Tribunal sent a copy of the decision to a party under paragraph (3)(a), that party may apply in writing for a direction that the decision does not apply to, and is not binding on the parties to, a particular related case.

(5) The Tribunal must give directions in respect of cases which are stayed under paragraph (2)(b), providing for the disposal of or further directions in those cases.

(6) If the lead case or cases lapse or are withdrawn before the Tribunal makes a decision in respect of the common or related issues, the Tribunal must give directions as to—

(a) whether another case or other cases are to be specified as a lead case or lead cases; and

(b) whether any direction affecting the related cases should be set aside or amended.

Transfer of cases

19.—(1) In addition to the Tribunal's power to transfer proceedings under rule 5(3)(k) (transfer of proceedings to another tribunal), the Tribunal may, at the request of the appellant, transfer the proceedings to a Pensions Appeal Tribunal appointed for Scotland or Northern Ireland if—

(a) the appellant did not reside in the United Kingdom when the proceedings were started; and

(b) the appellant has satisfied the Tribunal that—

  (i) the appellant has a closer connection with Scotland or with Northern Ireland than with England and Wales; or

  (ii) there is some other good reason for the appeal to be heard in Scotland or in Northern Ireland.

(2) If the Tribunal transfers the proceedings under paragraph (1) it must notify the parties and the tribunal to which it transfers the proceedings.

(3) If the Tribunal refuses a request to transfer the proceedings under paragraph (1) it must send written notice of reasons for such refusal to the appellant.

Expenses

20.—(1) The Tribunal must pay travelling expenses actually and reasonably incurred by, and a subsistence allowance at the prescribed rate to—

(a) an appellant attending a hearing or an examination under rule 24 (medical examinations);

(b) a relative or friend attending a hearing on behalf of an appellant who is unable to attend the hearing for reasons of health; or

(c) an appellant's attendant, if the appellant attending a hearing or an examination under rule 24 (medical examinations) requires for reasons of health to be accompanied by an attendant.

(2) The Tribunal may pay to a person mentioned in paragraph (1)(a) such allowance as the Tribunal considers reasonable for compensation for loss of time, if—

(a) the appeal was successful or there were reasonable grounds for the appeal; and

(b) the allowance does not exceed the prescribed maximum.

(3) The Tribunal may pay to an appellant such allowance as the Tribunal considers reasonable in respect of the expenses incurred in securing the attendance of a medical witness at a hearing or the provision of a medical report or certificate or other medical document for the case, if—

(a) the Tribunal considers that the attendance of such witness or provision of such document was reasonably necessary; and

(b) the allowance does not exceed the prescribed maximum.

(4) In this rule "prescribed" in relation to an amount or a rate means the amount or rate determined by the Lord Chancellor from time to time.

PART 3

Proceedings before the Tribunal

CHAPTER 1

Before the hearing

Notice of appeal(a)

21.—(1) An appellant must start proceedings by sending or delivering a notice of appeal to the decision maker so that it is received—

(a) in proceedings under section 5(1) of the Pensions Appeal Tribunals Act 1943, within 3 months after the date on which written notice of the decision being challenged was sent to the appellant; or

(b) in other cases under the Pensions Appeal Tribunals Act 1943, within 6 months after the date on which written notice of the decision being challenged was sent to the appellant.

(2) If the appellant provides the notice of appeal to the decision maker later than the time required by paragraph (1) the notice of appeal must include the reason why the notice of appeal was not provided in time.

(3) Subject to paragraph (4), where an appeal is not made within the time specified in paragraph (1), it will be treated as having been made in time if the decision maker does not object.

(4) No appeal may be made more than 12 months after the time specified in paragraph (1).

(5) The notice of appeal must be in English or Welsh, must be signed by the appellant and must state—

(a) the name and address of the appellant;

(b) the name and address of the appellant's representative (if any);

(c) an address where documents for the appellant may be sent or delivered;

(d) details (including the full reference) of the decision being appealed; and

(e) the grounds on which the appellant relies.

(6) The decision maker must refer the case to the Tribunal immediately if—

(a) the appeal has been made after the time specified in paragraph (1) and the decision maker objects to it being treated as having been made in time; or

(b) the decision maker considers that the appeal has been made more than 12 months after the time specified in paragraph (1).

(7) [Notwithstanding rule 5(3)(a) (case management powers) and rule 7(2) (failure to comply with rules etc.), the Tribunal must not extend the time limit in paragraph (4).]

Lapse of cases

22.—(1) If the decision maker revises the decision challenged—

(a) the proceedings shall proceed as if they had been brought in relation to the revised decision; and

(b) the appellant may make representations in relation to the revised decision within 42 days of the date on which notice of the revised decision was sent to the appellant.

(a) Rule 21(7) was inserted by S.I. 2009/1975.

(2) The appeal will lapse if the appellant—

(a) does not wish to proceed with the appeal and notifies the Tribunal accordingly; or

(b) subject to paragraph (3), does not make representations within the time specified in paragraph (1)(b).

(3) Paragraph (2)(b) does not apply if the appellant has no representations to make under paragraph (2)(b) and has notified the Tribunal accordingly.

Responses and replies

23.—(1) When a decision maker receives the notice of appeal or a copy of it, the decision maker must send or deliver a response to the Tribunal as soon as reasonably practicable after the decision maker received the notice of appeal.

(2) The response must state—

(a) the name and address of the decision maker;

(b) the name and address of the decision maker's representative (if any);

(c) an address where documents for the decision maker may be sent or delivered;

(d) the names and addresses of any other respondents and their representatives (if any);

(e) whether the decision maker opposes the appellant's case and, if so, the grounds for such opposition; and

(f) any further information or documents required by a practice direction or direction.

(3) The response may include a submission as to whether it would be appropriate for the case to be dealt with without a hearing.

(4) The decision maker must provide with the response—

(a) a copy of any written record of the decision under challenge, and any statement of reasons for that decision;

(b) copies of all documents relevant to the case in the decision maker's possession, unless a practice direction or direction states otherwise; and

(c) a copy of the notice of appeal, any documents provided by the appellant with the notice of appeal and, unless stated in the notice of appeal, the name and address of the appellant's representative (if any).

(5) The decision maker must provide a copy of the response and any accompanying documents to each other party at the same time as it provides the response to the Tribunal.

(6) The appellant and any other respondent may make a written submission and supply further documents in reply to the decision maker's response.

(7) Any submission or further documents under paragraph (6) must be provided to the Tribunal and to each other party within 1 month after the date on which the decision maker sent the response to the party providing the reply.

Medical examinations and commissioning of medical evidence etc.

24.—(1) An appropriate member of the Tribunal may make a medical examination of the appellant if—

(a) the proceedings relate to the appellant's disablement or incapacity for work; and

(b) the appellant consents.

(2) If the appellant lives outside the United Kingdom, the Tribunal may arrange a medical examination of the appellant.

(3) If a medical or other technical question arises in a case the Tribunal may—

(a) request a medical or other technical specialist to provide a report in relation to the question; and

(b) if the question is a medical one, arrange for the appellant to be examined for the purposes of the preparation of such a report.

(4) Subject to rule 14(2) (withholding documents or information likely to cause harm) the Tribunal must provide to each party a copy of any report obtained under this rule.

(5) If the Tribunal arranges a medical examination under paragraph (2) or requests a report under paragraph (3) the Tribunal may pay a fee to the medical or other technical specialist.

(6) Any fee paid under paragraph (5) must not exceed the maximum fee determined by the Lord Chancellor from time to time.

CHAPTER 2

Hearings

Decision with or without a hearing

25.—(1) Subject to the following paragraphs, the Tribunal must hold a hearing before making a decision which disposes of proceedings unless—

(a) each party has consented to, or has not objected to, the matter being decided without a hearing; and

(b) the Tribunal considers that it is able to decide the matter without a hearing.

(2) This rule does not apply to decisions under Part 4.

(3) The Tribunal may in any event dispose of proceedings without a hearing under rule 8 (striking out a party's case).

Entitlement to attend a hearing

26. Subject to rule 28(4) (exclusion of a person from a hearing), each party to proceedings is entitled to attend a hearing.

Notice of hearings

27.—(1) The Tribunal must give each party entitled to attend a hearing reasonable notice of the time and place of the hearing (including any adjourned or postponed hearing) and any changes to the time and place of the hearing.

(2) The period of notice under paragraph (1) must be at least 14 days except that the Tribunal may give shorter notice—

(a) with the parties' consent; or

(b) in urgent or exceptional circumstances.

Public and private hearings

28.—(1) Subject to the following paragraphs, all hearings must be held in public.

(2) The Tribunal may give a direction that a hearing, or part of it, is to be held in private.

(3) Where a hearing, or part of it, is to be held in private, the Tribunal may determine who is permitted to attend the hearing or part of it.

(4) The Tribunal may give a direction excluding from any hearing, or part of it—

(a) any person whose conduct the Tribunal considers is disrupting or is likely to disrupt the hearing;

(b) any person whose presence the Tribunal considers is likely to prevent another person from giving evidence or making submissions freely;

(c) any person who the Tribunal considers should be excluded in order to give effect to a direction under rule 14(2) (withholding information likely to cause harm); or

(d) any person where the purpose of the hearing would be defeated by the attendance of that person.

(5) The Tribunal may give a direction excluding a witness from a hearing until that witness gives evidence.

Hearings in a party's absence

29. If a party fails to attend a hearing the Tribunal may proceed with the hearing if the Tribunal—

(a) is satisfied that the party has been notified of the hearing or that reasonable steps have been taken to notify the party of the hearing; and

(b) considers that it is in the interests of justice to proceed with the hearing.

CHAPTER 3

Decisions

Consent orders

30.—(1) The Tribunal may, at the request of the parties but only if it considers it appropriate, make a consent order disposing of the proceedings and making such other appropriate provision as the parties have agreed.

(2) Notwithstanding any other provision of these Rules, the Tribunal need not hold a hearing before making an order under paragraph (1), or provide reasons for the order.

Notice of decisions

31.—(1) The Tribunal may give a decision orally at a hearing.

(2) Subject to rule 14(2) (withholding information likely to cause harm), the Tribunal must provide to each party as soon as reasonably practicable after making a decision which finally disposes of all issues in the proceedings (except a decision under Part 4)—

(a) a decision notice stating the Tribunal's decision;

(b) where appropriate, notification of the right to apply for a written statement of reasons under rule 32(2); and

(c) notification of any right of appeal against the decision and the time within which, and the manner in which, such right of appeal may be exercised.

Reasons for decisions

32.—(1) The Tribunal may give reasons for a decision which disposes of proceedings (except a decision under Part 4)—

(a) orally at a hearing; or

(b) in a written statement of reasons to each party.

(2) Unless the Tribunal has already provided a written statement of reasons under paragraph (1)(b), a party may make a written application to the Tribunal for such statement following a decision which finally disposes of all issues in the proceedings.

(3) An application under paragraph (2) must be received within 42 days of the date on which the Tribunal sent or otherwise provided to the party a decision notice relating to the decision which finally disposes of all issues in the proceedings.

(4) If a party makes an application in accordance with paragraphs (2) and (3) the Tribunal must, subject to rule 14(2) (withholding information likely to cause harm), send a written statement of reasons to each party within 28 days of the date on which it received the application or as soon as reasonably practicable after the end of that period.

PART 4

Correcting, setting aside, reviewing and appealing Tribunal decisions

Interpretation

33. In this Part—

"appeal" means the exercise of a right of appeal on a point of law under section 11 of the 2007 Act; and

"review" means the review of a decision by the Tribunal under section 9 of the 2007 Act.

Clerical mistakes and accidental slips or omissions

34. The Tribunal may at any time correct any clerical mistake or other accidental slip or omission in a decision, direction or any document produced by it, by—

(a) sending notification of the amended decision or direction, or a copy of the amended document, to all parties; and

(b) making any necessary amendment to any information published in relation to the decision, direction or document.

Setting aside a decision which disposes of proceedings

35.—(1) The Tribunal may set aside a decision which disposes of proceedings, or part of such a decision, and re-make the decision, or the relevant part of it, if—

(a) the Tribunal considers that it is in the interests of justice to do so; and

(b) one or more of the conditions in paragraph (2) are satisfied.

(2) The conditions are—

(a) a document relating to the proceedings was not sent to, or was not received at an appropriate time by, a party or a party's representative;

(b) a document relating to the proceedings was not sent to the Tribunal at an appropriate time;

(c) a party, or a party's representative, was not present at a hearing related to the proceedings; or

(d) there has been some other procedural irregularity in the proceedings.

(3) A party applying for a decision, or part of a decision, to be set aside under paragraph (1) must make a written application to the Tribunal so that it is received no later than 1 month after the date on which the Tribunal sent notice of the decision to the party.

Application for permission to appeal

36.—(1) A person seeking permission to appeal must make a written application to the Tribunal for permission to appeal.

(2) An application under paragraph (1) must be sent or delivered to the Tribunal so that it is received no later than 42 days after the latest of the dates that the Tribunal sends—

(a) written reasons for the decision;

(b) notification of amended reasons for, or correction of, the decision following a review; or

(c) notification that an application for the decision to be set aside has been unsuccessful.

(3) The date in paragraph (2)(c) applies only if the application for the decision to be set aside was made within the time stipulated in rule 35 (setting aside a decision which disposes of proceedings) or any extension of that time granted by the Tribunal.

(4) If the person seeking permission to appeal sends or delivers the application to the Tribunal later than the time required by paragraph (2) or by any extension of time under rule 5(3)(a) (power to extend time)—

(a) the application must include a request for an extension of time and the reason why the application was not made in time; and

(b) unless the Tribunal extends time for the application under rule 5(3)(a) (power to extend time) the Tribunal must not admit the application.

(5) An application under paragraph (1) must—

(a) identify the decision of the Tribunal to which it relates;

(b) identify the alleged error or errors of law in the decision; and

(c) state the result the party making the application is seeking.

(6) If a person makes an application under paragraph (1) when the Tribunal has not given a written statement of reasons for its decision—

(a) if no application for a written statement of reasons has been made to the Tribunal, the application for permission must be treated as such an application;

(b) unless the Tribunal decides to give permission and directs that this sub-paragraph does not apply, the application is not to be treated as an application for permission to appeal; and

(c) if an application for a written statement of reasons has been, or is, refused because of a delay in making the application, the Tribunal must only admit the application for permission if the Tribunal considers that it is in the interests of justice to do so.

Tribunal's consideration of application for permission to appeal

37.—(1) On receiving an application for permission to appeal the Tribunal must first consider, taking into account the overriding objective in rule 2, whether to review the decision in accordance with rule 38 (review of a decision).

(2) If the Tribunal decides not to review the decision, or reviews the decision and decides to take no action in relation to the decision, or part of it, the Tribunal must consider whether to give permission to appeal in relation to the decision or that part of it.

(3) The Tribunal must send a record of its decision to the parties as soon as practicable.

(4) If the Tribunal refuses permission to appeal it must send with the record of its decision—

(a) a statement of its reasons for such refusal; and

(b) notification of the right to make an application to the Upper Tribunal for permission to appeal and the time within which, and the method by which, such application must be made.

(5) The Tribunal may give permission to appeal on limited grounds, but must comply with paragraph (4) in relation to any grounds on which it has refused permission.

Review of a decision

38.—(1) The Tribunal may only undertake a review of a decision—

(a) pursuant to rule 37(1) (review on an application for permission to appeal); and

(b) if it is satisfied that there was an error of law in the decision.

(2) The Tribunal must notify the parties in writing of the outcome of any review, and of any right of appeal in relation to the outcome.

(3) If the Tribunal takes any action in relation to a decision following a review without first giving every party an opportunity to make representations, the notice under paragraph (2) must state that any party that did not have an opportunity to make representations may apply for such action to be set aside and for the decision to be reviewed again.

Power to treat an application as a different type of application

39. The Tribunal may treat an application for a decision to be corrected, set aside or reviewed, or for permission to appeal against a decision, as an application for any other one of those things.

Patrick Elias
Phillip Brook Smith Q.C. Lesley Clare
Douglas J. May Q.C.
Newton of Braintree
M.J. Reed Mark Rowland
Nicholas Warren

I allow these Rules

Signed by authority of the Lord Chancellor

Bridget Prentice
Parliamentary Under Secretary of State

9th October 2008 Ministry of Justice

EXPLANATORY NOTE

(This note is not part of the Rules)

Part 1 of the Tribunals, Courts and Enforcement Act 2007 (c.15) establishes a new tribunal structure comprising a First-tier Tribunal and an Upper Tribunal. Appeal functions of existing tribunals are being transferred to this structure and assigned to chambers within the new tribunals. These Rules govern the practice and procedure to be followed in the First-tier Tribunal in proceedings which have been allocated to the War Pensions and Armed Forces Compensation Chamber by the First-tier Tribunal and Upper Tribunal (Chambers) Order 2008(**a**).

Part 1 contains provisions for interpreting and applying the Rules and sets out the overriding objective of the Rules.

Part 2 contains general powers and provisions including the Tribunal's general case management powers, the giving of directions, the power to strike out a party's case, the service of documents and rules about evidence, submissions and witnesses.

Part 3 contains provisions on the notice of appeals and on responses and replies. It also makes provision for hearings and for decisions made by the Tribunal.

Part 4 deals with correcting, setting aside, reviewing and appealing against Tribunal decisions.

(**a**) S.I. 2008/2684.

Appendix 8

SI 2008 No 2698 (L 15)

The Tribunal Procedure (Upper Tribunal) Rules 2008

Version in force from 15th February 2010, showing amendments made by S.I. 2009/274, S.I. 2009/1975, S.I. 2010/43, S.I. 2010/44 and S.I. 2010/747. This document has been produced in order to assist users but its accuracy is not guaranteed and should not be relied upon. For a definitive version of the Rules, users should refer to the original statutory instruments.

Made - - - -	*9th October 2008*
Laid before Parliament	*15th October 2008*
Coming into force - -	*3rd November 2008*

CONTENTS

PART 3

[Procedure for cases in] the Upper Tribunal

PART 4

Judicial review proceedings in the Upper Tribunal

PART 5

Hearings

PART 6

Decisions

PART 7

Correcting, setting aside, reviewing and appealing decisions of the Upper Tribunal

[SCHEDULE 1

Procedure after the notice of appeal in appeals against decisions of traffic commissioners]

[SCHEDULE 2

Additional procedure in national security cases]

[SCHEDULE 3

Procedure in financial services cases]

After consulting in accordance with paragraph 28(1) of Schedule 5 to, the Tribunals, Courts and Enforcement Act 2007(**a**) the Tribunal Procedure Committee has made the following Rules in exercise of the power conferred by sections 10(3), 16(9), 22 and 29(3) and (4) of, and Schedule 5 to, that Act.

The Lord Chancellor has allowed the Rules in accordance with paragraph 28(3) of Schedule 5 to the Tribunals, Courts and Enforcement Act 2007.

PART 1

Introduction

Citation, commencement, application and interpretation(b)

1.—(1) These Rules may be cited as the Tribunal Procedure (Upper Tribunal) Rules 2008 and come into force on 3rd November 2008.

(2) These Rules apply to proceedings before the Upper Tribunal [except proceedings in the Lands Chamber].

(3) In these Rules—

"the 2007 Act" means the Tribunals, Courts and Enforcement Act 2007;

["appellant" means—

(a) a person who makes an appeal, or applies for permission to appeal, to the Upper Tribunal;

(b) in proceedings transferred or referred to the Upper Tribunal from the First-tier Tribunal, a person who started the proceedings in the First-tier Tribunal; or

---

(**a**) 2007 c.15.

(**b**) In rule 1(2) the words in square brackets were inserted by S.I. 2009/1975. In rule 1(3), S.I. 2009/274 substituted the definition of "appellant", omitted the definitions of "disability discrimination in schools case", "legal representative" and "special educational needs case" and paragraph (a)(ii) in the definition of "respondent", and inserted paragraph (ca) in the definition of "respondent". S.I. 2009/1975 inserted the definitions of "appropriate national authority", "authorised person" and "tribunal", and the words in square brackets in paragraph (b) in the definition of "respondent".

(c) a person substituted as an appellant under rule 9(1) (substitution and addition of parties);]

...

["applicant" means—

(a) a person who applies for permission to bring, or does bring, judicial review proceedings before the Upper Tribunal and, in judicial review proceedings transferred to the Upper Tribunal from a court, includes a person who was a claimant or petitioner in the proceedings immediately before they were transferred; or

(b) person who refers a financial services case to the Upper Tribunal;]

...

["appropriate national authority" means, in relation to an appeal, the Secretary of State, the Scottish Ministers or the Welsh Ministers, as the case may be;]

["asylum case" means proceedings before the Upper Tribunal on appeal against a decision in proceedings under section 82, 83 or 83A of the Nationality, Immigration and Asylum Act 2002**(a)** in which a person claims that removal from, or a requirement to leave, the United Kingdom would breach the United Kingdom's obligations under the Convention relating to the Status of Refugees done at Geneva on 28 July 1951 and the Protocol to the Convention;]

["authorised person" means an examiner appointed by the Secretary of State under section 66A of the Road Traffic Act 1988**(b)**, or a person acting under the direction of such an examiner, who has detained the vehicle to which an appeal relates;]

"dispose of proceedings" includes, unless indicated otherwise, disposing of a part of the proceedings;

"document" means anything in which information is recorded in any form, and an obligation under these Rules or any practice direction or direction to provide or allow access to a document or a copy of a document for any purpose means, unless the Upper Tribunal directs otherwise, an obligation to provide or allow access to such document or copy in a legible form or in a form which can be readily made into a legible form;

["fast-track case" means an asylum case or an immigration case where the person who appealed to the First-tier Tribunal—

(a) was detained under the Immigration Acts at a place specified in Schedule 2 to the Asylum and Immigration Tribunal (Fast Track Procedure) Rules 2005**(c)** when the notice of decision that was the subject of the appeal to the First-tier Tribunal was served on the appellant;

(b) remains so detained; and

(c) the First-tier Tribunal or the Upper Tribunal has not directed that the case cease to be treated as a fast-track case;] "hearing" means an oral hearing and includes a hearing conducted in whole or in part by video link, telephone or other means of instantaneous two-way electronic communication;

["financial services case" means a reference to the Upper Tribunal in respect of—

(a) a decision of the Financial Services Authority;

(b) a decision of the Bank of England;

(a) 2002 c. 41. Section 82 was amended by sections 26(2) and 31 of the Asylum and Immigration (Treatment of Claimants, etc.) Act 2004 (c. 19); sections 2, 11(6), 47(6), 57(2) and 61 of the Immigration, Asylum and Nationality Act 2006 (c. 13), and section 35(1) and (3) of the UK Borders Act 2007 (c. 30). Section 83A was inserted by section 1 of the Immigration, Asylum and Nationality Act 2006.

(b) 1988 c. 52. Section 66A was inserted by section 9(1) of the Road Traffic Act 1991 (c. 40) and amended by paragraph 11 of Schedule 7 to the Goods Vehicles (Licensing of Operators) Act 1995 (c. 23).

(c) S.I. 2005/560.

(c) a decision of the Pensions Regulator; or

(d) a decision of a person relating to the assessment of any compensation or consideration under the Banking (Special Provisions) Act 2008(**a**) or the Banking Act 2009(**b**).]

["immigration case" means proceedings before the Upper Tribunal on appeal against a decision in proceedings under section 40A of the British Nationality Act 1981(**c**), section 82 of the Nationality, Immigration and Asylum Act 2002, or regulation 26 of the Immigration (European Economic Area) Regulations 2006(**d**) that are not an asylum case;]

"interested party" means—

(a) a person who is directly affected by the outcome sought in judicial review proceedings, and has been named as an interested party under rule 28 or 29 (judicial review), or has been substituted or added as an interested party under rule 9 [(addition, substitution and removal of parties)];

(b) in judicial review proceedings transferred to the Upper Tribunal under section 25A(2) or (3) of the Judicature (Northern Ireland) Act 1978(**e**) or section 31A(2) or (3) of the Supreme Court Act 1981(**f**), a person who was an interested party in the proceedings immediately before they were transferred to the Upper Tribunal; [and

(c) in a financial services case, any person other than the applicant who could have referred the case to the Upper Tribunal and who has been added or substituted as an interested party under rule 9 (addition, substitution and removal of parties);]

"judicial review proceedings" means proceedings within the jurisdiction of the Upper Tribunal pursuant to section 15 or 21 of the 2007 Act, whether such proceedings are started in the Upper Tribunal or transferred to the Upper Tribunal;

...

"mental health case" means proceedings before the Upper Tribunal on appeal against a decision in proceedings under the Mental Health Act 1983(**g**) or paragraph 5(2) of the Schedule to the Repatriation of Prisoners Act 1984(**h**);

["national security certificate appeal" means an appeal under section 28 of the Data Protection Act 1998 or section 60 of the Freedom of Information Act 2000(**i**) (including that section as applied and modified by regulation 18 of the Environmental Information Regulations 2004(**j**)); and]

"party" means a person who is an appellant, an applicant, a respondent or an interested party in proceedings before the Upper Tribunal, a person who has referred a question [or matter] to the Upper Tribunal or, if the proceedings have been concluded, a person who was an appellant, an applicant, a respondent or an interested party when the Tribunal finally disposed of all issues in the proceedings;

"permission" includes leave in cases arising under the law of Northern Ireland;

(**a**) [2008 c.2]
(**b**) [2009, c.1]
(**c**) 1981 c. 61.
(**d**) S.I. 2006/1003.
(**e**) 1978 c.23. Section 25A was inserted by section 19(2) of the 2007 Act.
(**f**) 1981 c.54. Section 31A was inserted by section 19(1) of the 2007 Act.
(**g**) 1983 c.20.
(**h**) 1984 c.47.
(**i**) 2002 c. 41. Section 82 was amended by sections 26(2) and 31 of the Asylum and Immigration (Treatment of Claimants, etc.) Act 2004 (c. 19); sections 2, 11(6), 47(6), 57(2) and 61 of the Immigration, Asylum and Nationality Act 2006 (c. 13), and section 35(1) and (3) of the UK Borders Act 2007 (c. 30). Section 83A was inserted by section 1 of the Immigration, Asylum and Nationality Act 2006.
(**j**) S.I. 2004/3391.

"practice direction" means a direction given under section 23 of the 2007 Act;["relevant minister" means the Minister or designated person responsible for the signing of the certificate to which a national security certificate appeal relates;]

["reference", in a financial services case, includes an appeal;]

"respondent" means—

(a) in an appeal, or application for permission to appeal, against a decision of another tribunal, any person other than the appellant who—

(i) was a party before that other tribunal;

(ii) ...; or

(iii) otherwise has a right of appeal against the decision of the other tribunal and has given notice to the Upper Tribunal that they wish to be a party to the appeal;

(b) in an appeal against any other decision [except a decision of a traffic commissioner], the person who made the decision;

(c) in judicial review proceedings—

(i) in proceedings started in the Upper Tribunal, the person named by the applicant as the respondent;

(ii) in proceedings transferred to the Upper Tribunal under section 25A(2) or (3) of the Judicature (Northern Ireland) Act 1978 or section 31A(2) or (3) of the Supreme Court Act 1981, a person who was a defendant in the proceedings immediately before they were transferred;

(iii) in proceedings transferred to the Upper Tribunal under section 20(1) of the 2007 Act, a person to whom intimation of the petition was made before the proceedings were transferred, or to whom the Upper Tribunal has required intimation to be made.

[(ca) in proceedings transferred or referred to the Upper Tribunal from the First-tier Tribunal, a person who was a respondent in the proceedings in the First-tier Tribunal;]

(d) in a reference under the Forfeiture Act 1982**(a)**, the person whose eligibility for a benefit or advantage is in issue;

[(da) in a financial services case, the maker of the decision in respect of which a reference has been made; or]

(e) a person substituted or added as a respondent under rule 9 (substitution and addition of parties);

...

["tribunal" does not include a traffic commissioner;]

"working day" means any day except a Saturday or Sunday, Christmas Day, Good Friday or a bank holiday under section 1 of the Banking and Financial Dealings Act 1971**(b)**.

Overriding objective and parties' obligation to co-operate with the Upper Tribunal

2.—(1) The overriding objective of these Rules is to enable the Upper Tribunal to deal with cases fairly and justly.

(2) Dealing with a case fairly and justly includes—

(a) dealing with the case in ways which are proportionate to the importance of the case, the complexity of the issues, the anticipated costs and the resources of the parties;

(a) 1982 c.34.
(b) 1971 c.80.

(b) avoiding unnecessary formality and seeking flexibility in the proceedings;

(c) ensuring, so far as practicable, that the parties are able to participate fully in the proceedings;

(d) using any special expertise of the Upper Tribunal effectively; and

(e) avoiding delay, so far as compatible with proper consideration of the issues.

(3) The Upper Tribunal must seek to give effect to the overriding objective when it—

(a) exercises any power under these Rules; or

(b) interprets any rule or practice direction.

(4) Parties must—

(a) help the Upper Tribunal to further the overriding objective; and

(b) co-operate with the Upper Tribunal generally.

Alternative dispute resolution and arbitration

3.—(1) The Upper Tribunal should seek, where appropriate—

(a) to bring to the attention of the parties the availability of any appropriate alternative procedure for the resolution of the dispute; and

(b) if the parties wish and provided that it is compatible with the overriding objective, to facilitate the use of the procedure.

(2) Part 1 of the Arbitration Act 1996**(a)** does not apply to proceedings before the Upper Tribunal.

PART 2

General powers and provisions

Delegation to staff

4.—(1) Staff appointed under section 40(1) of the 2007 Act (tribunal staff and services) may, with the approval of the Senior President of Tribunals, carry out functions of a judicial nature permitted or required to be done by the Upper Tribunal.

(2) The approval referred to at paragraph (1) may apply generally to the carrying out of specified functions by members of staff of a specified description in specified circumstances.

(3) Within 14 days after the date on which the Upper Tribunal sends notice of a decision made by a member of staff under paragraph (1) to a party, that party may apply in writing to the Upper Tribunal for that decision to be considered afresh by a judge.

Case management powers(b)

5.—(1) Subject to the provisions of the 2007 Act and any other enactment, the Upper Tribunal may regulate its own procedure.

(2) The Upper Tribunal may give a direction in relation to the conduct or disposal of proceedings at any time, including a direction amending, suspending or setting aside an earlier direction.

(3) In particular, and without restricting the general powers in paragraphs (1) and (2), the Upper Tribunal may—

(a) 1996 c.23.
(b) Rule 5(3)(n) was substituted by S.I. 2009/1975.

(a) extend or shorten the time for complying with any rule, practice direction or direction;

(b) consolidate or hear together two or more sets of proceedings or parts of proceedings raising common issues, or treat a case as a lead case;

(c) permit or require a party to amend a document;

(d) permit or require a party or another person to provide documents, information, evidence or submissions to the Upper Tribunal or a party;

(e) deal with an issue in the proceedings as a preliminary issue;

(f) hold a hearing to consider any matter, including a case management issue;

(g) decide the form of any hearing;

(h) adjourn or postpone a hearing;

(i) require a party to produce a bundle for a hearing;

(j) stay (or, in Scotland, sist) proceedings;

(k) transfer proceedings to another court or tribunal if that other court or tribunal has jurisdiction in relation to the proceedings and—

    (i) because of a change of circumstances since the proceedings were started, the Upper Tribunal no longer has jurisdiction in relation to the proceedings; or

    (ii) the Upper Tribunal considers that the other court or tribunal is a more appropriate forum for the determination of the case;

(l) suspend the effect of its own decision pending an appeal or review of that decision;

(m) in an appeal, or an application for permission to appeal, against the decision of another tribunal, suspend the effect of that decision pending the determination of the application for permission to appeal, and any appeal;

(n) [require any person, body or other tribunal whose decision is the subject of proceedings before the Upper Tribunal to provide reasons for the decision, or other information or documents in relation to the decision or any proceedings before that person, body or tribunal].

[(4) The Upper Tribunal may direct that a fast-track case cease to be treated as a fast-track case if—

(a) all the parties consent;

(b) the Upper Tribunal is satisfied that there are exceptional circumstances which suggest that the appeal or application could not be justly determined if it were treated as a fast-track case; or

(c) the Secretary of State for the Home Department has failed to comply with a provision of these Rules or a direction of the First-tier Tribunal or the Upper Tribunal, and the Upper Tribunal is satisfied that the other party would be prejudiced if the appeal or application were treated as a fast-track case.]

[(5) In a financial services case, the Upper Tribunal may direct that the effect of the decision in respect of which the reference has been made is to be suspended pending the determination of the reference, if it is satisfied that to do so would not prejudice—

(a) the interests of any persons (whether consumers, investors or otherwise) intended to be protected by that notice; or

(b) the smooth operation or integrity of any market intended to be protected by that notice.

(6) Paragraph (5) does not apply in the case of a reference in respect of a decision of the Pensions Regulator.]

Procedure for applying for and giving directions

6.—(1) The Upper Tribunal may give a direction on the application of one or more of the parties or on its own initiative.

(2) An application for a direction may be made—

(a) by sending or delivering a written application to the Upper Tribunal; or

(b) orally during the course of a hearing.

(3) An application for a direction must include the reason for making that application.

(4) Unless the Upper Tribunal considers that there is good reason not to do so, the Upper Tribunal must send written notice of any direction to every party and to any other person affected by the direction.

(5) If a party or any other person sent notice of the direction under paragraph (4) wishes to challenge a direction which the Upper Tribunal has given, they may do so by applying for another direction which amends, suspends or sets aside the first direction.

Failure to comply with rules etc.

7.—(1) An irregularity resulting from a failure to comply with any requirement in these Rules, a practice direction or a direction, does not of itself render void the proceedings or any step taken in the proceedings.

(2) If a party has failed to comply with a requirement in these Rules, a practice direction or a direction, the Upper Tribunal may take such action as it considers just, which may include—

(a) waiving the requirement;

(b) requiring the failure to be remedied;

(c) exercising its power under rule 8 (striking out a party's case); or

(d) except in [a mental health case, an asylum case or an immigration case], restricting a party's participation in the proceedings.

(3) Paragraph (4) applies where the First-tier Tribunal has referred to the Upper Tribunal a failure by a person to comply with a requirement imposed by the First-tier Tribunal—

(a) to attend at any place for the purpose of giving evidence;

(b) otherwise to make themselves available to give evidence;

(c) to swear an oath in connection with the giving of evidence;

(d) to give evidence as a witness;

(e) to produce a document; or

(f) to facilitate the inspection of a document or any other thing (including any premises).

(4) The Upper Tribunal may exercise its power under section 25 of the 2007 Act (supplementary powers of the Upper Tribunal) in relation to such non-compliance as if the requirement had been imposed by the Upper Tribunal.

Striking out a party's case(a)

8.—[(1A) Except for paragraph (2), this rule does not apply to an asylum case or an immigration case.]

(1) The proceedings, or the appropriate part of them, will automatically be struck out if the appellant or applicant has failed to comply with a direction that stated that failure by the appellant or applicant to comply with the direction would lead to the striking out of the proceedings or that part of them.

(a) The words in square brackets in rule 8(7) and (8) were inserted by S.I. 2009/274.

(2) The Upper Tribunal must strike out the whole or a part of the proceedings if the Upper Tribunal—

(a) does not have jurisdiction in relation to the proceedings or that part of them; and

(b) does not exercise its power under rule 5(3)(k)(i) (transfer to another court or tribunal) in relation to the proceedings or that part of them.

(3) The Upper Tribunal may strike out the whole or a part of the proceedings if—

(a) the appellant or applicant has failed to comply with a direction which stated that failure by the appellant or applicant to comply with the direction could lead to the striking out of the proceedings or part of them;

(b) the appellant or applicant has failed to co-operate with the Upper Tribunal to such an extent that the Upper Tribunal cannot deal with the proceedings fairly and justly; or

(c) in proceedings which are not an appeal from the decision of another tribunal or judicial review proceedings, the Upper Tribunal considers there is no reasonable prospect of the appellant's or the applicant's case, or part of it, succeeding.

(4) The Upper Tribunal may not strike out the whole or a part of the proceedings under paragraph (2) or (3)(b) or (c) without first giving the appellant or applicant an opportunity to make representations in relation to the proposed striking out.

(5) If the proceedings have been struck out under paragraph (1) or (3)(a), the appellant or applicant may apply for the proceedings, or part of them, to be reinstated.

(6) An application under paragraph (5) must be made in writing and received by the Upper Tribunal within 1 month after the date on which the Upper Tribunal sent notification of the striking out to the appellant or applicant.

(7) This rule applies to a respondent [or an interested party] as it applies to an appellant or applicant except that—

(a) a reference to the striking out of the proceedings is to be read as a reference to the barring of the respondent [or interested party] from taking further part in the proceedings; and

(b) a reference to an application for the reinstatement of proceedings which have been struck out is to be read as a reference to an application for the lifting of the bar on the respondent [or interested party] taking further part in the proceedings.

(8) If a respondent [or an interested party] has been barred from taking further part in proceedings under this rule and that bar has not been lifted, the Upper Tribunal need not consider any response or other submission made by that respondent [or interested party, and may summarily determine any or all issues against that respondent or interested party].

[Addition, substitution and removal of parties(a)

9.—(1) The Upper Tribunal may give a direction adding, substituting or removing a party as an appellant, a respondent or an interested party.

(2) If the Upper Tribunal gives a direction under paragraph (1) it may give such consequential directions as it considers appropriate.

(3) A person who is not a party may apply to the Upper Tribunal to be added or substituted as a party.

(4) If a person who is entitled to be a party to proceedings by virtue of another enactment applies to be added as a party, and any conditions applicable to that entitlement have been satisfied, the Upper Tribunal must give a direction adding that person as a respondent or, if appropriate, as an appellant.]

(a) Rule 9 was substituted by S.I. 2009/1975.

[(5) In an asylum case, the United Kingdom Representative of the United Nations High Commissioner for Refugees ("the United Kingdom Representative") may give notice to the Upper Tribunal that the United Kingdom Representative wishes to participate in the proceedings.

(6) If the United Kingdom Representative gives notice under paragraph (5)—

(i) the United Kingdom Representative is entitled to participate in any hearing; and

(ii) all documents which are required to be sent or delivered to parties must be sent or delivered to the United Kingdom Representative.]

[Orders for costs(a)

10.—(1) The Upper Tribunal may not make an order in respect of costs (or, in Scotland, expenses) in proceedings [transferred or referred by, or on appeal from,] another tribunal except—

[(aa) in a national security certificate appeal, to the extent permitted by paragraph (1A);]

(a) in proceedings [transferred by, or on appeal from,] the Tax Chamber of the First-tier Tribunal; or

(b) to the extent and in the circumstances that the other tribunal had the power to make an order in respect of costs (or, in Scotland, expenses).

[(1A) In a national security certificate appeal—

(a) the Upper Tribunal may make an order in respect of costs or expenses in the circumstances described at paragraph (3)(c) and (d);

(b) if the appeal is against a certificate, the Upper Tribunal may make an order in respect of costs or expenses against the relevant Minister and in favour of the appellant if the Upper Tribunal allows the appeal and quashes the certificate to any extent or the Minister withdraws the certificate;

(c) if the appeal is against the application of a certificate, the Upper Tribunal may make an order in respect of costs or expenses—

(i) against the appellant and in favour of any other party if the Upper Tribunal dismisses the appeal to any extent; or

(ii) in favour of the appellant and against any other party if the Upper Tribunal allows the appeal to any extent.]

(2) The Upper Tribunal may not make an order in respect of costs or expenses under section 4 of the Forfeiture Act 1982**(b)**.

(3) In other proceedings, the Upper Tribunal may not make an order in respect of costs or expenses except—

(a) in judicial review proceedings;

(b) ...

(c) under section 29(4) of the 2007 Act (wasted costs);

(d) if the Upper Tribunal considers that a party or its representative has acted unreasonably in bringing, defending or conducting the proceedings; [or

(e) if, in a financial services case, the Upper Tribunal considers that the decision in respect of which the reference was made was unreasonable.]

(a) Rule 10 was substituted by S.I. 2009/274. The words in square brackets in rule 10(1) were substituted by S.I. 2009/1975, and paragraph (2)(b) was omitted by S.I. 2009/1975.

(b) 1982 c.34.

(4) The Upper Tribunal may make an order for costs (or, in Scotland, expenses) on an application or on its own initiative.

(5) A person making an application for an order for costs or expenses must—

(a) send or deliver a written application to the Upper Tribunal and to the person against whom it is proposed that the order be made; and

(b) send or deliver with the application a schedule of the costs or expenses claimed sufficient to allow summary assessment of such costs or expenses by the Upper Tribunal.

(6) An application for an order for costs or expenses may be made at any time during the proceedings but may not be made later than 1 month after the date on which the Upper Tribunal sends—

(a) a decision notice recording the decision which finally disposes of all issues in the proceedings; or

(b) notice of a withdrawal under rule 17 which ends the proceedings.

(7) The Upper Tribunal may not make an order for costs or expenses against a person (the "paying person") without first—

(a) giving that person an opportunity to make representations; and

(b) if the paying person is an individual and the order is to be made under paragraph (3)(a), (b) or (d), considering that person's financial means.

(8) The amount of costs or expenses to be paid under an order under this rule may be ascertained by—

(a) summary assessment by the Upper Tribunal;

(b) agreement of a specified sum by the paying person and the person entitled to receive the costs or expenses ("the receiving person"); or

(c) assessment of the whole or a specified part of the costs or expenses incurred by the receiving person, if not agreed.

(9) Following an order for assessment under paragraph (8)(c), the paying person or the receiving person may apply—

(a) in England and Wales, to the High Court or the Costs Office of the Supreme Court (as specified in the order) for a detailed assessment of the costs on the standard basis or, if specified in the order, on the indemnity basis; and the Civil Procedure Rules 1998(**a**) shall apply, with necessary modifications, to that application and assessment as if the proceedings in the tribunal had been proceedings in a court to which the Civil Procedure Rules 1998 apply;

(b) in Scotland, to the Auditor of the Court of Session for the taxation of the expenses according to the fees payable in that court; or

(c) in Northern Ireland, to the Taxing Office of the High Court of Northern Ireland for taxation on the standard basis or, if specified in the order, on the indemnity basis.]

Representatives(b)

11.—(1) A party may appoint a representative (whether a legal representative or not) to represent that party in the proceedings [save that a party in an asylum or immigration case may

(a) S.I. 1998/3132.

(b) In rule 11, paragraph (2) was amended and paragraphs (2A) and (9) were inserted by S.I. 2009/274. Paragraph (8)(b) was amended by S.I. 2009/1975.

not be represented by any person prohibited from representing by section 84 of the Immigration and Asylum Act 1999(a)].

(2) If a party appoints a representative, that party (or the representative if the representative is a legal representative) must send or deliver to the Upper Tribunal written notice of the representative's name and address.

[(2A) If the Upper Tribunal receives notice that a party has appointed a representative under paragraph (2), it must send a copy of that notice to each other party.]

(3) Anything permitted or required to be done by a party under these Rules, a practice direction or a direction may be done by the representative of that party, except signing a witness statement.

(4) A person who receives due notice of the appointment of a representative—

(a) must provide to the representative any document which is required to be provided to the represented party, and need not provide that document to the represented party; and

(b) may assume that the representative is and remains authorised as such until they receive written notification that this is not so from the representative or the represented party.

(5) At a hearing a party may be accompanied by another person whose name and address has not been notified under paragraph (2) but who, subject to paragraph (8) and with the permission of the Upper Tribunal, may act as a representative or otherwise assist in presenting the party's case at the hearing.

(6) Paragraphs (2) to (4) do not apply to a person who accompanies a party under paragraph (5).

(7) In a mental health case if the patient has not appointed a representative the Upper Tribunal may appoint a legal representative for the patient where—

(a) the patient has stated that they do not wish to conduct their own case or that they wish to be represented; or

(b) the patient lacks the capacity to appoint a representative but the Upper Tribunal believes that it is in the patient's best interests for the patient to be represented.

(8) In a mental health case a party may not appoint as a representative, or be represented or assisted at a hearing by—

(a) a person liable to be detained or subject to guardianship or after-care under supervision, or who is a community patient, under the Mental Health Act 1983; or

(b) a person receiving treatment for mental disorder at the same hospital [or] home as the patient.

[(9) In this rule "legal representative" means [a person who, for the purposes of the Legal Services Act 2007, is an authorised person in relation to an activity which constitutes the exercise of a right of audience or the conduct of litigation within the meaning of that Act], [a qualified person as defined in section 84(2) of the Immigration and Asylum Act 1999,] an advocate or solicitor in Scotland or a barrister or solicitor in Northern Ireland.]

[(10) In an asylum case or an immigration case, an appellant's representative before the First-tier Tribunal will be treated as that party's representative before the Upper Tribunal, unless the Upper Tribunal receives notice—

(a) of a new representative under paragraph (2) of this rule; or

(b) from the appellant stating that they are no longer represented.]

(a) 1999 c. 33.

Calculating time(a)

12.—(1) An act required by these Rules, a practice direction or a direction to be done on or by a particular day must be done by 5pm on that day.

(2) If the time specified by these Rules, a practice direction or a direction for doing any act ends on a day other than a working day, the act is done in time if it is done on the next working day.

(3) In a special educational needs case or a disability discrimination in schools case, the following days must not be counted when calculating the time by which an act must be done—

(a) 25th December to 1st January inclusive; and

(b) any day in August.

[(3A) In an asylum case or an immigration case, when calculating the time by which an act must be done, in addition to the days specified in the definition of "working days" in rule 1 (interpretation), the following days must also not be counted as working days—

(a) 27th to 31st December inclusive; and

(b) in a fast-track case, 24th December, Maundy Thursday, or the Tuesday after the last Monday in May.]

(4) Paragraph (3) [or (3A)] does not apply where the Upper Tribunal directs that an act must be done by or on a specified date.

[(5) In this rule—

"disability discrimination in schools case" means proceedings concerning disability discrimination in the education of a child or related matters; and

"special educational needs case" means proceedings concerning the education of a child who has or may have special educational needs.]

Sending and delivery of documents(b)

13.—(1) Any document to be provided to the Upper Tribunal under these Rules, a practice direction or a direction must be—

(a) sent by pre-paid post [or by document exchange, or delivered by hand,] to the address specified for the proceedings;

(b) sent by fax to the number specified for the proceedings; or

(c) sent or delivered by such other method as the Upper Tribunal may permit or direct.

(2) Subject to paragraph (3), if a party provides a fax number, email address or other details for the electronic transmission of documents to them, that party must accept delivery of documents by that method.

(3) If a party informs the Upper Tribunal and all other parties that a particular form of communication, other than pre-paid post or delivery by hand, should not be used to provide documents to that party, that form of communication must not be so used.

(4) If the Upper Tribunal or a party sends a document to a party or the Upper Tribunal by email or any other electronic means of communication, the recipient may request that the sender provide a hard copy of the document to the recipient. The recipient must make such a request as soon as reasonably practicable after receiving the document electronically.

(5) The Upper Tribunal and each party may assume that the address provided by a party or its representative is and remains the address to which documents should be sent or delivered until receiving written notification to the contrary.

(a) Rule 12(5) was inserted by S.I. 2009/274.
(b) Rule 13(1)(a) was amended by S.I. 2009/274.

[(6) Subject to paragraph (7), if a document submitted to the Upper Tribunal is not written in English, it must be accompanied by an English translation.

(7) In proceedings that are in Wales or have a connection with Wales, a document or translation may be submitted to the Tribunal in Welsh.]

Use of documents and information(a)

14.—(1) The Upper Tribunal may make an order prohibiting the disclosure or publication of—

(a) specified documents or information relating to the proceedings; or

(b) any matter likely to lead members of the public to identify any person whom the Upper Tribunal considers should not be identified.

(2) The Upper Tribunal may give a direction prohibiting the disclosure of a document or information to a person if—

(a) the Upper Tribunal is satisfied that such disclosure would be likely to cause that person or some other person serious harm; and

(b) the Upper Tribunal is satisfied, having regard to the interests of justice, that it is proportionate to give such a direction.

(3) If a party ("the first party") considers that the Upper Tribunal should give a direction under paragraph (2) prohibiting the disclosure of a document or information to another party ("the second party"), the first party must—

(a) exclude the relevant document or information from any documents that will be provided to the second party; and

(b) provide to the Upper Tribunal the excluded document or information, and the reason for its exclusion, so that the Upper Tribunal may decide whether the document or information should be disclosed to the second party or should be the subject of a direction under paragraph (2).

(4)

...

(5) If the Upper Tribunal gives a direction under paragraph (2) which prevents disclosure to a party who has appointed a representative, the Upper Tribunal may give a direction that the documents or information be disclosed to that representative if the Upper Tribunal is satisfied that—

(a) disclosure to the representative would be in the interests of the party; and

(b) the representative will act in accordance with paragraph (6).

(6) Documents or information disclosed to a representative in accordance with a direction under paragraph (5) must not be disclosed either directly or indirectly to any other person without the Upper Tribunal's consent.

(7) Unless the Upper Tribunal gives a direction to the contrary, information about mental health cases and the names of any persons concerned in such cases must not be made public.

[(8) The Upper Tribunal may, on its own initiative or on the application of a party, give a direction that certain documents or information must or may be disclosed to the Upper Tribunal on the basis that the Upper Tribunal will not disclose such documents or information to other persons, or specified other persons.

(9) A party making an application for a direction under paragraph (8) may withhold the relevant documents or information from other parties until the Upper Tribunal has granted or refused the application.

(a) In rule 14, paragraph (4) was omitted and paragraphs (8) to (11) were inserted by S.I. 2009/1975.

(10) In a case involving matters relating to national security, the Upper Tribunal must ensure that information is not disclosed contrary to the interests of national security.

(11) The Upper Tribunal must conduct proceedings and record its decision and reasons appropriately so as not to undermine the effect of an order made under paragraph (1), a direction given under paragraph (2) or (8) or the duty imposed by paragraph (10).]

Evidence and submissions

15.—(1) Without restriction on the general powers in rule 5(1) and (2) (case management powers), the Upper Tribunal may give directions as to—

(a) issues on which it requires evidence or submissions;

(b) the nature of the evidence or submissions it requires;

(c) whether the parties are permitted or required to provide expert evidence, and if so whether the parties must jointly appoint a single expert to provide such evidence;

(d) any limit on the number of witnesses whose evidence a party may put forward, whether in relation to a particular issue or generally;

(e) the manner in which any evidence or submissions are to be provided, which may include a direction for them to be given—

(i) orally at a hearing; or

(ii) by written submissions or witness statement; and

(f) the time at which any evidence or submissions are to be provided.

(2) The Upper Tribunal may—

(a) admit evidence whether or not—

(i) the evidence would be admissible in a civil trial in the United Kingdom; or

(ii) the evidence was available to a previous decision maker; or

(b) exclude evidence that would otherwise be admissible where—

(i) the evidence was not provided within the time allowed by a direction or a practice direction;

(ii) the evidence was otherwise provided in a manner that did not comply with a direction or a practice direction; or

(iii) it would otherwise be unfair to admit the evidence.

[(2A) In an asylum case or an immigration case—

(a) if a party wishes the Upper Tribunal to consider evidence that was not before the First-tier Tribunal, that party must send or deliver a notice to the Upper Tribunal and any other party—

(i) indicating the nature of the evidence; and

(ii) explaining why it was not submitted to the First-tier Tribunal; and

(b) when considering whether to admit evidence that was not before the First-tier Tribunal, the Upper Tribunal must have regard to whether there has been unreasonable delay in producing that evidence.]

(3) The Upper Tribunal may consent to a witness giving, or require any witness to give, evidence on oath, and may administer an oath for that purpose.

Summoning or citation of witnesses and orders to answer questions or produce documents(a)

16.—(1) On the application of a party or on its own initiative, the Upper Tribunal may—

(a) by summons (or, in Scotland, citation) require any person to attend as a witness at a hearing at the time and place specified in the summons or citation; or

(b) order any person to answer any questions or produce any documents In that person's possession or control which relate to any issue in the proceedings.

(2) A summons or citation under paragraph (1)(a) must—

(a) give the person required to attend 14 days' notice of the hearing or such shorter period as the Upper Tribunal may direct; and

(b) where the person is not a party, make provision for the person's necessary expenses of attendance to be paid, and state who is to pay them.

(3) No person may be compelled to give any evidence or produce any document that the person could not be compelled to give or produce on a trial of an action in a court of law In the part of the United Kingdom where the proceedings are due to be determined.

[(4) A person who receives a summons, citation or order may apply to the Upper Tribunal for it to be varied or set aside if they did not have an opportunity to object to it before it was made or issued.

(5) A person making an application under paragraph (4) must do so as soon as reasonably practicable after receiving notice of the summons, citation or order.

(6) A summons, citation or order under this rule must—

(a) state that the person on whom the requirement is imposed may apply to the Upper Tribunal to vary or set aside the summons, citation or order, If they did not have an opportunity to object to it before it was made or issued; and

(b) state the consequences of failure to comply with the summons, citation or order.]

Withdrawal

17.—(1) Subject to paragraph (2), a party may give notice of the withdrawal of its case, or any part of it—

(a) at any time before a hearing to consider the disposal of the proceedings (or, if the Upper Tribunal disposes of the proceedings without a hearing, before that disposal), by sending or delivering to the Upper Tribunal a written notice of withdrawal; or

(b) orally at a hearing.

(2) Notice of withdrawal will not take effect unless the Upper Tribunal consents to the withdrawal except in relation to an application for permission to appeal.

(3) A party which has withdrawn its case may apply to the Upper Tribunal for the case to be reinstated.

(4) An application under paragraph (3) must be made in writing and be received by the Upper Tribunal within 1 month after—

(a) the date on which the Upper Tribunal received the notice under paragraph (1)(a); or

(b) the date of the hearing at which the case was withdrawn orally under paragraph (1)(b).

(5) The Upper Tribunal must notify each party in writing of a withdrawal under this rule.

[(6) Paragraph (3) does not apply to a financial services case other than a reference against a penalty.]

(a) Rule 16(4) to (6) were substituted by S.I. 2009/274.

[Appeal treated as abandoned or finally determined in an asylum case or an immigration case

7A.—(1) A party to an asylum case or an immigration case before the Upper Tribunal must notify the Tribunal if they are aware that—

(a) the appellant has left the United Kingdom;

(b) the appellant has been granted leave to enter or remain in the United Kingdom;

(c) a deportation order has been made against the appellant; or

(d) a document listed in paragraph 4(2) of Schedule 2 to the Immigration (European Economic Area) Regulations 2006**(a)** has been issued to the appellant.

(2) Where an appeal is treated as abandoned pursuant to section 104(4) or (4A) of the Nationality, Immigration and Asylum Act 2002**(b)** or paragraph 4(2) of Schedule 2 to the Immigration (European Economic Area) Regulations 2006, or as finally determined pursuant to section 104(5) of the Nationality, Immigration and Asylum Act 2002, the Upper Tribunal must send the parties a notice informing them that the appeal is being treated as abandoned or finally determined.

(3) Where an appeal would otherwise fall to be treated as abandoned pursuant to section 104(4A) of the Nationality, Immigration and Asylum Act 2002, but the appellant wishes to pursue their appeal, the appellant must send or deliver a notice, which must comply with any relevant practice directions, to the Upper Tribunal and the respondent so that it is received within thirty days of the date on which the notice of the grant of leave to enter or remain in the United Kingdom was sent to the appellant.

(4) Where a notice of grant of leave to enter or remain is sent electronically or delivered personally, the time limit in paragraph (3) is twenty eight days.

(5) Notwithstanding rule 5(3)(a) (case management powers) and rule 7(2) (failure to comply with rules etc.), the Upper Tribunal must not extend the time limits in paragraph (3) and (4).]

Notice of funding of legal services

18. If a party is granted funding of legal services at any time, that party must as soon as practicable—

(a) (i) if funding is granted by the Legal Services Commission or the Northern Ireland Legal Services Commission, send a copy of the funding notice to the Upper Tribunal; or

(i) if funding is granted by the Scottish Legal Aid Board, send a copy of the legal aid certifcate to the Upper Tribunal; and

(b) notify every other party in writing that funding has been granted.

Confidentiality in child support or child trust fund cases

19.—(1) Paragraph (3) applies to an appeal against a decision of the First-tier Tribunal in proceedings under the Child Support Act 1991**(c)** in the circumstances described in paragraph (2), other than an appeal against a reduced benefit decision (as defined in section 46(10)(b) of the Child Support Act 1991, as that section had effect prior to the commencement of section 15(b) of the Child Maintenance and Other Payments Act 2008**(d)**).

(2) The circumstances referred to in paragraph (1) are that—

(a) S.I. 2006/1003.
(b) 2002 c.41. Section 104(4) was substituted by, and sectin 104(4A) to 94C) was inserted by, section 9 of the Immigration, Asylum and Nationality Act 2006
(c) 1991 c.48.
(d) 2008 c.6.

(a) in the proceedings in the First-tier Tribunal in respect of which the appeal has been brought, there was an obligation to keep a person's address confidential; or

(b) a person whose circumstances are relevant to the proceedings would like their address (or, in the case of the person with care of the child, the child's address) to be kept confidential and has given notice to that effect—

(i) to the Upper Tribunal in an application for permission to appeal or notice of appeal;

(ii) to the Upper Tribunal within 1 month after an enquiry by the Upper Tribunal; or

(iii) to the Secretary of State, the Child Maintenance and Enforcement Commission or the Upper Tribunal when notifying a change of address after proceedings have been started.

(3) Where this paragraph applies, the Secretary of State, the Child Maintenance and Enforcement Commission and the Upper Tribunal must take appropriate steps to secure the confidentiality of the address, and of any information which could reasonably be expected to enable a person to identify the address, to the extent that the address or that information is not already known to each other party.

(4) Paragraph (6) applies to an appeal against a decision of the First-tier Tribunal in proceedings under the Child Trust Funds Act 2004**(a)** in the circumstances described in aragraph (5).

(5) The circumstances referred to in paragraph (4) are that—

(a) in the proceedings in the First-tier Tribunal in respect of which the appeal has been brought, there was an obligation to keep a person's address confidential; or

(b) a person whose circumstances are relevant to the proceedings would like their address (or, in the case of the person with care of the eligible child, the child's address) to be kept confidential and has given notice to that effect—

(i) to the Upper Tribunal in an application for permission to appeal or notice of appeal;

(ii) to the Upper Tribunal within 1 month after an enquiry by the Upper Tribunal; or

(iii) to HMRC or the Upper Tribunal when notifying a change of address after proceedings have been started.

(6) Where this paragraph applies, HMRC and the Upper Tribunal must take appropriate steps to secure the confidentiality of the address, and of any information which could reasonably be expected to enable a person to identify the address, to the extent that the address or that information is not already known to each other party.

(7) In this rule—

"eligible child" has the meaning set out in section 2 of the Child Trust Funds Act 2004; and

"HMRC" means Her Majesty's Revenue and Customs.

Power to pay expenses and allowances(b)

20.—(1) In proceedings brought under section 4 of the Safeguarding Vulnerable Groups Act 2006**(c)**, the Secretary of State may pay such allowances for the purpose of or in connection with the attendance of persons at hearings as the Secretary of State may, with the consent of the Treasury, determine.

(a) 2004 c.6.
(b) Rule 20(1) was amended by S.I. 2009/274.
(c) 2006 c. 47.

(2) Paragraph (3) applies to proceedings on appeal from a decision of—

(a) the First-tier Tribunal in proceedings under the Child Support Act 1991, section 12 of the Social Security Act 1998(**a**) or paragraph 6 of Schedule 7 to the Child Support, Pensions and Social Security Act 2000(**b**);

(b) the First-tier Tribunal in a war pensions and armed forces case (as defined in the Tribunal Procedure (First-tier Tribunal) (War Pensions and Armed Forces Compensation Chamber) Rules 2008(**c**)); or

(c) a Pensions Appeal Tribunal for Scotland or Northern Ireland.

(3) The Lord Chancellor (or, in Scotland, the Secretary of State) may pay to any person who attends any hearing such travelling and other allowances, including compensation for loss of remunerative time, as the Lord Chancellor (or, in Scotland, the Secretary of State) may determine.

[Procedure for applying for a stay of a decision pending an appeal(d)

20A.—(1) This rule applies where another enactment provides in any terms for the Upper Tribunal to stay or suspend, or to lift a stay or suspension of, a decision which is or may be the subject of an appeal to the Upper Tribunal ("the substantive decision") pending such appeal.

(2) A person who wishes the Upper Tribunal to decide whether the substantive decision should be stayed or suspended must make a written application to the Upper Tribunal which must include—

(a) the name and address of the person making the application;

(b) the name and address of any representative of that person;

(c) the address to which documents for that person should be sent or delivered;

(d) the name and address of any person who will be a respondent to the appeal;

(e) details of the substantive decision and any decision as to when that decision is to take effect, and copies of any written record of, or reasons for, those decisions; and

(f) the grounds on which the person making the application relies.

(3) In the case of an application under paragraph (2) for a stay of a decision of a traffic commissioner—

(a) the person making the application must notify the traffic commissioner when making the application;

(b) within 7 days of receiving notification of the application the traffic commissioner must send or deliver written reason for refusing or withdrawing the stay—

(i) to the Upper Tribunal; and

(ii) to the person making the application, if the traffic commissioner has not already done so.

(4) If the Upper Tribunal grants a stay or suspension following an application under this rule—

(a) the Upper Tribunal may give directions as to the conduct of the appeal of the substantive decision; and

(b) the Upper Tribunal may, where appropriate, grant the stay or suspension subject to conditions.

(**a**) 1998 c.14.
(**b**) 2000 c. 19.
(**c**) S.I. 2008/2686 (L. 14)
(**d**) Rule 20A was inserted by S.I. 2009/1975.

(5) Unless the Upper Tribunal considers that there is good reason not to do so, the Upper Tribunal must send written notice of any decision made under this rule to each party.]

PART 3

[Procedure for cases in] the Upper Tribunal(a)

Aplicaion to the Upper Tribunal for permission to appeal(b)

21.—(1) ...

(2) A person may apply to the Upper Tribunal for permission to appeal to the Upper Tribunal against a decision of another tribunal only if—

(a) they have made an application for permission to appeal to the tribunal which made the decision challenged; and

(b) that application has been refused or has not been admitted.

(3) An application for permission to appeal must be made in writing and received by the Upper Tribunal no later than—

(a) in the case of an application under section 4 of the Safeguarding Vulnerable Groups Act 2006, 3 months after the date on which written notice of the decision being challenged was sent to the appellant;

[(aa) subject to paragraph (3A), in an asylum case or an immigration case where the appellant is in the United Kingdom at the time that the application is made—

(i) seven working days after the date on which notice of the First-tier Tribunals refusal of permission was sent to the appellant; or

(ii) if the case is a fast-track case, four working days after the date on which notice of the First-tier Tribunal's refusal of permission was sent to the appellant;

(ab) subject to paragraph (3A), in an asylum case or an immigration case where the appellant is outside the United Kingdom at the time that the application is made, fifty six days after the date on which notice of the First-tier Tribunal's refusal of permission was sent to the appellant; or]

(b) otherwise, a month after the date on which the tribunal that made the decision under challenge sent notice of its refusal of permission to appeal, or refusal to admit the application for permission to appeal, to the appellant.

[(3A) Where a notice of decision is sent electronically or delivered personally, the time limits in paragraph (3)(aa) and (ab) are—

(a) in sub-paragraph (aa)(i), five working days;

(b) in sub-paragraph (aa)(ii), two working days; and

(c) in sub-paragraph (ab), twenty eight days.]

(4) The application must state—

(a) the name and address of the appellant;

(b) the name and address of the representative (if any) of the appellant;

(c) an address where documents for the appellant may be sent or delivered;

(d) details (including the full reference) of the decision challenged;

(a) The heading of Part 3 was amended by S.I. 2009/274.
(b) Rule 21(1) was omitted by S.I. 2009/1975.

(e) the grounds on which the appellant relies; and

(f) whether the appellant wants the application to be dealt with at a hearing.

(5) The appellant must provide with the application a copy of—

(a) any written record of the decision being challenged;

(b) any separate written statement of reasons for that decision; and

(c) if the application is for permission to appeal against a decision of another tribunal, the notice of refusal of permission to appeal, or notice of refusal to admit the application for permission to appeal, from that other tribunal.

(6) If the appellant provides the application to the Upper Tribunal later than the time required by paragraph (3) or by an extension of time allowed under rule 5(3)(a) (power to extend time)—

(a) the application must include a request for an extension of time and the reason why the application was not provided in time; and

(b) unless the Upper Tribunal extends time for the application under rule 5(3)(a) (power to extend time) the Upper Tribunal must not admit the application.

(7) If the appellant makes an application to the Upper Tribunal for permission to appeal against the decision of another tribunal, and that other tribunal refused to admit the appellant's application for permission to appeal because the application for permission or for a written statement of reasons was not made in time—

(a) the application to the Upper Tribunal for permission to appeal must include the reason why the application to the other tribunal for permission to appeal or for a written statement of reasons, as the case may be, was not made in time; and

(b) the Upper Tribunal must only admit the application if the Upper Tribunal considers that it is in the interests of justice for it to do so.

Decision in relation to permission to appeal(a)

22.—(1) If the Upper Tribunal refuses permission to appeal, it must send written notice of the refusal and of the reasons for the refusal to the appellant.

(2) If the Upper Tribunal gives permission to appeal—

(a) the Upper Tribunal must send written notice of the permission, and of the reasons for any limitations or conditions on such permission, to each party;

(b) subject to any direction by the Upper Tribunal, the application for permission to appeal stands as the notice of appeal and the Upper Tribunal must send to each respondent a copy of the application for permission to appeal and any documents provided with it by the appellant; and

(c) the Upper Tribunal may, with the consent of the appellant and each respondent, determine the appeal withhout obtaining any further response.

(3) [Paragraph (4) applies where the Upper Tribunal, without a hearing, determines an application for permission to appeal—

(a) against a decision of—

(i) the Tax Chamber of the First-tier Tribunal;

(ii) the Health, Education and Social Care Chamber of the First-tier Tribunal;

[(iia) the General Regulatory Chamber of the First-tier Tribunal;]

(iii) the Mental Health Review Tribunal for Wales; or

(a) Rule 22(3) was substituted by S.I. 2009/274, and sub-paragraph (a)(iia) was inserted by S.I. 2009/1975.

(iv) the Special Educational Needs Tribunal for Wales; or

(b) under section 4 of the Safeguarding Vulnerable Groups Act 2006.]

(4) In the circumstances set out at paragraph (3) the appellant may apply for the decision to be reconsidered at a hearing if the Upper Tribunal—

(a) refuses permission to appeal; or

(b) gives permission to appeal on limited grounds or subject to conditions.

(5) An application under paragraph (4) must be made in writing and received by the Upper Tribunal within 14 days after the date on which the Upper Tribunal sent written notice of its decision regarding the application to the appellant.

Notice of appeal(a)

23.—[(1) This rule applies—

(a) to proceedings on appeal to the Upper Tribunal for which permission to appeal is not required, except proceedings to which rule 26A [or 26B] applies;

(b) if another tribunal has given permission for a party to appeal to the Upper Tribunal; or

(c) subject to any other direction by the Upper Tribunal, if the Upper Tribunal has given permission to appeal and has given a direction that the application for permission to appeal does not stand as the notice of appeal.

[(1A) In an asylum case or an immigration case in which the First-tier Tribunal has given permission to appeal, subject to any direction of the First-tier Tribunal or the Upper Tribunal, the application for permission to appeal sent or delivered to the First-tier Tribunal stands as the notice of appeal and accordingly paragraphs (2) to (6) of this rule do not apply.]

(2) The appellant must provide a notice of appeal to the Upper Tribunal so that it is received within 1 month after—

(a) the date that the tribunal that gave permission to appeal sent notice of such permission to the appellant; or

(b) if permission to appeal is not required, the date on which notice of decision to which the appeal relates was sent to the appellant.]

(3) The notice of appeal must include the information listed in rule 21(4)(a) to (e) (content of the application for permission to appeal) and, where the Upper Tribunal has given permission to appeal, the Upper Tribunal's case reference.

(4) If another tribunal has granted permission to appeal, the appellant must provide with the notice of appeal a copy of—

(a) any written record of the decision being challenged;

(b) any separate written statement of reasons for that decision; and

(c) the notice of permission to appeal.

(5) If the appellant provides the notice of appeal to the Upper Tribunal later than the time required by paragraph (2) or by an extension of time allowed under rule 5(3)(a) (power to extend time)—

(a) the notice of appeal must include a request for an extension of time and the reason why the notice was not provided in time; and

(b) unless the Upper Tribunal extends time for the notice of appeal under rule 5(3)(a) (power to extend time) the Upper Tribunal must not admit the notice of appeal.

(a) Rule 23(1), (2) and (6) were substituted by S.I. 2009/1975.

(6) [When the Upper Tribunal receives the notice of appeal it must send a copy of the notice and any accompanying documents—

(a) to each respondent; or

(b) in an appeal against the decision of a traffic commissioner, to—

(i) the traffic commissioner;

(ii) the appropriate national authority; and

(iii) in a case relating to the detention of a vehicle, the authorised person.]

Response to the notice of appeal(a)

24.—[(1) This rule and rule 25 do not apply to an appeal against a decision of a traffic mmissioner, in respect of which Schedule 1 makes alternative provision.

(1A) Subject to any direction given by the Upper Tribunal, a respondent may provide a response to a notice of appeal.]

(2) Any response provided under paragraph ([1A]) must be in writing and must be sent or delivered to the Upper Tribunal so that it is received—

(a) [if an application for permission to appeal stands as the notice of appeal, no later than one month after the date on which the respondent was sent notice that permission to appeal had been granted];

[(aa) in a fast-track case, one day before the hearing of the appeal; or]

(b) in any other case, no later than 1 month after the date on which the Upper Tribunal sent a copy of the notice of appeal to the respondent.

(3) The response must state—

(a) the name and address of the respondent;

(b) the name and address of the representative (if any) of the respondent;

(c) an address where documents for the respondent may be sent or delivered;

(d) whether the respondent opposes the appeal;

(e) the grounds on which the respondent relies, including [(in the case of an appeal against the decision of another tribunal)] any grounds on which the respondent was unsuccessful in the proceedings which are the subject of the appeal, but intends to rely in the appeal; and

(f) whether the respondent wants the case to be dealt with at a hearing.

(4) If the respondent provides the response to the Upper Tribunal later than the time required by paragraph (2) or by an extension of time allowed under rule 5(3)(a) (power to extend time), the response must include a request for an extension of time and the reason why the [response] was not provided in time.

(5) When the Upper Tribunal receives the response it must send a copy of the response and any accompanying documents to the appellant and each other party.

Appellant's reply

25.—(1) Subject to any direction given by the Upper Tribunal, the appellant may provide a reply to any response provided under rule 24 (response to the notice of appeal).

(a) In rule 24, paragraphs (1) and (1A) were substituted, and paragraphs (2)(a) and (3)(e) were amended, by S.I. 2009/1975. Paragraph (4) was amended by S.I. 2009/1975.

(2) [Subject to paragraph (2A), any] reply provided under paragraph (1) must be in writing and must be sent or delivered to the Upper Tribunal so that it is received within one month after the date on which the Upper Tribunal sent a copy of the response to the appellant.

[(2A) In an asylum case or an immigration case, the time limit in paragraph (2) is—

(a) one month after the date on which the Upper Tribunal sent a copy of the response to the appellant, or five days before the hearing of the appeal, whichever is the earlier; and

(b) in a fast-track case, the day of the hearing.]

(3) When the Upper Tribunal receives the reply it must send a copy of the reply for any accompanying documents to each respondent.

References under the Forfeiture Act 1982

26.—(1) If a question arises which is required to be determined by the Upper Tribunal under section 4 of the Forfeiture Act 1982, the person to whom the application for the relevant benefit or advantage has been made must refer the Upper Tribunal.

(2) The reference must be in writing and must include—

(a) a statement of the question for determination;

(b) a statement of the relevant facts;

(c) the grounds upon which the reference is made; and

(d) an address for sending documents to the person making the reference and each respondent.

(3) When the Upper Tribunal receives the reference it must send a copy of the reference and any accompanying documents to each respondent.

(4) Rules 24 (response to the notice of appeal) and 25 (appellant's reply) apply to a reference made under this rule as if it were a notice of appeal.

[Cases transferred or referred to the Upper Tribunal, applications made directly to the Upper Tribunal and proceedings without notice to a respondent(a)

26A.—[(1) Paragraphs (2) and (3) apply to—

(a) a case transferred or referred to the Upper Tribunal from the First-tier Tribunal; or

(b) a case, other than an appeal or a case to which rule 26 (references under the Forfeiture Act 1982) applies, which is started by an application made directly to the Upper Tribunal.]

(2) In a case to which this paragraph applies—

(a) the Upper Tribunal must give directions as to the procedure to be followed in the consideration and disposal of the proceedings; and

(b) the preceding rules in this Part will only apply to the proceedings to the extent provided for by such directions.

(3) If a case or matter to which this paragraph applies is to be determined without notice to or the involvement of a respondent—

(a) any provision in these Rules requiring a document to be provided by or to a respondent; and

(b) any other provision in these Rules permitting a respondent to participate in the proceedings does not apply to that case or matter.]

(a) Rule 26A was inserted by S.I. 2009/2741; paragraph (1) was substituted by S.I. 2009/1975.

[(4) Schedule 2 makes further provision for national security certificate appeals transferred to the Upper Tribunal.]

[Financial services cases

26B. Schedule 3 makes provision for financial services cases.]

PART 4

Judicial review proceedings in the Upper Tribunal

Application of this Part to judicial review proceedings transferred to the Upper Tribunal

27.—(1) When a court transfers judicial review proceedings to the Upper Tribunal, the Upper Tribunal—

(a) must notify each party in writing that the proceedings have been transferred to the Upper Tribunal; and

(b) must give directions as to the future conduct of the proceedings.

(2) The directions given under paragraph (1)(b) may modify or disapply for the purposes of the proceedings any of the provisions of the following rules in this Part.

(3) In proceedings transferred from the Court of Session under section 20(1) of the 2007 Act, the directions given under paragraph (1)(b) must—

(a) if the Court of Session did not make a first order specifying the required intimation, service and advertisement of the petition, state the Upper Tribunal's requirements in relation to those matters;

(b) state whether the Upper Tribunal will consider summary dismissal of the proceedings; and

(c) where necessary, modify or disapply provisions relating to permission in the following rules in this Part.

Applications for permission to bring judicial review proceedings(a)

28.—(1) A person seeking permission to bring judicial review proceedings before the Upper Tribunal under section 16 of the 2007 Act must make a written application to the Upper Tribunal for such permission.

(2) Subject to paragraph (3), an application under paragraph (1) must be made promptly and, unless any other enactment specifies a shorter time limit, must be sent or delivered to the Upper Tribunal so that it is received no later than 3 months after the date of the decision[, action or omission] to which the application relates.

(3) An application for permission to bring judicial review proceedings challenging a decision of the First-tier Tribunal may be made later than the time required by paragraph (2) if it is made within 1 month after the date on which the First-tier Tribunal sent—

(a) written reasons for the decision; or

(b) notification that an application for the decision to be set aside has been unsuccessful, provided that that application was made in time.

(4) The application must state—

(a) The words in square brackets in rule 23(2) were inserted by S.I. 2009/274.

(a) the name and address of the applicant, the respondent and any other person whom the applicant considers to be an interested party;

(b) the name and address of the applicant's representative (if any);

(c) an address where documents for the applicant may be sent or delivered;

(d) details of the decision challenged (including the date, the full reference and the identity of the decision maker);

(e) that the application is for permission to bring judicial review proceedings;

(f) the outcome that the applicant is seeking; and

(g) the facts and grounds on which the applicant relies.

(5) If the application relates to proceedings in a court or tribunal, the application must name as an interested party each party to those proceedings who is not the applicant or a respondent.

(6) The applicant must send with the application—

(a) a copy of any written record of the decision in the applicant's possession or control; and

(b) copies of any other documents in the applicant's possession or control on which the applicant intends to rely.

(7) If the applicant provides the application to the Upper Tribunal later than the time required by paragraph (2) or (3) or by an extension of time allowed under rule 5(3)(a) (power to extend time)—

(a) the application must include a request for an extension of time and the reason why the application was not provided in time; and

(b) unless the Upper Tribunal extends time for the application under rule 5(3)(a) (power to extend time) the Upper Tribunal must not admit the application.

(8) When the Upper Tribunal receives the application it must send a copy of the application and any accompanying documents to each person named in the application as a respondent or interested party.

Acknowledgment of service(a)

29.—(1) A person who is sent a copy of an application for permission under rule 28(8) (application for permission to bring judicial review proceedings) and wishes to take part in the proceedings must send or deliver to the Upper Tribunal an acknowledgment of service so that it is received no later than 21 days after the date on which the Upper Tribunal sent a copy of the application to that person.

(2) An acknowledgment of service under paragraph (1) must be in writing and state—

(a) whether the person intends to [support or] oppose the application for permission;

(b) their grounds for any [support or] opposition under sub-paragraph (a), or any other submission or information which it considers may assist the Upper Tribunal; and

(c) the name and address of any other person not named in the application as a respondent or interested party whom the person providing the acknowledgment considers to be an interested party.

(3) A person who is sent a copy of an application for permission under rule 28(8) but does not provide an acknowledgment of service may not take part in the application for permission, but may take part in the subsequent proceedings if the application is successful.

(a) The words in square brackets in rule 29(2)(a) and (b) were inserted by S.I. 2009/274.

Decision on permission or summary dismissal, and reconsideration of permission or summary dismissal at a hearing

30.—(1) The Upper Tribunal must send to the applicant, each respondent and any other person who provided an acknowledgment of service to the Upper Tribunal, and may send to any other person who may have an interest in the proceedings, written notice of—

(a) its decision in relation to the application for permission; and

(b) the reasons for any refusal of the application, or any limitations or conditions on permission.

(2) In proceedings transferred from the Court of Session under section 20(1) of the 2007 Act, where the Upper Tribunal has considered whether summarily to dismiss of the proceedings, the Upper Tribunal must send to the applicant and each respondent, and may send to any other person who may have an interest in the proceedings, written notice of—

(a) its decision in relation to the summary dismissal of proceedings; and

(b) the reasons for any decision summarily to dismiss part or all of the proceedings, or any limitations or conditions on the continuation of such proceedings.

(3) Paragraph (4) applies where the Upper Tribunal, without a hearing—

(a) determines an application for permission to bring judicial review proceedings and either refuses permission, or gives permission on limited grounds or subject to conditions; or

(b) in proceedings transferred from the Court of Session, summarily dismisses part or all of the proceedings, or imposes any limitations or conditions on the continuation of such proceedings.

(4) In the circumstances specified in paragraph (3) the applicant may apply for the decision to be reconsidered at a hearing.

(5) An application under paragraph (4) must be made in writing and must be sent or delivered to the Upper Tribunal so that it is received within 14 days after the date on which the Upper Tribunal sent written notice of its decision regarding the application to the applicant.

Responses

31.—(1) Any person to whom the Upper Tribunal has sent notice of the grant of permission under rule 30(1) (notification of decision on permission), and who wishes to contest the application or support it on additional grounds, must provide detailed grounds for contesting or supporting the application to the Upper Tribunal.

(2) Any detailed grounds must be provided in writing and must be sent or delivered to the Upper Tribunal so that they are received not more than 35 days after the Upper Tribunal sent notice of the grant of permission under rule 30(1).

Applicant seeking to rely on additional grounds

32. The applicant may not rely on any grounds, other than those grounds on which the applicant obtained permission for the judicial review proceedings, without the consent of the Upper Tribunal.

Right to make representations

33. Each party and, with the permission of the Upper Tribunal, any other person, may—

(a) submit evidence, except at the hearing of an application for permission;

(b) make representations at any hearing which they are entitled to attend; and

(c) make written representations in relation to a decision to be made without a hearing.

PART 5

Hearings

Decision with or without a hearing

34.—(1) Subject to paragraph (2), the Upper Tribunal may make any decision without a hearing.

(2) The Upper Tribunal must have regard to any view expressed by a party when deciding whether to hold a hearing to consider any matter, and the form of any such hearing.

Entitlement to attend a hearing

35.[—(1)] Subject to rule 37(4) (exclusion of a person from a hearing), each party is entitled to attend a hearing.

[(2) In a national security certificate appeal the relevant Minister is entitled to attend any hearing.]

Notice of hearings

36.—(1) The Upper Tribunal must give each party entitled to attend a hearing reasonable notice of the time and place of the hearing (including any adjourned or postponed hearing) and any change to the time and place of the hearing.

(2) The period of notice under paragraph (1) must be at least 14 days except that—

- (a) in applications for permission to bring judicial review proceedings, the period of notice must be at least 2 working days;
- [(aa) in a fast-track case the period of notice must be at least one working day; and]
- (b) [in any case other than a fast-track case] the Upper Tribunal may give shorter notice—
    - (i) with the parties' consent; or
    - (ii) in urgent or exceptional cases.

[Special time limits for hearing an appeal in a fast-track case

36A.—(1) Subject to rule 36(2)(aa) (notice of hearings) and paragraph (2) of this rule, where permission to appeal to the Upper Tribunal has been given in a fast-track case, the Upper Tribunal must start the hearing of the appeal not later than—

- (a) four working days after the date on which the First-tier Tribunal or the Upper Tribunal sent notice of its grant of permission to appeal to the appellant; or
- (b) where the notice of its grant of permission to appeal is sent electronically or delivered personally, two working days after the date on which the First-tier Tribunal or the Upper Tribunal sent notice of its grant of permission to appeal to the appellant.

(2) If the Upper Tribunal is unable to arrange for the hearing to start within the time specified in paragraph (1), it must set a date for the hearing as soon as is reasonably practicable.]

Public and private hearings(a)

37.—(1) Subject to the following paragraphs, all hearings must be held in public.

(2) The Upper Tribunal may give a direction that a hearing, or part of it, is to be held in private.

[(2A) In a national security certificate appeal, the Upper Tribunal must have regard to its duty under rule 14(10) (no disclosure of information contrary to the interests of national security) when considering whether to give a direction that a hearing, or part of it, is to be held in private.]

(a) In rule 37(4), paragraph (c) was amended by S.I. 2009/1975 and paragraph (e) was amended by S.I. 2009/274.

(3) Where a hearing, or part of it, is to be held in private, the Upper Tribunal may determine who is entitled to attend the hearing or part of it.

(4) The Upper Tribunal may give a direction excluding from any hearing, or part of it—

(a) any person whose conduct the Upper Tribunal considers is disrupting or is likely to disrupt the hearing;

(b) any person whose presence the Upper Tribunal considers is likely to prevent another person from giving evidence or making submissions freely;

(c) any person who the Upper Tribunal considers should be excluded in order to give effect to [the requirement at rule 14(11) (prevention of disclosure or publication of documents and information)];

(d) any person where the purpose of the hearing would be defeated by the attendance of that person[; or

(e) a person under the age of eighteen years.]

(5) The Upper Tribunal may give a direction excluding a witness from a hearing until that witness gives evidence.

Hearings in a party's absence

38. If a party fails to attend a hearing, the Upper Tribunal may proceed with the hearing if the Upper Tribunal—

(a) is satisfied that the party has been notified of the hearing or that reasonable steps have been taken to notify the party of the hearing; and

(b) considers that it is in the interests of justice to proceed with the hearing.

PART 6

Decisions

Consent orders(a)

39.—(1) The Upper Tribunal may, at the request of the parties but only if it considers it appropriate, make a consent order disposing of the proceedings and making such other appropriate provision as the parties have agreed.

(2) Notwithstanding any other provision of these Rules, the Tribunal need not hold a hearing before making an order under paragraph (1).

Decisions(b)

40.—(1) The Upper Tribunal may give a decision orally at a hearing.

(2) [Except where rule 40A (special procedure for providing notice of a decision relating to an asylum case) applies]The Upper Tribunal must provide to each party as soon as reasonably practicable after making a decision which finally disposes of all issues in the proceedings (except a decision under Part 7)—

(a) a decision notice stating the Tribunal's decision; and

(b) notification of any rights of review or appeal against the decision and the time and manner in which such rights of review or appeal may be exercised.

(a) Rule 39(2) was amended by S.I. 2009/274.

(b) In rule 40, paragraphs (2) and (3) were amended by S.I. 2009/274 and paragraphs (3) and (4) were amended by S.I. 2009/1975.

(3) [Subject to rule [14(11) (prevention of disclosure or publication of documents and information)],] the Upper Tribunal must provide written reasons for its decision with a decision notice provided under paragraph (2)(a) unless—

(a) the decision was made with the consent of the parties; or

(b) the parties have consented to the Upper Tribunal not giving written reasons.

(4) The [Upper] Tribunal may provide written reasons for any decision to which paragraph (2) does not apply.

[(5) In a national security certificate appeal, when the Upper Tribunal provides a notice or reasons to the parties under this rule, it must also provide the notice or reasons to the relevant Minister and the Information Commissioner, if they are not parties.]

[Special procedure for providing notice of a decision relating to an asylum case

40A.—(1) This rule applies to an appeal before the Upper Tribunal under section 11 of the 2007 Act in an asylum case where—

(a) the person who appealed to the First-tier Tribunal is in the United Kingdom; and

(b) the case is not a fast-track case.

(2) The Upper Tribunal must provide to the Secretary of State for the Home Department as soon as reasonably practicable—

(a) a decision notice stating the Upper Tribunal's decision; and

(b) a statement of any right of appeal against the decision and the time and manner in which such a right of appeal may be exercised.

(3) The Secretary of State must, subject to paragraph (5)—

(a) send the documents listed in paragraph (2) to the other party not later than 30 days after the Upper Tribunal sent them to the Secretary of State for the Home Department; and

(b) as soon as practicable after sending the documents listed in paragraph (2), notify the Upper Tribunal on what date and by what means they were sent.

(4) If the Secretary of State does not notify the Upper Tribunal under paragraph (3)(b) within 31 days after the documents listed in paragraph (2) were sent, the Upper Tribunal must send the notice of decision to the other party as soon as reasonably practicable.

(5) If the Secretary of State applies for permission to appeal under section 13 of the 2007 Act, the Secretary of State must send the documents listed in paragraph (2) to the other party no later than the date on which the application for permission is sent to the Upper Tribunal.]

PART 7

Correcting, setting aside, reviewing and appealing decisions of the Upper Tribunal

Interpretation(a)

41. In this Part—

"appeal"[, except in rule 44(2) (application for permission to appeal),] means the exercise of a right of appeal under section 13 of the 2007 Act; and

"review" means the review of a decision by the Upper Tribunal under section 10 of the 2007 Act.

(a) The words in square brackets in rule 41 were inserted by S.I. 2009/274.

Clerical mistakes and accidental slips or omissions

42. The Upper Tribunal may at any time correct any clerical mistake or other accidental slip or omission in a decision or record of a decision by—

(a) sending notification of the amended decision, or a copy of the amended record, to all parties; and

(b) making any necessary amendment to any information published in relation to the decision or record.

Setting aside a decision which disposes of proceedings

43.—(1) The Upper Tribunal may set aside a decision which disposes of proceedings, or part of such a decision, and re-make the decision or the relevant part of it, if—

(a) the Upper Tribunal considers that it is in the interests of justice to do so; and

(b) one or more of the conditions in paragraph (2) are satisfied.

(2) The conditions are—

(a) a document relating to the proceedings was not sent to, or was not received at an appropriate time by, a party or a party's representative;

(b) a document relating to the proceedings was not sent to the Upper Tribunal at an appropriate time;

(c) a party, or a party's representative, was not present at a hearing related to the proceedings; or

(d) there has been some other procedural irregularity in the proceedings.

(3) [Except where paragraph (4) applies,] A party applying for a decision, or part of a decision, to be set aside under paragraph (1) must make a written application to the Upper Tribunal so that it is received no later than 1 month after the date on which the Tribunal sent notice of the decision to the party.

(4) In an asylum case or an immigration case, the written application referred to in paragraph (3) must be sent or delivered so that it is received by the Upper Tribunal—

(a) where the person who appealed to the First-tier Tribunal is in the United Kingdom at the time that the application is made, no later than twelve days after the date on which the Upper Tribunal or, as the case may be in an asylum case, the Secretary of State for the Home Department, sent notice of the decision to the party making the application; or

(b) where the person who appealed to the First-tier Tribunal is outside the United Kingdom at the time that the application is made, no later than thirty eight days after the date on which the Upper Tribunal sent notice of the decision to the party making the application.

(5) Where a notice of decision is sent electronically or delivered personally, the time limits in paragraph (4) are ten working days.]

Application for permission to appeal(a)

44.—(1) A person seeking permission to appeal must make a written application to the Upper Tribunal for permission to appeal.

(2) Paragraph (3) applies to an application under paragraph (1) in respect of a decision—

(a) on an appeal against a decision in a social security and child support case (as defined

---

(a) Rule 44(2)(ba) was inserted by S.I. 2009/274.

in the Tribunal Procedure (First-tier Tribunal) (Social Entitlement Chamber) Rules 2008(**a**));

(b) on an appeal against a decision in proceedings in the War Pensions and Armed Forces Compensation Chamber of the First-tier Tribunal(**b**);

[(ba) on an appeal against a decision of a Pensions Appeal Tribunal for Scotland or Northern Ireland; or]

(c) in proceedings under the Forfeiture Act 1982.

(3) Where this paragraph applies, the application must be sent or delivered to the Upper Tribunal so that it is received within 3 months after the date on which the Upper Tribunal sent to the person making the application—

(a) written notice of the decision;

(b) notification of amended reasons for, or correction of, the decision following a review; or

(c) notification that an application for the decision to be set aside has been unsuccessful.

[(3A) An application under paragraph (1) in respect of a decision in an asylum case or an immigration case must be sent or delivered to the Upper Tribunal so that it is received within the appropriate period after the Upper Tribunal or, as the case may be in an asylum case, the Secretary of State for the Home Department, sent any of the documents in paragraph (3) to the party making the application.

(3B) The appropriate period referred to in paragraph (3A) is as follows—

(a) where the person who appealed to the First-tier Tribunal is in the United Kingdom at the time that the application is made—

(i) twelve days; or

(ii) if the party making the application is in detention under the Immigration Acts, seven working days; and

(b) where the person who appealed to the First-tier Tribunal is outside the United Kingdom at the time that the application is made, thirty eight days.

(3C) Where a notice of decision is sent electronically or delivered personally, the time limits in paragraph (3B) are—

(a) in sub-paragraph (a)(i), ten working days;

(b) in sub-paragraph (a)(ii), five working days; and

(c) in sub-paragraph (b), ten working days.]

[(3D) An application under paragraph (1) in respect of a decision in a financial services case must be sent or delivered to the Upper Tribunal so that it is received within 14 days after the date on which the Upper Tribunal sent to the person making the application—

(a) written notice of the decision;

(b) notification of amended reasons for, or correction of, the decision following a review; or

(c) notification that an application for the decision to be set aside has been unsuccessful.]

(4) Where paragraph (3), [(3A) or (3D)] does not apply, an application under paragraph (1) must be sent or delivered to the Upper Tribunal so that it is received within 1 month after the latest of the dates on which the Upper Tribunal sent to the person making the application—

(**a**) S.I. 2008/2685 (L. 13).

(**b**) The War Pensions and Armed Forces Compensation Chamber of the First-tier Tribunal is established by the First-tier Tribunal and Upper Tribunal (Chambers) Order 2008 (S.I. 2008/2684).

(a) written reasons for the decision;

(b) notification of amended reasons for, or correction of, the decision following a review; or

(c) notification that an application for the decision to be set aside has been unsuccessful.

(5) The date in paragraph (3)(c) or (4)(c) applies only if the application for the decision to be set aside was made within the time stipulated in rule 43 (setting aside a decision which disposes of proceedings) or any extension of that time granted by the Upper Tribunal.

(6) If the person seeking permission to appeal provides the application to the Upper Tribunal later than the time required by paragraph (3), [(3A), (3D)] or (4), or by any extension of time under rule 5(3)(a) (power to extend time)—

(a) the application must include a request for an extension of time and the reason why the application notice was not provided in time; and

(b) unless the Upper Tribunal extends time for the application under rule 5(3)(a) (power to extend time) the Upper Tribunal must refuse the application.

(7) An application under paragraph (1) must—

(c) identify the decision of the Tribunal to which it relates;

(d) identify the alleged error or errors of law in the decision; and

(e) state the result the party making the application is seeking.

Upper Tribunal's consideration of application for permission to appeal

45.—(1) On receiving an application for permission to appeal the Upper Tribunal may review the decision in accordance with rule 46 (review of a decision), but may only do so if—

(a) when making the decision the Upper Tribunal overlooked a legislative provision or binding authority which could have had a material effect on the decision; or

(b) since the Upper Tribunal's decision, a court has made a decision which is binding on the Upper Tribunal and which, had it been made before the Upper Tribunal's decision, could have had a material effect on the decision.

(2) If the Upper Tribunal decides not to review the decision, or reviews the decision and decides to take no action in relation to the decision or part of it, the Upper Tribunal must consider whether to give permission to appeal in relation to the decision or that part of it.

(3) The Upper Tribunal must send a record of its decision to the parties as soon as practicable.

(4) If the Upper Tribunal refuses permission to appeal it must send with the record of its decision—

(a) a statement of its reasons for such refusal; and

(b) notification of the right to make an application to the relevant appellate court for permission to appeal and the time within which, and the method by which, such application must be made.

(5) The Upper Tribunal may give permission to appeal on limited grounds, but must comply with paragraph (4) in relation to any grounds on which it has refused permission.

Review of a decision

46.—(1) The Upper Tribunal may only undertake a review of a decision—

(a) pursuant to rule 45(1) (review on an application for permission to appeal); or

(b) pursuant to rule 47 (reviews of decisions in proceedings under the Forfeiture Act 1982).

(2) The Upper Tribunal must notify the parties in writing of the outcome of any review and of any rights of review or appeal in relation to the outcome.

(3) If the Upper Tribunal decides to take any action in relation to a decision following a review without first giving every party an opportunity to make representations, the notice under paragraph (2) must state that any party that did not have an opportunity to make representations may apply for such action to be set aside and for the decision to be reviewed again.

Review of a decision in proceedings under the Forfeiture Act 1982

47.—(1) A person who referred a question to the Upper Tribunal under rule 26 (references under the Forfeiture Act 1982) must refer the Upper Tribunal's previous decision in relation to the question to the Upper Tribunal if they—

(a) consider that the decision should be reviewed; or

(b) have received a written application for the decision to be reviewed from the person to whom the decision related.

(2) The Upper Tribunal may review the decision if—

(a) the decision was erroneous in point of law;

(b) the decision was made in ignorance of, or was based on a mistake as to, some material fact; or

(c) there has been a relevant change in circumstances since the decision was made.

(3) When a person makes the reference to the Upper Tribunal, they must also notify the person to whom the question relates that the reference has been made.

(4) The Upper Tribunal must notify the person who made the reference and the person who to whom the question relates of the outcome of the reference.

(5) If the Upper Tribunal decides to take any action in relation to a decision following a review under this rule without first giving the person who made the reference and the person to whom the question relates an opportunity to make representations, the notice under paragraph (4) must state that either of those persons who did not have an opportunity to make representations may apply for such action to be set aside and for the decision to be reviewed again.

Patrick Elias
Phillip Brook Smith Q.C. Lesley Clare
Douglas J. May Q.C.
Newton of Braintree
M.J. Reed Mark Rowland
Nicholas Warren

I allow these Rules

Signed by authority of the Lord Chancellor

Bridget Prentice
Parliamentary Under Secretary of State

9th October 2008 Ministry of Justice

[SCHEDULE 1(a)

RULE 24(1)

Procedure after the notice of appeal in appeals against decisions of traffic commissioners

1. This Schedule applies to an appeal against the decision of a traffic commissioner.

2. The only parties to the appeal are the appellant and any person added as a party under rule 9 [(addition, substitution and removal of parties)].

3. On receipt of a copy of a notice of appeal under rule 23(6)(b), the traffic commissioner must send to the Upper Tribunal a copy (and, on request, further copies) of—

(a) a written record of the decision appealed against and reasons for the decision;

(b) all documents produced to the traffic commissioner in connection with the decision;

(c) if a public inquiry was held, the transcript of the inquiry or, if no such transcript was produced, the traffic commissioner's note of the inquiry; and

(d) in an appeal under section 50 of the Public Passenger Vehicles Act 1981**(b)** or section 37 of the Goods Vehicles (Licensing of Operators) Act 1995**(c)**, a list of the names and addresses of objectors and representors.

4. On receipt of a list under paragraph 3(d) the Upper Tribunal must send a copy of the notice of appeal—

(a) where the appellant had applied for, or for the variation of, an operator's licence, to each person who made an objection to the application;

(b) where the appellant had made an objection to an application for, or (in the case of a goods vehicle operator's licence) for the variation of, an operator's licence, to the person who made the application and to every other person who made an objection to the application; and

(c) in an appeal under section 37(5) of the Goods Vehicles (Licensing of Operators) Act 1995, each person who made representations under section 12(4) or 19(2) of that Act against the application for, or for the variation of, the operator's licence in question.

5. The appropriate national authority and any person to whom the Upper Tribunal has sent a copy of the notice of appeal under paragraph 4 may apply for a direction under rule 9(2) adding them as a respondent.

6. An application under paragraph 5 must be sent or delivered to the Upper Tribunal so that it is received within 14 days of the date that the Upper Tribunal sent a copy of the notice of appeal to the person making the application.

7. If a person specified in paragraph 8 makes an application in accordance with paragraphs 5 and 6, the Upper Tribunal must give a direction under rule 9(2) adding that person as a respondent.

8. The persons specified for the purposes of paragraph 7 are—

(a) the appropriate national authority;

(b) an objector who was sent a copy of the notice of appeal under paragraph 4(a) or (b); and

(c) a person who made an application and was sent a copy of the notice of appeal under paragraph 4(b).

(a) Schedule 1 was inserted by S.I. 2009/1975.

(b) 1981 c. 14. Section 50 was substituted by section 31 of the Transport Act 2985 (c. 67) and amended by section 65(2) of, and paragraph 7 of Schedule 14 to, the Deregulation and Contracting Out Act 1994 (c. 40).

(c) 1995 c. 23.

9. The Upper Tribunal must notify each other party of any application under paragraph 3 and the Upper Tribunal's decision in respect of each such application.

10. Any party may make a request to the Upper Tribunal for copies of specified documents provided by the traffic commissioner under paragraph 3.

11. On receiving a request under paragraph 9 the Upper Tribunal—

(a) must provide the requested copies unless it considers the request unreasonable; and

(b) if it considers the request unreasonable, give details of why it considers the request unreasonable.]

[SCHEDULE 2

RULE 26A(4)

Additional procedure in national security certificate cases

1. This Schedule applies only to national security certificate appeals.

2. Following the transfer of the appeal from the First-tier Tribunal, the Upper Tribunal must provide a copy of the notice of appeal to the respondent, the relevant Minister and the Information Commissioner.

3. The relevant Minister must send or deliver to the Upper Tribunal a copy of the certificate to which the appeal relates, and a response to the notice of appeal, not later than 42 days after the date on which the relevant Minister received a copy of the notice of appeal.

4. In an appeal under section 28(4) of the Data Protection Act 1998 or section 60(1) of the Freedom of Information Act 2000 (including that subsection as applied and modified by regulation 18 of the Environmental Information Regulations 2004), the relevant Minister's response must state whether the relevant Minister intends to oppose the appeal and, if so set out—

(a) a summary of the circumstances relating to the issue of the certificate;

(b) the reason for the issue of the certificate;

(c) the grounds on which the relevant Minister relies in opposing the appeal; and

(d) a statement of the evidence on which the relevant Minister relies in support of those grounds.

5. In an appeal under section 28(6) of the Data Protection Act 1998 or section 60(4) of the Freedom of Information Act 2000 (including that subsection as applied and modified by regulation 18 of the Environmental Information Regulations 2004), the relevant Minister's response must state whether the relevant Minister intends to make representations in relation to the appeal and, if so set out—

(a) the extent to which the relevant Minister intends to support or oppose the appeal;

(b) the grounds on which the relevant Minister relies in supporting or opposing the appeal; and

(c) a statement of the evidence on which the relevant Minister relies in support of those grounds.

6. The Upper Tribunal must—

(a) subject to paragraph 11, provide the relevant Minister's response and any other response to the appellant, the Information Commissioner and any respondent; and

(b) send a copy of any other response to the relevant Minister.

7. On grounds of the need to ensure that information is not disclosed contrary to the interests of national security, the relevant Minster may—

(a) object to the disclosure of the relevant Minister's response to the appellant, the Information Commissioner or any respondent, by sending a notice to the Upper Tribunal with the response; or

(b) object to the disclosure of any other response to the Information Commissioner or any respondent, by sending a notice to the Upper Tribunal within 42 days of the date on which the relevant Minister received a copy of the response.

8. A notice under paragraph 7 must—

(a) state the reason for the objection; and

(b) in the case of a notice under paragraph 7(a) and to the extent that it is possible to do so, be accompanied by a version of the relevant Minister's response in a form that can be shown to the appellant, the Commissioner or, as the case may be, a respondent.

9. Before the Upper Tribunal gives a direction, issues a summons or citation, or produces or publishes a written record of, or reasons for, a decision—

(a) the Upper Tribunal must notify the relevant Minister of the proposed action; and

(b) if the relevant Minister considers that the proposal would cause information that is or would be exempt by virtue of a provision in Part 2 of the Freedom of Information Act 2000 to be disclosed, the relevant Minister may object to the proposal by sending a notice to the Upper Tribunal [so that the Upper Tribunal receives the notice within 14 days of the date that the Minister received notice of the proposal].

10. When deciding whether to uphold an objection made by the relevant Minister—

(a) any hearing must take place in the absence of the parties;

(b) if the Upper Tribunal is minded to overrule the relevant Minister's objection, or to require the relevant Minister to provide a version of the relevant Minister's response in a form other than one provided under paragraph 8(b) above, the Upper Tribunal must invite the relevant Minister to make representations; and

(c) if the Upper Tribunal overrules an objection in relation to the disclosure of a response, the Tribunal must not disclose, or require the relevant Minister to disclose, any material the subject of the objection unless the relevant Minister relies upon that material in opposing the appeal.

11. Where the relevant Minister may object to the disclosure of a response or proposed action by the Upper Tribunal, the Upper Tribunal may not proceed with that disclosure or that proposed action unless—

(a) the time for the relevant Minister to object has expired; and

(b) the relevant Minister has not objected, or the Tribunal has overruled the relevant Minister's objection and, in the case of the disclosure of a response, may proceed with the disclosure under paragraph 10(c).]

["SCHEDULE 3

RULE 26B

Procedure in financial services cases

Interpretation

1. In this Schedule—

"further material" means documents which—

(a) were considered by the respondent in reaching or maintaining the decision to give the notice in respect of which the reference has been made; or

(b) were obtained by the respondent in connection with the matter to which that notice relates (whether they were obtained before or after giving the notice) but which were not considered by it in reaching or maintaining that decision;

but does not include documents on which the respondent relies in support of the referred action;

"reference notice" means the written notice required in making a reference in a financial services case;

"referred action" means the act (or proposed act) on the part of the respondent that gave rise to the reference; and

"the 2000 Act" means the Financial Services and Markets Act 2000(**a**).

Reference notice

2.—(1) A reference notice must be signed by or on behalf of the applicant and sent or delivered by the applicant to the Upper Tribunal.

(2) A reference notice must be received by the Upper Tribunal no later than 28 days after notice was given of the decision in respect of which the reference is made.

(3) The reference notice must state—

(a) the name and address of the applicant;

(b) the name and address of the applicant's representative (if any);

(c) if no representative is named under sub-paragraph (b), an address where documents for the applicant may be sent or delivered; and

(d) the issues that the applicant wishes the Upper Tribunal to consider.

(4) The applicant must send or deliver to the Upper Tribunal with the reference notice a copy of the notice of the decision in respect of which the reference has been made.

(5) At the same time the applicant must send a copy of the reference notice to the respondent.

Register of references and decisions

3.—(1) The Upper Tribunal must keep a register of references and decisions in financial services cases.

(2) The register must be open to inspection by any person without charge and at all reasonable hours.

(3) The Upper Tribunal may direct that the register is not to include particulars of a reference if it is satisfied that it is necessary to do so having regard in particular to any unfairness to the applicant or prejudice to the interests of consumers that might otherwise result.

(4) Upon receiving a reference notice, the Upper Tribunal must—

(a) subject to any direction given under sub-paragraph (3), enter particulars of the reference in the register; and

(b) notify the parties either that it has done so or that it will not include particulars in the register, as the case may be.

Respondent's statement of case

4.—(1) The respondent must send or deliver a written statement ("a statement of case") in support of the referred action so that it is received by the Upper Tribunal no later than 28 days after the day on which the respondent received from the Upper Tribunal the notification required by paragraph 3(4)(b).

(**a**) 2000 c.8.

(2) The statement of case must—

(a) identify the statutory provisions providing for the referred action;

(b) state the reasons for the referred action; and

(c) set out all the matters and facts upon which the respondent relies to support the referred action.

(3) The respondent must provide with the statement of case a list of—

(a) any documents on which the respondent relies in support of the referred action; and

(b) any further material which in the opinion of the respondent might undermine the decision to take that action.

(4) At the same time as it sends or delivers the statement of case, the respondent must send to the applicant a copy of the statement of case and of the list referred to in sub-paragraph (3).

Applicant's reply

5.—(1) The applicant must send or deliver a written reply so that it is received by the Upper Tribunal no later than 28 days after—

(a) he date on which the applicant received a copy of the statement of case; or

(b) f the respondent amends its statement of case, the date on which the applicant received a copy of the amended statement of case.

(2) The reply must—

(a) tate the grounds on which the applicant relies in the reference;

(b) dentify all matters contained in the statement of case which are disputed by the applicant; and

(c) tate the applicant's reasons for disputing them.

(3) The applicant must send with the reply a list of all the documents on which the applicant relies in support of his case.

(4) At the same time the applicant must send to the respondent a copy of the reply and of the list referred to in sub-paragraph (3).

Secondary disclosure by the respondent

6.—(1) After the applicant's reply has been sent or delivered, if there is any further material which might reasonably be expected to assist the applicant's case as disclosed by the applicant's reply and which is not listed in the list provided in accordance with paragraph 4(3), the respondent must send or deliver to the Upper Tribunal a list of such further material.

(2) Any list required to be sent or delivered by sub-paragraph (1) must be sent or delivered so that it is received no later than 14 days after the day on which the respondent received the applicant's reply.

(3) At the same time as it sends or delivers any list required by sub-paragraph (1) the respondent must send a copy to the applicant.

Exceptions to disclosure

7.—(1) A list provided in accordance with paragraph 4(3) or 6(1) need not include any document that relates to a case involving a person other than the applicant which was taken into account by the respondent in the applicant's case only for the purposes of comparison with other cases.

(2) A list provided in accordance with paragraph 4(3), 5(3) or 6(1) need not include any document that is material the disclosure of which for the purposes of or in connection with

any legal proceedings is prohibited by section 17 of the Regulation of Investigatory Powers Act 2000(**a**).

(3) A list provided in accordance with paragraph 4(3), 5(3) or 6(1) need not include any document in respect of which an application has been or is being made under sub-paragraph (4).

(4) A party may apply to the Upper Tribunal (without giving notice to any other party) for a direction authorising the party making the application not to include in the list required by paragraph 4(3), 5(3) or 6(1) a document on the ground that disclosure of the document—

(a) would not be in the public interest; or

(b) would not be fair, having regard to—

(i) the likely significance of the document to the applicant in relation to the matter referred to the Upper Tribunal; and

(ii) the potential prejudice to the commercial interests of a person other than the applicant which would be caused by disclosure of the document.

(5) For the purpose of deciding an application by a party under sub-paragraph (4), the Upper Tribunal may—

(a) require the document to be produced to the Upper Tribunal together with a statement of the reasons why its inclusion in the list would—

(i) in the case of an application under sub-paragraph (4)(a), not be in the public interest; or

(ii) in the case of an application under sub-paragraph (4)(b), not be fair; and

(b) invite any other party to make representations.

(6) If the Upper Tribunal refuses an application under sub-paragraph (4), it must direct the party—

(a) to revise its list so as to include the document; and

(b) to send or deliver a copy of the revised list to the Upper Tribunal and to any other party.

(7) A party who has sent or delivered a list under paragraph 4(3), 5(3) or 6(1) must, upon the request of another party, provide that other party with a copy of any document specified in the list or make any such document available to that party for inspection or copying.

(8) Sub-paragraph (7) does not apply to any document that is a protected item.

(9) In this paragraph "protected item" has the meaning provided by section 413 of the 2000 Act, section 311(2) of the Pensions Act 2004(**b**) or article 283(2) of the Pensions (Northern Ireland) Order 2005(**c**).

Subsequent notices in relation to the referred action

8. Where, after a reference notice has been sent or delivered, the respondent gives the applicant any further, amended or supplementary notice in relation to the referred action, the respondent must without delay send or deliver a copy of that notice to the Upper Tribunal.

References by third parties

9.—(1) In the case of any reference made by an applicant under section 393 of the 2000 Act (third party rights) these rules apply subject to the modifications set out in this paragraph.

(2) In this paragraph—

(**a**) 2000 c.23.
(**b**) 2004 c.35.
(**c**) S.I. 2005/255 (N.I. 1).

(a) if the reference was made under section 393(9) of the 2000 Act (reference to the Upper Tribunal by a third party to whom a decision notice was copied), the notice of the decision in respect of which the reference has been made is the decision notice which was copied to the applicant by the respondent; and

(b) if the reference was made under section 393(11) of the 2000 Act (reference to the Upper Tribunal by a third party who alleges that they were not given a copy of a decision notice), the notice of the decision in respect of which the reference has been made is the decision notice which the applicant alleges was not copied to them.

(3) If the reference was made under section 393(11) of the 2000 Act, paragraph 2(4) does not apply.

(4) The duties of the respondent to set out information under paragraph 4(2) or to list material under paragraph 4(3) or 6(1) apply only to information, documents or material which relate to the matters referred to the Upper Tribunal in accordance with section 393(9) or (as the case may be) section 393(11) of the 2000 Act.]

EXPLANATORY NOTE

(This note is not part of the Rules)

Part 1 of the Tribunals, Courts and Enforcement Act 2007 (c.15) establishes a new tribunal structure comprising a First-tier Tribunal and an Upper Tribunal. Appeal functions of existing tribunals are being transferred to this structure and assigned to chambers within the new tribunals. These Rules govern the practice and procedure to be followed in the Upper Tribunal.

Part 1 contains provisions for interpreting and applying the Rules and sets out the overriding objective of the Rules.

Part 2 contains general powers and provisions including the Upper Tribunal's general case management powers, the giving of directions, the power to strike out a party's case, the service of documents and rules about evidence, submissions and witnesses.

Part 3 contains provisions on permission for and notice of appeals and on responses and replies.

Part 4 contains provisions in relation to the Upper Tribunal's "judicial review" jurisdiction under sections 15 and 21 of the 2007 Act.

Parts 5 and 6 make provision for hearings and for decisions made by the Upper Tribunal.

Part 7 deals with correcting, setting aside, reviewing and appealing against decisions of the Upper Tribunal.

Appendix 9

SI 1996 No 1022

Lands Tribunal Rules 1996

(as amended by the Lands Tribunal (Amendment) Rules 1997 (SI 1997 No. 1965);the Lands Tribunal (Amendment) Rules 1998 (SI 1998 No. 22);the Lands Tribunal (Amendment) Rules 2003 (SI 2003 No. 2945);the Lands Tribunal (Amendment) Rules 2006 (SI 2006 No. 880); and the Transfer of Tribunal Functions (Lands Tribunal and Miscellaneous Amendments) Order 2009 (SI 2009 No. 1307)).

Note: Part IIA and Rule 26A were inserted and Rules 6(1) and (4), 26 and 32 were substituted by the Lands Tribunal (Amendment) Rules 1997, which also contained minor amendments to Rules 6(6)(a), 46(2) and 50(5). Rules 29A and 32(d) were inserted by the Lands Tribunal (Amendment) Rules 1998. Part IIA and rules 28(11) and 52(1) were amended by the Lands Tribunal (Amendment) Rules 2003. Part IIA was further amended and rules 6, 7 and 8 were amended and rule 35A was substituted by the Lands Tribunal (Amendment) Rules 2006. Rules 1(2), 2A, 6(1ZA), 10(6), (7) and (8) and Part 8A were inserted by the Transfer of Tribunal Functions (Lands Tribunal and Miscellaneous Amendments) Order 2009. Rules 3, 29(A), 30(2), 38(11), 52(1) and 54(4) were omitted and changes were made to Rule 5 by the Transfer Order which also made minor amendments to many other rules by substituting "Upper" *for "Lands" in "Lands Tribunal" and "Tribunal" for "President" and "Member" and removing reference to "the office*".

1 June 2009

ARRANGEMENT OF RULES

PART I

Preliminary

PART II

Composition and hearings of the Tribunal

PART IIA

Applications for permission to appeal

PART III

Appeals

PART IV

References

PART V

Applications under section 84 of the Law of Property Act 1925

(Relief from restrictive covenants affecting land)

PART VI

Applications under section 2 of the Rights of Light Act 1959

PART VII

References by consent

PART VIII

General Procedure

PART 8A

Permission to appeal to the Court of Appeal and review

Notes

PART I

Preliminary

1. Citation and commencement

(1) These Rules may be cited as the Lands Tribunal Rules 1996 and shall come into force on 1st May 1996.

(2) These Rules apply to proceedings which have been assigned to the Lands Chamber by the First-tier Tribunal and Upper Tribunal (Chambers) Order 2008(**a**)

2. Interpretation

(1) In these Rules -

"the Act" means the Lands Tribunal Act 1949;

the 1961 Act" means the Land Compensation Act 1961;

"appeal" except in Part 8A(**b**) means an appeal against a determination of any question by an authority in respect of whose decision an appeal lies to the Tribunal;

"authority" means the person or body in respect of whose decision an appeal is brought;

"compulsory" purchase compensation reference" means a reference of a question to the Tribunal

(a) under section 1 of the Land Compensation Act 1961;

(b) under section 11(4) of the Compulsory Purchase (Vesting Declarations) Act 1981(**c**); or

(c) to which the provisions of section 4 of the Land Compensation Act apply, with the exception of references

 (i) under section 16(7) of the City of London (Various Powers) Act 1967(**d**);

 (ii) under section 307(1) of the Highways Act 1986(**e**); and

 (iii) under regulation 96(2) of the Conservation (Natural Habitats, &c) Regulations 1994(**f**).

"party" in relation to an appeal, means the appellant, the authority and any person who has served notice of intention to respond in accordance with rule 7;

"proceedings" means proceedings before the Tribunal;

"rating appeal" means an appeal form the decision of a valuation tribunal in relation to non-domestic rating;

"the registrar" means the registrar of the Tribunal or, as respects any powers or functions of the registrar, a member of staff appointed under section 40(1) of the Tribunals, Courts and Enforcement Act 2007(**g**) (tribunal staff and services) and authorised by the Senior President of Tribunals;

"the Tribunal" means the Upper Tribunal;

"valuation officer" means a valuation officer appointed under section 61 of the Local Government Finance Act 1988 or any officer authorised by him in writing to act on his behalf.

(2) In these Rules, a form referred to by number alone means the form so numbered in Schedule 1 to these Rules.

(**a**) S.I. 2008/2684 as amended by the First-tier Tribunal and Upper Tribunal (Chambers) (Amendment) Order 2009 (S.I. 2009/196) and the First-tier Tribunal and Upper Tribunal (Chambers) (Amendment No. 2) Order 2009 (S.I. 2009/No. 1021).
(**b**) See Notes
(**c**) 1981 c.66
(**d**) 1967 c.42
(**e**) 1980 c.66
(**f**) SI 1994/2716
(**g**) 2007 c.15

2A. Delegation to staff

(1) Staff appointed under section 40(1) of the Tribunals, Courts and Enforcement Act 2007 (tribunal staff and services) may, with the approval of the Senior President of Tribunals, carry out functions of a judicial nature permitted or required to be done by the Tribunal.

(2) The approval referred to at paragraph (1) may apply generally to the carrying out of specified functions by members of staff of a specified description in specified circumstances.

(3) Within 14 days after the date on which the Tribunal sends notice of a decision made by a member of staff under paragraph (1) to a party, that party may apply in writing to the Tribunal for that decision to be considered afresh by a judge.

3. ------

PART II

Composition and hearings of the Tribunal

4. Notice of hearings and sittings of the Tribunal

(1) The registrar shall, as soon as practicable after the commencement of proceedings before the Tribunal, send to each party a notice informing him of the date, time and place of the hearing.

(2) Upon receipt of a notice of intention to respond from a person who is not already a party to the proceedings, the registrar shall send to that person a notice informing him of the date, time and place of the hearing.

5. Public and private hearings

(1) Subject to paragraph (1A) all hearings by the Tribunal shall be in public except where -

(a) it is acting as an arbitrator under a reference by consent under section 1(5) of the Act: or

(b) it is satisfied that, by reason of disclosure of confidential matters or matters concerning national security, it is just and reasonable for the hearing or any part of the hearing to be in private.

(1A) Any hearing in proceedings on a compulsory purchase compensation reference shall be in public

(2) A judge or other member of the Tribunal shall be entitled to attend a hearing whether or not it is in private, notwithstanding that they do not constitute the Tribunal for the purpose of the hearing

(3) The Tribunal, with the consent of the parties, may permit any other person to attend hearing which is held in private.

PART IIA

Applications for permission to appeal

5A. Application of Part IIA

Part IIA applies to an application to the Tribunal for permission to appeal

(a) under section 175 of the Commonhold and Leasehold Reform Act 2002, against a decision of the Leasehold Valuation Tribunal; or

(b) under section 231 of the Housing Act 2004, against a decision of the residential property tribunal.

5B. Interpretation

(A) In this Part first instance tribunal means

(a) in relation to an appeal under section 175 of the Commonhold and Leasehold Reform Act 2002, the Leasehold Valuation Tribunal; and

(b) in relation to an appeal under section 231 of the Housing Act 2004, the residential property tribunal.

(1) A respondent to an application for permission to appeal is any party in the proceedings before the first instance tribunal, other than the applicant, who was present or represented at the hearing before the first instance tribunal or, where the proceedings were determined without a hearing, made representations in writing to that tribunal.

(2) A respondent to an application for permission to appeal shall not be a respondent to any subsequent appeal unless he gives notice of intention to respond to the appeal in accordance with rule 7.

5C. Application for permission to appeal

(1) A person (the applicant') may only apply to the Tribunal for permission to appeal if he has made an application to the first instance tribunal for such permission and that application has been refused.

(2) An application for permission must be made to the Tribunal within 14 days of the date on which the decision of the first instance tribunal to refuse permission to appeal was sent to the applicant.

(3) The application for permission shall contain -

(a) the name and address of the applicant;

(b) the name and address of every respondent;

(c) the grounds of appeal against the decision in respect of which

permission to appeal is sought;

(d) where the applicant is represented, the name, address and profession

of the representative; and

(e) the signature of the applicant or his representative and the date the

application was signed.

(4) The application for permission shall be accompanied by -

(a) a copy of the decision against which permission to appeal is being

sought;

(b) a copy of the decision of the first instance tribunal refusing leave to

appeal;

(c) the fee payable to the Tribunal in respect of the proposed appeal.

(5) The applicant shall deliver or send the application for permission to appeal to the Tribunal together with sufficient copies for service upon each respondent.

(6) Upon receiving an application for permission to appeal the registrar shall -

(a) serve a copy of the application on each respondent;

(b) inform the applicant of the date on which this was done; and

(c) enter details of the application in the register of appeals.

(7) The registrar shall, when serving a copy of the application, notify each respondent of the

time limit specified by the Tribunal, within which any written representations relating to the application must be made to the Tribunal.

5D. Determination of application

(1) The Tribunal shall determine an application for permission without a hearing unless it considers that there are special circumstances which make a hearing necessary or desirable.

(2) The registrar shall serve on the applicant and each respondent a notice recording the decision of the Tribunal on the application for permission.

5E. Refusal of permission to appeal

If the Tribunal refuses permission to appeal the registrar shall refund to the applicant the fee paid in respect of the appeal.

5F. Permission to appeal

(1) If the Tribunal grants permission to appeal it may do so on such conditions as it thinks fit.

(2) The registrar shall note in the register of appeals that the appeal is proceeding unless the applicant notifies him, within 14 days of the date of service of the notice recording the decision to grant permission, that he does not wish to proceed with the appeal.

(3) The registrar shall serve notice on each respondent that the appeal is proceeding with details of the number of the appeal entered on the register which shall constitute the title of the appeal.

5G. Application of Part III (Appeals)

Where an appeal proceeds following the grant of permission to appeal under this Part

(a) rule 6 shall not apply to the appeal, and

(b) rule 7 shall apply as if the reference to the notice of appeal was a reference to the notice that the appeal is proceeding referred to in rule 5F(3).

5H. Application of Part VIII (General Procedure)

In Part VIII, reference to an appeal shall include reference to an application for permission to appeal under this Part.

PART III
Appeals

6. Notice of appeal

(1) An appeal to the Tribunal shall be made by sending to the registrar a written notice indicating an intention to appeal so that it is received by the registrar -

(a) within 28 days of the date on which the decision appealed against ('the disputed decision') was sent to the applicant, or within such other time as is prescribed by the enactment conferring the right to appeal, or

(b) subject to paragraph (1B), where the appeal is made following the grant of permission to appeal, within 28 days of the date on which the decision granting permission to appeal was sent to the applicant.

(1ZA) In an appeal under regulation 37(1) of the Non-Domestic Rating (Alteration of Lists and Appeals) (England) Regulations 2005**(a)** or regulation 37(1) of the Non-Domestic Rating

(a) SI 2005/659

(Alteration of Lists and Appeals) (Wales) Regulations 2005(**a**), for the purposes of paragraph (1) of this rule the date on which the disputed decision was sent includes -

(i) if an application for the disputed decision to be reviewed was made within the time specified in regulation 35(3) of either Regulations, the date on which notice of a decision not to undertake a review was served; or

(ii) the date on which notice was served of a decision not to set aside the disputed decision on a review under regulation 35(1) of either Regulations

(1A) Paragraph (1B) applies to

(a) an appeal under section 175 of the Commonhold and Leasehold Reform Act 2002 against a decision of the Leasehold Valuation Tribunal; or

(b) an appeal under section 231 of the Housing Act 2004 against a decision of the residential property tribunal.

(1B) Subject to rule 35A, if it is satisfied that it is in the interests of justice to do, the Tribunal may direct

(a) that a shorter period be substituted for the period of 28 days in paragraph (1)(b); or

(b) that the application to the first instance tribunal for permission to appeal shall stand as notice under paragraph (1).

(2) Where the notice referred to in paragraph (1) does not conform with the requirements set out in paragraph (3), the appellant shall, within such time as the registrar may direct. send to the registrar a notice which does so conform.

(3) The notice of appeal shall state that it is a notice of appeal and shall contain -

(a) the name and address of the appellant;

(b) the date and any reference number of the disputed decision and the name and address of the Authority;

(c) the grounds of appeal;

(d) where the appellant is represented. the name. address and profession of the representative: and

(e) the signature of the appellant or his representative and the date the notice was signed.

(4) The appellant shall attach to the notice of appeal -

(a) a copy of the disputed decision; and

(b) where the appeal is made following grant of permission to appeal by the authority, a copy of the decision granting permission to appeal; and

(c) where the appeal relates to a rating appeal, a copy of the proposal or determination that was the subject of the proceedings which led to the disputed decision.

(5) The appellant shall deliver or send the notice of appeal to the Tribunal together with sufficient copies for service upon each of the parties to the proceedings which led to the disputed decision and upon the authority, and where appropriate, the valuation officer.

(6) Upon receiving a notice of appeal the registrar shall -

(a) enter particulars of the appeal in the *register of appeals*;

(b) serve a copy of the notice on the parties to the proceedings which led to the disputed decision other than the appellant, on the authority and, where applicable, on the valuation officer and inform the appellant of the date on which this was done; and

---

(**a**) SI 2005/758

(c) inform the appellant and all persons on whom a copy of the notice of appeal is served of the number of the appeal entered on the Register which shall constitute the title of the appeal.

7. Notice of intention to respond

(1) If a person on whom a copy of the notice of appeal is served intends to respond he shall give written notice of his intention, signed and dated, stating -

(a) whether he intends to respond separately or jointly with some other person;

(b) the grounds on which he opposes the appeal; and

(c) an address for service of notices and other documents on him.

(2) Subject to paragraph (2B), the notice of intention to respond shall be served on the registrar and the appellant within 28 days of the date of service of the copy of the notice of appeal.

(2A) Paragraph (2B) applies to –

(a) an appeal under section 175 of the Commonhold and Leasehold Reform Act 2002 against a decision of the Leasehold Valuation Tribunal; or

(c) an appeal under section 231 of the Housing Act 2004 against a decision of the residential property tribunal.

(2B) Subject to rule 35A, if it is satisfied that it is in the interests of justice to do so, the Tribunal may direct that a shorter period be substituted for the period of 28 days in paragraph (2).

(3) Where the registrar receives more than one notice of intention to respond, he shall serve a copy of each such notice on all parties other than the appellant.

8. Statement of case

(1) A person giving notice of intention to respond is, in this rule, called a "respondent".

(2) Subject to paragraph (4B), within 28 days of service of a notice of intention to respond, the appellant shall serve on the respondent from whom it is received, a statement of his case, including full particulars of the facts relied upon and any points of law on which he intends to rely at the hearing.

(3) Subject to paragraph (4B), within 28 days of service of the appellant's statement, a respondent shall serve on the appellant a reply stating his case including full particulars of the facts relied upon and any points of law on which he intends to rely at the hearing.

(4) Subject to paragraph (4B), where a party receives from the registrar a copy of a notice of intention to respond from another party in accordance with rule 7(3), he shall, within 28 days of service of such notice on him, send to that other party a copy of the reply referred to in paragraph (3).

(4A) Paragraph (4B) applies to -

(a) an appeal under section 175 of the Commonhold and Leasehold Reform Act 2002 against a decision of the Leasehold Valuation Tribunal; or

(b) an appeal under section 231 of the Housing Act 2004 against a decision of the residential property tribunal.

(4B) Subject to rule 35A, if it is satisfied that it is in the interest of justice to do so, the Tribunal may direct that a shorter period be substituted for the period of 28 days in paragraph (2), (3) or (4).

(5) Where a party serves a statement or reply in accordance with paragraphs (2) or (3), he shall at the same time send a copy to the registrar with confirmation that the statement or reply has been served in accordance with this rule.

(6) A statement or reply served in accordance with this rule shall be accompanied by -

(a) every valuation which the party proposes to put in evidence (which shall include all particulars and computations in support of the valuation), or a statement of the value or values which the parties have agreed, and

(b) either

(i) full particulars of any comparable properties and transactions to which the party intends to refer at the hearing in support of his case and a statement of the purpose for which the comparison is made; or

(ii) a statement that no comparable properties or transactions will be referred to.

(7) If at the hearing of an appeal a party seeks to rely upon any valuation or other document which appears to the Tribunal not to have been served in accordance with this rule, it may adjourn the hearing on such terms as to costs or otherwise as it thinks fit.

PART IV

References

9. Application of Part IV

Part IV applies to any reference to the Tribunal other than an appeal, or an application to which Part V or VI applies.

10. Notice of reference

(1) A reference shall be made by sending to the registrar a notice of reference together with sufficient copies for service upon every other person named in the notice.

(2) The parties to the proceedings shall be the person lodging the notice of reference and the persons named in that notice.

(3) The notice of reference shall contain -

(a) the name and address of the person lodging the reference and, if he is represented, the name, address and profession of the representative;

(b) the name and address of every other person with an interest in the land to which the reference relates ("the land");

(c) the address or description of the land;

(d) the nature of the interest in the land of the person lodging the reference;

(e) the statutory provision under which the reference is made; and

(f) the signature of the person lodging the reference or his representative and the date the reference was signed.

(4) The person lodging the notice of reference shall attach to it

(a) where the matter relates to compensation payable on the compulsory acquisition of land -

(i) a copy of the notice to treat if one has been served;

(ii) a copy of the notice of entry if one has been served; and

(iii) any notice of claim and amendments of it delivered to the acquiring authority in pursuance of section 4 of the 1961 Act; and

(b) in any other case, a copy of the order or other document in consequence of which proceedings for the determination of the reference are instituted including a copy of any agreement conferring Jurisdiction on the Tribunal.

(5) A notice of reference in relation to the compensation payable on the compulsory acquisition of land shall not be given before the expiration of 28 days from the date of service or constructive service of the notice to treat, or where no such notice is served or deemed in accordance with the appropriate statutory provision to be served, of the notice of claim.

(6) In a reference under section 153(1) of the Town and Country Planning Act 1990**(a)**, the notice of reference must be given to the Tribunal within two months of the date of service of the counter-notice.

(7) In a reference under regulation 7(1) or 12(3) of the Town and Country Planning (Compensation and Certificates) Regulations 1974**(b)**, the notice of reference must be given to the Tribunal within 30 days of the issue of notice of the decision or findings to which the dispute relates.

(8) In a reference under regulation 15(1) of the Town and Country Planning (Compensation and Certificates) Regulations 1974 –

(a) the notice of reference must be given to the Tribunal within 30 days of the Secretary of State's determination; and

(b) the notice of reference must specify whether the objection is on ground (a) or ground (b) as set out in regulation 14(4) of those Regulations.

11. Entry of reference

(1) Upon receipt of a notice of reference, the registrar shall enter particulars of it in the Register of References and shall send a copy of the notice to every party to the, proceedings other than the applicant.

(2) The registrar shall inform all parties to the proceedings of the number of the reference which shall constitute the title of the proceedings.

PART V

Applications under section 84 of the Law of Property Act 1925 (Relief from restrictive covenants affecting land)

12. Interpretation

In this Part -

"section 84" means section 84 of the Law of Property Act 1925; and

"restriction" means a restriction, arising under a covenant or otherwise, as to the user of or building on any freehold land or any leasehold land held for a term of more than 40 years of which at least 25 years have expired.

13. Method of making application

(1) A person interested in land affected by a restriction who wishes to make an application under the section shall send to the registrar in duplicate an application which shall contain -

(a) the name and address of the person making the application and, if he is represented, the name, address and profession of the representative;

(b) the address or description of the land to which the application relates;

(c) the address or description of the land which is subject to the restriction;

(a) 1990 c.8
(b) SI 1974/1242

(d) the address or description of the land which, and the identity of any person (if known) who, has the benefit of the restriction or any person whom the applicant believes may have such benefit and the reasons for that belief;

(e) the ground or grounds in section 84 on which the applicant relies and the reason he considers that that ground or those grounds apply;

(f) a statement as to whether the applicant is applying to discharge the restriction wholly or for its modification, and if the latter the extent of the modification;

(g) a statement as to whether any planning permission has been applied for, granted or refused within the five years preceding the application in respect of the land the subject of the application;

(h) the signature of the person making the application or his representative and the date of the signature.

(2) The application referred to in paragraph (1) shall be accompanied by -

(a) a copy of the instrument imposing the restriction or, if this is not available, documentary evidence of the restriction; and

(b) a plan identifying the land to which the application relates and, so far as practicable, all the land which is subject to the restriction and the land which has the benefit of the restriction.

(3) An application may be made jointly by two or more persons whether the land in which they are interested is the same land or different parts of the land affected by the restriction.

14. Publication of notices

(1) Upon receipt of an application, the registrar shall determine what notices are to be given, and whether these should be given by advertisement or otherwise, to persons who appear to be entitled to the benefit of the restriction.

(2) For the purpose of paragraph (1), the registrar may require the applicant to provide any documents or information which it is within his power to provide.

(3) The notices shall require persons claiming to be entitled to the benefit of the restriction, who object to the discharge or modification of it proposed by the application, or who claim compensation for such modification or discharge, to send to the registrar and to the applicant notice of any objections they may have and of the amount of compensation they claim (if any).

(4) The notices to be given under paragraph (1) shall be given by the applicant who shall certify in writing to the registrar that directions as to the giving of those notices have been complied with.

15. Notice of objection

(1) A notice of objection to the application and a claim for compensation shall be in writing and shall be sent to the registrar and the applicant within 28 days from the publication of the notices referred to in rule 14.

(2) If the registrar requires, the person objecting shall submit a statement containing -

(a) his name and address and if he is represented the name, address and profession of the representative;

(b) the basis upon which he claims to be entitled to the benefit of the restriction;

(c) any ground of objection; and

(d) his signature or that of his representative and the date the statement was signed.

16. Suspension of proceedings

At any time after the registrar has received a notice of objection to the application the Tribunal -

(a) of its own motion may, or

(b) on the application of the applicant or of any person who has given a notice of objection, shall,

suspend the proceedings for such time as it may consider appropriate to enable an application to be made to the High Court for the determination of a question arising under subsection (2) of section 84.

17. Order without hearing etc

(1) If it appears to the Tribunal that, having regard to the applicant's interest in the land, the applicant is not a proper person to make the application, the Tribunal may dismiss it and shall inform the applicant of its reasons for doing so.

(2) Where -

(a) the registrar receives no notice of objection within the time allowed by rule 15(1), or

(b) all objectors have withdrawn their objections before a hearing has taken place,

the Tribunal may, with the consent of the applicant, determine the application without a hearing.

(3) Where at or after a hearing -

(a) all objectors withdraw their objections, or

(b) the Tribunal directs that no objector shall be admitted to oppose the application,

the Tribunal may, with the consent of the applicant, determine the application without any further hearing.

18. Power to direct additional notices

If it appears to the Tribunal at any time before the determination of the application that any person who has not received notice of the application otherwise than by advertisement should have received specific notice, the Tribunal may require the applicant to give notice to that person and may adjourn the hearing to enable that person to make an objection or a claim for compensation.

19. Enquiries of local authorities

If before or at the hearing of an application the Tribunal considers that enquiries should be made at any local authority within whose area the land affected by the restriction is situated, the Tribunal may direct those enquiries to be made and may adjourn the case until the local authority has replied.

20. Provisions as to orders

(1) Where the Tribunal orders the discharge or modification of a restriction subject to the payment of compensation. the discharge or modification shall not take effect until the registrar has endorsed on the order that the compensation has been paid.

(2) The Tribunal may direct that the compensation be paid within a specified time failing which the order shall cease to have effect.

(3) The Tribunal may determine that any compensation awarded shall be paid into the Court Funds Office of the Supreme Court.

PART VI

Applications under section 2 of the Rights of Light Act 1959

21. Form of application

(1) An application for a certificate of the Tribunal under section 2 of the Rights of Light Act 1959 shall be in Form 1.

(2) An application under paragraph (1) shall be accompanied by two copies of the application which the applicant proposes to make to the local authority in whose area the dominant building is situated.

22. Publicity

(1) Upon receipt of an application the registrar shall determine what notices are to be given, whether by advertisement or otherwise, to persons who appear to have an interest in the dominant buildings referred to in rule 21(2).

(2) For the purpose of paragraph (1), the registrar shall require the applicant to provide any documents or information which it is within his power to provide.

(3) The notices that the registrar determines shall be given under this rule shall be given by the applicant who shall notify the registrar in writing once this has been done setting out full particulars of the steps he has taken.

23. Issue of temporary certificate

(1) Where the Tribunal is satisfied that exceptional urgency requires the immediate registration of a temporary notice in the register of local land charges, it shall issue a temporary certificate in Form 2.

(2) A temporary certificate shall not last longer than six months.

24. Issue of definitive certificates

The Tribunal shall issue a certificate in Form 3 or, where a temporary certificate has been issued under rule 23, in Form 4, once it is satisfied that the notices which the registrar has determined shall be given under rule 22 have been duly given.

PART VII

References by consent

25. Application of Part VII

This Part applies to proceedings before the Tribunal where it is acting as arbitrator under a reference by consent under section 1(5) of the Act.

26. Application of Arbitration Act 1996

Unless otherwise agreed by the parties, the following provisions of the Arbitration Act 1996 shall apply to proceedings under this Part, in addition to those set out in rule

32 -

(a) section 8 (whether agreement discharged by death of a party);

(b) section 9 (stay of legal proceedings);

(c) section 10 (reference of interpleader issue to arbitration);

(d) section 12 (power of court to extend time for beginning arbitral proceedings, etc.);

(e) section 23 (revocation of arbitrator's authority);

(f) section 57 (correction of award or additional award) in so far as it relates to costs and so that the reference to 'award' shall include a reference to any decision of the Tribunal;

(g) section 60 (agreement to pay costs in any event).

26A. The person referring the matter to the Tribunal shall, at the time the reference is made, supply the Tribunal with copies of the arbitration agreement and any other written agreement relevant to the manner of arbitration.

PART VIII

General Procedure

27. Determination of proceedings without a hearing

(1) The Tribunal may, with the consent of the parties to the proceedings, order that the proceedings be determined without an oral hearing.

(2) Where the Tribunal makes an order under paragraph (1), any party to the proceedings may submit written representations to the Tribunal.

(3) On or after making an order under paragraph (1), the Tribunal shall give such directions relating to the lodging of documents and representations as it considers appropriate.

(4) Rule 42 shall apply to proceedings to which this rule applies as if references to the calling of witnesses and the hearing of evidence in that rule were references to representations.

(5) The Tribunal may at any time, on the application of a party to the proceedings or of its own motion, order that the proceedings should be heard and in that event may give directions for the disposal of the proceedings in accordance with these Rules.

28. Simplified procedure

(1) The Tribunal or the registrar may, with the consent of the applicant or appellant or, in relation to proceedings under Part IV, the consent of the person who is claiming compensation, direct that proceedings shall be determined in accordance with this rule.

(2) The registrar shall send a copy of any direction made under paragraph (1) on all the parties to the proceedings and any party who objects to the direction may, within 7 days of service of the copy on him, send written notice of his objection to the registrar.

(3) Rule 38(6) to (9) and (11) shall apply as appropriate where an objection is received by the registrar under paragraph (2).

(4) Paragraphs (5) to (12) shall apply to proceedings in respect of which the registrar has made a direction under paragraph (1).

(5) Where the proceedings relate to an appeal under Part III, rule 8 shall not apply.

(6) The registrar shall -

(a) give directions concerning the filing and contents of a statement of claim by the applicant or appellant and a reply by the other parties to the proceedings; and

(b) give the parties not less than 21 days notice of the day fixed for the hearing of the proceedings.

(7) The following directions shall take effect -

(a) each party shall. not less than 14 days before the date fixed for the hearing, send to every other party copies of all documents in his possession on which he intends to rely at the hearing; and

(b) each party shall not less than 7 days before the date fixed for the hearing send to the registrar and to every other party a copy of any expert report on which he intends to rely at the hearing and a list of the witnesses whom he intends to call at the hearing.

(8) The registrar may from time to time, whether on application or of his own motion, amend or add to any direction issued if he thinks it necessary to do so in the circumstances of the case.

(9) The hearing shall be informal and the Tribunal shall act as if it were an arbitrator and shall adopt any procedure that it considers to be fair.

(10) Strict rules of evidence shall not apply to the hearing and evidence shall not be taken on oath unless the Tribunal orders otherwise.

(11) No award shall be made in relation to the costs of the proceedings except in cases to which section 4 of the 1961 Act or subsections (6) and (7) of section 175 of the Commonhold and Leasehold Reform Act 2002 apply, save that the Tribunal may make an award of costs

(a) in cases where an offer of settlement has been made by a party and the Tribunal considers it appropriate to have regard to the fact that such an offer has been made; or

(b) in cases in which the Tribunal regards the circumstances as exceptional,

and if, exceptionally, an award of costs is made the amount shall not exceed that which would be allowed if the proceedings had been heard in a county court.

(12) The Tribunal may at any time, on the application of a party to the proceedings or of its own motion, order that this rule shall no longer apply to the proceedings and in that event may give directions for the disposal of the proceedings in accordance with these Rules.

29. Site inspections

(1) Subject to paragraph (2), the Tribunal may enter and inspect-

(a) the land or property which is the subject of proceedings, and

(b) as far as is practicable, any comparable land or property to which the attention of the Tribunal is drawn.

(2) When the Tribunal intends to enter any premises in accordance with paragraph (1) it shall give notice to the parties who shall be entitled to be represented at the inspection; where the Tribunal deems it appropriate, such representation shall be limited to one person to represent those parties having the same interest in the proceedings.

29(A) -------

30. Consolidation of proceedings

(1) Where two or more notices of appeal, references or applications have been made which -

(a) are in respect of the same land or buildings; or

(b) relate to different interests in the same land or buildings; or

(c) raise the same issues

the Tribunal may, on its own motion or on the application of a party to the proceedings, order that the appeals, references or applications be consolidated or heard together.

(2) An order may be made with respect to some only of the matters to which the appeals. references or applications relate.

31. Power to select test case in appeals or references

(1) Where the Tribunal is of the opinion that two or more appeals or references involve the same issues it may, with the written consent of all the parties to the appeals or references, select one or more appeal or reference to be heard in the first instance as a test case or test cases and the

parties to each appeal or reference shall be bound by the decision of the Tribunal on that appeal or reference.

(2) -------

32. Application of Arbitration Act 1996

The following provisions of the Arbitration Act 1996 shall apply to all proceedings as they apply to an arbitration -

(a) section 47 (awards on different issues, etc.), as if the words 'unless otherwise agreed by the parties' were omitted from subsection (1) and so that the reference to 'award' shall include a reference to any decision of the Tribunal;

(b) section 49 (interest) subject to any enactment that prescribes a rate of interest;

(c) section 57(3) to (7) (correction of award or additional award);

(d) section 66 (enforcement of the award).

33. Evidence

(1) Evidence before the Tribunal may be given orally and may be on oath or affirmation or, if the parties to the proceedings consent or the Tribunal so orders, by affidavit.

(2) Notwithstanding paragraph (1), the Tribunal may at any stage of the proceedings require the personal attendance of any deponent for examination or cross-examination.

(3) Paragraphs (2) to (7) of rule 38 shall apply to an application to the Tribunal for leave to give evidence by affidavit but as if for

(4) Nothing in the Civil Evidence Act 1972, or in rules of court made under it, shall prevent expert evidence from being given before the Tribunal by any party even if no application has been made to the Tribunal for a direction as to the disclosure of that evidence to any other party to the proceedings.

34. Power to order discovery etc

(1) The Tribunal, or subject to any directions given by the Tribunal, the registrar may, on the application of any party to the proceedings or of its or his own motion, order any party -

(a) to deliver to the registrar any document or information which the Tribunal may require and which it is in the power of the party to deliver;

(b) to afford to every other party to the proceedings an opportunity to inspect those documents (or copies of them) and to take copies;

(c) to deliver to the registrar an affidavit or make a list stating whether any document or class of document specified or described in the order or application is, or has at any time been in his possession. custody or power and stating when he parted with it;

(d) to deliver to the registrar a statement in the form of a pleading setting out further and better particulars of the grounds on which he intends to rely and any relevant facts or contentions;

(e) to answer interrogatories on affidavit relating to any matter at issue between the applicant and the other party;

(f) to deliver to the registrar a statement of agreed facts, facts in dispute and the issue. or issues to be tried by the Tribunal; or

(g) to deliver to the registrar witness statements or proofs of evidence.

(2) Where an order is made under paragraph (1) the Tribunal or registrar may give directions as to the time within which any document is to be sent to the registrar (being at least 14 days from the date of the direction) and the parties to whom copies of the document are to be sent.

(3) Rule 38 shall apply to this rule as appropriate both in relation to applications and where the registrar acts of his own motion.

35. Extension of time

(1) The time appointed by or under these Rules for doing any act or taking any steps in connection with any proceedings may be extended on application to the registrar under rule 38.

(2) The registrar may extend the time limit on such terms as he thinks fit and may order an extension even if the application is not made until after the time limit has expired.

35A. Shortening of time etc

(1) In this rule urgency direction means a direction under rule 6(1B), 7(2B) or 8(4B).

(2) The Tribunal may make an urgency direction

(a) on application of a party, or

(b) on its own initiative.

(3) Paragraphs (4) to (8) apply, and rule 38 does not apply, where a party applies for an urgency direction.

(4) The application shall be made in writing and shall state the title of the proceedings, and the grounds upon which the application is made.

(5) If the application is made with the consent of all parties, it shall be accompanied by consents signed by or on behalf of the parties.

(6) If the application is not made with the consent of every party the applicant shall serve a copy of the proposed application on every other party before it is made and the application shall state that this has been done.

(7) Subject to paragraph (8), the Tribunal shall give notice in writing to the parties other than the applicant inviting them to make representations in writing in relation to the application.

(8) Paragraph (7) does not apply where the Tribunal, having considered the application and the grounds upon which it is made, decides to refuse the application.

(9) Where the Tribunal proposes to make an urgency direction on its own initiative it shall give notice in writing to the parties

(a) of the direction which it proposes to make; and

(b) inviting the parties to make representations in writing in relation to the proposal.

(10) The notice given under paragraph (7) or (9) may specify a date by which representations are to be made.

(11) Before making an urgency direction the Tribunal shall consider all the representations that it has received.

36. Appellant limited to grounds of appeal

(1) On the hearing of an appeal under Part III or of an application under Part V, the appellant or applicant may rely only on the grounds stated in his notice of appeal, statement of case or application unless the Tribunal permits additional grounds to be put forward.

(2) If the Tribunal permits additional grounds to be put forward in accordance with paragraph (1) it may do so on such terms as to costs, adjournment or otherwise as it thinks fit.

37. Right of audience

(1) Subject to paragraph (2), in any proceedings a party may appear in person or be represented by counsel or solicitor or by any other person with the leave of the Tribunal, or, in the case of an interlocutory application, the leave of the registrar.

(2) Where a valuation officer is a party to proceedings, he may not appear in person except with the leave of the Tribunal or, in the case of an interlocutory application, the leave of the registrar.

38. Interlocutory applications

(1) Except where these Rules make other provision or the Tribunal otherwise orders, an application for directions of an interlocutory nature in connection with any proceedings shall be made to the registrar.

(2) The application shall be made in writing and shall state the title of the proceedings, and the grounds upon which the application is made.

(3) If the application is made with the consent of all parties, it shall be accompanied by consents signed by or on behalf of the parties.

(4) If the application is not made with the consent of every party the applicant shall serve a copy of the proposed application on every other party before it is made and the application shall state that this has been done.

(5) A party who objects to an application may, within 7 days of service of a copy on him, send written notice of his objection to the registrar.

(6) Before making an order on an application the registrar shall consider all the objections that he has received and may allow any party who wishes to appear before him the opportunity to do so.

(7) In dealing with an application the registrar shall have regard to the convenience of all the parties and the desirability of limiting so far as practicable the costs of the proceedings and shall inform the parties in writing of his decision.

(8) The registrar may refer the application to the Tribunal for a decision and he shall do so if requested by the applicant or a party objecting to the application.

(9) A party may appeal to the Tribunal from a decision of the registrar under this rule by giving written notice to the registrar within 7 days of service of the notice of decision or such further time as the registrar may allow.

(10) An appeal under paragraph (9) shall not act as a stay of proceedings unless the Tribunal so orders.

(11) --------

39. Pre-trial review

(1) The Tribunal and, subject to any direction given by the Tribunal, the registrar may, on the application of a party to the proceedings or of its or his own motion order a pre-trial review to be held and the registrar shall send to each party to the proceedings a notice informing him of the place and date of the pre-trial review.

(2) Unless the parties agree otherwise, the date of the pre-trial review shall be not less than 14 days from the making of the order that the pre-trial review should be held.

(3) The Tribunal or the registrar -

- (a) shall at the pre-trial review give any direction that appears necessary or desirable for securing the just, expeditious and economical disposal of the proceedings; and
- (b) shall at the pre-trial review endeavour to secure that the parties make all such admissions and agreements as ought reasonably to be made by them in relation to the proceedings;
- (c) may record in the order made on the review any admission or agreement made under sub-paragraph (b) or any refusal to make any admission or agreement.

(4) Where a party seeks a specific direction he shall, so far as is practicable, apply for such direction at the pre-trial review and shall give the registrar and every other party notice of his intention to do so.

(5) If an application which might have been made at the pre-trial review is made subsequently the applicant shall pay the costs of and occasioned by the application unless the Tribunal considers that there was sufficient reason for the application not having been made at the review.

(6) Paragraphs (6) to (10) of rule 38 shall apply to a pre-trial review as if it were an interlocutory application.

(7) If any party does not appear at the pre-trial review the Tribunal or the registrar may, after giving the parties the opportunity to be heard, make such order as may be appropriate for the purpose of expediting or disposing of the proceedings.

40. Certificates of value

A party may apply in writing to the registrar for a certificate of value under section 35 of the 1961 Act and shall provide the registrar, at his request, with the information necessary to enable the certificate to be given.

41. Administration of oaths

The registrar and the Tribunal shall have power to administer oaths and take affirmations for the purpose of affidavits to be used in proceedings or for the purpose of the giving of oral evidence at hearings.

42. Expert witnesses

(1) This rule applies to any proceedings except an application for a certificate under Part VI.

(2) Subject to paragraph (3), only one expert witness on either side shall be heard unless the Tribunal orders otherwise.

(3) Where the proceedings relate to mineral valuations or business disturbance, not more than two expert witnesses on either side shall be heard unless the Tribunal orders otherwise.

(4) An application for leave to call more than the number of expert witnesses permitted by this rule may be made to the registrar in accordance with rule 38, or to the Tribunal at the hearing.

(5) A party shall, within 28 days of receiving a request from the registrar, send to him and to the other parties to the proceedings a copy of each of the following documents relating to the evidence to be given by each expert witness -

- (a) the expert witness's report, including every plan and valuation of the land or property to which the proceedings relate (which shall include full particulars and computations in support of the valuation) which it is proposed to put in evidence; and
- (b) either -
  - (i) full particulars of any comparable properties and transactions to which the party intends to refer at the hearing in support of his case and a statement of the purpose for which the comparison is made; or
  - (ii) a statement that no comparable properties or transactions will be referred to.

(6) If -

- (a) an application for leave under paragraph (4) is made at the hearing and granted by the Tribunal; or
- (b) at the hearing any party seeks to rely on documents not sent to the registrar or to the other parties in accordance with paragraph (5);

the Tribunal may adjourn the hearing on such terms as to costs or otherwise as it thinks fit.

43. Preliminary issues

(1) The Tribunal may, on the application of any party to proceedings, order any preliminary issue in the proceedings to be disposed of at a preliminary hearing.

(2) If in the opinion of the Tribunal the decision on the preliminary issue disposes of the proceedings, it may order that the preliminary hearing shall be treated as the hearing of the case or may make such other order as it thinks fit.

(3) Paragraphs (2) to (7) of rule 38 shall apply to an application under paragraph (1) above as if for "registrar" in those paragraph there were substituted "Tribunal".

44. Sealed offers

(1) Where any party unconditionally offers or is ready to accept, any sum as compensation or by way of price, or to agree a rent or a rateable value, a copy of the offer or indication of the readiness to accept enclosed in a sealed cover may be sent to the registrar or delivered to the Tribunal at the hearing by the party who made the offer or indicated the readiness to accept and shall be opened by the Tribunal after it has determined the proceedings.

(2) An offer or an indication of readiness to accept which is sent to the registrar or delivered to the Tribunal in accordance with paragraph (1), shall not be disclosed to the Tribunal until it has decided the amount of such sum, rent or rateable value.

45. Withdrawal or dismissal of appeal etc, before hearing

(1) An appeal, reference or application may be withdrawn by sending to the registrar a written notice of withdrawal signed by all parties to the proceedings or by their representatives.

(2) A party may, at any time before the hearing of the proceedings, apply to the Tribunal for an order to dismiss the proceedings and the Tribunal may make such order as it thinks fit.

(3) Paragraphs (2) and (4) to (7) of rule 38 shall apply to an application under paragraph (2) as if for "registrar" there were substituted "Tribunal".

46. Failure to pursue proceedings or comply with Rules

(1) If it appears to the Tribunal that any party to proceedings has failed to send a copy of any document to any other party or to the registrar as required by these Rules, it may -

- (a) direct that a copy be sent;
- (b) adjourn the further hearing of the proceedings; and
- (c) require the party at fault to pay any additional costs occasioned as a result of the failure.

(2) Where a party has failed to pursue any proceedings with due diligence or has failed to comply with any of the provisions of these Rules the registrar or the Tribunal on the application of any party or of his or its own motion after giving the parties an opportunity to be heard may make -

- (a) an order that the proceedings be heard by the Tribunal; or
- (b) an order that the proceedings be dismissed or that any party be debarred from taking any further part in the proceedings; or
- (c) such other order as may be appropriate for expediting or disposing of the proceedings including an order for costs.

(3) Paragraphs (9) and (10) of rule 38 shall apply to any order made by the registrar under paragraph (2).

47. Failure to comply with the Rules not to render proceedings invalid

Any failure by any person to comply with these Rules shall not render the proceedings or anything done in pursuance of them invalid unless the Tribunal so directs.

48. Procedure at hearing

Subject to these Rules the procedure at the hearing of any proceedings shall be such as the Tribunal may direct.

49. Default of appearance at hearing

(1) If on an appeal under Part III or an application under Part V the appellant or applicant fails to attend or be represented at the hearing the Tribunal may dismiss the appeal or application.

(2) If any party to proceedings referred to in paragraph (1) other than the appellant or applicant, or any party to a reference under Part IV fails to attend or be represented at the hearing, the Tribunal may hear and determine the appeal, application or reference in his absence and may make such order as to costs as it thinks fit.

(3) Where proceedings have been dismissed or determined under this rule, the Tribunal may, on the application of the party who has failed to attend within 7 days of the dismissal or determination, if it is satisfied that he had sufficient reason for his absence, set aside the dismissal or determination on such terms as to costs as it thinks fit.

50. Decision of Tribunal

(1) Subject to paragraph (2), the decision of the Tribunal on an appeal, reference or application shall be given in writing, and shall state the reasons for the decision.

(2) The Tribunal may give its decision orally in cases where it is satisfied that this would not result in any injustice or inconvenience to the parties.

(3) The Tribunal may, and on the application of any party to the proceedings shall, issue an order incorporating its decision.

(4) Where an amount awarded or value determined by the Tribunal is dependent upon the decision of the Tribunal on a question of law which is in dispute in the proceedings, the Tribunal shall ascertain, and shall state in its decision, any alternative amount or value which it would have awarded or determined if it had come to a different decision on the point of law.

(5) The Tribunal**(a)** shall serve a copy of the decision or, where the decision is given orally an order stating its effect, on every party who has appeared before the Tribunal in the proceedings, and -

(a) in the case of an appeal against the decision of a valuation tribunal to the clerk of that tribunal and, if the appeal is a rating appeal, to the valuation officer;

(b) in the case of any other appeal under Part III, to the authority.

(6) If the Court of Appeal directs that any decision of the Tribunal which has been appealed to the Court of Appeal, should be amended the registrar shall send copies of the amended decision to every person who was notified of the original decision.

(7) Where the Tribunal has made an award in proceedings on a compulsory purchase compensation reference, on the application of any party the Tribunal must specify the amount awarded in respect of any particular matter the subject of the award.

51. Consent orders

Where the parties to proceedings have agreed the terms of an order to be made by the Tribunal, particulars of those terms signed by all the parties or by their representatives shall be sent to the registrar and an order may be made by the Tribunal in accordance with those terms in the absence of the parties.

52. taxation of costs

(1) ------

(2) The registrar may make an order as to costs in respect of any application or proceedings heard by him.

(a) See Notes

(3) A person dissatisfied with the order of the registrar under paragraph (2) may, within 10 days of the order, appeal to the Tribunal which may make such order as to the payment of costs including the costs of the appeal as it thinks fit.

(4) If the Tribunal directs that the costs of a party to the proceedings be paid by another party it may settle the amount of costs by fixing a lump sum or direct that the costs be taxed by the registrar on such basis as the Tribunal thinks fit, being a basis that would be applied on a taxation of the costs of High Court or county court proceedings.

(5) A party dissatisfied with a taxation of costs under paragraph (4) may, within 7 days of the taxation. serve on any other interested party and on the registrar written objection specifying the items objected to and applying for the taxation to be reviewed in respect of those items.

(6) Upon such application the registrar shall review the taxation of the items objected to and shall state in writing the reasons for his decision.

(7) A person dissatisfied with the decision of the registrar under paragraph (6) may, within 10 days of the decision, apply to the Tribunal to review the taxation and the Tribunal may make such order as it thinks fit including an order as to payment of the costs of the review.

(8) Paragraphs (8) and (10) of rule 38 shall apply to any application under this rule.

53. Solicitor to be on the record

(1) Where a solicitor commences or responds to proceedings on behalf of a party to those proceedings he shall be noted on the record of the Tribunal as acting for that party.

(2) A party who has previously carried on proceedings in person may appoint a solicitor at any time to act on his behalf and if he does so shall notify the Tribunal who shall note on the record that the solicitor is acting for that party.

(3) A party who has previously been represented by a solicitor may change his solicitor at any time, or may decide to continue the proceedings in person but unless such chance or decision is notified to the Tribunal the former solicitor shall be considered the representative of the party until the conclusion of the proceedings.

(4) The notifications referred to in paragraphs (2) and (3) may be given by the party or his solicitor and the person giving the notification shall send a copy to every other party to the proceedings.

(5) A solicitor who is on the record of the Tribunal as acting for a party shall be responsible for the payment of all fees of the Tribunal which are the responsibility of that party whilst he remains on the record.

54. Service of notices

(1) Every party to proceedings shall notify the registrar of an address for service of documents on him.

(2) Where a party to proceedings is represented by a person other than a solicitor he shall -

(a) send to the registrar written authority for that representative to act on his behalf; and

(b) notify the registrar if the representative ceases to act on his behalf and, if replaced, shall give the registrar details of the new representative together with the written authority for the new representative to act on his behalf.

(3) Any document to be served on any person under these Rules shall be deemed to have been served if sent by pre-paid post to that person at his address for service.

(4) ------

(5) Any application or communication to be made to the Tribunal in respect of any case shall be addressed to the registrar.

55. Change of address

A party to any proceedings may at any time by notice in writing to the registrar and to every other party to the proceedings change his address for service under these Rules.

56. Substituted service

If any person to whom any notice or other document is required to be sent under these Rules -

(a) cannot be found after all diligent enquiries have been made;

(b) has died and has no personal representative; or

(c) is out of the United Kingdom;

or for any other reason service upon him cannot readily be effected in accordance with these Rules, the Tribunal may dispense with service upon that person or make an order for substituted service in such other form (whether by advertisement in a newspaper or otherwise) as the Tribunal may think fit.

PART 8A

Permission to appeal to the Court of Appeal and review

57. Interpretation of Part 8A

In this Part –

"appeal" means the exercise of a right of appeal on a point of law under section 13 of the Tribunals, Courts and Enforcement Act 2007; and

"review" means the review of a decision by the Tribunal under section 10 of that Act.

58. Application for permission to appeal

(1) A person seeking permission to appeal must make a written application to the Tribunal for permission to appeal.

(2) An application under paragraph (1) must be sent or delivered to the Tribunal so that it is received within 28 days after the date on which the Tribunal sent a copy of the decision or an order stating its effect to the party making the application.

(3) If the person seeking permission to appeal provides the application to the Tribunal later than the time required by paragraph (2), or by any extension of time under rule 35 (extension of time)

(a) the application must include a request for an extension of time and the reason why the application was not provided in time; and

(b) unless the Tribunal decides to extend time for the application, the Tribunal must refuse the application.

(4) An application under paragraph (1) must

(a) identify the decision of the Tribunal to which it relates;

(b) identify the alleged error or errors of law in the decision; and

(c) state the result the person making the application is seeking.

59. Tribunal's consideration of application for permission to appeal

(1) On receiving an application for permission to appeal the Tribunal may review the decision in accordance with rule 60 (review of a decision), but may only do so if –

(a) when making the decision the Tribunal overlooked a legislative provision or binding authority which could have had a material effect on the decision; or

(b) since the Tribunal's decision, a court has made a decision which is binding on the Tribunal and which, had it been made before the Tribunal's decision, could have had a material effect on the decision.

(2) If the Tribunal decides not to review the decision, or reviews the decision and decides to take no action in relation to the decision or part of it, the Tribunal must consider whether to give permission to appeal in relation to the decision or that part of it.

(3) The Tribunal must send a record of its decision to the parties as soon as practicable.

(4) If the Tribunal refuses permission to appeal it must send with the record of its decision

(a) a statement of its reasons for such refusal; and

(b) notification of the right to make an application to the relevant appellate court for permission to appeal and the time within which, and the method by which, such application must be made.

(5) The Tribunal may give permission to appeal on limited grounds, but must comply with paragraph (4) in relation to any grounds on which it has refused permission.

60. Review of a decision

(1) The Tribunal may only undertake a review of a decision pursuant to rule 59(1) (review on an application for permission to appeal).

(2) The Tribunal must notify the parties in writing of the outcome of any review and of any rights of review or appeal in relation to the outcome.

(3) If the Tribunal decides to take any action in relation to a decision following a review without first giving every party an opportunity to make representations, the notice under paragraph (2) must state that any party that did not have an opportunity to make representations may apply for such action to be set aside and for the decision to be reviewed again.

Dated 27th March 1996 *Mackay of Clashfern, C.*

Notes

1. In Rule 2 (interpretation) the definition of appeal should read: "'apeal' except in Part 8A ..."

2. Rule 50(5) should read "the registrar shall" ...

Rule 2 Rule 21

Strike out words not applicable

Application for temporary certificate. Strike out if not applicable.

SCHEDULE 1

FORM 1

Application for Certificate under section 2 of the Rights of Light Act 1959

To:-The Registrar.

Upper Tribunal.

I/We ....

of ....

being [owner(s)][tenant(s) for a term of years certain expiring in 19] [mortgagee(s) in possession] of *(here describe the servient land)* ....

.... apply to the Upper Tribunal for the issue of a certificate that adequate publicity has been given to my/our proposed application for the registration in the register of local land charges of the .... Council of a notice under section 2 of the Rights of Light Act 1959.

I/We attach two copies of the proposed application.[I/We also apply for the issue of a certificate authorising the registration forthwithof the proposed notice as a temporary notice. The case is one of exceptional

urgency because *(here insert reasons)* ....

....

.... To the best of my/our knowledge persons likely to be affected by the registration of the notice are *(here insert names and addresses of all persons in occupation of the dominant building or having a proprietary interest in it)* ....

....

.... All communications regarding this application should be addressed to me/us at the address shown above [*or* to my/our solicitor/agent .... of ....
....]

Dated .... Signed ....

Rule 23

FORM 2

Temporary Certificate for Registration of a Notice under section 2 of the Rights of Light Act 1959

I hereby certify that for reasons of exceptional urgency a temporary notice may be registered by *(name of applicant)* ....

....

forthwith against the building specified in the attached Form of Application for the registration of a notice under section 2 of the Rights of Light Act 1959

A notice registered under the said application shall not have effect after the effluxion of .... months from the date of registration unless before the expiration of that period a further certificate of this Tribunal has been lodged with the registering authority stating that due publicity has been given to the proposed registration.

Dated .... Signed .... Registrar Upper Tribunal

Rule 24

FORM 3

Certificate for Registration of a Notice under section 2 of the Rights of Light Act 1959

I certify that adequate notice of the proposed application by *(name of applicant)* ....

a copy of which is attached to this certificate, to register a notice under section 2 of the Rights of Light Act 1959 against *(description of dominant building as specified in the application)* .... has been given to all persons who, in the circumstances existing at the present time appear to the Upper Tribunal to be persons likely to be affected by the registration of such a notice.

Dated .... Signed .... Registrar Upper Tribunal

Rule 24

Appendix 9

FORM 4

Certificate for Registration of a Notice under section *2 of the Rights of Light Act 1959 following Registration of a Temporary Notice*

I certify that adequate notice of the proposed application by *(name of applicant)* ....
....

to register a notice under section 2 of the Rights of Light Act 1959 against *(description of dominant building as specified in the application)* ....

....

has been given to all persons who, in the circumstances existing at the present time appear to the Upper Tribunal to be persons likely to be affected by the registration of such a notice.

A temporary certificate authorising the registration of a temporary notice was issued by the Upper Tribunal on ....

Dated .... Signed .... Registrar Upper Tribunal

Index

G

H

L

Q

R

V